W9-CJO-560

THE COMMUNIST INTERNATIONAL
1919-1943
DOCUMENTS

VOLUME I

THE COMMUNIST INTERNATIONAL

1919—1943

DOCUMENTS

SELECTED AND EDITED BY

JANE DEGRAS

THREE VOLUMES

VOLUME I

1919 — 1922

Originally issued under the auspices of the
Royal Institute of International Affairs

FRANK CASS & CO. LTD.

1971

Published by
FRANK CASS AND COMPANY LIMITED
67 Great Russell Street, London WC1B 3BT
by arrangement with Oxford University Press, London

All rights reserved

First edition   1956
New impression   1971

The Royal Institute of International Affairs is an unofficial body which promotes the scientific study of international questions and does not express opinions of its own. The opinions expressed in this publication are the responsibility of the author.

ISBN 0 7146 1554 4

Burgess
HX
11
.I5
A5314
1971

V. 1

*Printed in Great Britain by Clarke, Doble & Brendon Ltd.
Plymouth and London*

1982 OCT 11
IW

PREFACE

THE documents included in this volume fall roughly into four categories. There are first of all the programmatic and theoretical statements of the Communist International, enunciating its aims and objects and formulating general policy on particular questions, such as the Comintern Statutes and the theses on the national and colonial question. The selection here has been fairly wide; with the exception of theses on communist work among women and young people and in co-operative organizations, it includes all the important documents for the period covered. Secondly, there are statements on current events; here the selection represents a smaller proportion of those issued. On such questions as the Versailles treaty and the Washington conference, Comintern statements, reflecting and reinforcing the policies of the Soviet Government, were usually well-considered and instructive, and most of them are given here. It was also customary for the Comintern to make pronouncements, usually ill-informed and always repetitive, on events within the labour movement; only a small number of these are reproduced, since little further understanding of the Comintern's operations would have been gained by including more of them. Letters to and resolutions on the national communist parties form a third group. Obviously only a part of the correspondence has ever been made public, but even of that part it was impossible to include more than a few representative items, illustrating the attitude of the central body to its affiliated sections. Most of them concern the communist parties of Germany, Italy, and France, countries which seemed at the time to offer the most hopeful prospects for revolutionary work. The eastern countries, where the communist movement developed somewhat later than in Europe, will be represented in the second volume. Finally, there are documents referring to the internal organization of the Communist International. These are few in number but none of importance has been omitted. It was only towards the end of the period covered by this volume that the Comintern became a tightly organized body, with a large staff in Moscow operating its communications and maintaining the hierarchy of authority.

There would have been some gain from arranging the documents on these lines, but the advantages of chronological sequence seemed greater. It has not been possible to observe this strictly, since some documents were not dated at all, while others were obviously wrongly dated.

This first volume ends in December 1922, that is, after the fourth world congress of the Communist International. This was the last which Lenin attended, and the last at which discussion was fairly uninhibited. In later years debates were more constrained, and the disputes within the Russian Communist Party had marked repercussions on the Comintern. Moreover, with the fading of revolutionary hopes, the candour of the earlier years disappeared from Comintern statements as it did from the pronouncements of the Soviet Government. For both the heroic period had come to an end; Russia had survived without the aid of revolution in other countries, and had reassumed her position as a great power. The prestige and authority of the Bolsheviks, understandably great from the outset, was now virtually unchallenged. It became more than ever true that the test of a communist hinged on his attitude to the Soviet Union, and as, with the united front tactics, expediency replaced a fixed revolutionary standpoint, fidelity to the communist cause became a matter of discipline rather than principle.

The introductory remarks are intended to give briefly the context of the document and to bring together relevant comments on the questions at issue made at the time and subsequently by leading Comintern members. In writing them I have made use of the proceedings of the Comintern congresses, reports of meetings of the Executive Committee of the Communist International, the files of *Kommunisticheskii Internatsional* and of *Internationale Presse-Korrespondenz*, the notes to the protocols of congresses of the Russian Communist Party and to Lenin's collected works, and *Desiat Let Kominterna*. I have also drawn freely on the published memoirs of Angelica Balabanova, Klara Zetkin, and A. Rosmer, and have consulted in particular the third volume of Mr. E. H. Carr's *The Bolshevik Revolution*, O. Flechtheim's history of the German Communist Party, G. Walter's history of the French Communist Party, A. Rossi's *Rise of Italian Fascism*, and the studies of the Communist International by F. Borkenau, R. Fischer, and B. Lazitch.

The translations have been made from the German text of the reports of the four Comintern congresses of this period since it was the main language used, but wherever it was doubtful it has been compared with the Russian. There were many variations between the two, both verbal and in arrangement, but none that I have discovered of any substance. Conflicting figures are sometimes given for the number of delegates attending the congresses and the meetings of the enlarged Executive Committee.

It was customary for draft theses to be published before the opening of the congress; they were then debated at plenary sessions and, as a rule, referred back to a commission for detailed discussion and amendment. The revised theses were then reintroduced, debated, and voted upon. No reports of the meetings of the commissions were published, but the rapporteur frequently gave the congress a summary account of their work. Voting was as a rule individual, not by delegation.

I should like to thank Miss Violet Conolly and Mr. E. H. Carr for their help and advice; Mr. F. Carsten for the loan of books not otherwise available in this country, and Mr. R. Lowenthal for allowing me to use information collected for his forthcoming biography of Ernst Reuter.

J. D.

July 1955

CONTENTS

TABLE OF DOCUMENTS

1919

1921

INVITATION TO THE FIRST CONGRESS OF THE COMMUNIST
INTERNATIONAL

24 January 1919   *Borba Bolshevikov*, p. 113

[The foundation of a new international to replace the Second had been included in Lenin's April 1917 'theses' submitted to the central committee of the Bolshevik party, and the conference which followed resolved on 29 April 1917 that, 'It is the task of our party, acting in a country where the revolution has started earlier than in other countries, to take the initiative in creating a third international'. A further stimulus was provided by the formation in December 1918 of the German Communist Party.

The decision to convene an international conference of socialist parties and groups 'opposed to the Second International' with the object of establishing the new and revolutionary international was taken hurriedly, when it became known that an attempt to re-form the Second International was to be made, since this would mean a consolidation of the forces in the labour movement hostile to bolshevism. Hopes of wide representation were not entertained, since Russia was at the time virtually cut off from Europe, and the difficulties of communication and travel were very great. In the midst of civil war and intervention, and with no normal diplomatic channels at its command, the Bolshevik leaders resorted to transmission by radio for this as for other communications to the outside world.

Angelica Balabanova, the first secretary of the Communist International, wrote that it was realized at the time that a representative international congress could not possibly be held in Russia then, but it was considered essential to have some kind of gathering to offset the meeting to be held in Berne. The invitation was drafted by Trotsky, and approved by a small committee which included Lenin and Chicherin, at that time Commissar for Foreign Affairs; it was first published in *Pravda* on 24 January 1919. The lack of precision in the names of the parties and organizations to which it was addressed reflects both the confused state of labour organizations at the end of the 1914–1918 war, and the ignorance of the Bolshevik leaders about developments in other countries. The signatories were all in Moscow.]

The undersigned parties and organizations consider it urgently necessary to convene the first congress of a new revolutionary international. During the war and the revolution it became conclusively clear not only that the old socialist and social-democratic parties, and with them the Second International, had become completely bankrupt, not only that the half-way elements of the old social-democracy (the so called 'centre') are incapable of positive revolutionary action, but that the outlines of a real revolutionary international are already clearly defined. The gigantic pace of the world revolution, constantly presenting new problems, the danger that this revolution may be throttled by the alliance of capitalist States, which are banding together against the revolution under the hypocritical banner of the 'League of Nations', the attempts of the social-traitors' parties to get together and, having 'amnestied' each other, to help their governments and their bourgeoisie to deceive the working classes once more; finally, the extraordinarily rich revolutionary experience already gained and the internationalization of the entire revolutionary movement, compel us to take the initiative in placing on the order of the day the convening of an international congress of revolutionary proletarian parties.

I. AIMS AND TACTICS

In our opinion the new international should be based on the recognition of the following propositions, put forward here as a platform and worked out on the basis of the programme of the Spartakusbund in Germany and of the Communist Party (Bolsheviks) in Russia:

1. The present epoch is the epoch of the disintegration and collapse of the entire capitalist world system, which will drag the whole of European civilization down with it if capitalism with its insoluble contradictions is not destroyed.

2. The task of the proletariat now is to seize State power immediately. The seizure of State power means the destruction of the State apparatus of the bourgeoisie and the organization of a new proletarian apparatus of power.

3. This new apparatus of power should embody the dictatorship of the working class (and in some places also of the rural semi-proletariat, the village poor), that is, it should be the instrument for the systematic suppression of the exploiting classes and for their expropriation. Not false bourgeois democracy—that hypocritical form of the rule of the financial oligarchy—with its purely formal equality, but proletarian democracy, which gives the working masses the opportunity to make a reality of their freedom; not parliamentarianism, but self-government of these masses by their elected organs; not capitalist bureaucracy, but organs of administration created by the masses themselves, with the masses really taking part in the government of the country and in socialist construction—this should be the type of the proletarian State. Its concrete form is given in the regime of the Soviets or of similar organs.

4. The dictatorship of the proletariat must be the lever for the immediate expropriation of capital and for the abolition of private property in the means of production and their transformation into national property. The nationalization of large-scale industry (nationalization being understood as the abolition of private ownership and transference to the ownership of the proletarian State, to come under the socialist management of the working class) and of its organizing centres, the banks; confiscation of the estates of the large landowners and nationalization of capitalist agricultural production; monopoly of wholesale trade, nationalization of large

houses in towns and on large estates; introduction of workers' management and centralization of economic functions in the hands of agencies of the proletarian dictatorship—these are the essential problems of the day.

5. In order to safeguard the socialist revolution, to defend it against internal and external enemies, to give aid to other national sections of the fighting proletariat, etc., it is essential to disarm the bourgeoisie and their agents completely, and to arm the proletariat.

6. The world situation today demands the closest possible contact between the different sections of the revolutionary proletariat and a complete union of the countries where the socialist revolution has already triumphed.

7. The basic methods of struggle are mass actions of the proletariat right up to open armed conflict with the political power of capital.

2. ATTITUDE TO 'SOCIALIST' PARTIES

8. The old 'International' has broken down into three main groups: the avowed social-chauvinists, who throughout the imperialist war of 1914 to 1918 supported their own bourgeoisie and turned the working class into executioners of the international revolution; the 'centre', whose theoretical leader is Kautsky, consisting of those elements who are always vacillating, incapable of a firm line of conduct, and at times outright treacherous; finally there is the left revolutionary wing.

9. Towards the social-chauvinists, who everywhere at critical moments come out in arms against the proletarian revolution, no other attitude but unrelenting struggle is possible. As to the 'centre'—the tactics of splitting off the revolutionary elements, and unsparing criticism and exposure of the leaders. Organizational separation from the centrists is at a certain stage of development absolutely essential.

10. On the other hand, it is necessary to form a bloc with those elements in the revolutionary workers' movement who, although they did not formerly belong to socialist parties, now stand by and large for the proletarian dictatorship in the form of Soviet power. Chief among these are the syndicalist elements in the workers' movement.

11. Finally it is necessary to draw in all those proletarian groups and organizations which, although they have not openly attached themselves to the left revolutionary tendency, nevertheless appear to be moving in this direction.

12. In concrete terms, we propose that representatives of the following parties, groups, and trends shall take part in the congress (full membership of the Third International shall be open to those parties which stand completely on its platform):

1. The Spartakusbund (Communist Party of Germany)
2. The Communist Party (Bolsheviks) of Russia

3. The Communist Party of German-Austria
4. The Communist Party of Hungary
5. The Communist Party of Poland
6. The Communist Party of Finland
7. The Communist Party of Estonia
8. The Communist Party of Latvia
9. The Communist Party of Lithuania
10. The Communist Party of White Russia
11. The Communist Party of the Ukraine
12. The revolutionary elements in the Czech Social-Democratic Party
13. The 'narrow' Bulgarian Social-Democratic Party (Tesniaki)
14. The Rumanian Social-Democratic Party
15. The left wing of the Serbian Social-Democratic Party
16. The left Social-Democratic Party of Sweden
17. The Norwegian Social-Democratic Party
18. The 'Klassenkampen' group in Denmark
19. The Communist Party of Holland
20. The revolutionary elements in the Belgian Labour Party
21 and 22. The groups and organizations within the French socialist and syndicalist movement which by and large support Loriot
23. The left social-democrats of Switzerland
24. The Italian Socialist Party
25. The left elements in the Spanish Socialist Party
26. The left elements in the Portuguese Socialist Party
27. The left elements in the British Socialist Party (in particular the group represented by Maclean)
28. The Socialist Labour Party (England)
29. The I.W.W. (England)
30. The I.W. of Great Britain
31. The revolutionary elements among the Shop Stewards (Great Britain)
32. The revolutionary elements in the Irish workers' organizations
33. The Socialist Workers' Party of America
34. The left elements in the American Socialist Party (in particular the group represented by Debs and the League for Socialist Propaganda)
35. The I.W.W. (America)
36. The I.W.W. (Australia)
37. The Workers' International Industrial Union (America)
38. Socialist groups in Tokyo and Yokohama (represented by comrade Katayama)
39. The Socialist Youth International (represented by comrade Münzenberg)

3. THE QUESTION OF ORGANIZATION AND THE NAME OF THE PARTY

13. The basis of the Third International is already provided by the existence, in various parts of Europe, of groups and organizations of like-minded comrades which have a common platform and by and large use the same tactical methods. Chief among these are the Spartakists in Germany and the communist parties in many other countries.

14. The congress must establish a common fighting organ for the purpose of maintaining permanent co-ordination and systematic leadership of the movement, a centre of the communist international, subordinating the interests of the movement in each country to the common interest of the international revolution. The actual form to be taken by the organization, representation on it, etc., will be worked out by the congress.

15. The congress must assume the name of 'The first congress of the Communist International', and the individual parties shall become its sections. Marx and Engels had already found the name 'social-democrat' theoretically incorrect. The shameful collapse of the social-democratic 'International' also makes a break on this point necessary. Finally, the kernel of the great movement is already formed by a number of parties which have taken this name. In view of the above, we propose to all fraternal parties and organizations to discuss the question of the convening of the international communist congress. With fraternal greetings

> The Central Committee of the Russian Communist Party (LENIN, TROTSKY)
> The foreign bureau of the Communist Workers' Party of Poland (KARSKI)
> The foreign bureau of the Communist Party of Hungary (RUDNIANSKY)
> The foreign bureau of the Communist Party of German-Austria (DUDA)
> The Russian bureau of the Central Committee of the Latvian Communist Party (ROZIN)
> The Central. Committee of the Communist Party of Finland (SIROLA)
> The Executive Committee of the Balkan Revolutionary Social-Democratic Federation (RAKOVSKY)
> For the Socialist Workers' Party of America (REINSTEIN)

THE FOUNDATION CONGRESS OF THE COMMUNIST INTERNATIONAL

[The first congress of the Communist International was held in Moscow from 2 to 6 March 1919. It was to have opened on 15 February, but was postponed because of the difficulties of travelling to Russia. It was attended by 35 delegates with voting powers, representing 19 parties and organizations, and by 19 delegates, representing 16 organizations, with a consultative voice. Most of the delegates, Balabanova wrote later, 'had been hand-picked by the Russian central committee from so-called communist parties in these smaller nations which had formerly comprised the Russian empire . . . or they were war prisoners or foreign radicals who happened to be in Russia at the time'. Eberlein (Germany), Gruber (Austria), Stange (Norway), Grimlund (Sweden), and Rutgers (Holland), were the only delegates arriving from abroad especially for the meeting. Zinoviev was elected Chairman, and Balabanova and Vorovsky acted as secretaries.

The Russian Communist Party was represented by Lenin, Trotsky, Zinoviev, Bukharin, and Chicherin. Stalin's name was also included but there is no evidence, either in the records of the congress or in the accounts written by participants and observers, that he took any part in its meetings. No full stenographic record of the proceedings was made: German was the official language of the congress.

It was decided that no voting powers were to be exercised by those who had no mandates from their organizations, or were not its accredited representatives (Sadoul, for example, spoke as 'a French officer in the ranks of the Red Army').

The conference opened without any report in the press. Reports appeared first on 6 March, after the decision had been taken that the meeting be regarded as the foundation congress of the Third International. This had been opposed from the start by Eberlein, the German delegate, acting on instructions from his party. At a meeting on 1 March Lenin had tried to persuade Eberlein to agree to its foundation, but without success. It was then decided to consider the meeting as a preparatory conference which would draw up a platform and elect a working committee to make arrangements for a wider and more representative gathering.

The proceedings were opened by Lenin with a speech in which he said that the civil war had become a fact not only in Russia but in Germany, and that a practical form had to be found to enable the revolutionary opposition in the labour movement to give effect to its views.

Eberlein reported on the breakaway of the Spartakusbund from the German Independent Social-Democratic Party (USPD) and the formation of the German Communist Party (KPD) at the end of 1918. 'Unless all the signs are deceptive, the German proletariat is facing the last decisive struggle. However difficult it may be, the prospects for communism are favourable.'

Zinoviev reported for the Russian Communist Party. 'We consider it one of our primary duties to give as much material assistance as possible to the workers' movement in other countries. . . . We shall continue to regard it as our duty to help every workers' movement that acknowledges communist principles.'

Speaking on the situation in Finland, Sirola said that it needed only a shock to bring revolutionary tension there to the pitch of explosion.

Speaking nearly four years later, at the fourth congress, Radek said that the belief in an immediate world revolution held when the International was founded was shared by Lloyd George and Clemenceau.

Rutgers, the Dutch delegate to the first congress, was instructed to set up a west European bureau of the Comintern in Holland, because of Moscow's isolation. The bureau was established at the end of 1919 in Amsterdam.

The west European secretariat, also set up in the autumn of 1919, had its seat in Berlin and included Paul Levi among its members. It had been started by Thomas, a Bavarian, and Bronsky, a Pole who had served with the Soviet trade mission in Berlin.]

THESES ON BOURGEOIS DEMOCRACY AND PROLETARIAN DICTATORSHIP
ADOPTED BY THE FIRST COMINTERN CONGRESS

4 *March* 1919   *Protokoll*, i, p. 115

[These theses, written by Lenin, were adopted by the congress without discussion. In introducing them, as in his other speeches at the congress, Lenin expressed the belief, shared by the other delegates, that the capitalist world was rapidly approaching its end, and that the working class everywhere was moving towards revolution (he likened the shop stewards movement in England to the Soviets). Unless the proletariat seized power, the problems created by the imperialist war and its aftermath could not be solved. The chief danger lay in the attempt of the reformist socialist parties to hold the workers back, and win them for a policy of bourgeois reconstruction and Wilsonian reforms, by appealing to their loyalty to the old socialist organizations, and their attachment to democratic procedures.

The main emphasis of the congress was not on the struggle against capitalism, but on the struggle against the right wing in the labour movement. Speaking three years later, at the June 1922 meeting of the Executive Committee of the Communist International (ECCI), Zinoviev said: 'We were splitters when the Comintern began its work. At that time we could not act otherwise. We had to split the old socialist parties, rescue the best revolutionary elements of the working class, form a rallying point for communist parties in every country. . . . The split was historically necessary; it was a great step forward, a means of winning the masses.']

1. The growth of the revolutionary movement of the proletariat in all countries has provoked the bourgeoisie and their agents in the workers' organizations to convulsive efforts to find theoretical arguments in defence of the rule of the exploiters. Among these, particular emphasis is placed on the rejection of dictatorship and the defence of democracy. The falseness and hypocrisy of this argument, repeated in a thousand forms in the capitalist press and at the February 1919 Berne conference of the yellow international, is however clear to anyone who is unwilling to commit treachery to the principles of socialism.

2. In the first place, the argument uses abstract concepts of 'democracy' and 'dictatorship', without specifying what class is in question. Putting the question in this way, outside or above the class standpoint, as though it were valid as a standpoint of the entire people, is downright mockery of the basic theory of socialism, namely the theory of the class struggle, which is

still recognized in words, it is true, by the socialists who have gone over to the camp of the bourgeoisie, but judging by their deeds is forgotten. For in no civilized capitalist country is there 'democracy in the abstract', there is only bourgeois democracy, and the question is one not of 'dictatorship in the abstract', but of the dictatorship of the oppressed class, that is, of the proletariat, over the oppressors and exploiters, that is, the bourgeoisie, in order to overcome the resistance put up by the exploiters in the effort to maintain their rule.

3. History teaches us that an oppressed class has never and can never come to power without passing through a period of dictatorship, that is, without the conquest of political power and the forcible suppression of the most desperate and frenzied resistance, that shrinks from no crime, which is always put up by the exploiters. The bourgeoisie, whose rule is now defended by socialists who express hostility to 'dictatorship in general' and stand up body and soul for 'democracy in general', won their power in the civilized countries by a series of revolts, civil wars, the forcible suppression of monarchical rule, of the feudal lords and slave-owners, and of their attempts at restoration. Thousands and millions of times, in their books and pamphlets, their congress resolutions and speeches, socialists in every country have explained to the people the class character of these bourgeois revolutions. That is why the present defence of 'bourgeois democracy' in speeches about 'democracy', and the present outcry against the proletarian dictatorship in the clamour about 'dictatorship', is an outright betrayal of socialism, objectively a going over to the camp of the bourgeoisie, a denial of the right of the proletariat to its political revolution, a defence of bourgeois reformism, and this precisely at the historical moment when bourgeois reformism has gone to pieces throughout the world and when the war has created a revolutionary situation.

4. By recognizing the class character of bourgeois democracy, of bourgeois parliamentarianism, all socialists have articulated the ideas expressed with the greatest scientific precision by Marx and Engels when they said that even the most democratic bourgeois republic is nothing but the instrument by which the bourgeoisie oppress the working class, by which a handful of capitalists keeps the working masses under. There is not a single revolutionary or a single Marxist among those who now raise such an outcry against dictatorship and advocate democracy who has not loudly and solemnly sworn to the workers that he acknowledges this basic truth of socialism; but now, when ferment and movement have started among the revolutionary proletariat, aimed at breaking this machine of oppression and fighting for the dictatorship of the proletariat, these traitors to socialism present the case as though the bourgeoisie had made a gift of 'pure democracy' to the workers, as though the bourgeoisie renounced resistance and were ready to submit to a workers' majority, as though in

the democratic republic there were no State apparatus for the oppression
of labour by capital.

5. The Paris Commune, which everyone who wanted to be considered
a socialist extolled in words, for they knew that the working masses had
a great and genuine sympathy with it, proved particularly clearly the
historical conditioning and limited value of bourgeois parliamentarianism
and bourgeois democracy, which are highly progressive institutions in
comparison with the Middle Ages, but which in the epoch of proletarian
revolution inevitably require to be changed from the ground up. It was
Marx himself, who placed the highest value on the historical significance
of the Commune, who in his analysis of it demonstrated the exploiting
character of bourgeois democracy and bourgeois parliamentarianism,
under which the oppressed class is given the right, once in several years,
to decide which deputy of the possessing classes shall represent and betray
the people in Parliament. It is now, when the Soviet movement which is
seizing the entire world is carrying forward before all eyes the cause of the
Commune, that the traitors to socialism forget the practical experience and
the concrete lessons of the Paris Commune and repeat the old bourgeois
rubbish about 'democracy in general'. The Commune was not a parliamentary institution.

6. The significance of the Commune consists further in this, that it
made an attempt to destroy and utterly root out the bourgeois State
machine, the apparatus of officials, court, army, and police, and to replace
it by the self-governing mass organization of workers without any separation of legislative and executive powers. All bourgeois democratic republics
of our time, including the German, which the traitors to socialism, making
a mockery of truth, call proletarian, retain this bourgeois State apparatus.
That proves once more, and clearly and unmistakably, that the outcry in
defence of 'democracy' is nothing but defence of the bourgeoisie and their
privileges of exploitation.

7. 'Freedom of assembly' can be used as an example of the demand for
'pure democracy'. Every class-conscious worker who has not broken with
his class grasps immediately that it would be monstrous to promise the
exploiters freedom of assembly in times and situations in which they are
resisting their overthrow and defending their privileges. Neither in England
in 1649, nor in France in 1793, did the revolutionary bourgeoisie guarantee
freedom of assembly to the royalists and nobility when these summoned
alien troops to the country and 'assembled' to organize an attempt at
restoration. If the bourgeoisie of today, who have long since become reactionary, demand that the proletariat shall guarantee in advance that
'freedom of assembly' shall be assured to the exploiters regardless of the
resistance the capitalists put up to their expropriation, the workers will
only laugh at such bourgeois hypocrisy.

On the other hand the workers know very well that even in the most democratic bourgeois republic 'freedom of assembly' is an empty phrase, for the rich have the best public and private buildings at their disposal, have also enough leisure for meetings, and enjoy the protection of the bourgeois apparatus of power. The proletariat of town and country, as well as the small peasants, that is the overwhelming majority of the population, have neither the first nor the second nor the third. So long as this is true, 'equality', that is, 'pure democracy', is a deception. To win real equality, to make a reality of democracy for the workers, the exploiters must first be deprived of all public and private mansions, the workers must be given leisure and their freedom of assembly defended by armed workers and not by the offspring of the nobility or officers from capitalist circles in command of an intimidated rank and file.

Only after such changes is it possible to speak of 'freedom of assembly', of equality, without mocking the workers, the labouring people, the poor. But nobody can bring these changes about except the vanguard of the working people, the proletariat, by overthrowing the exploiters, the bourgeoisie.

8. 'Freedom of the press' is another leading watchword of 'pure democracy'. But the workers know, and the socialists of all countries have admitted it a million times, that this freedom is deceptive so long as the best printing works and the biggest paper supplies are in capitalist hands, and so long as capital retains its power over the press, a power which throughout the world is expressed more clearly, sharply, and cynically, the more developed the democracy and the republican regime, as for example in America. To win real equality and real democracy for the working masses, for the workers and peasants, the capitalists must first be deprived of the possibility of getting writers in their service, of buying up publishing houses and bribing newspapers. And for that it is necessary to throw off the yoke of capital, to overthrow the exploiters and to crush their resistance. The capitalists have always given the name of freedom to the freedom of the rich to make profits and the freedom of the poor to die of hunger. The capitalists give the name of freedom of the press to the freedom of the rich to bribe the press, the freedom to use wealth to create and distort so-called public opinion. The defenders of 'pure democracy' reveal themselves once more as defenders of the dirty and corrupt system of the rule of the rich over the means of mass education, as deceivers of the people who with fine-sounding but thoroughly false phrases divert them from the concrete historical task of liberating the press from capital. Real freedom and equality will be found in the system the communists establish, in which there will be no opportunity to get rich at the expense of others, no objective possibility of subjecting the press, directly or indirectly, to the power of money, where nothing will prevent the workers (or any large group of

workers) from having and employing equal rights to use the presses and paper belonging to society.

9. The history of the 19th and 20th centuries showed us, even before the war, what this much-praised 'pure democracy' really means under capitalism. Marxists have always maintained that the more developed, the more 'pure' democracy is, the more openly, sharply, and ruthlessly does the class struggle proceed, the more clearly does the oppression of capital and the dictatorship of the bourgeoisie come to light. The Dreyfus affair in republican France, the bloody collisions between striking workers and the mercenaries armed by the capitalists in the free and democratic republic of America, these and a thousand similar facts disclose the truth which the bourgeoisie try in vain to conceal, namely that in reality terror and a bourgeois dictatorship rule the most democratic republic, and come openly to the surface whenever it seems to the exploiters that the power of capital is endangered.

10. The imperialist war of 1914–18 exposed the true character of bourgeois democracy, once and for all, even to the backward workers, even in the freest republics, as the dictatorship of the bourgeoisie. To enrich a group of German and English millionaires and milliardaires, dozens of millions of men were killed and the military dictatorship of the bourgeoisie established in the freest republics. This military dictatorship still exists in the Entente countries even after the defeat of Germany. It was the war, more than anything else, that opened the eyes of working people, tore the false tinsel from bourgeois democracy, and revealed to the people the whole pit of speculation and greed for profits during the war and in connexion with the war. The bourgeoisie waged this war in the name of freedom and equality; in the name of freedom and equality the war contractors enormously increased their wealth. No efforts of the yellow Berne international will succeed in concealing from the masses the exploiting character of bourgeois freedom, bourgeois equality, and bourgeois democracy, now finally exposed.

11. In the country of Europe where capitalism has been most highly developed, that is, in Germany, the first months of full republican freedom which followed the downfall of imperialist Germany, showed the German worker and the entire world the real class-content of the bourgeois democratic republic. The murder of Karl Liebknecht and Rosa Luxemburg is an event of world-historical significance not only because the best people and leaders of the truly proletarian communist international perished tragically, but also because it finally showed up the class character of the leading European State, of, it can be said without exaggeration, the leading State in the world. If prisoners, that is, people who have been taken under protection by the State power, can be murdered with impunity by officers and capitalists under a government of social-patriots, the democratic

republic in which this can happen is a dictatorship of the bourgeoisie. Those who express indignation over the murder of Karl Liebknecht and Rosa Luxemburg but do not understand this truth only demonstrate their obtuseness or their hypocrisy. In one of the freest and most advanced republics of the world, in the German republic, there is freedom to kill the imprisoned leaders of the proletariat and to go unpunished. And it cannot be otherwise so long as capitalism remains, for the development of democracy does not blunt but sharpens the class struggle, which has now, as a result of the war and its consequences, reached boiling-point.

All over the civilized world bolsheviks are being deported, persecuted, imprisoned; in Switzerland, one of the freest bourgeois republics, and in America, there are pogroms against the bolsheviks. From the standpoint of 'democracy in general', or 'pure democracy', it is simply ludicrous that progressive, civilized, democratic countries, armed to the teeth, should fear the presence of a few dozen people from backward, hungry, ruined Russia, described as savages and criminals in millions of copies of bourgeois newspapers. It is obvious that a social system which can give rise to such glaring contradictions is in reality a dictatorship of the bourgeoisie.

12. In such a state of affairs the dictatorship of the proletariat is not merely wholly justified, as a means of overwhelming the exploiters and overcoming their resistance, but quite essential for the mass of workers as their only protection against the bourgeois dictatorship which led to the war and is getting ready for new wars.

The chief thing which the socialists do not understand, a failure which reflects their intellectual shortsightedness, their dependence on bourgeois prejudices, their political treachery to the proletariat, is that when, in capitalist society, the class struggle on which it rests becomes more acute, there is nothing between dictatorship of the bourgeoisie and dictatorship of the proletariat. The dream of another, third way is the reactionary lament of the petty bourgeoisie. Proof of this can be found in the experience of more than a hundred years of bourgeois democracy and the workers' movement in all advanced countries, and particularly the experience of the last five years. The same proof is furnished by economic theory, by the entire content of Marxism, which analyses the economic necessity of bourgeois dictatorship in every commodity economy, a dictatorship which can be abolished by none other than the class which through the development of capitalism itself develops and grows, becomes more organized and powerful, that is, by the class of proletarians.

13. The second theoretical and political mistake of the socialists is their failure to understand that the forms of democracy have inevitably changed in the centuries since it first appeared in the Ancient World, as one ruling class gave way to another. In the republics of Ancient Greece, in the medieval cities, in advanced capitalist States, democracy has different

forms and varying scope. It would be the greatest nonsense to assume that the most profound revolution in mankind's history, the first transference of power from the hands of the exploiting minority to the hands of the exploited majority, could take place within the framework of the old bourgeois parliamentary democracy, without the greatest changes, without the creation of new forms of democracy, new institutions, new conditions for their use, etc.

14. The dictatorship of the proletariat is like the dictatorship of other classes in that, like any dictatorship, it originates in the necessity of suppressing by force the resistance of the class which is losing its political power. The fundamental difference between the proletarian dictatorship and the dictatorship of other classes, that of the large landowners in the Middle Ages and that of the bourgeoisie in all civilized capitalist countries, consists in this, that while the dictatorship of the large landowners and the bourgeoisie forcibly suppresses the resistance of the overwhelming majority of the population, namely the working masses, the dictatorship of the proletariat is the forcible suppression of the resistance of the exploiters, that is, of the minority of the population, the large landowners and capitalists.

From this it follows further that the dictatorship of the proletariat must inevitably involve not only a change in the forms and institutions of democracy, but change of a kind which results in an extension of actual democratic usages, on a scale never before known in the world, to the working classes whom capitalism enslaved.

And in fact the forms taken by the dictatorship of the proletariat, which have already been worked out, that is, the Soviet power in Russia, the workers' councils in Germany, the shop stewards' committees, and other analogues of Soviet institutions in other countries, all these make a reality of democratic rights and privileges for the working classes, that is, for the overwhelming majority of the population; they mean that it becomes really possible to use these rights and privileges in a way and on a scale that was never even approximately possible in the best democratic bourgeois republic.

The essence of Soviet power lies in this, that the permanent and sole foundation of the entire State power, of the entire State apparatus, is the mass organization of those very classes which were oppressed by the capitalists, that is, the workers and semi-proletarians (peasants who do not exploit labour and who are always forced to sell at least part of their labour). The masses, who even in the most democratic bourgeois republics, where in law they had equal rights, but in fact were prevented by a thousand ways and tricks from taking part in political life and making use of democratic rights and liberties, are now drawn into continuous, unhampered, and decisive participation in the democratic administration of the State.

15. The equality of citizens, regardless of sex, religious belief, race, nationality, which bourgeois democracy always promised everywhere but in fact never carried out, and could not carry out because of the rule of capitalism, has been made a complete reality at one stroke by the Soviet regime, or the proletarian dictatorship, for only the power of the workers, who are not interested in private property in the means of production and in the struggle for their distribution and redistribution, is able to do this.

16. The old democracy, that is, bourgeois democracy and parliamentarianism, was so organized that it was the working classes who were most alien to the administrative machine. The Soviet power, the proletarian dictatorship, on the other hand, is so organized that it brings the working masses close to the administrative machine. The merging of legislative and executive power in the Soviet organization of the State serves the same purpose, as does the substitution of the production unit, the workshop or factory, for the territorial constituency.

17. The army was an instrument of oppression not only under the monarchy; it is still that in all bourgeois republics, even the most democratic. Only the Soviet power, as the only established State organization of the very classes oppressed by the capitalists, is in a position to abolish the dependence of the military on the bourgeois command and really fuse the proletariat with the military, to arm the proletariat and disarm the bourgeoisie, without which the victory of socialism is impossible.

18. The Soviet organization of the State is designed to give the proletariat, as the class which was most concentrated and educated by capitalism, the leading role in the State. The experience of all revolutions and all movements of enslaved classes, the experience of the world socialist movement, teaches us that only the proletariat is in a position to unite the scattered and backward strata of the working and exploited population and carry them along.

19. Only the Soviet organization of the State is able to destroy, at one stroke and completely, the old, that is, the bourgeois apparatus of bureaucracy and judiciary, which under capitalism, even in the most democratic republics, remained and had to remain, being in fact for the workers and the working masses the greatest obstacle to making democracy effective. The Paris Commune took the first world historical step in this direction, the Soviet regime the second.

20. The abolition of State power is the goal of all socialists, including and above all Marx. Unless this goal is reached true democracy, that is, equality and freedom, is not attainable. But only Soviet and proletarian democracy leads in fact to this goal, for it begins at once to prepare for the complete withering away of any kind of State by drawing the mass organizations of the working people into constant and unrestricted participation in State administration.

21. The complete bankruptcy of the socialists who met in Berne, the complete absence of understanding which they showed of the new, that is, proletarian democracy, can be seen very clearly from the following. On 10 February 1919 Branting declared the international conference of the yellow international in Berne closed. On 11 February 1919 its members in Berlin published an appeal of the 'Independents' to the proletariat in *Freiheit*. In this appeal the bourgeois character of Scheidemann's government was admitted. It was reproached for wanting to abolish the workers' councils, which were called 'bearers and defenders' of the revolution, and the proposal was made to legalize the councils, to give them statutory rights, to give them the right to veto the decisions of the National Assembly and refer the question at issue to a national referendum.

Such a proposal reflects the complete intellectual bankruptcy of the theoreticians who defend democracy and have not understood its bourgeois character. The ridiculous attempt to unite the system of councils, that is, the proletarian dictatorship, with the National Assembly, that is, the dictatorship of the bourgeoisie, finally exposes the mental poverty of the yellow socialists and social-democrats, and their reactionary petty-bourgeois policy, as well as their cowardly concessions to the irresistibly growing forces of the new proletarian democracy.

22. The majority of the yellow international in Berne, who condemned bolshevism but did not dare, for fear of the working masses, to vote formally for a resolution on these lines, acted correctly from the class standpoint. This majority is completely at one with the Russian mensheviks and social-revolutionaries and with the Scheidemanns in Germany. The Russian mensheviks and social-revolutionaries, who complain of persecution by the bolsheviks, try to conceal the fact that this persecution was provoked by their participation in the civil war on the side of the bourgeoisie against the proletariat. In precisely the same way the Scheidemanns and their party in Germany took part in the civil war on the side of the bourgeoisie against the workers.

It is therefore quite natural that the majority of those attending the yellow international in Berne should come out in favour of condemning the bolsheviks. But that did not represent a defence of 'pure democracy'; it was the self-defence of people who feel that in the civil war they are on the side of the bourgeoisie against the proletariat.

For these reasons the decision of the majority of the yellow international must be described as correct from the class point of view. But the proletariat should not fear the truth, but look it straight in the face and draw the political conclusions which follow.

On the basis of these theses and having heard the reports of the delegates from various countries, the congress of the communist international declares that the chief tasks of the communist parties in countries where Soviet power is not yet established are:

1. To explain to the broad masses of the working class the historical meaning of the political and practical necessity of a new proletarian democracy which must replace bourgeois democracy and parliamentarianism.

2. To extend and build up workers' councils in all branches of industry, in the army and navy, and also among agricultural workers and small peasants.

3. To win an assured, conscious communist majority in the councils.

RESOLUTION CONSTITUTING THE COMMUNIST INTERNATIONAL PASSED AT ITS FIRST CONGRESS

4 *March* 1919   *Protokoll,* i, p. 131

[Eberlein, the only German delegate at the conference, had been explicitly instructed to oppose the formation of the Third International as premature. His party, he said during the discussion, was not opposed in principle, but considered that the conference in Moscow should do no more than lay down principles and put forward a provisional platform, defining their goals and methods of attaining them, which could then be used to test the strength of the forces available in other countries and establish the foundations on which they could unite. What was missing at the conference, he said, was the whole of western Europe. The German communists wished to know in advance that a new international would have the forces with which to support the proletarian struggle. Because of the importance of the German party, the Russian delegates at first agreed to regard the meeting as a preliminary conference, although Zinoviev made it clear that they considered the time ripe.

Zinoviev, answering Eberlein's objections to the immediate establishment of a new international, asked why it should be postponed.

'We have a victorious proletarian revolution in a great country. We have a powerful revolution moving towards victory in two countries, and are we still to say that we are too weak? Our device is the international Soviet republic, and nobody can call that utopian. We are convinced that this is a question of the immediate future, and are we to shrink from creating in the Third International the instrument for creating an international Soviet republic. . . . You want communist parties to be first established officially in all countries? You have a victorious revolution, and that is more than any formal foundation. You have in Germany a party marching to power which in a few months will establish a proletarian government. And are we still to delay? Nobody would understand it.' The decision to transform the conference into the foundation congress of the new international was taken after the belated arrival of the Austrian delegate, who gave an extremely optimistic account of the progress of revolution in central Europe. The resolution was moved by Rakovsky, Gruber (Steinhardt), Grimlund, and Rudniansky. It was carried, with Eberlein abstaining.

Balabanova, Zinoviev, Rakovsky, Trotsky, Lenin, and Platten, in the name of the 'Zimmerwald left', declared that they regarded the Zimmerwald organization dissolved, since 'all that was truly revolutionary in it' had now been taken over by the Third International.]

The representatives of the Communist Party of German-Austria, of the left Social-Democratic Party of Sweden, of the Social-Democratic Revolutionary Workers' Federation of the Balkans, of the Communist Party of Hungary, move that the Communist International be founded.

1. The fight for the dictatorship of the proletariat requires a united, resolute, international organization of all communist elements which adopt this platform.

2. The foundation of the Communist International is the more imperative since now at Berne, and possibly later elsewhere also, an attempt is being made to restore the old opportunist International and to rally to it all the confused and undecided elements of the proletariat. It is therefore essential to make a sharp break between the revolutionary proletariat and the social-traitor elements.

3. If the conference now sitting in Moscow were not to found the Third International, the impression would be created that the communist parties are not at one; this would weaken our position and increase the confusion among the undecided elements of the proletariat in all countries.

4. To constitute the Third International is therefore an unconditional historical imperative which must be put into effect by the international communist conference now sitting in Moscow.

PLATFORM OF THE COMMUNIST INTERNATIONAL ADOPTED BY THE
FIRST CONGRESS

4 *March* 1919   *Protokoll*, i, p. 185

[The platform was drafted by Bukharin. In seconding it Eberlein, the German delegate, suggested that it should be discussed by the revolutionary parties and organizations in the various countries before the new international was established. When the decision to found the Third International was taken, the platform was adopted with one abstention (Norway).]

The contradictions of the capitalist world system, which lay concealed within its womb, broke out with colossal force in a gigantic explosion, in the great imperialist world war.

Capitalism tried to overcome its own anarchy by organizing production. Instead of numerous competing businessmen, powerful capitalist associations (syndicates, cartels, trusts) were formed; bank capital united with industrial capital; all economic life was dominated by the finance-capitalist oligarchy, who attained sole dominion by organizing on the basis of this power. Monopoly took the place of free competition. The individual capitalist became a trust-capitalist. Insane anarchy was replaced by organization.

But while in each country the anarchy of the capitalist mode of production was superseded by capitalist organization, the contradictions, the competitive struggle, and the anarchy in world economy grew ever sharper. The struggle between the largest organized robber States led with iron necessity to the monstrous imperialist world war. Greed for profits drove world capital to fight for new markets, new investment openings, new raw material sources, the cheap labour power of colonial slaves. The imperialist States which divided the entire world among themselves, which had changed many millions of African, Asiatic, Australian, and American proletarians and peasants into beasts of burden, had sooner or later to expose the true anarchist nature of capital in that tremendous conflict. This was the origin of the greatest of all crimes—the predatory world war.

Capitalism also tried to eliminate the contradictions in its social structure. Bourgeois society is a class society. In the greatest 'civilized' States capital wanted to gloss over social contradictions. At the expense of the plundered colonial peoples capital corrupted its wage slaves, created a community of interest between the exploited and the exploiters as against the oppressed colonies—the yellow, black, and red colonial peoples—and chained the European and American working class to the imperialist 'fatherland'.

But the same method of steady corruption which created the patriotism of the working class and its moral submission was changed by the war into its opposite. Physical annihilation, the complete enslavement of the proletariat, tremendous oppression, impoverishment and deterioration, world famine—these were the final fruits of civil peace. It broke down. *The imperialist war changed into civil war.*

A new epoch is born! The epoch of the dissolution of capitalism, of its inner disintegration. *The epoch of the communist revolution of the proletariat.*

The imperialist system is breaking down. Ferment in the colonies, ferment among the former dependent small nations, insurrections of the proletariat, victorious proletarian revolutions in some countries, dissolution of imperialist armies, complete incapacity of the ruling classes to continue to guide the destinies of the peoples—this is the state of affairs throughout the world today.

Humanity, whose entire civilization now lies in ruins, is threatened with complete annihilation. There is only one force that can save it, and that is the proletariat. The old capitalist 'order' no longer exists; it can no longer exist. The final outcome of the capitalist system of production is chaos. And this chaos can only be overcome by the largest class, the productive class, the working class. It must create genuine order, communist order.

It must destroy the rule of capital, make war impossible, abolish State frontiers, change the entire world into one co-operative community, make a reality of the brotherhood and freedom of the peoples.

On the other side, world capital is arming for the last fight. Under the cloak of the 'League of Nations', pouring out torrents of pacifist words, it is making its last efforts to patch together again the capitalist system, which is spontaneously breaking up, and to turn its forces against the steadily growing proletarian revolution. The proletariat must answer this new and monstrous conspiracy of the capitalist class by conquering power, turning this power against its class enemies and using it as a lever for starting the economic revolution. The final victory of the world proletariat means the beginning of the real history of liberated humanity.

1. THE CONQUEST OF POLITICAL POWER

The conquest of political power by the proletariat means the annihilation of the political power of the bourgeoisie. The bourgeoisie's most powerful means of exercising power is the bourgeois State machine with its bourgeois army led by bourgeois-junker officers, its police and gendarmerie, its prison governors and judges, its priests, officials, etc. The conquest of political power means not only a change in ministry personnel, but the annihilation of the enemy's State apparatus, the conquest of real strength, the disarming of the bourgeoisie, of the counter-revolutionary officers, of the white guards, and the arming of the proletariat, of the revolutionary soldiery, of the red workers' guard; the dismissal of all bourgeois judges and the establishment of proletarian courts; the abolition of the rule of reactionary State officials and the creation of new proletarian organs of administration. The victory of the proletariat lies in shattering the organization of the enemy power and organizing proletarian power; it consists in the destruction of the bourgeois State machine and the construction of the proletarian State machine. Only after the proletariat has won victory and broken the resistance of the bourgeoisie can it make its former enemies of use in the new order by bringing them under its control and gradually drawing them into the work of communist construction.

2. DEMOCRACY AND DICTATORSHIP

Like all States, the proletarian State is an instrument of repression, but it is directed against the enemies of the working class. Its purpose is to break the resistance of the exploiters, who use every means at their disposal in the desperate struggle to drown the revolution in blood, to make their resistance impossible. The dictatorship of the proletariat, which openly gives the proletariat a privileged position in society, is however a provisional institution. As the resistance of the bourgeoisie is broken, as they are expropriated, and changed gradually into a working stratum, the proletarian dictatorship disappears, the State withers away, and with the State classes themselves.

So-called democracy, i.e. bourgeois democracy, is nothing but the concealed dictatorship of the bourgeoisie. The much praised 'general will of the people' exists no more than 'the people' as a whole exists. What does really exist are classes with opposed and incompatible wills. But since the bourgeoisie are a small minority they need this fiction, this fraud of the national 'people's will', so that behind these high-sounding words they can consolidate their rule over the working classes and impose on them their own class will. As against this the proletariat, as the vast majority of the population, openly uses the class power of its mass organizations, its Soviets, to abolish the privileges of the bourgeoisie and to ensure the transition to the classless communist society.

In bourgeois democracy the emphasis lies in purely formal declarations of rights and liberties, though for the working people, for the proletarians and semi-proletarians without any material means, these are unattainable, while the bourgeoisie use their material resources, their press and their organizations, to cheat and deceive. As against this the Soviet system, this new type of State power, puts chief weight on giving the proletariat the opportunity of making a reality of its rights and liberties. The Soviet regime gives the best palaces, houses, printing works, paper stocks, to the people for their press, their meetings, their unions. Only in this way is it possible to have real proletarian democracy.

It is only on paper that bourgeois democracy with its parliamentary system gives the masses a share in the administration of the State. In fact the masses and their organizations are completely cut off from real power and the real State administration. In the Soviet system administration is through the mass organizations, and through them the masses themselves, as the Soviets draw ever-growing numbers of workers into the State administration; this is the only way in which the entire working people will gradually be drawn into the State administration. The Soviet system is thus based on the mass organizations of the proletariat, on the Soviets themselves, the revolutionary trade unions, co-operatives, etc.

By separating the legislative and executive powers, by the absence of the power to recall parliamentary mandates, bourgeois democracy and the parliamentary system widen the gulf between the masses and the State. The Soviet system, on the contrary, with its right of recall, its merging of legislative and executive power, the character of the Soviets as working collegia, unites the masses with the organs of administration; and the same object is promoted by the Soviet electoral system which is based, not on artificial territorial constituencies, but on the production unit.

Thus the Soviet system brings about genuine proletarian democracy,

democracy by and for the proletariat against the bourgeoisie. In this system the industrial proletariat is privileged as the leading, best-organized, and politically most mature class, under whose hegemony the level of the semi-proletarians and the small peasants is gradually raised. These temporary privileges of the industrial proletariat must be used to free the poorer petty-bourgeois masses in the countryside from the influence of the large peasants and the bourgeoisie, and to organize and train them for co-operation in building the communist system.

3. EXPROPRIATION OF THE BOURGEOISIE AND THE SOCIALIZATION OF PRODUCTION

In the given class relationships the dissolution of the capitalist order and of capitalist labour discipline makes it impossible to reconstruct production on its former basis. The workers' wage struggles, even when they are successful, do not bring the hoped-for improvement in their conditions of life, for soaring prices of all consumption commodities make every success illusory. The condition of life of the workers can be improved only if the proletariat, and not the bourgeoisie, controls production. The pressure of the mighty wage struggles of the workers in all countries, which clearly reflect their desperate plight, and which tend to become universal, makes the continuation of capitalist production impossible. To raise the productive forces, to break as quickly as possible the resistance of the bourgeoisie, which prolongs the death agony of the old society and hence threatens economic life with complete ruin, the proletarian dictatorship must expropriate the big bourgeoisie and the junkers and make the means of production and exchange the common property of the proletarian State.

Communism is now being born out of the ruins of capitalism; history offers no other way out for mankind. The opportunists who put forward the utopian demand for the reconstruction of capitalist society in order to postpone nationalization, only prolong the process of dissolution, which involves the danger of complete ruin. The communist revolution is both the best and the only method by which the most important productive force—the proletariat—and with it society itself, can be maintained.

Proletarian dictatorship does not by any means involve any sharing out of the means of production and distribution. On the contrary; its purpose is to centralize the forces of production even more and to subordinate production as a whole to a unified plan.

The first steps towards nationalization of the entire economy will include: The nationalization of the big banks, which now control production; the seizure of the economic organs of the capitalist State and their transference to the proletarian State power; taking over all municipal undertakings, the nationalization of industries organized in syndicates and trusts, and of those branches of industry in which the concentration and centralization of capital makes this technically feasible; the nationalization of large agricultural estates and their transformation into socially managed agricultural undertakings.

As to small concerns, the proletariat must gradually amalgamate them by ways appropriate to their size.

In this connexion it must be expressly emphasized that small properties will not be expropriated, and that proprietors who do not exploit any wage labour will not be subject to any coercive measures. This stratum is to be gradually drawn into socialist organization by example, by the practical demonstration of the advantages following from the new regime, a regime which will liberate the small peasants and the urban petty-bourgeoisie from the economic pressure of usury-capital and the junkers, from the burden of taxation (particularly by the cancellation of the public debt, etc.).

The task of the proletarian dictatorship in the economic sphere can only be accomplished in conditions which enable the proletariat to create centralized organs for the management of production and to make a reality of workers' management. In this work it will necessarily use those mass organizations which are most closely integrated with the production process.

In the field of distribution the proletarian dictatorship must replace trade by the correct distribution of goods; steps towards this include the following measures: the nationalization of wholesale businesses, the taking over by the proletariat of all bourgeois State and municipal distributive machinery, control of the large co-operative associations, whose organization will continue to play an important economic part in the transition epoch; the gradual centralization of all these organs and their transformation into a unified whole effecting a rational distribution of goods.

In distribution, as in production, all skilled technicians and specialists are to be used when their political resistance has been broken and they have learned to adapt themselves not to capital, but to the new system of production.

The proletariat will not oppress them, but will, for the first time, give them the opportunity of developing the most intensive creative work. The proletarian dictatorship will replace the separation of manual and mental work, which capitalism encouraged, by their co-operation and in this way unite science with labour.

In addition to the expropriation of factories, mines, estates, etc., the proletariat must also abolish the exploitation of the population by capitalist landlords, hand large houses over to the local workers' councils, move workers into bourgeois houses, etc.

During this period of great changes the Soviet power must continue steadily to centralize the entire administrative machinery, at the same time drawing ever larger sections of the working people into direct administration.

4. THE ROAD TO VICTORY

The revolutionary epoch demands that the proletariat use those methods of struggle which concentrate its entire energy, namely the methods of mass action leading logically to direct clashes with the bourgeois State machine in open struggle. All other methods, as for example the revolutionary use of bourgeois parliaments, must be subordinated to this purpose.

For success in this struggle it is necessary to break not only with the outright lackeys of capital and the hangmen of the communist revolution —the part played by the right-wing social-democrats—but also with the 'centre' (Kautskyites) which, in the most critical moments, deserts the proletariat in order to flirt with its avowed enemies.

On the other hand it is necessary to form a bloc with those elements in the revolutionary workers' movement who, although they did not formerly belong to the socialist party, now adhere by and large to the standpoint of proletarian dictatorship in the form of Soviet power, e.g. certain elements in syndicalism.

The growth of the revolutionary movement in all countries, the danger that the alliance of capitalist States will strangle this movement, the attempts of the parties of social traitors to unite (the formation of the 'yellow international' at Berne) in order to perform services for Wilson's League, finally the absolute necessity of co-ordinating proletarian action— all this must lead to the foundation of a truly revolutionary, truly proletarian, communist international.

The International, which subordinates so-called national interests to the interests of the international revolution, will embody the mutual aid of the proletariat of different countries, for without economic and other mutual aid the proletariat will not be in a position to organize the new society. On the other hand, in contrast to the yellow social-patriotic international, international proletarian communism will support the exploited colonial peoples in their struggles against imperialism, in order to promote the final downfall of the imperialist world system.

On the outbreak of war the capitalist criminals maintained that they were only defending their common fatherland. But by its bloody actions in Russia, in the Ukraine, in Finland, German imperialism quickly revealed its true predatory nature. Now the Entente States are being unmasked before the eyes of even backward strata of the population, and they are revealed as robbers and murderers of the proletariat. Together with the German bourgeoisie and social-patriots, with hypocritical words of peace on their lips, they are using their arms and their brutalized barbarous colonial troops to strangle the revolution of the European proletariat. Indescribable is the white terror of the bourgeois cannibals.

Innumerable are its victims in the working class. The best—Liebknecht, Luxemburg—are lost.

The proletariat must defend itself, at any cost. The communist international calls the entire world proletariat to this last fight, weapon against weapon, force against force.

Down with the imperialist conspiracy of capital!

Long live the international republic of proletarian soviets!

EXTRACTS FROM THE RESOLUTION OF THE FIRST COMINTERN CONGRESS
ON THE BERNE CONFERENCE OF THE PARTIES OF THE SECOND INTER-
NATIONAL

5 *March* 1919   *Protokoll*, i, p. 163

[This resolution was drafted by Zinoviev and passed unanimously. The Berne conference of parties of the Second International was held from 3 to 10 February 1919; it was attended by 98 delegates from 26 countries. The Italian, Swiss, Serbian, and Bulgarian socialist parties refused to attend because the congress was convened by 'reactionaries'; the Belgian because the Germans had been invited. Many delegates—in particular the French and Austrians—were profoundly critical of official social-democratic policy. It was proposed to send a delegation to Russia, to study the political and economic situation there and report back. Permission for their entry was given by the Soviet Government (against the opposition of some leading Bolsheviks, who argued that if such a delegation did not condemn the revolution they would be condemning themselves) but the proposal fell through. The congress elected a committee to make arrangements for the reconstitution of the Second International.]

I

As early as 1907, at the international socialist congress at Stuttgart which discussed questions of colonial policy and imperialist war, it was clear that more than half the Second International, and the majority of its leaders, held views on these questions much closer to those of the bourgeoisie than to those of Marx and Engels. Nevertheless the Stuttgart congress accepted an amendment moved by the representatives of the revolutionary wing, N. Lenin and Rosa Luxemburg, which ran as follows:

'If, however, a war should break out, socialists are obliged to intervene to bring it to an end as quickly as possible, and to exploit in every way the economic and political crisis created by the war to stir up the people and so to accelerate the overthrow of capitalist rule. . . .'

Even at the end of July and beginning of August 1914, 24 hours before the outbreak of the world war, the leading organs and bodies of the Second International continued to condemn the approaching war as the greatest crime of the bourgeoisie. The statements issued by the leading parties of the Second International at that time serve as the most eloquent accusation against its leaders.

At the first shot in the mass slaughter, the chief parties of the Second International betrayed the working class, and each of them, on the pretext of 'defence of the fatherland', went over to the side of 'its' bourgeoisie. . . . It was at that moment that the Second International finally reached bankruptcy and perished. . . .

Three basic trends were already visible within the Second International. In the course of the war, up to the beginning of the proletarian revolution in Europe, their outlines emerged with unmistakable clarity.

1. The social-chauvinist trend (the 'majority' trend), whose most typical representatives are the German social-democrats now sharing power with the German bourgeoisie, who were later to become the murderers of the leaders of the Communist International, Karl Liebknecht and Rosa Luxemburg. The social-chauvinists have now exposed themselves completely as class enemies of the proletariat, and are following the programme for 'liquidating' the war prescribed by the bourgeoisie: shunting the greater part of the tax burden on to the working masses; leaving private property untouched; leaving the army in the hands of the bourgeoisie; dissolving the workers' councils which are springing up everywhere; leaving political power in the hands of the bourgeoisie; supporting bourgeois democracy against socialism.

Although the communists have up to now fought vigorously against the 'majority socialists', the workers have not yet grasped the danger threatening the international proletariat from these traitors. One of the most important tasks of the international proletarian revolution is to open the workers' eyes to this Judas-work of the social-chauvinists, and with armed hand to make this counter-revolutionary party harmless.

2. The 'centrist' trend (social pacifists, Kautskyites, Independents). This trend began to be formed even before the war, chiefly in Germany. On the outbreak of war the 'centre' nearly everywhere occupied roughly the same ground as the social-chauvinists. The theoretical leader of the 'centre', Kautsky, came forward with a defence of the policy pursued by the German and French social-chauvinists. The International was only a 'peace-time instrument'. 'Fight for peace', 'the class struggle in peacetime'—these were Kautsky's slogans. After war broke out the 'centre' insisted on 'unity' with the social-chauvinists. After the murder of Liebknecht and Luxemburg the 'centre' again preached the same 'unity', that is, the unity of communist workers with the murderers of the communist leaders, Liebknecht and Rosa Luxemburg.

Early in the war the 'centre' (Kautsky, Viktor Adler, Turati, MacDonald), began to advocate a 'reciprocal amnesty', to be valid for the leaders of the social-chauvinist parties of Germany and Austria on the one side, and France and England on the other. The 'centre' is still advocating this amnesty today, after the war has ended, and thus prevents the workers getting a clear understanding of the causes of the breakdown of the Second International. The centre has sent its representatives to Berne, to the international conference of compromising socialists, and has thus made it easier for the Scheidemanns and Renaudels to deceive the workers.

It is absolutely essential to split the most revolutionary elements off from the 'centre'; this can be done only by the ruthless criticism and exposure of the 'centrist' leaders. The organizational break with the 'centre' is an absolute historical necessity. It is the task of the communists in each country to determine the moment for this break, according to the stage of development which the movement has reached there.

3. Communists. In the Second International, where this trend put forward communist-Marxist views on war and the tasks of the proletariat (the Lenin–Luxemburg resolution, Stuttgart, 1907), they remained a minority. The 'left radical' group (later the Spartakus group) in Germany, the Bolshevik party in Russia, the Tribunists in Holland, the youth group in Sweden, the left wing of the Youth International in a number of countries, formed the first kernel of the new international.

Faithful to the interests of the working class, this trend from the beginning of the war proclaimed as its slogan: Turn the imperialist war into a civil war. This trend has now constituted itself the Third International.

II

The Berne socialist conference of February 1919 was an attempt to galvanize the corpse of the Second International. The composition of the Berne conference shows clearly that the revolutionary proletariat of the world has nothing in common with this conference.

The victorious proletariat of Russia, the heroic proletariat of Germany, the Italian proletariat, the communist section of the proletariat of Austria and Hungary, the proletariat of Switzerland, the working class of Bulgaria, Rumania, Serbia, the left-wing workers' parties of Sweden, Norway, Finland, and the Ukraine, the Lettish and Polish proletariat, the best part of the organized English proletariat, the Youth International and the Women's International, demonstratively refused to take part in the Berne conference of social-patriots.

Of the participants, those who still have some contact with the real workers' movement of our time formed an opposition group, which, at least in the chief question—'Appraisal of the Russian Revolution'—opposed the doings of the social-patriots. The declaration of the French comrade Loriot, who scourged the majority of the Berne conference as servants of the bourgeoisie, represents the real opinion of all class-conscious workers throughout the world.

On the so-called 'guilt' question the Berne conference did not escape from the bourgeois ideological frame. The German and French social-patriots made the same charges against each other as the German and French bourgeoisie. The Berne conference lost its way in a flood of petty details about what this or that bourgeois minister had done before the war, and refused to see that capitalism, the finance-capitalists of both coalitions, and their social-patriot lackeys, are those primarily guilty. The social-patriot majority at Berne wanted to find out who were chiefly responsible for the war. They had only to look in a mirror, and they would have recognized themselves all as guilty. . . .

The most reactionary representative of the imperialist bourgeoisie, M. Clemenceau, acknowledged the service rendered to imperialist reaction by the Berne conference of social-patriots by receiving a delegation from the conference and suggesting that they take part in all the relevant commissions of the imperialist conference at Paris.

On the colonial question it emerged clearly that the Berne conference was at one with those liberal-bourgeois colonial politicians who find nothing wrong in the exploitation and enslavement of colonies by the imperialist bourgeoisie, but try to plaster it over with humanitarian and philanthropic phrases. The German social-patriots demanded that the German colonies should continue to belong to the German Reich, that is, that German capital should continue to exploit these colonies. The disagreements which thereupon came to light showed that the social-patriots of the Entente have the same slave-holders' attitude, and think it quite natural that French and English capital should continue to enslave French and English colonies. In this the Berne conference showed that it had completely forgotten the slogan: 'Clear out of the colonies.'

In its appraisal of the 'League of Nations' the Berne conference showed that it was treading in the footsteps of those bourgeois elements who want to use the deceptive illusion of the so-called League of Nations to conjure away the proletarian revolution which is advancing throughout the world. Instead of exposing the goings-on at the Paris conference as haggling with nations and economic areas, the Berne conference seconded Paris by degrading itself into its instrument. The obsequious attitude of the conference, which left to a bourgeois government conference in Paris the question of labour legislation, shows that the social-patriots were knowingly in favour of maintaining capitalist wage slavery and are ready to let the working class be put off with petty reforms.

It was only the efforts of the opposition which defeated the attempt, inspired by the policy of the bourgeoisie, to get the Berne conference to pass a resolution which would have provided a cover for any future armed intervention in Russia. This victory of the Berne opposition over the outspoken chauvinist elements provides indirect proof that the proletariat of western Europe sympathizes with the Russian proletarian revolution and is ready to fight against the imperialist bourgeoisie.

The fear that these lackeys of the bourgeoisie feel for the inevitable extension of the workers' council movement can be seen in their anxiety to avoid spending any time whatever on this world-historical phenomenon. The workers' councils are the most important phenomenon since the Paris Commune. By ignoring them, the Berne conference publicly proclaimed its moral poverty and theoretical bankruptcy.

The congress of the Communist International considers the 'International' which the Berne conference is trying to establish a yellow strike-breaking international, which is and will remain nothing but a tool of the bourgeoisie.

The congress calls on the workers of all countries to start a resolute fight against the yellow international and to warn the broad masses of the proletariat against this lying and fraudulent international.

EXTRACTS FROM THE APPEAL OF THE FIRST CONGRESS OF THE COMMUNIST INTERNATIONAL TO THE WORKERS OF ALL COUNTRIES

5 *March* 1919   *Protokoll*, i, p. 195

[The landing of Allied troops in Russia in the early summer of 1918 had given rise to a series of protests and appeals by the Soviet Government.

On 18 April 1919 Chicherin, Soviet Commissar for Foreign Affairs, issued an appeal 'to the workers of the Allied countries' to protest against the blockade of Russia, against intervention, and against support by the western governments of anti-Soviet plots in the countries bordering on Russia. 'It is none other than your rulers who are keeping civil war alive among us by giving help to the brutal counter-revolutionaries and creating hunger and unemployment by the criminal blockade of Soviet Russia.'

On 20 October 1919 Chicherin addressed a warning to the German Government, and to the governments of the European countries which had remained neutral in the war, that their agreement to the Allied request to join in the blockade would be considered a hostile act. In the absence of any official diplomatic contacts, these messages were sent out by radio. Statements such as the present appeal were widely used by the Soviet Government to announce and promote its policy. The Communist International provided a useful channel. The blockade was lifted in January 1920.]

The first congress of the Third International, assembled on 5 March 1919 in the Kremlin, expresses its grateful admiration to the Russian revolutionary proletariat and to its directing party, the Communist Party of Bolsheviks.

The great revolution, undertaken to guide socialist doctrine, so long corrupted by the opportunists, back to its original source, Marxism, the superhuman efforts made for nearly a year and a half to create, in the place of the old bourgeois world, a new communist social order, both in moral and intellectual culture, as well as in the material spheres, collective or individual, of political, economic, and social life, the help given at all times to the workers of all countries against their militarist and despotic governments—all this must call forth the universal and enthusiastic approval of the working class of all countries. . . .

It is not the fault of the Soviet system or of bolshevism that this goal has not yet been reached, that the population of Central Russia are suffering from hunger and from a growing shortage of finished products. On the contrary, it was only the Soviet system and bolshevism which made it possible to put a complete end to the anarchy and chaos provoked by Kerensky and bourgeois democracy; they alone enabled the country to keep economic life going at its present level.

The responsibility for the crisis rests solely on the internal and external enemies of the Soviet regime, for by sabotage, plots, and military intervention they compelled Russia to spend a great part of its strength, its man-power, and its resources on the creation of a new army.

Despite their burning desire for peace, the entire Russian people courageously recognized and accepted this necessity. Everybody knows with what extraordinary success the Soviet power managed to carry out this immense task. The blame may be put on bolshevism, but the best way of finding out whether it is to blame or not would be for the Entente Powers to cease forcing the Soviet power to defend itself by arms.

To do that they must not only stop sending armed forces to Russia and evacuate its ports; they must also refrain from exerting any pressure inside the country, they must cease to support with money, arms, and advisers the counter-revolutionary bands which without the help of the Entente would soon melt away of themselves.

Then the soldiers of the Red Army could return to their families, and the best workers, the most devoted organizers, the most skilled engineers would be at the disposal of the Soviet power. Their activities in peaceful economic labour would soon yield the most substantial results.

It should not be forgotten, however, that the young Russian industry never was able to manage without foreign assistance. The Entente is paralysing the new economic organization by forbidding the foreign specialists, who in fact used to manage Russian industry, to return to Russia. It is hampering the equipment and maintenance of the factories, the transport of raw materials and fuel; it is condemning industry to ruin and the people to unemployment by prohibiting the import into Russia of machinery, trucks, and locomotives. . . .

More than once the Soviet Republic has officially expressed its desire to continue to call on the help of foreign industry and specialists; it has stated its readiness to pay a high price for their services, which are at the present time indispensable to the prosperity of Russian economic life. But the Entente, without even troubling to answer these proposals, is operating a strict blockade, using threats and force against Russia and even against the Central Powers and neutral countries.

The working masses of all countries must demand of their governments a genuine renunciation of any direct or indirect intervention in Soviet Russian affairs. To give these demands a precise form, the congress of the Third International proposes to all peoples the following programme of action.

The honour, independence, and most elementary interests of the proletariat of all countries demand that they should immediately act and use all means at their disposal, if necessary, revolutionary means, to give effect to the following demands:

1. Non-intervention by the Entente in the internal affairs of Soviet Russia.
2. Immediate recall of all Allied European and Asiatic troops now in Russia.
3. Abandonment of any direct or indirect policy of intervention, whether it takes the form of provocation or of material and moral support for the Russian counter-revolutionaries or the reactionary border States.
4. Cancellation of treaties already concluded contemplating intervention by the given State, by Russian counter-revolutionaries, or by countries bordering on Russia, in the internal affairs of the Soviet Republic; immediate return to their countries of the diplomatic and military missions which the Entente governments dispatched to north and south Russia, to Rumania, Finland, Poland, and the Czech countries with the object of stirring up struggle against the Soviet Republics.
5. Recognition of the Soviet Government which after being eighteen months in existence is stronger and more popular than ever.
6. Re-establishment of diplomatic relations, carrying with it the sending of official representatives (socialists) to Russia and the recognition of Russian representatives abroad.
7. The admission to the peace conference of delegates of the Soviet Government as the representatives, and indeed the only representatives, of the Russian people. A European peace negotiated and concluded without Russia would be in the highest degree unstable. It would be odious and ridiculous to admit to the conference, in the absence of the bolsheviks, or even alongside them, as representatives of the whole of Russia or a part of Russia, those mountebanks

forming the various regional governments artificially created by the
Allies, existing only thanks to Allied support, and who, moreover,
stand for practically nothing but a few personal aspirations and
interests.

8. Cessation of the economic blockade which may soon condemn
   Russia to industrial ruin and hunger.
9. Resumption of tráde relations and conclusion of trade agreements.
10. Dispatch to Russia of a few hundred or rather a few thousand
    organizers, engineers, instructors, and skilled workmen, in particular
    metal workers, to give the young socialist republic real help in the
    industrial field, above all in carrying out the most important tasks,
    the restoration of rolling-stock and of the railways, and the organiza-
    tion of transport.

EXTRACTS FROM THE THESES ON THE INTERNATIONAL SITUATION AND
THE POLICY OF THE ENTENTE ADOPTED BY THE FIRST COMINTERN
CONGRESS

6 *March* 1919   *Beschlüsse des ersten Kongresses,* p. 53

[These theses were drafted by Obolensky-Osinsky, one of the non-voting Russian
delegates. A review of the international situation was customary at all communist party congresses. The invitation to all de facto Russian governments to
a conference at Prinkipo, suggested by Lloyd George, was supported by President Wilson and approved by the Council of Ten at the Paris peace conference.
The Soviet Government accepted the invitation, but the conference was not
held.]

The events of the world war exposed the imperialist policy of the bourgeois 'democracies' as the militant policy of the great Powers aimed at
carving up the world and consolidating the economic and political dictatorship of finance capital over the exploited and oppressed masses. The
killing and crippling of millions of men, the impoverishment and enslavement of the proletariat, the unparalleled enrichment of the upper strata of
the bourgeoisie through war contracts, loans, etc., the triumph of military
reaction in all countries—all this began to destroy the illusions of national
defence, of civil peace, and of 'democracy'. The 'peace policy' is revealing
the real aims of the bourgeoisie of all countries and making the exposure
final.

THE BREST-LITOVSK PEACE AND THE EXPOSURE OF GERMAN IMPERIALISM

The Brest-Litovsk peace, and subsequently the treaty of Bucharest,
revealed the predatory and reactionary character of the imperialism of the
Central Powers. The victors wrung indemnities and annexations from

defenceless Russia. They used the right of national self-determination as cover for an annexationist policy by creating vassal States whose reactionary governments promoted their predatory policy and suppressed the revolutionary movement of the working masses. . . .

THE VICTORY OF THE ENTENTE AND THE ALIGNMENT OF STATES

The victory of the Entente has divided the so-called civilized countries of the world into the following groups: the first group consists of the lords of the capitalist world, the victorious imperialist great Powers (England, America, France, Japan, and Italy). Opposed to them are the countries of defeated imperialism, broken by war and their structure shaken by the beginning of the proletarian revolution (Germany, Austria, Hungary, and their former vassals). The vassal States of the Entente Powers form the third group. It consists of the small capitalist States who fought the war on the side of the Entente (Belgium, Serbia, Portugal, etc.), and also of the recently created 'national' republics and buffer States (Czechoslovakia, Poland, Russian counter-revolutionary republics, etc.). The position of the neutral States is approximately that of the vassal States, but they are subject to heavy political and economic pressure which at times makes their position similar to that of the defeated States. The socialist republic of Russia is a workers' and peasants' State standing apart from the capitalist world and representing a tremendous social danger for victorious imperialism, the danger that all the fruits of victory will be lost in the flood of world revolution.

ENTENTE IMPERIALISM'S 'PEACE POLICY' AND ITS SELF-EXPOSURE

The 'peace policy' of the five ruling Powers was and is, when we regard it as a whole, one of continuous self-revelation.

Notwithstanding all the talk about their 'democratic foreign policy', it represents the complete triumph of secret diplomacy, deciding the fate of the world by arrangements between the agents of the financial trusts behind the backs and at the expense of the millions of workers of all countries. All important questions without exception are decided by the Paris committee of the five great Powers behind closed doors, in the absence of representatives of the defeated and neutral countries, and even of the vassal States.

The speeches of Lloyd George, Clemenceau, Sonnino, etc., frankly proclaim and justify the need for annexations and indemnities.

Regardless of lying words about the 'war for universal disarmament', the need for further armaments and in particular for the maintenance of British sea power, ostensibly 'to safeguard the freedom of the seas', is openly announced.

The right of national self-determination proclaimed by the Entente is publicly trampled under foot and for it is substituted the division of the disputed areas among the ruling States and their vassals.

Alsace-Lorraine has been incorporated in France without consulting its population; Ireland, Egypt, India, have no right of national self-determination; the Yugoslav State and the Czechoslovak Republic were established by armed force; shameless haggling is going on about the division of European and Asiatic Turkey, the distribution of the German colonies has in fact already begun, and so on.

The policy of indemnities has been pushed to the point of complete plundering of the defeated countries; they are not only presented with bills running into many milliards, they are not only deprived of all weapons, but the Entente countries are also taking their locomotives, railway trucks, ships, agricultural equipment, gold stocks, etc., and in addition the prisoners of war are to be made the slaves of the victors. Proposals for compulsory labour service for German workers are being discussed. The Allied Powers intend to impoverish them and make them the hungry slaves of Entente capital. . . .

Reaction is in the saddle both within the Entente countries themselves— France has reverted to the worst features of Napoleon III—as well as throughout the capitalist world which is under Entente influence. The Allies are strangling the revolution in the occupied areas of Germany, in Hungary, Bulgaria, etc.; they are inciting the bourgeois-opportunist governments of the defeated countries against the revolutionary workers by threatening the withdrawal of food supplies. The Allies have stated that they will sink all German ships which dare to raise the red flag of revolution; they have refused to recognize the German workers' councils; they have abolished the eight-hour day in the occupied parts of Germany. Quite apart from supporting reactionary policies in the neutral States and promoting them in the vassal States (the Paderewski regime in Poland), the Allies are inciting the reactionary elements in these countries (Finland, Poland, Sweden, etc.) against revolutionary Russia and demanding the intervention of German armed forces.

CONTRADICTIONS AMONG THE ENTENTE STATES

A number of profound contradictions are appearing among the great Powers who rule the capitalist world, despite the similarity of the basic features of their imperialist policy.

These contradictions are focused mainly on the peace programme of American finance capital (the so-called Wilson programme). The most important points in this programme are: 'freedom of the seas', 'the League of Nations', and 'internationalization of colonies'. The slogan of freedom of the seas—stripped of its hypocritical cloak—means in fact the abolition of the supremacy of some great Powers (primarily England) at sea and the opening of all sea routes to American trade. The League of Nations means that the European great Powers (primarily France) are refused the right of directly annexing the weaker States and peoples. The internationalization of colonies has the same significance in regard to colonial areas.

This programme derives from the fact that American capital . . . has no possibility of making direct annexations in Europe and therefore contemplates the exploitation of weak States and peoples by means of trade and capital investment. . . . In the field of economic exploitation highly-developed American finance capital will win hegemony and thus be able to secure for itself world economic and political supremacy.

The 'freedom of the seas' is in most acute conflict with the interests of England and Japan, and partly also of Italy (in the Adriatic). The 'League of Nations' and the 'internationalization of colonies' are most emphatically in conflict with the interests of France and Japan, and to a lesser extent with the interests of all other imperialist Powers. Imperialist France, where industrial development is weak and the forces of production have been completely shattered by the war, is resorting to the most desperate means to maintain the capitalist regime; these include the savage spoliation of Germany, the subjection and predatory exploitation of the vassal States (proposals for a Danubian federation, for a South Slav State), and the squeezing out by force of the debts incurred by Russian Tsarism to the French Shylock. . . .

While the interests of the great Powers conflict with those of America, they also conflict with one another. England fears a strengthening of France on the continent; in Asia Minor and Africa its interests are incompatible with French interests. Italy's interests in the Balkan peninsula and the Tyrol are in conflict with French interests. Japan disputes the Pacific islands with English Australia, etc.

GROUPS AND TRENDS WITHIN THE ENTENTE

These contradictions among the great Powers lead to various combinations within the Entente; the two principal combinations which have emerged are the French-English-Japanese combination, directed against America and Italy, and the Anglo-American, which is opposed to the other great Powers. . . .

The Anglo-American bloc is opposed to French priority in the spoliation of Germany and to its excessive intensity. It places certain limitations on the exaggerated annexationist demands of France, Italy, and Japan. It prevents the newly formed vassal States from being directly subjected to them. In the Russian question the Anglo-American combination is more peacefully inclined; it wants a free hand to complete the partition of the world, to strangle the European revolution, and then to turn to the suppression of the Russian revolution.

These two combinations of Powers correspond to two trends, one the extreme annexationist, the other the more moderate; the Wilson–Lloyd George combination supports the latter.

THE 'LEAGUE OF NATIONS'

Faced by the irreconcilable contradictions which have made their appearance within the Entente itself, the League of Nations—if it should come into formal existence—will only play the part of a Holy Alliance of the capitalists to suppress the workers' revolution. Propaganda for the 'League of Nations' is the best way of introducing confusion into the revolutionary consciousness of the working class. Instead of the slogan of an international union of revolutionary workers' republics, the slogan of an international association of sham democracies is put forward, to be attained by class collaboration between the proletariat and the bourgeoisie.

The 'League of Nations' is a delusive slogan by means of which the social-traitors, acting on behalf of international capital, split the forces of the proletariat and promote the imperialist counter-revolution.

The revolutionary proletariat of all countries of the world must wage an irreconcilable struggle against the idea of the Wilsonian 'League of Nations' and protest against entry into this League of robbery, of exploitation, and of imperialist counter-revolution.

FOREIGN AND DOMESTIC POLICY IN THE DEFEATED COUNTRIES

The crushing military defeat and the internal collapse of Austrian and German imperialism brought bourgeois-social-opportunist regimes to power in the first period of the revolution in the Central States. Behind the shield of democracy and socialism the German social-traitors are defending and restoring the economic rule and the political dictatorship of the bourgeoisie. In their foreign policy they are trying to re-establish German imperialism by demanding the return of the colonies and the admission of Germany to the predatory League of Nations. . . . At the same time the bourgeois-social-opportunist Government is undermining the international solidarity of the proletariat and separating the German workers from their brother workers, by carrying out the counter-revolutionary instructions of the Allies, and particularly, in order to please the Entente, by inciting the German workers against the Russian workers' revolution. The policy of the bourgeoisie and the social-opportunists in Austria and Hungary repeats, in an attenuated form, the policy of the bourgeois-opportunist bloc in Germany.

THE VASSAL STATES OF THE ENTENTE

In the vassal States and the republics newly created by the Entente (the Czechs, the South Slavs, and also Poland, Finland, etc.) Entente policy, relying on the ruling classes and the social nationalists, is designed to create centres for a national counter-revolutionary movement. This movement is to be directed against the defeated countries, to keep the forces of the newly arisen States in equilibrium and subordinate them to the Entente, to obstruct the revolutionary movements developing within the new 'national' republics, and finally to supply white guards for the struggle against the international, in particular the Russian revolution.

As to Belgium, Portugal, Greece, and other small countries allied with the Entente, their policy is wholly determined by the policy of the big robbers, to whom they are completely subject and whose help they solicit in getting their minor annexations and war indemnities. . . .

THE ENTENTE AND SOVIET RUSSIA

The predatory, misanthropic, and reactionary character of Entente imperialism is most clearly shown in relation to Soviet Russia. From the beginning of the November revolution the Entente Powers took the side of the counter-revolutionary parties and governments of Russia. With the help of bourgeois counter-revolutionaries they annexed Siberia, the Urals, the shores of European Russia, the Caucasus, and part of Turkestan. From the annexed areas they stole raw materials (timber, oil, manganese, etc.). With the help of bands of Czechoslovak mercenaries they seized the gold reserve of the Russian empire. Working under the English diplomat Lockhart, English and French spies plotted to blow up bridges, destroy railways, and hamper the movement of food supplies. With money and arms the Entente supported the reactionary generals Denikin, Kolchak, and Krasnov, who hanged and shot thousands of workers in Rostov, Yusovka, Novorossiisk, Omsk, etc. Through the mouth of Clemenceau and Pichon the Entente openly proclaimed the principle of 'economic encirclement', that is, of starving out and annihilating the republic of revolutionary workers and peasants, and promised 'technical assistance' to the bands of Denikin, Kolchak, and Krasnov. The Entente has rejected the repeated peace offers of the Soviet Government.

On 23 January 1919 the Entente Powers, among whom the more moderate tendency was at the time growing stronger, addressed a proposal to all Russian governments to send representatives to Prinkipo. This proposal undoubtedly had an element of provocation in it, in regard to the Soviet Government. But although the Entente received an affirmative answer from the Soviet Government on 4 February, in which the latter even stated its readiness to discuss annexations, indemnities, and concessions, in order to free the Russian workers and peasants from the war forced on them by the Entente, the Entente made no reply even to this Soviet Russian peace offer.

This confirms that the annexationist-reactionary tendencies in the ranks of the Entente imperialists have a sure hold. They threaten the socialist republic with further annexations and counter-revolutionary attacks.

In this the Entente 'peace policy' conclusively reveals to the international proletariat the nature of Entente imperialism in general. At the same time it shows that the imperialist governments are incapable of concluding a 'just' or a 'just and lasting' peace, and that finance capital is unable to restore the destroyed economy. The continued rule of finance capital would lead either to the complete destruction of civilized society, or to greater exploitation, to further enslavement, political reaction, and armaments, and finally to new destructive wars.

RESOLUTION OF THE FIRST COMINTERN CONGRESS ON THE ORGANIZATION OF THE EXECUTIVE COMMITTEE OF THE COMMUNIST INTERNATIONAL

6 *March* 1919   *Protokoll*, i, p. 200

[Moscow was the obvious choice for the headquarters of the new organization; between congresses, the Executive Committee was to act in its name. It is clear from speeches and articles by the Russian leaders at this time that they had every hope and intention of transferring the seat of the Executive to a western capital once conditions were favourable to such a move.

In moving the resolution Platten said the Executive would have the right to move its headquarters to another country. The Russian comrades would have to take over provisionally, because of the time that must elapse before the delegates reported back to their national parties and got representatives delegated to the ECCI.]

In order to start work without delay, the congress shall now elect the necessary bodies, believing that the definitive constitution of the Communist International should be decided at the next congress, on the report of the bureau.

The conduct of the business of the Communist International is entrusted to an Executive Committee. This shall be composed of one representative from each of the most important countries. The parties of the following countries shall immediately delegate their representatives to the first Executive Committee:

      Russia
      Germany

German-Austria
Hungary
The Balkan federation
Switzerland
Scandinavia

Parties of other countries which proclaim their adherence to the Communist International before the second congress shall have a seat on the Executive Committee.

Until the arrival of these representatives from abroad the comrades of the country where the Executive Committee has its seat shall take over the work.

The Executive Committee shall elect a bureau of five persons.

MANIFESTO OF THE COMMUNIST INTERNATIONAL TO THE PROLETARIAT
OF THE ENTIRE WORLD

6 *March* 1919   *Beschlüsse des ersten Kongresses*, p. 3

[The manifesto was written by Trotsky, and adopted unanimously by the congress at its last session.]

Seventy-two years have passed since the Communist Party announced its programme to the world in the form of a Manifesto written by the greatest teachers of the proletarian revolution, Karl Marx and Friedrich Engels. Even at that time communism, which had barely entered the arena of struggle, was beset by the baiting, lies, hatred, and persecution of the possessing classes, who rightly sensed in it their mortal enemy. In the course of those seven decades communism developed along complex paths, periods of stormy advance alternating with periods of decline; it has known successes, but also severe defeats. But essentially the movement proceeded along the path indicated in advance by the Manifesto of the Communist Party. The epoch of final, decisive struggle came later than the apostles of social revolution had expected and hoped. But it has come. We communists, the representatives of the revolutionary proletariat of various countries of Europe, America, and Asia, who have gathered in Soviet Moscow, feel and consider ourselves to be the heirs and executors of the cause whose programme was announced 72 years ago. Our task is to generalize the revolutionary experience of the working class, to cleanse the movement of the disintegrating admixtures of opportunism and social-patriotism, to mobilize the forces of all genuinely revolutionary parties of the world proletariat and thereby facilitate and hasten the victory of the communist revolution throughout the world.

Today, when Europe is covered with debris and smoking ruins, the most infamous incendiarists are busy seeking out the criminals responsible for the war. Behind them stand their professors, members of parliament, journalists, social-patriots, and other political pimps of the bourgeoisie.

For many years socialism predicted the inevitability of imperialist war, seeing its causes in the insatiable greed of the possessing classes of the two chief camps and, in general, of all capitalist countries. At the Basle congress, two years before the outbreak of war, responsible socialist leaders of all countries branded imperialism as originator of the impending war, and threatened the bourgeoisie with socialist revolution as the proletarian retribution for the crimes of militarism. Today, after the experience of the last five years, after history has laid bare the predatory appetites of Germany, and the no less criminal acts of the Entente, the State-socialists of the Entente countries continue together with their governments to expose the overthrown German Kaiser. On top of this, the German social-patriots who in August 1914 proclaimed the Hohenzollern diplomatic *White Book* to be the most sacred gospel of the peoples, are now, like vile toadies, following in the footsteps of the Entente socialists and accusing the overthrown German monarchy, which they had once slavishly served, as the chief criminal. They hope in this way that their own guilt will be forgotten and at the same time to earn the goodwill of the victors. But the light cast by unfolding events and diplomatic revelations shows up, alongside the toppled dynasties of the Romanovs, the Hohenzollerns, and the Habsburgs, and the capitalist cliques of their countries, the ruling classes of France, England, Italy, and the United States in all their boundless infamy.

English diplomacy did not raise its veil of secrecy up to the very moment when war broke out. The government of the financiers took care to make no unambiguous statement of its intention of entering the war on the side of the Entente in order not to frighten the Berlin Government. In London they wanted war. That is why they behaved in such a way that Berlin and Vienna counted on England's neutrality, while Paris and Petrograd relied firmly on England's intervention.

Matured by the entire course of events over decades, the war was unleashed through the direct and deliberate provocation of Great Britain. The English Government calculated on extending just enough aid to Russia and France to keep them going until, themselves exhausted, England's mortal enemy, Germany, was also crippled. But the power of the German military machine proved too formidable and demanded of England not token but actual intervention in the war. The role of *tertius gaudens* to which Great Britain, following ancient tradition, aspired, fell to the United States. The Washington Government reconciled itself the more easily to the English blockade, which unilaterally restricted American stock exchange speculation in European blood, since the countries of the Entente compensated the American bourgeoisie with fat profits for violations of 'international law'. But Germany's enormous military superiority compelled the Washington Government to abandon its fictitious neutrality. In relation to Europe as a whole, the United States assumed the role which England had taken in relation to the continent in previous wars and tried to take in the last war, namely: weakening one camp by helping the other, intervening in military operations only so far as to secure for itself all the advantages of the situation. According to American standards of gambling, Wilson's stake was not very high, but it was the final stake, and it secured him the prize.

The war has made mankind aware of the contradictions of the capitalist system in the shape of primitive sufferings, hunger and cold, epidemics, and moral savagery. This has settled once and for all the academic controversy within the socialist movement over the theory of impoverishment and the gradual undermining of capitalism by socialism. Statisticians and pedants of the theory that contradictions were being smoothed out have for decades been trying to dig out from every corner of the globe real or alleged facts testifying to the greater well-being of various groups and categories of the working class. It was assumed that the theory of impoverishment had been buried to the accompaniment of contemptuous jeers from the eunuchs of bourgeois professordom and the mandarins of socialist opportunism. Today this impoverishment, no longer only of a social kind, but also physiological and biological, confronts us in all its shocking reality.

The catastrophe of the imperialist war has swept away all the gains of the trade union and parliamentary struggle. For this war itself was just as much a product of the inherent tendencies of capitalism as were those economic agreements and parliamentary compromises which the war buried in blood and mud.

Finance capital, which plunged mankind into the abyss of war, has itself suffered catastrophic changes in the course of the war. The relation between paper money and the material foundation of production has been completely disrupted. Steadily losing significance as the means and regulator of capitalist commodity circulation, paper money has become an instrument of requisition, of robbery, and of military-economic violence in general. The complete debasement of paper money reflects the general mortal crisis of capitalist commodity exchange. In the decades preceding the war, free competition, as the regulator of production and distribution, had already been supplanted in the major fields of economic life by the system of trusts and monopolies; but the course of events during the war tore this role from the hands of these economic associations and transferred it directly to the military State power. The distribution of raw materials, the utilization of Baku or Rumanian oil, of Donetz coal and Ukrainian wheat, the fate of German locomotives, trucks, and automobiles, the provisioning of starving Europe with bread and meat—all these fundamental questions of the world's economic life are being settled not by free competition, nor by associations of national and international trusts and consortiums, but by the direct application of military power in the interests of its continued preservation. If the complete subjection of State power to the power of finance capital led mankind into the imperialist shambles, then through this mass slaughter finance capital has completely militarized not only the State but also itself, and it is no longer capable of fulfilling its cardinal economic functions otherwise than by means of blood and iron.

The opportunists, who before the world war appealed to the workers to practise moderation for the sake of the gradual transition to socialism, and who during the war demanded class docility in the name of civil peace and national defence, are now again demanding self-denial of the proletariat in order to overcome the frightful consequences of the war. If this sermon were to be obeyed by the working masses, capitalist development would celebrate its restoration in new, more concentrated and more monstrous forms on the bones of many generations, with the prospect of a new and inevitable world war. Fortunately for mankind this is no longer possible.

State control of economic life, which capitalist liberalism resisted so strongly, has become a fact. There is no return to free competition, nor even to the domination of trusts, syndicates, and other economic monsters. There is only one question: Who shall henceforth take charge of nationalized production—the imperialist State or the State of the victorious proletariat?

In other words: Shall all toiling mankind become the bond slaves of a victorious world clique who, under the name of the League of Nations and aided by an 'international' army and 'international' navy, will plunder and strangle in one place and cast crumbs elsewhere, while everywhere shackling the proletariat, with the sole object of maintaining their own rule; or shall the working class of Europe and of the advanced countries in other parts of the world themselves take in hand the disrupted and ruined economy in order to assure its reconstruction on socialist foundations?

It is possible to shorten the present epoch of crisis only by means of the proletarian dictatorship which does not look back to the past, which respects neither hereditary privileges nor property rights, but takes as its starting-point the need of saving the starving masses and to this end mobilizes all forces and resources, introduces universal labour conscription, establishes the regime of labour discipline, in order in the course of a few years not only to heal the gaping wounds inflicted by war but also to raise mankind to new and unimagined heights.

The national State, which imparted a mighty impulse to capitalist development, has become too narrow for the further development of productive forces. This makes still more untenable the position of the small States hemmed in by the major Powers of Europe and other continents. These small States, which arose at different times as fragments chipped from larger ones, as small change in payment for various services rendered, or as strategic buffers, have their own dynasties, their own ruling cliques, their own imperialist pretensions, their own diplomatic intrigues. Their illusory independence rested, before the war, on the same foundations as the European balance of power—the uninterrupted antagonism between the two imperialist camps. The war has disrupted this equilibrium. By giving an enormous preponderance to Germany in its early stages, the war forced the small States to seek salvation in the magnanimity of German militarism. When Germany was defeated, the bourgeoisie of the small States, together with their patriotic 'socialists', turned to the victorious Allied imperialists and began to seek guarantees for their continued independent existence in the hypocritical provisions of the Wilsonian programme. At the same time the number of small States increased; out of the Austro-Hungarian monarchy, out of parts of the former Tsarist empire, new State entities have been carved, which were no sooner born than they sprang at one another's throats over the question of State frontiers. Meanwhile the Allied imperialists are constructing combinations of small Powers, both old and new, bound to themselves by the pledge of mutual hatreds and common impotence.

While oppressing and coercing the small and weak peoples, condemning them to hunger and degradation, the Allied imperialists, like the imperialists of the Central Powers a short while ago, do not stop talking about the right of national self-determination, which is today trampled underfoot in Europe as in all other parts of the world.

The small peoples can be assured the opportunity of a free existence only by the proletarian revolution, which will liberate the productive forces of all countries from the constraint of the national State, unite the peoples in closest economic collaboration on the basis of a common economic plan, and afford even the smallest and weakest people the opportunity of conducting their national cultural affairs freely and independently, without detriment to the unified and centralized European and world economy.

The last war, which was not least a war for colonies, was at the same time a war fought with the help of colonies. The colonial populations were drawn into the European war on an unprecedented scale. Indians, Negroes, Arabs, and Madagascans fought on the European continent— for what? For their right to remain the slaves of England and France. Never before has the infamy of capitalist rule been shown up so clearly;

never before has the problem of colonial slavery been posed so sharply as it is today.

Consequently there has been a series of open insurrections, revolutionary ferment in all the colonies. In Europe itself Ireland reminded us by bloody street battles that it still remains and still feels itself an enslaved country. In Madagascar, Annam, and other countries the troops of the bourgeois republic had more than one revolt of colonial slaves to suppress during the war. In India the revolutionary movement has not subsided for a single day, and has lately led to the greatest workers' strike in Asia, which the British Government met by ordering its armoured cars into action in Bombay.

Thus the colonial question in its fullest extent has been placed on the agenda, not only on the order papers of the diplomats in congress in Paris, but also in the colonies themselves. Wilson's programme, at its best, is meant only to change the commercial label of colonial slavery. The emancipation of the colonies is possible only in conjunction with the emancipation of the metropolitan working class. The workers and peasants not only of Annam, Algiers, and Bengal, but also of Persia and Armenia, will gain their opportunity of independent existence only when the workers of England and France have overthrown Lloyd George and Clemenceau and taken State power into their own hands. Even now the struggle in the more developed colonies is more than the struggle for national liberation; it is assuming an explicitly social character. If capitalist Europe forcibly dragged the backward sections of the world into the capitalist whirlpool, then socialist Europe will come to the aid of liberated colonies with its technology, its organization, its spiritual forces, in order to facilitate their transition to a planned and organized socialist economy.

Colonial slaves of Africa and Asia! The hour of proletarian dictatorship in Europe will also be the hour of your own liberation!

The entire bourgeois world accuses the communists of abolishing freedom and political democracy. That is not true. Having taken power, the proletariat merely asserts the utter impossibility of employing the methods of bourgeois democracy, and creates the conditions and forms of a new and higher workers' democracy. The whole course of capitalist development, especially during its final imperialist epoch, has undermined political democracy not only by splitting nations into two irreconcilable classes, but also by condemning the numerous petty-bourgeois and semi-proletarian strata, as well as the lowest strata of the proletariat, to permanent economic deprivation and political impotence.

In those countries where history provided the opportunity, the working class utilized the regime of political democracy in order to organize the fight against capital. The same thing will happen in those countries where conditions for the workers' revolution have not yet matured. But the broad intermediate strata in the countryside as well as the town are being hampered by capitalism, and are behindhand in their historical development. The peasant in Baden and Bavaria who still cannot see beyond the spire of his village church, the small French wine producer who is being ruined by the large-scale capitalists who adulterate wine, and the small American farmer fleeced and cheated by bankers and Congressmen—all these social strata, thrust by capitalism out of the main stream of development, are ostensibly called on, under the regime of political democracy, to run the State. But in reality, on all the important questions which determine the destinies of the peoples, the financial oligarchy make the decision behind the back of parliamentary democracy. That was true above all on the question of war; it is true now on the question of peace.

When the financial oligarchy think it advisable to get parliamentary cover for their acts of violence, the bourgeois State has at its disposal for this purpose all the manifold instruments inherited from centuries of class rule and multiplied by all the miracles of capitalist technology—lies, demagogy, baiting, calumny, bribery, and terror.

To demand of the proletariat that like meek lambs they comply with the requirements of bourgeois democracy in the final life-and-death struggle with capitalism is like asking a man fighting for his life against cut-throats to observe the artificial and restrictive rules of French wrestling, drawn up but not observed by his enemy.

In this realm of destruction, where not only the means of production and exchange but also the institutions of political democracy lie in bloody ruins, the proletariat must create its own apparatus, designed first and foremost to bind together the working class and to ensure the possibility of its revolutionary intervention in the further development of mankind. This apparatus is the workers' Soviets. The old parties, the old trade unions, have in the persons of their leaders proved incapable of carrying out, even of understanding, the tasks presented by the new epoch. The proletariat has created a new kind of apparatus, which embraces the entire working class regardless of occupation or political maturity; a flexible apparatus capable of continual renewal and extension, of drawing broader and broader strata into its orbit, opening its doors to the working people in town and country who stand close to the proletariat. This irreplaceable organization of working-class self-government, of its struggle, and later of its conquest of State power, has been tested in the experience of various countries and represents the greatest achievement and mightiest weapon of the proletariat of our time.

In all countries where the masses have wakened to consciousness, Soviets of workers', soldiers', and peasants' deputies will continue to be built. To strengthen the Soviets, to raise their authority, to put them up in opposition to the State apparatus of the bourgeoisie—this is today the most important task of the class-conscious and honest workers of all countries. Through the Soviets the working class can save itself from the disintegration introduced into its midst by the hellish sufferings of war and of hunger, by the violence of the possessing classes and by the treachery of its former leaders. Through the Soviets the working class will be able most surely and easily to come to power in all those countries where the Soviets are able to rally the majority of the working people. Through the Soviets the working class, having conquered power, will manage all spheres of economic and cultural life, as is the case at present in Russia.

The collapse of the imperialist State, from the Tsarist to the most democratic, is proceeding simultaneously with the collapse of the imperialist military system. The multimillioned armies mobilized by imperialism could stand firm only so long as the proletariat remained obediently under the yoke of the bourgeoisie. The breakdown of national unity means also an inevitable breakdown of the army. This is what happened first in Russia, then in Austria-Hungary and Germany. The same thing may be expected to occur in other imperialist States. The revolt of the peasant against the landlord, of the worker against the capitalist, and of both against the monarchical or democratic bureaucracy, inevitably brings in its train the revolt of soldiers against the army command, and subsequently a sharp split between the proletarian and bourgeois elements of the army. The imperialist war, which pitted one nation against another, has passed and is passing over into civil war which pits one class against another.

The outcry of the bourgeois world against civil war and red terror is the most monstrous hypocrisy yet known in the history of political struggle. There would be no civil war if the clique of exploiters who have brought mankind to the very brink of ruin had not resisted every forward step of the working masses, if they had not instigated conspiracies and assassinations, and summoned armed assistance from without in order to maintain or restore their thievish privileges.

Civil war is forced on the working class by its arch-enemies. Unless it renounces itself and its own future, which is also the future of all mankind, the working class must give blow for blow. The communist parties, which never conjure up civil war artificially, try to shorten it as much as possible whenever with iron necessity it does break out, to reduce to a minimum the number of victims and, above all, to assure victory to the proletariat. Hence arises the necessity of disarming the bourgeoisie in time, of arming the workers, of creating a communist army to defend the proletarian power and the inviolability of its socialist construction. Such is the Red Army of Soviet Russia which arose to defend the conquests of the working class against all attacks from within and without. The Soviet Army is inseparable from the Soviet State.

Conscious of the world-historical character of their tasks, the enlightened workers, from the very beginning of their organized socialist movement, strove for association on an international scale. The foundation stone was laid in London in 1864 in the shape of the First International. The Franco-Prussian war, from which the Germany of the Hohenzollerns emerged, undermined the First International, while at the same time it gave an impetus to the development of national workers' parties. In 1889 these parties came together at a congress in Paris and created the organization of the Second International. But the centre of gravity of the workers' movement during this period remained wholly on national soil, wholly within the framework of national States, founded upon national industry and confined within the sphere of national parliamentarianism. Decades of reformist organizational activity created a generation of leaders the majority of whom recognized in words the programme of social revolution but denied it by their actions; they were bogged down in reformism and in adaptation to the bourgeois State. The opportunist character of the leading parties of the Second International was finally revealed, and it led to the greatest collapse in world history at a moment when the march of events demanded revolutionary methods of struggle from the working-class parties. If the war of 1870 dealt a blow to the First International, disclosing that there was as yet no resolute mass power behind its social-revolutionary programme, then the war of 1914 killed the Second International, disclosing that the working masses, though welded together, were dominated by parties which had become transformed into subsidiary organs of the bourgeois State!

This applies not only to the social-patriots who have today gone over openly to the camp of the bourgeoisie, who have become their favourite agents and the most reliable hangmen of the working class; it also applies to the amorphous, unstable socialist centre, which is now trying to re-establish the Second International, that is, to re-establish the narrowness, the opportunism, and the revolutionary impotence of its leading élites. The Independent Party of Germany, the present majority of the Socialist Party of France, the Menshevik group of Russia, the Independent Labour Party of England, and other such groups are actually trying to fill the place occupied before the war by the old official parties of the Second International by coming forward, as before, with ideas of compromise and unity, using all the means at their disposal to paralyse the energy of the proletariat, to prolong the crisis, and thus make Europe's calamities even greater. The struggle against the socialist centre is the indispensable premiss for the successful struggle against imperialism.

In rejecting the timidity, the lies, and the corruption of the obsolete official socialist parties, we communists, united in the Third International, consider that we are carrying on in direct succession the heroic endeavours and martyrdom of a long line of revolutionary generations from Babeuf to Karl Liebknecht and Rosa Luxemburg.

If the First International predicted the future course of development and indicated the roads it would take, if the Second International rallied and organized millions of proletarians, then the Third International is the International of open mass struggle, the International of revolutionary realization, the International of action.

The bourgeois world order has been sufficiently lashed by socialist criticism. The task of the international communist party consists in overthrowing that order and erecting in its place the edifice of the socialist order.

We summon the working men and women of all countries to unite under the communist banner under which the first great victories have already been won.

Proletarians of all countries! In the struggle against imperialist savagery, against monarchy, against the privileged estates, against the bourgeois State and bourgeois property, against all kinds and forms of social and national oppression—*Unite*!

Under the banner of workers' Soviets, under the banner of revolutionary struggle for power and the dictatorship of the proletariat, under the banner of the Third International—proletarians of all countries, unite!

Signed in Moscow, 6 March 1919, by:

MAX ALBERT [Hugo Eberlein] *for Germany*
N. LENIN *for Russia*
K. GRUBER *for German Austria*
A. RUDNIANSKY *for Hungary*
OTTO GRIMLUND *for Sweden*
FRITZ PLATTEN *for Switzerland*
B. REINSTEIN *for the United States*
C. RAKOVSKY *for the Balkan Federation*
J. UNSCHLICHT (*Yurovsky*) *for Poland*
YRJO SIROLA *for Finland*
SKRYPNIK *for the Ukraine*
K. GAILIS *for Latvia*
HANS PÖGELMANN *for Estonia*
HAIKUNI *for Armenia*
G. KLINGER *for the Volga German colonists*
ZHALYMOV *for the Eastern peoples of Russia*
HENRI GUILBEAUX *for the French Zimmerwald left*

MANIFESTO OF THE ECCI TO THE WORKERS AND SOLDIERS OF ALL
COUNTRIES ON THE HUNGARIAN REVOLUTION

28 *March* 1919   *Beschlüsse des ersten Kongresses*, p. 74

[The short-lived Soviet regime in Hungary was set up on 21 March 1919, following the resignation of the government because of unwillingness to accede to
Allied territorial demands, and to the request for the withdrawal of Hungarian
troops from the frontier. Count Michael Karolyi, provisional President, in the
statement on his resignation, said he was 'handing power over to the Hungarian
proletariat'. The new Government was a coalition of social-democrats and communists, under the premiership of Bela Kun, who had been a prisoner of war in
Russia. The Hungarian Communis Party was founded in November 1918,
largely from prisoners of war repatriated from Russia. With the consent of the
ECCI, the Hungarian Communist Party signed an agreement on 21 March
1919 with the Social-Democratic Party for complete amalgamation; 'in the
name of the proletariat the party immediately takes all power into its hands.
The dictatorship will be exercised through councils of workers, soldiers, and
peasants. The plan to convene a national assembly thereby becomes obsolete.
... To secure the power of the proletariat and offer resistance to allied imperialism, a complete and close military and moral alliance shall be concluded with
the Russian Soviet Republic.'

   Lenin concluded a letter to the Hungarian workers, dated 27 May 1919, with
the words: 'You have given the world a still finer example than Soviet Russia,
in that you have been able to unite all socialists from the outset on the platform
of a real proletarian dictatorship.']

Comrades!
   In Hungary all power has been transferred to the working class.
   The imperialists of the Entente countries sent a new ultimatum to
Hungary. They wanted to rob Hungary of all its food supplies. They
wanted to deprive it completely of its independence. They wanted to wage
war against Soviet Russia across Hungarian territory.
   The Entente imperialists thought that the Hungarian bourgeoisie
would yield to their new ultimatum. They thought the Hungarian pro-
letariat would be powerless to resist their bloodthirsty demands.
   But that is not what happened. Fearing the wrath of the people, the
Hungarian bourgeoisie decided not to accept the Entente imperialists'
ultimatum. Gritting their teeth, they had to yield power to the workers.
The Entente imperialists burnt their fingers. Their rapacious pressure on
Hungary only hastened the birth of the Socialist Soviet republic in Hungary.
When the Hungarian bourgeoisie thus confirmed their inability to save the
country from ruin, they gave particularly clear proof that the historic role
of the bourgeoisie has been played out, and that their gravedigger, the
proletariat, has come to take their place.
   The Entente imperialists, however, are not content—in Paris the

imperialist robbers are sharpening the knife to slaughter the young Hungarian Soviet republic.

There is no calumny which these bourgeois gentlemen have not invented against the Hungarian Socialist Soviet republic—just as they have done for sixteen months in regard to the Russian Soviet Republic. The French imperialist Government intends to send its soldiers into battle against the Hungarian workers, as well as Rumanian and Czechoslovak troops.

Will this infernal plan succeed? The fate of working Hungary in the immediate future depends on the answer, and to a great extent also the immediate fate of the proletarian revolution in all other European countries.

In the name of the Communist International we appeal to the workers of all countries to come to the help of our brothers, the workers and peasants of Hungary.

Workers and soldiers of France! The eyes of workers throughout the world are turned to you. At this moment the French bourgeoisie are the most reactionary in all Europe. The leader of the French imperialists, Clemenceau, is doing most to incite the 'Allies' to suppress the Russian and Hungarian revolution.

French workers and soldiers, you are to be driven to act as hangmen, to strangle the Hungarian socialist revolution. The French bourgeoisie want to use your hands to strangle the proletarian revolution in Budapest, and thus to avert the proletarian revolution which is maturing in Vienna, Berlin, Paris, and London. After the four and a half years' war which you fought for the bankers' interests, they now want to force you to become international gendarmes, hangmen of the proletarian revolution.

That will not happen. The French workers will not stain themselves with treachery, they will turn their bayonets against their own oppressors, against the French and all other imperialists.

Comrades! The proletarian revolution has broken out in the whole world. The Hungarian revolution is only the first flash of lightning splitting the threatening clouds.

The bourgeoisie of all countries, who exterminated twenty million men in the most bloody of all wars, will now have to account to us for this crime. Mankind has not yet gone mad. It will not leave power in the hands of those who led us into the imperialist blood bath.

Everybody to the aid of the Hungarian revolution!

Soldiers! Refuse obedience to those who send you against red Hungary. Rise, form your councils, and go over to the side of Soviet Hungary.

May the Hungarian socialist revolution be a threatening warning to the bourgeoisie of all countries! Hands off red Hungary! This cry shall sound throughout the world.

May the Hungarian socialist revolution be the beginning of a whole series of new proletarian revolutions. The end of bourgeois rule has come.

Long live the working class and the revolutionary soldiers of Hungary. Long live the Hungarian Communist Party! Long live the proletarian world revolution!

ECCI MESSAGE TO THE BAVARIAN SOVIET REPUBLIC

April 1919   *Beschlüsse des ersten Kongresses,* p. 78

[The assassination of Kurt Eisner, the socialist-pacifist Premier of Bavaria, at the end of February, was followed by a decision of the Munich Workers' and Soldiers' Council (carried by 234 to 70 votes, the communists opposing) to proclaim an independent socialist republic. A government of social-democrats was formed, the communists refusing to take part in a coalition. On 7 April 1919 Bavaria was proclaimed a Soviet republic; on 13 April, after the revolt of the Munich garrison, the communists joined the Government, which was overthrown by military action on 1 May.

Writing in *Izvestia*, Chicherin, the Soviet Commissar for Foreign Affairs, said that 'every blow aimed at the Bavarian republic is aimed at us. In absolute unity we carry on our revolutionary struggle.']

To the People's Commissar for Foreign Affairs,
Munich

On behalf of the Executive Committee of the Communist International I send my warmest greetings through you to the Bavarian proletariat, who have founded a Soviet republic. We are deeply convinced that the time is not far off when the whole of Germany will be a Soviet republic. The Communist International is aware that you in Germany are now fighting at the most responsible posts, where the immediate fate of the proletarian revolution throughout Europe will be decided.

Long live the German proletariat and its Communist Party!
Long live the communist world revolution!

President of the ECCI,
G. Zinoviev

EXTRACTS FROM AN ECCI MAY DAY MANIFESTO

20 *April* 1919   *K.I.,* 1, *May* 1919, p. 21

[In an article on 'The Perspectives of the Proletarian Revolution' published in the same issue of *Kommunisticheskii Internatsional* Zinoviev wrote: 'As these lines are being written the Third International already has as its main basis three Soviet republics, in Russia, Hungary, and Bavaria. But nobody will be surprised if by the time these lines appear in print we have not three but six or more Soviet republics. . . . Now it is abundantly clear that the movement in Europe is going ahead far more quickly than even the greatest optimist at the Moscow congress of the Third International expected. The flames of civil war are blazing throughout Europe. The victory of communism in all Germany is wholly inevitable. There will be a few isolated defeats. Here and there perhaps for a while the black will defeat the red. Nevertheless, it is to the red that final victory will fall. And that in the next few months, perhaps even weeks. The movement is advancing so dizzyingly fast that one can say with certainty in a year's time we will already begin to forget that there was a struggle for communism in Europe, for in a year's time the whole of Europe will be communist. And the struggle will have spread to America, perhaps to Asia too, and the other continents. It may perhaps be that in America capitalism can continue to exist for a couple of years alongside a communist Europe. It may perhaps be that even in England capitalism will continue to exist for a year or two alongside the communism which will have triumphed over the whole European continent. But for any length of time such a symbiosis is impossible.']

TO THE WORKING PEOPLE OF THE WHOLE WORLD

. . . Now that the imperialist war has ended the workers of all countries can count the number of its victims. Thirty million killed and crippled, countries laid waste, millions of people starving, milliards of new war debts. These are the results of the imperialist slaughter. The war has ended, and the bourgeoisie in those countries where they are still on their feet are not asking much of the working class—only that the workers themselves should fill the gaps in production left by the extermination of thirty million workers and peasants. . . .

The Second International is dead. It signed its own death warrant on 4 August 1914 when the German and French social-patriots, equally shameful, voted for the war credits, that is, for the support of the imperialist slaughter.

But the idea of the International is alive. Never before have the workers of all countries so passionately demanded international union as now. . . .

In Paris the imperialist extortioners are trying to create their own black 'international', the so-called League of Nations. Conscious workers throughout the world know perfectly well that the so-called League of Nations is in fact a league of bourgeois robbers for the oppression of nations, for the division of the world, for the enslavement of the workers, for strangling the proletarian revolution.

And the social-traitors, those people who in the name of 'socialism' betrayed the working class to the bourgeoisie and the landlords, in their turn tried to create their own yellow 'international' in Berne.

The attempt to revive the corpse of the Second International did not succeed. The revolutionary workers of all countries refused to take part in the abominable comedy at Berne. . . . The yellow Berne international is only a branch of the black Paris international. . . .

But in 1919 the red international was formed, the international of communism. Our Third International is an international fellowship of the proletarians of all countries which has set itself the task of overthrowing the bourgeoisie and establishing the international Soviet republic. Our Third Communist International is taking over the organization of the international May Day celebrations. . . .

In what circumstances do we greet the first May Day after the end of the war? All over Europe the ruins are smoking and millions of proletarian children are dying of hunger. . . . But on the ruins of the old a new world is being born. The more the bourgeoisie suppressed the workers' movement during the war, the stronger the revolutionary flame is now burning. The working class is taking revenge for the tortures it suffered at the hands of the bourgeoisie in alliance with official 'social-democracy'.

Communism has come out on to the streets. The communist revolution is growing before our eyes. A Soviet republic in Russia, a Soviet republic in Hungary, a Soviet republic in Bavaria—these are the results of the recent struggles of the working class.

The whole of Germany is shaking under the strain of civil war. In Germany there is not a single town where the working class has not risen in revolt against the power of the bourgeoisie and the social-democrats. . . .

In France huge workers' demonstrations have begun. . . . In Italy the struggle has reached boiling point and the communists are calling for the dictatorship of the proletariat. In England strikes have taken on an epidemic character. Here and there workers' soviets are being created. In America the working class has come out on to the streets and is getting ready for the decisive conflict. . . .

Before a year has passed, the whole of Europe will be Soviet. In every country the workers have realized that the decisive moment has come . . . .

The workers see that in all the leading bourgeois countries the much vaunted 'democracy' is nothing but the arbitrary and unrestrained dictatorship of a gang of robbers, bankers, and generals. . . . They see that the bourgeoisie of all countries are preparing with united forces to stifle the proletarian revolution in Russia, Hungary, and Bavaria, and the proletarian revolution which is beginning in Austria and Germany. . . . They know that the proletarian dictatorship can save mankind from the bloody horror into which they were plunged by the bourgeoisie of all countries. The workers know that the proletarian dictatorship leads to the triumph of socialism.

There is no middle way. Either the bloody dictatorship of hangmen-generals, killing hundreds of thousands of workers and peasants in the interests of a gang of bankers, or the dictatorship of the working class, that is, of the overwhelming majority of the working people, disarming the bourgeoisie, creating their own red army, and liberating the whole world from slavery.

Down with the autocracy of tsars and kings. That cry rang out in Russia in 1917 and echoed throughout Europe. . . .

Down with the autocracy of capital. This cry resounds now, when the workers of the majority of countries are beginning their second revolution, when they are rising for the second time, when they are getting ready for the last and decisive battle.

The eight-hour working day!—that was the May Day slogan in the past. The Soviet republics have already carried out this demand. . . .

Down with the imperialist war!—this was the cry of the workers of the whole world on the first of May. Down with *their* war, down with the war which the Allied imperialists want to declare on the Soviet republics of Russia and Hungary—that is what we say now. For the civil war, the only just war, in which the oppressed class fights against its oppressors. . . .

Down with the French imperialists, down with the bourgeois 'Alliance', down with the robbers who want to send their troops to Russia to give power back to the landlords, to re-establish the monarchy, to restore the bourgeoisie.

Workers and soldiers of France, England, America, Italy, Serbia, Rumania, Poland. Turn your weapons against your own bourgeoisie. Your enemy is in your own country. Stir up rebellion in the rear against your bourgeois governments. . . .

Workers and peasants of Germany and Austria. Turn your weapons against your own bourgeoisie and the 'social-democrats' who serve them. . . . You, only you, can save your country from the torments of hunger and unemployment. . . .

The storm is rising. The flames of the proletarian revolution are spreading all over Europe, and it is invincible. The moment is drawing near for which our predecessors and teachers waited. . . . That of which the best among mankind dreamed is becoming reality. Our banner, reddened with the heart's blood of whole generations of great fighters and martyrs of the working class, flies over the whole world. The last hour of our oppressors has struck. . . . In thunder and storm, in blood and tears, in hunger and unending suffering, the new world is being born, the bright world of communism, of the universal brotherhood of labour.

In 1919 the great Communist International was born. In 1920 the great International Soviet Republic will come to birth.

ECCI MANIFESTO ON THE VERSAILLES PEACE TERMS

13 *May* 1919   *Beschlüsse des ersten Kongresses*, p. 92

[The German Communist Party, in its theses on the peace treaty, stated that acceptance of the terms would be as catastrophic as their rejection. The arguments for or against, it was suggested elsewhere, depended entirely on the actual situation. For the proletariat the consequences would be the same, and the question was, which would do more to promote the revolution. Since its acceptance would give the bourgeoisie a much needed respite, rejection of the Versailles terms became one of the main planks in the KPD platform and the avowed basis of its 'eastward orientation', of its advocacy of a German alliance with Soviet Russia in opposition to western imperialism. In '*Left-wing*' *Communism*, however, Lenin wrote: 'One of the undoubted mistakes of the "lefts" in Germany is their stubborn insistence on non-recognition of the Versailles peace.' This, he argued, might have been possible in the early summer of 1919, when there was a Soviet Government in Hungary and the possibility of a Soviet revolution in Austria. 'But the position is now obviously such that the German communists should not tie their hands and promise positively and without fail to repudiate the Versailles peace in the event of the victory of communism. That would be foolish.' The right-wing socialists had by their actions hindered the chances of an alliance with Soviet Russia and Soviet Hungary. 'We Communists will do all we can to facilitate and pave the way for such an alliance', but it would be petty-bourgeois nationalism to give liberation from Versailles precedence over promotion of the international Soviet revolution. This argument was directed against the group of German communists, known as 'national bolsheviks', who were prepared to collaborate with the extreme nationalist right wing in Germany in opposition to the peace treaty.]

DOWN WITH THE VERSAILLES PEACE!
LONG LIVE THE COMMUNIST REVOLUTION!

To the working people of the world!

The governments which five years ago began the rapacious war are now trying to end it with a rapacious peace. In Versailles the English, French, and American bourgeoisie have handed the representatives of the German bourgeoisie the so-called peace conditions. Versailles has become a new Brest. Every stipulation in the Versailles peace is a noose for strangling one or another people.

The fury and vindictiveness of the imperialist bourgeoisie of the victorious coalition know no limits. While the Anglo-French and American bourgeoisie announce the foundation of the 'League of Nations', they are in fact trying to make a mockery of the will of all the nations inhabiting Europe. The bourgeoisie of the Entente countries are trying to break Germany into fragments. A whole series of territories is to be cut from Germany; Germany is to be robbed of coal and bread, of its merchant fleet; Germany is to be forced to pay staggering indemnities. The Entente bourgeoisie, who allegedly fought the war to prevent the annexation of foreign lands, are putting through a series of the most gross and most cynical annexations. The colonies which formerly belonged to Germany are being dealt in like cattle. The Entente imperialists have armed themselves with a large knife and are vivisecting the body of Germany.

But the rapacious conditions of peace dictated to Germany from Versailles are only one link in the chain of violence wrought by the Entente imperialists. While attempting to stifle and throttle Germany, they are also conducting a campaign against the Hungarian Soviet Republic.

These French and English bourgeois are inciting the Rumanian boyars to lead their white-guard troops against our brothers, the workers of Hungary. It is these representatives of enlightened French and English 'democracy' who are inspiring the heroes leading their infuriated gangs in pogroms against red Budapest.

It is they, too, who incite the Russian ultra-reactionaries, Kolchak, Denikin, Krasnov, in their bloody struggle against the Russian working class and peasantry. They also encouraged the German white guards, led by Noske, Ebert, and Scheidemann, to destroy the Bavarian Soviet Republic. The Entente imperialists openly stipulated that Scheidemann's Government should make the suppression of the Soviet regime in Munich their primary task.

It is they, the English, French, and American bankers and generals, who are disarming the revolutionary troops in Bulgaria. It is they who are strangling the revolutionary popular movement in Serbia and Slavonia.

International gendarmes—that is what the English, French, and American imperialists are, who pass themselves off as representatives of 'world democracy'.

All illusions are destroyed. Masks have fallen. Those who did not learn the lesson of the endless, terrible, imperialist war will be taught by the imperialist peace, with which mankind is to be blessed from Versailles. The governments which for four and a half years deluded their peoples into thinking that the war was being fought for 'national self-determination', for the 'independence' of small nations, for 'freedom and civilization', for 'democracy'—these governments are now revealed as hangmen, pitiless slave-owners maddened by anger.

The fairy-tale of the League of Nations is fading before it had time to blossom. Now that the terms of the Versailles peace are known, not many workers will be deluded by the League of Nations. The League of Nations, at whose cradle stands the butcher Clemenceau, is exposed to the whole world as a league of robbers out to crucify the many millions of the European labouring masses.

The entire weight of the Versailles peace falls in the first place on the German working class. If it were to endure for any length of time, it would mean that the German working class would have to groan under a double yoke—that of their own bourgeoisie and that of the foreign slave-holders.

There is no need to say that the sympathies of the Communist International, the sympathies of honest workers throughout the world, are on the side of the German working class. Communist workers in all countries feel the Versailles peace terms as an attack on the international proletariat, as a blow which can be parried only by the united forces of proletarians in all countries.

The present German Government, which protests in words against the Versailles peace, is in fact helping the Entente imperialists to carry out their devilish plan in regard to the German working class. In Germany the hangman Clemenceau has no servants more faithful than Scheidemann and Ebert. The party of Scheidemann and Ebert has from the first moment of the German revolution danced obediently to the tune of the Entente imperialists. At Clemenceau's instigation Scheidemann and Ebert sent and are still sending white-guard troops against Soviet Russia. To please the Entente imperialists the social-democrats led by Scheidemann and Ebert murdered Karl Liebknecht and Rosa Luxemburg, and suppressed with fire and sword the great movement of the German workers to establish the power of the workers' councils. In carrying out the orders of the London and Paris Stock Exchanges Scheidemann's Government has already wiped out many thousands of German communist workers. Whenever the waves of the working-class movement in Germany rose particularly high and seemed about to wash the government of treacherous social-democrats away, Scheidemann and Ebert frightened the hungry workers off with the argument that if the rule of the workers' councils were to be established in Germany the Entente Powers would cut off bread supplies to the German people.

The central committee of Scheidemann's Social-Democratic Party maintains in its appeal on the Versailles peace that the lesson of Versailles is the 'best proof of the correctness of the attitude taken by German social-democracy on the question of defence of the fatherland!'

'Socialists of all countries, have you at last understood the way we acted during the war?' says Scheidemann in the appeal.

Oh you hypocrites, oh you cynics!

In 1914 two thieves fell upon the same booty. One of them was more successful than the other. This criminal not only captured all the booty to which his competitor laid claim, but also picked his rival's pockets. Then the other thief, putting a good face on his loss and hypocritically assuming an air of injured innocence, appeals to all decent people: 'You see, the behaviour of my opponent has conclusively demonstrated the correctness of my tactics. Won't you at last also understand that the Scheidemanns are purer than the Alpine snow?'

The terms of the Versailles peace have proved something quite different to all honest workers. The class-conscious workers of the whole world take first of all into account that if the war had ended with a victory for the German imperialists they would have been as ruthless towards the defeated as their enemies now are to them. And then the Hendersons and Renaudels would no doubt have made use of the same false words as the Scheidemanns and Noskes are using today.

The Versailles peace terms have shown that so long as imperialism still exists, even if only in one country, force and robbery will also continue to exist. The Versailles peace terms have shown that the imperialism of whatever coalition is equally bloodthirsty. Whatever 'democratic' fig-leaves imperialism may use to cover itself, it remains the embodiment of barbarism and bloodthirstiness.

The Versailles peace terms have shown that the social-patriots of all countries have finally and for ever become the lackeys of the bourgeoisie. The Versailles peace terms have shown how pitiful are the dreams of the adherents of the yellow 'Berne' international (in particular the Kautskys and their friends), dreams of 'disarmament' while capitalism is maintained, of a kind and benevolent League of Nations protected by Wilson. The Versailles peace terms have shown that the bourgeoisie themselves have left only one road open to the workers of all countries, the road of world revolution, the road that leads over the corpse of capitalism.

Workers of France! Workers of England! Workers of America! Workers of Italy! The Communist International turns to you! On you the fate of millions of German and Austrian workers primarily depends now. You must now have your say. You must tear from the bloody hands of your governments the robber's knife which they are holding over the heads of the German and Austrian working class. You must show that the lessons of the five years of slaughter have not been lost on you. Not for a moment should you forget that the victory of the Entente imperialists over the German and Austrian working class means victory over you, victory over the workers of all countries, victory over socialism. It is chiefly you that hold in your hands the fate of international socialism. The class-conscious workers of the whole world rely on you. And we are convinced that you will do your duty, in defiance of the advice of your Scheidemanns.

Workers of Germany! Workers of Austria! Now you can see that you have no other choice but to overthrow at once the government of traitors who call themselves social-democrats but who are in fact the most shameful agents of the bourgeoisie. Now you can see where the policy of Scheidemann and Noske has led you. You see that your only hope is the proletarian world revolution.

But the Scheidemanns and Eberts oppose this proletarian revolution with all their strength. When the Scheidemanns and Noskes appeal in your name to the international proletariat they are met only with contempt.

The men who uttered no word of protest when Soviet Hungary was strangled by the troops of the landowners, the men who at Libau are fighting on the side of the German barons against the Lettish workers and farm labourers, these men cannot count on the support of the international proletariat.

Count Brockdorff von Rantzau, Landsberg the traitor, Noske and Scheidemann, the executioners, must not now speak in your name. So long as the present German Government is at the helm the conflict between Berlin and Paris remains only a legal dispute between the bourgeoisie of two coalitions. The entire power in your country must be taken over as soon as possible by the workers' councils. It is the communist workers who should speak in your name.

Then and only then will you be able to save your country and to count on the full support of the proletarians of all countries.

The time for hesitation is past. Now it is already clear to each one of you that nothing can be worse, that the government of social-traitors has led you to the brink of ruin.

Workers of Germany and Austria! You must realize that the proletariat of other countries will put no trust in German official social-democracy, that social-democracy which uttered not a word of protest when the government of Wilhelm of Hohenzollern imposed the Brest peace on Soviet Russia.

Workers of Germany and Austria! You must realize that if the Brest peace which was forced on Russia in 1918 came to an end so quickly, it was because the Russian workers and peasants overthrew the government of the bourgeoisie and social-traitors and took power in their own hands. Only for that reason did the Russian workers succeed in winning the confidence and sympathy of the proletarians of all countries. Only thanks to that did they succeed in breaking the Brest noose so quickly.

The proletarian world revolution—that is the only salvation for the oppressed classes of the entire world.

The dictatorship of the proletariat and the establishment of Soviet power—that is the only lesson of Versailles for the proletarians of the whole world.

So long as capitalism lives there can be no lasting peace. Lasting peace will be built on the ruins of the bourgeois order.

Long live the revolt of the workers against their oppressors! Down with the Versailles peace! Down with the new Brest! Down with the government of social-traitors!

Long live Soviet power throughout the world!

EXTRACTS FROM AN ECCI MANIFESTO ON INTERVENTION IN RUSSIA

18 *June* 1919   *Beschlüsse des ersten Kongresses*, p. 111

[The landing of Japanese troops at Vladivostok in April 1918 opened the period of Allied intervention in Russia. The British landed at Murmansk in June, the French and Americans in August. The period was brought to a close by the lifting in January 1920 of the blockade of Russia imposed by the Supreme Allied Council.

Writing in the October 1919 issue of *Kommunisticheskii Internatsional*, Chicherin, Soviet Commissar for Foreign Affairs, argued that in the past the working class could not take sides in disputes between capitalist States, or give any support to their policy. But, he continued, 'The situation is completely changed with the establishment of revolutionary Soviet governments of workers and peasants. For the first time, after a long interval, the revolutionary proletariat is again confronted with positive tasks in the field of foreign policy. For the first time there are, among existing governments, some in whose support the revolutionary international proletariat has an interest. These governments are becoming the centre of the entire world struggle between the oppressed and the oppressing countries and groups. Revolutionary proletarian parties and groups have a new task, to fight for the security and consolidation of the international status of the revolutionary Soviet governments . . . .']

To the working people of all countries.

The capitalist world, which was shaken to its foundations by the five-year war, is on the eve of final collapse. The world revolution is drawing near, approaching with the inevitability of fate.

Faced by this danger the international bourgeoisie are making desperate efforts to keep power in their hands, to destroy the socialist revolution which threatens their class rule. . . .

They organize counter-revolutionary insurrections and give all-out support to the embittered reactionaries who are trying to restore the power of the landowners and capitalists, hated by the peoples but dear to the hearts of the bourgeoisie throughout the world. They insolently reject the peace proposals of the genuinely popular governments, the Soviet governments, and conclude an alliance with the extreme counter-revolutionaries, the Tsarist Generals Kolchak and Denikin in Russia, the avowed monarchists Counts Karolyi and Andrassy in Hungary. They go so far as to use agents to destroy railway bridges and blow up waterworks, thus increasing immeasurably the sufferings of the labouring masses. . . .

By hypocritical and lying statements in parliament and press they try to muffle the vigilance of their peoples. Lloyd George and Clemenceau, Wilson and Scheidemann—they all with one voice give assurances that they have no intention of waging war against the Soviet republics, while at the same time they continue to send troops to Siberia and Archangel, to

Murmansk and the Danube, and continue to provide all the enemies of the Soviet Republics with arms and munitions; they stir up the Polish landlords, the Rumanian boyars, the Baltic barons, the Czech, Finnish, and Estonian counter-revolutionaries, against the peoples of Russia, Hungary, and the Ukraine.

A united front of the bourgeoisie of the whole world is being formed to fight socialism. Is it not astonishing how quickly and easily the enemies of yesterday are reconciled, once it is a question of the fight against the socialist revolution? The victors—the Allies—have not yet concluded peace with Germany, which they intended to plunder to the uttermost, but the German bourgeois–social-traitor Government is already on Allied instructions willingly playing the part of executioner by crushing the rebellious workers at home and sending its regular troops to occupy Latvia, Lithuania, White Russia.

The workers of all countries should bear clearly in mind that what is now at stake is not only the fate of the Soviet Republics of Russia, Hungary, the Ukraine, etc.; the fate of the world revolution is being decided in the Urals and before red Petrograd, in the Carpathians and on the Danube. If the imperialists of all countries now succeed in smothering the first flames of the communist revolution, the working-class movement in all countries of the world will be set back many decades. The entire burden of paying for the first great imperialist war will be thrown on to the labouring people, and not only in the defeated countries, but also in those of the victors. The eternal conflict over the division of the spoils will, however, soon lead to new, even more senseless and more bloody wars, and in the end the whole world will be plunged into hopeless misery and bondage.

The only way out and the only salvation is the socialist world revolution.

The Executive Committee of the Communist International summons the masses of all countries to the defence of the socialist world revolution. At the same time it notes with joy that the working masses of many countries have already grasped their duty and are protesting resolutely against the criminal plans of their governments. It welcomes most warmly the decision of the Italian, French, and English socialists to declare a general strike of protest.

The Executive Committee of the Communist International for its part proposes that the workers of all countries express their solidarity with the peoples of the Soviet republics by arranging an international demonstration against the attack of the imperialist Powers on Russia and Hungary.

The time for verbal protests is past; it is time to act. . . .

APPEAL OF THE ECCI ON BEHALF OF THE HUNGARIAN SOVIET REPUBLIC

July 1919   *Beschlüsse des ersten Kongresses*, p. 100

[Allied pressure combined with internal dissensions to weaken the position of the Hungarian Soviet Government. Lenin was anxious for the Red Army to make contact with the Hungarian forces, although the territory between was occupied by Polish troops. A note to an article by Trotsky written shortly afterwards says: 'Soviet Russia, surrounded by a ring of enemies, could not come to the help of Hungary.' The advance of Czech and Rumanian troops towards Budapest was followed by the opening of negotiations with the Allied Powers, undertaken by the social-democratic members of the Hungarian Government.]

To all! To all!

A monstrous crime is being committed, compared with which all misdeeds which the propertied classes committed during the war grow pale. The English and French imperialists are encircling the Hungarian Soviet Republic from all sides, in order to drown the Hungarian workers, the Hungarian socialist revolution, in blood.

The Rumanian feudalists are inciting the troops, deceived by the nobility, against Hungary. From two other directions the Czechoslovak and Yugoslav Governments are moving against Hungary, spurred on by the same French imperialists. The Hungarian Soviet Government had agreed to accept the most severe peace terms and to satisfy all the unheard-of demands of the reactionary Rumanian and Czechoslovak Governments. And still the reactionary armies of these Governments are continuing their offensive against Hungary.

The meaning of these events is clear. The Hungarian Soviet Republic did not and does not want war. The Hungarian Soviet Republic is carrying out the will of the Hungarian workers. The Hungarian workers overthrew the power of the capitalists—that is their only 'crime'!

The advance of the imperialists against socialist Hungary is taking place with the open sympathy and fairly certain support of the social-traitors who call themselves social-democrats. The conference of the yellow 'international' meeting in Amsterdam uttered not a single word of protest against the predatory campaign against Hungary.

The Executive Committee of the Communist International appeals to the Czechoslovak, Rumanian, and Yugoslav workers and soldiers. Comrades, stop playing the part of forced executioners of the Hungarian workers! Stretch out a fraternal hand to your brothers, the Hungarian soldiers and workers. The workers of the entire world turn away in contempt from those who at this great moment fail in their duty.

Workers and soldiers of France! The bourgeoisie of your State are most to blame for the hangmen's campaign against the Hungarian Soviet

Republic. Raise your voices in protest! Wrest power from the hands of the greatest evildoers the world has ever known. Strike from the hand of the murderers the knife they have drawn against our brothers, the Hungarian workers.

The class-conscious workers of the entire world are proud of the heroic deed of the Hungarian workers who established a republic of labour in Hungary. To you, Hungarian proletarians, surrounded on all sides by enemies, the communist workers of the world send ardent greetings. In the year and a half of their dictatorship the Russian proletariat have often been in as grave a position. And still they surmounted all difficulties. We are firmly convinced that you will steadfastly withstand the present test.

Down with the international robbers! Long live the Hungarian Soviet Republic!

EXTRACTS FROM AN ECCI MANIFESTO ON THE LUCERNE CONGRESS OF THE SECOND INTERNATIONAL

15 *July* 1919   *Beschlüsse des ersten Kongresses*, p. 119

[The Lucerne congress of parties of the Second International was held from 2 to 9 August 1919; the committee appointed at Berne reported on its preparations for a world congress. This was held in Geneva in July 1920; the chief parties represented were the British Labour Party, the German Social-Democratic Party, and the Belgian, Dutch, Swedish, and Danish Social-Democratic Parties.]

BOYCOTT THE YELLOW INTERNATIONAL

To the workers of all countries!

On 1 August the congress of the Second 'International' is to be held in Lucerne. . . . Who in fact has called this congress? Those parties and men who from the first day of the 1914 war placed themselves entirely at the disposal of 'their' imperialist governments. The same Scheidemann and Renaudel, Vandervelde, Huysman, Hyndman, and Henderson who for four years spoke of 'war to the victorious end', of 'defence of the fatherland', of whom some blessed General Hindenburg and others Marshal Foch, who helped the bourgeoisie to annihilate the flower of the working class. These men now want to build the Labour International again! . . .

In the eyes of the workers of all countries they are all equally criminal. They are bound by mutual pledges, all these Scheidemanns and Renaudels. They have to rehabilitate each other, they must pretend that nothing special has happened in the International during the four and a half years of war. For these gentlemen socialism has lived through no crisis and is not living through one now. There were only unimportant 'misunderstandings', which, however, cost the lives of millions of workers. Now that the masters have been reconciled, and the Versailles peace signed, the servants can also be reconciled. . . . In Lucerne these gentlemen intend to forgive each other their sins, to proclaim a general amnesty, to wash their hands in their own innocence, and to throw sand in the eyes of the workers of all countries, asserting that the Second International has been rebuilt. . . .

The proletarian revolution is spreading not only daily, but hourly, in all the countries of Europe and America. But what are the official social-democratic parties doing, which are now convening the Lucerne congress? These official parties, rotten to the core, are doing their best to choke the workers' movement. In France, in Germany, in Austria, in England— everywhere the old patriotic social-democracy comes forward to strangle the railwaymen's strikes and the strikes and revolts of all other categories of workers.

The imperialist governments of the Entente countries have opened a crusade against the Russian and Hungarian proletarians who seized power in their countries. Honest workers in the Entente countries express the deepest indignation about this crusade and are ready to come out in arms against their governments. But what part are the official social-traitors playing in this affair? The social-chauvinists of Germany as of France, of Austria as of England, are trying to damp down the workers' protest. By their action they are helping Kolchak, the Rumanian boyars, and all other stranglers of the Hungarian and Russian revolution.

The Second International died on 4 August 1914, at the moment when the German and French Social-Democratic Parties voted the war credits and went over to the side of their governments. Nobody can awaken the Second International to life. In 1915 Rosa Luxemburg called official German social-democracy a 'mouldering corpse'. The entire Second International has now become a mouldering corpse, a corpse which should be unceremoniously buried as quickly as possible, so that it does not infect the surrounding atmosphere.

On the ruins of the Second International there arose a new international working men's association: the Third, Communist International. Every-thing that is honest, steadfast, militant in the working class joins the ranks of the Third International. About twenty communist parties took part in its constituent congress. Only four months have passed since the Third International was founded in Moscow. In that time many new parties have joined the Third International: the Italian Socialist Party, the Serbian Revolutionary Social-Democrats, the Swedish and Norwegian comrades, the Bulgarian workers, the left wing of the American party and many other workers' organizations in Europe and America. The struggle is bursting into flame throughout the world. The tremendous strikes which are shaking Italy are pledges that the emancipation of the Italian prole-tariat is not far off. The political strike which is to take place in the Allied countries on 21 July in protest against intervention in Russian and

Hungarian affairs heralds an entire series of international battles which will inevitably end with the victory of the world proletariat over international capital.

The Executive Committee of the Communist International has unanimously decided to call on workers' organizations throughout the world to boycott the forthcoming despicable comedy in Lucerne. . . .

On that day the workers in all countries should demonstrate in every possible way against the yellow 'International' and give proof of their fidelity to the ideals of communism proclaimed by Marx and Engels. Come out on to the streets that day, comrade workers, fling your contempt and hatred in the face of the lackeys of capitalism, proclaim the principles for which Karl Liebknecht fought, rally your forces under the banner of the Third, Communist International!

ECCI STATEMENT ON THE FALL OF THE HUNGARIAN SOVIET REPUBLIC

5 *August* 1919   *Beschlüsse des ersten Kongresses*, p. 136

[The resignation of the Hungarian Soviet Government on 1 August 1919 followed an ultimatum by the Allied Powers, and military intervention by Czech, Rumanian, and Serbian forces. Subsequent accounts by communists attributed its fall primarily to the 'treachery' of the social-democrats in the Government, but in reporting to the second Comintern congress Rakosi said that the Communist Party and the Soviets were too small and weak to carry out their tasks. The failure of the international strike called in support of Soviet Russia and Soviet Hungary 'showed clearly that the proletariat of France and England were hostile to Soviet Russia and on the side of Clemenceau and Lloyd George'. The strike, called for 21 July 1919, was partially carried out only in Italy.]

Comrades!

The greatest treachery has been committed. The Soviet power in Hungary has collapsed under the pressure of the imperialist robbers and the monstrous treachery of the social-patriots. The leaders of the Second International, who supported the imperialist slaughter, broke the international protest strike. The imperialist robbers, led by Clemenceau and Wilson, have become quite shameless. The ultimatum they sent runs: 'Overthrow the Soviet Government, and we will leave you in peace!'

The wholly despicable character of the former Social-Democratic Party has also been shown up. It swore fidelity to the proletarian dictatorship. It signed the agreement with the Communist Party of Hungary. Then it united with that party. At solemn meetings, at the congress of Soviets, at the party congress, it declared that it would fight to the last drop of blood for communism and the revolution. By uniting with the communists, it adhered to the Third, Communist International.

The party now carries the mark of Cain on its forehead. It has sold out the proletariat, the revolution, the glorious party of Hungarian communists, the International. By concluding a secret treaty with the Versailles murderers and with their own counter-revolutionaries, supported by the gold of the imperialists and the bayonets of the executioners, it overthrew the government of the communist proletariat. These 'true socialists' are now restoring private property. The League of Nations Powers are each sending a regiment to support them. At the head of the government stands Peidl, a murderer of workers, the Hungarian Noske.

The treacherous character of the social-patriots has been exposed. Just as the Scheidemanns and Kautskys in Germany drowned the proletarian revolution in blood, just as the social-revolutionaries and mensheviks are objectively helping the Tsarist generals, just as the entire yellow Berne international is selling out the working class, wholesale and retail, to the predatory 'League of Nations', so the Hungarian social-traitors have surrendered the Hungarian Soviet Republic, the pride of the world proletariat, to be torn to pieces.

There is no place in the Third International for the provocateurs and paid hangmen of capital!

Let them go into the Second, with Branting and Thomas, Noske and Kautsky!

The Communist International, mourning the fall of the Soviet Republic in Hungary and the loss of its glorious leader Tibor Szamuely, calls on the proletarians of the world to rally still more closely under the communist banner, to strengthen still more the offensive against the fortress of capital.

In the greatest historical struggle of our day there will be great victories and cruel defeats. But the bloody experience of Finland and Siberia has shown us that in countries where once the Soviets have had power no lasting victory of the counter-revolution is possible. Everywhere the waves of insurrection are rising. Our final victory is as inevitable as the fall of the bourgeoisie and the social-traitors.

The Communist International calls on the Hungarian proletariat to stand firm in courage and fortitude. To work, comrades! Start at once the organization of an illegal communist party. The bloody lesson of Hungary has taught the entire world proletariat that there can be no coalition, no compromise, with the social compromisers! The stratum of opportunist contemptible leaders must be swept away. New men must come to the head of the movement. They will come from the working class. For it is to them and not their enemies that victory is assigned.

Soviet Hungary has fallen—long live Soviet Hungary!

Long live the Hungarian Communist Party!

Long live the workers' revolution of the world!

Long live communism!

EXTRACTS FROM AN ECCI CIRCULAR LETTER ON PARLIAMENT AND
SOVIETS

1 *September* 1919   *Beschlüsse des ersten Kongresses,* p. 139

[This circular opened the campaign against 'ultra-leftism' in the Comintern, and
was followed by Lenin's pamphlet *'Left-wing' Communism, an infantile disorder*.
The reluctance to take part in parliamentary elections and parliamentary work
was characteristic not only of the anarchist-syndicalist wing of the labour movement, but also of many members of the communist parties. The first congress of
the German Communist Party voted 62 to 23 against taking part in the elections
to the National Assembly.

The KPD congress at Heidelberg in October 1919 considered a set of theses
submitted by Paul Levi, after correspondence with Radek, which implied expulsion of those who were opposed to parliamentary activities and to work in the
reformist trade unions. Radek was not in favour of pushing matters so far; Levi's
theses were carried by 31 against 18 votes, and the minority left the congress,
taking with them nearly half of the total membership of roughly 50,000. In
April 1920 they founded the Kommunistische Arbeiterpartei Deutschlands
(KAPD). The question of parliamentary activities was not, however, at this stage,
elevated to a major issue.

In July 1919 Sylvia Pankhurst (for the British Socialist Workers' Federation)
had written to Lenin asking for his support for direct as opposed to parliamentary
action. Lenin's reply suggested that if unity on the question of Parliament could
not be achieved, it might be necessary to have two communist parties in Britain,
agreeing on the major issues of proletarian dictatorship and Soviet power, but
divided on the issue of parliamentary action.

The KAPD was in agreement with the dissident group of Dutch communists
led by Herman Gorter, who emphasized the differences between conditions in
Russia, where the nature of the party was determined by the preponderance of
peasants among the population, and in western Europe and America, where the
proletariat was a majority. The proletarian party in the west should have no
truck with the petty-bourgeoisie, parliaments, or reformist unions. In reply to
'Left-wing' Communism Gorter wrote an 'open letter' to Lenin putting forward his
views. He left the Communist Party in the autumn of 1921 and formed the Communist Labour Party of Holland, analogous to the KAP in Germany. He is
reported to have said, after a visit to Russia in 1920, that Lenin, thinking constantly of Russia, 'saw all things only from the Russian point of view', not in the
sense of Russian interests, but of the universal validity of Russian experience.]

Dear Comrades!

The present phase of the revolutionary movement has placed squarely
and sharply on the order of the day the question, among others, of parliamentarianism. In France, America, England, Germany, as the class
struggle grows more acute, all revolutionary elements are joining the communist movement by merging or co-ordinating their activities under the
slogan of Soviet power. The anarcho-syndicalist groups, and the groups

which just call themselves anarchist, are joining in the general trend. The ECCI welcomes them most cordially. . . .

These groups and tendencies have always come out actively against parliamentary methods of struggle. On the other hand those elements in the Communist Party which have come to it from the socialist parties are mostly inclined to recognize parliamentary action also (Loriot's group in France, the ASP in America, the ILP in England, etc.). All these tendencies, which should at all costs and as quickly as possible be united in the communist party, require a uniform tactic. The question must therefore be decided on a common basis, and the ECCI is sending this circular, which is devoted to this special question, to all fraternal parties.

At the present moment the universal and unifying programme is recognition of the struggle for the dictatorship of the proletariat in the form of Soviet power. History has posed this question in such a way that it acts as a demarcation line between the revolutionary proletariat and the opportunists, between communists and social-traitors of every variety. The so-called 'centre' (Kautsky in Germany, Longuet in France, the ILP and some elements of the BSP in England, Hillquit in America) is, despite all its assurances, objectively an anti-socialist tendency, because it cannot and does not want to fight for the Soviet dictatorship of the proletariat. On the other hand, those groups and parties which formerly rejected any political struggle (e.g. some anarchist groups) have, by recognizing Soviet power, the dictatorship of the proletariat, in fact renounced their previous anti-political character, because they have admitted the idea of the seizure of power by the working class, the power which is necessary to suppress bourgeois resistance. In this way, we repeat, a common programme has been found, the programme of struggle for Soviet dictatorship.

The old divisions in the international workers' movement have clearly become obsolete. The war created a new alignment. Many of the anarchists or syndicalists who rejected parliamentarianism, behaved just as contemptibly and treacherously during the five years of war as the old leaders of official social-democracy, who take the name of Marx in vain. Forces are being mobilized along a new line—on one side those who are for a proletarian revolution, for the Soviets, for the dictatorship, for mass action rising to armed insurrection; on the other hand those who are against this. This is the basic question of our day. This is the main criterion. This is the distinguishing characteristic which marks the new associations.

What is the relation between recognition of the Soviet idea and parliamentarianism? Here two questions must be kept quite separate, for logically they have nothing in common with one another: the question of parliamentarianism as a desirable form of the political regime, and the question of using parliament for the purpose of promoting the revolution. Comrades often confuse these two questions, and this has an extremely harmful effect on the entire practical struggle. We shall deal with each of these questions in turn and draw all the necessary conclusions.

What is the form of the proletarian dictatorship? We answer: Soviets. That has been proved by Russian experience, which has universal significance. Can Soviet power be reconciled with parliamentarianism? No, and again, no. It is absolutely irreconcilable with parliaments as they now exist, because the parliamentary machine embodies the concentrated power of the bourgeoisie. The deputies, the chamber of deputies, their newspapers, the system of bribery, the secret connexions between deputies and bankers, the connexion with the entire machinery of the bourgeois State—all these are chains for the working class. They must be broken. The bourgeois State machine, and consequently bourgeois parliaments, are to be broken, dissolved, destroyed, and on their ruins a new power is to be organized, the power of working-class bodies, of 'workers' parliaments', that is, of the Soviets. Only traitors to the working class can delude the workers with the hope of a 'peaceful' social revolution by means of parliamentary reforms. Such people are the fiercest enemies of the working class, and they must be fought pitilessly; no compromise with them can be allowed. Hence our slogan for every bourgeois country is: 'Down with parliament! Long live Soviet power!'

But the question may be asked: All right, you reject the power of present bourgeois parliaments; why then do you not organize a new and more democratic parliament based on genuine universal franchise? During the socialist revolution the struggle reaches such an acute pitch that the working class must act quickly and decisively, and not give the class enemies in its camp access to its power organization. These requirements are met only by the Soviets of workers, soldiers, sailors, peasants, elected in the factories, on the land, in the barracks. That is the way to put the question of the form of proletarian power. The government must be overthrown: kings, presidents, parliaments, chambers of deputies, constituent assemblies, all these institutions are our sworn enemies and must be abolished.

Now let us pass to the second basic question: can bourgeois parliaments be used to further the revolutionary class struggle? Logically, as we have said, this question is quite separate from the first one. We can help to abolish an organization by entering it, by 'exploiting' it. Our class enemies also realize this very well, and use the official social-democratic parties, the trade unions, and other such organizations, for their own purposes. Let us take the most extreme example. The Russian communists, the bolsheviks, took part in the elections to the Constituent Assembly. They attended its meetings. But they came there in order to disperse the Assembly after 24 hours and to establish the power of the Soviets. The party of the bolsheviks also had its deputies in the Tsarist Duma. Does that mean that at that time they 'recognized' the Duma as an ideal or at least a tolerable form of State organization? It would be madness to make that assumption. It sent its representatives to the Duma so that, from this direction too, it could oppose the apparatus of Tsarist power, and help forward the abolition of that same Duma. It was not for nothing that the Tsarist Government sentenced the bolshevik 'parliamentarians' to prison for 'State treason'. It was illegal work that the bolshevik leaders were doing when they used their 'immunity' to rally the masses to an attack on Tsarism.

Are we in favour of retaining bourgeois 'democratic' parliaments as the form of State administration?

No, in no circumstances. We are for Soviets.

But are we in favour of using these parliaments for our communist work, so long as we are not strong enough to overthrow them?

Yes, we are in favour of that, on a number of conditions.

We know very well that in France, America, and England, the workers have not yet produced from their ranks parliamentarians capable of this kind of action. In these countries, until now, we have had parliamentary treachery. But that is no proof of the incorrectness of the tactics which we consider right. It only means that they have had no revolutionary party of the proletariat such as the bolsheviks or the German Spartakists. When there is such a party, everything can become quite different. In particular it is necessary: (1) that the centre of gravity of the struggle shall be outside parliament (strikes, revolts, and other forms of mass struggle); (2) that action inside parliament shall be bound up with this struggle; (3) that the deputies shall also do illegal work; (4) that they shall act on the instructions of the central committee and subordinate themselves to it; (5) that in their actions they shall disregard parliamentary forms (not fearing outright collisions with the bourgeois majority, speaking 'over their heads', etc). Whether at any given moment to take part in elections, in the electoral campaign, depends on a number of concrete circumstances which must be very carefully considered in the given country at the given time. The Russian bolsheviks were in favour of boycotting the elections to the first Imperial Duma in 1906, and the same bolsheviks were in favour of taking part in the elections to the second Duma, when it became clear that the bourgeois-landowning power in Russia would still be ruling in Russia for many years. Before the elections to the German National Assembly in 1918 some Spartakists were in favour of participation, others against. But their party remained a united communist party.

We cannot, on principle, renounce the utilization of parliament. . . . We must leave ourselves elbow room on this question.

What we wish specially to emphasize is that in all cases the question is really solved outside parliament, on the streets. Now it is clear that strikes and revolts are the only decisive methods of struggle between labour and capital. Therefore comrades should concentrate chiefly on mobilizing the masses. Founding the party, forming their own groups in the trade unions and capturing the unions, organizing Soviets in the course of the struggle, leading mass struggles, agitating among the masses for revolution—all that comes first; parliamentary activities and participation in the electoral campaign are only auxiliary activities, nothing more.

If that is so, and it undoubtedly is, then it is obvious that it is not worth while splitting over differences of opinion on this subsidiary question. . . . Therefore we appeal urgently to all groups and organizations who are genuinely fighting for Soviets to proceed with the utmost unity, even if on this question they are not of one mind.

All who are for the Soviets and the proletarian dictatorship will unite as quickly as possible and form a unified communist party.

With communist greetings,

President of the ECCI,
G. ZINOVIEV

EXTRACTS FROM A LETTER FROM THE ECCI TO THE BOLOGNA CONGRESS
OF THE ITALIAN SOCIALIST PARTY

22 *September* 1919   *Beschlüsse des ersten Kongresses,* p. 150

[The Italian Socialist Party had been opposed to the war and welcomed the Russian revolution as a step towards peace. It had declared its adherence to the Communist International, although unable to send delegates to the first congress. At the meeting of the central committee held in Milan on 19 March 1919, the motion to leave the Second International and to join the Third was carried by 10 votes to 3.

The Bologna congress voted by a large majority for adherence to the Comintern, although it took no steps to expel the considerable minority, led by Turati, who opposed the motion. A single socialist list was put forward in the November 1919 elections, and gained roughly a third of the total of five million votes, and 156 out of a total of 508 seats (Mussolini, standing as an independent in Milan, was defeated, receiving fewer than 5,000 votes out of a total of more than 250,000).]

Dear Comrades:

The ECCI sends its fraternal greetings to your congress to be held on 27 September. During the four and a half years of the infamous imperialist butchery the Italian working class never ceased to hold aloft the red flag. From the first moment when the Second International collapsed, there were men in the Italian Socialist Party who continued in word and deed to serve the idea of the international brotherhood of the workers. . . . The Italian working class was the first to take up the fight against the Allied imperialists who were conducting a robber campaign against Soviet Russia. . . .

The Communist International is, naturally, sure of the sympathy of the Italian proletariat. But our new international association of workers needs more than sympathy. We need clarity of programme and of aim. The dictatorship of the proletariat, the Soviets as the form of that dictatorship, the abolition of bourgeois-democratic parliaments, which are tools of bourgeois dictatorship, creation of a Red Army—these are the tasks which should bring together the international revolutionary proletariat.

The Communist International will follow with intense interest the work of your congress. One of the leading places in the Third International belongs to you, comrades!

> President of the ECCI,
> G. ZINOVIEV
> Secretary, A. BALABANOVA

EXTRACTS FROM A LETTER FROM THE ECCI TO THE INDUSTRIAL WORKERS OF THE WORLD

January 1920   Beschlüsse des ersten Kongresses, p. 173

[A congress of left-wing groups and parties held at Chicago in September 1919 resulted in the formation of two communist parties—entitled respectively the Communist Labour Party and the Communist Party. Early in 1920 the ECCI, in consultation with representatives of both parties, worked out an agreement for their fusion. It added the comment: 'This is a model of how communists should act. If serious differences arise among them, the first thing they should do is to send representations of both points of view to the ECCI and try to settle their differences with the help of the CI. The decision of the CI is law for every communist organization.' The agreement was not put into effect, and both parties sent delegates to the second Comintern congress. Both were very small in numbers. The IWW was a larger organization, and far more proletarian in character. Its hostility to orthodox parliamentary socialism was at this time of greater importance to the Comintern than its anarcho-syndicalist leanings.]

Comrades,

The ECCI, which is meeting in Moscow, the heart of the revolution, sends greetings to the revolutionary proletariat of America in the person of the union of the Industrial Workers of the World (IWW).

World capitalism, disorganized by war, is now no longer able to keep under control the tremendous forces which it has itself called into being, and is approaching its collapse.

The hour of the working class has struck. The social revolution has begun, and here, on the plains of Russia, the first battle of the vanguard is being fought.

History does not ask whether we are in the right or not, whether we are ready for revolution or not. A favourable opportunity has occurred. Seize it, and the whole world will belong to the workers. If you let it pass, there may not be a second for a century.

This is not the time to talk of the 'building of a new social order within the shell of the old'. The old social order is splitting its shell. The workers must establish the dictatorship of the proletariat, which alone can build the new order. . . .

We understand and share your hatred of the principles and tactics of the yellow socialists, who have discredited even the name of socialism in all countries of the world. Our goal is the same as yours—a community without State, without government, without classes, in which the workers manage the means of production and distribution for the welfare of the entire people.

We are sending you this letter, comrades of the IWW, in recognition of your many years of heroic participation in the class struggle . . . to explain communist principles and the communist programme.

We call on you, who are revolutionaries, to join the Communist International, which was born in the dawn of the social revolution. . . .

The capitalists of the whole world—American, as well as French, Italian, English, German, etc.—are now making plans to chain the workers once for all to a new, complete, and final subjection.

Either this, or the dictatorship of the working class; there can be no third alternative. The workers must now decide.

Capitalism is making desperate efforts to re-establish its precarious rule. The workers must, therefore, seize State power, in order to transform the whole social order in their own interests. . . .

Will the capitalists succeed in their intentions?

They certainly will, unless the workers declare war on the entire capitalist system, overthrow the capitalist governments, and set up a government of the working class, which abolishes the institution of capitalist private property and makes all wealth the common property of the workers.

That is what the workers of Russia did, and that is the only way in which the workers of other countries can shake off industrial slavery and transform the world so that the workers get the benefit of everything they produce and no one can exploit the labour of others.

But the Russian revolution cannot survive if the workers of other countries do not rise against their capitalists. The capitalists of the whole world have grasped the danger that Soviet Russia's example offers, and have united to destroy it. The Allies quickly forgot their hatred of Germany and called on the German capitalists to join them in their common cause.

And the workers of other countries are beginning to understand. The revolutionary wave is rising in Italy, Germany, France, and England. . . . The social revolution has begun; the first battles are raging in Russia. It will not wait while the workers experiment with reforms. The capitalists have already overthrown Soviet Hungary. If they can keep their power and suppress the workers' movement in other countries, then the industrial slave State will inevitably follow. Before it is too late, the class-conscious workers of the world must prepare themselves to meet the capitalist offensive, to attack capitalism and abolish it, and to get rid of it for ever. . . .

In the place of the capitalist State the workers must build their own workers' State, set up the dictatorship of the proletariat. In order to destroy the capitalist State, to break the resistance of the capitalists, and to disarm the capitalist class, in order to seize the property of the capitalists and to hand it over to the entire working class—for all these tasks a government is necessary, a State, the dictatorship of the proletariat, through which the workers in their Soviets can eradicate the capitalist order with an iron hand.

That is just what is happening in Soviet Russia. But the dictatorship of the proletariat is only a temporary measure. We communists also want to abolish the State. The State can exist only as long as the class struggle lasts. . . .

Every worker knows that when there is a strike there must be a strike committee, a central body conducting the strike whose orders must be obeyed. This committee is elected and controlled by the ordinary workers. Soviet Russia is 'on strike' against the entire capitalist world. The social revolution is a general strike against the entire capitalist system. The dictatorship of the proletariat is the strike committee of the social revolution. . . .

As the most important revolutionary-syndicalist organization among the revolutionary industrial unions in America, the IWW should take the initiative in seeking a basis for the unification of all unions with a class-conscious, revolutionary character, of all workers who recognize the class struggle, such as the Union of Industrial Workers, the One Big Union, and the few revolutionary unions in the AFL. This is not the time to quarrel about names or minor organizational questions. The chief thing is to unite all workers who at the critical moment will be capable of revolutionary mass action.

As revolutionaries they should not repulse the attempts of the American communists to get agreement on joint revolutionary action. The political party and the industrial organization must work shoulder to shoulder for the common purpose—the abolition of capitalism by the dictatorship of the proletariat and the establishment of Soviets; the dissolution of classes and of the State.

The Communist International extends a brotherly hand to the IWW.

President of the ECCI,
G. ZINOVIEV

EXTRACTS FROM A LETTER FROM THE ECCI TO THE STRASBOURG CONGRESS OF THE FRENCH SOCIALIST PARTY

17 *January* 1920   *Beschlüsse des ersten Kongresses*, p. 194

[The Strasbourg congress voted 4,300 to 300 to leave the Second International, and 3,000 to 1,600 against joining the Third. Cachin and Frossard, representing the centre, were appointed as a delegation to visit Russia.]

The ECCI trusts that the pressure of the French working masses will induce the Strasbourg congress to break with the Second International. . . . It appeals to all communist elements in France to unite into one organization and to declare open war on the traitors to the proletariat.

Cleanse the proletarian ranks of the adherents of the yellow Second International. . . .

President of the ECCI,
G. ZINOVIEV

EXTRACTS FROM A LETTER FROM THE ECCI TO THE CENTRAL COMMITTEE OF THE GERMAN COMMUNIST PARTY AND THE PRESIDIUM OF THE GERMAN INDEPENDENT SOCIAL-DEMOCRATIC PARTY

5 *February* 1920   *Beschlüsse des ersten Kongresses*, p. 195

[A group of members of the German Social-Democratic Party (SPD) broke away in March 1916, as a left-wing anti-war opposition, and in the following year, at a congress in Gotha in April, formed the Independent Social-Democratic Party (USPD—the 'Independents'); among its leaders were Kautsky and Bernstein. It included, on the extreme left, the Spartakusbund, which later became the German Communist Party. 'We joined the USPD', said Liebknecht, 'in order to drive them forward, to have them within reach of our whip'. The USPD left the SPD-USPD coalition Government, formed in November 1918, at the end of that year.

At its Leipzig congress in December 1919 the USPD voted by 227 to 54 to leave the Second International, and by 169 to 114 against joining the Third. It suggested that a conference be called of the 'Third International and other socialist revolutionary organizations' to discuss the foundation of a comprehensive international to include them all.

In *Left-wing' Communism* Lenin wrote that the movement to the left in Germany had strengthened the USPD rather than the KPD. This made it the more necessary to win over the USPD. 'The USPD is obviously not homogeneous: alongside the old opportunist leaders . . . there has arisen in this party a left, proletarian wing which is growing with remarkable rapidity. . . . To fear a "compromise" with this wing of the party is positively ridiculous. On the contrary, it is the *duty* of the communists to seek *and to find* a suitable form of compromise with them, such a compromise as, on the one hand, would facilitate and accelerate the necessary complete fusion with this wing, and, on the other, would in no way hamper the communists in their ideological and political struggle against the opportunist right wing.'

This letter prefigures the '21 conditions of admission to the Communist International' adopted by its second congress later in the year.]

The last congress of the Independent Social-Democratic Party decided to propose to the Communist International and other 'social-revolutionary organizations' that they unite into a common international organization. The ECCI regards it as its duty to place this question before all revolutionary workers. It assumes that the open discussion of this question before the broad working masses of all genuinely revolutionary elements of the international army of the proletariat is the only possible course, and not an agreement come to behind the scenes. The following considerations are therefore a reply to Crispien's letter of 15 December 1919 to the ECCI which was published in the *Freiheit* of 2 January 1920.

1. THE WORKERS IN THE USPD AND THEIR LEADERS DURING THE REVOLUTION

The Communist International is well aware that the workers who belong to the Independent Party think quite differently from their right-wing leaders. This is the starting-point of our appraisal of the situation in the USPD. The Communist International regards the Leipzig resolution as a change in the political direction of this party made in response to the pressure of that part of the German working class organized inside the party. Learning from the experience of the revolution, this section of the working class is coming more and more to take up the standpoint of proletarian dictatorship and mass struggle for the dictatorship under the banner of the Communist International. The opportunist right-wing party élite is doing its best to hamper this movement by recognizing it in words but in fact doing everything it can to prevent the development of the revolution. These opportunist 'centrists' restrained the proletariat from any active mass action during the imperialist war, supported the treacherous policy of defence of the bourgeois 'fatherland', denied the necessity of an illegal organization, and shrank from the idea of civil war. When the revolution broke out they formed a government with the avowed traitors of the working class, sanctioned the disgraceful expulsion of the Berlin embassy of the Russian proletariat, and supported the policy of breaking diplomatic relations with the Soviet Republic. The right-wing leaders of the Independents have since the beginning of the German revolution preached orientation towards the Entente and opposed with all their strength the alliance between Germany and Soviet Russia. The right-wing leaders have systematically spread petty-bourgeois illusions among the German workers about the nature of Wilsonism. They praise Wilson, and describe him as the defender of a just peace and the representative of democracy. Thanks to their tactics the State machine of Wilhelm's Empire, which was kept out of sight behind republican flags, remained completely untouched.

At the decisive moment of struggle against the executioner of the working class, Noske, the right-wing leaders of the Independents adopted a conciliatory policy of dishonourable bargaining, weakened the revolutionary will of the workers, destroyed the unity of the proletariat in struggle, and thus promoted its defeat. . . .

It is now quite clear that the German revolution is taking such a painful course because the Scheidemanns have succeeded in disarming the people, because the beginning of the revolution did not lead to an association between Germany and Soviet Russia, because the old apparatus of power has remained intact. An enormous part of the guilt and responsibility for this rests on the right-wing leaders of the USPD.

To straighten the line again these mistakes must be understood and corrected. To straighten the party line, even if this is done over the heads of some leaders, is the primary task of the workers who belong to the party of the Independents.

2. THE CHIEF MISTAKES OF THE USPD AND OF CENTRIST PARTIES GENERALLY

The ideology of the leaders of the USPD is not a specifically German phenomenon. The followers of Longuet in France, the ILP in England, the ASP in America, and other parties have the same standpoint. Their characteristic feature is a constant vacillation between the open social-treachery of the Noske type and the policy of the revolutionary proletariat, i.e. of communism. These mistakes may be summarized as follows:

(1) The dictatorship of the proletariat means the overthrow of the bourgeoisie by a class, the proletariat, in fact by its revolutionary vanguard. It is a denial of the point of view of the dictatorship of the proletariat and the adoption of the point of view of bourgeois democracy to demand that the vanguard must first win over the majority of the people in elections to a bourgeois parliament or bourgeois constituent assembly, etc., that is, by an election when wage slavery is still in existence, when exploiters are still at large, and private property in the means of production still prevails. . . .

(2) The dictatorship of the proletariat means recognition of the necessity of forcibly suppressing the resistance of the exploiters, means the readiness, the ability, and the resolution to do this. The bourgeoisie, even the most republican and democratic (for example in Germany, Switzerland, or America) systematically resort to pogroms, to lynch justice, to murder, to armed violence, to terror against communists, and are in reality opposed to all revolutionary steps of the proletariat. In these circumstances to renounce the use of force and of terror is to act like a whining petty-bourgeois, to sow reactionary philistine illusions about social peace is, to put it concretely, to show fear of the officer's sword. . . .

(3) The same is true of the civil war. After the imperialist war, confronted with reactionary generals and officers who use terror against the proletariat, faced with the fact that new imperialist wars are already being prepared by the present policy of all bourgeois States, and not only deliberately prepared but following with objective inevitability from their entire policy—in these circumstances and in this situation to condemn civil war against the exploiters, to bemoan it and fear it is, in reality, to become a reactionary. It means fearing the victory of the workers which may cost 10,000 victims while accepting a new imperialist butchery which cost millions of victims yesterday and will cost as many tomorrow. . . .

(9) The Independents, the right wing, and the followers of Longuet, are not conducting any agitation in the army (in favour of entry into the army for the purpose of preparing it to go over to the side of the workers against the bourgeoisie). They are not creating any organization for this purpose. They are making no reply to the violence of the bourgeoisie, who are constantly over-stepping 'legality' (during the war as well as after it), by systematic propaganda of illegal organizations and the creation of such organizations. Unless legal work is combined with illegal work and legal organizations with illegal organizations there can be no truly revolutionary party of the proletariat, either in Germany or in Sweden, in England, in France, or in America.

(10) The basic question of the socialist revolution, the expropriation of the exploiters, is discussed by the right-wing leaders in terms of 'nationalization' and is put in a reformist and not in a revolutionary sense. The word nationalization glosses over the necessity for confiscation which arises from the unbearable burden of imperialist debts and the impoverishment of the workers, it glosses over the resistance of the exploiters and the necessity for revolutionary measures by the proletariat to suppress that resistance. It creates reformist illusions which are wholly incompatible with the dictatorship of the proletariat.

(11) The Communist International regards it as not only incorrect but as inadmissible in principle for the USPD, which has in fact taken over the fundamental ideas of the German Spartakists although it has

appropriated these ideas too slowly, too inconsistently and incompletely, to say nothing in the resolutions of its congresses about amalgamation with the Communist Party of Germany (with the Spartakusbund). The unity of the revolutionary proletariat demands this amalgamation, for it is impossible in fact to recognize the dictatorship of the proletariat and Soviet power without taking concrete, serious and deliberate steps in that direction, so that the vanguard of the proletariat of the country in question, which has demonstrated in prolonged and severe struggle (against the opportunists as well as against the syndicalists and the allegedly left-wing semi-anarchists) its capacity to lead the working masses towards dictatorship, shall be supported by all class-conscious workers, consolidate its authority, and carefully guard and develop its traditions. . . .

3. THE USPD AND THE INTERNATIONAL

The same petty-bourgeois cowardly policy is being pursued by the right-wing leaders of the USPD on the question of the international unification of the proletariat.

(1) The right-wing Independents and the followers of Longuet are not trying to deepen and develop in the masses a realization of the corruption and rottenness of the reformism which in fact prevailed in the Second International (1889–1914) and destroyed it; they are obscuring this realization and concealing the disease instead of exposing it. The question of the collapse of the Second International, a question which is of the greatest historical importance, the causes of that collapse, the chief mistakes and crimes of the Second International, the part it plays as a subsidiary branch of the 'League of Nations'—none of these questions has been discussed by the USPD, which means that they are concealing these crimes and befogging the class consciousness of the proletarian masses.

(2) The right Independents and the followers of Longuet do not understand and explain to the masses that the imperialist super-profits of the advanced countries enabled and enable them to bribe the upper strata of the proletariat, to throw them crumbs of these super-profits drawn from the colonies and from the financial exploitation of weak countries, to create a privileged section of skilled workers, etc.

Without exposing this evil, without fighting not only against the trade union bureaucracy but also against all petty-bourgeois manifestations of the craft and labour aristocracy, without the ruthless expulsion of the representatives of this attitude from the revolutionary party, without calling in the lower strata, the broad masses, the real majority of the exploited, there can be no talk of the dictatorship of the proletariat.

(3) The reluctance or the inability to break with the upper ranks of the workers who have been corrupted by imperialism is shown among the right-wing Independents and the followers of Longuet by their failure to

support outright and unconditionally all insurrections and revolutionary movements among the colonial peoples. In these circumstances the condemnation of colonial policy and imperialism is nothing but hypocrisy, or the meaningless sighs of thick-headed philistines. . . .

(4) While the leaders of the USPD, urged forward by the working masses, enter into negotiations with the Communist International, they also have dealings with the parties of the Second International (including Mannerheim's Finnish Social-Democratic Party). They refer to these parties as social-revolutionary and they suggest that the Communist International shall unite with these parties. This hopeless attempt to found a fourth bastard International without a clear programme, without defined tactics, without prospects for the future, without any perspective, is, of course, doomed to failure. But it shows that the right-wing leaders are sabotaging the decision of the Leipzig congress of their party and have no intention of making an honest alliance with the vanguard of the fighting international proletariat.

In this connexion the ECCI declares . . .

(b) The ECCI is of the opinion that it is not possible in the interests of success in the international proletarian struggle to allow the creation on whatever pretext of any new international association of workers, which could not in fact be in any circumstances revolutionary. Splintering of the forces of the international proletariat would only be to the advantage of capital and its servants among one-time socialists.

(c) The ECCI considers it highly desirable to enter into negotiations with the parties which declare themselves ready for a final break with the Second International. With this in view it requests the representatives of these parties to come to Russia, where the executive organ of the Communist International has its seat. However great the technical difficulties involved in crossing frontiers it is still quite possible, as experience has shown, for the delegates of the party to make this journey.

(d) The ECCI is aware that in consequence of the complex relations and the specific peculiarities of the development of the revolution, full account must be taken of these peculiarities. We are quite prepared to extend the Third International, to take into consideration the experience of the proletarian movement in all countries, to amend and extend the programme of the Third International on the basis of Marxist theory and the experience of the revolutionary struggle throughout the world.

We decisively reject any co-operation with the right-wing leaders of the Independents and the followers of Longuet who are dragging the movement back into the bourgeois swamp of the yellow Second International.

In welcoming that section of the decision of the Leipzig congress which refers to a breach with the Second International, the ECCI invites the USPD delegation to negotiate, and expresses the firm conviction that as a result of the growing revolutionary consciousness of the proletarian masses the leadership of the USPD will be cleaned up, the party will be brought to amalgamation with the Communist Party of Germany, and its best elements at last organized under the common banner of the Communist International.

The ECCI suggests to the advanced workers of Germany that this reply shall be discussed in open proletarian meetings and that precise and clear answers be requested from the USPD leaders to the questions which have been put.

ECCI MANIFESTO ON THE DANGER OF A RUSSO-POLISH WAR

17 *February* 1920   *Beschlüsse des ersten Kongresses*, p. 214

[In January 1920 the Council of People's Commissars proposed negotiations with Poland, and early in February the Central Executive Committee addressed a long appeal to the Polish people disclaiming any intention of planting communism on Polish soil by force. The Poles also made half-hearted overtures, but neither side had confidence in the other's intentions. Lloyd George informed the House of Commons that at the end of January he had told the Polish representatives that the British Government 'could not advise Poland to open war on Russia'.]

The French, English, and American Governments, which for four years conducted such a bloody war, ostensibly in the name of democracy, liberty, and the establishment of lasting peace among the peoples, are now inciting Poland to war against Soviet Russia, the same Poland which received its freedom and independence not from the hands of these imperialist Governments, but thanks only to the revolution in Russia and Germany. Clemenceau's political testament was the instruction to wage war against Soviet Russia to the last drop of blood of the last Polish soldier. Along the entire front where Poland has cut into Lithuania, White Russia, and the Ukraine, without taking any notice of the desires of the inhabitants of these countries, the Polish proletariat dressed in Scottish uniforms presented by the English benefactors, are conducting a bloody fight against Russian peasants and workers.

Now, after the final defeat of Yudenich, Kolchak, and Denikin, a Polish war against Russia seems at first glance unlikely. If these white generals who brought into action not only all the forces of the Russian bourgeoisie but also everything that was left over from the feudal, Tsarist regime under the device of 'Great Russia, one and indivisible', and who were supported not only by international capitalism but also by the burning hatred for the revolution of all bourgeois elements of old Russia—if they could not withstand the mighty onslaught of the Red Army, could Poland really dare with the tiny forces at its disposal to take up battle against the workers' and peasants' republic of Russia? If the Polish Government did that it would be a senseless, suicidal adventure.

And yet, comrades, we must openly admit that this adventure is possible and the workers throughout the world must do everything in their power to prevent it.

In the first place the Allies are doing their utmost to force Poland into this desperate venture. At Versailles they tried to annihilate Germany economically and to break Central Europe into pieces, to dismember it so that the financial sharks could more easily swallow the peoples of Germany, Austria, and the Balkans piecemeal. But the peoples of Europe are not Hindus and Negroes, and since the French capitalists know this they fear the consequences of their policy. They do not believe that the German people, throttled in the noose of Versailles, will quietly and patiently endure the yoke of a shameful servitude. Just as after the defeat of France in 1871 Bismarck lived in constant fear of the possibility of a Franco-Russian alliance against Germany, so today the rulers of France regard with fear the threatening spectre of revolt among the peoples of Central Europe. And in particular they fear the thought that the Russian people, once they have settled accounts with their innumerable enemies, will unite with the German people, emancipated from capital and from the Junkers, and will later give powerful assistance to the French and English workers against their oppressors.

But the French bourgeoisie have other fears also. They are afraid of a strong 'Great Russia', a Russia of landlords and capitalists. If reaction in Russia were to succeed with the help of the Allies in defeating workers' and peasants' Russia, Russian reaction would be driven in alliance with de-stroyed imperialist Germany to turn on its saviours in order to get for itself some of the booty which the French, English, American, and Japanese capitalists have divided up among themselves. For Russian reaction could only go on fooling the masses of workers and peasants by the glitter of external conquest, by the illusion of a 'Great Russia'. This fear of a future alliance of the revolutionary proletariats of Russia and Germany on the one hand, and the fear of a possible coalition of reactionary Germany and reactionary Russia on the other, determines the policy of the Allies, and particularly of bourgeois France, towards Poland. . . .

Since Poland is thrust like a wedge between Russia and Germany, French capital decided to make it into a military bulwark against Germany and a barrier against the East, in order to maintain in Europe a new balance of power that would be advantageous for bourgeois France. . . .

But it is not only against a possible future war with Germany that bour-geois France wants to use Poland. It wants to use Poland now as an execu-tioner, to force it to strangle the Soviet regime in Russia and to do this as quickly as possible, before the victory of the working class in Germany. If before that victory Soviet Russia has been swept away, then Marshal Foch, unopposed, can occupy the Rhine coal basin with his black and yellow troops and cut the proletarian revolution in Germany off from its most important sources of strength and life. And having settled one by one with the revolution in Russia and Germany, the French exploiters hope to be able to settle accounts with their own proletariat without any great difficulty.

That is why the French bourgeoisie are urging Poland on so feverishly to war with Soviet Russia. . . .

Soviet Russia has several times proposed peace negotiations to the Polish Republic, and has not only emphasized its unqualified recognition of Polish independence but also its complete willingness to settle all questions in dispute by peaceful means. It has done everything in its power to prevent a new war and further bloodshed.

Now it is up to you, comrades in all countries. The Polish workers have shown their opposition to the war in many demonstrations and strikes. Honour is due to the Polish workers who in these most difficult conditions have done their duty.

French and English workers, it is up to you to support the Polish proletariat which is fighting against the war. Save Poland from the horrors of war. Help the Polish workers to free their land from the yoke of the masters and the intrigues of the Entente; help Soviet Russia to avoid a new war.

EXTRACTS FROM AN ECCI MANIFESTO ON THE CIVIL WAR IN GERMANY

25 *March* 1920   *Beschlüsse des ersten Kongresses*, p. 241

[The Kapp *putsch*, a short-lived rebellion of officers and Freikorps against the Weimar Republic, opened on 13 March 1920 with the entry of troops under General von Lüttwitz into Berlin. The Government withdrew to Dresden and then Stuttgart, and von Lüttwitz set up a right-wing government of 'neutral experts' under Wolfgang Kapp. The Reichswehr refused to intervene. The trade union federation called a general strike. The Communist Party *Zentrale* (the small working committee of seven members of the Central Committee, permanently resident in Berlin, which later became the politburo) issued a statement disclaiming interest in the affair—'The proletariat will not lift a finger for the democratic republic'—contending that naked reaction made the real situation clearer. The rank and file of the communist party, however, followed the trade union lead, and on 15 March the KPD came out in support of the strike. Paul Levi, a member of the *Zentrale*, was in prison at the time of the *putsch*, and vigorously attacked the policy of the KPD *Zentrale*. The KPD congress which met shortly afterwards endorsed the condemnation. The strike was successful, and Kapp's government lasted only a few days, but severe reprisals were taken against the strikers in various parts of the country. In putting down the resistance of trade union and socialist organizations in the Ruhr, the Reichswehr was permitted by the Allies to enter the 'neutral zone' demilitarized by the Versailles treaty. In the report of the German party to the second Comintern congress it was stated that, 'It is well known, and has never been concealed, that in the situation created by the Kapp *putsch* the party leadership in a certain sense failed to act'. The party membership, however, ignoring the leadership, went into action. The KPD, which had led a more or less illegal existence since January 1919, became a legal party in April 1920.]

However the struggles which are now being fought out in the streets of German towns may end, the events now taking place are among the most significant in the history of the international proletarian revolution.

For a year and a half the white social-democratic Government, the murderers of Karl Liebknecht and Rosa Luxemburg, have systematically disarmed the German workers and armed the offspring of the German bourgeoisie. The white social-democrats cleared the road for the white generals, and when these white generals thought that they were sufficiently strong and the German revolution sufficiently demoralized by the treacherous social-democrats, they attempted to bring about a counter-revolutionary change in Germany.

But they miscalculated. The entire proletariat of Germany without exception sprang into action. The cowardly gang of Ebert and Noske fled from Berlin in fear of their own generals, but the heroic Berlin proletariat in one tremendous outburst thrust aside the government of the white generals which could only keep going for a few days. The generals' counter-revolution worked a miracle; it opened the eyes of even those backward strata of the workers who, demoralized by the propaganda of the yellow social-democrats, had formerly put their trust in the Government of Ebert and Noske. With one powerful blow the Berlin proletariat pushed the gangs of Lüttwitz and Kapp out of their town. The flame of the general strike has spread over practically the whole of Germany. . . .

The German workers have got arms, that is the chief thing, and there is no power on earth which can take these arms away from them, because they have realized that a military dictatorship is inevitable if the workers are once again disarmed. In incredibly difficult circumstances the Red Army is being formed in Germany and it is growing in spite of everything, to the horror of those who oppress the proletariat and the joy of the workers of all countries. The formation of a standing Red Army, however small in numbers for the time being, is of tremendous importance for the fate of the proletarian revolution in Germany. Nor is it of small value that the agricultural workers and farm labourers are joining the insurrectionary urban proletariat in great numbers, are arming themselves and hastening to the help of the advanced troops in the towns as a reserve.

The civil war in Germany will not end until victory is in the hands of the workers. Neither treachery by the trade union 'leaders' nor rotten compromises hatched out by the right wing of the Independents, who are no different from the Scheidemanns, can save the power of the bourgeoisie. The lesson was too clear, the impulse which set the whole of working Germany in movement was too strong. The German workers' road to power is covered with thorns; the bourgeoisie and their servants, the white social-democrats, are resisting stubbornly, but nothing can save bourgeois rule. The throne of the bourgeoisie is tottering in Germany also. Should the French and English capitalists send their troops tomorrow to tame the German workers they will on the following day see with horror that the soldiers they have sent are fraternizing with the German workers. Intervention by the French and English capitalists will carry the communist wave like an echo to England and France and accelerate the ripening revolution in those countries. The bourgeoisie cannot avoid their fate. The proletarian revolution and the establishment of Soviet power throughout Europe is as inevitable as that morning shall follow the dark night.

What has the attempt at counter-revolution in Germany shown to the workers of all countries? It has proved once again without any possibility of doubt how right the Communist International was when it declared time and time again that as the epoch of civil war opens there are only two dictatorships possible: either the dictatorship of the proletariat which liberates all mankind and rebuilds the whole of life on communist foundations, or the dictatorship of the most reactionary and brutal bourgeois and generals who draw the knots tighter round the neck of the working class and lead humanity into new wars. One dictatorship or the other; there is no third. . . .

The victory of Soviet power in Germany will give the cause of proletarian revolution in all countries a gigantic impulse forward. The league of two Soviet republics, Russia and Germany, will strengthen both of them and make it possible for the German and Russian workers to organize their economic life and to save the people from hunger. The league of two Soviet republics will act as a powerful magnet attracting the proletariat of the entire world, and to this league of two Soviet republics others will be added one by one as the proletarian dictatorship triumphs in other countries.

Workers of Germany! Now you can all see where the policy of white social-democracy leads. You can see quite clearly how Scheidemann and Ebert betrayed you to the German bourgeoisie. Now you can see how the gangs despatched by Ebert and Scheidemann are shooting down not only communists but also social-democratic workers who with arms in hand are taking up the fight against reaction. Arm yourselves, German proletarians; take arms wherever you can find them, set up your councils. The conditions which are now being created will put new life into the councils. Yellow social-democracy cannot strangle them now as it did a year ago. Build up your Red Army without a moment's delay wherever you can form red detachments. . . . French, English and Belgian soldiers, if you are sent against your brothers, the insurrectionary German workers, if you are ordered to turn your bayonets against the starving German proletarians, their wives and mothers, turn these bayonets against your own bourgeois authorities; go over to the side of the rebels and fraternize with them. Remember that for an honest worker there is no greater crime than to stain his hands with the blood of the workers of another country. Remember that the German workers are fighting for bread, for peace, for freedom. Remember that there will only be an end to war if with an iron hand we put an end to the power of the capitalists.

EXTRACTS FROM A MANIFESTO TO THE COMMUNIST PARTIES OF
BULGARIA, RUMANIA, SERBIA, AND TURKEY

5 *March* [*April*] 1920   *Beschlüsse des ersten Kongresses*, p. 229

[The Balkan Social-Democratic Federation was founded in 1910 at a conference in Belgrade attended by the social-democratic parties of Bulgaria, Serbia, Rumania, and Greece; in 1914 it came out against the war; in 1919, at a conference in Sofia, it changed its name to Balkan Communist Federation and decided to affiliate to the Third International. Its affiliation was accepted in 1920. Its object was to concert the activities of the Balkan communist parties on questions concerning the peninsula as a whole. The Turkish Communist Party was founded illegally in June 1920. In June 1919 the 'narrow' Bulgarian Socialists (Tesniaki) voted for affiliation to the Third International. The elections in Bulgaria gave the communists 50 seats out of a total of 229; the Agrarian Party won 110 seats, and the social-democrats 9. The elections were held on 28 March.]

The Communist International sends its joyful greetings to the communist movement in the Balkan countries. The brilliant victory of the Bulgarian Communist Party in the elections to the Sobranie, the mass strikes and demonstrations which have taken place recently in Bulgaria and which have often led to bloody encounters with the troops, the wave of economic and political strikes in Rumania during the past year, the action of the Bucharest proletariat in December 1918 that ended with the shooting down of dozens of workers, the official adherence of the Serbian Social-Democratic Workers' Party to the Third International—all these clearly indicate the revolutionary frame of mind of the Balkan proletariat who have shown their desire to follow in the footsteps of the Russian proletariat and to strive for the dictatorship and the establishment of Soviet power. . . .

The programme and the methods of struggle pursued by the Russian proletariat in the severe and bloody experience of three years of revolution are in conformity with the interests of the proletarian masses in all countries, including the countries of the Balkans and the Danube.

Because of their geographical and economic position the Balkan and Danubian countries were drawn long ago into the sphere of interests of the imperialist Powers. The pressure of Tsarist, capitalist Russia towards the Mediterranean, of imperial Austria and Germany to the shores of the Aegean, Asia Minor, and Mesopotamia; the struggle of England, France, and Italy to get the upper hand in the Mediterranean, in Egypt, and in Mesopotamia—all these strands met and interlocked in the Balkans, which is the focal point of the roads to the South and to the Near and Far East.

The bloody rivalry for the upper hand in the Balkans lasted for decades, but when these rivals out of sheer exhaustion ceased waging war the ruling classes of the Balkan countries who had become their agents and servants continued the war among themselves. The last imperialist war began in the Balkans; it had a prelude in the Balkan war of 1912–13 which ended without complete victory for any of the groups taking part and provided the occasion for the opening of the 1914 war among the imperialist great Powers, to settle finally the question who should rule the Balkan peninsula and control the main roads to Asia and the Mediterranean.

In order to draw the Balkan States into war against one another their imperialist patrons exploited the greed of the bourgeoisie for territorial conquest and enticed them with promises of a 'Great Bulgaria', 'Great Serbia', or 'Great Rumania'. They incited the different nationalities against each other, made loans for armaments, taking as pledge the mines and harbours, and in fact transforming these countries into their colonies. . . .

The struggle to take possession of the Rumanian oil fields waged by American capital on one side and Anglo-American capital on the other clearly proves that the Allies have no intention whatever of guaranteeing to the Balkan bourgeoisie the enjoyment of the fruits of their victory.

As a result of this policy the prospects for the future awaiting the Balkan peoples are even worse than their present situation. The new national divisions which followed the dismemberment of Austria-Hungary and the defeat of Bulgaria and Turkey have made the nationality problem in the Balkan peninsula even more complex than it was before the war. Under the rule of the victors far more people have acquired alien nationality, and the policy of national oppression, the policy of insatiable militarism awakens a still greater desire for emancipation, and this struggle for emancipation is taking on an ever larger scope. . . .

Only the proletariat can avert a new catastrophe by its victory and free the working and peasant masses from economic and national oppression. Only the victory of the proletarian dictatorship can unite the masses in a Balkan or Balkan and Danubian federal, socialist, Soviet republic, liberate them both from the feudal capitalist exploitation of their own and the foreign bourgeoisie as well as from colonial servitude and national dissensions. The communist party is called upon by circumstances to play an even greater part in the Balkan peninsula than in the capitalist countries where there are no nationality problems. All the efforts of the Balkan communist parties should be directed to fulfilling this great historical mission of communism in the Balkans.

In the present preparatory phase of the socialist revolution the Balkan communist parties must pay great attention to close association and co-ordination of the work of the different Balkan parties. The experience of the Hungarian Socialist Republic, which collapsed because it came into conflict with the white Governments of Rumania, Yugoslavia, and Czecho-slovakia instead of meeting with the support of the workers of those countries, should be a clear enough lesson that without the closest association among all the Balkan parties victory is impossible.

The second lesson which the Balkan and Danubian communist parties must take deeply to heart is the necessity of drawing into the communist movement the working peasantry, the poor and middle peasants as well as the industrial workers. The triumph and consolidation of Soviet power in Rumania, Bulgaria, Serbia, Greece, and Turkey will depend on the ability of the communists to extend the influence of their party to the peasant masses.

EXTRACTS FROM A LETTER FROM THE ECCI TO THE TRADE UNIONS OF
ALL COUNTRIES

April 1920

K.I., 10, col. 1677
May 1920

[The International Federation of Trade Unions was reconstituted at a conference in Amsterdam, July–August 1919. It adopted a resolution condemning the 'Labour Convention' (that is, Part XIII of the Versailles peace treaty) but decided that the trade unions should attend the first International Labour Conference, to be held in Washington, provided (inter alia) that their representatives were recognized as representing the labour movement. One of the first actions of the IFTU was to appeal to all trade unions for 'mass action' against the blockade of Russia.

The suggestion that a new trade union international should be founded was made by Zinoviev in March 1920 to the congress of the Russian Communist Party. No steps were taken immediately, but when in April the IFTU helped to organize the conference in Washington at which the ILO was founded, the Russian trade unions decided to join the Comintern and to appeal to other revolutionary trade unions to do the same. An international trade union council was formed at the time of the second Comintern congress to make preparations for 'an international congress of red trade unions'.]

. . . What is now to happen to the trade unions? Along what path will they travel? The old union leaders will again try to push the unions on to the bourgeois road. . . .

What was it in the old trade unions that in fact led to their capitulation to the bourgeoisie?

A narrow craft spirit. Division into small units. An exaggerated respect for bourgeois legality. Emphasis on the labour aristocracy and contempt for the mass of unskilled workers. High membership dues which an ordinary worker could not afford. The leadership of the unions concentrated in the hands of bureaucratic bosses who developed into a caste of officials. The advocacy of a 'neutral' attitude to political questions, which amounted in fact to support of bourgeois policy. A distortion of the collective agreement system which meant in fact that the agreements were concluded by the bureaucratic bosses, and kept the workers covered by the agreements in chains for several years. . . . Pushing to the front the charitable and mutual benefit activities of the unions as against strike funds. Regarding the unions as organizations designed to win partial improvements *within the capitalist system*, not as organizations aiming at the revolutionary overthrow of the entire capitalist system. . . .

Will the unions continue along this old reformist road? That is the question which the international labour movement has to answer. We are deeply convinced that the answer will be no.

A fresh wind is blowing through the musty trade union offices. Factory committees are being formed in England, production councils in Germany, new centres are crystallizing in the French unions, unions of unions like the triple alliance in England, new currents have set in in the American unions —all these are symptoms that a radical revaluation of values is taking place in the world trade union movement.

It is our belief that a *new* trade union movement is being formed.

What should be its characteristic features?

The new trade union movement should throw overboard all vestiges of the craft spirit. It should make its task the direct struggle—shoulder to shoulder with the communist parties—for the dictatorship of the proletariat and the Soviet system. . . . It should place in the foreground the weapon of the general strike and should prepare for combining a general strike with armed insurrection. The new unions should cover the entire mass of workers and not only the labour aristocracy. They should implement the principle of strict centralism and organization by industry, not by occupation. . . . The new unions should start a revolutionary struggle for the immediate nationalization of the most important industries, while remembering that unless the proletariat establishes a Soviet regime no genuine nationalization is possible. . . .

The tremendous wave of strikes spreading across the entire continent of Europe, as well as America and other parts of the world, is the best proof that the unions will not wither away, but very quickly take on new life. They cannot and will not stand aside from the immense problems on which the attention of the entire world is fastened and which divide the whole of mankind into two camps, the white and the red. . . .

The old unions are reshaping; within a year we shall not recognize them. The old bureaucrats will be generals without armies. The new era will advance a new generation of proletarian leaders to reshape the trade union movement. But, foreseeing this, the bourgeoisie are not dozing. Through their tried and trusted servants, the old trade union bosses, they are trying to get the unions into their hands again. At Amsterdam, as you know, a congress was held which called itself an International Trade Union Congress. . . . The illustrious League of Nations, which is in fact a league of imperialist robbers, convened in Washington, and later in Paris, a farcical conference on 'international labour protection', at which two-thirds of the votes were given to the bourgeoisie, and one-third to bourgeois agents like Legien, Jouhaux, and co., who call themselves the workers' representatives. . . . By the united efforts of bourgeois ministers and trade union bureaucrats they want to pin the workers' unions into the procrustean bed of petty-bourgeois reformism.

The Communist International calls on the proletariat organized in trade unions to put an end to this bourgeois mockery, to expose this shameful comedy. . . . Tell the whole world that you have nothing in common with these creatures of Clemenceau and Wilson. . . .

The Communist International considers that the time has come when the unions of producers, freed from bourgeois and social-traitor influence, should begin to create their international organization, both for industries and generally. In opposition to the yellow international of unions which the bourgeois agents are trying to re-create in Amsterdam, Paris, and Washington, we should put up a genuinely proletarian *red* international of trade unions, marching side by side with the Third International. . . .

The cause of working-class emancipation demands the concentration of *all* the organized forces of the proletariat. *All* kinds of weapons are necessary if we are to make a successful assault on capitalism. The Communist International . . . aims at the closest bonds with the revolutionary unions. It wishes to bring together not only the political organizations of the workers, but all workers' organizations which in fact and not only in words are out for revolutionary struggle and for the dictatorship of the working class. The Executive Committee of the Communist International suggests that not only the communist parties should attend the congresses of the Communist International but also those trade unions which have a revolutionary programme. Red trade unions should unite on the international level and become a part (section) of the Communist International.

We make this proposal to the workers organized in unions throughout the world. In the trade union movement there is impending that evolution and breakaway which occurred in the political parties of the proletariat. Just as all the most important workers' parties left the Second International, so all honest unions should break with the yellow Amsterdam trade union international.

EXTRACTS FROM AN ECCI MANIFESTO ON THE POLISH ATTACK ON
RUSSIA

18 *May* 1920
K.I., 11, col. 1861
June 1920

[Desultory fighting and reluctant armistice overtures preceded the opening of the Polish offensive, aimed at annexing part of the Ukraine, at the end of April 1920; the Polish army advanced rapidly, capturing Kiev early in May. In the south of Russia civil war flared up again between the Red Army and Wrangel's forces. Analysing the mistakes of the KPD during the Kapp *putsch*, Radek urged the German communists to bear in mind that 'the conflict between Soviet Russia and Poland opens new perspectives'. Paul Levi is said to have offered communist support to any German government that would support Russia in this conflict.]

TO THE PROLETARIAT OF ALL COUNTRIES

Workers of all countries! In the East blood flows again. Again vast areas are laid waste by military operations; again the Russian working masses, thirsting for peace and for the creative labour of reconstruction and regeneration, are compelled to take up arms.

The attack of capitalist and landlord Poland on Soviet Russia has interrupted the work of peaceful construction to which the Russian workers and peasants turned once they had defeated Kolchak, Denikin, and Yudenich. . . .

Who is responsible for these new hostilities? You know that the Soviet Government recognized the independence of the Polish Republic from the very first day. . . . You know that to spare the lives of Russian and Polish workers it was ready to make territorial and economic concessions. You know that, firmly convinced that the Polish workers, allies of the Russian proletariat, would sooner or later take power into their own hand, the Soviet Government was even ready to transfer for the time being to the

Polish ruling classes territory which, by the composition of its population, should not belong to Poland. . . . Poland replied to the Soviet Government's peace proposals by a treacherous attack on the Ukraine. . . .

But it is not only the Polish landlords and capitalists who are guilty of this war. The Entente governments are also responsible. They armed and are arming white-guard Poland. While negotiating with Soviet Russia about the resumption of trade relations, they have not given up hope of subduing the workers and peasants of Russia. . . . The French capitalists have sent to Poland not only enormous quantities of arms, but also 600 officers. With one word—'Enough of war, enough of destruction. The whole world needs Russia, as a source of grain and raw materials'—the English Government could have stopped this war. But Lloyd George's Government, which in its notes to the Soviet Government appeals to the sentiments of humanity and demands an amnesty for the Russian counter-revolutionaries in Archangel and the Crimea, never even thought of telling Poland that enough blood had been shed. . . . To a greater or less extent all the Entente governments are supporting the Polish invaders and robbers.

Workers of the world! Soviet Russia will settle with the shameless bandits of Polish imperialism, as it settled with Yudenich, Kolchak, and Denikin. . . . But the question is, how long will the war last, how much blood will be shed, how much wealth destroyed, how many more wounds will be inflicted on the Russian people? It depends on you, workers of all countries, whether the war will stop as early as possible with the defeat of the Polish capitalists and landlords.

Workers in the ammunition factories of France, England, Italy, and America. Do not turn out a single bullet, a single rifle, not a single gun for Poland.

Transport workers, railwaymen, dockers, seamen! Do not despatch supplies or food to Poland, for it will be used for the war against workers' and peasants' Russia.

Workers of all Allied countries! March out on to the streets, demonstrate and strike under the slogan: 'No more support for white-guard Poland'. . . .

German railwaymen! Do not pass trains through from France to Poland. Dockers of Danzig! Do not load ships destined for Poland. Austrian railwaymen! Not one train must get through from Italy to Poland. . . .

Workers of Poland! There is no need to remind you, who are bound to the Russian proletariat by thirty years of common struggle, of your duty. You will organize demonstrations and strikes on behalf of peace with Soviet Russia. . . . The International is convinced that you will now exert your utmost efforts to strike white Poland in the rear, so that together with the workers of Russia you will win victory over the Polish landlords and capitalists. You know that Soviet Russia brings Poland not oppression, but national freedom, freedom from the chains of Allied capital, help in the fight against your own capitalists. The victory of workers' and peasants' Russia will be the victory of the Polish proletariat, brothers and allies of the Russian workers and peasants. To the attack, Polish workers.

LETTER FROM THE ECCI TO THE PRESIDIUM OF THE GERMAN INDEPENDENT SOCIAL-DEMOCRATIC PARTY

27 *May* 1920   *Beschlüsse des ersten Kongresses*, p. 284

[Between the Leipzig and Halle congresses of the USPD the ECCI kept up a continuous stream of propaganda and appeals to the USPD. These negotiations between the ECCI and the USPD—by-passing the small German Communist Party—were pressed hard in the attempt to 'capture' an important mass organization in Germany (in the June 1920 elections the USPD received 4·9 million votes, while the KPD received fewer than half a million).]

Dear Comrades,

The ECCI notes with regret that the Presidium of the USPD has not replied to its letter of 5 February 1920. This letter dealt with all the questions in dispute between us and the USPD. A clear answer would have certainly helped to clear up the relations of the USPD Presidium with the Third International.

Even more than this failure to reply, the ECCI regrets that the Presidium found it possible to conceal our letter from the membership. The attitude of the USPD to the Communist International is the concern not only of the party Presidium but of the million German workers who support German social-democracy and whose energetic pressure forced the USPD Presidium to enter into relations with us. The opinion of the Independent working masses is decisive for the USPD attitude to the Communist International. For it is not the half dozen men and women who make up the Presidium that decides whether the USPD shall belong to the Communist International or not, but the million Independent workers who decide by their deeds. We are convinced that it is enough for the Independent workers to be brought to an understanding of the meaning of their struggle, for them to decide consciously in favour of the Communist International. To keep our letter secret is therefore objectively nothing but an attempt to delay the decision of the USPD masses in regard to their relations with the Communist International. Any attempt to excuse this sabotage of the Leipzig congress decision by the USPD Presidium, which has so far done nothing more to carry out the congress decision than send a single letter, by reference to external difficulties, the Kapp *putsch*, and preparations for the elections, is exploded by the simple fact that the question of international organization is a question of life and death for the struggle of the German working class. Quite apart from that, however, the publication of our letter by our West European Secretariat has shown that publication was technically possible.

Since we are aware of the serious desire of the great majority of the Independent workers to enter the Communist International we think it our duty, regardless of obstacles placed in the way of dealing with the question of the international unification of the proletariat by the USPD Presidium, to request you to send your representatives to Moscow so that we can inform them of the thesis of the ECCI on the tactical questions of the struggle for proletarian dictatorship, and clear up the question of the reasons why the USPD Presidium is delaying adherence to the Communist International. Then it will be the job of the Independent German workers to decide whether they are in agreement with the Presidium or with the ECCI.

There are no insuperable technical difficulties in the way of the USPD representatives making the journey. If it is possible for workers from South Africa, Australia, and America to get here, sometimes almost entirely of their own accord, then representatives of a party of one million can find their way here if they really look for it.

> With communist greetings, for the ECCI,
>
> K. RADEK, *Secretary*

EXTRACTS FROM AN OPEN LETTER FROM THE ECCI TO THE MEMBERS
OF THE GERMAN COMMUNIST LABOUR PARTY

2 *June* 1920   *Beschlüsse des ersten Kongresses,* p. 292

[Lenin regretted the split in the KPD which led to the formation of the KAPD, but had been unable to prevent it (communication between the two countries was slow and difficult). In a letter to the German central committee of 20 October 1919 he said he had learnt of the split from the official German news broadcast. 'If you are in agreement on basic questions (for Soviet power against bourgeois parliamentarianism) unification is, in my opinion, both possible and necessary.' In regard to the KAPD, as to the IWW, the ECCI was ready to be conciliatory, to overlook disagreements over secondary matters such as parliamentary activities, in order to win the support of organizations hostile to the Second International. At the foundation congress of the KAPD it was decided to apply for affiliation to the Comintern, and two delegates, Jung and Appelt, were sent to Moscow.

Laufenberg and Wolffheim had advocated 'National Bolshevism', i.e. cooperation with the right-wing nationalist German parties on an anti-Versailles, anti-west, anti-social-democratic programme. Their proposals, communicated to Radek, were rejected by Lenin, and the two were expelled from the KPD. In April 1920 the ECCI had dissolved the Amsterdam bureau of the Comintern, whose leaders were in sympathy with the KAPD, stating that 'on some highly important questions the Amsterdam bureau is following a line which departs in principle from the line of the ECCI. In these circumstances the Executive has no choice but to cancel the powers given to the group of Dutch comrades'.

The following resolution was unanimously adopted by the ECCI: 'We are convinced that the differences with the Dutch comrades will be quickly resolved. In contrast to the Second International, we do not conceal our differences nor do we permit ambiguous formulations. On a number of questions (trade unions, parliament), the Dutch bureau has adopted an attitude inconsistent with that of the Executive Committee. The Dutch bureau did not inform the Executive Committee of its differing point of view before convening the international conference in Amsterdam.

'In view of this the Executive Committee declares that the mandate of the Dutch bureau has lost validity and withdraws that mandate. The Executive Committee instructs the little bureau to send the Dutch comrades a full report on this matter. The functions of the Dutch bureau are transferred to the West European Secretariat.' The conference referred to met early in February 1920 and was attended by delegates from left-wing groups in Holland, Britain, France, Italy, Belgium, Germany, the Scandinavian countries, and America. Michael Borodin attended as ECCI delegate. The conference was dispersed by the Dutch police on the second day and accomplished nothing.]

Comrades,

On 4 April 1920 a congress was opened in Berlin on the initiative of a few groups of the 'left' opposition which proclaimed itself a new party, the Communist Labour Party. According to the organizers of the congress it represented about 38,000 members.

The ECCI only learned about this congress a few weeks after it took place. We received no information that it was to be held. The statement made by the organizers (see the minutes) that a representative of the West European Bureau of the Communist International was present at the congress is not correct.

The ECCI has received the report of the representatives of your Party Presidium on the foundation of the Communist Labour Party and has thoroughly examined it at a prolonged discussion, together with all the material relevant to the subject. The Executive Committee on the basis of a full knowledge of the facts then decided to address the present letter to you in order to explain the point of view which the Executive Committee takes up on the disputed questions of the German revolution.

We know that the overwhelming majority of the members of the German Communist Labour Party are honest, revolutionary-minded workers; we know that they are filled with a sacred desire to fight for the emancipation of the proletariat; we know that they are deeply convinced that they stand on the platform of the Communist International. We know that what we have to say about the attitude of the Communist Labour Party will cause them pain.

But in contrast to the Second International the directing body of the Third International regards conflicts within the individual parties not from a 'diplomatic' standpoint, and does not allow itself to be guided merely by considerations of a formal and organizational character. The ECCI sees it as its duty to be a guiding political centre for the workers' movement of all countries. In the present case it considers it its duty to speak clearly on the nature of the disputes and problems which have become so acute because of the communist split in Germany.

We are not by any means adherents of unity at any price. The ECCI is fully aware that there are situations in which it is the sacred duty of a revolutionary to split a party organization. Such cases occur when the old party organization has become unfaithful to the interests of the proletariat and is leading the proletariat along the path to ruin. The organizers of the new Communist Labour Party who took the initiative in splitting the German communists did not by any means, we are deeply convinced, find themselves in such a situation. On the contrary, the views which the German Communist Labour Party upholds in contrast to those of the old German Communist Party (Spartakusbund) are, in the opinion of the ECCI, an outright deviation from communism and will have unfortunate results for the new party.

The ECCI does not mean to imply that it is in absolute agreement on all details with the German Communist Party *Zentrale*, against which the German Communist Labour Party has raised the banner of revolt. For example, it is completely out of agreement with the reasons given by the Spartakusbund Centre in its well-known statement of 21 March 1920 on the possibility of forming a so-called 'purely socialist' government. It was incorrect to state that such a 'purely socialist' government could ensure a situation in which 'bourgeois democracy need not appear as a capitalist dictatorship'.

We also admit that the Spartakusbund Centre has not always been sufficiently careful and patient in its organizational struggle with the opposition elements and has thus driven a part of the workers into the arms of the anarcho-syndicalist ranters. But we must state with all firmness to all members of the German Communist Labour Party that on all those most important questions of principle and tactics which have now become the most burning question of the day in Germany and throughout the Communist International, it is not the German Communist Labour Party but the German Communist Party which is right.

Let us deal with these problems one by one.

The most important question in our opinion is that of communist participation in the trade unions and in the campaign for factory council elections. . . .

The Berlin congress of the Communist Labour Party officially confirmed the slogan that German communists should leave the 'free' trade unions. . . . The ECCI can in no circumstances agree with this slogan.

What reasons did the Berlin congress of the German Communist Labour Party give for urging communists to leave the free trade unions? It gave only one reason, unfortunately a wholly inadequate and absurd reason: the 'free' trade unions are reformist unions which remain willing tools in the hands of their bureaucratic leaders.

To deal with this question more fully. The membership of the 'free' German trade unions is growing with unexampled speed. At the beginning of the imperialist war they numbered 3 million, and during the war fell to $1\frac{1}{2}$ million. Now their membership has increased to nearly 8 million. German workers are streaming into the unions because they hope to find in them the means of satisfying their most elementary economic demands. Can the Communist Labour Party stand aside from organizations to which practically the entire working class in the country concerned belongs? In our opinion, no. . . .

The new epoch, the epoch of embittered class struggle which is changing before our eyes into civil war, also changes the 'free' trade unions into a new organization. Some of these unions we must split. Others will of themselves come over to us, either wholly or in a majority. The fires of the proletarian revolution which is breaking out will burn out the opportunist tendencies in all mass workers' organizations, including 'free' trade unions, and transform these organizations into pillars of the proletarian dictatorship. This process of transformation has already begun in the German unions. Many of them are already expelling the social-democratic leaders and replacing them by Independents and sometimes by communists. A vigorous process of differentiation has already begun among the masses of the trade union membership, which will with every day that passes strengthen the influence of communism in the trade unions.

It is true that this process is going on slowly, too slowly, much more slowly than we wished. The ordinary members of these unions will grasp through their own experience the treachery of their present leaders and the utter powerlessness of social-democratic tactics. The March events in Germany during the counter-revolutionary Kapp–Lüttwitz *putsch* proved once more what a tremendous force the trade unions now represent, what irreparable harm they do to the cause of the proletarian revolution because they follow the yellow social-democrats, and what a great force they could be if the communists succeeded in wresting the unions from social-democratic influence.

But events themselves will cure the ordinary trade union member of his confidence in the 'old', 'tried' social-democratic tactics. The lessons of experience are driven home too deeply. It is the mission of communists in Germany to facilitate and to accelerate the development which is already taking place. But that can only happen if they stay inside the 'free' trade unions, form communist fractions inside them, even if at the beginning they are only small, take an energetic part in the current daily work of the unions and expose the bankruptcy of the Legiens in their day-to-day work. . . .

It is a deep concern of the Communist International that the German communists shall make no irreparable mistake in the trade union question. At the present moment this question is of great international significance. The Second International, in so far as it is a political organization of the working class, has collapsed like a house of cards. But it is trying to establish itself again on the basis of the trade unions. The Amsterdam International of social-democratic unions is a far more serious opponent of the Communist International than the Brussels International Bureau of the Second International. The Second International can only re-establish itself if it succeeds in maintaining its influence on the trade unions. If it has any mass support in the working-class movement it is only because of the unions which we have not yet been able to wrest from the Second International, which we have not known how to rescue from the disintegrating influence of social-democracy. The most important current task of the proletarian revolution is to destroy the Amsterdam International of 'free' trade unions just as we destroyed the Brussels Second International. The bourgeoisie maintain themselves in power at the present time only because the Second International still has some influence. But the latter maintains itself only because it still has some influence on the 'free' trade unions. Communist mistakes in this field can have as their result nothing more nor less than a prolongation of the rule of the bourgeoisie. The German Communist Labour Party, without of course wishing to do so, is helping the bourgeoisie to maintain their rule over the working class, and that is something to which the Communist International can in no circumstances reconcile itself. . . .

The German Communist Labour Party split from the German Communist Party because it considered the Communist Party's tactics opportunist; at the same time it accepted as members Laufenberg and Wolff-heim . . . advocates of civil peace with the bourgeoisie if the bourgeoisie recognized the government of the workers' councils, before that bourgeoisie had been destroyed and broken by the proletariat. They advocated giving the franchise to all peasants regardless of the size of their holdings. Thus their policy amounted in fact to the establishment of a sham Soviet republic, for a genuine Soviet republic, a genuine proletarian dictatorship, can only be established if the proletariat has defeated the bourgeoisie in civil war. If they get power without this struggle, the fight still confronts them. While it would be pedantic to renounce power if the proletariat could seize it without large-scale struggles, it would be the first duty of the communist party in such a situation to warn the proletariat against placing any trust in the bourgeois elements which recognized their power in words. Laufenberg and Wolffheim did the exact reverse. They tried to direct the policy of the proletariat towards a sham Soviet republic because they needed such a republic, that is, a coalition with the nationalist bourgeoisie and the officers corps, for the purpose of fighting the Entente. War against the Entente is the alpha and omega of the policy of Laufenberg and his comrades. It may be that war with Entente capitalism will become a necessity for Soviet Germany if the workers in the Entente countries should not come quickly enough to the help of a victorious proletariat in Germany. But should this war have to be fought the German proletariat will find it more than ever necessary to defeat the German bourgeoisie, for the German bourgeoisie, the German counter-revolution, notwithstanding all the hymns of hate against France and England, will make common cause with Entente capital against the German proletariat. In their address Laufenberg and Wolffheim are spreading the poison of the illusion that the German bourgeoisie could, out of nationalist hatred, become allies of the proletariat. If the proletariat were to be befooled by this idea they would become cannon fodder for German capital which, under the flag of the sham Soviet republic, would use the proletariat for war against the Entente, and then discard the cloak and openly re-establish capitalist rule. The nationalist petty-bourgeois standpoint of Laufenberg and Wolffheim is bound to lead them to fight against the Communist International. Whoever has trust in their own bourgeoisie must distrust the international proletariat and the International. . . .

The ECCI has told your delegates that it cannot regard you as a serious revolutionary communist party so long as you . . . keep within your ranks people and organizations who trample under foot the principles of communism. Your representatives were obliged to recognize completely the correctness of the Communist International's attitude, were obliged to issue a statement that on their return to Germany they would ask for the expulsion of Laufenberg and Wolffheim and of the organizations which take up the same position. We welcome this awakening of a proletarian sense of honour and of proletarian insight in your delegates, and expect that you will carry out the obligations which they solemnly undertook and which clear your road to the Communist International. . . .

If you wish to attend the Communist International congress, if you wish to be accepted into the communist family—and we know that is what you want, otherwise there would have been no point in your sending delegates to Moscow—it is obvious that you must state in advance that you accept the decisions of the Communist International congress. The Communist International has broken decisively with the rotten habit of the Second International in collecting round itself parties which in reality do not belong together. The Communist International is not a bundle of parties loosely tied together with general phrases; it is a fighting association, and whoever wants to belong to it must subordinate himself to and act in accordance with the general rules laid down by the international congress. . . .

We repeat, we do not by any means defend every step taken by the Spartakusbund Centre. We know that that Centre has made many mistakes; we think one of its chief weaknesses was its hesitating attitude to the question of participation in the trade unions and failure to take up a firm position. We know that making a cult of 'the leader' is no business for a communist. We know very well that an entire generation of so-called 'leaders' shamelessly betrayed the cause of the working class. We know that there are cases when the struggle against the old leaders becomes an absolute necessity and it is impossible to advance to the creation of a true proletarian movement without 'dethroning' these leaders. The German Communist Labour Party, however, has only convinced us, in the programmatic statements we have had the opportunity of seeing, that its struggle against the Spartakusbund is not dictated by such considerations, but represents rather a certain vacillation in the direction of a petty-bourgeois anarchist policy. . . .

We suggest that before the congress you reach agreement with the German Communist Party Centre and establish a provisional organization bureau of the two centres with equal representation and under the chairmanship of a member of the ECCI. The German working class is living through a period in which any dispersal of communist forces may result in tremendous dangers for their struggle. We must do everything that we can to alleviate the ruinous consequences of the split.

Our practical suggestions are as follows: (1) Ratify immediately the statement of the delegates of your party that Laufenberg, Wolffheim and Rühle will be expelled. (2) State officially, what goes without saying, that you submit unconditionally to the decisions of the second congress of the Communist International. (3) Accept our proposal for the organization of a provisional bureau representing both Centres under our chairmanship. (4) Send your delegates to the second congress of the Communist International on 15 July 1920.

EXTRACTS FROM A LETTER FROM THE ECCI TO THE GERMAN
INDEPENDENT SOCIAL-DEMOCRATIC PARTY

21 *June* 1920
K.I., 12, col. 2257
July 1920

[The USPD sent four representatives to Moscow; they attended the second
Comintern congress, but without the right to vote. On their return, two advocated adherence to the Third International (Däumig and Stoecker), two opposed
affiliation (Crispien and Dittmann). The 21 conditions of admission to the
Comintern approved by the congress were designed to ensure that the right
wing would find them unacceptable. At the September 1920 conference of the
USPD the conditions were rejected.]

On 15 July, as you know, the second world congress of the Communist
International opens in Moscow. . . . It is already clear that our second
congress will really be a world congress of leading workers. The congress
will take stock of the experience of our struggle. It will point out to us the
road of our further struggle; the voice of the congress will be heard by the
working people of the entire world.

Comrades, are you really going to stand aside from this congress?

We know that you proletarians of the USPD are heart and soul with us.
We know that you long to enter the ranks of our international fellowship
of workers, the Third International; the less can it be tolerated that the
right-wing leaders of your central committee should frustrate your wish
and ours.

Under your pressure, under the pressure of the workers, the Leipzig
congress of the USPD decided to leave the Second International and to
establish relations with the Third. But your right-wing leaders in fact
sabotaged and are still sabotaging that decision. . . . We sent an open
letter to the USPD stating in detail and precisely the terms on which we
can accept your party, as well as other parties which up to now have
belonged to the centrist tendency. Your central committee did not even
publish the letter of the ECCI in Germany. It kept it and is still keeping it
out of sight. It is hiding it from you, but the communists have published
it. . . . Their conduct shows how right we were when we said that your
admission into the Third International was possible only over the heads
of your right-wing leaders.

In view of the above, we suggest that individual local and regional
organizations of the USPD which want to join the Third International at
once should immediately elect and send their delegates to our congress. . . .
The revolutionary workers of the USPD must be present at the world
congress of the Communist International. . . . Discuss our proposal at all

your workers' meetings. Publish it in your papers. Expose those who frustrate your wishes. Act.

With communist greetings:

> *President of the ECCI*: G. ZINOVIEV
> *Secretary*: K. RADEK

Members of the ECCI: SERRATI, BOMBACCI, GRAZIADEI (Socialist Party of Italy), LENIN, BUKHARIN, KARAKHAN, BALABANOVA, KLINGER (RCP)

EXTRACTS FROM A LETTER FROM THE ECCI TO THE CENTRAL COM-
MITTEE OF THE COMMUNIST PARTY OF AMERICA AND THE CENTRAL
COMMITTEE OF THE COMMUNIST LABOUR PARTY OF AMERICA

June 1920   *Beschlüsse des ersten Kongresses*, p. 266

[At a meeting of the ECCI in August 1920 it was decided to give the two American parties until 10 October to amalgamate on the basis of the decisions of the second Comintern congress. At a further meeting in September they were given until 1 January 1921. Amalgamation did not take place, and at a subsequent ECCI meeting in March 1921, at which representatives of both parties were present, the ECCI, observing that their refusal was tantamount to a crime against the Comintern, declared that unless the two parties amalgamated before the third world congress the ECCI would recommend that delegates from neither should be admitted. Amalgamation was effected at a congress held in May 1921.]

Dear Comrades,

From the reports of comrades who have arrived from America and who represent the two tendencies in American communism, the ECCI has had the opportunity of familiarizing itself with the differences among the American comrades which led to an open conflict and to the formation of two communist parties. The question was examined at an enlarged meeting of the Executive which consisted, in addition to members of the Executive, of representatives of the two American parties and of the communist organizations of France, Switzerland, Hungary, Finland, and Yugoslavia. The ECCI came to the following conclusions: The split is doing great harm to the communist movement in America. It disperses the revolutionary forces and leads to injurious parallelism, to unnecessary friction and to unjustifiable expenditure of strength on the internal struggle. And this at a time when the mobilization of the forces of the American bourgeoisie has taken on an unprecedented scope, when the class struggle is becoming more acute from day to day, requiring unexampled sacrifices on the part of the American proletariat; at a time when, because of the inevitable growth of the world revolution, the greatest opportunities and the most brilliant prospects are opening before the American working class.

Careful examination of all the material on both sides has convinced us that there are no serious programmatic differences between the two parties. There are certain conflicts on questions of organization. There were disputes about how to break with the old social-patriotic party, but that was all.

In such circumstances the split has no justification and must in all circumstances be eliminated. In so far as both parties adopt the standpoint of the Communist International, and we have no reason whatever to doubt that they do, the unity of the party is not only possible but unconditionally necessary. The Executive Committee insists most emphatically that this unity shall be immediately established.

The necessity of immediate unification is further dictated by the fact that to a certain extent the two parties represent different aspects of the communist movement in America, and can, therefore, complement each other. In the Communist Party of America there are to be found chiefly the foreign elements organized in the so-called national federations. The Communist Labour Party of America represents primarily American or English-speaking elements. If the first party has a better theoretic training and closer connexions with the traditions of the revolutionary struggle of the Russian working class, it is at the same time less closely connected with the mass movement and the mass organizations of the American workers, who are gradually finding their way to the class struggle. If the second party has not yet had such a theoretic training it has, on the other hand, this colossal advantage, that through it the communist party can more easily exert an influence on the broad masses of the native American workers, who in the forthcoming decisive class struggle will have the most important part to play. One party is better at propaganda, the other at agitation. . . .

As a means of effecting the earliest possible unification the ECCI proposes that a joint congress be called, whose decisions shall be binding on both sections. An organization bureau shall be set up to prepare and convene the congress and to co-ordinate the work of the two parties until they are amalgamated. This bureau shall consist of an equal number of representatives of the two parties. The basis of unification must be the principles set forth in the directives of the Communist International and the decisions of the ECCI. In addition the Executive wishes to state. . . .

(4) While promoting in every way the splitting of the American Federation of Labour and other similar craft unions, the party must work to establish the closest possible relations with those industrial organizations of the working class which represent the tendency towards industrial unionism (IWW, OBU, IUW, and unions which split off from the AFL). . . .

(7) The increasing persecution of communists in America raises the question of illegal work. The congress of the Communist International in March 1919 expressed itself quite clearly on this point. Illegal work is

essential because throughout the world the bourgeois democracies are in fact placing communist workers in a state of siege. Two or three years ago the idea of working illegally in a free country like England seemed ridiculous to our English comrades. Now the revolutionary English workers have learnt to do illegal work also. . . . Every smallest possibility of legal action must be exploited. At the same time we must learn to issue illegal leaflets, to organize illegal groups, if necessary create illegal factory committees, have an illegal central direction, etc.

The ECCI is convinced that you will show yourselves equal to the responsible tasks which await you. The fate of the international proletariat depends on the successes of communism in America.

With communist greetings,

The ECCI

EXTRACTS FROM THE ECCI CIRCULAR CONVENING THE SECOND
CONGRESS OF THE COMMUNIST INTERNATIONAL

June 1920   *Protokoll*, ii, p. 1

[Apart from Russia (represented by Balabanova, Berzin, Bukharin, Vorovsky, Klinger, and Zinoviev) the ECCI between the first and second congresses included representatives of the communist parties of Hungary, Poland, Yugoslavia, Finland, and Lithuania. The other parties nominated to the ECCI in March 1919 were only occasionally represented. At different times leading communists from other countries who were visiting Russia were drawn into its work. The bureau of the ECCI had met 56 times between the first and second congresses.]

TO ALL COMMUNIST PARTIES AND GROUPS, TO ALL RED TRADE UNIONS, TO ALL COMMUNIST WOMEN'S ORGANIZATIONS, TO ALL COMMUNIST YOUTH LEAGUES, TO ALL WORKERS' ORGANIZATIONS STANDING ON A COMMUNIST PLATFORM, TO ALL HONEST WORKING PEOPLE!

Comrades:

The Executive Committee of the Communist International has decided to convene the second congress of the Communist International on 15 July 1920 in Moscow. . . .

All communist parties, groups, and trade unions which have officially affiliated to the Communist International and are recognized by its Executive Committee are invited to attend the congress, with voting powers.

Those groups and organizations which accept the platform of the Communist International, but which are in opposition to the officially affiliated communist parties, are also invited to take part in the congress, which will itself decide the voting powers to which they shall be entitled.

An invitation is also extended to all groups of revolutionary syndicalists, the IWW unions, and other organizations with which the ECCI has entered into relations. . . .

If it is at all possible, the first international conference of red trade unions will be held in connexion with the congress.

All parties and organizations are invited to send to the congress as large a delegation as possible. . . .

The ECCI emphatically insists that all communist parties represented at the congress *must* nominate one of their delegates as permanent representative on the ECCI. The comrade selected must be in a position to spend a considerable time in Russia. . . .

The first congress of the Communist International raised the banner of communism. Today millions of class-conscious workers all over the world are already gathered under that banner. Now it is no longer merely a question of propaganda for the communist idea. Now the era is opening of organizing the communist proletariat and of the *direct struggle* for the communist revolution.

The Second International has collapsed like a house of cards. The efforts of a few 'socialist' diplomats to found a new bastard international to stand between the second and the third, are downright ridiculous, and are meeting with no support from the workers. Separated from each other by military censorship, by the state of siege, the slander campaign of the yellow social-democrats and the bourgeois press, the workers of all countries are still stretching out brotherly hands to each other. During the one year of its existence the Communist International has won a decisive moral victory among the working masses of the entire world. . . .

These ordinary workers should force their parties and organizations to choose, once and for all; they should put an end to the unworthy game being played by some of their old 'leaders', who are trying to keep the parties from joining the Communist International.

The members of the trade unions which formally still belong to the white-guard international organized in Amsterdam by the agents of capital . . . should strive to get their organizations to break with the traitors to the workers' cause and to send their delegates to the congress of the Communist International. . . .

Every workers' organization, every workers' circle, should discuss the agenda proposed by the ECCI. The workers themselves should send in their own resolutions on these questions, and in the next few weeks the entire communist press should open their columns to a discussion of the important problems confronting us. The preparatory work must be carried out with vigour and zeal. . . .

> With communist greetings:
> *President of the ECCI*: G. ZINOVIEV
> *Secretary of the ECCI*: K. RADEK

EXTRACTS FROM AN ECCI APPEAL ON THE FORTHCOMING CONGRESS
OF EASTERN PEOPLES AT BAKU

July 1920   *Beschlüsse des ersten Kongresses*, p. 367

[Reporting at the ECCI meeting of 20 September 1920, Zinoviev stated that the Baku Congress, called on the initiative of the ECCI, had been attended by 1,891 representatives of 32 nationalities. They came largely from the Caucasus and the Central Asian territories of Russia, but included also many Turks and Persians. Of the total, two-thirds were communists; there were 44 women delegates.

Zinoviev, Radek, and Bela Kun were the principal ECCI representatives. In his opening speech, Zinoviev referred constantly to the struggle against 'English imperialism'. 'We are ready to help any revolutionary struggle against the English Government. . . . Our task is to help the East to liberate itself from English imperialism. . . . Our task is to kindle a real holy war against the English and French capitalists.'

Radek told the delegates they 'need fear no enemy, nothing can stay the torrent of the workers and peasants of Persia, Turkey, India, if they unite with Soviet Russia. . . . Soviet Russia can produce arms and arm not only its own workers and peasants, but also the peasants of India, Persia, Anatolia, all the oppressed, and lead them in a common struggle and a common victory'. He contended that their common enemy gave them a common cause. 'The Eastern policy of the Soviet Government is thus no diplomatic manœuvre, no pushing forward of the peoples of the East into the firing line in order, by betraying them, to win advantages for the Soviet Republic. . . . We are bound to you by a common destiny: either we unite with the peoples of the East and hasten the victory of the western European proletariat, or we shall perish and you will be slaves.'

In the discussion following the two speeches a delegate from Turkestan said (to applause) it was the duty of the congress to say to the Soviet Government: 'Comrades, the Moslems will not desert the Soviets, but on condition that the peculiarities of the Eastern peoples are recognized,' and that the measures taken by the Soviet Government were realized in practice and not only on paper. The west accused the Bolsheviks of red imperialism. To answer that charge, the leaders of the Soviet Government and the communist party 'should come and see for themselves what is happening there, what the local authorities are really doing, whose policy is such that it repels the labouring masses from the Soviet Government'. He asked them 'to remove your colonizers, working behind the mask of communism'.

Bela Kun spoke on Soviets in the East: the Soviet system, he argued, could be established in pre-capitalist conditions, as the dictatorship of the poor peasantry. His theses on 'The Soviet system of government in the East' were adopted unanimously. In closing the congress, Zinoviev said they hoped to meet annually. Meanwhile they would elect a 'Council of Propaganda and Action of Eastern peoples', attached to the ECCI, which would issue a journal in three languages, conduct propaganda throughout the East, unite the local liberation movements, and establish a university of the social sciences for Eastern workers. 'All the work of the Council will be done under the guidance and control of the ECCI.' The Comintern representatives on the Council were Pavlovich, Orjonikidze, Eleeva, Kirov, Stasova, and Skachko. It was to meet at least four times a year in Baku, and have a permanent presidium of seven, to include two ECCI delegates. The manifesto to the peoples of the East issued by the congress, after listing Britain's misdeeds and cruelties, called on them 'to rise as one man for the holy war against the English conquerors. . . . Rise, all of you, against the common enemy, imperialist England.' The congress also issued a manifesto to the workers of Europe, America, and Japan, on the interdependence of the anti-imperialist struggles in the East and the West.

It was as a result of the Baku Congress that an Institute of Oriental Studies was established in Moscow in 1920, and in the following year the Communist University of Toilers of the East, where instruction in political work was given to the students, who came from other countries as well as from Russia, in their own languages. There is no record that the Council of Propaganda and Action ever met.

The first congress of the Persian Communist Party was held at Enzeli in July 1920, preparatory work having been done at Tashkent. Enzeli had been occupied by Soviet forces in May 1920, ostensibly to take over the Russian ships abandoned there by Denikin's forces. The congress was attended by 48 delegates claiming to represent 2,000 members and sympathizers; until the arrival of the Red Army it had consisted of two 'underground' groups in Resht with a total membership of 37. A congress resolution stated that it was the duty of the Persian Communist Party 'to fight jointly with Soviet Russia against world capitalism, and to support in Persia all forces opposed to the English and to the Shah's government'. Soviet forces were withdrawn when the Soviet-Persian treaty was signed in February 1921, and the Persian Communist Party moved its headquarters to Baku.]

TO THE OPPRESSED POPULAR MASSES OF PERSIA, ARMENIA, AND TURKEY

The ECCI is calling a congress of the peasants and workers of Persia, Armenia, and Turkey, to be held in Baku on 1 September.

What is the Communist International? The Communist International is the organization of millions of revolutionary workers in Russia, Poland, Germany, France, England, and America who, awakened by the thunder of war and driven by hunger, have risen up so that they may work no longer for the rich but for themselves, so that they may no longer turn their arms against their own brothers, against their own suffering and hungry brothers, but bear arms in their own defence against the exploiters. These working masses have realized that their only strength consists in their unity, and in the organization of their forces, that these are the pledge of their victory. Last year they created the organization which they needed for this purpose, the Communist International. Despite all the persecution of the capitalist governments it has become in the year and a half of its existence the moving spirit in the struggle for emancipation of the workers and the revolutionary peasants throughout the world.

Why is the Communist International convening a congress of Persian, Armenian, and Turkish peasants and workers? What can it give them? What does it ask of them? The militant workers and peasants of Europe and America turn to you because, like them, you are suffering under the yoke of world capital. Because, like them, you have to fight the exploiters, and because the amalgamation of the Persian, Turkish, and Armenian peasants and workers with the great army of the European and American proletariat will strengthen this front, hasten the death of capital, and so bring about the liberation of the workers and peasants of the entire world.

Peasants and workers of Persia. The Teheran Government of Hajjars and their followers the provincial Khans, have plundered and exploited you for centuries. The land which under Shariat law was common property has been expropriated by the lackeys of the Teheran Government. They deal with it as they will. They impose taxes on you as they think fit. When their mishandling of the land had gone so far that it no longer yielded them anything they sold Persia last year for £2 million to the English capitalists, who are to form an army in Persia which will oppress you even more than you have been oppressed up to now. In order to collect the taxes for the Khans and the Teheran Government they have sold to the English capitalists the rich oil resources of south Persia and are thus helping to plunder the country.

Peasants of Mesopotamia! The English have declared your country independent, but in your country there are 80,000 English soldiers who plunder and rob, who kill you and violate your wives.

Peasants of Anatolia! The English, French, and Italian Governments are keeping Constantinople within range of their guns. They have made the Sultan their prisoner; they are forcing him to agree to the dismemberment of purely Turkish land, they are forcing him to surrender the country's finances to foreign capitalists so that they can the better exploit the Turkish people who have been impoverished and beggared by six years of war. They have occupied the coal mines of Herakleia and they are sending their troops to your country and trampling down your fields; they are dictating their alien laws to the peaceful Turkish peasants; they want to make beasts of burden of you and put all loads on you. Some of the Effendis and Beys have sold themselves to the foreign capitalists; others have called you to arms and are organizing you for the fight against the foreign invaders; but they do not allow you to take the government of your country into your own hands, to take for yourselves the fields which the Sultan presented to his parasites; to grow corn in these fields and to feed yourselves. And tomorrow, if the foreign capitalists should grant your masters better peace terms, your present leaders with the help of the foreigners, will again put you in chains just as the large landlords and the former officials are doing in the areas where the foreign armies are in command.

Peasants and workers of Armenia! For years you have been victims of the intrigues of foreign capital, which protested loudly against the massacres of the Armenians by the Kurds, and stirred you up to fight against the Sultan only in order to get greater profits from your struggle. During the war they not only promised you independence, they incited your merchants, your teachers and your priests to demand the land of the Turkish peasants so that there should be unending hostility between the Armenian and Turkish peoples, a hostility from which they could draw unending profits. For so long as there is enmity between you and the Turks so long will the English, French, and American capitalists be able to keep the Turks on a leash, threatening them with the danger of Armenian revolt and intimidating the Armenians with the danger of a Kurd pogrom.

Peasants of Syria and Arabia! Independence was promised you by the English and the French, but now their armies are occupying your country, now they are dictating their laws to you, while you who freed yourselves from the Turkish Sultan and the Constantinople Government are now the slaves of the Paris and London Governments, who differ from the Sultan's Government only by being stronger and better able to exploit you.

You understand this very well. The Persian peasants and workers have risen against the treacherous Teheran Government. The peasants of Mesopotamia are rebelling against the English troops and the English newspapers announce the losses which they have suffered in the fighting with the masses at Baghdad.

Peasants of Anatolia! You have already been called to the standard of Kemal Pasha, to fight the foreign invaders, but at the same time we know that you are trying to form your own people's and peasants' party, which will be able to fight on alone even if the Pashas make peace with the Entente despoilers.

There is no peace in Syria, and you, Armenian peasants, who are being starved to death by the Entente, despite all their promises, so that they can keep better control over you, you are coming to see more and more clearly that hope and salvation are impossible with the Entente capitalists, that even your bourgeois government, the government of the Dashnaks, of the lackeys of the Entente, is compelled to turn to the workers' and peasants' Government of Russia with the request for peace and assistance. Now that we see that you are yourselves beginning to understand your own interests we, as representatives of the European workers who have valuable experience, turn to you in order to help you in your struggle. We see that the time when European and American capitalists could oppress you with the help of their troops has passed. Everywhere in Europe the workers are rising, they are arming against the capitalists, they are marching to battle. . . .

Peasants and workers of the Near East, if you organize, if you arm yourselves, if you unite with the Russian workers' and peasants' Red Army, then you will be able to defy the French, English, and American capitalists, then you will be free of your oppressors, then you will have the opportunity in free alliance with the workers' republics of the world to take care of your interests. Then the wealth of your country will be yours. In your own interests and in the interests of the workers of the entire world the products of labour will be equitably exchanged and we shall help each other. We will discuss all this with you at the congress.

Spare no effort to come to Baku on 1 September in as large numbers as possible. Every year you make a pilgrimage across deserts to the Holy Places. Now make your way across desert and mountain and river to meet together, to deliberate together, how you can free yourselves from the chains of servitude, how you can join in brotherly union and live as free and equal men.

THE SECOND CONGRESS OF THE COMMUNIST INTERNATIONAL

[The congress was attended by 217 delegates from 41 countries, of whom 169 had voting powers. Of these, 136 represented communist parties, which also had 15 delegates with consultative voice. The principal non-communist parties represented were the German Independent Social-Democrats and the French Socialist Party, and various British organizations. The KAPD sent two delegates, Rühle and Merges, but they stayed only a few days and appear to have made no attempt to put their party's views to the congress. The congress opened on 19 July 1920 in Petrograd, and then adjourned to Moscow, where the proceedings lasted from 23 July to 7 August.

The second congress, Zinoviev said in his report to the third, had to fight leftism as represented by the unwillingness of British comrades to work in the Labour Party and of the Italian comrades to work in Parliament. At the time it was held, his view of the prospects before the International were bright. In a speech to a joint meeting of the congress delegates, the Central Executive Committee of the Soviets, the Moscow Soviet and trade union and factory committees held on 7 August 1920, he said: 'I am deeply convinced that the second world congress of the CI is the precursor of another world congress, the world congress of Soviet republics.' At the same meeting Trotsky said: 'If, since the first congress, the world proletariat has suffered defeats and has sometimes had to retreat, that was because it did not follow the road pointed out by the CI.' He paid tribute to the support given to Russia in its struggles. 'Every strike, every protest, every revolt in any town of Europe, America or Asia . . . gave us the certainty that we were on the right road, and enabled us in the darkest hours, when we were encircled on all sides, when it seemed we would be strangled, to stand up and say: We are not alone, the proletariat of Europe and Asia and the whole world are with us; we shall not yield, we shall stand fast.' He added:

'There is no doubt that the proletariat would be in power in all countries if there were not still, between them and the masses, between the revolutionary mass and the advanced groups of the revolutionary mass, a large, powerful, and complex machine, the parties of the Second International and the trade unions, which in the epoch of the disintegration, the dying of the bourgeoisie, placed their machine at the service of that bourgeoisie. . . . From now on, from this congress on, the split in the world working class will proceed with tenfold greater rapidity. Programme against programme; tactic against tactic; method against method.]

EXTRACTS FROM AN APPEAL OF THE SECOND COMINTERN CONGRESS
TO THE WORLD PROLETARIAT ON THE RUSSO-POLISH WAR

19 *July* 1920   *Protokoll,* ii, p. 51

[In June the fortunes of war changed and the Red Army recaptured the ground gained earlier by the Poles; at the time the second Comintern congress opened the Soviet forces were approaching Warsaw. Their success affected the negotiations going on at the time with Britain; in a note of 12 July Lord Curzon made the conclusion of an armistice with Poland a condition of their continuation. (It was in connexion with this note that the ethnographic line traced by the experts at Versailles the year before became known as the Curzon line.) Trotsky and Radek were opposed to the plan to follow up the retreating Polish forces into Polish territory; Lenin's argument, which prevailed, was that the advance of the Red Army would provoke revolution in Poland, and have repercussions in Germany. In a conversation with Klara Zetkin a year later he said: 'In the Red Army the Poles saw enemies, not brothers and liberators. . . . The revolution in Poland on which we counted did not take place'. The Polish counter-offensive opened in the middle of August and an armistice was concluded in October 1920.

The appeal was introduced by Paul Levi who said that, despite the sympathy of the European proletariat for the Russian revolution and the Red Army, it was German proletarians who were used to enforce the Brest-Litovsk treaty, and European proletarians who fought the revolution in the Baltic, the Ukraine, and south Russia. Now was the time for them to show that they could go beyond sympathy to action. Däumig (USPD) said 'every mile that the Red Army advances is a spur to revolution, a step towards the revolution in Germany'. In his speech at the meeting on 7 August Trotsky said that the liberation of Poland from Tsarism had opened the first pages of the history of the First International. 'Now a Russia freed from Tsarism is fulfilling its great historical mission and giving crucified and violated Poland back to the Polish workers and peasants.'

The optimism engendered by the Red Army's advance set the tone for the entire proceedings. The theses and resolutions, as Varga said at the fourth congress, were adopted in the belief that the revolution was about to spread to eastern and central Europe. Zinoviev described the scene in his report to the tenth congress of the Russian Communist Party on 16 March 1921. 'In the hall of the congress hung a large map. Every day we marked on it the

advance of our forces, and every day with breathless interest the delegates
examined the map. . . . All of them understood that if the military objectives
of our troops were reached it would mean an immense acceleration of the
international proletarian revolution. All of them understood that on every
step forward of our Red Army depended in the literal sense of the word the
fate of the international proletarian revolution. . . . We had to discuss as a
practical matter whether a victorious workers' republic could carry socialism
into other countries at the point of bayonets. There were differences of opinion.
Unfortunately the question is no longer a practical one, and we can continue
the discussion on a theoretical level.']

TO THE PROLETARIANS OF ALL COUNTRIES

Working men and women!
The second world congress of the Communist International is meeting
at a moment when, under the heavy blows of the Red Army of the Russian
workers and peasants, white Poland, the bulwark of world capitalist reaction, is collapsing. What all revolutionary workers of the entire world have
ardently longed for has come about.

The Russian workers and peasants rose against the insolent Polish
white guards as mightily as they rose against the Russian counter-revolution, to defeat the armies of Yudenich, Kolchak, and Denikin. The Polish
capitalists and junkers who scorned Soviet Russia's honest peace proposals
and flung their troops against Soviet Russia, hoping for help from world
capital and convinced that Soviet Russia had exhausted all its strength in
the struggle against counter-revolution, are now facing a great military
defeat. Their armies have retreated in panic from the Ukraine and White
Russia, followed closely by the Soviet armies. The bandits of capital, the
Polish junkers and capitalists, are now raising a loud lament—Poland is in
great danger.

They are appealing to the governments of capitalist countries for immediate help, otherwise European civilization will be destroyed by the
barbarians of the Russian revolution, and we see how the English Government, which armed the Poles for their campaign against Soviet Russia, and
together with its allies refused to restrain the Poles when on 8 April Soviet
Russia proposed negotiations in London, we see how this same capitalist
England is impudently threatening Soviet Russia with a new attack
organized by all the Allies if it does not conclude an armistice with the
Polish invaders. . . .

Men and women workers of the world! We do not need to tell you that
Soviet Russia does not harbour any plans of conquest against the Polish
people. . . . Soviet Russia was even ready to make peace with the Polish
capitalists, and for the sake of achieving peace not only recognized Poland's
independence, but even yielded up large frontier areas. Soviet Russia

counts in its ranks thousands of brave Polish fighters; it is bound closely to the Polish working masses by decades of common struggle; for Soviet Russia the right of the Polish people to self-determination is a sacred and inviolable right, and even if Poland were not defended by a single soldier Polish soil would remain the property of the Polish people, and the Polish people could freely decide their own destiny.

But so long as Poland is ruled by the clique of capitalist and junker adventurers who dragged Poland into the criminal war, so long as Entente capital provides Poland with arms, Soviet Russia is fighting a defensive war. If today Soviet Russia gives the Polish white guards a breathing space, if it lets them reorganize their shattered army, re-equip that army with the help of the Entente, tomorrow it will again be compelled to call up hundreds of thousands of its best sons from field and factory, and send them into battle in a new war of defence.

Men and women workers! When the capitalist canaille of the whole world shout about the threat to Poland's independence, in order to prepare a new campaign against Soviet Russia, remember one thing: Your slave-holders are trembling lest one of the pillars of their rule, of their world system of reaction, exploitation, and slavery, should fall: they fear that if white-guard Poland breaks under the blows of the Red Army and the Polish workers seize power it will be easier for the German, Austrian, Italian, and French workers to free themselves from their exploiters, and that then the workers of England and America will follow. If the capitalist canaille rage and storm about Poland's threatened independence, they do so for fear that your bondage and your dependence may give place to emancipation from the shackles of capitalist slavery. That is why it is the duty of the proletarians of all countries to do everything they can to make it impossible for the governments of England, France, America, and Italy to give help to the Polish white guards. Proletarians of the Entente countries! Your governments will again deceive you, they will say as they have said before that they are not supporting Poland. It is your duty to keep watch in all ports and at all frontiers, so that not a single train or a single ship leaves with munitions or food for Poland. Be on the look-out; do not let yourselves be deceived by false statements about the destination of those supplies; they can be sent to Poland by a detour, and if the governments or private capitalists do not yield to your protests, go on strike, get down to action, for in no circumstances should you help the Polish junkers and capitalists to slaughter your Russian brothers. . . .

Men and women workers of Germany! The hour has struck in which you can make a reality of what you have acclaimed a thousand times in great demonstrations: to stand by your Russian brothers and together with them to fight for your liberation. Do not let any attempts be made on German soil in support of white-guard Poland; do not let any more mercenaries be recruited on German soil. Keep a sharp watch on all trains going east, keep a sharp watch on Danzig and do everything that the situation demands. No truck, no ship, should leave Germany for Poland.

Proletarians of all other countries! Remember: White Poland is now the enemy. To destroy it is the duty of the hour.

Proletarians of all countries. Do not let yourselves be misled by any fine words of the treacherous or vacillating labour leaders, or soothed by government promises. Now is the time to act, now is the time to rally all your forces to blockade white-guard Poland, to rally all your forces to make a reality of the solidarity of the world proletariat with Soviet Russia.

Men and women workers! Solidarity with Soviet Russia is one with solidarity with the Polish proletariat. Under the leadership of the communist party the Polish proletariat has fought steadfastly against the war on Soviet Russia. The prisons of Poland are filled with our Polish brothers, with Polish communists. The defeat of the Polish white guards aroused the greatest enthusiasm in the hearts of the Polish workers. A wave of strikes swept over Poland. The Polish workers are trying to exploit the defeats of their exploiters in order to give the weakened class enemy the last blow, in order to unite with the Russian workers in the common struggle for emancipation.

The blockade of Poland is of direct help to the Polish workers in their struggle for freedom; it is the road which leads to Poland's freedom from the chains by which it is bound to the chariot of the victorious capitalists of London and France, the road to its development as an independent republic of the Polish workers and peasants.

The second world congress of the Communist International calls on you, proletarian men and women of all countries: go out on to the streets and show your governments that you will not let any help be given to white Poland, that you will not allow any intervention against Soviet Russia. Stop all work, stop all transport, if you see that despite your protests the capitalist cliques of your countries are preparing a new intervention against Soviet Russia. Do not allow a single train, a single ship, through to Poland. Show that proletarian solidarity exists in action and not only in words!

Long live Soviet Russia! Long live the Red Army of the Russian workers and peasants! Down with white Poland! Down with intervention! Long live Soviet Poland!

THESES ON THE BASIC TASKS OF THE COMMUNIST INTERNATIONAL
ADOPTED BY THE SECOND COMINTERN CONGRESS

19 *July* 1920   *Protokoll*, ii, p. 746

[These theses were drafted by Lenin and introduced on the opening day of the congress with the remark that the basic tasks of the Comintern contained nothing essentially new; in the main they were merely the extension to a number of west European countries of some of the cardinal lessons of Russian revolutionary experience. He argued that, as the living conditions of the masses became steadily more intolerable, while the handful of victorious Powers themselves were caught in a process of decline and decay, the prerequisites of world revolution were being created. Whether the crisis were successfully exploited depended on the revolutionary parties. The leaders of the centrist parties not merely failed to understand this, but were reluctant to exploit the crisis for revolutionary purposes. 'Opportunism is our chief enemy. . . . Without the support of the opportunist leadership the bourgeoisie could not maintain themselves in power.' But he went on to criticize those communists who asserted that there was 'absolutely no way out for capitalism'. 'There are no absolutely hopeless situations. The bourgeoisie . . . are committing one stupidity after another, thus making the situation worse and accelerating their own downfall. This is true, but . . . the attempt to "prove" in advance the "absolute" hopelessness of their position is sheer pedantry, a game with ideas and words. Only experience can provide a real "proof" in this and other questions. Over the whole world the bourgeois system is now going through an extreme revolutionary crisis. Now it is up to the revolutionary parties to "prove" that they are conscious enough, that their organization, their ties with the exploited masses, their resolution and intelligence are great enough to exploit this crisis for a successful, for a victorious revolution. It is largely to prepare this "proof" that we have assembled at the present congress of the Communist International.' The theses were passed against two votes and one abstention. The debate was concerned largely with the failure of the Italian Socialist Party to expel its right wing, and with the recommendation to British communists to work within the Labour Party. The recommendation was supported by the delegates representing the British Socialist Party, and opposed by the shop stewards, the Socialist Labour Party, and the Socialist Workers' Federation.]

1. It is characteristic of the present moment in the development of the international communist movement that in all capitalist countries the best representatives of the revolutionary proletariat have reached a thorough understanding of the most important principles of the Communist International, the dictatorship of the proletariat and Soviet power, and that they have enthusiastically come over to the side of the Communist International. It is a still bigger and more important step forward that everywhere, not only among the broadest masses of the urban proletariat, but also among the more advanced rural workers, unreserved sympathy with these most important principles is clearly apparent.

On the other hand, two errors or weaknesses have emerged in this international movement, which is growing with such unusual rapidity. One very serious mistake, which is of the greatest immediate danger to the success of the cause of proletarian emancipation, arises from the fact that some of the old leaders and old parties of the Second International, in part half unconsciously yielding to the wishes and the pressure of the masses, in part deceiving them in order to maintain their former role as agents and assistants of the bourgeoisie within the workers' movement, proclaim their conditional or even unconditional adherence to the Communist International, while in fact they remain, in all their practical party activities and political periormances, on the level of the Second International. Such a state of affairs is quite intolerable, for it creates confusion among the masses, hampers the formation and development of a strong communist party, diminishes respect for the Communist International, and threatens a repetition of the treachery committed by the Hungarian social-democrats, who hastened to don the red garb of communism. Another, but far less important error, which is rather a growing sickness in the movement, consists in the anxiety to be 'radical'; this leads to an incorrect appreciation of the role and tasks of the party in relation to the class and the masses and of the obligation of revolutionary communists to work in bourgeois parliaments and reactionary trade unions.

It is the duty of communists not to hush up the weaknesses of their movement, but to criticize them openly, in order the more quickly and thoroughly to eradicate them. For this purpose it is necessary, firstly, to define the concepts of 'proletarian dictatorship' and 'Soviet power' more concretely, using, in particular, practical experience; secondly, to state in what the immediate preparatory work for the realization of these slogans can and should consist in all countries; thirdly, to indicate ways and means of curing our movement of its defects.

I. THE NATURE OF PROLETARIAN DICTATORSHIP AND SOVIET POWER

2. The victory of socialism (as the first stage of communism) over capitalism requires the proletariat, as the only truly revolutionary class, to carry out the following three tasks. First: to overthrow the exploiters, and above all others the bourgeoisie, as their chief economic and political representatives; to crush their resistance, to make impossible any attempt on their part to restore the capitalist yoke and wage-slavery. Second: to attract not only the entire proletariat, or its overwhelming majority, but also the entire mass of working people and of those exploited by capital, and to bring them into position behind the revolutionary vanguard of the proletariat, the communist party; to educate, organize, train, and discipline them in the course of unflagging, bold, and relentless struggle against the exploiters; to rescue this overwhelming majority of the population in all capitalist countries from dependence on the bourgeoisie; to instil in them, through practical experience, belief in the leading role of the proletariat and of its revolutionary vanguard. The third task consists in neutralizing, in making harmless, the inevitable waverings between bourgeoisie and proletariat, between bourgeois democracy and Soviet power, of the class of small proprietors in agriculture, in industry, and in

trade, a class which is still fairly numerous in all advanced countries, even though they do not form the majority of the population, and also in neutralizing the vacillations among that section of the intellectuals and white-collar workers associated with this class.

The first and second tasks are independent in character, and each requires special measures to be taken in regard to both the exploiters and the exploited. The third follows from the first two, and requires only a skilful, timely, and flexible combination of the measures designed for the first two, according to the concrete circumstances of each particular case of vacillation.

3. In the concrete situation created throughout the entire world, and particularly in the most advanced, most powerful, most enlightened and free capitalist States, by militarism, imperialism, the oppression of the colonies and weak countries, the imperialist world slaughter and the Versailles 'peace', any concession to the idea that the capitalists will peacefully submit to the will of the exploited majority, the idea of a peaceful reformist transition to socialism, is not merely proof of extreme petty-bourgeois stupidity, but is a direct deception of the workers, a gilding of capitalist wage-slavery, a concealment of the truth. The truth is this, that the bourgeoisie, even the most enlightened and democratic, already shrink from no fraud and no crime, nor from the murder of millions of workers and peasants, to save private property in the means of production. Only the forcible overthrow of the bourgeoisie, the seizure of their property, the destruction of the entire bourgeois State machine from top to bottom—parliamentary, judicial, military, bureaucratic, administrative, municipal, etc.—going as far as the exile or internment of the most dangerous and stubborn exploiters, keeping a strict watch over them to combat the inevitable attempts at resistance and to restore capitalist slavery—only by such measures can the real submission of the entire exploiting class be attained and secured.

There is another idea which whitewashes capitalism and bourgeois democracy and deceives the workers: that is the opinion common among the old parties and old leaders of the Second International, that the majority of the working people and the exploited are able, in the conditions of capitalist slavery and under the yoke of the bourgeoisie—which assumes countless different forms, both more refined and more cruel and ruthless the more civilized the country is—to acquire for themselves a completely clear socialist consciousness, firm socialist convictions and attitudes. In reality the education, training, and organization of the working and exploited masses under the influence and guidance of communists, their liberation from egoism, from sectionalism, from the vices and weaknesses engendered by private property, their transformation into a free union of free workers—all that is possible only in the actual course of the most acute class struggles, only when the vanguard of the proletariat, supported by all or by a majority of this class, which is the only revolutionary class, has overthrown and suppressed the exploiters, freed the exploited from their position of slavery and improved their conditions of life at the expense of the expropriated capitalists.

4. To win victory over capitalism there must be the right relation between the communist party, as leader, the revolutionary class, the proletariat, on the one hand, and the masses, that is, all the working people and the exploited, on the other. Only if the communist party is really the vanguard of the revolutionary class, if it includes all the best representatives of that class, if it consists of thoroughly conscious and devoted communists, trained and steeled by the experiences of stubborn revolutionary struggle, only if the party has been able to tie itself indissolubly to the entire life of its class, and hence to the entire masses of the exploited, and enjoys the complete confidence of that class and those masses, only then is the party in a position to lead the proletariat in the unrelenting, decisive, last battle against all the forces of capitalism. On the other hand, it is only under the leadership of such a party that the proletariat is able to develop the full force of its revolutionary assault—which, because of the economic structure of capitalist society, is immeasurably greater than would correspond with the proportion of the total population represented by the proletariat—and to nullify the inevitable apathy and in part also the resistance of the small minority of the labour aristocracy, the old trade union and co-operative leaders, etc., corrupted by capitalism. Finally, it is only when the masses, i.e. all the working and exploited people, are really liberated from the yoke of the bourgeoisie and the bourgeois State machine, and have been given the opportunity to organize themselves freely in Soviets, that they will be able in their millions, for the first time in history, to develop all the initiative and energy suppressed by capitalism. Only when the Soviets have become the sole machinery of State can there be real participation in government by the entire mass of the exploited, who, even under the most enlightened and free bourgeois democracy, have in reality always been ninety-nine per cent. excluded from participation in government. Only in the Soviets do the exploited masses begin to learn, not from books but from their own practical experience, how to set about the work of socialist construction, of the creation of a new social discipline, a free union of free workers.

2. PREPARATION FOR THE DICTATORSHIP OF THE PROLETARIAT; WORK THAT MUST BE CARRIED OUT EVERYWHERE WITHOUT DELAY

5. It is a distinguishing feature of the present moment in the development of the international communist movement that in the great majority of capitalist countries the preparations of the proletariat to bring its

dictatorship into being have not been completed, indeed in many cases have not even been systematically begun. It does not follow that the proletarian revolution is impossible in the immediate future. It is quite possible, for the entire economic and political situation is unusually rich in inflammable material and in reasons for its suddenly catching fire. A further prerequisite of revolution, apart from the preparation of the proletariat, namely, a general state of crisis in all ruling and all bourgeois parties, is also present. But from what has been said it follows that for the communist parties the immediate task is to accelerate the revolution, taking care not to provoke it artificially before adequate preparations have been made. The preparation of the proletariat for the revolution must be promoted by action. On the other hand the history of many socialist parties, previously referred to, makes it essential to see that recognition of the dictatorship of the proletariat does not remain an empty word.

From the standpoint of the international proletarian movement, therefore, the chief task of the communist parties at the present moment is to rally the scattered communist forces, to create a united communist party in each country (or the consolidation and regeneration of the parties already in existence), to multiply tenfold the work of preparing the proletariat for the conquest of State power in the form of the dictatorship of the proletariat. The socialist work usually done by groups and parties which recognize the dictatorship of the proletariat has not yet by a long way been subjected to that radical transformation and regeneration which are essential if it is to be regarded as communist work, corresponding to the tasks on the eve of the proletarian dictatorship.

6. The conquest of political power by the proletariat does not put an end to its class struggle against the bourgeoisie; on the contrary, it makes this struggle particularly comprehensive, acute, and unrelenting. Because the struggle has reached a pitch of the utmost intensity, all groups, parties, and active participants in the workers' movement which are wholly or partly reformist or 'centrist' in character move inevitably either to the side of the bourgeoisie or to the side of the waverers, or (what is most dangerous) they join the unreliable friends of the victorious proletariat. That is why preparation for the dictatorship of the proletariat requires not only an intensified struggle against reformist and 'centrist' tendencies, but also a change in the character of that struggle. It must not be restricted to explaining the incorrectness of these tendencies, but must mercilessly and ruthlessly expose every leading individual in the workers' movement who displays these tendencies, for otherwise the proletariat cannot learn with whom to act in the decisive struggle against the bourgeoisie. This struggle is of such a character that it may at any moment replace the weapon of criticism by the criticism of weapons, and, as experience has already shown, it not only may, but does. Any inconsistency or weakness in expos-

ing those who turn out to be reformists or 'centrists' directly increases the danger of the overthrow of the power of the proletariat by the bourgeoisie, who will tomorrow make use of what today seems to shortsighted people nothing but a 'theoretical difference of opinion'.

7. In particular it is not enough to be content with the usual rejection in principle of any co-operation between proletariat and bourgeoisie, any 'class collaboration'. In conditions of the proletarian dictatorship—which will never be able to abolish private property completely at one blow—the simple defence of 'freedom' and 'equality' changes, while private property in the means of production is maintained, into 'co-operation' with the bourgeoisie, which directly undermines the power of the working class. For the dictatorship of the proletariat means that the entire apparatus of State power is used to establish and secure 'unfreedom' for the exploiters to carry on their work of oppression and exploitation, 'inequality' between property owners (that is, those who appropriate for their own use the means of production created by social labour) and the propertyless. What seems, before the victory of the proletariat, nothing but a theoretical difference of opinion about 'democracy' inevitably becomes, on the morrow of victory, a question to be decided by force of arms. Consequently, without a fundamental change in the entire character of the struggle against the 'centrists' and the 'defenders of democracy' even a preliminary preparation of the masses for the realization of the proletarian dictatorship is impossible.

8. The dictatorship of the proletariat is the most determined form of the class struggle of the proletariat against the bourgeoisie. This struggle can only be successful if the revolutionary vanguard is supported by the overwhelming majority of the proletariat. Preparation for the proletarian dictatorship therefore demands not only explaining the bourgeois character of any kind of reformism, any defence of democracy that involves the maintenance of private property in the means of production, not merely exposing those tendencies which mean in fact that the bourgeoisie are defended within the workers' movement; it also requires that the old leaders shall be replaced by communists in absolutely every kind of proletarian organization, not only political, but also trade union, co-operative, educational, etc. The longer bourgeois democracy has prevailed in a country, the more complete and well established it is, the more successful have the bourgeoisie of that country been in getting into those leading positions people who are reared in bourgeois democracy, saturated in its attitudes and prejudices, and very frequently bribed by it, whether directly or indirectly. These representatives of the labour aristocracy, or of workers who have become bourgeois in outlook, must be pushed out of all their positions a hundred times more boldly than ever before, and replaced even by inexperienced workers, so long as they are closely tied to the exploited masses and enjoy their confidence in the struggle against the

exploiters. The dictatorship of the proletariat will make it necessary to appoint such inexperienced workers to the most responsible offices of State, otherwise the power of the workers' government will be ineffective and will not be supported by the masses.

9. The dictatorship of the proletariat is the most complete realization of the leadership of all working and exploited people, who have been enslaved, downtrodden, oppressed, intimidated, disunited, and deceived by the capitalist class, by the one class which the entire history of capitalism has prepared for this leading part. Consequently the work of preparing for the dictatorship of the proletariat must be everywhere undertaken without delay, along the following lines:

In all organizations, unions and associations of the working and exploited masses without exception, first in the proletarian and then in the non-proletarian (political, trade union, military, co-operative, educational, sport, etc.), groups or cells of communists must be formed, chiefly open in character, but also secret, the latter being obligatory wherever their dissolution, or the arrest or deportation of their members by the bourgeoisie, is likely; these cells, closely connected with each other and with the party centre, shall pool their experience, carry on propaganda, agitation, and organizational work, adapting themselves to absolutely every sphere of public life and to every kind and group of the working masses, and by this varied work systematically train themselves, the party, the class, and the masses.

In this connexion it is of the utmost importance to work out and to develop the methods necessary for all these activities: the leaders or responsible representatives hopelessly corrupted by petty-bourgeois or imperialist prejudices must be mercilessly exposed and driven out of the workers' movement. In regard to the masses, however, who, particularly after the imperialist slaughter, are largely inclined to give a hearing to and to accept the theory of the necessity of the rule of the proletariat as the only way out of capitalist slavery, particular patience and caution must be shown in studying and allowing for the peculiarities and particular psychological features of every section, every occupation, etc.

10. There is *one* communist group or cell which deserves the party's particular attention and care; that is the parliamentary fraction, the group of members of parliament, deputies to bourgeois representative bodies (particularly in central, but also in local and municipal government). These bodies are of particularly great importance in the eyes of the backward working masses saturated in petty-bourgeois prejudices. Therefore communists must from that very tribune carry on the work of propaganda, agitation, and organization, and explain to the masses why it was legitimate in Russia (and in due course will be legitimate in any country) for the Soviet congress to dissolve the bourgeois parliament. On the other hand

the entire course of bourgeois democracy has turned parliament, particularly in the advanced countries, into the main or one of the main centres for incredible swindles, for the financial and political deception of the people, for careerism, hypocrisy, and the oppression of the working people. That is why the burning hatred of parliament felt by the best representatives of the revolutionary proletariat is fully justified. That is why communist parties, and all parties of the Communist International—particularly if they were founded not by breakaways from the old parties, and in protracted and stubborn struggles with them, but as a result of the old parties going over (often in appearance only) to new political positions—must be specially strict in their attitude to their parliamentary fractions. The fractions must be completely subject to the control and direction of the central committee of the party; they must consist largely of revolutionary workers; their speeches in parliament must be carefully analysed from the communist standpoint in the party press and at party meetings; members of parliament must be detailed for agitational work among the masses, and any member of the fraction who shows Second International tendencies must be expelled.

11. One of the chief difficulties encountered by the revolutionary workers' movement in the advanced capitalist countries arises from the fact that capital, thanks to colonial possessions and the surplus profits of finance capital etc., is able to detach a comparatively broad and stable stratum, the labour aristocracy, which is a small minority of the working class. They enjoy good wages and are most deeply imbued with a narrow craft spirit and with petty-bourgeois and imperialist prejudices. They represent the real social 'pillars' of the Second International of reformists and 'centrists', and at the present moment are almost the sole social mainstay of the bourgeoisie. It is impossible even to begin to prepare the proletariat for the overthrow of the bourgeoisie without an immediate, systematic, comprehensive, and open struggle against this stratum which—as experience has already clearly demonstrated—will undoubtedly provide the bourgeois white guard with not a few recruits after the victory of the proletariat. All parties adhering to the Communist International must, at whatever cost, carry through the slogan 'deeper into the masses', 'closer contact with the masses', meaning by the masses all working people and all who are exploited by capital, particularly those who are least organized and least enlightened, most deeply oppressed and least accessible to organization.

The proletariat becomes revolutionary only in so far as it does not lock itself up in narrow craft limits, only in so far as it takes part in all activities and all spheres of public life as leader of all the working and exploited masses, and it is impossible for it to achieve its dictatorship if it is not ready and able to make the greatest sacrifices for the sake of victory over the bourgeoisie. In this respect Russia's experience is of both theoretical and practical significance. There the proletariat could not have established its dictatorship, could not have won the respect and confidence of all the working masses, if it had not made greater sacrifices and suffered greater hunger than any other section of the masses, in the most difficult periods of attack, of war, and of the blockade by the world bourgeoisie.

The communist party and the entire advanced proletariat must, in particular, give all-round and self-denying support to the broad and spontaneous mass strike movement, which alone is able really to rouse the masses under the yoke of capital, to get them into action, to educate and organize them, and to foster in them complete confidence in the leading role of the revolutionary proletariat. Without this preparation no dictatorship of the proletariat is possible, and people who come out openly against strikes, like Kautsky in Germany and Turati in Italy, can in no circumstances be tolerated in parties which adhere to the Communist International. This of course applies in still greater degree to the trade union and parliamentary leaders who often betray the workers by using the experience of strikes to preach reformism and not revolution, for example Jouhaux in France, Gompers in America, J. H. Thomas in England.

12. In all countries, even the freest, most 'legal' and most 'peaceful'—that is, where the class struggle is least acute—the time has come when it is imperative for every communist party systematically to combine legal with illegal work, legal with illegal organization. For even in the most enlightened and free countries with the most 'solid' bourgeois-democratic regime the governments are already beginning, despite their own false and hypocritical statements, to keep regular secret lists of communists, to resort to violations of their own constitution, to half-secret and secret support of the white guards, and to the murder of communists in every country, to secret preparation for the arrest of communists, to smuggling *agents provocateurs* into communist circles, etc. Only the most reactionary petty-bourgeois, however fine the 'democratic' and pacifist phrases he may use, can deny these facts or the conclusion which necessarily follows from them—the necessity for all communist parties to establish without delay illegal organizations to carry on systematic illegal work and make thorough preparations for the day when bourgeois persecution comes out into the open. This illegal work is particularly necessary in the army, the navy, and the police, for after the great imperialist slaughter all governments have begun to fear national armies which are open to the worker and the peasant, and have begun in secret to single out from among the troops detachments recruited from the bourgeoisie and provided with special and technically superior equipment.

On the other hand it is also necessary, in all cases without exception, not to restrict oneself to illegal work but to carry out legal work, to overcome all obstacles, to found legal press organs and legal organizations under the most varied names, and when necessary to change the names frequently. This is being done by the illegal communist parties in Finland and Hungary, and to some extent in Germany, Poland, Latvia, etc. This must also be done by the IWW in America, and by all legal communist parties, if the public prosecutor finds it convenient to use decisions of the congresses of the Communist International to start persecuting them.

The imperative necessity, as a matter of principle, of combining illegal with legal work, is determined not merely by the totality of the special features of the present period, on the eve of the proletarian dictatorship, but also by the need to demonstrate to the bourgeoisie that there is not and cannot be any sphere of activity which the communists cannot conquer, and still more by the existence everywhere of broad strata of the proletariat, and even more of the non-proletarian working and exploited masses, who still have faith in bourgeois-democratic legality and whom it is very important for us to convince of the contrary.

13. The position of the workers' press in the most advanced capitalist countries shows particularly clearly both the entire mendacity of freedom and equality in a bourgeois democracy, and the necessity of systematic combination of legal and illegal work. In both defeated Germany and victorious America the entire power of the bourgeois State apparatus, and all the tricks of its financial tycoons, are used to deprive the workers of their press—prosecution in the courts and the arrest (even the murder by hired assassins) of its editors, the prohibition of distribution through the post, refusal of paper supplies, etc. Moreover, the news reports which are necessary for a daily paper are controlled by bourgeois press agencies, and the advertisements without which a large newspaper cannot pay its way are at the 'free' disposition of capitalists. In these ways, by fraud and by the pressure of capital and of bourgeois rule, the bourgeoisie deprive the revolutionary proletariat of its press.

To combat this the communist parties must start a new kind of periodical press for mass distribution among the workers; first, legal publications which, without calling themselves communist or referring to their adherence to the party, must learn to take advantage of the slightest legal opportunities, as the Bolsheviks did after 1905 under the Tsar; secondly, illegal papers, even if they are only very small and are published only irregularly, but which can be reproduced in small printing shops by the workers (either secretly, or if the movement has become strong enough, by the revolutionary seizure of printing presses), and which give the proletariat revolutionary information and revolutionary watchwords.

Without a revolutionary struggle for the freedom of the communist press which carries the masses along with it, preparation for the dictatorship of the proletariat is impossible.

3. CORRECTING THE POLICY AND PARTLY ALSO THE COMPOSITION OF THE PARTIES WHICH HAVE JOINED OR WISH TO JOIN THE COMMUNIST INTERNATIONAL

14. The degree to which the proletariat in the countries which are most important from the standpoint of world economy and world politics is prepared for the realization of its dictatorship is indicated with the greatest objectivity and precision by the breakaway of the most influential parties in the Second International—the French Socialist Party, the Independent Social-Democratic Party of Germany, the Independent Labour Party in England, the American Socialist Party—from that yellow International, and by their decision to adhere conditionally to the Communist International. This shows that not only the vanguard but the majority of the revolutionary proletariat, convinced by the course of events, have begun to come over to our side. The chief thing now is to know how to make this change complete and to consolidate what has been attained in lasting organizational form, so that progress can be made along the whole line without any hesitation.

15. The entire activity of the parties mentioned (to which the Swiss Socialist Party will most probably be added) shows, and their periodical press clearly confirms, that this activity is not yet communist and not infrequently is frankly incompatible with the basic principles of the Communist International, namely, recognition of the dictatorship of the proletariat and of Soviet power instead of bourgeois democracy.

Therefore the second congress of the Communist International has decided that it does not consider it possible to accept these parties immediately; that it approves the answer given by the ECCI to the German 'Independents', that it confirms its readiness to conduct negotiations with any party which leaves the Second International and wishes to approach the Communist International; that it grants delegates of such parties a consultative voice at all its congresses and conferences; that it makes the following conditions for the complete unification of these (and similar) parties with the Communist International:

(i) Publication of all decisions of all congresses of the Communist International and of its Executive Committee in all the party's periodicals.

(ii) Discussion of these decisions at special meetings of all sections or local groups of the party.

(iii) The convening, after such discussion, of a special congress of the party to draw the conclusions. This congress must be called as early as possible and in any case not later than four months after the second congress of the Communist International.

(iv) The party to be cleansed of all elements which continue to act in the spirit of the Second International.

(v) All party periodicals to be put in the hands of exclusively communist editorial boards.

(vi) Parties which now wish to enter the Communist International but have not yet made a radical break with their old tactics must ensure that two-thirds of the membership of their central committees and central bodies consist of comrades who, before the second congress, came out openly in favour of adherence to the Communist International. Exceptions can be made only with the consent of the ECCI.

(vii) Members of the party who reject the conditions and theses adopted by the Communist International must be expelled. The same applies to members of the extraordinary congress.

The second congress of the Communist International instructs the Executive Committee to accept the parties mentioned, and similar parties, into the Communist International, after satisfying itself that all these conditions have really been fulfilled and the party's activity has become communist in character.

16. As to the question how communists, who are now in the minority, should behave when they occupy responsible positions in the said parties, the second congress of the Communist International has decided that, in view of the present rapid growth in the revolutionary spirit of the masses, it is not desirable for communists to leave these parties so long as they have the opportunity of working in them for the recognition of the proletarian dictatorship and the Soviet power, and of criticizing the opportunists and centrists who still remain in these parties. Whenever the left wing of a centrist party has become strong enough, and the development of the communist movement requires it, it may leave the party in a body and form a communist party.

At the same time the second congress of the Communist International is in favour of the affiliation of communist or sympathizing groups and organizations in England to the Labour Party, although the Labour Party belongs to the Second International. For so long as this party allows the organizations affiliated to it their present freedom of criticism and freedom to engage in propaganda, agitation, and organization for the proletarian dictatorship and the Soviet power, so long as this party retains the character of an association of all trade union organizations of the working class, communists must do everything they can, and even make certain organizational compromises, to have the possibility of exercising influence on the broad working masses, of exposing their opportunist leaders from a high tribune visible to the masses, of accelerating the transference of political power from the direct representatives of the bourgeoisie to the 'labour lieutenants of the capitalist class', in order to cure the masses quickly of their last illusions on this score.

17. As to the Italian Socialist Party, the second congress of the

Communist International recognizes that the revision of the programme decided on at the Bologna congress of this party last year marks a very important stage in this party's road to communism, and that the proposals put forward by the Turin section to the National Council of the party and published in *L'Ordine Nuovo* of 8 May 1920 are in conformity with all the basic principles of the Communist International. The congress requests the Italian Socialist Party at its next congress, which is to be held in accordance with its own statutes and the conditions of admission to the Communist International, to examine the said proposals and all the decisions of the two congresses of the Communist International, particularly with respect to the parliamentary fraction, the trade unions, and noncommunist elements in the party.

18. The second congress of the Communist International judges as incorrect the views about the relation of the party to the class and the masses, about communist party participation in bourgeois parliaments and in reactionary trade unions held and defended in their most thoroughgoing form by the Communist Labour Party of Germany (KAPD), and in part by the Communist Party of Switzerland, and in *Der Kommunismus*, organ of the East European secretariat of the Communist International in Vienna, by some Dutch comrades, and by some communist organizations in England, for example the Socialist Workers' Federation and the Shop Stewards' Committee, and by the IWW in America; these views have been refuted in detail in special resolutions of the second congress.

Nevertheless the second congress of the Communist International considers both possible and desirable the immediate affiliation to the Communist International of such of these organizations as have not yet officially joined, for in these cases—particularly the IWW in America and Australia, and the shop stewards in England, we are dealing with a profoundly proletarian mass movement, whose principles really correspond to the basic principles of the Communist International. In such organizations the incorrect views about participation in bourgeois parliaments derive not so much from the influence of members of bourgeois origin, who bring their basically petty-bourgeois outlook into the movement—an outlook which anarchists often share—as from the lack of political experience of thoroughly revolutionary proletarians who are closely bound to the masses.

The second congress of the Communist International therefore requests all communist organizations and groups in the Anglo-Saxon countries, even if the IWW and the shop stewards should not immediately join, to pursue a friendly policy towards these organizations, to draw closer to them and to the masses who sympathize with them, and to explain to them, in the light of the experiences of all revolutions and particularly of the three Russian revolutions of the twentieth century, in a most friendly way the incorrectness of their views in this respect, and not to desist from repeated attempts to unite with these organizations into a single communist party.

19. In this connexion the congress directs the attention of all comrades, particularly in the Latin and Anglo-Saxon countries, to the deep theoretical cleavage that has been taking place since the war among anarchists throughout the world on the question of their attitude to the proletarian dictatorship and the Soviet power. The proletarian elements, who were frequently driven to anarchism by a wholly natural hatred of the opportunism and reformism of the parties of the Second International, have a particularly good grasp of these principles, which is growing as they become more familiar with the experience of Russia, Finland, Hungary, Latvia, Poland, and Germany.

The congress therefore thinks it the duty of all comrades to support to the utmost the movement of all mass proletarian elements from anarchism towards the Communist International. The congress declares that the success of the work of genuine communist parties can be measured among other things by the extent to which they succeed in attracting from anarchism to their side all the mass proletarian elements.

THESES ON THE ROLE OF THE COMMUNIST PARTY IN THE PROLE-
TARIAN REVOLUTION ADOPTED BY THE SECOND COMINTERN CONGRESS

24 *July* 1920   *Protokoll*, ii, p. 113

[These theses were drafted and introduced by Zinoviev; after discussion in the congress, and amendment in the commission, they were unanimously adopted. They were designed primarily to counteract syndicalist and 'direct action' tendencies, which were prevalent in France and Spain, as well as among the American IWW and the British shop stewards. The Russian party, Zinoviev said, had learnt from experience that it was essential to have a centralized organization imposing iron military discipline. Among the most outspoken critics of this attitude was Tanner (shop stewards), who suggested that Russia had something to learn from the west as well as something to teach. The parties should agree on all basic questions, but for the rest might be left to act on their own. The Second International had been too formless and characterless, but the Third was going to the opposite extreme and being too dogmatic. He questioned whether the dictatorship of the communist party and the dictatorship of the proletariat were identical. Wijnkoop (Holland) also suggested a less dogmatic approach, since conditions varied so widely. Lenin reacted sharply to the charge of dogmatism; if each party were allowed to do as it pleased, the International was unnecessary. Zinoviev said that 'the International must be a single communist party with sections in the different countries'; the dictatorship of the party was 'a function, a sign, and an expression of the dictatorship of the working class'. Trotsky made the same point by a topical example. 'Today we received peace proposals from the Polish Government. Who decides this question? We have the Council of People's Commissars, but that too must be subject to a certain control. Whose control? That of the working class as a formless, chaotic mass? No. So we convened the central committee of the party to discuss the proposal and decide on the answer. . . . The same is true of the agrarian question, the food question, and all other questions.']

Decisive struggles confront the world proletariat. The epoch in which we are now living is the epoch of open civil wars. The decisive hour is approaching. In practically every country where there is a substantial labour movement the working class, arms in hand, is faced by a series of bitter struggles.

More than ever before the working class needs strict organization. It must now work indefatigably to make itself ready for these struggles without losing a single precious hour.

If at the time of the Paris Commune (1871) the working class had had a disciplined communist party, however small, the first heroic rising of the French proletariat would have had far greater weight, and many mistakes and weaknesses could have been avoided.

The struggles which the proletariat is now facing, in a different historical situation, will be far more fateful than that of 1871. Therefore the second world congress of the Communist International directs the attention of the revolutionary workers of the entire world to the following:

1. The communist party is a *part* of the working class, the most advanced, most class-conscious, and hence most revolutionary part. By a process of natural selection the communist party is formed of the best, most class-conscious, most devoted and far-sighted workers. The communist party has no interests other than the interests of the working class as a whole. The communist party is differentiated from the working class as a whole by the fact that it has a clear view of the entire historical path of the working class in its totality and is concerned, at every bend in this road, to defend the interests not of separate groups or occupations, but of the working class in its totality. The communist party is the organizational and political lever which the most advanced section of the working class uses to direct the entire mass of the proletariat and the semi-proletariat along the right road.

2. Until the proletariat has seized State power and consolidated its rule once for all, and made it secure against a bourgeois restoration, the communist party will have in its ranks only a minority of the workers. Before the seizure of power, and in the transition period, the communist party can, in favourable circumstances, exercise an undivided intellectual and political influence on all proletarian and semi-proletarian strata of the population, but it cannot unite them all organizationally in its ranks. Only after the proletarian dictatorship has deprived the bourgeoisie of such

powerful means of exerting influence as the press, the schools, parliament, the church, the administrative machine, etc., only after the final defeat of the bourgeois order has become clear to everybody, only then will all or practically all the workers begin to enter the ranks of the communist party.

3. A sharp distinction must be made between the concepts of party and class. The members of the 'Christian' and liberal trade unions of Germany, England, and other countries are undoubtedly parts of the working class. The more or less numerous groups of workers who still follow Scheidemann, Gompers, and their like, are undoubtedly part of the working class. In certain historical circumstances it is even quite possible for the working class to include very numerous reactionary elements. It is the task of communism not to adapt itself to these backward sections of the working class but to raise the entire working class to the level of the communist vanguard. Confusion of these two concepts—party and class—can lead to the greatest mistakes and bewilderment. It is for example clear that in spite of the sentiments and prejudices of a certain section of the working class during the imperialist war, the workers' party had at all costs to combat those sentiments and prejudices by standing for the historical interests of the proletariat which required the proletarian party to declare war on the war.

Thus, on the outbreak of the imperialist war in 1914 the parties of the social-traitors in all countries, when they supported the bourgeoisie of their 'own' countries, always and consistently explained that they were acting in accordance with the will of the working class. But they forgot that, even if that were true, it must be the task of the proletarian party in such a state of affairs to come out against the sentiments of the majority of the workers and, in defiance of them, to represent the historical interests of the proletariat. In the same way, at the beginning of this century, the Russian mensheviks of that time (the so-called Economists) rejected open political struggle against Tsarism on the ground that the working class as a whole had not yet reached an understanding of the political struggle.

In the same way the right wing of the German Independents always insist, when acting irresolutely and inadequately, on 'the will of the masses', without understanding that the party is there to lead the masses and show them the way.

4. The Communist International adheres unshakeably to the conviction that the collapse of the old 'social-democratic' parties and the Second International should in no circumstances be presented as the collapse of the proletarian party system in general. The epoch of direct struggle for the dictatorship of the proletariat brings a *new* party of the proletariat to birth, the communist party.

5. The Communist International decisively rejects the view that the proletariat can accomplish its revolution without having an independent

political party of its own. Every class struggle is a political struggle. The goal of this struggle, which is inevitably transformed into civil war, is the conquest of political power. Political power cannot be seized, organized, and operated except through a political party. Only if the proletariat has as leader an organized and experienced party with clearly defined aims and a practical programme of immediate measures both for internal and external policy, will the conquest of political power turn out to be not an accidental episode, but the starting-point of an enduring communist structure of society built by the proletariat.

The same class struggle likewise demands the centralization and unified direction of the most varied forms of the proletarian movement (trade unions, co-operatives, factory councils, educational work, elections, etc.). Only a political party can be such a co-ordinating and guiding centre. The refusal to create and to strengthen such a party and to subordinate oneself to it implies the rejection of unity in the direction of the different fighting forces of the proletariat acting on the various fields of battle. The class struggle of the proletariat needs concentrated agitation which illuminates the various stages of the struggle from a single standpoint and directs the attention of the proletariat whenever the occasion demands to definite tasks common to the whole class. That cannot be done without a centralized political machinery, i.e. without a political party. The propaganda conducted by the revolutionary syndicalists and adherents of the Industrial Workers of the World (IWW) against the necessity for an independent workers' party objectively therefore helped and helps only to support the bourgeoisie and the counter-revolutionary 'social-democrats'. In their propaganda against a communist party, which they want to replace by trade unions alone or by formless 'general' workers' unions, the syndicalists and IWW come close to the avowed opportunists. After the defeat of the 1905 revolution the Russian mensheviks for many years advocated the idea of a so-called workers' congress which was to replace the revolutionary party of the working class. The 'yellow labourites' of every kind in England and America preach to the workers the creation of formless workers' unions or vague, purely parliamentary associations, to take the place of a political party, and at the same time put through a thoroughly bourgeois policy. The revolutionary syndicalists and IWW are anxious to fight against the dictatorship of the bourgeoisie, but do not know how. They fail to grasp that without an independent political party the working class is a body without a head.

Revolutionary syndicalism and industrialism mark a step forward only in comparison with the old, musty, counter-revolutionary ideology of the Second International. But in comparison with revolutionary Marxism, i.e. with communism, syndicalism and industrialism are a step backward. The declaration of the 'left' KAPD at its foundation congress in April, that it was founding a party, but 'not a party in the traditional sense', is an ideological surrender to these reactionary aspects of syndicalism and industrialism.

The working class cannot win victory over the bourgeoisie by the general strike alone, by the tactics of folded arms. The proletariat must resort to armed insurrection. Whoever has grasped that must also understand that an organized political party is essential, that formless workers' unions are not enough.

The revolutionary syndicalists often speak of the great part that can be played by a determined revolutionary minority. A really determined minority of the working class, a minority that is communist, that wants to act, that has a programme, that is out to organize the struggle of the masses —that is precisely what the communist party is.

6. The most important task of a genuine communist party is to keep always in *closest touch* with the broadest masses of the proletariat.

In order to do that, communists can and should also be active in associations which, though they do not have the character of political parties, have large proletarian groups among their members, such as the associations of disabled ex-servicemen in various countries, the 'Hands off Russia' committees in England, proletarian tenants' leagues, etc. The Russian example of the so-called 'non-party' workers' and peasants' conferences is particularly important. These conferences are organized in practically every town, in every working-class district, and also in the countryside. The broadest masses of even the backward workers take part in the elections to these conferences. The most pressing questions are placed on the agenda —food supplies, housing, the military situation, schools, the current political tasks, etc. The communists exercise a most active influence on these 'non-party' conferences, and with the greatest success for the party.

Communists consider it their most important task to carry on the work of organization and instruction in a systematic fashion within these wider workers' organizations. And in order to do this successfully, in order to prevent the enemies of the revolutionary proletariat from taking possession of these broad workers' organizations, the advanced communist workers must form their own independent tightly-knit communist party, which acts always in an organized way and which is able, at every turn of events and whatever form the movement takes, to look after the general interests of communism.

7. Communists do not by any means shun mass workers' organizations which have a non-political character, even when these are of an outright reactionary character (yellow or Christian unions, etc.); they do not shrink from taking part in them and using them. Within these organizations the communist party constantly carries on its propaganda and indefatigably persuades the workers that the idea of non-partisanship as a

principle is deliberately encouraged among the workers by the bourgeoisie and their hacks in order to divert them from organized struggle for socialism.

8. The old 'classic' division of the workers movement into three—party, trade union, and co-operative—is clearly obsolete. The proletarian revolution in Russia has created the basic form of the proletarian dictatorship, the soviets. The new division, which we are approaching everywhere, is: 1. party, 2. workers' councils (soviets), 3. producers' associations (trade unions). But both the councils and the unions must be constantly and systematically guided by the party of the proletariat, that is, by the communist party. The organized vanguard of the working class, the communist party, which *must direct* the struggles of the entire working class in the economic and the political field, as well as in the sphere of education, must be the animating spirit within the unions and the workers' councils, as well as in every other kind of proletarian organization.

The rise of soviets as the historical basic form of the dictatorship of the proletariat does not in any way diminish the leading role of the communist party in the proletarian revolution. When the German 'left' communists say (see their appeal to the German proletariat of 14 April 1920, signed 'Communist Labour Party of Germany') that 'the party too is *more and more adapting itself to the Soviet idea* and assuming a proletarian character' (*K[ommunistische] A[rbeiter] Z[eitung]* no. 54), that is a confused expression of the idea that the communist party must *merge* in the soviets, as though the soviets could *replace* the communist party.

This idea is basically wrong and reactionary. There was a period in the history of the Russian revolution when the soviets were opposed to the proletarian party and supported the policy of the agents of the bourgeoisie. The same was true of Germany. The same is possible in other countries also. If the soviets are to do justice to their historical mission, a strong communist party is essential, a party which does not simply 'adapt' itself to the soviets, but is able to ensure that the soviets do not 'adapt' themselves to the bourgeoisie and to white-guard social-democracy, a party which through its fractions in the soviets is able to take them in tow.

Whoever suggests that the communist party should 'adapt' itself to the soviets, whoever sees in such an adaptation a strengthening of the 'proletarian character' of the party, is doing both the party and the soviets a highly questionable service, and has failed to grasp the significance either of the party or of the soviets. The stronger the party that we create in any country, the sooner will the 'Soviet idea' triumph. Many 'Independents' and even right-wing socialists now pay lip-service to the 'Soviet idea'. We shall be able to prevent these elements from distorting the Soviet idea only if we have a strong communist party which is able to exercise a decisive influence on the policy of the soviets.

9. The working class needs the communist party not only up to the seizure of power, not only during the seizure of power, but also after the transfer of power to the working class. The history of the Communist Party of Russia, which has been in power nearly three years, shows that the importance of the communist party after the working class has seized power does not diminish but, on the contrary, grows enormously.

10. When the proletariat seizes power its party remains, as before, only a part of the working class—precisely that part of the working class which organized victory. For two decades in Russia, and for some years in Germany, the communist party has been fighting not only the bourgeoisie, but also those 'socialists' who transmit bourgeois influences to the proletariat; it took into its ranks the staunchest, most far-sighted, and most advanced fighters of the working class. Only if there is such a disciplined organization of the working class élite is it possible to surmount all the difficulties confronting the workers' dictatorship on the morrow of victory. In the organization of a new proletarian red army, in the real destruction of the bourgeois State apparatus and its replacement by the beginnings of a new proletarian State apparatus, in the fight against narrow craft tendencies among groups of workers, in the struggle against local and regional 'patriotism', in clearing the way for the creation of a new labour discipline—in all these fields the communist party has the decisive word. By their own example its members must inspire and lead the majority of the working class.

11. The need for a political party of the proletariat disappears only with the complete disappearance of classes. On the road to this final victory of communism it is possible that the historical importance of the three basic forms of proletarian organization today (party, soviet, producers' union) will change, and that gradually a single type of workers' organization will crystallize out. But the communist party will only *merge completely in the working class* when communism ceases to be a goal to be fought for and the entire working class has become communist.

12. The second congress of the Communist International not only re-affirms the historical mission of the communist party in general, but indicates to the international proletariat, although only in broad outline, what kind of communist party we need.

13. The Communist International is of the opinion that, particularly in the period of the proletarian dictatorship, the communist party must be built on foundations of iron proletarian centralism. In order to lead the working class successfully in the difficult and prolonged civil war the communist party must establish iron military discipline in its own ranks. The experience of the communist party which for three years has led the working class in the Russian civil war has shown that without the strictest discipline, without complete centralization, and without the fullest

comradely confidence of all party organizations in the party centre, the victory of the workers is impossible.

14. The communist party must be built on the basis of democratic centralism. The basic principles of democratic centralism are that the higher party bodies shall be elected by the lower, that all instructions of the higher bodies are categorically and necessarily binding on the lower; and that there shall be a strong party centre whose authority is universally and unquestioningly recognized for all leading party comrades in the period between congresses.

15. A number of communist parties in Europe and America have been compelled, as a result of the 'state of siege' decreed by the bourgeoisie against communists, to lead an illegal life. It must be borne in mind that in such a state of affairs the principle of election cannot be strictly observed and the leading party bodies must be given the right of co-opting members, as was done at one time in Russia. Under a 'state of siege' the communist party is unable to make use of a democratic referendum about every serious question; rather it is compelled to give its central body the right in emergencies to take important decisions for all party members.

16. At the present time the advocacy of broad 'autonomy' for the local party organizations only weakens the ranks of the communist party, undermines its capacity for action, and favours petty-bourgeois, anarchist tendencies, tendencies making for a loose structure.

17. In countries in which the bourgeoisie or the counter-revolutionary social-democracy are still in power, the communist parties must learn how to combine legal and illegal activity in an organized manner. Legal work must always be under the practical supervision of the illegal party. The communist parliamentary fractions, in both central and local government, must be completely under the control of the party, regardless of whether the party is at the given moment legal or illegal. Deputies who refuse, in whatever manner, to subordinate themselves to the party must be expelled from the party.

The legal press (newspapers and publishing houses) must be completely and unconditionally subordinate to the entire party and its central committee. No concessions are admissible on this point.

18. The basis of the entire organizational activity of the communist party must be, in all cases, the creation of a *communist cell*, however small the number of proletarians and semi-proletarians it consists of. In every soviet, in every trade union, in every co-operative, in every factory, in every tenants' council, wherever there are even three people who sympathize with communism, a communist cell must be formed immediately. It is only the strict organization of the communists which enables the vanguard of the working class to carry the entire working class with them. All communist party cells working in non-party organizations are

unconditionally subordinate to the party organization as a whole, regardless of whether the party is at the given moment working legally or
illegally. Communist cells of all kinds must be subordinate to each other in
a strictly hierarchical order of rank as precisely as possible.

19. Almost everywhere the communist party arises as an *urban* party, a
party of industrial workers living mainly in towns. To facilitate and hasten
the victory of the working class the communist party must become the
party not only of the towns, but also of the villages. The communist party
must carry its propaganda and its organizing work to the agricultural
workers and the small and medium peasants. The communist party
must pay particular attention to organizing communist cells in the
countryside.

The international organization of the proletariat can be strong only if,
in all countries where communists live and fight, the ideas about the role
of the communist party here formulated take firm hold. The Communist
International invites to its congress every trade union which recognizes
its principles and is ready to break with the yellow International. The
Communist International will organize an international section of red
trade unions which acknowledge communist principles. The Communist
International will not refuse to co-operate with any non-party workers'
organization which is willing to wage a serious revolutionary struggle
against the bourgeoisie. In doing so, however, the Communist International will declare to the proletariat of the entire world:

1. The communist party is the chief and primary weapon for the liberation of the working class. We must now have in every country not mere
groups or tendencies, but a communist party.

2. There shall be in each country only one single unified communist
party.

3. The communist party shall be built on the principle of the strictest
centralization, and in the epoch of civil war military discipline is to pre-
vail in its ranks.

4. Wherever there are a dozen proletarians or semi-proletarians, the
communist party must have an organized cell.

5. In every non-party institution there must be a communist party cell
which is strictly subordinate to the party.

6. While adhering firmly and unyieldingly to the programme and
revolutionary tactics of communism, the communist party must always be
connected as closely as possible with the broad workers' organizations,
avoiding sectarianism as much as unprincipled opportunism.

EXTRACTS FROM A LETTER FROM THE ECCI TO THE FRENCH SOCIALIST
PARTY

26 *July* 1920   *K.I.*, 13, col. 2369, *September* 1920

[The Strasbourg congress of the French Socialist Party in January 1920 had voted 4,300 against 300 to leave the Second International, and had resolved to enter into negotiations with the responsible authorities of the Third International; it had also agreed to work, in conjunction with the German Independent Social-Democratic Party and the Italian and Swiss Socialist Parties, for a conference which should bring together with the parties of the Third International all those parties adhering to the traditional principles of socialism.

Cachin and Frossard left for Moscow before the second Comintern congress was convened, and attended two sessions of the ECCI. (Rosmer was present as delegate of the 'Committee for the Third International' set up in France in May 1919.)

Cachin and Frossard were authorized by the national committee of their party, on a vote of 2,735 against 1,632 abstentions, to attend the second Comintern congress. It was the critical and ambiguous attitude of the French and USPD delegates which prompted the ECCI to formulate the conditions of admission so strictly.

The report on France given to the second congress by an unofficial member of the French Socialist Party asserted that a genuinely revolutionary situation existed, but could not be exploited because there were no organized revolutionary cadres who knew what to do.]

By a large majority the last congress of the French Socialist Party decided to withdraw from the Second International . . . the same congress, by a majority of roughly two-thirds, rejected immediate adherence to the Third International; in an ambiguous resolution, it decided to enter into relations with the Third International and, at the same time, to organize the parties which stand between the Second and the Third. . . .

In our judgment of the situation of the Socialist Party in France we are guided by two vital considerations: First, the part now being played in the world by the French bourgeoisie; and, second, the situation within the French Socialist Party.

The French bourgeoisie are at present playing the most reactionary of all roles. They have become the rampart of world reaction; French imperialist capitalism has, in the eyes of the entire world, assumed the part of international gendarme. More than any other, the French bourgeoisie worked to crush the proletarian republic in Hungary. The French bourgeoisie have always played and are still playing the chief part in organizing the war of brigandage against Soviet Russia. . . . It is they who were chiefly responsible for drawing up the predatory Versailles treaty. They send Negro troops to occupy German towns. In fact, they have entered into an alliance with the German bourgeoisie against the German working class. There is no monstrous crime that the government of the French bourgeoisie would not commit. The world revolution knows no more cruel enemy than the government of French capitalists.

This imposes on French workers and on their party an extremely important international duty. . . . But the ECCI notes with regret that the situation within the French Socialist Party is not at all favourable to the fulfilment of the historic mission which the course of events imposes on you. . . .

The work of your parliamentary fraction in the Chamber of Deputies is neither revolutionary, nor socialist, nor proletarian. Every socialist deputy does as he pleases. The parliamentary fraction as a whole does not follow party instructions except when it pleases it to do so. . . . It does not denounce the crimes of the French Government. It does not conduct propaganda among the millions of ex-service men. . . . It does not concern itself with the arming of the proletariat. In short, it not only fails to prepare the proletarian revolution; in fact it does everything to sabotage it. . . .

Your attitude to the trade unions is thoroughly equivocal. Not only are you failing to conduct a systematic struggle against the social-patriot ideas of the leaders of the CGT, you conceal them. . . . You have not made it your task to wrest the unions from the pernicious influence of the agents of capital. . . .

Your attitude towards the communist left wing in your own party leaves much to be desired. You are not trying to draw closer to them; on the contrary, you are organizing a struggle against them. You have put entry into the Communist International on the agenda but at the same time you are doing nothing to bring about a fraternal rapprochement with the communist elements of your own country. . . .

And now as to your attitude to the International. . . . In the report made to us in Moscow by your representative Frossard you still explain your non-adherence to the Third International by the fact that the strongest parties of western Europe have not yet joined. But you should not forget that if, by the strongest parties, you mean the parties contaminated by social-patriotism, we would reply that we do not need them and will never admit them to the ranks of the Communist International. The truly revolutionary parties of Europe and America are in our ranks. The Communist International has become such a great force that for certain socialists it has become the fashion. . . . We shall not allow our organization to be diluted. The Communist International must remain the *fighting* international association of communist workers.

Now let us deal with the question which your representative Frossard put to us in his first written report.

You ask what our attitude is to the French trade unions. . . . We are opposed to revolutionaries and communists leaving the unions. . . .

Revolutionaries and communists must be where the working masses are. . . .
We ask our adherents in France not to leave the unions in any circumstances.
On the contrary, if they are to perform their duty towards the Communist
International they must intensify their work within the unions. . . . The
Second International, which was a political organization, has collapsed
like a house of cards. The new Amsterdam international of yellow trade
unions is at the present time more dangerous and more harmful to the
world revolution than the League of Nations. . . . Whatever the cost, we
must wrest these unions from the control of the capitalists and social-
traitors, and to do that we must be in the unions; to do that we must direct
our best forces there. In every union and in every branch we must organize
a communist group . . . we must open the eyes of the members and get rid
of the social-patriot leaders. . . .

Red trade unions are beginning to be organized on an international
level . . . an international congress of red trade unions is to be convened
for August or September, in opposition to the Amsterdam international
of yellow unions. Support this move in France. Get your unions to associate
themselves with the international of red unions and to break, once and for
all, with the yellow unions. This is the task of the revolutionaries in France.

THESES ON THE NATIONAL AND COLONIAL QUESTION ADOPTED BY
THE SECOND COMINTERN CONGRESS

28 *July* 1920   *Protokoll*, ii, p. 224

[In his speech on the international situation at the opening session of the congress, Lenin said: 'The imperialist war drew the dependent peoples into world
history; it is one of our most important tasks to find out how we should set about
organizing the soviet movement in the non-capitalist countries. Soviets are possible there too; they will not be workers' soviets, but soviets of peasants, or of
labouring people. . . . The second congress must work out practical instructions
for making the work which has up to now been carried on among hundreds of
millions of people in an unorganized fashion organized, uniform, and systematic.
. . . The soviet movement has begun throughout the entire east, over the whole
of Asia, among all colonial peoples.'

At the eighth congress of the Russian Communist Party, held immediately
after the foundation of the Third International, Bukharin said: 'If we propound
the solution of the right of self-determination for the colonies . . . we lose nothing
by it. On the contrary, we gain. . . . The most outright nationalist movement . . .
is only water for our mill, since it contributes to the destruction of English
imperialism.'

The theses were drafted and introduced by Lenin, and adopted with three
abstentions (Serrati, Pestaña, and Graziadei). The thesis of Lenin's speech was
the division of the world into oppressing and oppressed nations; this and the

hostility of imperialist countries to Russia and to the soviet movement determined the world system of State relationships. Nationalist movements were bound to have a bourgeois character, because the vast majority of the population of the backward countries were peasants, a group characteristic of bourgeois-capitalist relations. The differences of opinion in the commission on the question whether the Comintern should or should not support bourgeois-democratic movements in backward countries had been resolved by the verbal expedient of calling them 'national-revolutionary', thus distinguishing them from reformist movements which were inclined to collaborate with the imperialists against local revolutionary movements. Communists could support bourgeois liberation movements in the colonies if they were genuinely revolutionary and were not opposed to the communists organizing and training the peasantry and the exploited masses on revolutionary lines. 'The idea of the Soviet form of organization is a simple one that can be applied not only to proletarian conditions, but also to feudal and semi-feudal peasant conditions. . . . Peasant soviets, soviets of the exploited, are suitable for pre-capitalist conditions also.' The commission had also discussed whether the backward countries would have to go through a period of capitalist development, and had decided that this was not necessary. 'If the victorious revolutionary proletariat organizes systematic propaganda and the Soviet governments give them all the help they can, it is incorrect to assume that such peoples must pass through the capitalist stage of development.' In the commission, Lenin reported, Quelch of the British Socialist Party had said that the ordinary English worker would regard it as treason to help the dependent peoples to rebel against British rule. Radek replied to this that the British proletariat itself would never be free of the capitalist yoke unless it actively supported the colonial revolutionary movement. The Comintern would judge the British comrades not by their articles in favour of liberation, but by the number of them imprisoned for agitation in Ireland, Egypt, or India, and among the troops despatched to suppress risings in these countries. The colonies were the Achilles heel of British imperialism.

A set of supplementary theses was written and introduced by M. N. Roy, the Indian delegate, who reminded the congress of the rapid industrial development of India that had taken place in recent years, which was giving rise to a revolutionary movement among the exploited that was quite independent of the middle-class nationalist movement; this would bring about the downfall of European imperialism, and was therefore of tremendous importance to the European proletariat; he also placed great emphasis on the struggle of the landless peasantry in colonial countries, which provided the mass basis for communist activity. Roy's theses were adopted unanimously, but were rarely referred to afterwards by the Comintern, which took Lenin's theses as a guide to its activities.]

1. An abstract or formal conception of equality in general, and of national equality in particular, is characteristic of the very nature of bourgeois democracy. Under a show of the equality of the human personality in general, bourgeois democracy proclaims the formal equality in law of property owners and proletarians, of exploiters and exploited, thereby deeply deceiving the oppressed classes. The idea of equality, which is itself

a reflection of the conditions of commodity production, is turned by the bourgeoisie, using the pretext of the alleged absolute equality of the human personality, into an instrument for combating the abolition of classes. The true meaning of the demand for equality resides solely in the demand for the abolition of classes.

2. As the conscious expression of the proletarian class struggle to shake off the yoke of the bourgeoisie, the communist party, in accordance with its chief task—which is to fight bourgeois democracy and expose its falseness and hypocrisy—should not advance abstract and formal principles on the national question, but should undertake first of all a precise analysis of the given environment, historical and above all economic; secondly, it should specifically distinguish the interests of the oppressed classes, of the workers and the exploited, from the general concept of so-called national interests, which signify in fact the interests of the ruling class; thirdly, it should as precisely distinguish the oppressed, dependent nations, unequal in rights, from the oppressing, exploiting nations with full rights, to offset the bourgeois-democratic lies which conceal the colonial and financial enslavement of the vast majority of the world's population by a small minority of the wealthiest and most advanced capitalist countries that is characteristic of the epoch of finance-capital and imperialism.

3. The imperialist war of 1914 demonstrated with the greatest clarity to all enslaved nations and oppressed classes of the entire world the falseness of bourgeois-democratic phraseology. Both sides used phrases about national liberation and the right of national self-determination to make good their case, but the treaties of Brest-Litovsk and Bucharest on one side, and the treaties of Versailles and St. Germain on the other, showed that the victorious bourgeoisie quite ruthlessly determine 'national' frontiers in accordance with their economic interests. Even 'national' frontiers are objects of barter for the bourgeoisie. The so-called League of Nations is nothing but the insurance contract by which the victors in the war mutually guarantee each other's spoils. For the bourgeoisie, the desire to re-establish national unity, to 're-unite with the ceded parts of the country', is nothing but an attempt of the defeated to assemble forces for new wars. The reunification of nations artificially torn apart is also in accordance with the interests of the proletariat; but the proletariat can attain genuine national freedom and unity only by means of revolutionary struggle and after the downfall of the bourgeoisie. The League of Nations and the entire post-war policy of the imperialist States disclose this truth even more sharply and clearly, everywhere intensifying the revolutionary struggle of the proletariat of the advanced countries and of the labouring classes in the colonies and dependent countries, accelerating the destruction of petty-bourgeois national illusions about the possibility of peaceful co-existence and of the equality of nations under capitalism.

4. From these principles it follows that the entire policy of the Communist International on the national and colonial question must be based primarily on bringing together the proletariat and working classes of all nations and countries for the common revolutionary struggle for the overthrow of the landowners and the bourgeoisie. For only such united action will ensure victory over capitalism, without which it is impossible to abolish national oppression and inequality of rights.

5. The world political situation has now placed the proletarian dictatorship on the order of the day, and all events in world politics are necessarily concentrated on one central point, the struggle of the world bourgeoisie against the Russian Soviet Republic, which is rallying round itself both the soviet movements among the advanced workers in all countries, and all the national liberation movements in the colonies and among oppressed peoples, convinced by bitter experience that there is no salvation for them except in union with the revolutionary proletariat and in the victory of the Soviet power over world imperialism.

6. At the present time, therefore, we should not restrict ourselves to a mere recognition or declaration of the need to bring the working people of various countries closer together; our policy must be to bring into being a close alliance of all national and colonial liberation movements with Soviet Russia; the forms taken by this alliance will be determined by the stage of development reached by the communist movement among the proletariat of each country or by the revolutionary liberation movement in the undeveloped countries and among the backward nationalities.

7. Federation is a transitional form towards the complete union of the working people of all nations. Experience has already shown the expediency of federation, both in the relations of the Russian Socialist Federal Soviet Republic with other Soviet republics (the Hungarian, Finnish, and Latvian in the past, the Azerbaijan and Ukrainian at the present time), as also within the RSFSR itself in regard to the nationalities which had neither independent political existence nor self-government (for example the Bashkir and Tatar autonomous republics of the RSFSR, which were established in 1919 and 1920).

8. On this question it is the task of the Communist International not only to promote further development in this direction, but also to study and examine the experiences of these federations which have arisen on the basis of the Soviet system and the Soviet movement. While recognizing federation as a transitional form to complete union, efforts must be made to bring about an ever closer federal association, consideration being given to the following: first, it is impossible for the Soviet republics, surrounded by the imperialist States of the entire world, which are far stronger from the military point of view, to hold out unless they are closely allied with other Soviet republics; secondly, the necessity for a close economic association

among the Soviet republics, without which it is impossible to restore the productive forces destroyed by imperialism or to ensure the welfare of the working people; thirdly, the movement towards the creation of a unified world economy on a common plan controlled by the proletariat of all nations. This tendency has already become clearly manifest under capitalism, and socialism will without any doubt carry forward and complete its development.

9. In regard to relations within States, the Communist International's national policy cannot confine itself to the bare and formal recognition of the equality of nations, expressed in words only and involving no practical obligations, to which bourgeois democracies—even if they call themselves 'socialist'—restrict themselves.

Offences against the equality of nations and violations of the guaranteed rights of national minorities, repeatedly committed by all capitalist States despite their 'democratic' constitution, must be inflexibly exposed in all the propaganda and agitation carried on by the communist parties, both inside and outside parliament. But that is not enough. It is also necessary: first, to make clear all the time that only the Soviet system is able to ensure real equality for the nations because it unites first the proletarians, and then all the masses of the working people, in the struggle against the bourgeoisie; secondly, communist parties must give direct support to the revolutionary movements among the dependent nations and those without equal rights (e.g. in Ireland, and among the American Negroes), and in the colonies.

Without this last particularly important condition the struggle against the oppression of the dependent nations and colonies, and the recognition of their right to secede as separate States, remains a deceitful pretence, as it is in the parties of the Second International.

10. To acknowledge internationalism in words only, while in fact adulterating it in all propaganda, agitation, and practical work with petty-bourgeois nationalism and pacifism, is a common characteristic not only of the parties of the Second International, but also among those which have left the Second International. This phenomenon even occurs not infrequently among parties which now call themselves communist. The fight against this evil, against deeply rooted petty-bourgeois national prejudices which make their appearance in every possible form, such as race hatred, stirring up national antagonisms, anti-semitism, must be brought into the foreground the more vigorously, the more urgent it becomes to transform the dictatorship of the proletariat from a national dictatorship (i.e. a dictatorship existing in one country alone, and incapable of conducting an independent world policy) into an international dictatorship (i.e. a dictatorship of the proletariat in at least a few advanced countries, which is capable of exercising decisive influence in the political affairs of

the entire world). Petty-bourgeois nationalism calls the mere recognition of the equality of nations internationalism, and (disregarding the purely verbal character of such recognition) considers national egoism inviolable. Proletarian internationalism on the other hand demands: 1. Subordination of the interests of the proletarian struggle in one country to the interests of the struggle on a world scale; 2. that the nation which achieves victory over the bourgeoisie shall display the capacity and readiness to make the greatest national sacrifices in order to overthrow international capitalism.

That is why, in the States where capitalism is fully developed and which have workers' parties which really are the vanguard of the proletariat, the struggle against opportunist and petty-bourgeois pacifist distortions of the idea and policy of internationalism is the primary and most important task.

11. In regard to the more backward States and nations, primarily feudal or patriarchal or patriarchal-peasant in character, the following considerations must be kept specially in mind:

a. All communist parties must support by action the revolutionary liberation movements in these countries. The form which this support shall take should be discussed with the communist party of the country in question, if there is one. This obligation refers in the first place to the active support of the workers in that country on which the backward nation is financially, or as a colony, dependent.

b. It is essential to struggle against the reactionary and medieval influence of the priesthood, the Christian missions, and similar elements.

c. It is necessary to struggle against the pan-Islamic and pan-Asiatic movements and similar tendencies, which are trying to combine the liberation struggle against European and American imperialism with the strengthening of the power of Turkish and Japanese imperialism and of the nobility, the large landlords, the priests, etc.

d. It is particularly important to support the peasant movement in the backward countries against the landlords and all forms and survivals of feudalism. Above all, efforts must be made to give the peasant movement as revolutionary a character as possible, organizing the peasants and all the exploited wherever possible in soviets, and thus establish as close a tie as possible between the west European communist proletariat and the revolutionary peasant movement in the East, in the colonies and backward countries.

e. A resolute struggle must be waged against the attempt to clothe the revolutionary liberation movements in the backward countries which are not genuinely communist in communist colours. The Communist International has the duty of supporting the revolutionary movement in the colonies and backward countries only with the object of rallying the constituent elements of the future proletarian parties—which will be truly communist and not only in name—in all the backward countries and

144 THE COMMUNIST INTERNATIONAL

educating them to a consciousness of their special task, namely, that of fighting against the bourgeois-democratic trend in their own nation. The Communist International should collaborate provisionally with the revolutionary movement of the colonies and backward countries, and even form an alliance with it, but it must not amalgamate with it; it must unconditionally maintain the independence of the proletarian movement, even if it is only in an embryonic stage.

f. It is essential constantly to expose and to explain to the widest masses of the working people everywhere, and particularly in the backward countries, the deception practised by the imperialist Powers with the help of the privileged classes in the oppressed countries in creating ostensibly politically independent States which are in reality completely dependent on them economically, financially, and militarily. A glaring example of the deception practised on the working classes of an oppressed nation by the combined efforts of Entente imperialism and the bourgeoisie of that same nation is offered by the Zionists' Palestine venture (and by Zionism as a whole, which, under the pretence of creating a Jewish State in Palestine in fact surrenders the Arab working people of Palestine, where the Jewish workers form only a small minority, to exploitation by England). In present international conditions there is no salvation for dependent and weak nations except as an alliance of Soviet republics.

12. The centuries-old enslavement of the colonial and weak peoples by the great imperialist Powers has left behind among the working masses of the enslaved countries not only feelings of bitterness but also feelings of distrust of the oppressing nations as a whole, including the proletariat of these nations. The despicable treachery to socialism committed by the majority of the official leaders of that proletariat in the years 1914–1919, when the social-patriots concealed behind the slogan of 'defence of the fatherland' the defence of the 'right' of 'their' bourgeoisie to enslave the colonies and plunder the financially dependent countries—such treachery could only strengthen that quite natural distrust. Since this distrust and national prejudice can only be eradicated after the destruction of imperialism in the advanced countries and after the radical transformation of the entire foundations of economic life in the backward countries, the removal of these prejudices can proceed only very slowly. From this it follows that it is the duty of the class-conscious communist proletariat of all countries to be especially cautious and particularly attentive to the national feelings, in themselves out of date, in countries and peoples that have been long enslaved; it is also their duty to make concessions in order to remove this distrust and prejudice the more quickly. Unless the proletariat, and all the working masses of all countries and nations of the entire world, themselves strive towards alliance, and unite as one, the victory over capitalism cannot be pursued to a completely successful end.

EXTRACTS FROM THE THESES ON THE TRADE UNION MOVEMENT, FAC-
TORY COUNCILS, AND THE COMMUNIST INTERNATIONAL, ADOPTED BY
THE SECOND COMINTERN CONGRESS

July 1920   *Protokoll*, ii, p. 526

[The theses were introduced by Radek in a speech in which he argued that,
although capitalism could no longer ensure a rising standard of life for the
workers, it was wrong to say that the economic struggle was pointless. It kept
the working classes in fighting trim, and they would only be convinced by
experience that capitalism had nothing to offer them. Communist policy was to
give support to all factory organizations which helped to break the power of the
trade union bureaucracy; so long as the unions were controlled by the reformist
bureaucracy, the factory committees should not be incorporated in the unions.
'We go into the unions in order to overthrow the bureaucracy and if necessary
to split the unions. We go into the unions in order to make them instruments of
struggle. We shall try to turn the unions into fighting organizations; but if the
resistance of the bureaucracy should be stronger then we assume, we shall not
hesitate to destroy them, for we know that it is not the form that is most important, but the capacity of the workers to organize, and their will to organize the
revolutionary struggle.'
It was in connexion with communist work in the unions, whose leaders, he
thought, would do their best to exclude them, that Lenin wrote, shortly before
the second congress: 'One must know how to resist all this, to accept any and
every sacrifice, even—in case of necessity—to resort to every kind of trick, cunning, illegal expedient, concealment, suppression of the truth, in order to penetrate into the trade unions, to remain in them, to conduct in them, at whatever
cost, communist work.'
Objections to the theses were raised by most of the British and United States
delegates. Sceptical of the possibility of winning the existing unions for a revolutionary policy, they advocated the formation of new unions. In the debate on
the Statutes Gallacher asserted that the British trade unions could never be won
for communism; on the contrary, they were the strongest bulwark of capitalism
against the social revolution. The unions could not be won for communism, but
office in the unions would corrupt communists.
The commission to which the theses were referred held six long sessions, but
the conflict was unresolved. When the question came again before the congress,
the discussion was closed on a motion put forward by Zinoviev and carried by
50 votes to 25. The theses were carried by 64 votes; there were 13 abstentions,
including the British and United States delegates.]

I

1. . . . The trade unions, which catered primarily for the skilled and
best-paid workers, who were limited by their craft narrowness, bound by
the bureaucratic machinery which cut them off from the masses, and
misled by their opportunist leaders, have betrayed not only the cause of

social revolution, but even the cause of the struggle for an improvement in the conditions of life of their own members. They deserted the platform of trade union struggle against the employers and adopted in its place a programme of peaceful agreement with the capitalists at any price. This policy has been followed not only by the liberal unions in England and America, and by the allegedly 'socialist' free trade unions in Germany and Austria, but also by the syndicalist unions in France. . . .

2. In order to wage their economic struggles successfully, the broad working masses are now streaming into the ranks of the trade unions. In all capitalist countries the membership of the trade unions is increasing by leaps and bounds; the unions no longer organize only the advanced sections, but the great mass of the proletariat, who are trying to turn them into their own fighting weapon. The greater acuteness of class contradictions forces the unions to lead the strikes which are spreading in a broad wave over the entire capitalist world and constantly interrupting the process of capitalist production and exchange. As prices rise and their own exhaustion grows, the working masses raise their demands and thus destroy the basis of all capitalist calculations, which are the essential prerequisite of any orderly economy. The trade unions, which during the war became channels for influencing the working masses in the interests of the bourgeoisie, are now becoming organs for the destruction of capitalism.

3. This change in the character of trade unions is being hampered in every way by the old trade union bureaucracy and the old organizational forms of the trade unions. The old union bureaucracy is trying to maintain the unions as organizations of the labour aristocracy; it retains the rules and regulations which make it impossible for the badly paid working masses to join the unions. Even now the old trade union bureaucracy is trying to substitute for the strike struggle of the workers, which with every day takes on more and more the character of a revolutionary struggle between proletariat and bourgeoisie, a policy of agreement with the capitalists, a policy of long-term agreements which, with the uninterrupted mad rise in prices, are utterly meaningless. It is trying to force on the workers the policy of collaboration with the employers, of joint industrial councils, and to make the conduct of strikes more difficult from the legal point of view, with the help of the capitalist State. . . .

4. Since powerful working masses are streaming into the unions, and since the economic fight which these masses are waging, in opposition to the trade union bureaucracy, has an objectively revolutionary character, communists in all countries must join the trade unions, in order to turn them into conscious fighting organs for the overthrow of capitalism and for communism. They must take the initiative in forming trade unions where these do not exist.

All voluntary abstention from the unions, all artificial attempts to create separate trade unions, unless compelled thereto either by extraordinary acts of violence on the part of the trade union bureaucracy (such as the dissolution of revolutionary branches of the unions by the opportunist union headquarters), or by their narrow policy of serving only the labour aristocracy which makes it impossible for the masses of less skilled workers to join the union, are extremely dangerous for the communist movement. They involve the danger that the masses, who are on the road to communism, will be separated from the most advanced and class-conscious workers and surrendered to the opportunist leaders who work hand in glove with the bourgeoisie. The indecision of the working masses, their intellectual irresolution, their susceptibility to the specious arguments of the opportunist leaders, can be overcome only in the course of the sharpening struggle, to the extent that the broadest strata of the proletariat learn from their own experience, from their victories and defeats, that it is no longer possible within a capitalist economic system to get human conditions of life, to the extent that the advanced communist workers learn to act, in the economic struggle, not only as heralds of the ideas of communism, but as the most determined leaders of the struggle and of the trade unions. Only in this way will it be possible to get rid of the opportunist union leaders. Only in this way can the communists get at the head of the trade union movement and make of it an organ of revolutionary struggle for communism. . . .

5. Since communists attach more importance to the goal and nature of trade unions than to their form, they should not shrink from a split in the union organizations if the refusal to split would be tantamount to abandoning revolutionary work in the unions, abandoning the attempt to make them instruments of revolutionary struggle and to organize the most exploited sections of the proletariat. But even if such a split should prove to be necessary, it should be effected only if the communists succeed in convincing the broad working masses, by constant struggle against the opportunist leaders and their tactics, by the most vigorous participation in the economic struggle of the broad working masses, that the split is to be made not for the sake of distant revolutionary aims which they do not yet understand, but for the sake of the most immediate practical interests of the working class in the development of their economic struggle. . . .

6. Where splits between opportunist and revolutionary trade union leadership have already occurred, where, as in America, there are, in addition to the opportunist unions, unions with revolutionary if not communist tendencies, communists are obliged to support these revolutionary unions, to help them free themselves of syndicalist prejudices and adopt a communist standpoint, which can alone serve as a reliable compass in the perplexities of the economic struggle. Where there are factory organizations, whether part of or outside the trade unions, such as shop stewards

and factory committees, whose object is to fight the counter-revolutionary tendencies of the trade union bureaucracy and support the spontaneous direct actions of the proletariat, communists must of course support these organizations with the utmost energy. But support for revolutionary unions should not mean that communists leave the opportunist unions which are in a state of ferment and are moving towards advocacy of the class struggle. On the contrary, in seeking to accelerate this development of the mass unions which are on the road to revolutionary struggle, communists will be able to play the part of an element uniting the workers in the unions, theoretically and organizationally, for the common struggle for the abolition of capitalism.

7. In the epoch of capitalist decay the economic struggle is transformed into a political struggle far more quickly than could have happened in the age of peaceful capitalist development. Any large-scale economic conflict may confront the workers with the question of revolution. It is therefore the duty of communists, at all stages of the economic struggle, to point out to the workers that the struggle can be successful only if the working class defeats the capitalist class in open battle and embarks on the work of socialist construction by means of dictatorship. With this in mind, the communists must try to establish complete unity as widely as possible between the trade unions and the communist party, subordinating the unions to the leadership of the party as the vanguard of the workers' revolution. For this purpose communists must form communist party fractions in all trade unions and factory committees and with their help take over and lead the trade union movement.

II

1. The economic struggle of the proletariat for higher wages and better living conditions generally for the working masses is getting deeper into a blind alley every day. The economic disorder which is enveloping one country after another shows even the backward workers that it is not enough to fight for higher wages and a shorter working day, that with every day the capitalist class is less and less able to restore economic life and to ensure for the workers even the standard of life they enjoyed before the war. From this growing recognition arise the efforts of the working masses to create organizations which can take up the struggle to rescue economic life by workers' control, exercised through the control of production by the factory committees. . . . It is therefore a mistake to want to organize factory committees only of those workers who have already adopted the programme of proletarian dictatorship. On the contrary, because of this economic disorder, it is the duty of the communist party to organize *all* workers, and to arm them for the struggle for the proletarian

dictatorship by extending and deepening the struggle, which they all understand, for workers' control over production.

2. The communist party will be able to accomplish this task if, in the struggle of the factory committees, it intensifies the awareness of the masses that the planned restoration of economy on a capitalist basis, which would mean the further subjugation of the workers by the State for the benefit of the capitalist class, is now impossible. The organization of economic life in the interests of the working masses is possible only when the State is in the hands of the workers, when the strong hand of the workers' dictatorship starts on the abolition of capitalism and on socialist reconstruction.

3. The struggle of the factory committees against capitalism has as its immediate general object workers' control over production. . . . The committees in the different factories will soon be faced with the question of workers' control over entire branches of industry and industry as a whole. But since any attempt by the workers to supervise the supply of raw materials and the financial operations of the factory owners will be met by the bourgeoisie and the capitalist government with the most vigorous measures against the working class, the fight for workers' control of production leads to the fight for the seizure of power by the working class. . . .

5. Factory committees cannot replace the trade unions. Only in the course of the struggle can the committees step outside the limits of the individual factory or workshop and unite on the basis of an entire industry, establishing machinery for the conduct of the struggle as a whole. The trade unions are already centralized fighting organs, although they do not include such great working masses as the factory committees can, which are looser organizations accessible to all the workers in an undertaking. This division of function between factory committee and trade union is a result of the historical development of the social revolution. Trade unions organize the working masses for struggle on the basis of the demands for higher wages and a shorter working day throughout the country. Factory committees are organized for workers' control over production, for the fight against economic chaos; they cover all the workers in the factory, but their struggle can only gradually assume a nation-wide character. Only in so far as the trade unions overcome the counter-revolutionary tendencies of their bureaucracy, deliberately become organs of revolution, should communists support the effort to turn factory committees into factory branches of the trade union. . . .

III

. . . The opportunist trade union leaders, who during the war acted as lackeys of the bourgeoisie, are now trying to re-establish the trade union international and make of it a weapon for international world capital in its fight against the proletariat. Led by Legien, Jouhaux, and Gompers, they are forming a 'labour office' attached to the League of Nations, that organization of the international system of capitalist robbery. In all countries they are trying to throttle the strike movement by legislation which will compel the workers to submit to courts of arbitration composed of representatives of the capitalist State. Everywhere they are trying to reach agreement with the capitalists on granting concessions to the skilled workers, seeking in this way to shatter the growing unity of the working class.

With every day the economic struggle of the proletariat in every country is becoming more revolutionary. Therefore the trade unions must consciously use all their power to support every revolutionary struggle, in other countries as well as their own. For this purpose they must not only strive to bring about the greatest possible centralization of the struggle in their country, but they must do this on an international scale by entering the Communist International, uniting with it into an army whose various parts carry on the struggle in common by reciprocal support.

EXTRACTS FROM THE THESES ON COMMUNIST PARTIES AND PARLIAMENT ADOPTED BY THE SECOND COMINTERN CONGRESS

2 *August* 1920   *Protokoll*, ii, p. 466

[The historical introduction to these theses was written by Trotsky; the theses themselves were drafted and introduced by Bukharin. In the commission they were adopted against 2 votes (Switzerland and the IWW); theses submitted to the commission by Bordiga (Italy), urging abstention from Parliament, received 2 votes. Bukharin's theses were adopted by the congress against 7 votes, with 11 abstentions. In his introductory speech Bukharin said the theses were directed against the parliamentarians who became part of the bourgeois State machine, and the anti-parliamentarians 'on principle', the anarchists and abstentionists who believed that in the given conditions of class struggle participation in Parliament was a mistake. Gallacher (shop stewards), supported by a German syndicalist, Suchi, thought the theses opportunist; they would discourage a revolutionary spirit among the workers, and parliamentary activities would corrupt those who were elected. Murphy disagreed with Gallacher, and supported the theses.

Lenin maintained that Parliament, reflecting class conflicts and interests, was an arena of the class struggle. It could be used in a revolutionary way, which would itself contribute to the destruction of Parliament.]

I. THE NEW EPOCH AND THE NEW PARLIAMENTARIANISM

From the very first, at the time of the First International, the attitude of socialist parties towards parliament was to utilize bourgeois parliaments for purposes of agitation. Participation in parliament was viewed from the standpoint of developing class consciousness, that is, of awakening the class hostility of the proletariat towards the ruling class. This attitude changed under the influence, not of theory, but of political developments. . . .

The attitude of the Communist International towards parliament is determined not by any new theory, but by the change in the role of parliaments themselves. In the preceding epoch parliament, as the instrument of developing capitalism, accomplished work which was to a certain extent historically progressive. In present conditions of unbridled imperialism, however, parliament has become an instrument of falsehood, deception, and violence, an enervating talk-shop. In the face of the devastation, looting, violence, robberies, and destruction committed by imperialism, parliamentary reforms, lacking system, durability, and order, lose all practical significance for the working masses. . . .

Socialists who, while inclined towards communism, point out that the moment for revolution has not yet come in their country, and refuse to break away from the parliamentary opportunists, are in fact arguing from a conscious or semi-conscious assessment of the approaching epoch as one of relative stability of imperialist society, and assuming, on this basis, that practical results can be obtained by a coalition with the Turatis and Longuets in the fight for reform. But communism must start from a clear theoretical analysis of the character of the present epoch (the culmination of capitalism, imperialist self-negation and self-destruction, uninterrupted spread of civil war, etc.). The forms of political relations and groupings may be different in different countries, but their essential nature is the same everywhere. For us the question is the immediate political and technical preparation of the insurrection of the proletariat for the destruction of bourgeois power and the establishment of the new proletarian power.

For communists, parliament today can in no circumstances serve as the centre of the struggle for reforms, for improving the lot of the working class, as it did at certain times in the preceding epoch. The centre of gravity of political life has now been completely and finally removed beyond the confines of parliament. On the other hand the bourgeoisie are compelled, in virtue not only of their relation to the working masses, but also of the involved inter-relationships within the bourgeois classes, to put some of their measures into effect, in one way or another, through parliament, where the various cliques bargain for power, display their strength and betray their weakness, show themselves up as they really are, etc.

Therefore it is the immediate historical task of the working class to wrench this machine from the hands of the ruling classes, to destroy and annihilate it, and to put in its place new proletarian organs of power. At the same time however the revolutionary general staff of the working class has a strong interest in having reconnaissance units in the parliamentary institutions of the bourgeoisie, to facilitate the work of destruction. From this emerges clearly the fundamental difference between the tactics of communists, who enter parliament with revolutionary aims, and the tactics of the socialist parliamentarians. . . . The disgusting traditions of the old parliamentary tactics have however impelled some revolutionary elements into the camp of opponents of parliament in principle (the IWW, the revolutionary syndicalists, KAPD). The second congress therefore puts forward the following theses:

2. COMMUNISM, THE FIGHT FOR THE DICTATORSHIP OF THE PROLETARIAT, AND THE UTILIZATION OF BOURGEOIS PARLIAMENTS

I

1. Parliamentarianism as a State system became a 'democratic' form of the rule of the bourgeoisie who, at a certain stage of development, needed the fiction of a popular representative body, which from the outside seems to be an organization of the 'popular will' standing outside classes, but is in essence an instrument of oppression and subjection in the control of ruling capital.

2. Parliamentarianism is a particular form of the *State* order; hence it cannot be the form of communist society, in which there are neither classes nor class struggle, nor any State power.

3. Nor can parliament serve as the form of proletarian State administration in the transition period from the dictatorship of the bourgeoisie to the dictatorship of the proletariat. When the class struggle has come to a head, in the civil war, the proletariat must build up its State organization as a *fighting organization* to which representatives of the former ruling classes are not admitted. At this stage the fiction of the 'popular will' is directly harmful to the proletariat. The proletariat needs no parliamentary division of powers, which is harmful to it. The form taken by the proletarian dictatorship is the Soviet republic.

4. Bourgeois parliaments, one of the most important pieces of machinery in the bourgeois State apparatus, cannot as such be won permanently, just as the proletariat cannot win the bourgeois State. The task of the proletariat is to shatter the bourgeois State machine, to destroy it, and to destroy with it parliamentary institutions, whether republican or deriving from a constitutional monarchy. . . .

6. Consequently, communism repudiates parliamentarianism as the form of the future society, as the form of the class dictatorship of the proletariat. It denies the possibility of winning parliament over permanently; its object is to destroy parliamentarianism. It follows that communism can be concerned only with exploiting bourgeois State institutions

with the object of destroying them. In this way, and only in this way, can the question be conceived.

II

7. Every class struggle is a political struggle, for in the final analysis it is a struggle for power. Any strike which spreads over the whole country endangers the bourgeois State and therefore assumes a political character. . . .

8. Consequently the question of political struggle is by no means identical with the question of the attitude to parliament. The first is a general question of the proletarian class struggle, in which small and partial struggles mount up to the general struggle for the overthrow of the capitalist order as a whole.

9. . . . Civil war is war. In this war the proletariat must have its courageous political officers' corps, its strong political general staff, directing all the operations of the struggle in every field.

10. The mass struggle is an entire system of developing actions which become more and more acute in form and logically lead to insurrection against the capitalist State. In this mass struggle which develops into civil war, the leading party of the proletariat must as a rule secure all legal positions, using them as auxiliary centres of its revolutionary activity and incorporating them in its main plan of campaign, the campaign of mass struggle.

11. One such auxiliary centre is the rostrum of the bourgeois parliament. It is no argument against participation in the parliamentary struggle that parliament is a bourgeois State institution. The communist party does not enter this institution to function there as an organic part of parliament, but in order by action inside parliament to help the masses to shatter the State machine and parliament itself. . . .

12. This activity inside parliament, which consists chiefly in revolutionary agitation from the parliamentary tribune, in exposing enemies, in the ideological mobilization of the masses, who, particularly in the backward areas, are still encumbered with democratic illusions and look to the parliamentary rostrum, must be wholly and completely subordinate to the aims and tasks of the mass struggle outside parliament.

Participation in the electoral struggle and revolutionary propaganda from inside parliament are particularly important in the political approach to those sections of the working class, such as the agricultural working masses, who have up to now been remote from political life. . . .

III

16. 'Anti-parliamentarianism' on principle, that is, the absolute and categorical rejection of participation in elections and in revolutionary

parliamentary activity, is therefore a naïve and childish doctrine which is beneath criticism, a doctrine which is occasionally founded on healthy disgust with paltry parliamentary politicians, but which is at the same time blind to the possibility of revolutionary parliamentarianism. Moreover, this doctrine is frequently connected with a wholly false idea of the role of the party, which pictures it not as the centralized vanguard of the workers, but as a decentralized system of loosely-connected groups.

17. On the other hand it does not at all follow from the theoretical admission of parliamentary activity that participation in actual elections and in actual parliamentary sessions is *in all circumstances* absolutely necessary. That depends on a whole series of specific conditions. In certain circumstances it may be necessary to walk out of parliament. The Bolsheviks did that when they left the pre-parliament in order to destroy it. . . . In certain circumstances it may be necessary to boycott elections and to remove by force both the entire bourgeois State apparatus, as well as the bourgeois parliamentary clique, or it may be necessary to take part in elections while boycotting parliament itself, etc.

18. . . . The boycotting of elections or of parliament, as well as walking out of parliament, are permissible primarily when the conditions for the immediate transition to armed struggle for power are at hand.

19. The comparative unimportance of this question should always be borne in mind. Since the centre of gravity lies in the struggle for State power waged outside parliament, it is obvious that the question of the proletarian dictatorship and of the *mass struggle* for that dictatorship cannot be placed on the same footing as the question of the utilization of parliament.

20. That is why the Communist International emphasizes most strongly that it considers any split or any attempt at a split within the communist party solely on this question a serious error. . . .

3. REVOLUTIONARY PARLIAMENTARIANISM

. . . 2. After elections, the organization of the parliamentary fraction must be completely in the hands of the central committee of the communist party, whether or not the party as a whole is at the time legal or illegal. The chairman and presidium of the communist parliamentary fraction must be confirmed in their office by the central committee. The central committee must have a permanent representative in the fraction, with the right of veto and, on all important political questions, the fraction must seek in advance guidance from the party central committee. The central committee has the right and the duty, when the communist fraction in parliament is about to undertake an important step, to appoint or to contest the spokesman for the fraction and to require that the outline of his

speech or the speech itself be submitted for approval by the central committee, etc. Every communist candidate must officially give a written
undertaking that he is ready to resign from parliament at the first request
of the party central committee, so that in any given situation resignation
from parliament can be carried out in unison. . . .

4. A communist member of parliament is obliged, on the decision of the
central committee, to combine legal with illegal work. In those countries
where communist deputies enjoy immunity under bourgeois law, this
immunity must be used to support the party's illegal activities in the fields
of organization and propaganda.

5. Communist deputies must subordinate all their activities in parliament to party action outside parliament. Demonstrative legislative proposals should be regularly submitted on the instructions of the party and
its central committee, not with the idea that they will be accepted by the
bourgeois majority, but for purposes of propaganda, agitation, and
organization. . . .

8. Every communist member of parliament must bear in mind that he
is not a legislator seeking agreement with other legislators, but a party
agitator sent into the enemy camp to execute party decisions. The communist deputy is responsible not to the loose mass of the electors, but to
his communist party, legal or illegal.

9. The speeches of communist deputies in parliament must be readily
understandable to every ordinary worker, every peasant, every washer-
woman, every shepherd, so that the party can issue his speeches as leaflets
for distribution in every corner of the country. . . .

11. Communist deputies must use the parliamentary rostrum to expose
not only the bourgeoisie and their avowed followers, but also the social-
patriots and reformists, to expose the indecisiveness of the 'centrist' politicians and other opponents of communism, and to conduct propaganda
for the ideas of the Communist International.

EXTRACTS FROM THE THESES ON THE AGRARIAN QUESTION ADOPTED
BY THE SECOND COMINTERN CONGRESS

4 *August* 1920   *Protokoll*, ii, p. 767

[These theses, drafted by Lenin, were to have been introduced by Markhlevsky,
who was, however, 'prevented from speaking by the gratifying progress of the
Red Army'. (Markhlevsky, Dzerzhinsky, F. Kon, and Unschlicht were in
Bialystok as a kind of provisional revolutionary government, ready to take over
in Poland should Warsaw fall.)

Serrati, of the Italian Socialist Party, who abstained from voting, spoke
against the theses, arguing that they did not correspond with the needs of the

revolution in western countries, and ignored both the existing peasant parties and peasant mentality.]

1. Only the urban industrial proletariat led by the communist party can liberate the working masses of the countryside from the yoke of capital and large landownership, or protect them from decline and from the imperialist wars which are forever unavoidable so long as the capitalist system is maintained. The masses working on the land cannot find salvation otherwise than in alliance with the communist proletariat, and in all-out support of its revolutionary struggle for the overthrow of the junkers (large landowners) and the bourgeoisie. On the other hand the industrial workers cannot accomplish their world-historical mission of emancipating humanity from the shackles of capital and war if they shut themselves up within the circle of narrow craft trade unionist interests, and self-complacently restrict themselves to efforts to improve their more or less tolerable petty-bourgeois position. But that precisely is what is being done in many advanced countries by the 'labour aristocracy', which forms the basis of the allegedly socialist parties of the Second International, but which is in reality the worst enemy of socialism, its betrayers, petty-bourgeois chauvinists and agents of the bourgeoisie within the labour movement. The proletariat is a genuinely revolutionary class, a class acting in genuinely socialist fashion, only when it comes forward and acts as the vanguard of all working and exploited people, as leader in the struggle for the overthrow of the exploiters. But this cannot be put into effect without the class struggle being carried over on to the land, without rallying the working masses of the countryside, without the communist party of the urban proletariat, without the training of the rural by the urban proletariat.

2. The working and exploited rural masses whom the urban proletariat must lead in the fight or at least attract to its side, are represented in capitalist countries by the following groups:

First: the agricultural proletariat, the wage-workers (seasonal, migrant, and daily labourers), who get their living by wage labour in agricultural undertakings and the industrial concerns connected with them. To organize this class, including forestry workers, artisans on large estates, etc., independently of other groups of the rural population (politically and militarily, in trade union, co-operative, and educational organizations), to intensify propaganda and agitation among this group and to draw them over to the side of Soviet power and the dictatorship of the proletariat—that is the basic task of the communist party in all countries.

Second: the semi-proletariat, the dwarf-holders, that is, those who earn their living partly by wage-labour in agricultural, industrial, and capitalist undertakings, and partly by drudgery on a plot of land which they own or rent, and which yields only part of the food required by their families.

In all capitalist countries this part of the working rural population is very large; their existence, however, and their situation is ignored by the representatives of the bourgeoisie and the socialists who belong to the Second International. This is done in part deliberately, to mislead the workers, and in part as a result of the common petty-bourgeois view which confuses this group with the mass of the peasantry as a whole. This method of misleading the workers is most in evidence in Germany and France, but can also be seen in America and other countries. If the communist party does its work correctly this group can become reliable adherents of the party, for the lot of these semi-proletarians is very hard, and the advantages they would gain from Soviet power and the proletarian dictatorship are great and would come into effect immediately.

In some countries the first and second group are not sharply separated from each other. In special circumstances therefore they may be organized jointly.

Third: the small peasants, that is, those who work small farms, their own or rented, which just cover the requirements of their family and which need no hired labour. This section undoubtedly gains by the victory of the proletariat, which brings them: (a) freedom from the payment of rent or part of the harvest to the landowner (e.g. the *métayers* in France and Italy); (b) freedom from mortgage payments and redemption dues; (c) freedom from the various forms of dependence on the large landowners (use of woods and commons, etc.); (d) immediate help for their farm from the proletarian State (the opportunity to use agricultural machinery and part of the arable land of the large capitalist farms expropriated by the proletariat; immediate transformation by the proletarian State of consumers' and agricultural co-operatives from organizations which under capitalism served primarily the wealthy and powerful peasants, into organizations which primarily serve the poor, i.e. the proletarians, semi-proletarians, and small peasants).

At the same time the communist party must bear in mind that in the transition period from capitalism to communism, that is, during the period of the proletarian dictatorship, waverings in at least part of this stratum towards complete freedom of trade and the free disposal of private property are inevitable. For this stratum, which on a small scale at any rate has a food surplus to sell, is tied to customs and habits of trade and property. With a firm proletarian policy, with a resolute settling of accounts between the victorious proletariat and the large landowners and large peasants, the vacillation of this stratum need not be significant. Nor can it change the fact that the small peasants as a whole will stand on the side of the proletarian revolution.

3. Taken together, these three groups represent, in all countries, the majority of the rural population. Therefore the final triumph of the

proletarian revolution is ensured not only for the towns, but also for the countryside. The contrary opinion is widespread, but it is only kept alive, firstly by the systematic deception practised by bourgeois science and statistics, which use every means to conceal the deep abyss between these three strata and the exploiters, the landowners and capitalists, and that between the semi-proletarians and small peasants on the one hand, and the large peasants on the other; and secondly, by the inability and reluctance of the heroes of the Second International and the 'labour aristocracy', demoralized by imperialist privileges, to carry out genuinely proletarian, revolutionary propaganda and agitational and organizational work among the rural working population. The entire attention of the opportunists was and is directed to reaching a theoretical and practical understanding with the bourgeoisie, including the large and middle peasantry, and not to the revolutionary overthrow by the proletariat of the bourgeois government and the bourgeoisie. Thirdly, this false opinion is kept alive by a stubborn prejudice which goes with all bourgeois-democratic and parliamentary prejudices. This prejudice holds out against a truth thoroughly demonstrated by theoretical Marxism and fully confirmed by the experience of the proletarian revolution in Russia, namely, that with the exception of the rural workers who are already on the side of revolution, the dispersed, oppressed, intimidated rural population in the groups referred to, who are condemned in all countries, even the most advanced, to semi-barbaric living conditions, groups which are economically, socially, and culturally interested in the victory of socialism, can give decisive support to the revolutionary proletariat only after the proletariat has seized political power, after it has finally settled accounts with the large landowners and capitalists, and after these groups have seen from experience that they have an organized leader and defender who is powerful and resolute enough to help them and put them on the right road.

4. The middle peasants, using the term in an economic sense, include the small farmers, that is, owners or tenants of farms which as a rule, under capitalism, not only support the family but also yield a small surplus which, at least in good years, can be changed into capital; many of these farms also employ outside labour. As an example of the middle peasantry in an advanced capitalist country we can take the group of German farmers with 5 to 10 hectares of land who, according to the 1907 figures, employed agricultural wage labourers totalling one-third their own number. In France, where special crops (e.g. vines) are cultivated which require a great deal of labour, this group probably employs an even larger number of hired workers.

The revolutionary proletariat cannot undertake, at least in the immediate future and in the early stage of the proletarian dictatorship, to attract this group to its side. Rather it must restrict itself to the job of neutralizing them, that is, preventing them from giving active help to the bourgeoisie in their struggle with the proletariat. The vacillations of this group are unavoidable, and at the opening of the new epoch they will tend to lean, in the developed capitalist countries, towards the bourgeoisie, for the outlook and feelings of proprietors are turned very markedly in the direction of private capital. The victorious proletariat will improve the condition of this group by cancelling rent and mortgage debts, by providing machinery and installing electricity, etc. The question of the immediate abolition of private property by the proletarian regime does not arise in most capitalist States. But the proletarian State power will annul all the obligations imposed on this group which arise from private property. In any case, the proletarian regime will guarantee the small and middle peasantry not only the retention of their land, but also that it will be increased by all the land they hitherto rented (by the abolition of rent).

The combination of such measures with the implacable struggle against the bourgeoisie guarantees the success of the policy of neutralization. The transition to collective farming among the middle peasantry, without the use of any compulsion, can be effected by the proletarian State only gradually and with the greatest caution, by the force of example (provision of machinery, the introduction of technical improvements, electrification).

5. The large peasants are represented by capitalist undertakings in agriculture, employing as a rule several wage labourers, and connected with the peasantry only by their cultural level, their manner of living, and by personal, physical co-operation on the farm.

This is the most numerous of the bourgeois strata, who are openly and definitely hostile to the revolutionary proletariat. The work of the communist party in the countryside must have as its main object the emancipation of the working and exploited majority of the rural population from the moral and political influence of these exploiters, the struggle against this group.

After the victory of the proletariat in the towns this group will inevitably resort to every kind of resistance and sabotage of a counter-revolutionary character, even to armed resistance. Therefore the revolutionary proletariat must immediately begin the intellectual and organizational training of the forces necessary to disarm this stratum and at the first sign of resistance to deal it, when the industrial capitalists are overthrown, a decisive, ruthless, annihilating blow. For this purpose the agricultural proletariat must be armed and organized in soviets (estate councils) in which there should be no place for exploiters, and which must assure overwhelming influence to the proletarians and semi-proletarians.

The expropriation of the large peasants should not, however, be the direct task of the victorious proletariat, for the material prerequisites, in particular the technical as well as the social, for the socialization of these farms are not yet at hand. In individual cases, which will probably be exceptional, those parts of their land which are rented out, or for which there is a particular need among the small peasant population of the neighbourhood, will be expropriated. These small peasants must also be guaranteed the free use on certain conditions of part of the agricultural machinery of the large peasants. In general the proletarian State power can leave the large peasants their land, and expropriate it only if resistance is shown to the rule of the working and exploited people. The experience of the proletarian revolution in Russia, where the struggle against the large peasants was extremely complex and long drawn out because of a number of exceptional circumstances, showed that this stratum is capable, if it gets a proper lesson at the least sign of resistance, of loyally meeting the demands of the proletarian State power, and even begins to feel respect for that power which protects every worker and ruthlessly pursues the wealthy idlers. . . .

6. The revolutionary proletariat must at once expropriate, without exception and without compensation, all the land belonging to the large landowners and proprietors of estates and all who, whether directly or through leasing land, systematically exploit the labour power of wage-workers and the neighbouring small (frequently also middle) peasantry, and do not themselves work. . . . In the most advanced capitalist countries the Communist International recognizes that it is correct to maintain the majority of large-scale agricultural undertakings and to run them on the lines of the State farms in Russia. It will also be appropriate to encourage the formation of collective undertakings (co-operative estates, communes). The maintenance of large agricultural undertakings is the best way of taking care of the interests of the revolutionary section of the rural population, the propertyless land workers and the semi-proletarian dwarf-holders, who earn their living largely by wage labour in large concerns. Moreover, the nationalization of these large estates makes the urban population at least partly independent of supplies from the peasantry. . . .

In countries and regions where large-scale agriculture is of comparatively insignificant proportions, but where there are large numbers of small peasant proprietors who hope to receive land, the division among them of the land of the large proprietors will be the most certain means of winning the peasantry for the revolution. . . .

7. . . . It is urgently necessary that the conditions of the rural working masses, the most exploited of them, should be immediately and appreciably improved, by the victory of the proletariat, at the expense of the exploiters, for without that the industrial proletariat could not rely confidently on support from the countryside or on the provisioning of the towns with food.

8. The tremendous difficulty of organizing the masses of the rural population, who have been kept by capitalism intellectually undeveloped,

scattered, suppressed, and frequently in a state of semi-medieval dependence, and of training them as revolutionary fighters, requires the communist party to pay particular attention to the strike movement in agriculture, and to give wholehearted support and every encouragement to mass strikes of the rural proletariat and semi-proletariat. . . .

The congress of the Communist International denounces as traitors and deserters those socialists—to be found, unfortunately, not only in the Second International, but also in the parties, particularly important for Europe, which have left that International—who manage not merely to regard the rural strike movement with indifference but (like the trade union bureaucracy, the Scheidemanns and Kautskys) come out against the strikes because they look at them only from the standpoint of the danger of a decrease in food production. No programme and no declaration, however solemn, is of the slightest value if it is not demonstrated in deed that the communists and the workers' leaders place the development of the proletarian revolution and its victory above everything else, that they are ready to make the greatest sacrifices for it and that there is no other way and no other means of getting rid of hunger and ruin for ever and preventing new imperialist wars. The communist parties must make the utmost efforts to prepare for the establishment in the countryside of soviets, estate councils, composed in the first place of representatives of wage-labourers and semi-proletarians. Propaganda should also be carried out for the formation of small-peasant councils. Only in association with the mass strike movement and together with the most oppressed class will the soviets be able to carry out their task and consolidate their position, to get the small peasants under their influence and later bring them into the land workers' councils. But so long as the strike movement is not strong enough, and the organization of the agricultural proletariat is still weakly developed, so long as the landlords and large peasants still exert great pressure and the industrial workers and their organizations give inadequate support, the formation of soviets in the countryside requires long preparation. This preparation must be effected by the creation of communist party cells, however small to begin with, by active propaganda which explains communist demands in everyday language and illustrates the different methods of exploitation and enslavement by practical examples, by regular agitation tours of the rural areas by industrial workers, etc.

STATUTES OF THE COMMUNIST INTERNATIONAL ADOPTED AT THE
SECOND COMINTERN CONGRESS

4 *August* 1920   *Protokoll*, ii, p. 599

[Kabakchiev reported on the Statutes, which were put forward by the ECCI and adopted unanimously. Unlike the Second International, which exercised no authority over the programme and activities of the affiliated parties, the Third International was to be as highly centralized and disciplined as the party which had overthrown capitalism in Russia. To the objection urged in the commission that too much emphasis was laid in the statutes on armed struggle and illegal organization, Kabakchiev replied that their concealment would not save communists from persecution. Could they shrink from talking of armed struggle at a time 'when the victorious Red Army is inflicting deadly blows on Entente imperialism and clearing the road for the world revolution', and when civil war was raging in a number of countries? 'This diplomatic prudence is dangerous, for today the illegal is as important as the legal organization. And not only important, but indispensable. . . . It is not by omitting from the statutes the article about illegal organization that we shall parry the blows of the bourgeoisie, but by learning, by getting used to creating illegal organizations which elude the investigations and vigilance of the bourgeois authorities.' Zinoviev said that it was not the form of communist work but the work itself that the bourgeoisie were fighting. Illegal organizations were essential because in times of crisis legal parties would be suppressed. Wijnkoop said article 8 would mean not an international, but an enlarged Russian executive; this might be unavoidable but if so it should be frankly admitted. Levi also expressed misgivings on this point; it would mean that delegates from the national sections would lose touch with their own parties. Reed and Fraina (United States) objected to article 14, which left the unions too little autonomy.]

In 1864 the International Workingmen's Association, the First International, was founded in London. Its provisional rules ran as follows:

That the emancipation of the working classes must be conquered by the working classes themselves; that the struggle for the emancipation of the working classes means not a struggle for class privileges and monopolies, but for equal rights and duties, and the abolition of all class rule;

That the economical subjection of the man of labour to the monopolizer of the means of labour, that is the sources of life, lies at the bottom of servitude in all its forms, of all social misery, mental degradation, and political dependence;

That the economical emancipation of the working classes is therefore the great end to which every political movement ought to be subordinate as a means;

That all efforts aiming at that great end have hitherto failed from the want of solidarity between the manifold divisions of labour in each country, and from the absence of a fraternal bond of union between the working classes of different countries;

That the emancipation of labour is neither a local nor a national, but a social problem, embracing all countries in which modern society exists, and depending for its solution on the concurrence, practical and theoretical, of the most advanced countries;

That the present revival of the working classes in the most industrious countries of Europe, while it raises a new hope, gives solemn warning against a relapse into the old errors and calls for the immediate combination of the still disconnected movements.

The Second International, founded in Paris in 1889, undertook to carry on the work of the First International. But in 1914, at the beginning of the world slaughter, it suffered complete breakdown. Undermined by opportunism and shattered by the treachery of its leaders, who went over to the side of the bourgeoisie, the Second International collapsed.

The Communist International, founded in March 1919 in the capital of the Russian Federal Soviet Republic, Moscow, solemnly declares before the entire world that it undertakes to continue and to carry through to the end the great work begun by the First International Workingmen's Association.

The Communist International was formed after the conclusion of the imperialist war of 1914–18, in which the imperialist bourgeoisie of the different countries sacrificed 20 million men.

'Remember the imperialist war!' These are the first words addressed by the Communist International to every working man and woman; wherever they live and whatever language they speak. Remember that because of the existence of capitalist society a handful of imperialists were able to force the workers of the different countries for four long years to cut each other's throats. Remember that the war of the bourgeoisie conjured up in Europe and throughout the world the most frightful famine and the most appalling misery. Remember, that without the overthrow of capitalism the repetition of such robber wars is not only possible, but inevitable.

It is the aim of the Communist International to fight by all available means, including armed struggle, for the overthrow of the international bourgeoisie and for the creation of an international Soviet republic as a transitional stage to the complete abolition of the State. The Communist International considers the dictatorship of the proletariat the only possible way to liberate mankind from the horrors of capitalism. And the Communist International considers the Soviet power the historically given form of this dictatorship of the proletariat.

The imperialist war bound the destinies of the proletariat of each country very closely to the destinies of the proletariat of all other countries. The imperialist war once again confirmed what was written in the statutes of the First International: the emancipation of the workers is not a local, nor a national, but an international problem.

The Communist International breaks once and for all with the traditions of the Second International, for whom in fact only white-skinned people existed. The task of the Communist International is to liberate the working people of the entire world. In its ranks the white, the yellow, and the black-skinned peoples—the working people of the entire world—are fraternally united.

The Communist International supports to the full the conquests of the great proletarian revolution in Russia, the first victorious socialist revolution in world history, and calls on the proletariat of the entire world to take the same path. The Communist International undertakes to support every Soviet republic, wherever it may be formed.

The Communist International recognizes that in order to hasten victory, the Workingmen's Association which is fighting to annihilate capitalism and create communism must have a strongly centralized organization. The Communist International must, in fact and in deed, be a single communist party of the entire world. The parties working in the various countries are but its separate sections. The organizational machinery of the Communist International must guarantee the workers of each country the opportunity of getting the utmost help from the organized proletariat of other countries at any given moment.

For this purpose the Communist International ratifies the following statutes:

1. The new international association of workers is established to organize joint action by the proletariat of the different countries which pursue the one goal: the overthrow of capitalism, the establishment of the dictatorship of the proletariat and of an international Soviet republic which will completely abolish all classes and realize socialism, the first stage of communist society.

2. The new international association of workers is called 'The Communist International'.

3. All parties belonging to the Communist International bear the name 'Communist Party of such and such a country (section of the Communist International)'.

4. The supreme authority in the Communist International is the world congress of all the parties and organizations which belong to it. The world congress meets regularly once a year. The world congress alone is empowered to change the programme of the Communist International. The world congress discusses and decides the most important questions of programme and tactics connected with the activities of the Communist International. The number of votes to which each party or organization is entitled shall be fixed by special congress decision.

5. The world congress elects the Executive Committee of the Communist International, which is the directing body of the Communist International in the period between its world congresses. The Executive Committee is responsible only to the world congress.

6. The seat of the Executive Committee of the Communist International

shall be determined on each occasion by the world congress of the Communist International.

7. An extraordinary world congress of the Communist International may be convened either by a decision of the Executive Committee or at the request of half the parties which belonged to the Communist International at the time of its preceding world congress.

8. The chief work of the Executive Committee falls on the party of that country where, by decision of the world congress, the Executive Committee has its seat. The party of the country in question shall have five representatives with full voting powers on the Executive Committee. In addition the ten to thirteen most important communist parties, the list to be ratified by the regular world congress, shall each have one representative with full voting powers on the Executive Committee. Other organizations and parties accepted by the Communist International have the right to delegate to the Executive Committee one representative each, with consultative voice.

9. The Executive Committee conducts the entire work of the Communist International from one congress to the next, publishes, in at least four languages, the central organ of the Communist International (the periodical *Communist International*), issues any necessary appeals in the name of the Communist International, and issues instructions which are binding on all parties and organizations belonging to the Communist International. The Executive Committee of the Communist International has the right to demand that parties belonging to the International shall expel groups or persons who offend against international discipline, and it also has the right to expel from the Communist International those parties which violate decisions of the world congress. These parties have the right to appeal to the world congress. Should the need arise the Executive Committee shall set up in the various countries its technical and other auxiliary bureaus, which are wholly subordinate to the Executive Committee. The representatives of the Executive Committee shall carry out their political tasks in closest contact with the party centre of the country concerned.

10. The Executive Committee of the Communist International has the right to co-opt on to the committee, with consultative voice, representatives of organizations and parties which, while not belonging to the Communist International, sympathize with and stand near to it.

11. The press organs of all parties and all organizations which belong to the Communist International, and those which are recognized as sympathizing parties and organizations, are bound to publish all official decisions of the Communist International and its Executive Committee.

12. The general situation all over Europe and America compels communists throughout the world to create illegal communist organizations side by side with the legal organization. The Executive Committee is obliged to see that this is put into effect everywhere.

13. As a rule political communication between the individual parties belonging to the Communist International will be conducted through the ECCI. In urgent cases communication may be direct, but the ECCI shall be simultaneously informed.

14. Trade unions adhering to the communist platform and organized internationally under the leadership of the Communist International, shall form a trade union section of the Communist International. These trade unions shall send their representatives to the world congresses of the Communist International through the communist parties of the countries concerned. The trade union section of the Communist International shall have one representative with full voting powers on the ECCI. The ECCI has the right to send one representative with full voting powers to the trade union section of the Communist International.

15. The Communist Youth International is, like all other members of the Communist International, subordinate to the Communist International and its Executive Committee. The Executive Committee of the Communist Youth International has one representative with full voting powers on the ECCI. The ECCI has the right to send one representative with full voting powers to the Executive Committee of the Communist Youth International.

16. The ECCI confirms the appointment of the international secretary of the communist women's movement and shall organize the women's section of the Communist International.

17. When moving from one country to another every member of the Communist International shall receive the fraternal help of the local members of the Communist International.

CONDITIONS OF ADMISSION TO THE COMMUNIST INTERNATIONAL
APPROVED BY THE SECOND COMINTERN CONGRESS

6 *August* 1920   *Protokoll*, ii, p. 387

[Neither the first congress, nor the ECCI in the interval between the first and second congresses, had laid down conditions of admission to the Communist International. These conditions (or rather 19 of them) were drafted by Lenin, amended and supplemented in the commission, and debated at two sessions on 29 and 30 July. Zinoviev and Meyer (KPD) acted as reporters. Zinoviev, who described them later as 'a bulwark against centrism', said they were designed to establish 'what the CI is and what it wants to be'. In March 1919 it was nothing but a propagandist society, and it had remained that for a whole year. Now they had to become a fighting organization. The defeat in Hungary was due in part to the amalgamation of the Hungarian Communist Party (with the consent of the ECCI) with the social-democrats, who at the decisive moment went over to the bourgeoisie. There could in future be no co-operation with those who did not wholeheartedly accept the CI platform. The USPD and the Scandinavian, French, and Italian Socialist Parties would have to choose between the CI and the reformist and opportunist elements in their own ranks. But, whatever their choice, 'the hearts of the workers in all countries belong to us, and more so with every day, because the last hour of the bourgeoisie and of the semi-bourgeois Second International has struck'. To those (such as Crispien of the USPD and Serrati of the Italian Socialist Party) who suggested that it should be left to the parties themselves to determine the appropriate moment for splitting from the right wing, Lenin replied that there could never be an inappropriate moment for splitting from the MacDonalds and Kautskys. Serrati contended that conditions of admission could be laid down only after a programme had been adopted, otherwise what were they being admitted to?

Surveying the work of the congress at the meeting of 7 August, Zinoviev said: 'Just as it is not easy for a camel to pass through the eye of a needle, so, I hope, it will not be easy for the adherents of the centre to slip through the 21 conditions. They were put forward to make clear to the workers in the USPD and in the Italian and French Socialist Parties, and to all organized workers, what the international general staff of the proletarian revolution demands of them.' A split was to be preferred to diluted theory or lax discipline.

The most severe critics of the 21 conditions were Crispien and Dittmann, two of the USPD delegates. 'I can imagine conditions,' said Crispien 'in which a split is necessary. The USPD is a proof of that. It was a bitter necessity. But, before splitting, you must try to win the workers to a clear position of principle. And for that you need time and patience. It is much easier to split the workers in Germany than to win them for the revolution, and keep them together.'

The USPD had also criticized the use of terror (as opposed to force). 'Here too, as in the question of dictatorship, the specifically Russian form is raised to a principle for the entire international proletariat. Content is stifled by form, and this makes the course of the revolution more difficult, for not enough consideration is given to circumstances which, within a different sociological frame, may also require a different form of revolution.' Lenin did not reply to this charge, but said that Crispien's attempt to distinguish between terror and force might do for a textbook on sociology, but did not work in practical politics.

It was during this interchange with the USPD delegates that they were attacked for their attitude in November 1918, when the offer of Soviet grain, 'made as a gesture of solidarity to show that the fate of the Russian and German revolutions was linked together', was refused for fear of offending the Allies, and for not having prevented the expulsion of the Soviet diplomatic representative Joffe. The United States, Dittmann replied, had promised sufficient grain to maintain the rations. They were grateful for the Russian offer, but Russia itself was short of food, and they had to think of the danger of starvation in Germany. As to the expulsion of Joffe, that had been decided before the socialist government (consisting of three members of the SPD and three of the USPD) had taken office, and the USPD was unable to persuade the SPD to cancel the order, although they had urged that the charge against Joffe of intervention in domestic affairs was a formal one which they, as revolutionary socialists, could not endorse.

The conditions were carried against two votes.]

The first congress of the Communist International did not draw up any precise conditions for the admission of parties to the Third International. When the first congress was convened there were in the majority of countries only communist *trends* and *groups*.

The second congress of the Communist International is meeting in different circumstances. At the present time there are in most countries not only communist trends and tendencies, but communist *parties* and *organizations*.

Application for admission to the Communist International is now frequently made by parties and groups which up to a short time ago still belonged to the Second International, but which have not in fact become communist. The Second International has finally broken down. The in-between parties and the centrist groups, seeing the utter hopelessness of the Second International, are trying to find a support in the Communist International, which is growing steadily stronger. But in doing so they hope to retain enough 'autonomy' to enable them to continue their former opportunist or 'centrist' policy. The Communist International is becoming, to some extent, fashionable.

The desire of some leading 'centrist' groups to join the Communist International indirectly confirms that it has won the sympathies of the overwhelming majority of the class-conscious workers of the entire world and that with every day it is becoming a more powerful force.

The Communist International is threatened by the danger of dilution by unstable and irresolute elements which have not yet completely discarded the ideology of the Second International.

Moreover, in some of the larger parties (Italy, Sweden, Norway, Yugoslavia, etc.) where the majority adhere to the communist standpoint, there still remains even today a reformist and social-pacifist wing which is only waiting a favourable moment to raise its head again and start active sabotage of the proletarian revolution and so help the bourgeoisie and the Second International.

No communist should forget the lessons of the Hungarian revolution. The Hungarian proletariat paid a high price for the fusion of the Hungarian communists with the so-called 'left' social-democrats.

Consequently the second congress of the Communist International thinks it necessary to lay down quite precisely the conditions of admission of new parties, and to point out to those parties which have already joined the duties imposed on them.

The second congress of the Communist International puts forward the following conditions of adherence to the Communist International:

1. *All propaganda and agitation* must be of a genuinely communist character and in conformity with the programme and decisions of the Communist International. The entire party press must be run by reliable communists

who have proved their devotion to the cause of the proletariat. The dictatorship of the proletariat is to be treated not simply as a current formula learnt by rote; it must be advocated in a way which makes its necessity comprehensible to every ordinary working man and woman, every soldier and peasant, from the facts of their daily life, which must be systematically noted in our press and made use of every day.

The periodical press and other publications, and all party publishing houses, must be completely subordinated to the party presidium, regardless of whether the party as a whole is at the given moment legal or illegal. Publishing houses must not be allowed to abuse their independence and pursue a policy which is not wholly in accordance with the policy of the party.

In the columns of the press, at popular meetings, in the trade unions and co-operatives, wherever the adherents of the Communist International have an entry, it is necessary to denounce, systematically and unrelentingly, not only the bourgeoisie, but also their assistants, the reformists of all shades.

2. Every organization which wishes to join the Communist International must, in an orderly and planned fashion, remove reformists and centrists from all responsible positions in the workers' movement (party organizations, editorial boards, trade unions, parliamentary fractions, co-operatives, local government bodies) and replace them by tried communists, even if, particularly at the beginning, 'experienced' opportunists have to be replaced by ordinary rank and file workers.

3. In practically every country of Europe and America the class struggle is entering the phase of civil war. In these circumstances communists can have no confidence in bourgeois legality. They are obliged everywhere to create a parallel illegal organization which at the decisive moment will help the party to do its duty to the revolution. In all those countries where, because of a state of siege or of emergency laws, communists are unable to do all their work legally, it is absolutely essential to combine legal and illegal work.

4. The obligation to spread communist ideas includes the special obligation to carry on systematic and energetic propaganda in the army. Where such agitation is prevented by emergency laws, it must be carried on illegally. Refusal to undertake such work would be tantamount to a dereliction of revolutionary duty and is incompatible with membership of the Communist International.

5. Systematic and well-planned agitation must be carried on in the countryside. The working class cannot consolidate its victory if it has not by its policy assured itself of the support of at least part of the rural proletariat and the poorest peasants, and of the neutrality of part of the rest of the rural population. At the present time communist work in rural areas is acquiring first-rate importance. It should be conducted primarily with

the help of revolutionary communist urban and rural workers who have close connexions with the countryside. To neglect this work or to leave it in unreliable semi-reformist hands, is tantamount to renouncing the proletarian revolution.

6. Every party which wishes to join the Communist International is obliged to expose not only avowed social-patriotism, but also the insincerity and hypocrisy of social-pacifism; to bring home to the workers systematically that without the revolutionary overthrow of capitalism no international court of arbitration, no agreement to limit armaments, no 'democratic' reorganization of the League of Nations, will be able to prevent new imperialist wars.

7. Parties which wish to join the Communist International are obliged to recognize the necessity for a complete and absolute break with reformism and with the policy of the 'centre', and to advocate this break as widely as possible among their members. Without that no consistent communist policy is possible.

The Communist International demands unconditionally and categorically that this break be effected as quickly as possible. The Communist International is unable to agree that notorious opportunists, such as Turati, Modigliani, Kautsky, Hilferding, Hilquit, Longuet, MacDonald, etc., shall have the right to appear as members of the Communist International. That could only lead to the Communist International becoming in many respects similar to the Second International, which has gone to pieces.

8. A particularly explicit and clear attitude on the question of the colonies and the oppressed peoples is necessary for the parties in those countries where the bourgeoisie possess colonies and oppress other nations. Every party which wishes to join the Communist International is obliged to expose the tricks and dodges of 'its' imperialists in the colonies, to support every colonial liberation movement not merely in words but in deeds, to demand the expulsion of their own imperialists from these colonies, to inculcate among the workers of their country a genuinely fraternal attitude to the working people of the colonies and the oppressed nations, and to carry on systematic agitation among the troops of their country against any oppression of the colonial peoples.

9. Every party which wishes to join the Communist International must carry on systematic and persistent communist activity inside the trade unions, the workers' councils and factory committees, the co-operatives, and other mass workers' organizations. Within these organizations communist cells must be organized which shall by persistent and unflagging work win the trade unions, etc., for the communist cause. In their daily work the cells must everywhere expose the treachery of the social-patriots and the instability of the 'centre'. The communist cells must be completely subordinate to the party as a whole.

10. Every party belonging to the Communist International is obliged to wage an unyielding struggle against the Amsterdam 'International' of the yellow trade unions. It must conduct the most vigorous propaganda among trade unionists for the necessity of a break with the yellow Amsterdam International. It must do all it can to support the international association of red trade unions, adhering to the Communist International, which is being formed.

11. Parties which wish to join the Communist International are obliged to review the personnel of their parliamentary fractions and remove all unreliable elements, to make these fractions not only verbally but in fact subordinate to the party presidium, requiring of each individual communist member of parliament that he subordinate his entire activity to the interests of genuinely revolutionary propaganda and agitation.

12. Parties belonging to the Communist International must be based on the principle of *democratic centralism*. In the present epoch of acute civil war the communist party will be able to fulfil its duty only if its organization is as centralized as possible, if iron discipline prevails, and if the party centre, upheld by the confidence of the party membership, has strength and authority and is equipped with the most comprehensive powers.

13. Communist parties in those countries where communists carry on their work legally must from time to time undertake cleansing (re-registration) of the membership of the party in order to get rid of any petty-bourgeois elements which have crept in.

14. Every party which wishes to join the Communist International is obliged to give unconditional support to any Soviet republic in its struggle against counter-revolutionary forces. Communist parties must carry on unambiguous propaganda to prevent the dispatch of munitions transports to the enemies of the Soviet republics; they must also carry on propaganda by every means, legal or illegal, among the troops sent to strangle workers' republics.

15. Parties which still retain their old social-democratic programmes are obliged to revise them as quickly as possible, and to draw up, in accordance with the special conditions of their country, a new communist programme in conformity with the decisions of the Communist International. As a rule the programme of every party belonging to the Communist International must be ratified by the regular congress of the Communist International or by the Executive Committee. Should the programme of a party not be ratified by the ECCI, the party concerned has the right to appeal to the congress of the Communist International.

16. All the decisions of the congresses of the Communist International, as well as the decisions of its Executive Committee, are binding on all parties belonging to the Communist International. The Communist International, working in conditions of acute civil war, must be far more

centralized in its structure than was the Second International. Consideration must of course be given by the Communist International and its Executive Committee in all their activities to the varying conditions in which the individual parties have to fight and work, and they must take decisions of general validity only when such decisions are possible.

17. In this connexion, all parties which wish to join the Communist International must change their names. Every party which wishes to join the Communist International must be called: *Communist* party of such and such a country (section of the Communist International). This question of name is not merely a formal matter, but essentially a political question of great importance. The Communist International has declared war on the entire bourgeois world and on all yellow social-democratic parties. The difference between the communist parties and the old official 'social-democratic' or 'socialist' parties, which have betrayed the banner of the working class, must be brought home to every ordinary worker.

18. All leading party press organs in all countries are obliged to publish all important official documents of the Executive Committee of the Communist International.

19. All parties belonging to the Communist International and those which have applied for admission, are obliged to convene an extraordinary congress as soon as possible, and in any case not later than four months after the second congress of the Communist International, to examine all these conditions of admission. In this connexion all party centres must see that the decisions of the second congress of the Communist International are made known to all local organizations.

20. Those parties which now wish to join the Communist International, but which have not radically changed their former tactics, must see to it that, before entering the Communist International, not less than two-thirds of the members of their central committee and of all their leading central bodies consist of comrades who publicly and unambiguously advocated the entry of their party into the Communist International before its second congress. Exceptions can be made with the consent of the Executive Committee of the Communist International. The ECCI also has the right to make exceptions in the case of representatives of the centre mentioned in paragraph 7.

21. Those members of the party who reject in principle the conditions and theses put forward by the Communist International are to be expelled from the party.

The same applies in particular to delegates to the extraordinary congresses.

EXTRACTS FROM THE MANIFESTO OF THE SECOND WORLD CONGRESS
OF THE COMMUNIST INTERNATIONAL

8 *August* 1920   *Protokoll*, ii, p. 718

[This manifesto was delivered as a speech by Trotsky at the open meeting held
at the conclusion of the congress.]

... The economic restoration of Europe, about which its statesmen talk,
is a lie. Europe is being ruined and the whole capitalist world along with it.

On capitalist foundations there is no salvation. The policy of imperialism
does not lead to the abolition of want but to its aggravation, because
existing reserves are plundered. The question of fuel and raw materials is
an international question which can be solved only on the basis of universally planned socialist production.

It is necessary to cancel State debts. It is necessary to emancipate labour
and the fruits of labour from the monstrous tribute paid to world plutocracy. It is necessary to overthrow this plutocracy. It is necessary to remove the State barriers which atomize world economy. The Supreme
Economic Council of the Entente imperialists must be replaced by the
Supreme Economic Council of the world proletariat, to effect the centralized exploitation of all the economic resources of mankind.

Imperialism must die, that mankind may live.

III

THE BOURGEOIS REGIME AFTER THE WAR

The entire energy of the propertied classes is concentrated upon two
questions: to maintain themselves in power in the international struggle,
and to prevent the proletariat from becoming the master of the country.
In these tasks the former political groupings of the bourgeoisie have wasted
their powers. Not only in Russia, where the banner of the Cadet Party
became at the decisive stage of struggle the banner of all the property
owners against the workers' and peasants' revolution, but even in countries
with an older and higher political culture, the former programmes which
used to separate the different sections of the bourgeoisie disappeared without a trace, even before the revolutionary onslaught of the proletariat.

Lloyd George steps forward as the spokesman for the amalgamation of
the Tories, Unionists, and Liberals for a joint struggle against the rising
power of the working class. This hoary demagogue singles out the benedic-
tion of the holy church as the central power station whose current feeds
equally all the parties of the propertied classes.

In France the epoch of anti-clericalism, so lively only a brief while ago,
seems like an antediluvian ghost. The Radicals, Royalists, and Catholics

now form a bloc of national order against the rising proletariat. Ready to extend its hand to every reactionary force, the French Government supports the arch-reactionary Wrangel and re-establishes diplomatic relations with the Vatican.

Giolitti, champion of neutrality and Germanophile, has taken the helm of the Italian Government as the joint leader of interventionists, neutralists, clericals, and Mazzinists. He is ready to tack and veer on the subordinate questions of domestic and foreign policy in order all the more ruthlessly to repel the offensive of the revolutionary proletarians of city and country. Giolitti's Government rightfully considers itself the Italian bourgeoisie's last court card.

The policy of all German Governments and government parties since the downfall of the Hohenzollerns has been to create, in concert with the Entente ruling classes, an atmosphere of hatred of Bolshevism, that is, of the proletarian revolution. While the Anglo-French Shylock is tightening the noose around the neck of the German people more and more savagely, the German bourgeoisie, regardless of party, entreat their enemy to loosen the cords just enough to enable them to strangle the vanguard of the German proletariat with their own hands. This is the gist of the periodic conferences and agreements on disarmament and the delivery of war material.

In America the line of demarcation between the Republicans and the Democrats has been completely erased. These two powerful political organizations of the exploiters, adapted to the hitherto narrow circle of American relations, revealed their total hollowness when the American bourgeoisie entered the arena of world plunder.

Never before have the intrigues of individual leaders and cliques—in the opposition and in the Ministries alike—been marked by such cynical frankness as now. But at the same time all the leaders, cliques, and parties of the bourgeoisie are building a united front against the revolutionary proletariat.

Whilst the social-democratic philistines persist in advocating the road of democracy in opposition to the violent road of dictatorship, the last vestiges of democracy are being trampled underfoot and destroyed in every State throughout the world. Since the war, during which the national assemblies played the part of powerless but noisy patriotic screens for the ruling imperialist cliques, parliaments have fallen into a state of complete impotence. All important issues are now decided outside parliament. Nothing is changed in this respect by the apparent extension of parliamentary rights, so solemnly proclaimed by the imperialist clowns of Italy and other countries. The real masters and rulers of State destinies—Lord Rothschild and Lord Weir, Morgan and Rockefeller, Schneider and Loucheur, Hugo Stinnes and Felix Deutsch, Rizello and Agnelli, the gold, coal, oil, and metal kings—operate behind the scenes and send their second-rank lieutenants into parliament to carry out their work.

The French parliament, more discredited than any other by its false rhetoric and cynical corruption, whose chief amusement lies in the procedure of reading the most insignificant legislative bills several times, suddenly learns that the four milliards voted for the restoration of the devastated regions of France had been expended by Clemenceau for entirely different purposes, in particular to create more devastated regions in Russia.

The overwhelming majority of members of the supposedly all-powerful English parliament are scarcely better informed about the real intentions of Lloyd George and Lord Curzon with regard to Soviet Russia, or even France, than are the old women in the villages of Bengal.

In the United States, Congress is a docile or disgruntled chorus for the President, who is himself a servant of the electoral machine, which is in its turn the political apparatus of the trusts, incomparably more so now after the war than ever before.

Germany's belated parliamentarianism, an abortion of the bourgeois revolution, which is itself an abortion of history, suffers in its infancy from every disease peculiar to cretins in their senility. The-most-democratic-in-the-world Reichstag of Ebert's republic is impotent, not only before the Marshal's baton of Foch, but even before the stock market manipulations of its own Stinneses, and the military plots of its officer clique. German parliamentary democracy is a void between two dictatorships.

The very composition of the bourgeoisie has undergone profound modifications in the course of the war. Against the background of universal impoverishment, the concentration of capital made a sudden and colossal leap forward. Firms hitherto standing in the shadows have stepped to the forefront. Solidity, stability, the inclination to make reasonable compromises, the observance of a certain decorum both in exploitation and in the enjoyment of its fruits—all this has been washed away by the torrents of the imperialist flood.

To the foreground have stepped the newly rich, war contractors, disgusting speculators, upstarts, international adventurers, smugglers, criminals bedecked with diamonds, the unbridled scum greedy for luxury and capable of any brutality against the proletarian revolution from which they can expect nothing but the hangman's rope.

The existing system stands before the masses in all its nakedness as the rule of the rich. In America, in France, in England, indulgence in postwar luxury has become an orgy of perversity. Paris, jammed with international patriotic parasites, resembles, as *Le Temps* says, Babylon on the eve of its destruction.

Politics, courts, the press, the arts, and the church fall into line behind the bourgeoisie. All restraint has been cast aside. Wilson, Clemenceau, Millerand, Lloyd George, and Churchill do not shrink from the most brazen deceit and the crudest lie, and when convicted of falsity they calmly go on to new criminal feats. The classical rules of political duplicity as expounded by old Machiavelli become the innocent aphorisms of a provincial simpleton in comparison with those principles which guide bourgeois governments today. The courts, which formerly concealed their bourgeois essence under democratic tinsel, have now become avowed organs of class contempt and counter-revolutionary provocation. The judges of the Third Republic, without blinking an eye, acquitted the murderer of Jaurès. The courts of Germany, which has proclaimed itself a 'socialist republic', give encouragement to the murderers of Liebknecht, Rosa Luxemburg, and other martyrs of the proletariat. The tribunals of bourgeois democracy have become instruments for the solemn legalization of all the crimes of the white terror.

The bourgeois press carries the stamp of venality, like a trade mark, on its forehead. The leading newspapers of the world bourgeoisie are monstrous factories of falsehood, calumny, and spiritual poison. . . .

The programme of ameliorating antagonisms, the programme of class collaboration, parliamentary reforms, gradual socialization, and national unity appears tragic tomfoolery in the light of the bourgeois regime as it has emerged from the world war.

The bourgeoisie have entirely abandoned the idea of conciliating the proletariat by means of reforms. They demoralize a small and dwindling upper group with a few gifts and force the great mass into obedience by blood and iron.

There is not a single serious issue today which could be decided by the vote. Of democracy nothing remains save its memory in the minds of reformists. The State organization is reverting more and more to its original form, i.e. detachments of armed men. Instead of counting votes, the bourgeoisie are busy counting the bayonets, machine guns, and cannon which will be at their disposal when the question of power and property is at the point of decision.

There is no longer room for collaboration or mediation. Only the overthrow of the bourgeoisie will bring salvation. But this can be achieved only by the insurrection of the proletariat. . . .

At a time when national interests clash with imperialist encroachments and are a source of incessant conflicts, uprisings, and wars throughout the world, socialist Russia has shown that the workers' State is able to reconcile national and economic requirements without suffering, by purging the former of chauvinism and by liberating the latter from imperialism. Socialism wants to bring about a union of all regions, all provinces, and all nationalities in a unified economic plan. Economic centralism, freed from the exploitation of one class by another, and of one nation by another, and therefore equally beneficial to all, is compatible with real freedom of national development.

The experience of Soviet Russia is enabling the peoples of Central Europe, of the south-eastern Balkans, of the British possessions, all the oppressed nations and tribes, the Egyptians and the Turks, the Indians and the Persians, the Irish and the Bulgarians, to convince themselves that the fraternal collaboration of all the national units of mankind can be realized only through a union of Soviet Republics.

The revolution created in Russia the first proletarian State. In the three years of its existence its boundaries have undergone constant change. They have shrunk under the external military pressure of world imperialism. They expanded whenever this pressure relaxed.

The struggle for Soviet Russia has merged with the struggle against world imperialism. The question of Soviet Russia has become the touchstone by which all the organizations of the working class are tested. The German Social-Democrats committed their second most infamous treachery —the first was on 4 August 1914—when, at the head of the German State, they sought the protection of Western imperialism instead of seeking an alliance with the revolution in the East. A Soviet Germany united with Soviet Russia would have been stronger than all the capitalist States put together!

The Communist International has proclaimed the cause of Soviet Russia as its own. The world proletariat will not sheathe its sword until Soviet Russia is one member in the World Federation of Soviet Republics. . . .

V

THE PROLETARIAN REVOLUTION AND THE COMMUNIST INTERNATIONAL

Civil war is on the order of the day throughout the world. Its device is the Soviet power.

Capitalism has proletarianized immense masses of mankind. Imperialism has thrown these masses out of balance and brought them into revolutionary movement. The very concept of the term 'masses' has undergone a change in recent years. What used to be regarded as the masses in the era of parliamentarianism and trade unionism have now become the upper crust. Millions and millions of those who formerly stood outside political life are being transformed today into the revolutionary masses. The war has roused everybody; it has awakened the political interest of even the most backward; it aroused in them illusions and hopes and it has deceived them.

Craft exclusiveness among the workers, the relative stability of living standards among the upper proletarian strata, the dumb and apathetic hopelessness among the lower, these social foundations of the old forms of the labour movement have receded beyond recall into the past. New millions have been drawn into the struggle. . . . In different countries the struggle has passed through different stages. But it is the final struggle. Not infrequently the waves of the movement flow into obsolete organizational forms, lending them temporary vitality. Here and there old labels and half-obliterated slogans come to the surface. Minds are still filled with much error, confusion, prejudice, and illusion. But the movement as a whole is of a profoundly revolutionary character. It is all-embracing and irresistible. It spreads, strengthens and purifies itself; it casts off all the old rubbish. It will not halt before the rule of the world proletariat has been attained.

The basic form of this movement is the strike, of which the primary and most potent cause is the rising cost of living. Not infrequently the strike arises out of isolated local conflicts. It breaks out as an expression of the masses' impatience with the parliamentary socialist tussle. It combines economic and political slogans. It originates in the feeling of solidarity with the oppressed in their own and other countries. In it are not infrequently combined fragments of reformism with slogans of the programme of social revolution. It dies down, ceases, and rises again, disturbing production, keeping the State apparatus under constant strain, driving the bourgeoisie out of their wits and taking every opportunity to send greetings to Soviet Russia. The premonitions of the exploiters are not unfounded. This inchoate strike is in reality the signal of the social revolution, the mobilization of the international proletariat.

The profound interdependence between one country and another, which was so catastrophically revealed during the war, invests with particular significance those industries which serve to connect the various countries, and puts the railroad workers and transport workers in general as it were into first place. The transport proletarians have had occasion to display some of their power in the boycott of white Hungary and white Poland. The strike and the boycott, methods applied by the working class at the dawn of its trade union struggles, i.e. even before it began utilizing parliament, now have a far wider field of play and a new and menacing significance, like the artillery bombardment before the final attack.

The growing helplessness of the individual before the onslaught of historic events has driven into the unions not only new strata of working men and women but also white-collar workers, officials, and petty-bourgeois intellectuals. Until the proletarian revolution leads of necessity to the creation of soviets, which will immediately assume ascendancy over all of the old workers' organizations, the working people are streaming into the traditional trade unions, tolerating for the time being their old forms, their official programme, their bosses, but introducing into these organizations an increasing revolutionary impulse of the many-millioned masses.

The most lowly—the rural proletarians, the agricultural labourers—are raising their heads. In Italy, Germany, and other countries we observe a magnificent growth of the revolutionary movement among the agricultural workers and their fraternal rapprochement with the urban proletariat.

The attitude towards socialism of the poorest among the peasantry is changing. The parliamentary reformists flirted unsuccessfully with the property superstitions of the peasants, but the genuine revolutionary movement of the proletariat and its implacable struggle against the oppressors has brought a glimmer of hope into the hearts of the most backward and benighted peasants, ruined and chained to the soil.

The ocean of human misery and spiritual darkness is bottomless. Under every social layer that rises there is another layer that is about to rise. But the vanguard does not have to wait for a large following before engaging in battle. The work of awakening, uplifting, and educating its most backward sections will be accomplished by the working class only *after* it has won power.

The working people of the colonial and semi-colonial countries have awakened. In the vast areas of India, Egypt, Persia, over which the gigantic octopus of English imperialism sprawls—in this immeasurable human ocean internal forces are constantly at work, throwing up huge waves that cause tremors in the City's stocks and hearts.

In the movement of colonial peoples, the social element is combined in diverse forms with the national element, but both are directed against imperialism. The road from the first stumbling steps to the mature forms of struggle is being traversed by the colonies and backward countries in general through a forced march, under the pressure of modern imperialism and under the leadership of the revolutionary proletariat.

The promising rapprochement of the Moslem and non-Moslem peoples who are welded together by the common shackles of British and foreign domination, the purging of the movement internally, the elimination of the influence of the clergy and of chauvinist reaction, the simultaneous struggle against foreign oppressors and their native rulers—the feudal lords, the priests, and the usurers—all this is transforming the growing army of the colonial insurrection into a great historical force, into a mighty reserve for the world proletariat. The pariahs are rising. Their awakened minds ardently gravitate to Soviet Russia, to the barricades in the streets of German cities, to the growing strike struggles in Great Britain, to the Communist International.

The socialist who directly or indirectly helps to perpetuate the privileged position of one nation at the expense of another, who accommodates himself to colonial slavery, who makes distinctions between peoples of different race and colour in the matter of rights, who helps the bourgeoisie of the metropolis to maintain their rule over the colonies instead of aiding the armed uprising of the colonies; the British socialist who fails to support by all possible means the uprisings in Ireland, Egypt, and India against the London plutocracy—such a socialist deserves to be branded with infamy, if not with a bullet, but in no case merits either the mandate or the confidence of the proletariat.

More, the proletariat is being thwarted in its international revolutionary actions not so much by the half-destroyed barbed-wire entanglements that still remain, in many places, from the war, as by the egotism, conservatism, stupidity, and treachery of the old party and trade union organizations which rose on the backs of the workers during the preceding epoch.

The leaders of the old trade unions use every means to counteract and to obstruct the revolutionary struggles of the working masses, or, if they cannot do it otherwise, they take charge of strikes in order all the more surely to strangle them by underhand machinations behind the scenes.

The historical treachery perpetrated by international social-democracy is unequalled in the history of oppression and struggle. It was shown most clearly and terribly in Germany. The collapse of German imperialism occurred at the same time as the collapse of the capitalist system of economy. Save for the proletariat there was no class that could pretend to State power. The success of the socialist insurrection was amply assured by the development of technology and by the numerical strength and the high cultural level of the German working classes. But German social-democracy blocked the road by which this mission could be accomplished. By means of intricate manœuvres in which cunning vied with stupidity, it deflected the energy of the proletariat from its natural and necessary goal—the conquest of power. Over a number of decades social-democracy had won the confidence of the masses only in order to place—when the critical moment came and the fate of bourgeois society was in the balance —its entire authority at the disposal of the oppressors.

The treachery of liberalism and the collapse of bourgeois democracy was less important than the monstrous treachery of the socialist parties. Even the part played by the Church, the central powerhouse of conservatism, as Lloyd George called it, recedes into the background against the anti-socialist role of the Second International. . . .

The governmental and semi-governmental socialists of various countries have no lack of pretexts on which to ground the charge that the communists by their intransigent tactics provoke the counter-revolution into action, and help it to consolidate its forces. This political accusation is nothing but a belated echo of the grievances of liberalism. The latter maintained that the independent struggle of the proletariat drives the propertied classes into the camp of reaction. This is incontestable. If the working class refrained from encroaching upon the foundations of capitalist rule, the bourgeoisie would have no need of repressive measures. The very concept of counter-revolution would never have arisen if revolutions were unknown to history. That the uprisings of the proletariat inevitably entail the organization of the bourgeoisie for self-defence and counter-attack, simply means that the revolution is the struggle between two irreconcilable classes which can end only with the final victory of one of them.

Communism rejects with contempt the policy which consists in keeping the masses inert by intimidating them with the whip of counter-revolution. To the disintegration and chaos of the capitalist world, whose death agony threatens to destroy human civilization, the Communist International opposes the united struggle of the world proletariat, the abolition of private ownership of the means of production, and the reconstruction of national and world economy on the basis of a single economic plan, instituted and carried out by a community of producers acting in solidarity.

Rallying millions of working people in all parts of the world round the banner of the dictatorship of the proletariat and the Soviet system, the Communist International purifies, builds up, and organizes its own ranks in the fire of struggle. The Communist International is the party of the revolutionary insurrection of the world proletariat. It rejects all those groups and organizations which openly or covertly stupefy, demoralize, and weaken the proletariat; it exhorts the proletariat not to kneel before the idols which adorn the façade of the dictatorship of the bourgeoisie: legalism, democracy, national defence, etc. Neither can the Communist International admit into its ranks those organizations which, while recognizing the dictatorship of the proletariat in their programme, continue to conduct a policy which counts on a peaceful solution of the historical crisis. Mere recognition of the Soviet system settles nothing. The Soviet form of government does not possess any miraculous powers. Revolutionary power lies within the proletariat itself. It is absolutely necessary for the proletariat to rise and to fight for power; only then does the Soviet organization reveal its qualities as the irreplaceable weapon in the hands of the proletariat. The Communist International demands the expulsion from the ranks of the workers' movement of all those leaders who are directly or indirectly implicated in collaboration with the bourgeoisie, who directly or indirectly afford any political aid to the bourgeoisie. We need leaders who have no other attitude toward the bourgeoisie than that of deadly hatred, who rouse and lead the proletariat in indefatigable struggle, who are ready to lead an insurgent army into battle, who will not stop half-way in fear and who, whatever happens, will not shrink from punishing ruthlessly all those who may try to hold them back. The Communist International is the world party of proletarian revolt and proletarian dictatorship. It has no aims and tasks other than those of the entire working class. The pretensions of tiny sects, each of which wants to save the working class in its own manner, are alien and hostile to the spirit of the

Communist International. It does not possess any universal panacea or magic formula, but bases itself on the past and present international experience of the working class; it purges that experience of all blunders and deviations; it generalizes the results and recognizes and adopts only such formulas as are the formulas of mass action.

Trade union organization, the economic and political strike, the boycott, parliamentary and municipal elections, the parliamentary tribune, legal and illegal agitation, secret footholds in the army, work in the co-operatives, barricades—the Communist International rejects none of the forms of organization or of struggle created in the development of the workers' movement, nor does it single out any one of them as a panacea.

The Soviet system is not an abstract principle opposed by communists to the principle of parliamentarianism. The Soviet system is a class apparatus which is to do away with and replace parliamentarianism during the struggle and as a result of the struggle. While waging an implacable struggle against reformism in the trade unions and against parliamentary cretinism and careerism, the Communist International condemns sectarian appeals to leave the ranks of the multimillioned trade unions or to refuse to work in parliamentary and municipal institutions. Communists do not separate themselves in any way from the masses who are being deceived and betrayed by the reformists and the patriots, but engage the latter in an irreconcilable struggle within the mass organizations and institutions established by bourgeois society, in order by this struggle to overthrow bourgeois society more surely and more quickly.

Under the aegis of the Second International, the methods of class organization and of class struggle, which were almost exclusively of a legal character, turned out to be, in the last analysis, subject to the control and direction of the bourgeoisie, whose reformist agents acted as a brake on the revolutionary class. The Communist International wrenches this brake out of the hands of the bourgeoisie, wins over all the organizations, unites them under revolutionary leadership, and through them puts before the proletariat one single goal, namely, the conquest of power for the abolition of the bourgeois State and for the establishment of communist society.

In all his work, whether as leader of a revolutionary uprising, or as organizer of underground groups, as secretary of a trade union, or as agitator at mass meetings, as member of parliament or co-operative worker or barricade fighter, the communist always remains true to himself as a disciplined member of the communist party, an unrelenting fighter, a mortal enemy of capitalist society, its economic foundation, its State forms, its democratic lies, its religion, and its morality. He is a self-sacrificing soldier of the proletarian revolution and an untiring herald of the new society.

Working men and women! On this earth there is only one banner under which it is worth fighting and dying: It is the banner of the *Communist International*!

The Second World Congress of the Communist International

EXTRACTS FROM AN ECCI APPEAL TO THE WORKERS OF ENGLAND AND
FRANCE ON THE RUSSO-POLISH WAR

August 1920   *K.I.*, 13, col. 2601, *September* 1920

[The Polish counter-offensive opened on 16 August and the Soviet army was soon in full retreat. Strikes had occurred in Germany and Britain against the loading of munitions for Poland, and the central Council of Action in London had sent a deputation to the Prime Minister threatening more drastic action if Britain gave direct support to Poland or to Wrangel. The French granted Wrangel *de facto* recognition on 12 August. Desultory negotiations for an armistice had been going on at Minsk between Russia and Poland.]

The war between white Poland and Soviet Russia is a war between the bourgeoisie and the proletariat of the whole world. That has become clear to every conscious worker. The outcome of that war depends above all on the actions of the workers of England and France. . . .

When the Polish white armies got into an extremely difficult position, the English Government came out with a whole series of ultimatums to Soviet Russia, broke off the peace negotiations with the Russian delegation in London, and has not yet resumed them, in order to exert pressure on the Russian Soviet Government.

The reactionary French bourgeoisie act even more openly. From every one of its hundred mouths the entire French press repeats again and again that the fate of bourgeois Poland is the fate of all bourgeois Europe. As one man the French bourgeoisie declare frankly that the cause of the Polish landlords and capitalists is their cause and that they will support with all their forces the continuation of the Polish robber campaign against Soviet Russia. . . .

At this moment, when the Communist International addresses these words to you, it is not yet clear whether the English and French capitalists will succeed in provoking a new slaughter and organizing a crusade against the first workers' republic. The troops of white Poland, with powerful support from English and French capital, have passed to the counter-attack against the red Soviet forces. At the first glimmer of military success the Polish capitalists are beginning to disrupt the negotiations for peace and are clearly anxious to prolong the war. . . .

What is the proletariat of Europe doing in these circumstances, and what should it do? That is the burning question of the day.

With great joy the Communist International notes that in England a magnificent workers' movement has begun, which is with every day taking on a more explicitly revolutionary character. For the first time after long years of crisis the English working class is beginning to play a revolutionary part. . . . In France the workers are only just beginning to stir . . . but even in France one trade after another has proposed replying with a general strike if the French bourgeoisie should dare to continue and extend offensive action against Russia.

Under the pressure of the proletarian masses the old leaders of the moribund trade unions seem to be beginning to move to the left. . . . The Communist International considers it its duty to warn you, French and English comrades. Of course, if the leaders of the Council of Action in England, and the councils which are beginning to be formed in other countries, really carry out their duty to the proletariat, if words do not take the place of deeds, if they remain true to the movement to the end, we shall be the first to welcome such a fulfilment of duty. But we must remember what happened in the past. We must not ignore the lessons of last year's strike called for 21 July. We remember that under mass pressure the French and English opportunists came out in favour of the strike, but when they took the lead in the movement they did so in order to betray it at the decisive moment. The partisans of the Second International took control of the growing movement in order to sabotage it from within. In July 1919 the international situation was such that the treachery of the Second International leaders was paid for with the heads of the Hungarian Soviet Republic. Now, in the late summer of 1920, such treachery might cost the international proletariat a much heavier price. . . .

Workers of England and France! Without any exaggeration, you hold in your hands the fate of Europe, the fate of the proletarian revolution. Be firm, be vigilant, rely only on yourselves. Watch every act of these newly made advocates of the revolutionary struggle, who only yesterday were sabotaging every genuinely revolutionary movement. . . . Remember that meetings and resolutions of protest will not by themselves accomplish anything serious in the way of results. The general strike is not the last but only the first word in the struggle which is impending. Armed insurrection, the dictatorship of the proletariat, the establishment of the Soviet regime— these are the real means with the help of which the working class can change the present situation in Europe and in the whole world.

EXTRACTS FROM A MANIFESTO TO ALL TRADE UNIONS ON THE
DECISION TO FOUND A RED TRADE UNION INTERNATIONAL

August 1920   *K.I.*, 13, col. 2361, *September* 1920

[In supporting the trade union theses at the second congress Zinoviev reported
on the preliminary steps taken on 15 July to found the Red International of
Labour Unions (Profintern or RILU). Russian, Italian, Bulgarian, and French
delegates, claiming to represent eight million members, had formed an international trade union council with the declared objects of fighting the IFTU, of
overthrowing bourgeois society, and establishing the dictatorship of the proletariat by winning the trade unions for the communist cause. He added that
they must 'split Amsterdam' and draw the workers away. 'We can now say to
every union: "Leave the Amsterdam International. You now have an international of red unions, and you should join it".' Tanner argued that it was
inconsistent to urge the workers to stay in the unions, but to split them internationally. The council was to convene an international congress of revolutionary trade unions, and the ECCI was to issue an appeal to all trade unions
to send delegates. The delegates of the British shop stewards and of the IWW
did not sign the declaration. At the ECCI in September 1920 Zinoviev, asserting
that the right wing were calling for the expulsion of communists from the unions,
added: 'This proves that our plan arouses fear among these gentlemen, that we
are on the right road. Of course, the trade unions cannot be won in a day. It
will take months, perhaps years. But when we have won the unions the victory
of the world revolution will be assured.'

Rosmer recalls that after the theses had been adopted John Reed said to him:
'We cannot go back to America with a decision like that. In the American
unions the Comintern has friends only in the IWW, and we are being sent into
the AFL, where it has nothing but bitter enemies.' The International Federation
of Trade Unions (IFTU) had been revived in July 1919 with its headquarters
in Amsterdam. In April 1920 it took an active part in the conference at which
the ILO was established. In January 1921 the ECCI discussed the work of the
international trade union council set up at the time of the second congress, and
put forward proposals for the agenda of the conference that was to be called
later in the year of all trade unions and trade union minority organizations
hostile to the IFTU.]

Workers, members of the trade unions of all countries!

The most backward worker, the most backward workers' organization,
must now recognize that the bourgeois world is crumbling in ruins. The
old social relations are destroyed, the stability of the bourgeois order is
seen to be an illusion. The bourgeoisie cannot restore the economy
destroyed by the war. In bloody civil war there is being born the new free
world of labour and true brotherhood.

The whole of mankind is divided into two parts: on one side the bourgeoisie, well-organized, the master of all the technical resources at the disposal of the modern State, and keenly class-conscious; on the other, less conscious than the bourgeoisie, less well-organized than its enemy, and, most important of all, too loosely bound together on the international level, the proletariat. . . .

This high degree of class consciousness, the awareness of common interests, and the excellence of organization, are the basic strength of the bourgeoisie in their struggle against the working class. But this alone does not explain the victories of the bourgeoisie on every international front except the Russian. They owe their strength also . . . to the inadequate consciousness and the backwardness of the workers, and to the fact that in their fight against the revolution they can rely on some workers' organizations. This is monstrous, but it is an historical fact which cannot be disputed. It is enough to think of the chief countries of Europe and America to be convinced that the strength of the bourgeoisie and their victories rest on the trade unions of these countries.

In the war years the trade unions of almost all countries acted as pillars and strongholds of their governments' war policy. Who advanced and supported the idea of a class truce? The non-political trade unions. Who during the war persuaded the workers to refrain from any revolutionary offensive and even from any industrial strikes? The free social-democratic unions. Who advocated a longer working day, the greater exploitation of the labour of women and children, the surrender of hard-won rights? . . . And if the war dragged on endlessly . . . if during the course of that war the bourgeoisie succeeded in bringing into subjection hundreds of millions of people and making untold millions in profits from the mutual exhaustion of the nations, then the overwhelming share of the responsibility for this falls on those leaders of the trade union movement who forgot the first principles of international class solidarity. . . .

When the war ended these leaders started to create international organizations which were to consolidate on the international level what they had done in their own countries during the truce between proletariat and bourgeoisie. Two institutions were created for this purpose by the experienced traitors of the working class, the Labour Office of the League of Nations, and the International Federation of Trade Unions. . . .

The Amsterdam Federation is an agency of the bourgeoisie in the workers' camp. And the working class should therefore realize that the class struggle today consists not only in fighting against the ruling classes, but primarily and above all in an unrelenting and pitiless struggle against the 'lieutenants of capital' in their own midst. . . .

Throughout the world there are 30 million workers organized in unions. This is a gigantic army, and the fate of mankind depends on the direction its activities take. If this army were imbued with the spirit of revolutionary class struggle, it could overturn the entire world ... but it is still influenced and run by leaders who have gone over to the side of the bourgeoisie. ...

Why are the unions backward? Why in most countries do they continue to act as a barrier to the social revolution? Because ... they have retained their old machinery, their old forms of organization, their old habits, their old outworn leaders. ... The working masses are for the revolution, the old trade union organizations are against it. ...

The second congress of the Communist International is perfectly well aware of the value of the yellow leaders and the extent of their treachery. Nevertheless it came out sharply and categorically *against* leaving the workers' mass organizations. Communists must be where the working masses are. Every worker must realize and remember that in western Europe and America no social revolution is possible without the trade union army of millions, and therefore it is necessary to expel from the ranks of the working class, from its organizations, those elements which at the moment of the most acute conflict between labour and capital will play the part of strikebreakers. ... This struggle against the treacherous policy of the trade union bosses must be fought by means of the factory committees. These committees must be won over, brought under the influence of communist and revolutionary parties. ...

But the socialist revolution is international; the conflict between labour and capital, which begins in each separate country, can be resolved only when our international organizations are filled with revolutionary energy and communist determination to overthrow international capital. Therefore, besides winning the trade unions in each country, the union members in all countries have the task of creating an international centre for the trade union movement which, together with the Communist International, will make one whole, a single steel block. This task will be accomplished when the unions reject the Labour Office ... and turn their backs on the yellow Amsterdam trade union federation, which is bound ideologically and materially to the capitalist world.

The Communist International summons all workers who stand for the social revolution and the proletarian dictatorship to fight vigorously for the adherence of their unions to the International Council of Trade Unions established in Moscow on 15 July by the unions of Russia, England, Italy, Spain, Yugoslavia, Bulgaria, France, and Georgia. ...

The programme of the International Council is the programme of the Communist International, that is, the revolutionary overthrow of the bourgeoisie, the establishment of the proletarian dictatorship, the creation of a world republic of Soviets, and a close and indestructible alliance between the communist parties and the trade unions. Hence it follows that the Amsterdam centre ... must be destroyed. All revolutionary class unions must become, through their International Council, an indissoluble part of the Third, Communist International.

Trade union members, communists, revolutionaries!

The second world congress of the Communist International summons you to active struggle for the unions. Take into your own hands these powerful organizations, not shrinking from the most resolute struggle against those who are distorting the workers' organizations into instruments of bourgeois policy. They try to frighten you with splits and expulsions. But only the weak-willed and passive will be frightened by expulsions or splits. The Communist International does not want to split the trade union movement, does not aim at it, but does not fear it either. . . . The unions, like other workers' organizations, are not an end in themselves, but a means to an end. And therefore neither a split nor unity is an absolute. It is not necessary to split the unions, but it is necessary to expel from them the treacherous group of leaders who are making the unions into a plaything of the imperialists.

EXTRACTS FROM AN ECCI LETTER TO THE ITALIAN SOCIALIST PARTY

27 *August* 1920   *K.I.*, 13, col. 2605, *September* 1920

[Serrati, editor of *Avanti*, and delegate from the Italian Socialist Party to the second Comintern congress, concluded his report with the words: 'Thus the political and economic conditions in Italy are such that they inevitably drive towards revolution. The party is so powerful that it may be said that the Italian proletariat is almost ready to seize power, establish a dictatorship and then institute the Soviet system.' He added that its military forces were, however, very weak, while the bourgeoisie were already organizing their white guards.

During the debate on the 21 conditions at the second world congress Serrati had argued that if, as seemed likely, a new wave of reaction was rising in Italy, it would be inappropriate for the Socialist Party to split or to expel part of its membership. At its meeting after the second congress, the new ECCI discussed with the Italian delegates the question of expelling the reformists; Serrati said he was in favour of this course, but it had to be done in a way that would not alienate the masses.]

TO THE CENTRAL COMMITTEE AND ALL MEMBERS OF THE ITALIAN SOCIALIST
PARTY
TO THE REVOLUTIONARY PROLETARIAT OF ITALY

The Executive Committee wishes, with complete proletarian candour, to direct the attention of all members of the Italian party to some deficiencies in the party's policy. The EC considers this not only its right but its duty. . . .

The Italian proletariat and its party are in the front ranks of the international attack on capital. Your party was one of the first to adhere to the Third International. This makes it the more essential to overcome as quickly as possible that harmful resistance which arises from the voluntary and involuntary mistakes of the party. . . .

Capitalist Poland's war on proletarian Russia, in which Poland is supported by the entire capitalist world, will inevitably be transformed into an all-European conflict of labour and capital. Therefore it is the duty of every party which stands for the dictatorship of the proletariat, not in words but in fact, to get ready to throw into the scales at the right moment the entire weight of the revolutionary energy of the proletariat.

An attitude of indefinite waiting for the revolution in other countries is profoundly mistaken. If some Italian comrades say that it is necessary to wait for the revolution in Germany or in England, because Italy cannot live without importing coal, the same argument can be used in other countries—power should not be seized in Germany because the Entente will attack; it should not be seized in Austria because America and the colonies will refuse to trade, etc. It is obvious that this is equivalent to arranging mutual insurance for the capitalists against the revolution and delaying the international revolution at the very moment when it is essential to unleash and expand it.

The Executive Committee knows that there are circumstances in which it is more advantageous for the proletariat to wait, until its own forces are stronger and those of the bourgeoisie weaker. But it should not be forgotten that every hour's respite will be used by the bourgeoisie in their turn to rally their forces, to form a bourgeois white guard. . . .

It is clear to everybody that the Italian bourgeoisie are already not quite so helpless as they were a year ago. The Italian bourgeoisie are feverishly organizing their forces, arming. And at the same time they are trying to break up and demoralize the Italian proletariat by means of the reformists. The danger is great. If the Italian bourgeoisie get a little stronger, they will show their teeth.

If certain Italian leaders are using the Entente to frighten the Italian workers they are, consciously or unconsciously, leading the Italian working class into error. The Entente *will not be able* to send its troops against the Italian working class. . . . The events in England in connexion with the attempt of the English imperialists to give active support to white Poland, clearly prove this. . . . The French bourgeoisie *will not be able* to send their troops to 'pacify' the proletarian revolution in Italy. And if they should risk sending them they will break their own necks. . . .

It is quite clear that nowhere in the world is the victory of the proletariat possible without suffering and deprivation for the workers. . . . If the revolution does not come quickly in other countries also it is possible that the Italian proletariat will have to travel the same hard and painful road as the Russian proletariat. . . . But it is far more likely that the Italian revolutionary road will not be so difficult. Soviet Russia had for years to fight *alone* against the entire bourgeois world. The Italian proletarian revolution will not in any case stand alone.

The Italian working class shows astonishing unaniminity—the Italian proletariat is as one *for* the revolution. The Italian bourgeoisie cannot count on their regular troops, who will at the decisive moment go over to the rebels, and the greater part of the peasantry are for the revolution. It is now up to the Italian workers' party. . . .

In this situation the confused attitude, the hesitations, the indecision within the party can bring incalculable misfortune on the working class. . . .

We repeat that we are opposed to artificially provoked 'putsches', we are opposed to actions which have not been thought out in advance. But we are equally opposed to the proletarian party turning itself into a fire brigade, which puts out the flame of the revolution, when that flame is breaking through every crevice in capitalist society.

In Italy there are at hand all the most important conditions for a *genuinely popular, great proletarian revolution*. This must be understood. This must be the starting point. This is the contention of the Third International. The Italian comrades themselves must determine the next steps.

We suggest that from this point of view the Italian Socialist Party has acted and is acting too irresolutely. Every day brings news of disturbances in Italy. All eye-witnesses—including the Italian delegates—assert and reiterate that the situation in Italy is profoundly revolutionary. Nevertheless in many cases the party stands aside, without attempting to *generalize the movement, give it watchwords, give it a more systematic and organized character, turn it into a decisive offensive on the bourgeois State*. . . .

The basic reason for this is contamination of the party by reformist and liberal bourgeois elements who at the moment of civil war become outright agents of the counter-revolution, class enemies of the proletariat. It is naïve and foolish to mix up the subjective honesty and decency of these people with their objectively dangerous rôle . . . they may be personally honest but objectively they are enemies of the revolution for whom there can be no place in the party of the communist proletariat. . . .

The position is even worse in regard to the trade unions. Unless these mass organizations are correctly led by the party the proletariat cannot be victorious. . . . The Italian unions, which are allied with your party, are still members of the treacherous yellow Amsterdam International. . . . Their leaders like d'Aragona and other reformists collaborate with the bourgeoisie on committees created by the capitalists to fight the revolution. Such a state of affairs is absolutely intolerable. . . .

The Executive Committee thinks it necessary to state that it must put the question of cleansing the party and all the other conditions of admission as an *ultimatum*, as it cannot otherwise take responsibility before the world proletariat for its Italian section. . . .

We are not out for numbers alone—we do not want weights on our feet —we shall not allow reformists into our ranks. . . .

The decisive struggle is approaching. Italy will be Soviet. The Italian party will be a *communist* party. The Italian proletariat will be the best detachment in the international proletarian army.

President of the ECCI, G. ZINOVIEV
Members of the ECCI, N. BUKHARIN
N. LENIN

ECCI APPEAL ON THE RUSSIAN PEACE PROPOSALS TO POLAND

13 *September* 1920   *K.I.*, 15, col. 3371, *December* 1920

[The armistice between Poland and Russia was signed on 12 October; it gave Russia a far less favourable frontier than that proposed by the Allied Supreme Council (the Curzon line). There is some confusion of dates here. The resolution of the Central Executive Committee was passed on 25 September, that is, twelve days after the date given to the present document.]

TO ALL COMMUNIST PARTIES, ALL COMMUNIST YOUTH ORGANIZATIONS, TO ALL UNIONS ADHERING TO OR SYMPATHIZING WITH THE COMMUNIST INTER-NATIONAL, TO THE WORKERS AND PEASANTS OF THE WHOLE WORLD

Comrades!

The Russian Socialist Federal Soviet Republic, the republic of workers and peasants, has in the three years of its existence never for a moment ceased to struggle for peace and quiet. In the days of most bitter trial, as in the days of brilliant success over the enemies of the working class and of the government of workers and peasants, it had one care, one desire, one thought—peace.

In order to demonstrate once more its devotion to peace, the All-Russian Central Executive Committee, the highest legislative authority of the republic, took on 23 September a decision of tremendous historical importance: to avoid the impending winter campaign, which would have claimed thousands of new victims from the Russian and Polish peoples, the Soviet Government is prepared to make a heavy sacrifice and offer the Polish Government a frontier more advantageous than that defined for the Polish State by the Allied Supreme Council, if it concludes peace with Soviet Russia by 5 October this year. The Polish Government, supported by the English and French imperialists, will probably reject this generous proposal. If it does so, it will prove to the entire world, and in particular to all the oppressed and the dispossessed, that it is fighting not for Polish independence, but for the destruction of the Russian Soviet Republic, fighting against the Russian revolution, the centre and light of the world revolution.

Comrade workers of Poland, England, France, America, Germany, Italy . . . you must not allow this crime to be committed. You must rise as one man, and with all the means at your command insist on your governments using their influence on the Polish Government to persuade it to cease shedding the blood of the Polish people for alien interests, to accept Soviet Russia's proposal. By protests, meetings, and strikes proclaim to the entire world the will of the working people—peace with Russia. The Polish Government and the Anglo-French imperialists must be made aware of your wishes, your will, your strength.

Do not delay. Hurry. On you depends the peace of Europe; on your decision depends the fate of the world revolution, your own emancipation.

Prove, comrades, not in words but in actions, your fraternal solidarity with the Russian workers and peasants who have for three years been fighting not only for their own but also for your liberation from the yoke of bloodthirsty capitalism. Act!

> Down with international imperialism!
> Long live international peace!
> Long live the international revolution.

EXTRACTS FROM AN ECCI LETTER TO THE ITALIAN PROLETARIAT

22 *September* 1920   *K.I.*, 14, col. 2939, *November* 1920

[The disorders and strikes of the post-war period in Italy became more widespread and acute in the second half of 1920. A lock-out of engineering workers in Milan in August was answered by the trade union with an order to its members to remain in the factories. The lock-out was made national, and all over the country workers, acting unofficially, and numbering all together some 600,000, 'occupied' the factories, that is, attempted to run them independently of the employers. Most of the technical and clerical staffs left. The resolution of the third world congress on the report of the ECCI observed that the attitude of Serrati's group after the second congress showed that they were not seriously intending to implement the congress decisions. In an article in *Avanti* on 5 October 1920, Serrati referred to the 'draconian conditions dictated by comrades' who were too far off to grasp the situation correctly. Lenin replied in an article in *Pravda* that unity with the reformists would be a catastrophe, since they were bound to sabotage the revolutionary movement. At critical moments the loss of hesitating and reluctant leaders does not weaken, but strengthens the party, the movement, and the revolution. Such a moment had now come in Italy.]

Strike after strike, rising after rising, are breaking out in Italy. Matters have gone as far as the mass seizure of factories, houses, etc., by the workers. The labour movement in Italy is faced by decisive conflicts. As in every severe crisis, its course reveals clearly the strength and weakness of the movement.

The Italian bourgeoisie are retreating, and their most skilful man of affairs, an experienced swindler, Signor Giolitti, pretends to make concessions to you. He is playing for time; he is trying to localize the movement. He wants to discredit the movement, to put it in a Procrustean bed. . . .

The Italian reformists, as was to be expected, are betraying you. Their leader, Signor d'Aragona, following Giolitti, suggests that you restrict yourselves to economic demands and . . . abandon the seizure of factories and workshops.

The ECCI sends you this message: You cannot win by the seizure of factories and workshops alone. The bourgeoisie will leave you without raw materials, without money, without orders, without markets. They will try to compromise the movement, to provoke disappointment among the workers.

We do not conclude from this that you should abandon the seizure of factories and workshops. We conclude that the scope of this movement must be *extended, generalized*, that the question be raised to a general political level, in other words, that the movement be broadened into a general uprising with the object of overthrowing the bourgeoisie by the seizure of power by the working class, and the organization of the proletarian dictatorship.

This is the only way to salvation; otherwise the disintegration and collapse of the mighty and magnificent movement that has begun is inevitable. . . . Italian proletarians, you should now, by quick and energetic action, be in a position to cover the whole of Italy with councils of workers', peasants', soldiers', and sailors' deputies. You should begin at once to arm. You should drive out the representatives of the reformists. You should mobilize all the genuinely revolutionary forces of the country.

The Italian party should become a communist party in the full sense of the word, that is, a party taking the road to insurrection and leading the insurrection. Your fight must be unified and centralized. . . . You must have your general staff. This general staff is a reorganized communist party cleansed of reformists. The councils of workers' deputies should be led by communists. . . . Time will not wait. The movement that has begun must be expanded.

Clear the traitors and reformists out of the way.

EXTRACTS FROM AN ECCI–RILU MANIFESTO TO THE WORKERS OF
FRANCE ON THE FRENCH TRADE UNION CONGRESS

September 1920   *K.I.*, 14, col. 2927, *November* 1920

[The fifteenth congress of the CGT (Confédération Générale du Travail) was held
at Orléans from 27 September to 2 October 1920. The minority resolution condemned CGT participation in the ILO and proposed adherence to the Moscow
trade union centre; it mustered 658 votes against 1,485, with 54 abstentions.
By the time of the next congress, held at Lille from 25 to 30 June 1921, the left
wing had greatly increased their strength, having in the interval organized
themselves into 'revolutionary trade union committees'. Feeling at Lille ran
high, and shots (none fatal) were exchanged. The minority resolution protested
against the expulsion of local revolutionary unions from the CGT and advocated
adherence to the RILU. The voting was 1,556 for the CGT, 1,348 for the
minority, and 46 abstentions. At the end of the congress the minority met independently to consider future action, and convened a conference for December
1921.

The CGT denounced the congress as a split, and announced that any organization taking part would thereby place itself outside the ranks of the CGT.
Some half-hearted negotiations between the IFTU and the RILU broke down.
The congress set up a provisional administrative commission which issued membership cards and collected dues. In March 1922 it claimed a membership of
337,000. At the congress in St. Etienne in June 1922 where the opposition
founded the CGTU (Confédération Générale du Travail Unitaire), the proposal
to affiliate to the RILU was passed by 783 to 406 votes. Among the resolutions
passed by the congress was one condemning the persecution of anarchists,
even by the Soviet Government.

The ECCI wrote to the French party that the existence of the CGTU must
be explained to the French masses not as an end in itself, but 'only as a means
to attain the earliest possible unification of the trade union movement'.

At the fourth Comintern congress, Lauridan, of the French Communist Party,
supported by Rosmer, criticized the CPF attitude to the trade unions very
sharply. The provisional committee of the CGTU had submitted a syndicalist
platform expressing hostility to *any* State, and the party had not even convened
a meeting of the communist fraction in the CGTU before the St. Etienne congress. Rosmer added that the party made no attempt to influence the CGTU,
but merely followed and supported it. The attitude of the two speakers was
endorsed by Lozovsky, who had attended the St. Etienne congress, when wind-
ing up the debate on the trade union question.]

. . . Your present congress was provoked by the failure of the railwaymen's strike and the general strike which was to have been called in support, and it is meeting in the shadow of that failure, just as last year's
congress met under the shadow of the failure of the general strike called for
21 July. Failure after failure. Why? . . . The French proletariat can no

longer tolerate being led from defeat to defeat. It must seek out the reasons and act accordingly.

Well-meaning people, who preach reformism at a time when the bourgeoisie are getting machine guns ready, not reforms, the old and the new advocates of social peace, at a time when social peace is impossible, accuse the Communist International of wanting deliberately to provoke a split in the workers' forces. . . .

The Communist International does not want to split the workers' ranks. It does not advise the creation of revolutionary unions side by side with reformist unions. It has said to the communists, and it repeats, that they are obliged to remain and fight inside the reformist unions, and it has rebuked the German comrades who with the best intentions took the opposite course. But at the same time it stigmatizes the Amsterdam International as 'yellow' and, as a counterweight to this caricature of an international, which is nothing but a section of the League of Nations, it has created a genuine International. . . .

French imperialism acts so boldly and aggressively and provocatively . . . only because it knows how greatly the vacillations of those who are at the head of the trade unions have disordered and harassed the French workers' movement. . . .

The Communist International trusts that the workers' organizations, realizing that the choice must now be made between Amsterdam and Moscow, will accept the resolution of the Paris congress minority which declares that there is only one international of the revolution, that is, the Third, Moscow International. . . .

ZINOVIEV
ROSMER

EXTRACTS FROM AN OPEN LETTER FROM THE ECCI TO ALL MEMBERS
OF THE USPD

28 *September* 1920   *K.I.*, 14, col. 2901, *November* 1920

[During the debate on the 21 conditions at the second Comintern congress Lenin, Levi, Radek, and Rakovsky were among the most bitter critics of the USPD. Radek said they acted as a brake on the German workers' militancy; Rakovsky held them responsible for the collapse of the revolutionary movement, for by their collaboration with the right-wing socialists they deceived and misled the German workers. Levi said that their boast of being always at one with the masses revealed their cardinal error—they were weak when the masses were unconscious of their strength; they did not understand the role of leadership that had to be played by a revolutionary party. Lenin said that, whatever their intentions and subjective honesty, their entire way of thought was opportunist.

In a series of letters to the USPD after its Leipzig congress the ECCI analysed the differences between them, discussed the attitude of the four USPD delegates to the second world congress, and elaborated on the 21 conditions of admission to the Comintern to which two of the four had agreed. At the time of the Halle congress the USPD membership was about 800,000 and it controlled 55 daily papers; 81 of its members were in the Reichstag.

The USPD congress was held in Halle from 12 to 17 October; the debate on affiliation to the Third International lasted four days.

The voting was 236 in favour of the Third International against 156; Zinoviev addressed the congress in a speech which lasted four hours. Most of the Reichstag members and the control of most of the papers remained with the USPD, which continued as an independent party until September 1922, when it amalgamated with the SPD. About 300,000 USPD members joined the KPD which at that time had fewer than 50,000 members.

The Halle congress, Zinoviev wrote, showed how right the Comintern was to adopt the 21 conditions of admission. 'It made the reformists and the semi-reformists show their true colours. If the Third, Moscow, International had not been so strict, then some of these semi-reformist elements would have preferred to slip through the half-open door of the Third International, to continue their opportunist activities there. The Third International had to take precautions against this possibility. It must be an unadulterated organization, all of one piece.' The right-wing leaders of the USPD had said that they would continue as before to demonstrate their solidarity with the Soviet Government. 'But that is not true. A socialist who today comes out against the Third International will tomorrow come out against the Soviet Government also!' Hilferding, one of the principal speakers against affiliation, accused the Comintern of exploiting the socialist and colonial independence movements in the interests of the Russian State, citing the Baku congress as a flagrant example.

In a message to all socialist parties which had left the Second International (and which was signed also by the central committee of the KPD and the USPD majority) Zinoviev wrote that Halle had shown that it was unnecessary to make any concession to the reformists. Economic conditions in Germany were ripe for revolution, but the movement had been held back and checked by the right wing.]

Comrades,

Your congress at Halle is to take a decision of historical importance. For some weeks your entire party press has been discussing the conditions of admission to the Communist International. . . . The ECCI considers it its duty to address to you this letter on the results of our conversations with your central committee and the arguments with which your press has been and still is filled. . . .

In the centrist parties—in your Independent party in Germany, in the French Socialist Party, the Socialist Party of America, etc.—a process of extremely rapid differentiation is going on. More and more the proletarian elements in the party are liberating themselves from the ruinous and rotten ideas of the 'centre'. At the same time the leading party organs remain, because of inertia, in the hands of the right-wing leaders who will do anything, fair or foul, to retain their power in the party.

It is the task of the Communist International to accelerate and strengthen this process of differentiation, to help free the proletarian elements from the mouldering influence of reformism.

That is precisely why we cannot accept into the Communist International all those who express the desire to join it. To a certain extent the Communist International has become the fashion. We do not want our Communist International to resemble the bankrupt Second International. We open our doors wide to every *mass proletarian* revolutionary organization, but we think it over ten times before opening the doors of the Communist International to newcomers from the camp of the petty-bourgeois, bureaucratic, opportunist leaders like Hilferding and Crispien. . . .

Remember what happened in the German revolution, beginning with its very first steps. How often the German working class has paid, with the lives of hundreds and thousands of its best fighters, because at the decisive moment the forces of the party were not organized and the working class had no unified centre. The experience of the great Russian revolution showed that without a centralized and powerful communist party the working class cannot win the civil war. . . .

The principle of centralism, valid for every party separately, remains valid on an international scale. The Communist International will exist as a centralized association of organizations, or it will not exist at all. It is a single universal workers' party which has its sections in different countries. . . . The imperialist war created a situation in which the working class of every single country cannot take any serious step that does not have repercussions throughout the entire movement and the entire struggle of the working class of every other country.

Every basic question of our life is now decided on an international scale. We need an International which acts as the international general staff of the proletarians of all countries. We cannot change the Communist International into a mere post office, like the Second International. . . . The war between Soviet Russia and the Polish bourgeoisie in Lithuania and White Russia brought about the establishment of the Council of Action in London. This one example shows how closely the workers' movement in one country is bound to the workers' struggle throughout the world. . . .

There has been a great deal of discussion among the Independents of the question of illegal organization. In our very first letter to the USPD six months ago we dealt with the necessity of forming an illegal organization at a time when the bourgeoisie placed force on the order of the day. . . . The working class should cherish no illusions about the permanency of bourgeois legality. The working class must make use of every slightest legal opportunity, but at the same time it must have its illegal organization. . . .

There are historical situations in which splitting is the sacred duty of every revolutionary. This is when the leaders are deceiving the party and betraying the working class. . . . To split away from your right-wing leaders is necessary not in the interests of some mythical 'Russian dictatorship', but in the interests of your own German working-class movement. . . . It is a vital necessity if we want, when the decisive moment comes, to be firm, united, resolute. If we keep the reformists and centrists in our ranks, we are keeping enemies within our own house, we are deliberately preparing our own defeat. Whether to cleanse the party or to split—that now still depends on you, workers in the Independent party. If you are able, firmly and unanimously, to impose your will on your leaders, if you can remove those who are incorrigible, who belong to the bourgeois rather than the proletarian camp, then a split will not be necessary, but if part of the workers are still so blind, after all the dreadful lessons they have had, as to follow leaders like Hilferding and Crispien, then you will have to split. And the sooner, the more resolutely you do this, the sooner will their eyes be opened, and the sooner will they return to you. . . .

You must break with the vacillating right-wing elements and unite with the entire international revolutionary proletariat, or unite with the faltering elements of the petty-bourgeois centre and break with the international revolutionary proletariat. That is how the question stands. German workers, choose.

EXTRACTS FROM A LETTER FROM THE ECCI TO THE CONGRESS OF THE GERMAN COMMUNIST PARTY

October 1920   *K.I.*, 14, col. 2925, *November* 1920

[The fifth congress of the KPD was held early in November, primarily to discuss the question of amalgamation with the USPD after the Halle congress.]

The Communist Party of Germany has achieved most important results. The reformist and semi-reformist elements in the USPD have been excluded, the best part of the workers in the USPD are on our side, on the side of communism. The job now is to take the lead in the large united communist party that is being formed, to bring to it communist clarity of thought. Everything else is of secondary importance. Recalling the past may only hamper the essential fusion and theoretical understanding.

We also ask you to show more toleration than before to the KAPD. The KAPD has . . . given serious proof of its desire to fight against nationalist infection. Some leaders of the KAPD still show a non-Marxist and non-communist attitude on trade union and parliamentary questions . . . but just the same there are in the ranks of the KAPD serious and excellent proletarian revolutionaries. We must at all costs attract them into our ranks, and it is essential to meet them half way.

The amalgamation of all communist elements in Germany into a large united party is an event of world historical importance. The Spartakusbund has fulfilled its mission. Its task at the given moment is to merge into the new great united party and to be the moving force in communist unification.

A new struggle confronts you, new sacrifices, new sufferings. The Russian Communist Party, the entire Communist International are completely confident that the German working class will be able to shoulder these gigantic tasks.

EXTRACTS FROM AN ECCI APPEAL TO ALL MEMBERS OF THE ITALIAN SOCIALIST PARTY AND THE ITALIAN TRADE UNIONS

November 1920   *K.I.*, 15, col. 3395, *December* 1920

[Under an agreement made in 1918 between the Italian unions and the Socialist Party, the party was to take over 'political' as distinct from industrial strikes. The national council of the trade union federation, meeting in September 1920, decided that the 'occupation of the factories' did not constitute a political movement; the employers, anxious to take over their factories again, consented to the negotiation of collective agreements, and to a vague formula giving the unions a share in the management of industry.

At the third Comintern congress Trotsky attributed the failure of the strikes in Italy in the autumn of 1920 to the influence of the right wing in the Socialist Party. The resolution on the report of the ECCI took the same line. The Comintern leaders exaggerated both the extent and the strength of the movement. In a speech two years later, a few days before the march on Rome, Trotsky said: 'In September 1920 the working class of Italy had in effect gained control of the State . . . but there was no organization capable of consolidating the victory . . . and since then the working class of Italy has been retreating.' At the end of September the Central Committee of the Italian Socialist Party met in Milan; while agreeing to accept the 21 conditions of admission to the Comintern, it was divided on the question of expelling the right wing. The right wing then met separately at Reggio Emilia, the left at Imola, where it was decided to break with the reformists at the next party congress. Serrati's centrist group, meeting at Florence, wished to apply the 21 conditions at a suitable time in accordance with 'prevailing historical circumstances.']

With unflagging attention the ECCI is following every step of your heroic struggle. Communists all over the world see in you one of the best and toughest detachments of the international proletarian revolution. The proletarian revolution is knocking at your door. You are at the moment closer to victory than the workers of any other country. In Italy practically all the prerequisites for a victorious proletarian revolution are at hand. The working class is unanimous in its readiness to overthrow capitalism. A significant part of the peasantry is on your side; a good part of the army is with you. Up to the very latest moment the bourgeoisie were demoralized. The Entente will not have the forces to maintain a blockade of red Italy. And if they should try they will break their necks. Grain from Soviet Russia for red Italy is assured. Ardent fraternal support from the French workers for a Soviet Italy is also assured.

The prerequisites for victory are practically all there—all except one; that is the state of organization among yourselves. We do not say that you are not organized. The working class of Italy is organized. But your organizations are not homogeneous. Reformists have found refuge there, that is, people who at bottom share the views not of the communist proletariat but of the liberal bourgeoisie. Reformist influence in the Italian workers' organizations is the principal brake on your movement, the curse which weighs it down. . . .

It is self-evident that the seizure of factories and workshops without a parallel struggle for the proletarian dictatorship cannot bring victory to the working class. But it was a superb beginning from which a genuinely revolutionary mass movement might grow. Victory was in your hands. Who snatched it from you? The reformists. The bourgeoisie were powerless to take up open struggle. Giolitti was forced to resort to the method of 'strategic retreat', as the Italian bourgeois press said. . . .

Through its agents the bourgeoisie injected the poison of reformism into the Italian workers' organizations, above all into the unions. . . . The reformists at the head of the Italian unions advanced the slogan of establishing commissions composed of representatives of the workers' 'leaders' and capitalists on a parity basis to work out the principles and methods of control over production. This was the high-class funeral arranged by the reformists for your revolutionary movement. . . . The Italian capitalists were saved by the efforts of d'Aragona, Turati, Modigliani, Dugoni and other agents of capital. The Italian bourgeoisie received a new lease of life.

Now, when d'Aragona and Co. have done their job . . . the bourgeoisie have begun to arrest hundreds of the best leaders of the Italian working class. They are filling the prisons with our best fighters. Having introduced confusion into our ranks through their reformist agents, the bourgeoisie now think they are strong enough to resort to force.

The immediate future, we are convinced, will show them that they are cruelly mistaken in thinking surgical methods appropriate to cure their ills. Counter-revolutionary surgery will rebound *against* the Italian bourgeoisie.

But, comrades, we must just the same learn from our mistakes, we must be able to draw the practical conclusions from the great lessons of your movement.

What is the lesson of the autumn movement? That so long as there are reformists and semi-reformists in our ranks, so long as we tolerate disguised bourgeois at the head of the unions, our victory over capitalism is impossible.

Of late there have been in evidence in Italy every possible kind of 'uniter', frightening you and trying to convince you that a break with the reformists would weaken us. That is nonsense. Not every split is harmful to the working class. Splitting away from the agents of capital is not harmful but good for us. . . .

The Italian party at one time reached an agreement with the Confederation of Labour that during strikes and other revolutionary movements the Confederation would acknowledge the leadership of the party. But we have seen that at the decisive moment the reformists, while observing the letter of the agreement, in fact broke it. That will happen whenever serious issues are at stake. We must relentlessly eject from the party and the unions the reformist leaders. Only then will it be possible to think seriously of decisive battles with the bourgeoisie.

To effect the break with the agents of capital, to defend honestly and sincerely all the decisions of the second congress of the Communist International, our Italian friends have organized themselves in a communist fraction. Its leading paper is the Turin *Avanti* and the periodical *Communist* published in Bologna. All honest and consistent partisans of the Comintern are asked to support this fraction, and only this fraction. To all other fractions we say: whoever is not with us is against us.

Comrades, if the Italian bourgeoisie have now passed so rapidly from defence to attack, it is because they rely on the demoralizing work of the reformists. . . . Our answer must be the following: while fighting back against the capitalists with one hand, we must with the other, and without losing an hour, carry out to the end that cleansing of our organizations of reformists and semi-reformists without which our organizations cannot become organs of the proletarian masses.

The lawyer-reformists, who occupy so many seats in the parliamentary fraction of the Italian Socialist Party . . . are trying to present the entire dispute with the Communist International as turning on organizational questions. This is the favourite method of all opportunists. It was resorted to by the socialist renegades among the right wing Independents in Germany. Comrades, do not believe them. These are far more than organizational questions. The Communist International does not encroach on the autonomy of the individual workers' parties, it is well aware that there is a large field in which each party must act independently. It has declared more than once that it takes binding decisions only in regard to questions where such decisions are possible. Our dispute with the reformists and semi-reformists is *not* about the necessity or otherwise of accepting the 21 conditions, or 18, or two and a half. Our fight with the reformists turns on the question whether our party is to be the militant vanguard of the proletariat in its struggle for communism, or whether it is to remain, as the reformists would have it, a plaything in the hands of petty-bourgeois patchers-up of the capitalist regime.

We are divided from the reformists and semi-reformists not by mere organizational differences. No, it is a case of two philosophies, two camps, two classes, two programmes. . . .

We appeal to all members of the Italian Socialist Party and trade unions . . . our ranks must be cleansed of the ulcer of reformism. This must be done as quickly as possible, and at whatever cost. *With* the leaders, if they want to; *without* the leaders if they hesitate and hold back; *against* the leaders if they interfere with our carrying out this work.

EXTRACTS FROM AN ECCI LETTER TO ALL LEFT-WING MEMBERS OF THE USPD, TO THE KPD, AND THE KAPD

November 1920   *K.I.*, 15, col. 3401, *December* 1920

[The sixth congress of the KPD was held early in December 1920, and effected amalgamation with the section of the USPD which had broken away at Halle. Of the 485 delegates, 349 were from the USPD; of the seven principal platform speakers, two were from the USPD. Representation on the *Zentrale* was equal.]

What happened at the Halle congress is of immense importance not only for the members of the USPD, but for all socialists, for the entire German working class, and for the world proletariat. . . . The German labour movement is breaking away from the moribund ideology of the 'centre' and is rejecting, once and for all, the counter-revolutionary ideas of Kautskyianism.

Practically all over Europe the forces of the working class at the present moment are so great that the victory of the proletariat over the bourgeoisie would present little difficulty *if* the working class were sufficiently prepared to carry out its historical mission. What the working class chiefly lacks at the moment is its own clear, theoretical orientation, the consciousness of its aims, a clear understanding of its revolutionary road. The chief obstacle to our victory is among us ourselves. . . . In a country like Germany it is particularly obvious that the opportunist 'leaders', the reactionary trade union officials, the labour aristocracy and bureaucracy, are incomparably more dangerous to the workers' movement than the avowed white guards of the armed bourgeoisie. In the German trade union movement there are in round figures about 100,000 'officials', that is, employees of the unions. *These form the chief white-guard detachment of the bourgeoisie.* These people came from our ranks, the ranks of the workers. These 'leaders' know the strengths and weaknesses of the labour movement. Everything that is good in the worker—his energy, his fortitude, his knowledge of life—these opportunist leaders have placed at the service of the bourgeoisie. This stratum of opportunist leaders, born and reared in the working class in the preceding period of the peaceful organic development of the labour movement, are the biggest counter-revolutionary force of our time. To liberate the labour movement from the influence of this stratum is to clear the road for the victory of the proletarian revolution.

And that is precisely what happened at Halle. Only from this point of view can the real historical meaning of what happened there be fully understood. In Germany a mass communist workers' party is being created which will from the first include some hundreds of thousands who have overcome their illusions and grasped the necessity of breaking not only with the open social-chauvinists but with the centre which hides behind left phrases. . . .

The German workers now see clearly that we fought the right-wing Independents not on the question of one or another of the 21 conditions of admission to the Communist International, but on the question whether they are partisans or enemies of the proletarian dictatorship, friends of Soviet Russia or its secret foes. . . .

The clearing of the ground has created the conditions for the formation of a united and mighty mass communist party in Germany. The central committee of the left Independent and the communist parties in Germany have already agreed to convene a joint congress early in December for the establishment of a united German communist party. Those members of the KAPD who wish to join this united party are also invited to the congress. . . . Old personal and petty differences must be forgotten. Differences on particular questions must be relegated to the rear, as against what now unites all those in the left USPD, the KPD, and the KAPD. . . .

Among the right-wing Independents there are some workers who only yielded to the demagogy of the right-wing leaders because they believed their stupid assertions that the Communist International wants to deprive the German party of its autonomy, that 'Moscow' wants to impose its views by force on the workers of other countries. To these proletarian elements we say, shake off the lies and the demagogy, and look at the facts . . . the gulf that divides the right-wing leaders from the Third International is one of principle. They are opponents of the world revolution and they do not believe either in the dictatorship of the proletariat or in the conquest of Soviet power in Germany.

EXTRACTS FROM AN OPEN LETTER FROM THE ECCI AND THE
INTERNATIONAL TRADE UNION COUNCIL TO THE IFTU

November 1920   *K.I.*, 15, col. 3409, *December* 1920

[The IFTU congress in London in 1920 was a special one to discuss the programme for economic reconstruction drafted by the Management Committee.
The programme adopted by the congress was designed 'to combat reaction and
the danger of a new world war, and . . . to contribute to the establishment of a
new system which would form a sound basis for world economic restoration'.

In his memoirs Rosmer, the French representative on the council which
organized the formation of the RILU, deplores the 'stupidity and vulgarity' of
Zinoviev's manifestoes against 'yellow Amsterdam', which betrayed in his view
a complete ignorance of the nature of trade unionism in western Europe and of
the kind of propaganda required.]

TO THE WORLD CONGRESS OF THE YELLOW LEADERS OF THE TRADE UNIONS
IN LONDON

Citizens!

You call your congress a world trade union congress. In fact it will be
a congress of *yellow leaders*, betraying at every step the true interests of the
labour movement in general and the trade unions in particular. We know
that you will at once cry that this letter is an insult to tens of millions of
workers in the unions. Shout as much as you like. We are not insulting the
workers in the unions. It is not their fault that it is still possible for you,
yellow leaders, to speak in the name of workers' organizations. We know
very well that among the millions and millions whom you 'represent' there
are many honest and conscious workers who are not yet organized adequately enough to expel you. But rest assured that the time will soon
come. . . .

What did you do in the war, yellow leaders? You were the worst traitors
to the working class. Legien and Co. incited the German workers against
the French. Jouhaux and Co. equally cynically stirred up the French
workers against the Germans. And now these traitors meet and absolve
each other of their sins, proclaim a mutual amnesty, and conclude an
alliance to go on deceiving the workers. . . . Equally with the imperialist
executioners, you are responsible for the millions of corpses, for the tens of
millions of crippled lives, for the hunger and cold, for the wretchedness and
savagery which accompanied the imperialist war, which you called the
'great war of liberation'. . . .

You have declared war on the Communist International. Yes, that war
will be fought. In that war the organized workers can lose nothing but the
shackles on their feet, and you are those shackles. In fighting the capitalists
we must also fight their agents, and that is you, gentlemen.

You are hated by the workers as they hate the leaders of international imperialism. Conscious workers despise you yellow leaders even more than they despise the kings of the stock exchange and the magnates of capital. These at least do not hide behind socialist slogans. They do not call themselves leaders of the working class—they are our avowed enemies.

Many of you, gentlemen, at one time belonged to the workers. Many of you were brought up in poor homes. Many of you came from among us. Until now many in the working class trusted you. You have mocked everything that is sacred to the working class. You broke all your promises and betrayed the workers at the very time when the fate of the working class was being decided. You are the most dangerous enemies of the proletariat. . . .

You are the chief bulwark of capitalism, now living out its last days— you are the watchdogs of capital, barking furiously at all those who approach your master's lair. You are the last bourgeois barricade which the revolutionary working class must storm to clear the road to a new life, to happiness and to true freedom. . . .

Your yellow Second International has finally perished as a political organization. You are now trying to take revenge in the trade union field. In Amsterdam and London you are trying to revive the trade union 'International'. Rest assured that this last attempt, too, will fail.

The conscious workers have formed in Moscow an international council of genuinely proletarian red trade unions. By furious slander and lies you will perhaps for a time succeed in restraining the workers from entering this real proletarian international of red unions, but your game is played out. Labour kulaks, labour reactionaries, such as you all are, cannot deceive the proletarian masses much longer. The more you rage against the Communist International the worse for you, the sooner will the workers throw you where you belong—in the bourgeois cesspool. . . .

Pygmies! Just as a tattered handkerchief cannot hide the sun, so your manifestoes, patched together with lies and hypocrisy, cannot vanquish the Communist International. The Communist International is the sun of the working class. This sun is shining more and more ardently over the entire earth, over all the oppressed and exploited, over all the working masses you have deceived and betrayed.

Soon, from the throats of these millions and millions of workers in the unions whom you claim to represent there will arise one cry: down with the yellow traitors, down with the enemies of the international fellowship of workers, long live the Communist International.

ECCI: ZINOVIEV, LENIN, BUKHARIN, RADEK, STEINHARDT, QUELCH, TSKHAKAYA, BELA KUN, RUDNIANSKY

International T.U. Council: TOMSKY LOZOVSKY, ROSMER, SHABLIN, MILKICH.

EXTRACTS FROM AN ECCI RESOLUTION ADMITTING THE GERMAN COM-
MUNIST LABOUR PARTY TO THE COMMUNIST INTERNATIONAL AS A
SYMPATHIZING PARTY

28 *November* 1920   *K.I.*, 15, col. 3368, *December* 1920

[The resolution admitting the KAPD as a sympathizing party was passed with
one abstention. Two sessions of the Executive had been devoted to this question,
to meet the objections of the central committees of the KPD and the USPD (not
yet amalgamated). The January 1921 meeting of the ECCI considered a protest
from the central committee of the German Communist Party against the admission of the KAPD as a sympathizing party on the grounds that it was not a
revolutionary party, that it was a dying party to which the ECCI had given an
artificial stimulus, and that the KPD, in its fight against the incorrect ideas of
the KAPD, was deprived of its chief weapon, the authority of the International.
Levi, who had been largely responsible for the split in 1919 which led to the
formation of the KAPD, was particularly incensed by the Executive's action.
Zinoviev replied that the ECCI action was in accordance with the decisions of
the second Comintern congress; the KAPD consisted of genuinely revolutionary
workers, and the KPD must be patient and tolerant in its conduct. The ECCI
passed a resolution, one delegate voting against and one abstaining, confirming
its previous decision.]

Having once more, in conjunction with delegates of the KAPD, subjected the question of the KAPD to a thorough examination, the ECCI
resolves:

The only section of the Comintern in Germany with full rights is the
United Communist Party of Germany [VKPD] now being formed.

We once again suggest that all members of the KAPD join this united
communist party and fight within it for their views. The ECCI trusts that
the KAPD organizations will take part in the joint congress of the KPD
and the left USPD in Berlin on 4 December 1920.

The ECCI again declares that the KAPD tactics, particularly in reference to trade unions and parliament, are mistaken, and suggests that the
comrades of the KAPD submit to international proletarian discipline and
the decisions of the second world congress of the Comintern.

To facilitate the unification of all communist elements in Germany and
to meet halfway the best proletarian elements in the KAPD, the ECCI
declares its readiness to accept the KAPD temporarily into the Communist
International as a sympathizing party with consultative voice.

This acceptance obliges the KAPD to insert regularly in its press all the
manifestoes and resolutions of the ECCI. It also obliges the KAPD to
render fraternal support to the Communist Party of Germany in all its
actions.

LETTER FROM THE ECCI TO THE CONGRESS OF THE FRENCH SOCIALIST
PARTY AT TOURS

December 1920   *K.I.*, 16, col. 3803, *March* 1921

[In May 1919 the left-wing opposition in the French Socialist Party, which had
in 1915 constituted themselves as 'the Committee to re-establish international
relations' on an anti-war platform, was renamed the 'Committee for adherence
to the Third International'. The Tours congress was attended by 285 delegates
holding 4,574 mandates. Klara Zetkin attended the congress as ECCI delegate.
The voting gave 3,028 for adherence to the Third International, against 1,022.
A *comité directeur* was elected, including Frossard as secretary, Loriot as international secretary, and Cachin as editor of *Humanité*. The majority included
13 deputies.]

Dear Comrades,

The ECCI will follow with intense interest the course of your congress,
which will undoubtedly occupy a prominent place in the history of the
French workers' movement.

We have read the draft of the resolution bearing the signatures of comrades Loriot, Monatte, Souvarine, Cachin, Frossard, and others. With the
exception of certain points (for example, the question of the name of the
party) we can agree with this resolution.

We have also read the draft of the resolution signed by Jean Longuet,
Paul Faure, and others. This resolution is permeated through and through
with the spirit of reformism and the most pettifogging diplomacy. The
theses approved by the second congress of the Communist International
permit certain exceptions to be made in regard to those reformists who now
submit to the decisions of the Communist International and renounce
their former opportunism. The resolution signed by Longuet and Faure
shows that Longuet and his group have no desire to be exceptions in the
reformist camp. They were and are outright conductors of bourgeois influence into the proletariat. Their resolution is unmistakable, not only on
the points it deals with, but even more on those about which its authors
keep silent. On the world revolution, the proletarian dictatorship, the
Soviet system, Longuet and his friends prefer to say nothing, or to utter
the most banal ambiguities. The Communist International can have
nothing in common with the authors of such a resolution.

The worst service that could be done to the French proletariat in the
present state of affairs would be to think up some kind of confusing compromise which would then turn out to be shackles on the feet of your
party. We are deeply convinced that the majority of the conscious workers
of France will not allow such a despicable compromise with the reformists,

but will at last create at Tours a strong and united genuine communist party free of reformist and semi-reformist elements.

In this spirit we greet your congress and wish it success.

Long live the communist party of France!

Long live the French proletariat!

On behalf of the ECCI,

G. ZINOVIEV

EXTRACTS FROM AN ECCI LETTER TO THE CONGRESS OF THE ITALIAN SOCIALIST PARTY

January 1921   *K.I.*, 16, col. 3805, *March* 1921

[The Leghorn congress of the Italian Socialist Party, which opened on 15 January 1921, was attended by Rakosi and Kabakchiev for the ECCI, and by Paul Levi as a fraternal delegate from the German Communist Party. The resolution introduced by Bordiga for unconditional acceptance of the 21 conditions of admission to the Comintern received 59,000 votes, against 98,000 for Serrati's motion of conditional acceptance, and 15,000 for Turati's motion of rejection. Serrati was willing to accept the conditions, but not to proceed to the expulsion of the right wing which they implied; Levi disapproved of the insistence of the ECCI representatives on effecting the break. The left wing of the congress seceded and formed the Italian Communist Party. At the third Comintern congress Terracini declared that the left were not thinking of a split, only of expelling the reformists; Serrati was therefore responsible for the split. But it is clear from the proceedings of the ECCI in November 1920 that the break with Serrati had been determined beforehand.

At the meeting in November Zinoviev suggested that no further concessions should be made to Serrati, who had failed both in his attitude to the reformists, and in his conduct during the autumn strikes. 'That was the beginning of the revolution; the workers seized the factories and started to organize their own red guard; the movement was not defeated by force, it was broken by the opportunists.' Serrati and his friends had remained silent while the old reformist leaders were collaborating with the Italian Government in pacifying the workers with promises. After the Leghorn congress the Socialist Party reaffirmed its adherence to the Third International, but reserved 'independence in the interpretation of the 21 conditions'; it was expelled by the ECCI.]

The congress of your party, being held at a moment when the proletarian revolution is knocking on your country's door, will be of tremendous importance for the fate of the international revolution. The Italian proletariat has at last fully grasped the need of creating a communist party cleansed of reformist and semi-reformist elements. The entire Italian situation cries out against any compromise of principle whatever with the reformists. The deepest and most vital interests of the Italian proletariat and the world revolution demand a complete and unreserved break with reformism as a tendency.

We have received your central committee's reply of 31 October 1920 to the ECCI letter sent to your party in August. We tell you frankly, comrades, that the reply seemed extremely unsatisfactory to us. One example will serve our purpose. In its letter the central committee still thinks it possible to take up the defence of the reformist leaders of the Confederation of Labour. . . .

The Amsterdam International is part of the Second International . . . it is at present the chief instrument of the bourgeoisie in their struggle against the proletariat. D'Aragona and co. still find it possible to belong to this organization, and your central committee finds it possible to tolerate this.

We think it necessary to say to you once again, dear comrades, that the Communist International has and wishes to have nothing in common with people belonging to the reformist camp. We tell you, firmly and clearly: You must choose between Turati, d'Aragona and co., and the Third International. . . .

The ECCI, attaching great importance to your congress, intended to send two delegates from Moscow to attend it. Unfortunately, because of circumstances outside our control, this has not been possible. . . .

On behalf of the ECCI,

G. ZINOVIEV

EXTRACT FROM AN ECCI STATEMENT ON THE VIENNA CONFERENCE
OF SOCIALIST PARTIES

15 *January* 1921   *K.I.*, 16, col. 3799, *March* 1921

[The International Union of Socialist Parties, usually referred to as the Vienna Union or the Two-and-a-half International, was founded at a conference held in Vienna from 22 to 27 February 1921. There were 80 delegates from 13 countries, claiming a following of 10 million members. The negotiations which led to its foundation had been started in April 1920 between the Swiss Socialist Party and the Independent Labour Party. It included the Austrian, French, and Swiss Socialist Parties, the Independent Social-Democratic Party of Germany, the British Independent Labour Party, the Russian mensheviks, and a number of smaller parties and groups, which had dissociated themselves from the Second International but were unwilling to join the Third. At the invitation of the Labour Party, representatives of the Vienna Union met the Labour Party in London on 20 October 1921 to discuss the question of fusion with the Second International. After the meeting the Vienna Union published a statement rejecting fusion. At its meeting in Frankfurt, the Vienna Union approved the fusion of the USPD–SPD which had been agreed at Nuremberg on 24 September 1922. After the Hague conference of December 1922 the Second International and the Vienna Union agreed on fusion, and the constitution of the

Labour and Socialist International (LSI) was adopted at a congress held in Hamburg in May 1923. Radek, writing on the foundation of the Vienna Union, asserted that it was an organization without ideas or programme of its own, but if the development of the revolutionary movement in Europe were slowed down, it would be able to deter workers, who were still hesitating at the cross-roads, from joining the Third International.]

A NEW ATTEMPT AT INTERNATIONAL DECEPTION
THE 'TWO-AND-A-HALF INTERNATIONAL'

The Second International collapsed like a house of cards. Conscious workers of the whole world refer to it in disgust as the gendarme international. Larger and larger contingents of conscious workers are joining the ranks of the Third International.

But the 'leaders' they leave behind cannot reconcile themselves to this state of affairs. And so the supporters of this 'centre' have evolved a plan to build a 'new' international, neither the Second nor the Third, but the Two-and-a-half. . . .

In the guise of forming an allegedly 'new' international, an attempt is being made to reconstruct the Second International. An entire 'international conference' is being called for this purpose in the near future in Vienna.

Who will take part in this conference? Renner, Bauer, & co.; that is, gentlemen who are in no decisive respect distinguished from Scheidemann and Noske. . . . This one fact is eloquent enough testimony to the character of the forthcoming conference. . . .

Germany will be represented by Messrs. Dittmann and Crispien, also former ministers of the German bourgeoisie. Rejected by the German workers, these gentlemen are moving further to the right every day, and soon it will be impossible to distinguish even with a magnifying glass between Dittmann and Scheidemann.

France, apparently, will be represented by citizen Longuet's party. . . . Even in the Second International you do not often meet such dirty and abject traitors as these gentlemen. . . .

Russia will be represented at the forthcoming 'international' conference by M. Martov and other mensheviks. Rejected and despised by the whole Russian working class, Martov and co. will make notable members of the future Two-and-a-half International. . . . The Russian mensheviks, who betrayed the interests of the proletarian revolution in Russia from the very day of its outbreak, who joined the governments of Miliukov, Kerensky, and Kolchak, who even helped the Tsarist government at the beginning of the imperialist war—these Russian mensheviks are quite worthy of being leaders of the Two-and-a-half 'International'. . . .

Conscious workers of the whole world should know that the right-wing German Independents, the French Longuetists, the Austrian social-democrats, are enemies of the proletarian revolution, that their press violently slanders Soviet Russia, that their leaders more and more cynically help the bourgeoisie against the workers. Conscious workers of the whole world should heap on the forthcoming Vienna conference of deceivers and traitors the contempt it deserves. They should boycott the Two-and-a-half 'International' just as they boycotted the Second.

ECCI RESOLUTION ON THE RESIGNATION OF FIVE MEMBERS FROM THE CENTRAL COMMITTEE OF THE GERMAN COMMUNIST PARTY

March 1921   *K.I.*, 17, col. 4071, *June* 1921

[Levi's support of Serrati at the Leghorn congress had brought him into conflict with the ECCI delegates (at the third Comintern congress later in the year Zinoviev accused Levi of 'conspiring with Serrati'), and on their return via Berlin Rakosi and Kabakchiev asked the German central committee to condemn his action. The resolution; moved by Thalheimer at a meeting on 24 February, was passed by 28 votes to 23, whereupon Levi, Zetkin, and three other members resigned from the central committee.

Reporting on the Comintern to the tenth congress of the Russian Communist Party in March 1921, Zinoviev assured his audience that Klara Zetkin's resignation was a temporary affair, an episode that would soon be settled, whereas Levi's attitude showed his steady drift towards reformism. The congress did not discuss Zinoviev's report, but passed a resolution approving the action of the RCP delegates on the ECCI, with particular reference to Italy and Germany.

It was in the debate on the report of the ECCI to the third Comintern congress that Koenen (Germany), referring to Klara Zetkin's statement that, once convinced she was wrong, she was willing to accept correction, but 'I would feel humiliated and unworthy if I ever did anything against my convictions', said, 'Of course, one must act even against one's convictions, if it is in the interests of the party. In certain circumstances it is possible to settle conflicts of conscience only by making the alternative clear: For the party or out of the party'.]

Five members of the CC of the VKPD have resigned from the central committee because of their dissatisfaction with the attitude of the Executive Committee towards the split in the Italian Socialist Party.

For any thinking communist it is enough that the centrist group of leaders, faced with the necessity of choosing between the reformists and the communists, broke with the 60,000 communist proletarians of Italy in favour of Serrati and 12,000 reformists. This fact is of greater weight than all the long-winded speeches about the tactless conduct of one or another representative of the Communist International. That should have been clear to all members of the German central committee. In a communist party the leaders, placed there by the workers, have as little right to leave their posts without permission of the party as a soldier in the Red Army has to leave his sentry box. Only in bourgeois and opportunist parties does a leader think he has the right to act independently, against the will of the members of the party. In any case, these five comrades were bound, out of respect for international discipline, to inform the Executive Committee of the Communist International of their intention to leave the central committee. The ECCI regrets the departure of these comrades and sees in it:

1. Inadequate discipline among the leading elements of the VKPD;
2. Proof of the fact that among the leaders of the VKPD there are signs of the formation of a right wing.

The Executive Committee adheres to the opinion that the reason why comrade Levi and his group left the central committee of the VKPD was not the Italian question, but opportunist vacillations concerning German and international policy.

It should be clear to all conscious German communists that the ECCI has as its aim the formation in each country not of a sect, but of an active communist revolutionary mass party. The efforts of the Executive Committee to unite in Germany the Spartakusbund, the USPD, and the KAPD, into a powerful mass communist party, is sufficient proof of this.

The attempt of some comrades to represent the events in the Italian party as a 'mechanical split' shows either that they are inadequately informed about the real situation in the Italian party, or that they are yielding to menshevik-reformist tendencies.

The ECCI directs the attention of all German communists to the fact that in the past few months there have been signs of an attempt to form a communist right wing. Therefore communists should close their ranks and nip these tendencies in the bud. Comrade Levi's statement of 23 March shows that he has already reached a complete break with the Communist International. This should show the comrades who formerly declared their solidarity with Levi where his road leads, and help them to recognize their error.

EXTRACTS FROM AN ECCI MANIFESTO ON THE KRONSTADT RISING

March 1921   *K.I.*, 17, col. 4299, *June* 1921

[The policies of war communism, in particular the requisitioning of grain, had aroused deep discontent among the peasants, and the severe shortage of food and fuel supplies was felt in the towns, where real wages had fallen far below the pre-war level. With the ending of the civil war in November 1920 the unrest and resentment came to the surface. The strike movement was most marked in Petrograd; it spread to the Putilov works on 28 February 1921 and a state of emergency was declared. The Kronstadt garrison expressed full sympathy with the strikers, and put forward a programme which amounted to an attack on the monopolist position of the communist party within the State and on the economic policies of war communism, and called for new elections to the soviets. The crisis interrupted the deliberations of the tenth congress of the Russian Communist Party, in session at the time, and the delegates were sent to Petrograd to assist the army. Kronstadt was besieged and surrendered after ten days of fighting. Speaking to the fourth Comintern congress at the end of 1922, Lenin said that 'in 1921 . . . we felt the impact of a grave—I think it was the gravest—internal political crisis in Soviet Russia, which caused discontent among considerable numbers of the peasantry, and even of the workers.' That had happened because 'we had advanced too far in our economic offensive.']

THE SECOND AND TWO-AND-A-HALF INTERNATIONALS AS ACCOMPLICES OF THE
COUNTER-REVOLUTION

The victories of the Red Army, and the steadily growing movement of protest among English and French workers, have forced the Entente to cease open warfare against Soviet Russia. The leading power in world counter-revolution, England, was compelled to sign a trade agreement with Soviet Russia because the English workers looked to it to reduce unemployment. So now the Entente States are seeking out all kinds of other methods of overthrowing the Soviet Government. Entente agents are roaming all over Russia trying to stir up peasant revolts.

They tell the peasants that their land is no longer threatened by the nobles or by the white generals, and that they have no need to supply the industrial workers with grain. Peasant revolts are to cut railway communications between the industrial centres and the grain areas, and hunger will then force the backward working masses to rise against the Soviet Government—this is the Entente's plan. The capitalist counter-revolution is counting on . . . a number of workers being so exhausted and harassed that they will be inclined to yield to the enticements of the counter-revolution. Working side by side with the usual Entente spies and the agents of monarchist organizations to these ends are the underground organizations of the Social-Revolutionary Party, and also part of the mensheviks, who belong to the Second International.

Their agitation was successful in provoking a rising among some of the Kronstadt sailors on 2 March. To explain the mere possibility of such a rising, it should be borne in mind that the old sailors of Kronstadt, the heroes of the October revolution, either fell on one of the many fronts of the civil war or are occupying responsible posts in the Red Army or in Soviet institutions. The Kronstadt garrison consisted in large part of peasants from the south of Russia, and of sons of bourgeois and petty-bourgeois families of technicians who had not finished their education, who had joined the navy, attracted by the comparatively good conditions of life it offered.

Dissatisfied, and irritated by the discipline prevailing in the fortress and on board ship . . . these sailors allowed themselves to be enticed by the S.R.s, anarchists, and monarchists who pursued their secret purposes under the apparently innocent slogans of new elections to the soviets. That they did not dare to proceed under the device of the Constituent Assembly or of restoration of the monarchy, shews that they realized that even these backward sailors would on no account consciously serve the cause of counter-revolution. . . . Behind the backs of the sailors they turned for help to capitalist governments and to counter-revolutionary organizations abroad. . . . Russian banks abroad, headed by the monarchist leader Guchkov and the former Tsarist minister Kokovtsov, immediately sent large sums to Finland for the support of the Kronstadt movement. The French and American Governments also at once mobilized support for Kronstadt under the flag of the Red Cross. This help, however, did not arrive quickly enough. The red troops, commanded by communists, went into action before the emigré counter-revolutionaries succeeded in reaching Kronstadt through Finland with their supplies. The Kronstadt counter-revolutionary attack was liquidated, and besides the many lessons which it taught the international working class, it succeeded at last in tearing the mask from the Second and Two-and-a-half Internationals. The entire Second International press stood on the side of the counter-revolution. . . . If these enemies of the proletarian dictatorship came out in favour of the Kronstadt sailors, who were allegedly calling for a genuine Soviet government, it was because they clearly understood that, should the Russian Soviet Government fall, the Vanderveldes and Scheidemanns would see the realization of their dream of the return to Russia of the only legal bourgeois government.

Far more important for an appraisal of the real state of affairs in the international labour movement is the fact that the press of the Two-and-a-half International, which in words supported the Russian revolution, the proletarian dictatorship, the Soviet Government, in fact also sang the praises of the Kronstadt rising. At a time when conscious Russian proletarians were falling in their thousands on the ice of the gulf of Finland, in the battle against the heavy artillery of the Kronstadt forts, and filling with their bodies the breach made by the Kronstadt revolt in the rampart which protects Petrograd from the Entente, the USPD *Freiheit* found nothing better to say than to denounce Comrade Zinoviev as the destroyer of the Russian proletariat and thus to surround the Kronstadt counter-revolutionary rising with a halo of martyrdom.

Jean Longuet in his organ *Populaire* published an article in honour of the Kronstadt rising. The Vienna *Arbeiterzeitung*, organ of Bauer and Friedrich Adler, was firmly on the side of the Kronstadt sailors. Thus, at a moment of world-historical importance, when the capitalist counter-revolution was striking a new blow, Hilferding, Crispien, Dittmann, Jean Longuet, Friedrich Adler, Otto Bauer, stood hand in hand with Wrangel, Miliukov, Kokovtsov, and the heroes of English and French espionage. This fact must penetrate the consciousness of the broad proletarian masses of the entire world. They will certainly now understand that the rising favoured by the entire Russian counter-revolutionary movement . . . is a counter-revolutionary rising, even though it hoisted the red flag and used the slogans which were used in Russia in 1917 when the power of the bourgeoisie was overthrown. . . .

Therefore down with the Second and the Two-and-a-half Internationals! Down with the open and the masked lackeys of the bourgeoisie!

ECCI STATEMENT ON THE MARCH ACTION IN GERMANY

6 *April* 1921   *K.I.*, 17, col. 4317, *June* 1921

[Rioting in the Mansfeld area of central Germany led on 16 March 1921 to the intervention of the Reichswehr. On the following day the central committee of the KPD called for open insurrection; although there was little response to this summons, it was followed a few days later by a call for a general strike, which brought members of the German Communist Party into conflict with their fellow workers as well as with the police and troops. There were many casualties, and thousands of arrests. On 31 March the action was called off.

Of the March action Trotsky wrote later that the German CP mistook its own impatience for a mature revolutionary situation. At the time Bela Kun and two less well-known Comintern emissaries were in Berlin, and the resignation of the five moderate members of the central committee enabled them to carry proposals for a more active policy. This was, both at the time and later, interpreted by many as action designed to help Russia, profoundly shaken in March 1921 by the Kronstadt revolt. Heckert, the German delegate to the Russian congress of trade unions in May 1921, said: 'These German communists let themselves be shot and thrown into prison because they were conscious that, in raising the standard of revolt, they were rendering aid to the Russian proletariat.'

At the third Comintern congress in the following summer Klara Zetkin said that 'the ECCI bore at any rate a great share of responsibility . . . for the incorrect slogans and incorrect political attitude of the central committee'. The question of ECCI responsibility was shelved at the congress, presumably because leading members of the ECCI were involved.

Zinoviev wrote later in the year: 'The leaders of the KPD made, it is true, only one mistake: they made an incorrect estimate of the situation.'

In the debate on the tactical theses at the third congress Trotsky said that the German workers must be told that the March action was a mistake; a repetition might really put an end to the party. 'We consider the philosophy of the offensive as the greatest danger and its practical application as the greatest political crime.' In the same debate Lenin said that in spite of faulty leadership and the absence of preparation for an offensive, the action marked a great step forward, because hundreds of thousands of workers had fought heroically against the bourgeoisie.

Trotsky replied to the assertion that, because of the serious Russian situation, the Comintern provoked in other countries revolutionary action which bore no relation to the situation there. 'If we were capable of such treachery, we would all deserve to be lined up against the wall and shot down one by one.'

Zinoviev's figure, given in the ECCI report to the third congress, of half a million workers drawn into the action, was disputed by some of the German delegates, who placed it, as a maximum, at 200,000. In the discussion Thalheimer said that although the March action was a defeat for the proletariat, it was not a defeat for the party; 'for the party it was a victory in the sense that it emerged from the struggle strengthened by the masses'. Communist party membership after the March action fell from over 400,000 to 180,000.

At the meeting of the ECCI in December 1921 Zinoviev began his report with Germany 'because the revolution is nearest there'. The March action, he said, was a heroic measure designed to counteract passivity and reformism in the working class, although it was not wholly free of irresponsibility and adventurism.

Radek, in an article published at the end of the year on 'The tasks of the Communist International', wrote that 'The mistakes of the March action were that the party used the methods appropriate to the final struggle for a partial struggle forced on them—armed insurrection when at the best the situation called for a mass strike'. He attributed this to the influence of the ex-USPD membership, who still entertained putschist ideas, and who, acting on 'the theory of the offensive', and in an attempt to avoid defeat, 'resorted to terrorist acts which repelled the masses'. The evidence about communist terrorism published by *Vorwärts* at the end of 1921 was followed by the resignation of Ernst Reuter, at that time secretary of the KPD, and some other prominent members.

In a speech to the Moscow communists shortly before the opening of the fourth Comintern congress Trotsky said: 'These two retreats of ours [in 1921], the one in the economic field and the other in the political field in Europe, are intimately linked, because we could have developed war communism into complete socialism and communism without retreating, on one condition, namely, that the proletariat of Europe seized power in 1919 and 1920. . . . The signal for a review of the international tasks of communism was given by the March 1921 events in Germany. . . . During the March days of 1921 in Germany we saw a communist party—devoted, revolutionary, ready for struggle—rushing forward, but not followed by the working class. . . . Because of its revolutionary impatience this most revolutionary section of the working class came into collision with the rest and tried, mechanically as it were, and here and there by force, to draw them into the struggle. . . . The party incurred the risk of shattering itself not so much against the resistance of the bourgeoisie, as against the resistance of four-fifths or two-thirds of the working class itself. But at that moment the International sounded the alarm, proclaiming a new stage.']

For the first time since the January and March days of 1919 the revolutionary proletarians of Germany have entered into battle against the capitalist government, not only for a piece of bread, not only as a protest against the violence of the white gangs, but in an attempt to bring to an end the rule of the German exploiters. For the first time they took up the struggle as a strongly fused mass moved by one will. They showed the whole of Germany that millions of proletarians are ready to sacrifice their lives to win freedom from the rule of capital.

This first organized assault of the revolutionary German proletariat was not crowned with success. The proletariat suffered defeat thanks to the *unconscionable treachery* of the German Socialist Party, whose members—all those Hörsings and Severings—are playing Noske's part even now, under a purely bourgeois government. Further, thanks to the open going over of the Independent Socialist Party of Germany to the camp of the counter-revolution, the proletariat could not establish a united front against the united bourgeoisie. Relying more on the disarray among the proletariat than on their own bayonets, the German bourgeoisie are again celebrating a victory. But their rejoicings will be short-lived. The proletariat gained a great deal of experience in the struggle. It will know better how to prepare for the forthcoming struggle, and its call to arms will find a response among broader and broader masses, for the bourgeoisie will be less inclined and less able than ever to satisfy even the most trifling demands of the proletariat.

Hörsing triumphed, but Foch is on the Rhine; and the victors in the field of civil war are feeling round their necks the noose of victorious world capital. The bourgeoisie, aware that they cannot rely on the defeated working masses, will yield to the demands of victorious world capital in order to unload all the burdens imposed by the Entente on to the backs of the German proletariat.

The moment will soon draw near when the workers, basely deceived by the SPD and the USPD and the trade union bureaucrats, will understand that they have to choose between shameful apathy under the double yoke of German and Entente capital, and a bold united struggle for power, for a Soviet Germany. We, together with you, mourn the heroic victims who have fallen in the struggle for proletarian liberation. We, together with you, think with anger and bitterness of the sufferings of our arrested comrades at the mercy of the harsh and arbitrary jurisdiction of the democratic courts-martial. The first assault of the German proletarian vanguard has suffered defeat. The bourgeoisie and their lackeys will try to bring disorder into the ranks of the retreating troops.

The Communist International says to you: You acted rightly! The working class can never win victory by a single blow. You have turned a new page in the history of the German working class. Prepare for new struggles. Study the lessons of your past struggles. Learn from your experience. Close your ranks, strengthen your organization, legal and illegal, strengthen proletarian discipline and communist unity in struggle.

> Long live the united communist proletariat of Germany!
> Long live the proletarian revolution in Germany!
> Long live the Communist International!

ECCI STATEMENT ON THE EXPULSION OF PAUL LEVI

29 *April* 1921   *K.I.*, 17, col. 4295, *June* 1921

[Paul Levi was in Austria when the March action began. He returned to Germany, and on 29 March wrote to Lenin describing it as a 'putsch'. His pamphlet *Unser Weg*, attacking the action and those responsible for it, was sent to the press on 3 April, and he was expelled from the KPD on 15 April. In his pamphlet he described the action as 'war by the communist party on the working class'. The initial impulse had come from persons without any understanding of the situation, and the ECCI must be held at least partly responsible because it interpreted the strong anti-putschist tendencies in the KPD as opportunism. ECCI delegates, he said, 'never work with, but always behind and frequently against the central committee of the country to which they are sent. . . . The ECCI acts like a Cheka projected beyond the Russian frontiers.' He was bitterly critical of the 'irresponsible game' being played with the existence of the party, and with the life and fate of its members.

In conversation with Klara Zetkin, Lenin said that Levi's criticism of the March action was entirely negative, and embittered his colleagues more by its tone than by its content. 'You know how highly I value Paul Levi. . . . Ruthless criticism of the March action was necessary, but what did Paul Levi give? He tore the party to pieces. . . . He gave nothing to which the party could usefully turn. He lacks the spirit of solidarity with the party, and it was that which has made the rank and file . . . deaf and blind to the great deal of truth in Levi's criticism, particularly to his correct political principles. . . . The "leftists" have to thank Paul Levi that up to the present they have come out so well, much too well.'

At the third congress Klara Zetkin defended Levi. He wrote his pamphlet, she asserted, only because the party centre was persisting in its incorrect line. Levi was being made the whipping boy; he had acted honestly, to save the proletariat. To Radek's interjection that Levi's pamphlet had supplied material for the public prosecutor, she replied that the manifestoes and articles in the *Rote Fahne* had supplied him with even more. 'I can take 20 lines from anybody's writings and bring him to the gallows.'

After his expulsion, Levi formed a new Reichstag fraction, the Kommunistische Arbeitsgemeinschaft (KAG), which was joined by other dissident members of the KPD fraction, including Däumig.

In a letter to the Jena congress of the German Communist Party in August 1921 Lenin explained that he 'defended Paul Levi so long at the third congress because . . . *in essentials*, much of Levi's criticism of the March uprising in Germany was *right*', but his criticism 'was clothed in an impermissible and harmful form'.

After the disclosures in *Vorwärts* about organized terrorist action by the KPD during the March action, a central committee resolution attacking the KAG prohibited communist party members from giving it any direct or indirect support.

At its conference on 19 February 1922 the USPD agreed on the admission of the KAG.]

The ECCI at its meeting on 29 April held a thorough discussion of the situation created in the United Communist Party of Germany. In regard to the celebrated pamphlet by Paul Levi there was complete unanimity. All members of the ECCI spoke of it with burning indignation. The general opinion was—Paul Levi is a traitor. In the name of the small bureau and the entire ECCI, comrade Zinoviev declared, 'It is an abominable lie that the ECCI or its representatives provoked the March rising. This fable was needed by the German counter-revolution, on whose side Levi stood.'

Sentiments of ardent sympathy and affection were expressed for our German brothers, fighting and languishing in prison.

At the end of the discussion the following resolution was unanimously adopted:

Having examined the situation created in the VKPD by the March action, the ECCI declares:

1. In regard to the tactical differences arising in connexion with the March action, the ECCI thinks it necessary, because of the great international importance of the question, to submit the question to the third congress of the Communist International and asks the German comrades to see that all the material shall be made available to the third world congress.

2. The ECCI is not in a position to decide whether or not the VKPD shall hold an extraordinary congress before the third world congress. It suggests, however, that with the white terror now prevailing in Germany, serious preparations for a congress, and the work of the congress itself, may perhaps be impossible to carry out. If the central committee of the VKPD shares this opinion, the ECCI invites all German comrades to adhere to this decision.

3. Having read Paul Levi's pamphlet *Unser Weg wider den Putschismus*,

the ECCI ratifies the decision to expel Paul Levi from the United Communist Party of Germany and, consequently, from the Third International. Even if Paul Levi were nine-tenths right in his views of the March offensive, he would still be liable to expulsion from the party because of his unprecedented violation of discipline and because, by his action, *in the given circumstances*, he dealt the party a blow in the back.

4. In view of the persecution of the party by the Government, the ECCI considers it the unconditional duty of all members of the VKPD, notwithstanding all their differences, to enter with closed ranks and maintaining strict discipline, into implacable struggle against the reaction now raging.

President: G. ZINOVIEV

ECCI: Russia: LENIN, TROTSKY, BUKHARIN, RADEK
France: ROSMER
England: QUELCH, BELL
Hungary: BELA KUN, RUDNIANSKY, VARGA
Poland: WALECKI
Bulgaria: DIMITROV, POPOV, SHABLIN
Finland: KUUSINEN, MANNER, RAHIA
Norway: FRIIS
Austria: STEINHARDT
Holland: JANSEN
Georgia: TSKHAKAYA
Latvia: STUCHKA
Switzerland: ITSCHNER
Persia: SULTAN-ZADE
Communist Youth International: SHATSKIN

EXTRACTS FROM AN ECCI MANIFESTO ON THE PAYMENT OF
REPARATIONS BY GERMANY

7 *May* 1921   *K.I.*, 17, col. 4311, *June* 1921

[After prolonged disputes and correspondence between the German and Allied Governments and the reparations commission, and appeals from Germany to the League of Nations, the Pope, and President Harding, the Allied Governments drew up a new schedule of reparations payments, which was on 5 May 1921 sent to the German Government with a six-day ultimatum threatening further sanctions (three towns in the Ruhr had been occupied in March) if the new terms were not accepted. On 11 May the Reichstag voted 225–172 to accept the schedule. The minority vote included the communist and the right-wing parties.

At the third congress Kolarov (Bulgaria) complained that during the reparations crisis the French and German communist parties had pursued different policies, and the Executive had failed to lay down a clear line.]

TO THE PROLETARIANS OF ALL COUNTRIES
WORKING MEN AND WOMEN!

The Entente, led by the French Government, is preparing to draw the noose round the neck of Germany in order to compel it to agree to demands which would amount to the economic suicide of sixty million people.

The German bourgeoisie, covetous, bloodthirsty, and brutally cruel when, protected by cannon, they lorded it over almost half the world, are not now in a position to defend the vital interests of the German people. Not only because they cannot reject the Entente's demands . . . but primarily because they fear the unarmed German workers even more than they fear the troops of the Entente, armed from head to foot; because, having waded knee deep in the blood of the German proletarians, they know that the workers of other countries also hate them. If they accept the conditions put forward by the Entente usurers, Germany's economic situation will get so much worse that the workers, driven to desperation, will be forced to rise against the robber Entente and its German underlings.

We do not yet know whether the German bourgeoisie have already submitted to the Entente in order to avert the occupation of the Ruhr. Perhaps the blow has already fallen. . . .

German workers! If you continue to put up with the Government of capitalists and junkers, you will at the same time be helping the robbers of the imperialist Entente to rivet Germany in the chains of slavery. . . . The Russian people not only found in themselves the strength to defend their rights against the Entente, but also attracted to their side the workers of the whole world. . . . Only by breaking the class Government of Stinnes, by establishing the rule of the working class, and by forming an alliance between Soviet Germany and Soviet Russia can the proletariat find salvation, if it does not want to perish in the dual fetters of the German and Entente bourgeoisie.

To you, proletarians of France, England, and all the vassal States of the Entente . . . we say: rise vigorously against the robber campaign plotted by your governments—not for the sake of bourgeois junker Germany, but for your own sakes. . . .

If you allow Germany to be strangled, it will not be long before the sweated labour of the German helots will force your bosses to reduce your wages. . . .

When the German proletariat comes out with the slogans:

Down with the German capitalist Government!
Long live Soviet Germany!
Long live the alliance with Soviet Russia!

let the echo sound from the Vistula to the Elbe, from the Rhine and the Channel

Down with the Versailles robbers!
Peace to the cottages—war on the palaces!

EXTRACTS FROM AN ECCI CIRCULAR ON THE AGENDA OF THE THIRD
COMINTERN CONGRESS

May 1921   *K.I.*, 17, col. 4031, *June* 1921

[At the time of the congress, Rakosi claimed in an article in *Pravda*, the International had 51 sections with a total membership of 2,800,000; of these the Russian party accounted for 550,000, the German and Czechoslovakian parties for 300,000 each, the French 130,000, Norway 97,000, Yugoslavia 85,000, and Italy 70,000; the Youth International had an affiliated membership of 800,000. Of the 646 daily newspapers, 500 were published in Russia, 45 in the Ukraine, and 33 in Germany.]

TO ALL PROLETARIAN ORGANIZATIONS BELONGING TO OR WISHING TO JOIN
THE COMINTERN

The third world congress of the Communist International will open in Moscow on 1 June 1921. We have called the conference two months earlier than laid down in the statutes, and are sure that the parties affiliated to the Comintern will agree with us that the interests of the cause require the date to be put forward.

In the nine months which have passed since the second world congress broad discussions have taken place in a whole series of parties on all the questions resolved at the second congress. In a number of countries differentiation has reached the point at which at last there is an open break between the communists and the followers of the 'centre'. In Germany, in France, England, Sweden, Norway, Rumania, Yugoslavia, Greece, Switzerland, Belgium, and other countries the rupture between the communists and the adherents of the intermediate Two-and-a-half 'International' is an accomplished fact. . . .

During that time the ECCI had to make a number of most important decisions, on which it will have to report to the entire Communist International.

The third congress will first of all have to satisfy itself in regard to the extent to which each of the affiliated parties has in fact carried out all the conditions advanced by the second congress. An important period of Comintern activity is drawing to an end. Up to its first congress the Communist International went through its gestatory, preparatory period. Between the first and the second congress the Comintern lived through its initial period of agitation. At that time it was not yet a formal international organization. It was only a banner. The period between the second and third congress was a period of greater differentiation, and of the formation of genuine communist parties. The third congress will draw up the balance sheet of all the work done and give the Comintern a finished organization and clearcut tactics. . . .

The Comintern must lay down a firm and definite rule: the ECCI is entirely responsible to the regular world congress. Appeals can be made to the world congress against an ECCI decision. But between one congress and the next the entire conduct of affairs is in the hands of the ECCI. Its decisions must be carried out. Without that the Comintern cannot exist as a centralized and disciplined international organization. If the Communist International is not to call itself the international of action in vain, then as a fighting organization it must have a general staff and there must be certainty that discipline will be maintained not only in words but in fact.

The tactics of forming communist cells inside the trade unions, put forward by the second congress, have been justified. They have had considerable success in Germany, France, England, and other countries. The first substantial blows have been struck against the yellow Amsterdam federation. The yellow leaders vacillate from side to side. Today they are prepared to make concessions, tomorrow they start excluding from the unions all supporters of the Comintern. This is a certain sign of their complete future bankruptcy. . . .

The Comintern has had its first successes in work among the Eastern peoples. The Baku congress of the peoples of the East was of great and undoubted historical importance. The congress of the peoples of the Far East which is to be held will also play its part. The third congress will have to deal with the Eastern question not only theoretically, as at the second congress, but as a practical matter. Without a revolution in Asia there will be no victory for the world proletarian revolution. This too must be firmly grasped by every proletarian communist. Only then will the worker communists be adequately armed ideologically against the 'European' opportunism of Herr Hilferding and other heroes of the Two-and-a-half International, who have in stock nothing but disdainful smiles for the oppressed peoples of the East.

The question of the Italian Socialist Party, the tenth item on the agenda, will be of the greatest importance. The Italian Socialist Party formerly belonged to the Comintern. Under the influence of Serrati's 'centrist' agitation the congress of that party at Leghorn refused in fact to apply the 21 conditions put forward by the second Comintern conrgess for all parties. . . . The worker-communists formed an independent communist party. In these circumstances the ECCI considered it its duty to recognize the young Italian Communist Party as the *only* section of the Comintern in Italy, and to expel from the Comintern Serrati's party, which had in fact repudiated the second congress decisions. The Italian Socialist Party protested against this and appealed from the ECCI to the Comintern congress. . . .

In a special letter to the central committee of the Italian Socialist Party the ECCI wrote: 'We invite you to the third congress, but we ask (1) that your delegates should be fully empowered to give definite answers to the congress, (2) that you answer clearly and precisely whether you agree to the expulsion from a Comintern party of the group of Turati, Treves & co.'

The Italian question has assumed international importance. In January Levi's group, which had long been anxious to create some kind of a right wing in the Comintern, seized on the Italian dispute, asserting that the ECCI had made 'tactical' mistakes and was advocating 'mechanical' splits and so on. . . .

We ask all parties and unions belonging to or wishing to join the Comintern to open immediately the widest possible discussion of the third congress agenda in their press and at meetings. We ask them further to deal at once with the question of electing delegates to the congress. The ECCI unanimously agreed to suggest to all parties: (1) that the delegation to the congress should be as large as possible; (2) that one-third of the delegation should be members of the central committee, the other two-thirds to be drawn from the most important *local* organizations and be most closely connected with the working masses. We attach particularly great importance to this last point.

With communist greetings,
President of the ECCI

THE THIRD CONGRESS OF THE COMMUNIST INTERNATIONAL

[The third Comintern congress, held from 22 June to 12 July 1921, was attended by 509 delegates from 48 countries, of whom 291 had full voting rights. Its meetings were dominated by the discussion of the March action in Germany. This, the Kronstadt rising, and the New Economic Policy in Russia, brought to a close the first period of the Comintern's history. 'With the third congress', Trotsky wrote later, 'it is realized that the post-war revolutionary ferment is over. . . . The turn is taken to winning the masses, using the united front, that is, organizing the masses on a programme of transitional demands'. The broad revolutionary perspectives opened by the war and its consequences had not led to the victory of the proletariat, he said, because of the absence of revolutionary parties able and willing to seize power.

Comparing the second and third congresses, Lenin, using Japanese action at Port Arthur as an analogy, said that the Comintern had passed from the tactics of assault to the tactics of siege, infiltration taking the place of open armed struggle.

Zinoviev, at the end of the year, wrote that the third congress had to take note of a slower rate of development in the proletarian revolution than the first congress assumed. The Comintern's task now was to win positions from the social-democrats and the reformist unions, using the tactics of siege, not of assault. Thus, although Levi had been expelled for attacking the policy of artificially creating revolutionary situations, it was his policy which was in fact adopted; the question was thoroughly debated in the Politburo of the Russian Communist Party before the congress.

In his closing speech Zinoviev singled out as the two chief events of the congress the tactical theses and the expulsion of the Italian Socialist Party. The tactical theses made it clear that in Europe and America the enemy was stronger, cleverer, and better prepared for struggle than the enemy the Bolsheviks had to face in Russia in 1917; therefore the work and preparation of the parties for the struggle must be careful, thorough, and solid.

The expulsion of the Italian Socialist Party re-defined the attitude to centrists. 'Who is not with us is against us.' But they would continue to agitate among the membership over the heads of the leaders.

At the subsequent congress Trotsky said: 'At the third congress the over-whelming majority called to order those elements in the International whose views involved the danger that the vanguard might by precipitate action be shattered against the passivity and immaturity of the working masses, and against the strength of the capitalist State. That was the greatest danger. . . . In so far as there was a retreat, it ran parallel with the economic retreat in Russia.'

In the discussion of Lenin's report on the tactics of the Russian Communist Party, Sachs (KAPD) argued that agreements and treaties which contributed to Russia's economic progress also strengthened capitalism in the countries with which the treaties were concluded. The International had not given thought to this conflict of interests. Sachs referred to an interview given by Krasin to the *Rote Fahne* in which the British miners' strike was said to have interfered with the execution of the Anglo-Soviet trade agreement.

Radek and Bukharin, in reply, derided the idea that Soviet purchases in western Europe could halt the economic crisis. Radek in his speech contended that any measure 'which is a necessity from the standpoint of Soviet Russia is also a necessity from the standpoint of the world revolution'. Real help could not be given to the British miners because the Comintern was not in a position to persuade the German and American miners' unions to prevent the export of coal to the United Kingdom. Bukharin added that trade with Russia intensified competition among the capitalist States, and consequently heightened the political antagonisms between them; and, finally, that the balance of advantage was to Russia, which got more economic benefit from the trade and concessions than capitalism did.

The discussion of the 'question of the Orient' was opened by Mann (CPGB) with a short tub-thumping speech; the Turkish delegate spoke of the persecution of communists by Kemal Pasha (the Turkish Communist Party held its first congress in Baku); nevertheless the communists supported his movement because it was anti-imperialist, and the defeat of imperialism was the beginning of the world revolution. M. N. Roy, the Indian delegate, used the five minutes allotted to him to make 'an energetic protest' against the opportunist way in which the Eastern question was discussed. No attention had been paid to it during the congress and when, the previous day, the commission had at last met not a single member of the European or American delegations had attended. The Chinese delegate also urged the International and the national sections to pay more attention and give more support to the movement in the Far East. Roy's protest was supported by a French delegate, who alleged that the Eastern bureau of the Comintern had made no approach to the communist parties of the western countries.

Debates on the Italian Socialist Party and the KAPD also occupied a large amount of the congress's time. The KAPD delegates to the third congress were Bergmann, Hempel, Sachs, and Seemann. They were the only delegation to support the 'workers' opposition' in the debate on the Russian Communist Party. They complained that the Russian and Comintern press gave misleading accounts of the KAPD, and refused to publish their corrections. The congress declared that the KAPD, having been given sufficient time, must now either join the KPD or be expelled. The KAPD rejected amalgamation with the KPD. Expulsion followed at the ECCI meeting held after the congress, in a resolution which asserted that the KAPD had published a number of pamphlets and articles 'of a counter-revolutionary character'. The ECCI considered 'any association with the KAPD impossible until that party publicly renounces those counter-revolutionary ideas'.]

EXTRACTS FROM THE RESOLUTION OF THE THIRD COMINTERN
CONGRESS ON THE REPORT OF THE EXECUTIVE COMMITTEE

29 *June* 1921   *Protokoll*, iii, p. 408

[The discussion of the ECCI report, given by Zinoviev, lasted for three sessions; it was concerned chiefly with the German situation. Zinoviev stated that since the second congress the Executive had held 31 sessions, and had set up an inner bureau of 7 members to deal, inter alia, with secret and illegal activities; it had met 39 times. He emphasized that while the Executive was always subject to the next congress, it had complete control of the conduct of the Comintern between congresses, and its decisions must be carried out. Not all parties had sent their representatives to the ECCI. It was essential to have the best comrades on the ECCI, so that it could act as the general staff of the revolution. The adherence of the USPD had been the greatest success achieved since the second congress; he asserted that after Halle he had warned the German party not to allow itself to be provoked prematurely, but the March action was not a putsch; it was a revolutionary episode, a defensive, not an offensive action. The charge that control from Moscow was too tight was unjustified. 'On the contrary, we have been a much too loose organization. . . . We must be much more centralized. Our contacts must be firmer and tighter than before. A lot of nonsense is being talked about the dictatorship of Moscow; in fact the only charge that can be levelled against us is that we were not centralist enough, not tightly enough organized.' It was in the discussion of Zinoviev's report that the Dutch and KAPD delegates voiced their misgivings about the influence of Russian interests on Comintern policy. Zinoviev had referred to an article by Gorter urging the political and organizational separation of the Comintern from the system of Russian State policy—'we must aim at this goal if we are to do justice to the conditions of the west European revolution'—and had said that they would be only too glad if a revolution in Germany enabled them to transfer the centre of the world movement to Berlin. The argument was reiterated by the KAPD delegates at the congress. 'We do not for a moment forget the difficulties into which Russian Soviet power has fallen owing to the postponement of world revolution. But we also see the danger that out of these difficulties there may arise an apparent or real contradiction between the interests of the revolutionary world proletariat and the momentary interests of Soviet Russia.'

Another KAPD delegate objected to the ECCI treating every criticism as counter-revolutionary. 'This means the throttling of all opposition, and proves that the need for an opposition is not understood; without it an organization as great as the International is condemned to stagnation.'

The French delegation asked for a full statement from the Executive on the March action before voting on the report, but their proposal was rejected after a heated discussion.

The paragraph on work in the Near and Far East was put forward as an amendment by the delegates from those areas. The 'national and colonial question' was scarcely touched on in the proceedings of the congress; M. N. Roy, the Indian delegate, criticized this as 'sheer opportunism' (a reference to the Soviet-British trade agreement, which stipulated that the contracting parties would refrain from hostile propaganda, and to the agreements concluded by Russia in the spring of 1921 with Persia, Turkey, and Afghanistan). At the end of the discussion the resolution was taken paragraph by paragraph; the Yugoslav delegation abstained from voting on the paragraph concerning Germany, and the Mexican delegation on the paragraph concerning the KAPD; the resolution as a whole was passed unanimously.]

The congress takes cognizance with satisfaction of the report of the Executive and states that the policy and activity of the Executive over the past year were aimed at carrying out the decisions of the second congress. The congress approves in particular the application by the Executive of the 21 conditions drawn up by the second congress to the various countries; likewise it approves the actions of the Executive directed to the formation of large communist mass parties and to the relentless combating of the opportunist tendencies manifested in these parties.

1. In Italy the attitude of the Serrati group of leaders showed, directly after the second congress, that they were not seriously concerned with the decisions of the world congress and the Communist International. Above all, the part played by this group in the September struggles, their attitude at Leghorn, and even more their subsequent policy, proved clearly that they want to use communism only as a sham façade for their opportunist policy. In these circumstances the split was unavoidable. The congress welcomes the firm and resolute action of the Executive in this matter, which is of fundamental importance. It approves the decision of the EC, which recognized the Communist Party of Italy as the only communist section in that country.

After the communists had left the Leghorn congress, it passed the following resolution. . . . 'In once again fully confirming its adherence to the Communist International, the congress submits the conflict to the forthcoming congress of the Communist International, and in doing so undertakes to abide by and to carry out its decision.'

The third congress of the Communist International is convinced that this decision of the Serrati group of leaders was forced on them by the pressure of the revolutionary workers. The congress expects that these revolutionary elements in the working class will do everything in their power, now that the third world congress has made its decisions, to put them into effect.

In reply to the address of the Leghorn congress to the third world congress, the third world congress declares, by way of ultimatum:

So long as the Socialist Party of Italy does not expel those who took part in the reformist conference in Reggio Emilia and their followers, the SPI cannot belong to the CI.

If this condition should be fulfilled, the third world congress instructs the Executive to see that the necessary steps are taken to amalgamate the SPI, purged of its reformist and centrist elements, with the CPI into a unified section of the Communist International.

2. In Germany the congress of the USPD in Halle, held as a result of the decisions of the second world congress, took stock of the development of the workers' movement. The attitude of the Executive was designed to promote the formation of a strong CP in Germany, and experience has shown that this policy was correct.

The congress also fully approves the attitude of the Executive to the subsequent events within the VKPD. The congress trusts that in the future too the Executive will strictly apply the principles of international revolutionary discipline.

3. The admission of the KAPD to the CI as a sympathizing party was intended to test whether the KAPD would develop in the direction of the CI. The waiting period has been long enough. Now the KAPD must be

asked for its hitherto delayed adherence to the VKPD; otherwise it will be expelled as a sympathizing party from the CI.

The congress welcomes the manner in which the Executive applied the 21 conditions to the French party, which detached large masses of workers, who are on the road to communism, from the influence of Longuet, the opportunists and centrists, and accelerated their development. The congress trusts that in future too the Executive will actively promote the development of the French party into a militant and clear-principled party. . . .

In approving the work of the Executive in the Near and Far East, the congress welcomes the broadly conceived agitation carried on there, and thinks it essential that organizational work shall now be undertaken in these countries.

Finally, the congress rejects the objections to a strict international centralization of the communist movement raised by open and concealed enemies of communism. Rather it expresses its conviction that the parties must place their best forces at the disposal of the Executive in order to obtain an even more militant central political leadership of communist parties held together in one unbreakable union. The lack of central leadership has been shown, for example, in the questions of the unemployed and of reparations, where the Executive did not act quickly and effectively enough. The congress trusts that the Executive, with the greater co-operation of the member parties, will work out an improved machinery for maintaining contact and will, with greater participation by the parties in the Executive, be in the position to carry out its constantly growing tasks to an even greater extent than formerly.

EXTRACTS FROM THE THESES ON THE WORLD SITUATION AND THE TASKS OF THE COMINTERN ADOPTED BY THE THIRD COMINTERN CONGRESS

4 July 1921   *Thesen und Resolutionen*, iii, p. 7

[In a long speech on 23 June on the world economic crisis and the new tasks of the Comintern, Trotsky, who with Varga drafted the theses, which were designed to combat the 'theory of the offensive', surveyed the various defeats suffered by revolutionary movements since 1919 and proceeded to an analysis of the economic position of the leading powers, world trade, the prospects of economic recovery, the social changes effected by the war, and the international political scene, particularly Anglo-American rivalry. He concluded that capitalism had managed to restore a temporary and uncertain equilibrium, while the situation remained at bottom revolutionary. 'Whether slow or quick—we will not argue about the rate of development, after history deceived us so badly on this question

—the development is towards revolution. . . . We are not now confronted with the chaotic and elemental assault that we witnessed in Europe in 1918–1919. . . . At that time it seemed to us, with some historical justification, possible that the assault would mount and move forward in higher and higher waves . . . and that the working class would in a year or two achieve State power. It was a historical possibility, but it did not happen. . . . History has given the bourgeoisie a fairly long breathing spell. . . . The revolution is not so obedient, so tame, that it can be led on a leash, as we imagined. It has its ups and downs, its crises and booms.' After a brief discussion, in which a KAPD delegate criticized the theses, they were passed unanimously.]

1. The revolutionary movement at the end of the imperialist war and after it was marked by an amplitude unprecedented in history. . . . It did not, however, end with the overthrow of world capitalism, or even of European capitalism.

2. During the year which has passed between the second and third congresses of the Communist International, a series of working class risings and struggles have ended in partial defeat (the advance of the Red Army on Warsaw in August 1920, the movement of the Italian proletariat in September 1920, the rising of the German workers in March 1921).

The first period of the post-war revolutionary movement, distinguished by the spontaneous character of its assault, by the marked imprecision of its aims and methods, and by the extreme panic which it aroused among the ruling classes, seems in essentials to be over. The self-confidence of the bourgeoisie as a class, and the outward stability of their State organs, have undeniably been strengthened. The panic fear of communism has abated, even if it has not altogether disappeared. The leaders of the bourgeoisie are even boasting of the power of their State machine and have gone over to an offensive against the workers in all countries both on the economic and the political front.

3. Consequently the Communist International puts to itself and to the entire working class the following questions: To what extent do the new relations between the bourgeoisie and the proletariat correspond with the real relation of forces? Are the bourgeoisie really about to re-establish the social equilibrium destroyed by the war? Are there reasons for thinking that after the political upheavals and class struggles a new and prolonged epoch of the restoration and expansion of capitalism is about to open? Does it not follow from this that the programme and tactics of the Communist International should be revised? . . .

5. The period of demobilization, when the massacre that had been prolonged for four years had ceased, the period of transition from a state of war to a state of peace, inevitably accompanied by an economic crisis arising from the exhaustion and chaos of war, rightly appeared most dangerous in the eyes of the bourgeoisie. In fact in the two years following

its end the countries which had been ravaged by war became the scene of powerful proletarian movements.

The fact that a few months after the war it was not the apparently inevitable crisis but economic recovery which set in was one of the chief reasons why the bourgeoisie retained their dominant position. This period lasted about a year and a half. Industry absorbed practically all the demobilized workers. Although as a rule wages did not catch up with food prices, they rose enough to create a mirage of economic gain. It was precisely the favourable economic circumstances of 1919–1920 which, by ameliorating the most acute phase of liquidation of the war, encouraged the self-confidence of the bourgeoisie, and raised the question of the opening of a new epoch of organic capitalist development. At bottom, however, the recovery of 1919–1920 did not mark the beginning of the restoration of capitalist economy after the war; it only continued the artificial prosperity created by the war. . . .

8. At the cost of the further organic dislocation of the economic system (increase in fictitious capital, currency depreciation, speculation instead of rehabilitation), the bourgeois governments, acting in concert with the banks and the industrial trusts, succeeded in staving off the outbreak of the economic crisis until the political crisis brought about by demobilization and the first post-war squaring of accounts had subsided. Having gained a substantial respite, the bourgeoisie imagined that the danger of a crisis had been averted for an indefinite time. They became extremely optimistic. It seemed that the needs of reconstruction would open a prolonged era of industrial and commercial prosperity and above all of successful speculation. The year 1920 shattered these hopes. . . .

9. Thus the crisis of 1920, and this is essential to a correct understanding of the world situation, was not an ordinary phase of the 'normal' industrial cycle, but rather a profound reaction to the fictitious prosperity of wartime and the two years after the war, a prosperity based on destruction and exhaustion. The normal sequence of boom and crisis used to occur on a rising curve of industrial development. During the last seven years, however, European production, instead of rising, has fallen steeply. . . . In these circumstances periods of prosperity can only be of short duration, and largely speculative in character; crises will be prolonged and severe. The present crisis in Europe is a crisis of under-production. . . .

12. The illusory character of the boom is most evident in Germany. Over a period of a year and a half, in which prices increased sevenfold, production steadily declined. Germany's ostensibly successful participation in post-war international trade was paid for both by squandering the country's basic capital and by a further decline in the working classes' standard of life. . . . The German workers are becoming the coolies of Europe. . . .

14. Developments in the United States during the war were in certain respects the opposite of those in Europe. . . . Before the war it exported primarily agricultural products and raw materials which accounted for two-thirds of its total exports. Now, on the contrary, it exports primarily industrial products which account for sixty per cent. Before the war America was a debtor country; now it has become the creditor of the entire world. About half of the total world's gold reserve has been concentrated in the United States, and gold continues to flow steadily towards America. The determining role of the pound sterling on the world market has passed to the dollar.

15. But even American capitalism has been shaken out of its equilibrium. The immense expansion of American industry was determined by a singular combination of circumstances, by the absence of European competition, and above all by the European demand for war supplies. Ruined Europe has not been able even after the war to regain its position as a competitor with America on the world market, while as a market for American goods it cannot have anything like the importance which it had formerly. . . . In the United States the crisis is the beginning of a deep-seated and lasting disruption of the economy resulting from the war in Europe. That is the result of the destruction of the former world division of labour.

16. Japan also profited from the war to expand its place on the world market. Its development was incomparably smaller than that of the United States and in a number of industries has a purely hothouse artificial character. While its productive forces were great enough to win markets deserted by competitors, they are insufficient to retain them in the struggle with more powerful capitalist countries. Hence the severe crisis, which in fact began in Japan. . . .

18. Thus whether we examine production, trade, or credit, and not only in Europe but on all world markets, we find no reason to affirm that any stable equilibrium is being restored. Europe's economic decline continues, but the full extent of the destruction of the foundations of European economy will be revealed only in the years to come. The world market is disorganized. Europe needs American products but has nothing to offer in return. Europe is suffering from anaemia; America from plethora. The gold standard has gone. The depreciation of European currencies (which has in some cases reached ninety-nine per cent) presents the most serious obstacle to international trade. The unceasing and violent fluctuations in the exchanges transform capitalist production into wild speculation. The world market has no universal standard of value. The gold standard can be re-established in Europe only by increasing exports and reducing imports. But ruined Europe is incapable of making this change. America, on the other hand, is protecting itself against European dumping by raising its tariff barriers. Europe remains a lunatic asylum. Most of the countries

prohibit exports and imports and multiply their protective tariffs. England is taking measures against German exports and the entire economic life of Germany is at the mercy of a gang of Allied speculators, particularly the French. The territory of Austria-Hungary has been cut by a dozen tariff barriers. . . .

19. The disappearance of Soviet Russia, both as a market for industrial products and as a supplier of raw materials, helped appreciably to shatter the world economic equilibrium. Russia's return to the world market cannot in the near future make any great change. . . .

20. The war, which destroyed productive forces to a degree unprecedented in history, did not arrest the process of social differentiation. On the contrary, the proletarianization of the large middle strata, including the new middle class (employees and civil servants, etc.) and the concentration of property in the hands of small cliques (trusts, cartels, consortiums, etc.) have made enormous progress in the last seven years in the countries which suffered most from the war. . . .

Thus in regard to material resources Europe has been set back decades, while social tensions have become more acute; far from being arrested, their growth has been greatly accelerated. This cardinal fact is by itself enough to belie any hope of prolonged and peaceful development on a democratic basis. Progressive differentiation on the one hand, and, on the other, proletarianization and pauperization caused by economic decline will give the class struggle a tense, bitter, and convulsive character. In this respect the crisis only continues the work of the war and post-war speculative boom. . . .

22. The fall in the purchasing power of money has hit public and private employees more severely as a rule than the proletariat. The lower and middle ranks, their security shattered, have become an element of political unrest which undermines the structure of the State they serve. The new middle class, which, according to the reformists, was the pillar of conservatism, may rather become during the epoch of transition a revolutionary factor.

23. Capitalist Europe has finally lost its predominant economic position. That was the foundation of its relatively stable class structure. All the efforts of the European countries (England and to some extent France) to restore that situation can only aggravate the chaos and insecurity.

24. While in Europe the concentration of property has been based on general impoverishment, in the United States both this concentration and the greater acuteness of class antagonisms have reached an extreme degree on the basis of a feverish expansion of wealth. The sudden changes in the economic situation because of the general uncertainties of the world market give to the class struggle in America an extremely tense and revolutionary character. A period of capitalist expansion unprecedented in

history is bound to be followed by an unusual outburst of revolutionary struggle.

25. The emigration of workers and peasants has always acted as a safety valve for the capitalist regime in Europe. It rose during periods of prolonged depression and after the defeat of revolutionary movements, but now America and Australia are putting more and more checks on immigration. The safety valve is no longer working.

26. The vigorous development of capitalism in the East, particularly in India and China, has created new social bases there for the revolutionary struggle. The bourgeoisie of these countries tightened their bonds with foreign capital, and so became an important instrument of its rule. Their struggle against foreign imperialism, the struggle of a very weak rival, is essentially half-hearted and feeble in character. The growth of the indigenous proletariat paralyses the national revolutionary tendencies of the capitalist bourgeoisie, but at the same time the vast peasant masses are finding revolutionary leaders in the person of the conscious communist vanguard. The combination of military oppression by foreign imperialism, of capitalist exploitation by the native and the foreign bourgeoisie, and the survival of feudal servitude creates favourable conditions for the young proletariat of the colonies to develop rapidly and to take its place at the head of the revolutionary peasant movement. The popular revolutionary movement in India and in other colonies has now become as integral a part of the world revolution as the uprising of the proletariat in the capitalist countries of the Old and the New World.

27. The general world economic situation, and above all the decline of Europe, will give rise to a long period of grave economic difficulties, of shocks, of partial and general crises. The international relations established as a result of the war and the treaty of Versailles make the situation even more difficult. Imperialism was born of the pressure of the productive forces to abolish national frontiers and to create a single economic territory in Europe and in the world. The result of the conflict of hostile imperialisms has been to create in central and eastern Europe new frontiers, new tariffs, and new armies. In the economic and political sense Europe has relapsed into the Middle Ages. Its exhausted and devastated territory has now to support armies one and a half times as large as in 1914, that is, at the height of the 'armed peace'.

28. French policy on the European continent has two aspects: one, testifying to the blind rage of the usurer ready to strangle his bankrupt debtor, and the greed of rapacious heavy industry out to create with the help of the coalfields of the Saar and the Ruhr, and of Upper Silesia, the requisite conditions for industrial imperialism to replace bankrupt financial imperialism. The second tendency is directed against England. England's policy is to keep German coal apart from French ore, but the union of

these two is one of the most important prerequisites of European reconstruction.

29. The British Empire seems to be at the height of its power. It has
maintained its former possessions and gained new ones. But it is precisely
now that the contradiction between England's predominant position in the
world and its real economic decline becomes apparent. Germany, where
capitalism is incomparably more advanced in technology and organization, has been laid low by armed force, but a triumphant rival more
dangerous than Germany has arisen—the United States, in the economic
field the master of both Americas. Because of its better organization and
technology the productivity of labour in American industry is substantially
greater than in England. . . . In the industrial field Great Britain has gone
over to the defensive, and on the pretext of fighting cut-price German
competition is shielding itself with protectionist measures against the
United States. While England's navy, which has a great many obsolete
units, has been arrested in its development, Harding's Government has
taken up Wilson's programme of naval construction which in two or three
years will give naval mastery to the American flag.

England therefore will either be automatically pushed into the background and, despite its victory over Germany, become a second-class
power, or it will in the near future be forced to engage all the forces it has
acquired in the past in a life-and-death struggle with the United States.
It is with this in mind that England is maintaining its alliance with Japan,
and trying by a policy of concessions to gain French support or at least
French neutrality. France's growing importance in Europe in the past year
is due, not to a strengthening of France, but to a weakening of England.
Germany's capitulation last May on the question of war indemnities represented however a temporary victory for England and entails further economic decline for central Europe, without excluding the possibility that in
the near future France will occupy the Ruhr and Upper Silesia.

30. The hostility between Japan and the United States, temporarily disguised by their joint participation in the war against Germany, is now in
full swing. Japan has drawn nearer to the American coast by getting
strategically important islands in the Pacific. The Japanese industrial
crisis has made the question of emigration more acute. Japan, a country
with a dense population and poor in natural resources, must export either
goods or men, and in either case it comes into collision with the United
States. . . . Japan is spending more than half its budget on the army and
navy. In the struggle between England and America, Japan will have to
play at sea the part played on land by France in the war against Germany.
Japan is profiting momentarily from the antagonism between England and
America, but the decisive struggle between these two giants for the domination of the world will be fought out at its cost.

31. The last great war was European in origin and the chief belligerents were European. The axis of the struggle was the antagonism between England and Germany. American intervention merely widened the frame of the struggle but did not change its basic character; the European conflict was resolved on a world scale. The war which in a fashion resolved the differences between England and Germany and between the United States and Germany, not only failed to settle the relations between the United States and England, but, on the contrary, brought them for the first time into the very foreground as the fundamental question of world politics. It made the question of the relations between the United States and Japan secondary. The last war was thus the European prelude to the real world war, the war to decide which imperialism shall predominate.

32. But that is only one axis of world politics. There is a second. The Russian Soviet Federation and the Third International were born of the last war. The group formed by the international revolutionary forces is hostile in principle to all imperialist groups. The maintenance of the alliance between England and France or its disruption is, from the standpoint of the interests of the proletariat and the securing of peace, in the same category as the renewal or denunciation of the Anglo-Japanese alliance, the entry of the United States into the League of Nations or its refusal to enter; the proletariat can see no security in the ephemeral, fraudulent, rapacious, and perfidious alliances of capitalist States whose policy, revolving more and more around the Anglo-American antagonism, makes it more acute and prepares a new bloody conflagration.

The conclusion by some capitalist countries of treaties of peace and commercial agreements with Soviet Russia does not mean that the world bourgeoisie have abandoned the idea of destroying the Soviet Republic. It is probably no more than a temporary change in the forms and methods of struggle. . . .

It is absolutely clear that the more slowly the world proletarian revolutionary movement develops, the more inescapably will international economic and political antagonisms drive the bourgeoisie into seeking a new decision by force of arms. That would mean that the attempt to restore capitalist equilibrium after the new war would be made amidst economic impoverishment and cultural desolation in comparison with which the present European situation would seem the height of well-being. . . .

34. In the last analysis the question of restoring capitalism on the foundations outlined above can be summarized in this way: Is the working class ready, in the incomparably more difficult conditions of today, to make the sacrifices required to restore stable conditions for its own slavery, more harsh and more cruel than those which prevailed before the war? To restore European economy and to replace the productive apparatus destroyed during the war, an immense amount of new capital is necessary. That can only

be created if the proletariat is ready to work harder at much lower wages. This is what the capitalists are asking and this is what the treacherous leaders of the yellow International are recommending—first help to re-build capitalism, and only then fight for an improvement in the workers' lot. But the European proletariat is not ready to sacrifice itself. It demands an improvement in its lot, which is at present absolutely incompatible with the objective possibilities of capitalism. Hence the endless strikes and uprisings and the impossibility of restoring European economy. For many European countries—Germany, France, Italy, Austria-Hungary, Poland, the Balkans—currency stabilization requires, first of all, getting rid of debts which it is beyond their capacity to pay, that is, declaring themselves bankrupt. But this means giving a powerful impulse to the class struggle for the division of the national income. Currency stabilization means further reducing State expenditure at the cost of the masses (abandoning the minimum wage and price control); it means preventing the import of cheap goods from abroad, and increasing exports by reducing the cost of production, that is, again, primarily by intensifying the exploitation of the working masses. Any serious step to restore capitalist equilibrium shakes the equilibrium of classes, already disrupted, and gives a new impetus to revolutionary struggle. The question whether capitalism can be regenerated thus becomes a question of struggle between living forces, between classes and parties. If, of the two primary classes, the bourgeoisie and the proletariat, one, the proletariat, abandons the revolutionary struggle, the other will in the end undoubtedly achieve a new capitalist equilibrium, an equilibrium of material and moral decay by means of new crises, new wars, the impoverishment of whole countries and the death of millions of workers. But the frame of mind of the international proletariat provides absolutely no ground for such a prognosis.

35. The elements of stability, conservative in their social import, have lost much of their authority over the minds of the working masses. If social-democracy and the trade unions still preserve some influence over a considerable part of the proletariat, thanks to the organizational machine they inherited, that influence has already been deeply undermined. The war changed not only the state of mind but the very composition of the proletariat, and these changes are wholly incompatible with pre-war organizational gradualism. . . .

36. . . . The crisis fell on the proletariat of the entire world with a terrify-ing force. Wages fell more than prices. The number of unemployed and semi-employed is greater than it has ever been in the history of capitalism. The frequent changes in living conditions exercise a very unfavourable influence on the productivity of labour and make it impossible to estab-lish class equilibrium on a firm basis, that is, on the basis of production. Uncertainty in the conditions of life, reflecting the general economic

instability, national and universal, is the most revolutionary factor at work at the present time.

37. The war did not end directly with a proletarian revolution. With some justification, the bourgeoisie regard this as a major victory. But only petty-bourgeois blockheads can interpret the fact that the European proletariat did not overthrow the bourgeoisie during the war or immediately after it as the failure of the Communist International's programme. The line of the Communist International is not set for the appearance of the proletarian revolution on a certain date fixed dogmatically beforehand, or by a mechanical policy of carrying through the revolution within a given time. The revolution was and is a struggle of living forces in given historical conditions. The destruction by war of capitalist equilibrium throughout the world creates favourable fighting conditions for the forces of social revolution. All the efforts of the Communist International were and are designed to exploit this situation to the full.

The differences between the Communist International and the social-democrats of both groups do not consist in our having fixed a date for the revolution, while they reject utopianism and putschism. The difference is that the social-democrats obstruct real revolutionary development by doing all they can, whether in the government or in opposition, to help re-establish the stability of the bourgeois State, while the communists take advantage of every opportunity and of every means to overthrow or to destroy the bourgeois State.

In the two and a half years which have passed since the end of the war, the proletariat of many countries has shown more energy, militancy, and devotion, than would have been required for a victorious revolution if at the head of the working class there had been a strong international communist party centralized and ready for action. But for a number of historical reasons it was the Second International which stood at the head of the proletariat during and immediately after the war, and that organization was and still is an invaluable political instrument in the hands of the bourgeoisie. . . .

39. It cannot be denied that the open revolutionary struggle of the proletariat for power is at the present moment slackening and slowing down in many countries. But after all it could not be expected that the post-war revolutionary offensive, once it failed to win an immediate victory, would follow an unbroken upward curve of development. Political movements also have their cycles, their ups and downs. The enemy does not remain passive; he fights. If the proletarian attack is not crowned with success, the bourgeoisie pass at the first chance to the counter-attack. The loss of some positions, won without difficulty, is followed by a temporary depression among the proletariat. But it is equally undeniable that the curve of capitalist development is downwards, with a few passing upward

movements, while the curve of revolution is rising although it shows a few
falls. . . .

Capitalism can be restored only by infinitely greater exploitation, by the
loss of millions of lives, by the reduction of the standard of living of other
millions below the minimum, by perpetual uncertainty, and this makes for
constant strikes and revolts. It is under this pressure and in these struggles
that the mass will to overthrow capitalist society grows.

40. The chief task of the communist party in the present crisis is to
direct the defensive struggles of the proletariat, to broaden and deepen
them, to link them together and, in harmony with the march of events, to
transform them into decisive political struggles for the final goal. But if
events develop more slowly and a period of recovery follows in a greater
or lesser number of countries the present economic crisis, that would not
in any way mean the beginning of an 'organic' epoch. So long as capitalism
exists, recurrent fluctuations are inevitable. They will characterize capitalism in its death agony as they did in its youth and its maturity. . . .

41. Whether the revolutionary movement in the forthcoming period
advances more rapidly or slows down, in either case the communist party
must remain the party of action. It stands at the head of the fighting
masses, formulating clearly and vigorously the watchwords of the battle,
exposing the evasive slogans of social-democracy, designed for compromise.
Throughout the changing course of the struggle, the communist party
strives to consolidate its organizational footholds, to train the masses in
active manœuvring, to arm them with new methods aimed at open conflict with the forces of the enemy. Utilizing every respite to assimilate the
lessons of the preceding phase, the communist party strives to deepen and
extend class conflicts, to co-ordinate them nationally and internationally
by unity of aim and action, and in this way, as spearhead of the proletariat,
to sweep aside every obstacle on the road to its dictatorship and to the
social revolution.

RESOLUTION OF THE THIRD COMINTERN CONGRESS ON THE SITUATION
IN THE GERMAN COMMUNIST PARTY

9 *July* 1921   *Protokoll*, iii, p. 945

[The resolution was intended as a compromise; the danger of a further split in
the KPD, in which the conflicts of policies and personalities had become extremely bitter, was to be avoided by a conciliatory tone towards the left,
although their policy was rejected.

In the debate on the tactical theses Zinoviev had said that it was less important to distribute praise or blame than to look ahead to what should be done.
'There can only be one answer. In no circumstances must there be a further

split in the KPD. I really do not know whether our party can bear another split. Nor are there any reasons for one, now that the [tactical] theses put forward by our Russian delegation have found general acceptance. . . . The *Zentrale* has in many respects acknowledged the mistakes it made. Through Comrade Zetkin the opposition has declared that it now sees that the struggle had great historical significance.'

The resolution was proposed by Zinoviev in the name of the Russian delegation. Although passed unanimously, the opposition delegates of the German party, including Klara Zetkin, put in a statement, not to be voted on but for the record, which, they claimed, distributed light and shadow more correctly than the resolution.

In the course of the congress a 'peace treaty' was agreed between the different German groups. Three letters were sent to the subsequent congress of the KPD at Jena, one from the ECCI, one from Lenin, and one from Radek. The ECCI letter contained an attack on the 'ultra-left', and in his letter Lenin singled out one of its leaders, Maslow, for attack (he was elected by the congress as deputy member of the central committee of the KPD). The left wing, according to Ruth Fischer, had established friendly relations with leading members of the 'workers' opposition' in the Russian Communist Party. The resolution of the Jena congress on the decisions of the third Comintern congress noted that 'in his criticism of the March action comrade Trotsky had failed to mention that it was due not only to a mistaken "philosophy of the revolutionary offensive" but also to the former passivity of the party'.

At the fourth congress the dispute between the right and left wings in the KPD was brought before a commission which included, for the Russians, Lenin, Trotsky, Zinoviev, Bukharin, and Radek. Ernst Meyer, of the German right wing, asked for disciplinary action against the left, but the commission supported Lenin's rejection of this demand.]

The third world congress notes with satisfaction that all the most important resolutions, and particularly the section of the resolution on tactics dealing with the hotly-debated March action, were passed unanimously, and that the representatives of the German opposition themselves, in the resolutions they put forward on the March action, adopted by and large the same position as the congress. In this the congress sees proof that united and concentrated work within the VKPD on the basis of the decisions of the third congress is not only desirable but also practicable. The congress considers any further disintegration of forces within the VKPD, any factionalism—not to speak of a split—as the greatest danger for the entire movement.

The congress expects the *Zentrale* and the majority in the VKPD to deal tolerantly with the former opposition, and expects the opposition to carry out loyally the decisions of the third congress, and is convinced that the *Zentrale* will do everything possible to rally all the forces of the party. The congress demands of the former opposition the immediate dissolution of any fractional organization, the complete and absolute subordination of the parliamentary fraction to the party *Zentrale*, the complete subordination of the press to the relevant party bodies, the immediate cessation of any political collaboration with persons expelled from the party and the Communist International (in their newspapers, for example).

The congress instructs the Executive to observe carefully the further development of the German movement and in the event of the slightest breach of discipline to take immediately the most energetic steps.

EXTRACTS FROM THE THESES ON TACTICS ADOPTED BY THE THIRD
COMINTERN CONGRESS

12 *July* 1921   *Thesen und Resolutionen*, iii, p. 31

[These theses were drafted by the Russian delegation in consultation with the German delegation, and introduced by Radek. He argued that if, as Trotsky's analysis showed, the capitalists had won a respite, Comintern tactics must be concerned not with direct preparations for civil war, but with organization and agitation. In the discussion, which occupied four sessions and was concerned chiefly with the March action, Lenin explained that the theses were a compromise (Trotsky added later that it was a compromise which favoured the left, the maximum concession that could be made to those who supported the theory of the offensive); the German, Italian, Austrian, and youth delegations had wished to amend them in a 'left' direction.

'The first stage in our struggle', Lenin said, 'was to create a genuine communist party, so that we could know with whom we were talking and in whom we could have complete confidence. At the first and second congresses we said: "Out with the centrists!" . . . But now we have to go a bit further. The second stage, after we have created the party, must be to learn how to prepare the revolution. In many countries we have not even begun to learn how to win the leadership. . . . We have not only condemned the centrists, but chased them out. Now we must turn against the other side, which we think is also dangerous . . . these comrades must learn to wage a really revolutionary struggle. . . . Hundreds of thousands of proletarians fought heroically [in the March action]. Anyone who comes out against this fight must be immediately expelled. But after that . . . we must learn, learn from our mistakes to make better preparation for the struggle. We must not be afraid of exposing our mistakes in front of the enemy. Whoever fears that is no revolutionary.'

In dealing with the attempts of German delegates to amend the theses, Trotsky explained that, in describing the March action as a step forward, what was meant (or at least what he understood it to mean) was that the communist party was no longer an opposition within the USPD or a propagandist organization, but a 'homogeneous, independent, resolute, centralized party' able to intervene independently in the struggle, and that this had happened for the first time in the March action. It was not meant as a defence of the March action. 'The congress must tell the German workers that it was a mistake, and that the party's attempt to play a leading part in a great mass movement was an unhappy one, in the sense that, should it be repeated, it might really destroy this fine party.'

The 'open letter' referred to in section 3 was sent by the VKPD to the SPD, USPD, and the trade unions, proposing joint action on wages, workers' control, trade with Russia, etc. In an article published in *Inprekorr* on the last day of 1921, Radek explained that the split at Halle had alienated a number of German workers, who could be reconciled if they saw that the KPD was prepared to join with the other parties in the practical daily struggle; in the course of that struggle they would learn that reformism could not give them what they wanted. The 'open letter' was drafted by Radek, in agreement with Paul Levi, apparently to counter the 'putschism' of a section of the German party favoured by Zinoviev. The move was supported by Lenin, and the letter was published in the *Rote Fahne* on 8 January 1921; the proposal was rejected.]

1. THE DEFINITION OF THE QUESTION

'The new international association of workers is established to organize joint action by the proletariat of the different countries which pursue the one goal: the overthrow of capitalism, the establishment of the dictatorship of the proletariat and of an international Soviet republic which will completely abolish all classes and realize socialism, the first stage of communist society.' This definition of aims recorded in the Statutes of the Communist International clearly delimits all the tactical questions which are to be solved. They are the tactical questions of our fight for the proletarian dictatorship. They refer to the means for winning the majority of the working class for the principles of communism and to the means for organizing the socially decisive sections of the proletariat for the struggle to bring it into being; they refer to our attitude to the proletarianized petty-bourgeois strata, to the ways and means for the most rapid disintegration of the organs of bourgeois power, their destruction, and the final international struggle for the dictatorship. The question of the dictatorship itself, as the only road to victory, is outside discussion. The development of the world revolution has demonstrated beyond the shadow of a doubt that in the given historical situation there is only one alternative, capitalist dictatorship or proletarian dictatorship. The third congress of the Communist International takes up anew the examination of tactical questions at a time when, in a number of countries, the objective situation has become acutely revolutionary and a number of mass communist parties have been formed which, however, nowhere yet possess the actual leadership of the majority of the working class in real revolutionary struggle.

2. TOWARDS NEW STRUGGLES

The world revolution, that is, the downfall of capitalism and the concentration of the revolutionary energy of the proletariat, its organization into an attacking and victorious power, will require a fairly long period of revolutionary struggle. The variety in the degree of acuteness reached by contradictions in different countries, the variety in their social structure and in the obstacles to be surmounted, the high level of organization of the bourgeoisie in the highly developed capitalist countries of west Europe and North America, meant that the world war did not issue immediately in the victory of the world revolution. Communists were therefore right when they said, even during the war, that the epoch of imperialism would develop into the epoch of social revolution, that is, into a long series of civil wars in various capitalist States, and of wars between the capitalist States on one side and proletarian States and the exploited colonial peoples on the other. The world revolution is not an undeviating process advancing along a straight line; in the period of chronic capitalist decay, the continuous revolutionary sapping comes at times to a head in an acute crisis. . . .

The world economic crisis which began in the middle of 1920 and spread over the whole world, increasing unemployment everywhere, proves to the international proletariat that the bourgeoisie are unable to rebuild the world anew. . . . The illusions which international social-democracy and the trade union bureaucracy used to restrain the working masses from revolutionary struggle, the illusion that by renouncing the conquest of political power in revolutionary struggle they could gradually and peacefully achieve economic power and self-government, is fading away. . . .

3. THE MOST IMPORTANT TASK TODAY

The most important question before the Communist International today is to win predominating influence over the majority of the working class, and to bring its decisive strata into the struggle. For despite the objectively revolutionary situation, political and economic . . . the majority of the workers are not yet under communist influence; this is particularly true of those countries where finance capital is very powerful and where consequently large strata of workers are corrupted by imperialism (e.g. England and America), while real revolutionary mass propaganda has only just begun. From the day of its foundation the Communist International has clearly and unambiguously made its goal the formation not of small communist sects, trying by propaganda and agitation only to establish their influence over the working masses, but participation in the struggle of the working masses, the direction of this struggle in a Communist spirit, and the creation in the course of this struggle of experienced, large, revolutionary, mass communist parties. . . . At its second congress the Communist International publicly rejected sectarian tendencies in its resolutions on the trade union question and on parliament. The experience of two years of struggle by the communist parties has fully confirmed the correctness of this position. By its policy the Communist International succeeded in a number of countries in detaching the revolutionary workers not only from the avowed reformists but also from the centrists. . . . Thanks to the tactics of the Communist International (revolutionary work in the trade unions, the open letter, etc.) communism in Germany, from being the mere political tendency which it represented in the January and March struggles of 1919, has become a great revolutionary mass party. It has won an influence in the trade unions which has induced the trade union bureaucrats, fearing the revolutionary effect of communist trade union work, to expel many communists from the unions and forced them to take on themselves the odium of splitting the unions. . . . In France the communists have won the majority of the Socialist Party. In England the communist groups are consolidating themselves on the basis of the tactical platform of the Communist International, and their growing influence is forcing the social-traitors to try to make their affiliation to the Labour Party impossible. Sectarian communist groups (like the KAPD) on the other hand, have had not the slightest success. The theory of strengthening communism by propaganda and agitation alone, by the foundation of separate communist trade unions, has suffered complete shipwreck. Nowhere has it been possible to found an influential communist party by these means.

4. THE SITUATION IN THE COMMUNIST INTERNATIONAL

The Communist International has not everywhere advanced far enough in forming mass communist parties by these means. Indeed, in two of the most important countries of victorious capitalism everything still remains to be done in this respect.

In the United States where, for historical reasons, there was no broad revolutionary movement even before the war, the communists are still only on the threshold of the first stage of forming a communist nucleus and establishing contact with the working masses. The economic crisis, which has thrown five millions out of work, provides a very favourable soil for this work. Conscious of the threatening danger that the workers' movement will become more radical and be influenced by the communists, American capital is trying by the most barbarous persecution to break the young communist movement, to annihilate it and drive it underground, where, it is hoped, lacking contact with the masses, it will degenerate and wither away. . . .

Nor, despite the concentration of its forces into a single communist party, has the English communist movement succeeded in becoming a mass party. The prolonged dislocation of English economy, the unprecedented acuteness of the strike movement, the growing discontent among the broadest masses of the people with Lloyd George's Government, the possibility that the Labour Party and Liberal Party will win the next general election —all this opens new revolutionary perspectives and confronts English communists with questions of the utmost importance. The cardinal task of the Communist Party of Great Britain is to become a mass party. . . . The powerful strike movement is testing the capacity, the reliability, the steadfastness and conscientiousness of the trade union apparatus and leaders before the eyes of millions of workers. In these circumstances communist work in the trade unions is of decisive importance. No criticism from outside can influence the masses to anything remotely like the extent of the influence which can be exerted by the steadfast day-to-day work of the communist trade union cells, by the work of exposing and discrediting the trade union traitors and philistines who, in England more than in any other country, are the political pawns of capital. . . .

The mass communist parties of central and western Europe are working out appropriate methods of revolutionary agitation and propaganda, elaborating methods of organization which correspond to their fighting character, and are passing over from agitation and propaganda to action. This process is hampered by the fact that in a number of countries the movement of the workers into the communist camp took place under leaders who had not overcome their centrist tendencies, and are unable to conduct genuinely communist popular agitation and propaganda, or who fear it because they know that it will carry the parties on to revolutionary struggles.

In Italy these centrist tendencies have led to a split in the party. The party and trade union leaders around Serrati, instead of transforming the spontaneous movements of the working class and their growing activity into a conscious struggle for power, for which conditions in Italy were ripe, let these movements peter out. . . . Since they differed from the reformists neither in word nor deed, they did not wish to separate themselves from them, but preferred to separate from the communists. The Serrati policy, which strengthened the influence of the reformists, also created the danger of anarchist and syndicalist influence in the party, and of the growth of anti-parliamentary, sham-radical tendencies. The split at Leghorn, the formation of the Italian Communist Party, the concentration of all genuinely communist elements, on the platform of the decisions of the second Comintern congress, into a communist party, will make communism a mass force in Italy if the party, while fighting steadily and unyieldingly against the opportunist Serrati policy, is at the same time able to link itself with the proletarian masses in the trade unions, in their strikes, in the fight against the counter-revolutionary fascist movement, to fuse and to transform the spontaneous actions of the workers into carefully prepared struggles.

In France, where the chauvinist poison of 'national defence' and the subsequent frenzy of victory were stronger than in any other country, the reaction against the war developed more slowly than elsewhere. . . . The

French Socialist Party majority developed in a communist direction before the march of events raised the decisive questions of revolutionary action. The French Communist Party will be able to exploit this situation more fully and more advantageously, the more decisively it eliminates from its own ranks, and particularly from its leadership, the survivals, still very strong, of national-pacifist and parliamentary-reformist ideology. . . . In its parliamentary struggle the party must make a decisive break with those hypocritical formalities and false personal courtesies of French parliamentary life which the bourgeoisie deliberately encourage in order to intimidate and hypnotize the workers' deputies. Communist party deputies, in their strictly supervised action in parliament, must seek to expose the deception of nationalist democratism and traditional revolutionism, and present every question as one of class interests and inexorable class struggle. . . .

The attempts of impatient and politically inexperienced revolutionary elements to resort to the most extreme methods, which by their very nature imply the decisive revolutionary uprising of the proletariat, for particular problems and tasks (such as the proposal that this year's conscripts shall resist the call-up) contain elements of the most dangerous adventurism and may, if they are employed, frustrate for a long time the genuinely revolutionary preparation of the proletariat for the seizure of power. The French Communist Party, like the parties of other countries, must reject these extremely dangerous methods. This, however, must in no circumstances be used as a pretext for inactivity.

Strengthening the party's contact with the masses means above all closer links with the trade unions. In this field the task of the party does not consist in a mechanical external subordination of the unions to the party, and their renunciation of the autonomy required by the character of their work; it means that the truly revolutionary elements inside the unions, brought together and directed by the communist party, themselves give union work a direction in conformity with the general interests of the proletariat in its fight to capture power. Bearing this in mind, the Communist Party of France must, in a friendly but clear and resolute fashion, criticize those anarcho-syndicalist tendencies which reject the proletarian dictatorship and deny the necessity of the organization of the proletarian vanguard in a single centralized directing body, that is, in a communist party. . . .

The dislike of petty politicians characteristic of French syndicalism is primarily the expression of a perfectly natural hatred of traditional 'socialist' parliamentarians. The genuinely revolutionary character of the communist party will create the possibility of convincing all revolutionary elements of the necessity of political organization if the working class is to seize power.

The amalgamation of the revolutionary-syndicalist and the communist

organizations into one is an essential prerequisite for any serious struggle
by the French proletariat. . . .

The United Communist Party of Germany . . . although it is already a
mass party, has the great task of increasing and consolidating its influence
on the broad masses, of winning the proletarian mass organizations and
the trade unions, of destroying the influence of the social-democratic party
and trade union bureaucracy, and of becoming the leader of the mass
movement in the coming struggles of the proletariat. This, its main task,
means that all the work of agitation and organization must be directed to
winning the sympathy of the majority of the working class, without which,
in view of the strength of German capital, no victory for communism in
Germany is possible. Neither in the extent nor in the content of its agitation has the party up to now been equal to this task. Nor did it consistently
pursue the policy indicated in the 'open letter', of putting forward the
practical interests of the proletariat in opposition to the treacherous policy
of the social-democratic parties and trade union bureaucracy. . . . Centrist
tendencies, not yet completely overcome, meant that the party, faced with
the necessity of struggle, went into it rashly, without sufficient preparation,
and without maintaining the essential moral contact with the non-communist masses. . . .

The active tasks which will soon confront the VKPD, because of the
breakdown of the German economy and the capitalist threat to the very
existence of the working masses, can only be accomplished if the party,
instead of opposing the tasks of organization and agitation to those of
action, of the deed, keeps constantly on the alert the spirit of militancy in
its organizations, makes its agitation really popular in character, and builds
its organizations in such a way that, through its close ties with the masses,
it develops the ability to weigh up situations carefully, to determine the
moment for fighting, and to prepare thoroughly for the fight.

The parties of the Communist International will become revolutionary
mass parties only if they overcome opportunism, its survivals and traditions, in their own ranks by seeking to link themselves closely with the
working masses in their struggle, deriving their tasks from the practical
struggles of the proletariat, and in these struggles rejecting both the opportunist policy of self-deception, of hushing up and smoothing over the
unbridgeable contradictions, and the use of revolutionary phrases which
obscure a clear view into the real relation of forces and ignore the difficulties of the struggle.

The communist parties arose out of a split in the old social-democratic
parties. . . . The watchwords and the principles of the communist parties
provide the only ground on which the working masses can again unite, for
they express the necessities of the proletarian struggle. Since that is so, it is
now the social-democratic and centrist parties and groups which reflect

the dispersal and division of the forces of the proletariat, while the communist parties represent the element of concentration.

5. PARTIAL STRUGGLES AND PARTIAL DEMANDS

Communist parties can develop only in struggle. Even the smallest communist parties should not restrict themselves to mere propaganda and agitation. They must form the spearhead of all proletarian mass organizations, showing the backward vacillating masses, by putting forward practical proposals for struggle, by urging on the struggle for all the daily needs of the proletariat, how the struggle should be waged, and thus exposing to the masses the treacherous character of all non-communist parties. Only by placing themselves at the head of the practical struggles of the proletariat, only by promoting these struggles, can they really win over large masses of the proletariat to the fight for the dictatorship.

The entire agitation and propaganda, all the work of communist parties, must be informed with the consciousness that no lasting improvement in the position of the proletarian masses is possible on a capitalist basis. . . . But this should not imply a renunciation of the struggle for the practical, urgent needs of the proletariat until it is ready to fight for the dictatorship. Social-democracy, which today, in the period of capitalist collapse and decay . . . puts forward the old social-democratic programme of peaceful reforms, of reforms to be effected by peaceful means within the framework of bankrupt capitalism, is deliberately deceiving the working masses. Not only is capitalism in decay incapable of ensuring the workers decent living conditions, but the social-democrats, the reformists of all countries, are proving every day that they do not want to wage any struggle even for the most modest demands put forward in their own programme. Equally deceptive is the demand put forward by the centrist parties for the socialization or nationalization of the most important industries. The centrists have misled the masses by trying to persuade them that the most important industries can be wrested from capital before the bourgeoisie have been defeated; moreover, they try to deflect the workers from the real vital struggle for their immediate needs with the hope of gradually taking possession of one industry after another, to be followed by 'planned' economic construction. Thus they get back to the social-democratic minimum programme of the reform of capitalism, which has become notoriously a counter-revolutionary deception. . . . The communist parties do not put forward any minimum programme to strengthen and improve the tottering structure of capitalism. The destruction of that structure remains their guiding aim and their immediate mission. But to carry out this mission the communist parties must put forward demands whose fulfilment is an immediate and urgent working-class need, and they must fight for these demands in mass struggle, regardless of whether they are compatible with the profit economy of the capitalist class or not.

It is not the viability and competitive capacity of capitalist industry, nor the profitability of capitalist finance to which communist parties should pay regard, but the poverty which the proletariat cannot and should not endure any longer. If the demands correspond to the vital needs of broad proletarian masses and if these masses feel that they cannot exist unless these demands are met, then the struggle for these demands will become the starting-point of the struggle for power. In place of the minimum programme of the reformists and centrists, the Communist International puts the struggle for the concrete needs of the proletariat, for a system of demands which in their totality disintegrate the power of the bourgeoisie, organize the proletariat, represent stages in the struggle for the proletarian dictatorship, and each of which expresses in itself the need of the broadest masses, even if the masses themselves are not yet consciously in favour of the proletarian dictatorship. . . .

The task of the communist parties is to extend, to deepen, and to unify this struggle for concrete demands. Every partial action undertaken by the working masses to achieve a partial demand, every serious strike mobilizes the entire bourgeoisie, who as a class rally to the threatened section of the employers. . . . The bourgeoisie also bring into action their entire State machine in the struggle against the workers. . . . The workers who fight for partial demands will be automatically forced into a struggle against the entire bourgeoisie and their State apparatus. To the extent that the struggles for partial demands, and the partial struggles of particular groups of workers develop into a general struggle of the working class against capitalism, the communist party must also intensify and generalize its slogans, bringing them together under the single slogan of the direct defeat of the enemy. These partial demands, anchored in the needs of the broadest masses, must be put forward by the communist parties in a way which not only leads the masses to struggle, but by its very nature also organizes them. Every practical slogan which derives from the economic needs of the working masses must be channelled into the struggle for the control of production, not as a plan for the bureaucratic organization of the national economy under the capitalist regime, but through the factory councils and revolutionary trade unions. Only by building such organizations, linked together by industry and area, can the struggle of the working masses be organizationally unified and resistance put up to the splitting of the masses by social-democracy and the trade union leaders. The factory councils will accomplish these tasks only if they arise in the struggles for economic ends which are common to the broadest working masses. . . .

Every objection to the putting forward of such partial demands, every charge of reformism on this account, is an emanation of the same inability to grasp the essential conditions of revolutionary action as was expressed in the hostility of some communist groups to participation in the trade unions, or to making use of parliament. It is not a question of proclaiming the final goal to the proletariat, but of intensifying the practical struggle which is the only way of leading the proletariat to the struggle for the final goal. . . . The revolutionary character of the present epoch consists precisely in this, that the most modest conditions of life for the working masses are incompatible with the existence of capitalist society, and that therefore the fight for even the most modest demands grows into the fight for communism.

While the capitalists use the growing army of the unemployed to reduce the wages of organized labour, the social-democrats, the Independents, and the official trade union leaders keep themselves in cowardly fashion aloof from the unemployed, regarding them merely as the object of official and trade union charity, and politically as the lumpen-proletariat. Communists must realize that in present circumstances the army of the unemployed is a revolutionary factor of immense significance, and they must assume the leadership of this army. Exerting pressure on the trade unions through the unemployed, communists must bring fresh life into the unions and hasten their emancipation from their treacherous leaders. . . .

The more unemployed and short-time workers there are, the more do their interests become the interests of the working class as a whole, to which the temporary interests of the labour aristocracy must be subordinated. . . . As representative of working class interests as a whole, the communist party cannot restrict itself to their recognition and their use in propaganda. It can only represent them effectively if, when circumstances warrant, it leads the masses of the most oppressed and impoverished workers into the struggle, regardless of the resistance of the labour aristocracy.

6. PREPARING FOR THE STRUGGLE

The character of the transitional epoch makes it obligatory for all communist parties to raise to the utmost their readiness for struggle. Any struggle may turn into a struggle for power. . . .

Where communist parties represent a mass force, where their influence extends beyond their own party organization to the broad working masses, they must by action rouse the working masses to struggle. Powerful mass parties cannot confine themselves to criticizing other parties and putting forward communist demands in opposition to theirs. On them, as mass parties, rests the responsibility for the development of the revolution.

Wherever the position of the working masses becomes more and more intolerable, the communist parties must do their utmost to get them to fight for their interests. Since, in western Europe and America, where the

working masses are organized in political parties and trade unions, spontaneous movements are for the time being unlikely except in very rare
cases, the communist parties must try, by exerting their influence in the
unions, by increasing their pressure on other parties supported by the
working masses, to get joint action in the struggle for the immediate interests of the proletariat; should the non-communist parties be forced into the
struggle, the communists must warn the working masses from the outset
of the possibility of treachery by the non-communist parties at a subsequent stage of the struggle, must do their utmost to make the situation
more acute and push it further, in order to be able if necessary to continue
the struggle independently (e.g. the open letter of the VKPD, which can
serve as a model starting-point for action on these lines). If communist
party pressure in the unions and the press does not suffice to get the proletariat into a united front in the struggle, it is the duty of the communist
party to try on its own to lead large sections of the working masses into
struggle. An organized fighting proletarian minority must be used to
counteract mass passivity.

This independent policy of defending the vital interests of the proletariat
by its most active and class-conscious section will be successful, and will
spur on the backward masses, if its goals derive from the actual situation,
if they are intelligible to the broad masses, if the masses see in them their
own goals, even though they are not yet capable of fighting for them.

But the communist party must not restrict itself to defence against the
dangers threatening the proletariat. . . . In the epoch of world revolution
it is by its very nature an attacking party, on the offensive against capitalist
society; it is obliged, whenever a defensive struggle grows in depth and
extent, to turn it into an attack on capitalist society. It is also obliged to do
everything it can to lead the workers into this attack whenever the conditions for this are at hand. Whoever is opposed on principle to the policy
of the offensive against capitalist society is retreating from the principles
of communism.

These conditions are, firstly, the sharpening of the struggle within the
bourgeois camp itself, nationally and internationally. If the struggles in
the bourgeois camp have become so great that there are prospects that the
working class will have to deal with an enemy whose forces are broken up
and divided, the party must seize the initiative in leading the masses into
struggle after careful political and, so far as possible, organizational preparation. The second condition for offensive action on a broad front is
great discontent among the decisive categories of the working class. . . .
While the movement is advancing, the slogans must be stepped up, but
should the movement recede, it is the duty of the communist leadership to
withdraw the fighting masses from the struggle in as orderly and united a
fashion as possible.

Whether the communist party wages an offensive or defensive struggle depends on the actual circumstances. What is most important is that it should be imbued with a spirit of militancy and fighting readiness, and overcome the centrist passivity which necessarily diverts even party propaganda into semi-reformist channels. . . . The period of capitalist decay must be shortened if the material foundations of communism are not to be destroyed and the energy of the working masses crushed.

7. THE LESSONS OF THE MARCH ACTION

The March action was a struggle forced on the VKPD by the Government's attack on the proletariat of central Germany.

In this first great struggle since its foundation, the VKPD made a number of mistakes, of which the most important was that it did not clearly emphasize the defensive character of the struggle, but by the call to an offensive gave the unscrupulous enemies of the proletariat, the bourgeoisie, the SPD, and the USPD, the opportunity to denounce the VKPD to the proletariat as a plotter of putsches. This mistake was aggravated by a number of party comrades who represented the offensive as the primary method of struggle for the VKPD in the present situation. Official party organs, and the party chairman comrade Brandler, came out against these mistakes.

The third congress of the Communist International considers the March action of the VKPD as a step forward. It was a heroic struggle by hundreds of thousands of proletarians against the bourgeoisie. By assuming leadership of the defence of the workers of central Germany, the VKPD showed that it was the party of the revolutionary German proletariat. The congress is of the opinion that the VKPD will in the future be in a position to carry through its mass actions more successfully the better it adapts its fighting slogans to the real situation, the more thoroughly it studies the situation, and the greater the extent of agreement to carry the action through.

In making a thorough examination of the possibilities of struggle, the VKPD must carefully note the circumstances and opinions which indicate difficulties, and subject the reasons advanced against an action to searching inquiry, but once action has been decided on by the party authorities all comrades must obey the decisions of the party and carry the action through. Criticism of the action should begin only after the action itself is ended, it should be made only in party organizations and bodies, and must take account of the situation of the party in relation to the class enemy. Since Levi disregarded these obvious requirements of party discipline and the conditions of party criticism, the congress confirms his expulsion from the party and considers it impermissible for any member of the Communist International to collaborate with him.

8. FORMS AND MEANS OF DIRECT STRUGGLE

The forms and means of struggle, its extent, are, like the question of offensive or defensive action, dependent on definite conditions which cannot be arbitrarily created. Previous revolutionary experience shows various forms of partial action.

1. Partial action by a particular stratum of the working class (the miners, railwaymen, etc., in Germany and England).

2. Partial action by the entire working class for limited objectives (action during the Kapp days, action by English miners against military intervention by the English Government in the Russo-Polish war).

... The communist party must strive to transform every important local struggle into a general struggle. Just as it is obliged wherever possible to summon the entire working class to the defence of the fighting workers in one industry, so it must whenever possible bring out the workers of other industrial centres in defence of the fighting workers in one area. Revolutionary experience shows that the larger the field of battle, the greater the prospects for victory. The bourgeoisie in their struggle against the expanding world revolution rely partly on their white-guard organizations and partly on the dispersal of the workers' forces, the delay in forming the united proletarian front. The greater the masses drawn into the struggle, the broader the field of battle, the more must the enemy divide and split his forces. ...

The bourgeoisie, who boast of their power and their stability, know perfectly well, in the person of their leading Governments, that they only have a breathing space, and that in present conditions any mass strike has the tendency to develop into civil war and into a direct struggle for power.

In the proletarian struggle against the capitalist offensive it is the duty of communists not only to occupy the front rank and to instil an understanding of the basic revolutionary tasks, but to create their own workers' detachments and defence organizations, relying on the best and most active elements in the factories and trade unions, to resist the fascists and dissuade the *jeunesse dorée* of the bourgeoisie from exasperating the strikers. Because of the extraordinary importance of the counter-revolutionary shock troops the communist party, acting primarily through its trade union cells, must devote special attention to this question, organize a comprehensive information and contact service, keep under constant observation the forces of the white guard, their headquarters, arms depots, connexions with the police, the press, and the political parties, and work out in advance all the details of defence and counter-attack. ...

Against the acts of white terrorism and the fury of white justice, the communist party must keep alive in the minds of the proletariat the idea that at the time of insurrection it must not let itself be deluded by the enemy's appeals to its clemency. It will set up people's courts, and with proletarian justice settle accounts with the torturers of the proletariat. But when the proletariat is only beginning its march to battle, when it is only beginning to rally its forces by strikes, agitation, and political campaigns, the use of weapons and acts of sabotage have a purpose only if they serve to obstruct the transport of troops intended for use against the fighting proletarian masses or to wrest important positions from the enemy in direct struggle. Individual acts of terrorism, clear symptoms of revolutionary indignation though they are, and however natural when employed against the lynch justice of the bourgeoisie and their social-democratic lackeys, are in no way fitted to strengthen proletarian discipline and militancy, for they arouse among the masses the illusion that individual acts of terrorism can take the place of the revolutionary struggle of the proletariat.

9. ATTITUDE TO THE PROLETARIAN MIDDLE STRATA

In western Europe there is no large class apart from the proletariat which might become a decisive factor in the world revolution, as was the case in Russia, where from the first war and land hunger made the peasantry as well as the industrial workers a decisive factor in the revolutionary struggle. But even in western Europe the conditions of life of parts of the peasantry, large parts of the urban petty-bourgeoisie, and the broad stratum of the so-called new middle classes, white collar workers, etc., are becoming more and more intolerable. Under the pressure of the rising cost of living, of the housing shortage, of insecurity, a ferment is at work among these masses which is shaking them out of their political indifference and drawing them into the fight between revolution and counter-revolution. The bankruptcy of imperialism in the defeated countries, and of pacifism and social-reformism in the victor countries, drives one section of these middle strata into the counter-revolutionary and another into the revolutionary camp. The communist party must give constant attention to these strata. Winning the small peasants for the ideas of communism, and winning over and organizing the agricultural labourers, is one of the most important prerequisites for the victory of the proletarian dictatorship, for it makes it possible to carry the revolution from the industrial centres to the countryside and helps to solve the question of food supplies, which is a question of life and death for the revolution. . . . By energetically taking up the economic demands of the lower and middle ranks of the civil service, regardless of the state of public finances, communist parties are working effectively for the destruction of bourgeois State institutions and preparing for the construction of the proletarian State.

10. INTERNATIONAL CO-ORDINATION OF ACTION

In order to bring to bear all the forces of the Communist International to effect a breach in the international counter-revolutionary front, in order to accelerate the victory of the revolution, it is essential to exert the utmost effort to bring about a unified international leadership of the revolutionary struggle.

The Communist International imposes on all communist parties the duty of rendering one another the most vigorous support in the struggle. Whenever possible, the proletariat of other countries should immediately intervene when economic struggles are developing in one country. Communists must try to get the trade unions to prevent the despatch of strike-breakers, and also to prevent exports to countries where large sections of the proletariat are engaged in struggle. Where the capitalist government of one country resorts to coercive measures against another country, with the object of plundering or subjecting it, communist parties should not content themselves with protests, but do everything possible to obstruct their government. The third congress of the Communist International welcomes the French communist demonstrations as the beginning of increasing activity against the counter-revolutionary rôle of French capitalist exploitation. It reminds them of their duty to do everything they can to make the French soldiers in the occupied zone understand the part they are playing as policemen for French capital and reject the shameful task assigned to them. . . . The presence of black troops in France and the occupied zone imposes special tasks on the French Communist Party. It provides the French party with the opportunity of approaching these colonial slaves and explaining to them that they are serving their own torturers and exploiters, of rallying them to the struggle against the colonial regime, and through them getting into touch with the peoples of the French colonies.

In its activities the German Communist Party must make the German proletariat understand that a struggle against Entente capitalist exploitation is impossible unless the German capitalist Government is overthrown, for despite its clamour against the Entente it acts as overseer and deputy boss for Entente capital. Only if it proves by forceful and unrelenting struggle against the German Government that it is not trying to save bankrupt German imperialism but to clear the ground of the ruins of German imperialism, can the VKPD intensify among the French proletarian masses the will to fight French imperialism. . . .

The German working class can help the Russian workers in their difficult struggle only if they hasten by their own victorious battle the union of agricultural Russia with industrial Germany. . . . Unconditional support of Soviet Russia remains as before the cardinal duty of the communists of all countries. Not only must they vigorously oppose any attack on Soviet Russia, but they must fight energetically to clear away all the obstacles which the capitalist States place in the way of Soviet Russian trade on the world market and with other nations. Only if Soviet Russia succeeds in restoring its economy, in alleviating the terrible distress caused by three years of imperialist war and three years of civil war, in increasing the working capacity of the masses, will it be able in future to help the victorious proletarian States of the west with food and raw materials and protect them from strangulation by American capital. . . .

It is impossible to predict where the proletarian breakthrough is going to take place. Therefore it is the duty of the Communist International to intensify its efforts on all sectors of the proletarian world front, and it is the duty of the communist parties to do their utmost, with all the means at their disposal, in support of the decisive struggles of any section of the Communist International. Whenever a large-scale dispute breaks out in one country, the communist parties in other countries should try to bring all internal conflicts to a head.

II. THE DECAY OF THE SECOND AND TWO-AND-A-HALF INTERNATIONALS

. . . Although the parties of the centre and of social-democracy differ only in the words they use, the union of the two into one International has not yet taken place. Indeed, in February the centrist parties formed a separate international union with its own platform and statutes. On paper this Two-and-a-half International is trying to hover between democracy and proletarian dictatorship. In fact it is helping the capitalist class in every country by encouraging a spirit of irresolution among the working class. . . . The basic similarity in the political character of the reformists and centrists is shown in their common defence of the Amsterdam trade union International, the last stronghold of the world bourgeoisie. Wherever they have influence in the unions, the centrists unite with the reformists and the trade union bureaucracy to fight the communists, to reply to the attempts to revolutionize the unions by expelling communists and splitting the unions, so proving that just like the social-democrats they are opponents of the proletarian struggle and pace-makers of the counter-revolution.

EXTRACTS FROM THE THESES ON THE STRUCTURE OF COMMUNIST PARTIES AND ON THE METHODS AND CONTENT OF THEIR WORK, ADOPTED BY THE THIRD COMINTERN CONGRESS

12 *July* 1921   *Thesen und Resolutionen*, iii, p. 105

[In introducing these theses on 10 July, Koenen admitted that they had been hastily drafted, and they were referred without further discussion to a commission. Two days later they were passed unanimously, without discussion. The theses were intended to impose greater uniformity of structure on the parties. Although conditions varied from country to country, the aim of the communist party was everywhere the same, and the enemy was the same. The parties were to make factory cells their basic unit; members who could not be organized into these were to be formed into working groups on a local basis.

Koenen emphasized the importance of trade union work; the communist cells in these were 'to annoy, to torment, and to drive to desperation' the trade union bureaucracy. Where communist parties were illegal, they must establish legal 'sympathizing' organizations through which the illegal party could exert its influence.

It was of these theses that Lenin said, at the fourth congress: 'At the third congress in 1921 we adopted a resolution on the structure of communist parties and the methods and content of their activities. It is an excellent resolution, but it is almost entirely Russian, that is to say, everything in it is taken from Russian conditions. That is its good side, but it is also its bad side, bad because scarcely a single foreigner—I am convinced of this, and I have just re-read it—can read it. Firstly, it is too long, fifty paragraphs or more. Foreigners cannot usually read items of that length. Secondly, if they do read it, they cannot understand it, precisely because it is too Russian . . . it is permeated and imbued with a Russian spirit. Thirdly, if there is by chance a foreigner who can understand it, he cannot apply it. . . . My impression is that we committed a gross error in passing that resolution, blocking our own road to further progress. As I said, the resolution is excellent, and I subscribe to every one of the fifty paragraphs. But I must say that we have not yet discovered the form in which to present our Russian experience to foreigners, and for that reason the resolution has remained a dead letter. If we do not discover it, we shall not go forward.' He returned to the same point later: 'The foreign comrades must learn to understand what we have written about the organizational structure of the communist parties, which they have signed without reading and understanding. This must be their first task. That resolution must be carried out. It cannot be carried out overnight. . . . The resolution is too Russian, it reflects Russian experience. That is why it is quite unintelligible to foreigners, and they cannot be content with hanging it in a corner like an ikon and praying to it. . . . They must digest a good slice of Russian experience. How they will do this I do not know. . . . We Russians must also find ways and means of explaining the principles of this resolution to the foreigners.']

I. GENERAL

1. The organization of the party must be adapted to the conditions and the purpose of its activity. . . .

2. There can be no one absolutely correct and unalterable form of organization for the communist parties. The conditions of the proletarian class struggle are subject to change in an unceasing process of transformation and the organization of the proletarian vanguard must always seek the appropriate forms which correspond to these changes. Similarly, the parties in the different countries must be adapted to the historically determined peculiarities of the country concerned.

But this differentiation has definite limits. Despite all peculiarities there is a *similarity* in the conditions of the proletarian class struggle in the different countries and in the various phases of the proletarian revolution which is of fundamental importance for the international communist movement. It creates a common basis for the organization of communist parties in all countries. . . .

4. Any joint action requires *leadership* and this is necessary above all in the greatest struggle in world history. The organization of the communist party is the organization of communist leadership in the proletarian revolution. . . .

5. . . . Successful leadership presupposes moreover the closest contact with the proletarian masses. Without such contact the leaders will not lead the masses but, at best, only follow them. These organic contacts are to be sought in the communist party organization through democratic centralism.

II. ON DEMOCRATIC CENTRALISM

6. Democratic centralism in the communist party organization should be a real synthesis, a fusion of centralism and proletarian democracy. This fusion can be attained only on the basis of constant common activity, of constant struggle of the entire party organization.

Centralism in the communist party organization is not formal and mechanical but the centralization of communist activity, that is, the formation of a strong, militant, and at the same time flexible leadership.

Formal or mechanical centralization would be the centralization in the hands of a party bureaucracy of 'power' to dominate the other members or the masses of the revolutionary proletariat outside the party. But only enemies of communism can maintain that the communist party wants to dominate the revolutionary proletariat by its leadership of the proletarian class struggle and by the centralization of this communist leadership. That is a lie. Equally incompatible with the principles of democratic centralism adopted by the Communist International is a conflict of power or a struggle for domination within the party.

The organizations of the old non-revolutionary labour movement developed an all-pervading dualism, such as that which arose in the organization of the bourgeois State, the dualism between bureaucracy and 'people'. Under the ossifying influence of the bourgeois environment their officials became estranged and a living labour community was replaced by a purely formal democracy and the splitting of the organization into active functionaries and passive masses. To a certain degree, the revolutionary workers' movement has unavoidably inherited this tendency to formalism and dualism from the bourgeois environment. . . .

7. . . . If centralization is not to remain a dead letter, if it is to be really

carried out, this must be done in such a way that the members feel it to be an objectively justified strengthening and development of their common activity and fighting strength. Otherwise it will appear to the masses as a bureaucratization of the party which will conjure up an opposition to any centralization, to any leadership, to any strict discipline. Anarchism is the obverse of bureaucratism. . . .

III. THE COMMUNISTS' OBLIGATION TO WORK

8. The communist party must be a working school of revolutionary Marxism. Organic links between the various parts and between the individual members will be forged by daily common work in the party organizations.

In the legal communist parties there is still no regular participation of the majority of the members in daily party work. This is the chief defect of these parties and the cause of constant uncertainty in their development. . . .

10. A communist party, if it is to have only truly active members, must demand of *everyone* in its ranks that he shall devote his strength and his time, in so far as they are at his disposal, to the party and always give his best in its service. . . .

11. To carry out daily party work every member should as a rule belong to a small working group, a committee, a commission, a fraction, or a cell. Only in this way can party work be distributed, conducted, and carried out in an orderly fashion.

It goes without saying that all members should take part in the general membership meetings of the local organizations. It is not good to wish to replace these periodic meetings in conditions of legality by local delegate meetings; rather *all* members should be *obliged* to attend these meetings regularly. But that is far from enough. The proper preparation of these meetings presupposes work in smaller groups or work by designated comrades, as does the preparation for the effective utilization of general workers' meetings, demonstrations, and mass actions by the working class. The manifold tasks involved can be examined with care and carried out only if prepared by small groups. Unless this detailed work is constantly carried out by the entire membership and distributed among small working groups, even our most zealous efforts to participate in the class struggles of the proletariat will only lead to vain and powerless attempts to influence these struggles and not to the necessary concentration of all living revolutionary forces of the proletariat into a unified communist party capable of action.

12. Communist *nuclei* should be formed for the day-to-day work in the various spheres of party activity: house-to-house agitation, party studies, literature distribution, information services, liaison service, etc.

Communist *cells* are nuclei for day-to-day communist work in factories and workshops, in trade unions, in proletarian co-operatives, in military detachments, etc., wherever there are at least a few members or candidates of the communist party. If there are several party members in one factory or trade union branch, etc., the cell is extended to a fraction whose work is directed by the nucleus.

Whether circumstances demand the formation of a wider opposition fraction, or participation in an already existing opposition, communists must try to bring it under the leadership of their cell. The question whether a communist cell should come out openly as communist can be decided only after a thorough examination of the dangers and advantages of such a course in the given situation.

13. . . . It is particularly important that this reorganization shall from the outset be carried out with great care and after comprehensive deliberation. It is easy to distribute the members in any organization into small cells and groups according to a formal scheme and then without further ado require them all to undertake daily party work. But that would be worse than not beginning at all. It would very soon provoke dissension and aversion among the party members to this important innovation. . . .

16. Our entire party work consists of practical or theoretical struggle or preparation for struggle. Until now specialization in this work has for the most part been very defective. There are some important fields in which the party has only accidentally done any work—for example, the legal parties have done practically nothing in the special struggle against the political police. As a rule, the instruction of party comrades happens only casually and incidentally, and moreover so superficially that the greater part of the most important theoretical decisions of the party, even the party programme and the resolutions of the Communist International, remains wholly unknown to large sections of the party membership. The work of instruction must be systematically organized throughout the entire system of party organization, in all the party's working groups, and must be carried on unceasingly; this will also enable the party to reach a higher level of specialization.

17. The obligation to work necessarily involves the obligation to report. This applies both to all organizations and organs of the party, as well as to each individual member. . . .

18. The party makes a regular quarterly report to the leadership of the Communist International. Every organization in the party must report to its immediately superior committee (for example, the local organization must send in a monthly report to the appropriate committee).

Every cell, fraction, and working group must report to that party body under whose actual direction it stands. Individual members report (say weekly) to the cell or working group to which they belong, and on the fulfilment of special commissions to the party organ from which they were received.

The report should always be given at the *first* opportunity. It is to be given verbally unless the party has asked for a written report. Reports should be brief and objective. Those who receive the reports are responsible for the safe keeping of those reports which it would be unwise to publish, as well as for transmitting important reports *without delay* to the relevant leading party body.

19. . . . In all communist cells, fractions, and working groups the reports made, as well as the reports to be made, should be discussed. Discussion must become a customary practice.

Cells and working groups must see that individual party members, or groups of members, are regularly given special instructions to observe and to report on hostile organizations, particularly petty-bourgeois organizations and, above all, 'socialist' party organizations.

IV. PROPAGANDA AND AGITATION

20. Our general task in the period before open revolutionary insurrection is revolutionary propaganda and agitation. This activity and its organization is still often pursued to a large extent in the old formal manner by casual intervention from outside at mass meetings and without special attention to the concrete revolutionary content of speeches and writings.

Communist propaganda and agitation must take root in the very centre of the proletariat. It must grow out of the actual life of the workers, out of their common interests and aspirations, and particularly out of their common struggles.

The most important aspect of communist propaganda is its *revolutionary content*. It is from this point of view that the slogans and attitudes on concrete questions in different situations must be most carefully examined. This requires constant and detailed instruction, not only for professional propagandists and agitators but also for all other party members.

21. The principal forms of communist propaganda and agitation are: verbal personal persuasion, participation in the struggles of the trade union and political workers' movement; and through the party press and party literature. Every party member, whether in a legal or illegal party, is to take regular part in this activity.

Verbal personal propaganda must be conducted primarily as a systematically organized house-to-house agitation by working groups set up for that purpose. No house in the area covered by the local party organization should be omitted. In larger towns specially organized street agitation with posters and leaflets can bring good results. In addition regular personal agitation combined with literature distribution should be organized by the cells or fractions at their places of work.

In countries where there are national minorities it is the duty of the party to devote the necessary attention to agitation and propaganda among the proletarian sections of these minorities. This should of course be carried on in the language of the minority and for this purpose an appropriate party organ must be created.

22. Improved methods of work must be constantly sought in conducting communist propaganda in capitalist countries where the great majority of the proletariat still has no conscious revolutionary inclinations; it must be adapted to the understanding of workers who are not yet revolutionary but who are beginning to be revolutionized, and open the door for them into the revolutionary movement. Communist propaganda with its slogans should encourage in the different situations it encounters the budding, unconscious, hesitating, and semi-bourgeois tendencies towards revolution which wrestle in their minds against bourgeois traditions and sympathies.

At the same time communist propaganda should not limit itself to the restricted demands and vague hopes of the proletarian masses today. The revolutionary kernel of these demands and hopes only provides an opening for our influence, for the proletariat can be brought nearer to an understanding of communism only by seizing on these links.

23. Communist agitation among the proletarian masses must be conducted in such a way that our communist organization will be recognized by the fighting proletariat as the courageous, far-sighted, loyal, and energetic leader of their own movement.

To accomplish this communists must take part in all the spontaneous struggles and movements of the working class and lead the workers' cause in all conflicts with the capitalists about hours of work, wages, labour conditions, etc. Communists must concern themselves actively with the concrete questions of the workers' life; they must help them to disentangle these questions, direct their attention to the most important abuses; help them to formulate their demands in a precise and practical form; endeavour to develop among the workers the sense of solidarity, awaken in them the consciousness of their common interests and of the common cause of all workers of the country as a single working class which is one section of the world army of the proletariat.

It is only by this daily detailed work, by constant devoted participation in all the struggles of the proletariat that the communist party can develop into a *communist* party. Only in this way will it distinguish itself from the obsolete socialist parties, whose activity consists in nothing but recruiting members, talking about reforms, and exploiting parliamentary possibilities. The conscious and devoted participation of the entire mass of the party membership in the school of the daily struggles and disputes of the exploited against the exploiters, is the indispensable prerequisite, not only for the seizure of power, but even more for carrying out the dictatorship of the proletariat. It is only leadership of the working masses in the un-ending small-scale wars against the onslaughts of capital that will enable communist parties to become the vanguard of the working class, learning in practice how to lead the proletariat and gaining the ability to make deliberate preparation for the elimination of the bourgeoisie.

24. It is particularly important to mobilize the membership to take part in the workers' movement when there are strikes and lockouts and other mass dismissals.

It is the *greatest mistake* for communists to remain *passive* and disdain-ful or even hostile to the present struggles of the workers for small improvements in their working conditions by appealing to the communist programme and the final revolutionary armed struggle. However small and modest the demands may be for which the workers are ready today to fight the capitalists, that must never be a reason for communists to stand aside from the struggle. Our agitation should not, it is true, give the im-pression that we communists blindly stir up senseless strikes and other thoughtless action, but among the fighting workers communists must earn the reputation of being the ablest fighting comrades.

25. In their work in the *trade union movement* the communist cells and fractions are frequently perplexed by the simplest questions on the agenda. It is easy but useless just to go on preaching the general principles of com-munism, while falling into the negative attitude of a vulgar syndicalism when confronted by concrete questions. That only makes the work of the yellow Amsterdam leadership easier. Instead of that, communists should determine their revolutionary attitude according to the objective content of every question that comes up—for example, instead of contenting themselves with opposition in principle to all wage agreements, they should fight the actual provisions of the agreements recommended by the Amsterdam leaders. Every brake on the militancy of the proletariat is to be condemned and vigorously contested; it is well known that the object of the capitalists and their Amsterdam assistants in every wage agreement is to tie the hands of the fighting workers, so that it is obviously the duty of communists to expose this aim to the workers. Such an exposure can as a rule be brought about by proposing an agreement which does not tie the workers down in any way. . . .

26. In the struggle against the social-democratic and other petty-bourgeois trade union leaders as well as the various workers' parties there is no point in trying persuasion. Against them an energetic struggle must be organized. But they can only be fought successfully by detaching their adherents from them, by convincing the workers that the social-traitor leaders are just the errand boys of capitalism. Therefore these leaders

should whenever possible be placed in situations in which they are forced to expose themselves and then they can be attacked in the sharpest fashion.

It is not enough to damn the Amsterdam leaders merely as 'yellow'. Their yellow character must be demonstrated all the time by practical examples. Their activity in joint industrial councils, in the International Labour Office of the League of Nations, in bourgeois ministries and administrations, the treacherous words in their speeches at conferences and in parliament, illuminating extracts from their soothing articles in hundreds of newspapers, and in particular their hesitating and reluctant attitude in preparing and carrying out even the smallest wage struggle, offer daily opportunities to expose in simply formulated resolutions and clear speeches the unreliable and treacherous activities of the yellow Amsterdam leaders. . . .

27. The fractions and working groups must carefully prepare in advance communist work in trade union meetings and conferences—for example, draft their own resolutions, choose speakers, nominate capable, experienced, and energetic comrades for election. Similarly communist organizations through their working groups must make careful preparations for all workers' meetings, election meetings, demonstrations, and similar events arranged by hostile parties. When communists themselves convene general workers' meetings, as many communist working groups as possible should co-operate in advance to run the meetings on an organized basis and follow them up.

28. Communists must learn how to bring unorganized and unconscious workers under lasting party influence. Our cells and fractions should persuade these workers to join the unions and to read our party papers. Other workers' associations (co-operatives, disabled ex-servicemen, educational and study groups, sports associations, theatre groups, etc.) can also be used to transmit our influence. Where the communist party has to work illegally such workers' associations can, with the consent and under the supervision of the leading party organs, be founded outside the party on the initiative of party members (associations of sympathizers). . . .

29. In order to win the semi-proletarian strata of the working population as sympathizers of the revolutionary proletariat, communists must exploit their special conflicts of interest with the landlords, capitalists, and the capitalist State, and by constant persuasion rid these middle strata of their mistrust of the proletarian revolution. That may frequently require prolonged association with them. Their confidence in the communist movement will be promoted by a sympathetic interest in their daily needs, by the provision of information and help without charge in their difficulties, by drawing them into special associations which further their education, etc. In this connexion it is necessary to work cautiously and untiringly against those hostile organizations and persons who have authority in the

locality or who have influence on the working peasant, home workers, and other semi-proletarians. The nearest enemy, whom the exploited know as their oppressor from their own experience, must be exposed as the representative and personification of the entire body of capitalist criminals. All the daily events in which the State bureaucracy comes into conflict with the ideals of petty-bourgeois democracy and the rule of law must be intensively exploited in communist propaganda and agitation in a way which makes them intelligible to everyone. . . .

30. A special study must be made in each country of the best methods to be used in propaganda in the *army and the navy* of the capitalist State. Anti-militarist agitation in the pacifist sense is extremely harmful and only nourishes the efforts of the bourgeoisie to disarm the proletariat. The proletariat rejects in principle and combats most energetically all the militarist institutions of the bourgeois State and the bourgeois class. On the other hand, these institutions (army, rifle clubs, territorials) can be used to give the workers practice in the use of arms for their revolutionary struggles. Consequently intensive agitation must be directed not against the military training of the youth and the workers but against the military order and the autocracy of the officers. Every opportunity of getting weapons into the hands of the proletariat must be vigorously exploited.

The class contradiction shown in the material privileges for officers and the bad treatment of the rank and file must be brought home to the rank and file. They must also be brought to understand how closely their entire future is bound up with the fate of the exploited class. When the revolutionary ferment has reached an advanced stage, agitation for the democratic election of all commanding officers by the soldiers and sailors and for the establishment of soldiers' councils, can be very effective in undermining the foundations of capitalist class rule.

The greatest vigilance and vigour is always necessary in agitation against the special class-war troops of the bourgeoisie, particularly against their armed bands of volunteers. Wherever their social composition and corrupt behaviour makes it possible, social disintegration must at the proper time be systematically introduced into their ranks. Where they have a uniform bourgeois class character, as for example in the officers' corps, they must be exposed to the entire population and made so detestable and hated that the isolation in which they find themselves will act as a disintegrating force from within.

V. THE ORGANIZATION OF POLITICAL STRUGGLES

31. For a communist party there is no time in which the party organization cannot be politically active. The organizational exploitation of every political and economic situation and of every change in the situation must be developed into organizational strategy and tactics.

Even if the party is weak, it can still always make use of events which cause political excitement or large-scale strikes which shake the entire economic life by conducting radical propaganda which has been carefully and systematically organized. When a party has decided on such action it must direct all the energy of its members and sections into the campaign.

If the party cannot organize its own meetings suitable comrades must speak at general meetings of the fighting proletariat when they are on strike or in other actions, and take the lead in the discussion.

If there is a prospect of winning the majority or a great part of the meeting for our slogans, every effort must be made to get these embodied in well-formulated and well-argued motions and resolutions. If such resolutions are passed the attempt should be made to get the same or similar resolutions passed at all meetings in the same locality or in other localities involved in the same movement, or at least to get the support of strong minorities for them. . . .

As circumstances require, posters and small leaflets can be used to bring our practical slogans to the knowledge of the workers concerned, or more detailed leaflets can be handed out which enlighten them about the situation and with the help of suitable slogans help them to understand communism. The use of posters requires specially organized groups who choose the best places and times for putting up the posters. The distribution of leaflets in and outside factories, at the places where the workers involved in the movement meet, at traffic centres, labour exchanges, railway stations, etc., should as far as possible be used in conjunction with popular discussion of the kind which gets home to the working masses. . . .

34. Should the communist party make the attempt to take over the leadership of the masses at a time of political and economic tension which promises to lead on to the outbreak of new movements and struggles, special demands need not be put forward but appeals can be made directly to the members of socialist parties and trade unions in simple and popular language not to shrink from the struggles which their needs and the increasing oppression of the employers make necessary, even if this should be opposed by their bureaucratic leaders, otherwise they will be driven into complete ruin. The party press and, in particular, its daily newspapers, must in these circumstances emphasize and demonstrate every day that the communists are ready to intervene as leaders in the present and forthcoming struggles of the impoverished proletariat, that they are whenever possible prepared to come to the help of all the oppressed in the present tense situation. It must be proved every day that without these struggles the condition of the working class will become impossible and that nevertheless the old organizations avoid these struggles and try to prevent them. . . .

As the struggles increase in extent and become general it will be necessary to establish unified organs for directing the struggle. If the bureaucratic strike leaders in many unions abandon the struggle prematurely, timely efforts must be made to get them replaced by communists who must ensure strong and resolute leadership. . . .

If, as a result of the extension of the movement and of the intervention of employers' organizations and public authorities, it should take on a political character, propaganda and preparations must be made for the possible eventual election of workers' councils. In these cases all party organs must do their utmost to spread the idea that it is only through such working-class bodies arising directly in the course of the struggle that the real emancipation of the working class can be effected with the necessary ruthlessness, in defiance of the trade union bureaucracy and their socialist party satellites.

35. . . . Unless the party organization maintains the closest relations with the proletarian masses in the large and middle-sized factories, the communist party will not be able to carry through large-scale mass actions and genuine revolutionary movements. If the undoubtedly revolutionary rising which took place in Italy last year, and which was expressed most boldly in the occupation of the factories, collapsed prematurely, it was partly because of the treachery of the trade union bureaucracy and the inadequacy of the political party leadership, but also partly because there was no close and organized contact between the party and the factories through politically informed shop stewards interested in party life. The great English miners' strike this year also undoubtedly suffered because of this defect. . . .

VII. ON THE GENERAL STRUCTURE OF THE PARTY ORGANISM

43. In extending and consolidating the party a formal scheme based on geographical divisions should be avoided. The real economic, political, and communication structure of the area should be taken into account. The chief emphasis should be laid on capital cities and on the centres of large-scale industry. . . .

46. The party as a whole is under the leadership of the Communist International. The directives and resolutions of the international leadership in matters affecting an affiliated party shall be sent to (1) the central committee of the party, or (2) through the central committee to the chief committee in charge of a special activity, or (3) to all party organizations.

Directives and decisions of the International are binding on the party and of course on every individual party member.

47. The central leadership of the party (central committee and advisory council or committee) is responsible to the party congress and to the leadership of the Communist International. The smaller committee as well as

the larger committee and advisory council is as a rule elected by the party congress. If the congress considers it expedient it may instruct the central committee to elect from its own membership a smaller committee consisting of the members of the political and organizational bureaux. The policy and current activities of the party are directed by the smaller committee through these two bureaux. The smaller committee convenes regular plenary sessions of the party central committee to decide on matters of greater importance and larger scope. In order to gain a thorough knowledge of the political situation as a whole, and to be able to have continually in view a living picture of the party and its capacities, it is necessary, when electing the central committee, to bear in mind the different areas of the country if suitable candidates are available. For the same reasons differences of opinion on tactical questions which are of a serious character should not be suppressed in the election of the central committee. On the contrary, their representation on the central committee by their best advocates should be facilitated. The smaller committee, however, should, whenever this is feasible, be like-minded in their views and they must be able, if they are to provide strong and confident leadership, to rely not only on their authority but also on a clear and numerically strong majority in the leadership as a whole.

A broad constitution of this kind in the central party leadership will in particular enable the legal mass parties to create the best foundations for the work of the central committee, firm discipline and the unqualified confidence of the membership. It will also bring to light the weaknesses and ailments which may afflict party functionaries and enable them to be quickly cured and overcome. This will make it possible to avoid any serious accumulation of such maladies in the party and their perhaps catastrophic removal by surgery at subsequent party congresses. . . .

49. The central leadership of the party and of the Communist International are at all times entitled to demand exhaustive reports from all communist organizations, from their subsidiary bodies, and from individual members. The representatives and delegates of the central leadership are entitled to attend all meetings and sessions with a consultative voice and the right of veto. The central party leadership must always have their delegates (commissars) available in order to be able to give responsible instruction and information to district and area committees, not only by political and organizational circulars and correspondence but also by direct word of mouth. Attached to every central committee and district committee must be a revision committee, composed of tried and expert party comrades, to supervise the book-keeping and audit the accounts. It should report regularly to the full committee or advisory council.

Every organization and every party body as well as every individual member is entitled at any time to put his wishes and proposals, his comments or complaints, direct to the central committee of the party or to the International.

50. The directives and decisions of the leading party bodies are binding on subordinate organizations and on all individual members. . . .

51. In their public appearances party members are obliged to act always as disciplined members of a militant organization. Should differences of opinion arise as to the correct method of action, these should as far as possible be settled beforehand within the party organization and then action must be consistent with this decision. In order that every party decision shall be carried out by all party organizations and members with the maximum energy, the widest circle of the party membership must whenever possible be drawn into the examination and decision of every question. Party organizations and committees also have the duty of deciding whether and to what extent and in what form questions shall be discussed by individual comrades in public (the press, lectures, pamphlets). But, even if the decisions of the organization or of the party leadership are in the opinion of other members mistaken, these comrades must in their public appearances never forget that the worst offence in regard to discipline and the worst mistake in regard to the struggle is to disturb or break the unity of the common front.

It is the supreme duty of every party member to defend the communist party and above all the Communist International against all the enemies of communism. Whoever forgets this and publicly attacks the party or the International is to be treated as an enemy of the party.

52. . . . The decisions of the Communist International are to be carried out by affiliated parties without delay even in those cases where the requisite changes in the existing statutes and party decisions can only be made subsequently.

VIII. ON THE COMBINATION OF LEGAL AND ILLEGAL WORK

53. . . . At bottom there is no essential difference in the kind of party structure which should be aimed at by a legal or an illegal party.

The party should be organized in such a way that it is always in a position to adapt itself quickly to changes in the conditions of struggle.

The communist party must develop into a fighting organization capable, on the one hand, of avoiding open encounters with the enemy in a field where he has concentrated overwhelmingly superior forces, and, on the other, of exploiting the enemy's difficulties in order to fall on him when and where he least expects it. It would be the greatest mistake in building the party organization to calculate exclusively on insurrections and street battles, or even on conditions of extreme oppression. In their revolutionary work communists must prepare for every situation, and always be ready for struggle, for it is often almost impossible to foresee the alternation from periods of insurrection to periods of calm, and even in cases where it is possible, this foresight cannot as a rule be used to reorganize the party, because the change usually takes place in a very short time, often indeed with great suddenness.

54. Legal communist parties in capitalist countries have not yet as a rule fully understood their task of learning how the party should arm itself for revolutionary risings, for the armed struggle, or for the illegal struggle in general. The party organization leans far too heavily on the assumption of permanent legality and is constructed according to the requirements of day-to-day legal work.

In the illegal parties, on the other hand, the possibilities of legal activity are not sufficiently exploited, nor the party organization built in a way which maintains living contact with the revolutionary masses. In these cases party work shows a tendency to become a labour of Sisyphus or a powerless conspiracy.

Both are mistaken. Every legal communist party must know how to ensure the greatest possible militancy if it should have to go underground, and in particular it must be equipped for the outbreak of revolutionary risings. Every illegal communist party must energetically exploit the opportunities provided by the legal workers' movement to make itself by intensive party work the organizer and the real leader of the great revolutionary masses.

The direction of legal and of illegal work must always be in the hands of the same single central party committee.

55. Among some members in both the legal and illegal parties, illegal communist organizational work is often understood as the foundation and maintenance of a closely knit and exclusively *military* organization isolated from other party work and party organizations. That is completely wrong. On the contrary, in the pre-revolutionary period our fighting organization must be primarily the result of general communist party work. The entire party should be trained as a fighting organization for the revolution.

Isolated revolutionary military organizations, established far too soon before the revolution, are liable to early dissolution and demoralization because they do not engage in directly useful party work.

56. It is of course of decisive importance for an illegal party in all its activities to protect its members and organs from discovery and not to endanger them by membership registration, careless collection of dues, or distribution of literature. It cannot therefore use open forms of organization for conspirative purposes to the same degree as a legal party, but it can learn to do so to an increasing extent.

All precautionary measures must be taken to prevent the penetration of dubious or unreliable elements into the party. The methods to be used will depend very largely on whether the party is legal or illegal, persecuted or tolerated, growing rapidly or stagnant. One method which has proved successful in certain circumstances is the system of candidature. Under this system an applicant for membership in the party is at first admitted as a candidate on the proposal of one or two party comrades and it depends on the way the work entrusted to him is carried out whether he is accepted as a member.

It is inevitable that the bourgeoisie should attempt to get spies and *provocateurs* into the illegal organizations. This must be fought with the utmost care and patience. One method is to combine legal with illegal activity. Prolonged legal revolutionary activity is the best way of finding out who is reliable, courageous, conscientious, energetic, capable, and accurate enough to be entrusted according to his capacity with important commissions concerned with illegal work. . . .

58. It has often been observed in revolutionary situations that the central revolutionary leadership showed itself incapable of carrying out its tasks. In the revolution the proletariat may achieve great things . . . while disorder, bewilderment, and chaos reign at headquarters. . . .

Nor can it be otherwise if the leading revolutionary party has not organized *in advance* the special activities which will be required; for example . . . a system of secret communication can only work quickly and reliably if it has been in regular operation for a long time. In all these spheres of specialized revolutionary activity every legal communist party needs to make secret preparations, if only on a small scale. . . .

59. The communist organizer regards every party member and every revolutionary worker from the outset in his future historical rôle as a soldier in our fighting organization at the time of revolution. Accordingly he introduces him in advance into *that* nucleus and *that* work which best corresponds with his future position and weapon. His activity today must also be useful in itself, necessary for today's struggle, not merely an exercise which the practical worker today does not understand. This activity is however training for the important demands of tomorrow's final struggle.

EXTRACTS FROM THE RESOLUTION ON THE ORGANIZATION OF THE EXECUTIVE COMMITTEE OF THE COMMUNIST INTERNATIONAL ADOPTED BY THE THIRD COMINTERN CONGRESS

12 *July* 1921   *Thesen und Resolutionen*, iii, p. 144

[This was originally part of the theses on the structure of communist parties, and was separated in the commission. Paragraph 5 had been adopted in the commission by 'a large majority'; at the plenary session there was a protracted discussion on the question whether the little bureau should be drawn only from members of the Executive Committee. A resolution submitted by Souvarine at the final session of the congress on behalf of the French, Spanish, Swiss, Yugoslav, Austrian, and Australian delegations, that the members of the little bureau must be members of the Executive, was opposed by Radek. Elasticity, he argued, was particularly necessary in illegal work and furthermore the bureau might be hampered in its work when some members were in other countries, if it could not co-opt freely. The hands of the ECCI should not be tied. The resolution was defeated, and the compromise formula that exceptions could be made only in special cases was then passed without further discussion against one vote.

At the meeting held immediately after the third congress the ECCI elected the small bureau (renamed presidium at the end of August 1921), consisting of Zinoviev, Bukharin, Gennari, Heckert, Radek, Bela Kun, and Souvarine. The secretaries were Humbert-Droz, Kuusinen, and Rakosi. A committee was appointed to organize a conference on the Far East (to offset the Washington conference to which Russia was not invited). The following were appointed as the editorial board for *International Press Correspondence* (*Inprekorr*): Bukharin, Radek, Varga, Zinoviev, Bela Kun, Preobrazhensky, Shatskin, Kuusinen, E. Drahn. It was to appear three times a week in the German edition, and twice weekly in English and French.]

The ECCI shall be constructed in such a way as to make it possible for it to define its attitude on all questions of proletarian action. In addition to the general manifestoes issued hitherto on critical questions, the Executive shall devote itself more and more to finding ways and means of taking the practical initiative in instituting common organizational and propagandist activities of the various sections in international questions. The CI must mature into an international of the deed, an international leadership of the common daily struggle of the revolutionary proletariat of all countries. The prerequisites for this are:

1. The parties affiliated to the CI must do their utmost to maintain the closest and most active contact with the Executive. They must not only send their best representatives to the Executive but keep it constantly supplied with reliable information so that it can take up its position on any political problems which arise on the basis of factual documents and detailed material. In order to use this material fruitfully the Executive must establish departments for all special spheres. Furthermore an international economics and statistics institute for the workers' movement and communism shall be established and attached to the Executive.

2. Affiliated parties must maintain the closest contact with each other in regard to information and organization, particularly when they are neighbours and therefore equally interested in the political conflicts which arise out of capitalist contradictions. Reciprocal attendance at the most important conferences and the exchange of well-chosen members is at present the most suitable means of establishing these relations. This exchange of suitable members must be made a permanent arrangement in all sections where it can in any degree be executed.

3. The Executive shall promote the necessary fusion of all national sections into a single international party of common proletarian propaganda and action by publishing in West Europe a political correspondence in all the most important languages which will help to give steadily greater uniformity and clarity to the communist idea and which, by providing reliable and regular information, will create the basis for vigorous and simultaneous action by the various sections.

4. By sending authorized representatives to the sections the Executive can effectively support the efforts for a genuine international of the common daily struggle of the proletariat of all countries. It is the task of these delegates to inform the Executive of the special conditions in which the communist parties of the capitalist and colonial countries have to fight. They must also see that these parties remain in the closest contact, both with the Executive and with each other, in order to raise the fighting potential of both. The Executive as well as the parties must see that communication between the ECCI and the affiliated parties proceeds more frequently and more quickly than has been the case hitherto, both personally through agents as well as in writing, so that a unanimous attitude can be arrived at on all important political questions.

5. In order to be able to undertake this greatly extended activity the Executive must be greatly enlarged. The sections assigned forty votes by the congress as well as the Executive of the Young Communist International shall each have two votes in the Executive, and the sections assigned thirty and twenty votes at the congress shall each have one. As before, the Communist Party of Russia shall have five votes. Representatives of other sections have consultative voice. The President of the Executive is elected by the congress. The Executive is instructed to appoint three secretaries who are if possible to be drawn from different sections. In addition to them, members sent by the sections to the Executive are obliged to take part in dealing with the current work of their special national department or to take over work in a special field as *rapporteurs*. The members of the smaller working bureau shall as a rule be selected by the Executive from among the Executive members. Exceptions are permissible in special cases.

6. The Executive has its seat in Russia, the first proletarian State. The Executive shall however seek to extend its sphere of action by organizing conferences outside Russia in order to centralize more strongly the organizational and political leadership of the entire international.

EXTRACTS FROM THE THESES ON THE COMMUNIST INTERNATIONAL
AND THE RED INTERNATIONAL OF LABOUR UNIONS ADOPTED BY THE
THIRD COMINTERN CONGRESS

12 *July* 1921   *Thesen und Resolutionen*, iii, p. 70

[In introducing the theses, Zinoviev said that the fight against the IFTU was not
a fractional fight within the socialist movement, but a class fight. He claimed a
membership of 18 million for the RILU—a figure which included 6½ million
for Russia, 2 million for Germany, 2–3 million for Italy, nearly a million for
Spain—but suggested that the figures should be treated with caution. (The
RILU congress opened on the same day as the theses were discussed, 3 July
1921.) Communist parties should not attempt to interfere in the details of trade
union work, but should influence their general policy and, on important political
questions, intervene through their fractions in the unions. The RILU as a whole
was also to enjoy 'a certain independence', because of the great variety within
the world trade union movement, but political leadership of the RILU remained with the Communist International. Once they had won the majority in
the unions, they would have destroyed the last bastion of the bourgeoisie.
Heckert, co-reporter with Zinoviev, argued that since capitalism was in decline
and could not assure a minimum existence for the workers, the job of the trade
unions was to hasten its end, whereas the IFTU directed its efforts to rescuing
the economy from decline and decay. In the discussion Bergmann (KAPD) contended that since, in the industrially developed countries, the trade unions regarded it as their job to improve the workers' standards of life within capitalism,
they could not be used for revolutionary purposes. He claimed the support of the
British shop stewards, the American IWW and the syndicalist organizations
of France, Italy, and Spain for this view. The revolutionary movement would
have to create its own factory organizations, apart from the unions. The new
revolutionary unions would be built up from below.

In the discussion the delegates of the American Communist Party attacked
Haywood and the IWW because of its anarchist tendencies.

The theses were passed with one abstention.

The trade union commission, presided over by Heckert and Rosmer, met
jointly with the parallel RILU congress commission.

The first RILU congress, held from 3 to 19 July 1921, was attended by 380
delegates from 41 countries; most of the delegates represented minority or
opposition groups within their unions. The debate on the relations between the
RILU and the Comintern lasted for three days; the French delegates, the IWW,
and the German and Spanish syndicalists, advocated complete separation. A
compromise was reached which gave the Profintern organizational independence, but provided for close collaboration and reciprocal representation.]

I

The bourgeoisie hold the working class in slavery not only by means of
naked force, but also by the most cunning fraud. Schools, church, parliament, art, literature, the press—all these in the hands of the bourgeoisie

become powerful means of deluding the working masses, of transmitting bourgeois ideas to the proletariat.

Among the bourgeois ideas with which the ruling class has succeeded in inoculating the working masses is the idea of the neutrality of the trade unions, the idea of their a-political, non-party character.

In the last decades, and particularly since the end of the imperialist war, the trade unions throughout Europe and America have become the most comprehensive organizations of the proletariat, in some countries embracing the entire working class. The bourgeoisie are well aware that the immediate future of the capitalist system depends on the extent to which the trade unions will be able to emancipate themselves from bourgeois influences. Hence the intense efforts of the entire world bourgeoisie and their assistants the social-democrats, to keep the trade unions at any cost within the pale of bourgeois–social-democratic ideas.

The bourgeoisie cannot openly appeal to the workers' trade unions to support bourgeois parties. They therefore appeal to them to support no party; their object is to prevent the unions giving support to the party of communism.

The idea of neutrality, of a-political trade unions, has a long history behind it. . . . But in reality the trade unions were never neutral, and with the best will in the world could not have been. Trade union neutrality is not only harmful to the working class; it cannot be put into operation. In the struggle between labour and capital no mass workers' organization can remain neutral. Consequently the trade unions cannot maintain an attitude of neutrality as between bourgeois parties and the party of the proletariat. The leaders of the bourgeoisie understand this very well. But, just as it is essential to the bourgeoisie that the masses should believe in another life, so it is essential to them that they should believe it possible for the trade unions to be a-political and neutral towards the workers' communist party. To maintain their rule and to extract surplus profits from the workers, the bourgeoisie need not only priests, police, army, and police spies, but also the trade union bureaucrats, the 'labour leaders' who preach trade union neutrality and non-participation in the political struggle.

The falseness of the idea of neutrality was becoming clearer and clearer to the most advanced proletarians of Europe and America even before the imperialist war. As class contradictions became more acute its falseness became even more obvious. When the imperialist murder began, the old leaders of the trade unions were forced to let the mask of neutrality fall, and to come out openly on the side of 'their own' bourgeoisie. . . .

Now that the imperialist war has ended the same social-democratic and syndicalist trade union leaders are trying to put on again the mask of non-political neutrality. The war emergency is over, and these agents of the bourgeoisie are anxious to adapt themselves to the new situation, and to deflect the workers from the road of revolution on to the road which is of advantage only to the bourgeoisie.

Economics and politics are always bound to each other by ties that cannot be torn. The connexion between the two is particularly strong in times like the present. . . . At a time when the fight against hunger and the impoverishment of many million unemployed is on the order of the day, when the question of requisitioning the houses of the bourgeoisie to alleviate the housing shortage for the proletariat must be put as a practical question, when broader and broader masses of the workers are being forced by their own experience to consider the question of the arming of the proletariat, when the workers, now in one country, now in another, occupy the factories—to maintain at such a time that the trade unions should not intervene in the political struggle and should remain neutral in regard to all parties, means in fact to enter the service of the bourgeoisie.

With all their variety of names, political parties in Europe and America can, in essentials, be divided into three groups: 1. bourgeois parties; 2. petty-bourgeois parties (primarily the social-democrats); 3. the party of the proletariat. Those trade unions which proclaim themselves non-political, and neutral as between these three groups, are in reality supporting the parties of the petty-bourgeoisie and the bourgeoisie.

II

The Amsterdam International Federation of Trade Unions is the organization in which the Second and Two-and-a-half Internationals met and clasped hands. The entire international bourgeoisie regard this organization with trust and confidence. The chief idea of the Amsterdam IFTU is the neutrality of the trade unions. It is no accident that the bourgeoisie and their servants, the social-democrats and the right-wing syndicalists, are anxious to rally broad masses of the west European and American workers behind this slogan. . . . Under the flag of neutrality the Amsterdam International, obeying the instructions of the bourgeoisie, carries out the dirtiest and most difficult jobs. . . .

At the present time the IFTU is the chief mainstay of international capital. Whoever has not grasped the necessity of fighting the false idea of non-political, neutral trade unionism cannot fight successfully against this capitalist fortress. The elaboration of appropriate methods of struggle against the yellow Amsterdam International requires, first and foremost, a clear and explicit definition of the mutual relations between the party and the trade unions in each individual country.

III

The communist party is the vanguard of the proletariat, that part of the proletariat which has understood how the proletariat is to be liberated from the capitalist yoke and therefore consciously adopted the communist programme.

The trade unions are mass proletarian organizations, aiming at the inclusion of all workers in the given industry, not only the consciously communist workers, but also the middle and even the most backward strata of the proletariat, who only gradually approach communism as they learn the lessons of their daily life. The role of the trade unions in the period preceding the proletarian struggle for the seizure of power, in the period of that struggle itself, and in the period after the seizure of power, varies in many respects, but at all times the trade unions are a broader and more universal organization than the party, reaching greater masses; in relation to the party they play to some extent the role of periphery in relation to the centre. . . . In all three phases of the struggle the trade unions must support the proletarian vanguard, the communist party, which is the leader of the proletarian struggle in all its stages. To achieve this aim communists and elements sympathetic to the communists must organize their communist cells within the trade unions; these cells are subordinate in all respects to the communist party as a whole. . . . Communists must explain to the proletarians that salvation is to be found not in leaving the old trade unions and remaining unorganized, but in revolutionizing the trade unions, ridding them of the spirit of reformism and of the treacherous reformist leaders, and so transforming the unions into real mainstays of the revolutionary proletariat.

IV

In the forthcoming period the chief task for all communists is to work steadily, energetically, and stubbornly to win the majority of the workers in all unions, not to let themselves be discouraged by the present reactionary mood in the unions, but to seek, despite all resistance, to win the unions for communism by the most active participation in their day-to-day struggles.

The best measure of the strength of any communist party is the influence it really exercises over the working masses in the trade unions. *The party must learn to exercise decisive influence in the unions without subjecting them to petty control.* It is the union cell, not the union as such, which is under the authority of the party. It is only by patient, devoted, and intelligent work by the cells in the unions that the party will be able to bring about a state of affairs in which the unions as a whole will readily and joyfully follow party advice. . . .

V

These considerations determine the relations to be established between the Communist International on the one side and the Red International of Labour Unions on the other.

It is the Communist International's mission to conduct not only the political struggle of the proletariat, in the narrow sense of the word, but its entire struggle for emancipation, whatever form it may take. The Communist International cannot be the mere arithmetical total of the central committees of the various communist parties. It must inspire and co-ordinate the work of all proletarian organizations, both the purely political as well as the trade union, co-operative, soviet, and cultural organizations.

In contrast to the yellow International, the RILU cannot adopt an a-political or neutral standpoint. An organization which wished to remain neutral as between the Second, Two-and-a-half, and Third Internationals would inevitably become a pawn in the hands of the bourgeoisie. The programme of the Red International of Labour Unions . . . will in fact be defended only by the communist parties, only by the Communist International. For this reason, if for no other, the red trade unions, if they are really to revolutionize the trade union movements in every country, if they are really to carry out in a rigorous fashion the new revolutionary tasks falling on the unions, will be forced to work hand in hand, in the closest contact, with the communist party of the country in question, and the red trade union International will at every step have to bring its work into harmony with that of the Communist International.

Objectively, the prejudice in favour of neutrality, of 'independence', of a-political non-partisanship, which infects certain genuinely revolutionary syndicalists in France, Spain, Italy, and other countries, is nothing but a tribute paid to bourgeois ideas. The red unions cannot defeat yellow Amsterdam, and consequently capitalism also, unless they reject once and for all this bourgeois idea of independence and neutrality. From the point of view of economizing forces and concentrating blows, the ideal would be to establish a single International embracing, in addition to the political parties, other forms of working-class organization, and there is no doubt that the future belongs to this type of organization. But in the present transitional period, with the great variety of trade union organizations in different countries, it is essential to create a separate international association of red trade unions, which by and large adhere to the platform of the Communist International, although they accept members more freely than the Communist International can. . . .

In the opinion of the Communist International the programme of action which the foundation congress of the red trade unions should adopt should be approximately as follows:

PROGRAMME OF ACTION

1. The acute economic crisis . . . the aggressive policy of the bourgeoisie towards the working class . . . and the helplessness of the trade unions with their obsolete methods confront the revolutionary trade unions

of all countries with new tasks. New methods of economic struggle are required when capitalism is in decay, an aggressive policy on the part of the trade unions is necessary to repel the capitalist offensive and, when the old positions have been consolidated, to advance to the attack.

2. The foundation of trade union tactics is the direct action of revolutionary masses and their organizations against capital. All achievements of the workers are in direct proportion to direct action and to the exercise of revolutionary pressure by the masses. Direct action covers all forms of the exercise of direct pressure by the workers on the employers and the State, including boycotts, strikes, street action, demonstrations, occupation of factories, forcible resistance to the despatch of goods from factories, armed insurrection and other revolutionary actions calculated to unite the working class for the fight for socialism. It is therefore the task of the revolutionary trade unions to make direct action into an instrument for training and preparing the working masses for the struggle for the social revolution and the proletarian dictatorship.

3. . . . The fact that workers in a single undertaking are divided among several unions weakens them in their struggle. . . . The amalgamation of related unions into one union must be effected by revolutionary means; the question must be raised in the first place among union members in the factories, then at district and regional level, and finally at the national congresses of the unions.

4. Every factory and every plant should become a revolutionary stronghold. The old form of relations among the ordinary union members (treasurer, chairman, delegates and others) must be replaced by the factory committee. Factory committees must be elected by all the workers in the undertaking irrespective of their political allegiance. The task of the adherents of the RILU is to persuade all the workers in the undertaking concerned to take part in electing the body which is to represent them. Any attempt to restrict factory committee elections to meetings of likeminded comrades, to carry through an exclusively party line, and thus to exclude the broad non-party masses from the elections, must be categorically condemned. That would make it a cell, not a factory committee. The revolutionary section of the workers must exercise their influence on the general meeting and on the factory committee it elects through their cell, through their committee of action, and finally through each individual member.

5. The first demand to put to the factory committee is provision at the cost of the factory for workers dismissed as a result of unemployment. In no circumstances should the factory be allowed to throw workers on to the streets without bearing any of the consequences. The employer must be obliged to pay the unemployed full wages. This is the platform on which to organize, not primarily the unemployed, but those at work in the factory, explaining to them that the problem of unemployment cannot be

solved within the framework of the capitalist order, and that the best antidote to unemployment is the social revolution and the proletarian dictatorship.

6. The closing down of undertakings and short-time working are today among the most important means in the hands of the bourgeoisie for reducing wages, lengthening hours of work, and nullifying collective agreements. . . . Therefore the workers must fight against the closing down of factories, and demand investigation of the reasons for such action. For this purpose special control commissions must be set up, to supervise raw materials, fuel, orders. . . . Specially elected control commissions must thoroughly investigate the financial relations between the concern in question and other concerns, to do which it will be necessary to suggest to the workers as an immediate practical task to put an end to commercial secrecy.

7. One of the methods of fighting against the mass closing down of factories, wage cuts, and worsened conditions is occupation of the factory by the workers, who will continue production against the wishes of the employer. With the prevailing hunger for goods, the continuation of production is particularly important and therefore the workers should not permit the deliberate closing down of factories. . . .

8. . . . Capitalist arguments about foreign competition should be in all circumstances disregarded. The revolutionary unions must consider questions of wages and labour conditions not from the standpoint of competition between the robbers of different countries, but from the standpoint of maintaining and protecting labour power.

9. If there is an economic crisis in the country and the capitalists employ the tactics of pressure on wages, it is the duty of the revolutionary unions to prevent piecemeal reductions in one industry after another, that is, they must not allow themselves to be split into several groups. The workers in the most essential industries—miners, railwaymen, electricians, etc.—must from the first be drawn into the struggle. . . .

10. The trade unions must make it one of their practical tasks to prepare and organize international strikes embracing a particular industry . . . and never for a moment lose sight of the fact that attack on an international scale, of whatever kind, will be possible only when genuinely revolutionary international unions have been formed, which have nothing in common with the yellow Amsterdam International.

11. . . . Collective agreements are nothing but an armistice. The employers always violate collective agreements when they have the least opportunity to do so. The religious attitude towards collective agreements shows that the leaders of the working class are deeply imbued with bourgeois ideology. Revolutionary unions should not reject collective agreements, but should recognize that they have only a relative value and

should always keep clearly in view the question of ways of breaking the agreement if it should be of advantage to the working class.

12. . . . Every important strike must not only be well prepared by the workers beforehand; when it breaks out special cadres must be formed to fight strike-breakers and to resist the various provocations of the white-guard organizations encouraged by the bourgeois governments. The Italian fascists, the German technical emergency relief, the white-guard organizations composed of former officers and non-commissioned officers in France and England—all these organizations have as their object to disorganize and to break every workers' action not only by acting as black-legs but also by bringing about the material ruin and the death of the workers' leaders. . . .

13. These newly-formed fighting organizations should not only resist the attacks of the employers and strike-breakers, but also take the initiative in preventing the despatch of goods to and from the factory where the workers are on strike. . . .

14. The entire industrial struggle of the working class in the immediate future should be concentrated around the party slogan: 'workers' control of production', and this control must be established before the government and the ruling classes have created substitutes for control. . . .

18. Every economic struggle is at the same time a political struggle, that is, a general class struggle. . . . The theory and practice of splitting the class struggle of the workers into two independent parts is, especially at the present stage of the revolution, extremely harmful. Every action demands the utmost concentration of forces, the exertion of the utmost revolutionary energy of the working class. . . . Unity of action and the organic alliance of the communist party and the unions are essential prerequisites for success in the fight against capitalism.

EXTRACTS FROM A MANIFESTO OF THE ECCI ON THE CONCLUSION OF THE THIRD COMINTERN CONGRESS

17 *July* 1921   *Thesen und Resolutionen*, iii, p. 184

[In a letter to the KPD written immediately after the congress Lenin wrote: 'The third congress had to start on positive activities; it had to decide concretely, on the basis of the practical experience of the communist struggle which had already begun, how tactical and organizational work was to be carried further. We have now taken the third step. We have a communist army throughout the world. It is still badly trained and badly organized. It would do the greatest injury to our cause if we were to forget this or were afraid to admit it.' Lenin went on to attack the prevalent 'exaggeration' of the fight against centrism, which came from some of the best and most devoted elements. Reporting to the eleventh congress of the Russian Communist Party, Zinoviev said that since the Comintern now had to face a prolonged period of organizational work, greater attention would have to be paid to homogeneity. Anarchists and others who had been admitted earlier in the hope that the post-war crisis would clear their minds could no longer be retained in the Comintern.

In an unsigned editorial article published in the second number of *Inprekorr* entitled 'Co-ordination of Action', it was stated that 'The third congress laid it down that unreserved support of Soviet Russia must remain the primary and most important international obligation of communists of all countries' because it was the first outpost of the world revolution. 'When the fate of Soviet Russia is at stake, no sacrifice can be too great, no burden too heavy. That is a categorical imperative for every communist.'

The first meeting of the Executive after the third congress admitted the Communist Party of Argentina, which was asked to set up a propaganda bureau for Latin America. The same meeting instructed the German, Czech, and Polish Communist Parties of Czechoslovakia to convene a unity congress. It also considered the situation in the Finnish Communist Party; this party had been founded in August 1918, and its leaders took refuge in Petrograd after their defeat in the civil war in Finland. In April 1920 the ECCI 'at the request of the Finnish communists' appointed a provisional central committee. Zinoviev reported that the ECCI presidium had 'really conducted the work of the Finnish central committee'. What he referred to as 'tactical differences' led to a fight on 31 August 1920 in which eight leading members of the Finnish Communist Party, including two members of the central committee, had been killed, and twelve wounded.

Other subjects discussed were the famine in Russia, the Washington conference, the KAPD, and the French section. It was decided to set up a joint ECCI-RILU bureau in Berlin as a propaganda and information centre for famine relief work.]

TO THE PROLETARIANS OF ALL COUNTRIES

The third congress of the Communist International has ended. The great review of the communist proletariat of all countries has been concluded. It showed that in the course of the past year communism has become in a number of countries, where formerly it was only in its earliest stages, a mighty power which moves the masses and threatens capital. The Communist International, which at its foundation congress represented, apart from Russia, only small groups of comrades, which at its second congress last year was only seeking the road by which mass parties could be created, now disposes, not only in Russia but also in Germany, Poland, Czechoslovakia, Italy, France, Norway, Yugoslavia, and Bulgaria, of parties about whose banner great masses rally. The third congress calls upon the communists of all countries to continue further along this road and to do everything to mobilize into the ranks of the Communist International further millions of working men and women. For the power of capital can only be broken if the idea of communism is embodied in the stormy pressure of the great majority of the proletariat led by mass communist parties which must form the iron clamp holding together the fighting proletarian class. *To the masses*—that is the first battle-cry of the third congress to the communists of all countries. . . .

BUILD THE UNIVERSAL FIGHTING FRONT OF THE PROLETARIAT

The world bourgeoisie are incapable of guaranteeing work and bread, homes and clothing to the workers, but they are showing great capacity in organizing war against the world proletariat. From the moment of their first great disorientation, from the moment that they overcame their great fear of the workers returning from the war, from the moment that they managed to drive the workers back into the factories and to defeat their first revolts, managed to prolong the alliance with the social-democratic and trade union traitors to the proletariat and so to split the proletariat, they have devoted all their forces to the organization of white guards and to the disarming of the proletariat. The world bourgeoisie, armed to the teeth, are not only prepared to oppose every revolt of the proletariat by armed force, but are ready when necessary to provoke premature risings of the proletariat which is preparing for the struggle and to defeat them before the universal and invincible proletarian front has been erected. To this strategy of the world bourgeoisie the Communist International must oppose its own strategy. . . .

If millions and millions move into battle in closed ranks the tricks of the bourgeoisie will misfire and their power fail. The railways on which the white-guard troops are moved against the proletariat will stop. . . . If the proletariat is led into battle united then capital, the world bourgeoisie, will lose the most important prerequisite of victory, the belief in victory, which was restored to them only by the treachery of social-democracy and the splitting of the working masses. Victory over world capital, the road to victory against world capital, is gained by gaining the hearts of the majority of the working class. The third world congress of the Communist International calls on the communist parties of all countries and on communists in the trade unions to direct all their strength and all their efforts to wresting the broadest working masses from the influence of the social-democratic parties and the treacherous trade union bureaucracy. . . . We must show the broad working masses that it is only the communists who fight for an improvement in their position and that social-democracy and the reactionary trade union bureaucracy would let the proletariat die of hunger rather than fight. The traitors to the proletariat, the agents of the bourgeoisie, will be beaten not by theoretical arguments about democracy and dictatorship, but on the question of bread, of wages, of clothes and homes for the workers. The first and most important field of battle on which they must be beaten is the trade union field. The fight against the yellow Amsterdam trade union International, the fight for the Red International of Labour Unions: that is the fight to capture the enemy fortress in our own camp, to build a fighting front before which world capital must retreat. . . .

But this proletarian front will grow strong only if it is held together by communist parties whose spirit is single and firm, whose discipline is iron. Therefore the third world congress, while calling on all communists to build a single proletarian front, must add: 'Keep your ranks free of those elements which may demoralize the fighting spirit and the fighting discipline of the shock troops of the world proletariat, the communist parties.'

The congress of the Communist International ratifies the expulsion of the Italian Socialist Party until it shall have broken with the reformists and excluded them from its ranks. . . . Armies which tolerate leaders who are seeking reconciliation with the enemy will be betrayed and sold by those leaders to the enemy. . . .

OPPOSE PROLETARIAN STRATEGY TO CAPITALIST STRATEGY
PREPARE YOUR STRUGGLES

The enemy is strong because he has centuries of the exercise of power behind him which have given him a consciousness of power and the will to maintain it. The enemy is strong because for centuries he has learned how to split the proletarian masses, how to keep them down and defeat them. The enemy knows how the civil war should be fought and therefore the third world congress of the Communist International warns the communist parties of all countries of the dangers arising from the expert strategy of the ruling and possessing classes and from the defective strategy, which is only now beginning to take shape, of the working class in its struggle for power.

The March events in Germany showed the great danger that the front ranks of the working class, the communist vanguard of the proletariat, may be forced by the enemy into battle before the great proletarian masses have begun to move. The Communist International rejoiced that hundreds of thousands of workers throughout Germany hastened to the help of the threatened workers of central Germany. In this spirit of solidarity, in the rising of the proletarians of the whole country, indeed of the whole world, in defence of one threatened section of the proletariat, the Communist International sees the road to victory. It rejoiced that the United Communist Party of Germany placed itself at the head of the working masses who hastened to the defence of their threatened brothers. But at the same time it is the duty of the Communist International to say clearly and openly to the workers of all countries: even if the vanguard is not able to avoid struggles, and although these struggles are capable of accelerating the mobilization of the entire working class, the vanguard must never forget that it should not let itself be forced into decisive struggles alone and isolated, that if forced isolated into the struggle the vanguard of the proletarian army must avoid armed encounter with the enemy, for it is the mass weight of the proletariat which is the source of its victory over the armed white guards. If it does not march out as an overwhelming mass, then the vanguard should avoid encountering the armed enemy as an unarmed minority. The March struggles taught another lesson which the Communist International brings to the attention of the proletarians of all countries. The broadest working masses must be prepared for the coming struggles by unceasing daily agitation on an ever broadening and more intense scale, and the battle must be entered under watchwords which are clear and intelligible to the broadest masses of the proletariat. The proletarian strategy opposed to the enemy strategy must be well thought out and skilful. The militancy of the front ranks, their courage and resolution, are not enough. The struggle must be prepared and organized in a way which carries along with it the broadest masses, who will rally to it because it appears as the struggle for their own vital interests. The more precarious the position of world capital, the greater will be its efforts to frustrate the future victory of the Communist International by isolating the vanguard from the masses and attacking it. . . .

The third world congress of the Communist International realizes that it is only by experience in the struggle that the working class will be able to produce communist parties which are capable of attacking the enemy immediately he is in difficulties and avoiding him when he is superior. Therefore it is the duty of proletarians of all countries to study and to use all the lessons won by the working class of one country through great sacrifices.

THESES OF THE ECCI ON THE FORTHCOMING WASHINGTON CONFERENCE

15 *August* 1921   *Inprekorr*, i, 22, p. 203, 12 *November* 1921

[The Washington conference met from 12 November 1921 to 6 February 1922. Despite its protests, as a Power with Far Eastern interests, against exclusion, Soviet Russia was not invited to the conference, although an unofficial delegation from the Far Eastern Republic (later incorporated into the RSFSR) was present. At the session of the ECCI which drew up the theses on Washington it was decided to convene a congress of 'Toilers of the Far East' (originally planned immediately after the Baku congress in September 1920), which met in Moscow in January 1922.

Analyses by leading communists of the relations among the Powers at Washington went to extreme lengths of implausibility. Radek, for example, discussing Anglo-French rivalry, wrote that 'French militarism is becoming a greater and greater threat to England. It may become even more dangerous for England than German militarism was in its time. . . . With American support, France could even invade England.' France's aim was to get support from the United States for its Versailles policy; it would offer in return bases in the Channel, on the African coast, and in Indochina. Neumann also wrote on the possibility of an American-French alliance against Britain, which had only been averted by American support for the construction of the British naval base at Singapore, in return for the dropping of the alliance with Japan.

In these and other articles it was asserted that no world settlement could be effected without the participation of Russia and Germany. Versailles and Washington could not solve the world's problems, but only accelerate the next war. The real questions at issue in the Far East—such as immigration and the exploitation of China—were not dealt with, although it was the imperialists' fear of war which had led them to try to establish a balance and to delimit their interests.

Russia's position was in fact strengthened by the Washington conference, at which Japan was persuaded to withdraw its remaining troops from Siberia, while the termination of the Anglo-Japanese alliance gave Russia a freer field of action in the Far East.

The first congress of communist and revolutionary organizations of the Far East was held in Moscow in January 1922. The voting delegates included 52 from Korea, of whom 42 were communists, 37 from China, of whom 14 were communists, 73 from Japan, of whom 9 were communists, and 14 from Mongolia. Two delegates from India were present with a consultative voice. The Korean Communist Party had been founded in Moscow among Korean emigrés. The Japanese Communist Party had been founded in April 1921, the initial steps being taken by Japanese in the United States. The Chinese Communist Party, one of its delegates reported, consisted of a secretariat in Shanghai, with branches in Peking, Hankow, and Canton.

The object of the conference, according to Voitinsky, was to bring together the working masses of the Far East in a fraternal alliance against the imperialists. In his opening speech Zinoviev was particularly critical of the nationalists in China and Korea who still looked hopefully to the United States for help in the struggle for national independence. Of Mongolia (where Soviet troops were stationed), he said it would be unrealistic to ask for its return to China until China had driven the imperialists from its own territory. Japan, he concluded, was the key to the Far Eastern situation. Unless there were a revolution in Japan, revolution in the Far East would remain a local phenomenon, a relatively insignificant storm in a relatively small teacup.

The congress endorsed the theses of the second Comintern congress on the national and colonial question. The theses on the tasks of communists in the Far East adopted by the congress urged them to support every national revolutionary movement, but at the same time to expose the bourgeois half-heartedness and timidity of those who were willing to do deals with competing imperialist groups. Communists must win the leadership of the national revolutionary movements and advocate the Soviet system, which was suitable for peasant as well as proletarian revolutions. The congress also issued a 'manifesto to the Peoples of the

Far East' declaring war to the death, under the banner of the Comintern, on Japanese, American, British, and French imperialists, and 'their lackeys in China'.

In an article summarizing the results of the conference Katayama wrote that the conference was agreed that Japan was the greatest danger to peace in the Far East, and that the proletariat of China and Korea could not be free until Japanese imperialism was destroyed. Mongolia was threatened both by Japanese and by Chinese capitalism, but China itself was the object of western capitalist rivalries.]

I. THE WASHINGTON CONFERENCE

The conference to be held in Washington, called by the American Government to settle the problems of East Asia and the restriction of armaments, is the latest in the series of unsuccessful attempts undertaken by capitalist society to find a way out of the insoluble contradictions upon which the imperialist war threw such a glaring light, and which it proved incapable of resolving. The idea of 'Mittel-Europa' and the idea of a League of Nations have one after the other suffered bankruptcy. English and German capitalism, one after the other, have proved themselves incapable of organizing the world on a basis which, while the exploitation of one nation by another still remains, would nevertheless eliminate armaments and the danger of war. Today, three years after the ending of the war and two years after the conclusion of peace, Europe may be likened to a cage wherein beasts are brawling over a gnawed bone, watched by tamers who from time to time throw them a fresh bone, from time to time whip them. After victorious capitalism has so brilliantly demonstrated its qualifications as organizer of the world, the United States of America, which was a party to the Versailles attempt to form the League of Nations, and which then refused to join this League, its own handiwork, is for the second time taking the initiative in settling the problems of the Pacific Ocean, which are of the greatest importance to it, or in other words, the conflicts of East Asia. Then, leaving the shores of the Pacific, it wants to take up the question of disarmament, as one of worldwide significance. All this is to be done at the Washington conference. But this attempt, like all previous attempts, will fail. At best, it can but end with a regrouping of the various Powers and with an intensification of existing differences. This is obvious from an enumeration of the driving forces behind the United States, England, and Japan, and a survey of the contradictions among them.

II. THE RETURN OF THE UNITED STATES TO EUROPE

The United States withdrew from the League of Nations, first, because England, with six votes at its disposal, put the English stamp upon the

League; secondly, because the capitalists of America did not feel inclined to guarantee the territorial frontiers of the world patched together at Versailles; and thirdly, because the capitalist clique as represented by the Republican party wished to exploit the fact that the petty-bourgeois masses had grown tired of Europe to take over from the capitalist clique represented by the Democratic party the disposal of government patronage. The United States could not withdraw from world politics, however, because European capitalists and the Allies owe it 20 milliard dollars. The outcome of the conflicts in Europe will decide not only whether the debtors will be able to pay their debts, but also whether or not the United States will be able to keep going the industry developed during the war. In 1919 not all American capitalists believed that their prosperity depended on the economic development of Europe, but the raging crisis of 1920/21 proved even to the American farmers that America cannot export its products to Europe if European economy continues to decay. For this reason the United States has already taken part in settling the question of German reparations; it is now participating in the settling of the Upper Silesian question by the Supreme Council; it has taken a stand on the famine problem of Russia. In short, the United States has rejoined the true representative of victorious world capitalism, the Supreme Council, which has made a puppet of the Council of the League of Nations. The United States is now endeavouring to gain control of the Supreme Council and is exploiting the present difficult situation of its English competitor to this end.

III. ENGLAND'S SITUATION

In order to win, English imperialism was obliged to draw its colonies into the war, in the course of which they grew stronger economically. In 1917 they were given a voice in deciding British foreign policy. Now this nominal right must be made a reality, because English imperialism is unable to bear alone the cost of the naval armaments which it must keep up both against the United States and against its allies, France and Japan, as well, and because it must consider the colonies as factors in the power situation. Great Britain has now been replaced by a federation of Great Britain and its self-governing capitalist English colonies, whose foreign interests are not identical with those of their mother country. English imperialism wants to maintain the alliance with Japan in order to have an ally in case of conflict with the United States, and in order to play the part of arbitrator between American and Japanese imperialism, after having stirred up American-Japanese differences. But youthful Canadian capitalism which, by reason of its proximity, is becoming more and more dependent upon the United States, cannot afford a disturbance of relations with its powerful neighbour. At the recent Imperial conference,

Canada opposed renewal of the alliance with Japan and declined to be bound by an eventual renewal. Australia, whose only possible enemy is Japan, would in the event of a conflict with that country find an ally in the United States. The farmers of South Africa want to have nothing to do with world political conflicts. This attitude of its most important colonies has deprived English imperialism of freedom of movement in regard to the United States.

In this atmosphere of unsettled world political differences the increasing economic competition between Great Britain and the United States raises for both countries the question whether or not it will eventually lead to an increase of competitive armaments which might lead to a new world war. In such a war Great Britain would be in a more dangerous position than in the war of 1914–18, because while on the one hand it could not wholly rely on its colonies it would, on the other hand, probably have as an enemy France, whose attempt to dominate continental Europe by a network of vassal States, Poland, Czechoslovakia, and Rumania, and whose policy in the Near East, place it more and more in opposition to Great Britain. English imperialism has helped to destroy not only the naval, but also the military strength of German capitalism. The disarming of German capitalism has established French militarism as the deciding factor on the European continent. The development of long-distance weapons and of aircraft and submarines would, in case of war, enable France, in alliance with the United States, not only to blockade England, but to mount an invasion as well. This situation is compelling the English Government to try to come to an understanding with the United States. The object of this understanding is the formation of an Anglo-Saxon capitalist trust. The United States will be the centre of gravity of this trust while Japan is to foot the bill.

IV. THE ISOLATION OF JAPAN

Japanese imperialism at very little expense to itself amassed riches during the war by supplying the Allies and by exploiting England's inability to furnish its colonies with enough manufactured goods. Having at the beginning of the war shrewdly prevented China from participating in it, Japan forcibly took Kiaochow and the Province of Shantung from German imperialism and put herself in its place. It exacerbated China's difficulties and in the guise of organizer exploited them in order to gain mastery over the vast empire which, under the leadership of the bourgeois South, is slowly groping its way from feudal disunity to unity. The results of the war threaten to deny to the Japanese the fruits of their victory. Germany's defeat, and the disappearance of Russia as an imperialist factor which could join Japan in pillaging expeditions, reduce Japan to reliance upon England alone for assistance against the United States.

V. THE PLANS OF THE UNITED STATES IN EAST ASIA

The United States sees in China and in Russia (especially Siberia) the markets to satisfy its gigantic need for economic expansion, and the fields to be won for American capital investment. The monopoly position enjoyed by the United States as the world's creditor and, further, the ability of American industry to compete not only with Japanese industry but also with English, prompt the United States to oppose all the imperialist privileges formerly acquired in China by the older imperialist States, France, England, and Japan, or those which they might now acquire in Siberia. The United States, under the slogan of the 'open door in China' coined by the American Secretary of State John Hay as far back as 1900, is trying to force Japan back; its treatment of the question of the Chinese wireless stations on the island of Yap goes far to prove that it is determined to take up the battle along the whole front. This policy threatens English interests, though to a far less degree than the Japanese. Not only because England is a better match for American competition than Japan, but also because the Pacific question, vital for Japan, is only one of England's preoccupations. Hence Japan can rely upon England only to a certain extent. Obliged to choose between Japan and the United States, England will side with the latter. The Washington conference therefore represents a diplomatic attempt on the part of the United States to snatch the fruits of victory from Japan.

VI. PROSPECTS FOR THE WASHINGTON CONFERENCE

Any agreement on the limitation of armaments in the Pacific, or on its division into areas where each Power has supremacy, depends on the outcome of the diplomatic negotiations on the disputed Pacific problems. England will side with Japan and endeavour to bring about a compromise between the United States and Japan, enabling it to continue the alliance with Japan by the formal inclusion of the United States. The military value of the alliance with Japan in case of war with the United States is not to be underestimated. The compromise is to be brought about either by Japan receiving compensation in Siberia or by the United States being given concessions in China, the right to share in the exploitation of Mesopotamia's oil, etc. etc. If England succeeds in bringing about this compromise, it will, within the English-Japanese-American alliance, endeavour to maintain especially close relations with Japan. Thereafter an agreement will be arrived at by the three contracting powers fixing naval armaments at a level that will not be considered dangerously competitive. If the powers are unable, however, to reach an agreement on the points under discussion, the economic struggle and armaments competition will proceed unrestricted. In the first case, the United States and England will act in combination to deprive Japan of part of the fruits of its victory in favour of the United States and at the expense of China and, perhaps, Soviet Russia. An agreement of this kind would prove to be the starting point of diplomatic regroupings and new world political conflicts, after the fashion of the peace of Shimonoseki when Russia, Germany, and France endeavoured to snatch from Japan the fruits of its victory over China in 1894. In the second case, the process of intensification of the existing conflicts will develop more rapidly, but in no circumstances will they disappear. Then the economic conflict between England and America will continue to be the foremost world problem. The Anglo-Japanese conflict remains, as does the Anglo-French. In the background of these conflicts dividing the world of capitalist victors looms their conflict with the defeated capitalist countries, and, further, with the colonial peoples and, finally, with Soviet Russia, who represents a breach in the system of capitalist States.

VII. THE WASHINGTON CONFERENCE AND THE COMMUNIST INTERNATIONAL

The attempt to settle the international question of limitation of armaments on the European continent as well is doomed to failure. Even though, since the complete disarmament of Germany, French security would not be endangered if France abandoned its military preparations, France would not give up the position of first military power in Europe, because it is the policy of French imperialism to dominate the European continent. Aside from France, there exist its vassal States, all of which by the peace of Versailles and the succeeding treaties were allotted territories inhabited by alien and hostile populations. Poland has a great many Ukrainian, Little Russian, and German inhabitants, while Czechoslovakia may be likened to the former Austrian Empire, because, apart from Czechoslovakians, it is populated by Germans and Hungarians. A great many Hungarians and Bessarabians have been enslaved by Rumania. Large numbers of Bulgarians have been brought under Rumanian and Yugoslav rule. The status quo in central, southern, and eastern Europe rests today on bayonets. In the Near East, France, from her African possessions and from Syria, is endeavouring to outflank England at its most sensitive spot, the Suez Canal. This is intended to hamper the English policy of establishing—by means of the territory of a great Arab state dependent upon English imperialism—the lines of communication between Egypt and India. In order to compel France to forgo its armaments in such a situation, England must come to an agreement with France on all world problems.

How little the capitalist powers themselves believe in the likelihood of disarmament is shown by the fact that, having cordially welcomed Harding's proposal to discuss disarmament at Washington, the English

Government immediately afterwards decided to spend £30 million on building new warships. It justified this by pointing out that Japan is building eight dreadnoughts to be finished by 1925 and has already made appropriations for another series of eight, and that in 1925 the United States would possess 12 superdreadnoughts.

The Executive of the Communist International maintains that the Washington conference can result neither in disarmament nor in the establishment of peace among the nations, and that it represents only an attempt to reconcile the interests of the great Anglo-Saxon imperialist robbers at the expense of the weaker robber, Japan, of China, and of Soviet Russia. Emphasis is lent to this analysis of the character of the Washington conference by the fact that Russia has not been invited to it, in order to make it impossible for it to expose the shameful game being played at Washington with the fates of peoples.

The Executive of the Communist International warns the working masses and enslaved colonial peoples against harbouring the hope that any diplomatic combination whatever arrived at in Washington could free them from the menace of a heavily armed capitalist world and from exploitation by capitalist States. The Executive of the Communist International calls upon all communist parties and all trade unions affiliated to the Red Trade Union International to intensify the agitation and the struggle against the imperialist governments whose conflicting interests are certain to result in a new world-wide clash, unless the proletarian revolution disarms the capitalist class and thus creates the prerequisite for a true world-wide federation of all toiling peoples. The Executive draws the attention of the working class throughout the world to the intrigues that are being spun at Washington against Soviet Russia. It calls upon the masses in China, Korea, and Eastern Siberia to adhere more closely to Soviet Russia, the only State in the world willing to render assistance upon a basis of equality and of fraternal help to the peoples of the Orient who are being menaced by world imperialism.

EXTRACTS FROM A LETTER FROM THE ECCI AND THE EXECUTIVE
COMMITTEE OF THE RILU TO THE WORKERS OF GREAT BRITAIN

September 1921   *Inprecorr*, i, 1, p. 5, 1 *October* 1921

[On his return from Moscow at the end of 1920 J. T. Murphy, of the shop stewards movement, established a 'British bureau' of the RILU in England, whose propaganda was to be 'directed towards persuading the British trade unions to sever their connexion with the IFTU . . . and affiliate to the Moscow trade union International'. The 'Minority Movement' in the British trade unions was started in 1923 and held its first congress in 1924.

This letter was sent to coincide with the opening of the trade union congress in Cardiff on 5 September. Dissatisfaction with the work of British communists in the trade unions had been expressed at the third world congress. A British delegate, replying to Radek's criticism of the attitude of the CPGB during the miners' strike, said: 'If comrade Radek knows the history of the English trade union movement . . . he must know that it would be sheer folly for the English communist party to try to influence or advise the miners, who have $1\frac{1}{4}$ million men in their union.']

The working-class of Great Britain is in a position bordering on despair. Divided into a multitude of unions, federations, loose alliances, committees, councils, parties, and devoid of unified and militant leadership, the British labour movement of today is a vast confusion and chaos. Eight million organised workers, a mighty army indeed, cannot point out a single victory won by labour in recent years. The history of the labour movement, especially since the outbreak of the war and after the armistice, has been a record of blunders and defeats. Separate groups of workers, unaided and unsupported by the rest of the working-class, have, time and again, put up the most stubborn and the most heroic fights, but the working class as a whole has repeatedly suffered itself to be tricked and fooled by the bourgeoisie and labour politicians, has meekly and obediently accepted broken promises and downright betrayals, has submitted to threats and intimidations.

And what is the result? Millions of unemployed, hundreds of thousands of workers on short-time, a general insecurity of work, a continuous decline and fall in the standard of living. . . .

The capitalist system, which is responsible for the present crisis and all its attendant evils of unemployment, misery, and privations, is unable to extricate itself from the economic chaos of its own creation. It is not only unable to solve the unemployment problem, but to insure its own continued existence it is compelled to degrade the working class and reduce it still further to servitude. The universal economic chaos, to which imperialist capitalism has brought the world, threatens profits, and the bourgeoisie wishes to recoup itself at the expense of the meagre wages of the workers. Thus, the present crisis is being utilised by the capitalist class in a ruthless and ferocious attack on the standard of living of the proletariat. To maintain the profits of capitalism, the workers must starve. . . .

How is it that the British proletariat suffers itself to be thus cowed and beaten into submission without putting up a united and determined fight to a finish? This is the foremost question which the workers must raise before the Trade Union Congress and give a satisfactory answer. We on our part have this to say: The workers of Great Britain are organised in trade unions but not organised as a class. *They possess no class organisation capable of leading the whole of the working class to victory.* The trade unions form federations and alliances, or belong to the Trade Union Congress or Labour Party, but in spite of this multitude of organisations, the proletariat is not organised as a class. The bourgeoisie looks to the Federation of British Industries for aid and action. When in need, it has Parliament to fall back upon and a National Government is always at its disposal. The bourgeoisie is indeed organised as a class, but the workers alone are split and torn asunder into a multitude of petty unions, federations, alliances with high-sounding and imposing names, but none of them representing the working class as a whole and with neither authority nor power to act. ... That's why it has been beaten and crushed time and again, so badly. It is high time for Labour to recognize the painful truth that it is divided against itself, no matter how much it may profess class solidarity, and in spite of its deep conviction that 'an injury to one is an injury to all'. Class-solidarity, to be effective, must find its expression through class organisation and so long as labour remains disunited, it will be beaten.

The capitalist class and the Government know well that so long as they can keep labour in the present state of disorganisation and chaos, their rule is unassailable and unshakeable. As to the revolt of separate groups of labour, as in the case of the miners, there is nothing much for the bourgeoisie to fear. These can be crushed with comparative ease, and what is more, crushed by the aid of other groups of the working class which, while the struggle goes on, supply the enemy with the sinews of war to be used against their fellow workers. For, and let us not deceive ourselves on that score, when a million miners are engaged in a deadly grip with the employers, and the rest of the workers stand at their benches, drive engines and load cars, they help the enemy to beat the miners. ...

THE TRADE UNION CONGRESS

The Trade Union Congress, loose and involuntary as it has been till now, is not the organization capable of leading the working class to victory over the bourgeoisie, or even to defend the workers from capitalist aggression. The annual meetings of the Trade Union Congress only afford an additional platform to a few labour leaders to give vent to their eloquence before a labour audience. Its practical work results in a multitude of resolutions and recommendations and that is all.

The leaders of the Trade Union Congress readily turned into diplomats of the working class and concluded peace with the bourgeoisie and the Government by voluntarily assigning to them the rights of labour on empty promises for the future, but did nothing to compel the Government and the bourgeoisie to fulfil them. When the industries and the soldiers were demobilised, and hundreds of thousands of men and women were thrown out of work to become a public charge; when every promise made to the workers during the war was broken soon after, what did the Trade Union

Congress do to show to the capitalists and the Government that Labour cannot and will not be trifled with? It did nothing except silently witness the dignity of Labour being gradually degraded and dragged into the mire. Was the Trade Union Congress of any assistance to the workers in 1919? Did it bring active pressure of the whole working class to bear upon the Government to yield to the railwaymen? No, it did not. Did the Trade Union Congress help the miners to secure nationalisation at a time when the position of Labour was most favourable? No, it did not. Its threat of direct action remained on paper, notwithstanding the fact that over four million workers voted for direct action. Was the Trade Union Congress of any practical use in the Labour disputes of 1920? No, it was not. . . . Is it not then correct, fellow workers, to say that Labour has not found in the Trade Union Congress the class organization it needs, and is it not high time that every worker realises this before the capitalist class has got you securely by the throat. . . .

The present position of British Labour is such that we are quite justified in pointing out to every worker the immediate need for a centralised, efficient and militant class organisation. In fact the workers themselves realised that the present state of affairs in the labour movement is intolerable, and that drastic changes are needed immediately to avoid further and more crushing defeat. . . .

We must never for a moment forget that the leaders, such as Thomas and his like, do not want a real union of Labour, for that means that the large masses of the workers will be involved into a direct struggle with the Capitalist class. This is precisely what the leaders do not want. Did not Thomas state during the lockout of the miners that nobody could foretell the consequences of a combined strike of the Triple Alliance and other bodies of Labour, and did he not say that whichever side would win, the nation would lose? That means that even if the workers won, the Nation would lose? And so Thomas is against common action by the workers because the Nation, that is to say the capitalist class, would lose. . . .

Both the petty leaders and the leaders of national fame, those who represent labour in the bourgeoisie newspapers, in the Trade Union Congress and in Parliament, those who are hailed as the leaders of the future Labour Government will with a few exceptions oppose a centralised and disciplined organisation of the whole of the working class, because such an organisation would destroy their power of aiding the bourgeoisie and the Government to play off one group of workers against the other; it would eliminate that chaos in the Labour movement which heretofore afforded to them the very excellent opportunity of keeping Labour under their domination, and thus preventing every attempt on the part of the workers to revolt against the capitalist system. Their object is, as Thomas has more than once declared, to 'keep the ring' in the big battles of Labour and Capital. Their object can be best attained by holding the working class disunited, disorganised and discentralised.

To insure ourselves against the tricks and machinations of the leaders who will make every attempt to reduce the whole question of the unification of the Labour Movement to a mere change in the names of the old organizations, leaving everything else as it existed heretofore, the workers must take the work of unification into their own hands and see to it that first of all the shops and the works are united, along the lines of industry. The Workers' Committee is the foundation of working class unity. The Workers' Committee and the Trade Unions must form the Local Trades and Labour Councils with authority to act as the General Staff of Labour for the given locality. Finally, the Trades and Labour Congress must be representatives of the whole of the working class and responsible only to the working class. Unity in the factory, in the pit, and so on, unity on the point of production, unity in the locality, Working class unity in the whole country. It unites all the workers at the point of production irrespective of grade, craft, colour or sex.

The creation of directing staffs in the English Labour movement is only one part of the problem. What will the Executive Organs, invested with authority, do? Will they, like the general staffs of the Trade Union movement in other countries, look for salvation in collaboration with the bourgeoisie or will they carry on a revolutionary struggle against it? Will the new staff spend the revolutionary energy of the working class in bartering, or will it, clearly understanding the contradictions which tear apart the existing capitalist society, struggle with all its organised power for the overthrow of capitalism and the establishment of the power of the toilers? Here are the questions that are of the utmost interest to every proletarian, to every worker of Great Britain. You have witnessed the great struggles and social conflicts of the last years. The workers were being vanquished not only because they were poorly organised but also because they were striving for sectional aims. The bourgeoisie had triumphed over you not only because it is better organised than you, but also because it understands its class interests better than the working class. It never pursues merely economic problems. It always regards its problems as class problems and all its activities are permeated with the spirit of its class. Being numerically weaker than the working class it succeeds by the strength of its organisation and class consciousness.

If the General Staff of the English Labour movement will be permeated with the spirit of hatred against the dominating class, if each little conflict, each skirmish, will serve for the education of the masses, for the single aim of the overthrow of bourgeois domination, your staff will be worthy of the confidence of the English Labour movement, and will be worthy of its great mission. The victory in the social struggle belongs to the class which is not only better organised, but which is more conscious, to the class which can marshall all the might of its organisation and all its experience for the accomplishment of its class task.

APPEAL OF THE ECCI, THE EXECUTIVE OF THE RILU, AND THE YCI ON THE DANGER OF WAR AGAINST RUSSIA

October 1921   *Inprekorr*, i, 7, p. 57, 8 *October* 1921

[In the spring of 1921, Poland and Rumania, with French approval, concluded a treaty of alliance. In September 1921 the Russian Foreign Affairs Commissariat stated that the French Government had proposed joint action by itself and the two allies against Russia. According to Radek, it was the French Ambassador who had invited the Polish Government to send its 'ultimatum' of 18th September, charging Russia with non-fulfilment of the Riga treaty. The French, he argued, hoped that with sufficient pressure Russia would be forced to recognize the pre-war debts. The British note of 7 September charged Russia with violating the pledges given in the Anglo-Soviet agreement of March 1921 to refrain from hostile propaganda. In its reply of 27th September the Foreign Affairs Commissariat wrote that the 'mere facts of the Third International having for obvious reasons chosen Russia as the seat of its executive committee as the only land which allows full freedom to the spreading of communist ideas and personal freedom to communists, and of some of the members of the Russian Government in their individual capacity belonging to the executive committee', did not justify the identification of the Third International with the Russian Government. Later in the year the ECCI issued another manifesto which referred to the danger of a Franco-Polish attack on Russia. 'Harassed from the left by the growing revolutionary wave and from the right by the frightened bourgeoisie trembling for their power, the military oligarchy of Poland is preparing to proclaim its dictatorship in the interior and to drown the proletarian movement in blood, and at the same time, if it only can, to prepare for *war against Soviet Russia*. It is speculating upon the possibility that the French Government will add further sums to the 20 milliard francs that it has thrown into the jaws of Polish militarism, in order to obtain payment for its earlier sacrifices by putting a white-guard government in the saddle in Russia, which would immediately begin to extort the interest on the Tsarist debts from the Russian people. The Polish Government has protected itself in the event of war by an agreement with the Rumanian Bojars, and it has recently signed an agreement with the Czecho-slovakian bourgeoisie, which assures it the free passage of munitions. These criminal plans must be opposed with all the energy at our disposal. The workers of all countries, above all those which are Poland's neighbours, must do everything in their power so that *not a single railway waggon, not a single ship with war equipment shall enter Poland* this winter and spring.']

TO THE PROLETARIANS OF ALL COUNTRIES!

WORLD CAPITAL IS PREPARING A POLISH-RUMANIAN CAMPAIGN AGAINST
STARVING SOVIET RUSSIA

In our first appeal about the famine in Russia we warned you not to place confidence in the humanitarian speeches and declarations of readiness to help made by the capitalist States. We told you that now as formerly world capital sees in Soviet Russia the centre of world revolution, and it will exploit the famine caused by the drought and intensified by the consequences of intervention to prepare a new onslaught on Soviet Russia. Our prophecies are already being fulfilled. While real help for the hungry is being given only to a minimum extent, while France, making a mockery of the need of the Russian people, wanted to put the work of relief in the hands of Noulens, the organizer of the Russian counter-revolution, while the Allied Commission under the leadership of the same Noulens tried to turn the relief organization into an espionage organization in Russia, the French Government, working behind a diplomatic screen, is taking preparatory steps to organize war on Soviet Russia. On 3rd September it asked the Polish Government to present Soviet Russia with an ultimatum under which the Soviet Government was to make immediately the payments due under the Riga treaty, otherwise Poland would sever diplomatic relations with Soviet Russia. Since Soviet Russia ceased making payments under this provision because Poland supplied arms to Savinkov's white-guard bands who attacked Russia, burnt the crops and destroyed railways, it was clear that it could not meet these demands of the Polish Government. France promised Poland military help and the support of Rumania. The Polish Government which rejected the French request was overthrown. Marshal Pilsudski took over the helm. It was he who organized the attack on Soviet Russia last year, and the Polish Government has now sent the ultimatum asked for by France. It went even further than the French demands by including a number of demands which from the outset could not be met. At the same time the Polish Government is beginning to organize frontier conflicts in order to create the necessary atmosphere in Poland. In Poland, where the bourgeois regime is on the point of falling, because of its own incapacity, and where one wave of strikes succeeds another, nationalist instincts have to be whipped up to get control of the masses and to suppress any revolutionary movement by the establishment of a military dictatorship. France hopes by overthrowing the Soviet Government in war or by diplomatic intimidation to squeeze out the old Tsarist debts from a country where the economic chaos was caused largely by French intervention.

At first it seemed that France was acting alone but the last few days have shown that that is not the case. On 7th September, four days after the French action in Warsaw of which ostensibly it knew nothing, the English Government decided to demand that the Soviet Government cease all revolutionary propaganda in the East. It despatched a note in which, as the ECCI has ascertained, it made its complaint on the basis of forgeries manufactured by the dirtiest German gang of spies left over from Ludendorff's police and reinforced by a band of international adventurers. This English démarche means that the clique of the English war minister Winston Churchill, who has not for a moment ceased to rage against Soviet Russia, is getting ready to tow English policy out of peaceful channels into French channels, that is, into war. For the time being the English Government is using its forgeries and threats only with the object of crippling Soviet Russia in the East. But this makes no difference. The result of Lloyd George's yielding to warmonger Churchill encourages France in its criminal game. If, with French help, Poland begins war on Soviet Russia, Churchill will have the opportunity to carry England along in this policy.

Together with the representatives of the RILU, the ECCI has examined the situation closely and considers it necessary to tell you that the international situation is in the broadest meaning of the word serious. Even if the exposure of France's secret steps in Poland and of Lord Curzon's shameless forgeries were for a time to dam the interventionist currents, the French campaign and the English forgeries have shown that powerful forces are at work preparing for further intervention. Once again stirred up and urged on by the French imperialist bourgeoisie, munitions and transports are reaching Poland and Germany, once again in the central European States arms are being manufactured for Poland or delivered from existing stocks. The attack on Soviet Russia is being systematically prepared. The ECCI and the RILU call on the workers of all countries without distinction of party, who would without any doubt consider it a crime to give the hungry millions lead instead of bread, to take up the struggle against these preparations on the widest scale.

We call on you to organize meetings and demonstrations in every country under the slogans—Help for Soviet Russia—Down with the criminals who are preparing an offensive against Soviet Russia.

Stop the transport of arms to Poland, Rumania, Estonia, Latvia, and Finland.

In every country, strengthen your influence among the soldiers so that they will not let themselves be misused as cannon fodder for international capital against Soviet Russia.

Make your rulers realize that you will use every means at your disposal to counter every threat and every pressure against Soviet Russia.

Bread and peace for the hungry Russian people.

Fight to the last against any threat to Soviet Russia.

ECCI RESOLUTION ON MEMBERS' CONTRIBUTIONS

4 *December* 1921   *Inprekorr*, i, 38, p. 339, 20 *December* 1921

The Executive Committee in its session of 4 December unanimously adopted the following draft prepared by a subcommission concerning the introduction of membership dues for the Communist International:

1. The ECCI resolves that all members of the Communist International shall pay international membership dues.

2. The yearly dues in each of the sections affiliated to the Communist International shall be fixed at the average monthly dues of the respective section.

3. International membership dues are to be paid quarterly in four equal instalments against the issue of a special international dues stamp. The dues stamps are to be printed by each section according to a uniform design decided upon by the ECCI and counter-stamped by the national section.

4. In all affiliated parties working legally the dues stamp is to be pasted in the membership book. On moving from the territory of one section to that of another, the rights accorded to a member by the statutes of the Comintern will be granted only upon proof of the payment of the international dues.

5. The international membership dues are to be transmitted to the ECCI through the central committees of the communist parties. The sections are obliged to settle their accounts quarterly, at the latest before the end of the next quarter. Neither groups nor sections have the right to charge expenditure made for or in the name of the Comintern against the international contribution. The international contribution must unconditionally and in all circumstances be paid by the sections directly to the Comintern.

6. The Executive Committee of the Comintern is obliged to submit accounts to the world congress, after a previous audit by the control commission.

7. The purpose of this decision is threefold. The international contribution will help to cover the increasing expenses of the central apparatus of the Comintern.

8. It will enable the materially better situated sections to support the weaker ones. This applies especially in cases of important political and economic actions.

9. It will also aid materially in establishing a more intimate contact between the Comintern and the individual sections.

The Comintern is no loose structure of affiliated sections, but the unified party of the communist workers of the entire world. This unity, of course, is expressed primarily in its policy and in the co-ordination of all proletarian action. It should, however, also be manifested by every communist being materially bound to this international party by the link of his individual membership dues. Therefore this decision is not only an organizational, but also a political measure.

The contribution shall come into effect on 1 January 1922.

APPEAL OF THE ECCI FOR HELP FOR THE FAMINE-STRICKEN AREAS OF RUSSIA

4 *December* 1921   *Inprekorr*, i, 39, p. 348, 22 *December* 1921

[The first ECCI appeal for famine relief for Russia was published in July 1921, and the communist press for the rest of that year and throughout 1922 continued to publish appeals and to report on the action taken in response to them. In an article published in October 1921 Radek wrote that 'the association of capitalists which calls itself the League of Nations' no longer thought of sending millions of men to fight Russia, believing that hunger would force the Soviet Government to agree to their terms. Help came from a number of quarters; the American Relief Administration and the Red Cross contributed large sums and sent relief missions to the stricken areas. In August 1921 the IFTU allocated a million marks for relief, and by October its affiliated organizations had contributed a further £50,000. The British Government supplied food and medical stores to the value of £200,000, and the American Government contributed $20 million for relief work.

At the fourth congress at the end of 1922 Münzenberg reported that the relief campaign had raised sums equivalent to two and a half million dollars. Zinoviev at the same congress accused the Second International of using the famine as an excuse for an anti-communist campaign which had made some headway among inexperienced workers.]

PROLETARIANS OF ALL COUNTRIES! TO THE AID OF THE RUSSIAN PROLETARIAT

Workers! Over the whole world capitalism is moving towards the attack. The more the capitalist world decays, the higher the wave of unemployment and crisis rises, rolling like an avalanche from country to country, the more impudently capital attacks your organizations, the louder it boasts of its strength and its power. But its foremost heralds and trumpeters, ministers and presidents, bankers and kings, are preparing new wars for humanity and are working out new armament programmes, pushing all the countries of the world into a war which will be more destructive, inhuman, and horrible than its predecessor. It will leave nothing standing and will kill and cripple millions of human beings—workers and peasants, the productive population of city and country.

Comrades! All of you, without distinction of party, must realize this. You must all understand that the only guarantee for your victory is your own strength, your own proletarian power. Who at the present time holds in check the insane plans of the capitalists? Who fills them with terror and fear?

Your Soviet Russia! For every capitalist government fears the armed Russian workers. For every capitalist government understands that Soviet Russia is to-day the chief instrument, *the main weapon in the hands of the world proletariat.*

Imagine that Soviet Russia has fallen. Then the wave of bloody reaction would overwhelm the entire world. Capitalism would then stride in a triumphal march over the skulls of the working-class. It would consolidate its position for long, long, years.

THEREFORE HELP SOVIET RUSSIA!

Help its workers who have borne the brunt of the first combined blows of the capitalist governments.

IN YOUR OWN INTERESTS HASTEN TO THE ASSISTANCE OF THE FIRST SOVIET STATE

The Russian workers have only now won the possibility of building up their economy. Only now is production beginning to rise, are the chimneys of its factories beginning to smoke.

But the drought is clipping the wings of the Russian proletariat. In the rich Volga region the grain has completely withered. Millions of human beings are dying in horrible agony. Sickness and starvation are mowing down old and young, and little children are dying with a cry for help on their lips. The situation is serious. The misfortune is great.

PROLETARIANS, HURRY TO THE AID OF SOVIET RUSSIA!

A number of workers' organizations have already given their mite for the Russian workers and peasants. The communists have collected 100,000,000 marks. Other workers' organizations have also given much help. This enables us to feed about 50,000 persons.

BUT THAT IS NOT ENOUGH! HASTEN, FRIENDS OF THE WORKING CLASS

Especially you, workers of North and South America, Australia, and South Africa. You have not yet gone through the bloody battle with capital. You have not yet been drawn into the final conflict. But the capitalist monster is already grasping you by the throat. It is already throwing millions of workers on to the streets. It is ready to deal you too the final blow.

HURRY TO THE ASSISTANCE OF YOUR CHIEF FORTRESS, SOVIET RUSSIA!

Help it to grow strong and to consolidate. You will be repaid a hundred-fold. Together, in serried battle ranks, enter the struggle against the famine in Russia.

Long live the solidarity of the workers who will not let down their brothers in distress and misery!

EXTRACTS FROM A LETTER FROM THE ECCI TO THE MARSEILLE CONGRESS OF THE FRENCH COMMUNIST PARTY

5 *December* 1921　　　　　　　　　　*Inprekorr*, i, 43, p. 378, 31 *December* 1921

[This was the first congress of the French Communist Party; it claimed a membership of 120,000. During its first year of existence it had suffered a series of internal crises and conducted a number of disputes with the ECCI. The French delegation at the third world congress had been severely criticized for tolerating attacks on the ECCI by the right wing.

Souvarine, French representative on the ECCI, was considered to have inspired these criticisms; Fabre's *Journal du Peuple* described them as 'Souvarine's ukases'. He was defeated in the elections to the central committee, and four elected members (Loriot, Treint, Dunois, Vaillant-Couturier) resigned in protest.]

One year separates us from the Tours congress. Today there is no longer a single revolutionary who regrets the work of splitting and cleansing which was carried out there. . . .

The CI warmly welcomes the results of your efforts to regroup and to reorganize your federations, to build a great party of 130,000 members and to improve your press. It is only the communist party and its press which can organize resistance to imperialism and reaction, whose stoutest pillars throughout the world are the French bourgeoisie. In this past year the party succeeded in winning steadily growing influence among the working masses and the small peasants of France.

These results, which give us great satisfaction, should not however blind us to the weaknesses and defects displayed during this first year. . . . The CI must do more than send greetings and good wishes to its sections. It is its duty to point out in a fraternal fashion their weaknesses and, guided solely by the interests of the world revolution, in closest collaboration with them to find ways of eliminating these weaknesses. In appraising the work of this first year we do not ignore the situation in which the party was left by the split at Tours. We know that a party which was brought into such confusion during the war cannot become communist overnight by passing resolutions at a congress. The voting at Tours indicated the will of the party to become a communist party. Therefore this first year had to display a constant effort and steady work to impart to the party a communist character. The efforts of the party were great but not great enough. Together with you we want to discover the reasons for this, convinced that the Marseille congress is anxious to do everything in its power to continue the work begun at Tours, to take into consideration the suggestions of the International designed to reinforce the communist character of the party and of its policy.

The party has suffered from weakness of leadership. The central committee spent too much time on administrative work but was unable to give the party firm political leadership. In its daily work it was not guided by the idea of developing party activity. It did not create a collective consciousness. The party has suffered from the absence of an agrarian policy, a trade union policy, and an electoral policy. The central committee left the examination and solution of all these problems to the Marseille congress, fearing that the federations would accuse it of dictatorship if it settled these problems itself. But every revolutionary will understand that the leadership of a communist party elected by the congress and so enjoying the confidence of the party must have the most comprehensive powers if it is to conduct the party's policy in accordance with the resolutions and decisions of the national and international congresses. A far stronger leadership must come from the Marseille congress, able to exercise political leadership, effectively to supervise and influence the party press, guide its parliamentary work and define its position day by day on all questions of French and international policy.

We think it would be useful to transfer minor administrative affairs to a special secretariat and to appoint from the central committee a central bureau of at least five members whose most important task will be this daily guidance of party work and thought. Side by side with building a stronger leadership it is necessary to develop a spirit of greater discipline in the party. Communists must think of themselves primarily as members of the party and must act as such throughout their public and private lives.

The question of trade union policy is certainly the most important and most difficult confronting the Marseille congress and the one where the absence of a policy was most felt during the past year. If the communist party wants to be the spearhead and champion of the social revolution it must give serious thought to trade union questions. There are no questions of concern to the workers which do not also concern the party. The party must therefore keep to a steady policy on trade union questions. It must loudly assert before the working class its right and its duty to concern itself actively with these questions. It must demand of its members to be as communist in the trade unions as they are in the party. A communist party cannot allow its members to go on supporting the policy of Jouhaux and the Amsterdam International. It must say clearly to all those who agree with Jouhaux that their place is in the party of Renaudel, Albert Thomas, and Longuet.

Similarly the party must energetically combat the anarchist and syndicalist ideas which deny the rôle of the party in the revolution. Nobody must be left in doubt that it is not the desire of the party and of the CI to subordinate the trade unions to the party; it is anxious to ensure that all party members play their part in the struggle of the trade union minority in France. . . . The party must seek to collaborate as closely as possible with those syndicalists who have revised their revolutionary ideas as a result of the history of the last few years. By discussing with them in a fraternal way all revolutionary problems, the party must try to get them to define clearly their present attitude, and it must combat their old anarcho-syndicalist traditions. We do not doubt that the party, if it becomes a truly revolutionary and communist party, will not only win the sympathy and confidence of the proletarian masses in France but will also be able to win into its ranks the syndicalist-communist comrades who still mistrust it. It will win these elements by a policy that is not opportunist and not vacillating. The draft thesis on the trade union question worked out by your central committee is only the first outline of a clarification of this fundamental question.

Those who say that the economic struggle does not concern the party are either hopeless fools or they are making fun of communism. The party must draw to itself all the best elements of the working classes and it must on the theoretical side inspire all forms of the proletarian struggle, including the economic struggle.

The trade union, as trade union, is not subordinate to the party as party. In this sense the trade unions are autonomous. The communists who are active in the trade unions must however always act as disciplined communists.

As a result of a number of special circumstances, there are still today outside the ranks of the French Communist Party a number of valuable revolutionary elements who regard themselves as syndicalists. We must come to an understanding with them and sooner or later unite with them in the ranks of the single communist party, but we cannot and must not encourage syndicalist prejudices against parties and against political action.

When the French party delegation was in Moscow for the third congress the ECCI called their attention to the necessity of central committee supervision of the unofficial party press. The ECCI was thinking primarily of Brizon's *Vague* and Fabre's *Journal du Peuple*, both of which were conducting a policy incompatible with the policy of the party and the International. The unequivocal theses of the second congress laid it down that no party member can claim for himself a so-called press freedom in order to publish a journal which is not under the complete control of the party. With the unanimous consent of the French delegation, the Executive passed a resolution on this question and informed the French central committee, but it has received no official reply. It asks the Marseille congress to give the Executive the party's answer to this question, which it regards as a most fundamental question of communist discipline which should have been decided by the party leadership. The delay is the more regrettable as, since the decision was taken, the opportunist tendency has crystallized around the *Journal du Peuple*, regretting the split at Tours, bemoaning the expulsion of dissidents and of Serrati, and even advocating open collaboration with bourgeois parties in the form of the left bloc. It is not surprising that these comrades who are pursuing a policy so wholly inconsistent with communist principles should feel themselves injured by our resolution and should try to shift responsibility on to the French representative on the Executive.

We hope that the party at Marseille will clearly express its hostility to such a policy and will summon this group of comrades back to communist discipline.

It seems necessary to us that the French party should try to remain in the closest and most continuous contact with the workers in the factories. Far too often the party press has a discontented rather than a proletarian revolutionary character. Nor are there enough factory workers in the party leadership. It seems to us necessary to increase the working-class element when the new central committee is elected.

The French party has always stood too much aside from the life of the International. We hope that in future there will be closer and more frequent contacts, enabling the French party to take an active and fruitful share in the life of the Communist International.

As we consider French questions to be questions for the whole International so we hope that the French workers will regard all questions which concern the proletariat of Germany, Russia, America, etc., as their own, and will by discussion take an active part in the work and the struggle of all sections of the International.

ECCI CIRCULAR TO ALL SECTIONS ON FORWARDING OF MATERIAL

15 *December* 1921   *Inprekorr*, i, 39, p. 350, 22 *December* 1921

TO THE PARTIES AFFILIATED TO THE COMMUNIST INTERNATIONAL

The question of the transitional demands of the communist parties was before the third congress of the Communist International. But it could only be dealt with hastily, for the attention of the congress was concentrated primarily upon the problems raised by the March action. In the meanwhile, the question of transitional demands has become more important. With every day the communist parties have to give more and more time to the questions posed by current policy. They must define their attitude to the concrete measures of bourgeois governments and must place concrete remedial proposals before these governments. The Executive must study all these questions as a whole in order to assist the communist parties by enabling them to benefit from each other's experiences. It therefore requests all communist parties to collect and send to the Executive all the material upon their previous statements and demands on social and economic policy, taxes, judicial and constitutional questions, in short, all the material relating to our demands upon the bourgeois governments. Material referring to the past as well as the present activity of the party should be sent.

EXTRACTS FROM THE DIRECTIVES ON THE UNITED FRONT OF THE WORKERS AND ON THE ATTITUDE TO WORKERS BELONGING TO THE SECOND, TWO-AND-A-HALF, AND AMSTERDAM INTERNATIONALS, AND TO THOSE WHO SUPPORT ANARCHO-SYNDICALIST ORGANIZATIONS, ADOPTED BY THE ECCI

18 *December* 1921   *Protokoll*, iv, p. 1019

[In his speech of 4 December 1921 at the meeting of the ECCI which issued these theses, Zinoviev said that the war and the struggles of the immediate post-war period had left the working class exhausted and passive. They attributed their defeats to disunity, and a united front policy would win their allegiance. There was no contradiction, he said, between a united front policy and the policy of attracting unions from the IFTU into the RILU, since united front action could not be taken except on communist terms. To the question, if you want a united front, why split, he said: 'This is a dialectical question which every communist must understand. Precisely because it is an epoch of splits, and because we have now become a force, we can on certain conditions work together with the Second and Two-and-a-half Internationals, in order to draw the masses over to the side of communism most quickly. But if we had not made the split, we would not be the factor which we now are, and could not carry this manœuvre through. It is possible that we shall have to carry out many more splits, and we shall still go to the socialists and say: "Yes, we want unity; unity on this platform." ' At the end of the year, in a long article on 'The tasks of the Communist International', Radek wrote that reformist hostility to the united front policy showed how right it was. If it succeeded, they would have won the ear of the social-democratic workers and pushed their leaders to the left; if it failed, the leaders would be exposed. 'The new tactic therefore has such indisputable advantages and opens such favourable perspectives for international communism, for the class struggle of the proletariat, that it will certainly become the common property of all communist parties.' It corresponded with certain general changes in the international situation. Until 1920 they had used other methods of struggle, the methods of assault. 'At that time we not only did not propose joint action with the social-democratic parties, but sought by all means in our power to force a split in them. We placed in the foreground the slogan of Soviet dictatorship, while now . . . we place in the foreground concrete transitional demands.' An international explosion could not be expected, but only the slow ripening of the revolution. The programme therefore was not the assault itself, but the accumulation of forces for the assault, and this could be done inter alia by work inside the social-democratic parties, with the object of winning or splitting them. At the meeting of the enlarged ECCI in February 1922, Zinoviev said: 'Had the Red Army in 1920 taken Warsaw, the tactics of the CI to-day would be other than they are. . . . The strategic setback was followed by a political setback for the whole workers' movement. The Russian proletarian party was compelled to make extensive concessions. . . . That slowed down the tempo of the proletarian revolution, but the reverse is also true; the setback which the proletariat of the western European countries suffered from 1919 to 1921 influenced the policy of the first proletarian State and slowed down the tempo in Russia.'

Meyer (KPD) echoed the same thought: 'The slowing down of revolutionary tempo in central and western Europe forced Soviet Russia to a policy of concessions, as shown most recently in its agreement to participate in the Genoa conference. The new course in Soviet Russia and the new tactics of the International since the third congress are most closely connected; both are a consequence of the changes in the international situation.' At the fourth world congress Radek said: 'We entered on this road not because we want to merge with the social-democrats, but in the knowledge that we shall stifle them in our embrace.' In 1924, at the fifth world congress, Zinoviev said: 'The tactics of the united front were in reality . . . an expression of our consciousness, first, that we have not yet a majority of the working class, secondly, that social-democracy is still very strong, thirdly, that we occupy defensive positions, and . . . fourthly, that the decisive battles are still not yet on the immediate agenda.'

The theses aroused deep and prolonged controversy within the International. They were discussed by the French central committee in January at three meetings. It adopted (with one abstention) a resolution, to be submitted to a special delegate conference, asserting that the united front tactics could not be applied in France, instructing the French delegates to the special ECCI conference to be held in February to vote in this sense and to ask that the question be put on the agenda of the fourth Comintern congress. The special delegate conference endorsed the committee's resolution by a vote of 46 to 12.

At the first enlarged plenary session of the ECCI, which met from 21 February to 4 March 1922, and consisted of 105 delegates from 36 parties, the French, Italian, and Spanish delegations opposed the united front theses, which were adopted by 46 votes to 10. The chief argument of the opponents was that, having emphasized in all their propaganda that the social-democrats were the worst enemies of the working class, the new tactics would only bewilder and confuse the workers. The congress of the Italian Communist Party in Rome at the end of March 1922 passed, against 8 votes, a resolution put forward by Bordiga which rejected the application of united front tactics in the political field, while accepting them for trade union work.

Cachin, speaking at the February meeting, asked the ECCI to take note that three delegations—the French, Italian, and Spanish—had expressed reservations about the new tactics; the French party would, however, observe discipline and carry out ECCI decisions. But at the meeting of the national council of the CPF on 22–23 April 1922, a resolution was adopted that the party was bound to maintain until its next congress the objections previously put forward, while 'proclaiming its firm determination to fight as a whole alongside the CI.' It was opposed to any understanding with the reformist and syndicalist leaders and regretted that in some countries the communist parliamentary fractions were co-operating with the socialists. It regretted the joint activities with the Second and Two-and-a-half Internationals. 'The national council', it added, 'notes the resolution of the enlarged ECCI, but states that only the fourth world congress can finally decide the question at issue with the necessary authority.'

At the June 1922 meeting of the ECCI French and Italian opposition was maintained, but the internal conflict was covered by a resolution (formulated by Trotsky in the French commission) and passed by the ECCI without discussion, which asserted that the united front did not imply any abatement of hostility to reformism and instructed the Executive to work out instructions appropriate to each country. At French insistence the question was put on the agenda of the fourth world congress.]

1. The international labour movement is passing at present through a peculiar transition stage, which presents both the Communist International as a whole and its individual sections with new and important tactical problems.

The chief characteristics of this stage are: The world economic crisis is growing more acute. Unemployment is increasing. In practically every country international capital has gone over to a systematic offensive against the workers, as shown primarily in the fairly open efforts of the capitalists to reduce wages and to lower the workers' entire standard of life. The bankruptcy of the Versailles peace has become ever more apparent to the broadest strata of the workers. The inevitability of a new imperialist war, or even of several such wars, is clear, unless the international proletariat overthrows bourgeois rule. . . .

The 'democratic' and reformist illusions which, after the end of the imperialist slaughter, were reborn among the workers (the better-off workers on the one hand, and the most backward and politically inexperienced on the other) are fading before they reached full bloom. The 'labours' of the Washington conference will shake these illusions even more. If, six months ago, it was possible to speak with some justification of a general swing to the right among the working masses in Europe and

America, there is no doubt that today, on the contrary, the beginning of a swing to the left can be observed.

2. On the other hand, under the influence of the mounting capitalist attack there has awakened among the workers a spontaneous *striving toward unity* which literally cannot be restrained, and which goes hand in hand with a gradual growth in the confidence placed by the broad working masses in the communists. . . .

3. Communist parties can and should now gather the fruits of the struggle which they waged earlier on when conditions were most unfavourable because of the indifference of the masses. But while the workers are coming to feel greater and greater confidence in the uncompromising and militant elements of the working class, in the communists, they are as a whole moved by an unprecedented urge towards unity. Those strata of the workers now awakening to active life but with little political experience are dreaming of the unification of all workers' parties and even of all workers' organizations in general, hoping by this means to increase their power of resisting the capitalists. . . . Considerable sections belonging to the old social-democratic parties also are no longer content with the campaign of the social-democrats and centrists against the communist vanguard, and are beginning to demand an understanding with the communists. But at the same time they have *not yet* lost their belief in the reformists, and considerable masses still support the parties of the Second and the Amsterdam Internationals. These working masses do not formulate their plans and aspirations clearly enough, but by and large the new mood can be attributed to the desire to establish the united front and to attempt to bring about joint action by the parties and unions of the Second and Amsterdam Internationals with the communists against the capitalist attack. To that extent this mood is progressive. In essentials the belief in reformism has been undermined. In the general situation in which the labour movement now finds itself any serious mass action, even if it proceeds only from partial demands, inevitably brings to the forefront more general and fundamental questions of the revolution. The communist vanguard can only gain if new sections of workers are convinced by their own experience of the illusory character of reformism and compromise.

4. In the early stage of germination of a conscious and organized protest against the treachery of the leaders of the Second International these latter had the entire apparatus of the workers' organizations in their hands. They ruthlessly used the principle of unity and proletarian discipline to stifle the revolutionary proletarian protest and to eliminate any resistance to their placing the entire power of the workers' organizations at the service of national imperialism. In these circumstances the revolutionary wing was forced to win at any cost freedom of agitation and propaganda, i.e. freedom to explain to the working masses the unexampled historical

treachery committed and still being committed by the parties created by the working masses themselves.

5. Having secured organizational freedom to influence the working masses by their propaganda, the communist parties of all countries are now trying to achieve the broadest and most complete unity possible on practical action. The Amsterdamers and the heroes of the Second International preach this unity in words, but in their actions work against it. Having failed to suppress organizationally the voice of the proletariat and of revolutionary agitation, the reformist compromisers of Amsterdam are now seeking a way out of the deadlock for which they themselves are responsible by initiating splits, by disorganizing and sabotaging the struggle of the working masses. It is at present one of the most important tasks of the communist party to expose publicly these new forms of an old treachery.

6. Profound internal processes are however forcing the diplomats and leaders of the Second, Two-and-a-half, and Amsterdam Internationals to push the question of unity into the foreground. But while, for those sections of the working class with little experience who are only beginning to awaken to class-conscious life, the slogan of the united front expresses a most genuine and sincere desire to mobilize the forces of the oppressed classes against the capitalist onslaught, the leaders and diplomats of these Internationals advance that slogan only in a new attempt to deceive the workers and to entice them by new means on to the old road of class collaboration. The approaching danger of a new imperialist war (Washington), the growth of armaments, the new imperialist secret treaties concluded behind closed doors—all this will not induce the leaders of the three Internationals to beat the alarm in order to bring about the international unification of the working class not only in words, but also in fact; on the contrary, it will provoke inevitable friction and division within the Second and Amsterdam Internationals, roughly of the same kind as that apparent in the camp of the international bourgeoisie. This phenomenon is inevitable because the solidarity of the reformist 'socialists' with the bourgeoisie of their 'own' countries is the cornerstone of reformism. . . .

7. Confronted by this situation, the ECCI is of the opinion that the slogan of the third world congress of the Communist International 'To the Masses', and the interests of the communist movement generally, require the communist parties and the Communist International as a whole to *support the slogan of the united front of the workers* and to take the initiative in this matter. The tactics of each communist party must of course be worked out concretely in relation to the conditions in each country.

8. In *Germany* the communist party at its last national conference supported the slogan of a workers' united front and declared its readiness to support a workers' government which was willing to take up with some seriousness the struggle against the power of the capitalists. The ECCI

considers this decision completely right and is convinced that the KPD, while maintaining in full its independent political attitude, is in a position to permeate broad sections of the workers and strengthen the influence of communism on the masses. In Germany more than anywhere else the broad masses will be daily more convinced how right the communist vanguard were when at the most difficult time they did not want to lay down their arms and steadily emphasized the worthlessness of the reformist actions proposed, since the crisis could be resolved only by the proletarian revolution. By pursuing those tactics the party will in time also rally round itself the revolutionary elements among the anarchists and syndicalists who now stand aside from the mass struggle.

9. In *France* the communist party has a majority among the politically organized workers. Hence the united front question has a different bearing there from what it has in other countries. But even there it is necessary that the entire responsibility for the split in the united workers' camp should fall on our opponents. The revolutionary section of the French syndicalists are rightly fighting against a split in the French unions, that is, fighting for the unity of the working class in the economic struggle against the bourgeoisie. But the workers' struggle does not stop in the factories. Unity is necessary also in the face of growing reaction, of imperialist policies, etc. The policy of the reformists and centrists, on the other hand, led to the split in the party and now also threatens the unity of the trade union movement, which shows that Jouhaux just like Longuet objectively serves the cause of the bourgeoisie. The slogan of the united front of the proletariat in the economic and the political struggle against the bourgeoisie remains the best means of counteracting these splitting plans.

Even though the reformist CGT, led by Jouhaux, Merrheim and Co., betrays the interests of the French working class, French communists and the revolutionary elements among the French working class in general must, before every mass strike, every revolutionary demonstration, or any other revolutionary mass action, propose to the reformists support for such action, and if they refuse to support the revolutionary struggle of the workers they must be exposed. This will be the easiest way of winning the non-party working masses. In no circumstances, of course, must the Communist Party of France allow its independence to be restricted, e.g. by supporting the 'left bloc' during election campaigns, or behave tolerantly towards those vacillating communists who still bemoan the break with the social-patriots.

10. In *England* the reformist Labour Party has rejected communist party affiliation although other workers' organizations are accepted. Under the influence of the growing desire among the workers for the united front, the London workers' organizations recently passed a resolution in favour of the affiliation of the CPGB to the Labour Party.

England is of course in this respect an exception because as a result of peculiar circumstances the English Labour Party is a kind of general workers' association for the entire country. It is the task of the English communists to begin a vigorous campaign for their acceptance by the Labour Party. The recent treachery of the union leaders during the miners' strike, the systematic capitalist pressure on wages, etc. have stirred up a deep ferment among the English proletariat, who are becoming more revolutionary. English communists should make every effort, using the slogan of the revolutionary united front against the capitalists, to penetrate at all costs deep into the working masses.

11. In *Italy* the young communist party is beginning to conduct its agitation according to the slogan of the proletarian united front against the capitalist offensive, although it is most irreconcilably opposed to the reformist Italian Socialist Party and the social-traitor labour confederation, which recently put the finishing touch to their open treachery to the proletarian revolution. The ECCI considers this agitation by the Italian communists completely correct and insists only that it shall be intensified. The ECCI is convinced that with sufficient foresight the CP of Italy can give an example to the entire International of militant Marxism which mercilessly exposes at every step the half-heartedness and the treachery of the reformists and centrists who clothed themselves in the mantle of communism, and at the *same time* conduct an untiring and ever-mounting campaign among ever broader masses *for the united front of the workers against the bourgeoisie.*

The party must of course do its utmost to draw all the revolutionary elements among the anarchists and syndicalists into the common struggle. . . .

16. In a number of other countries the position differs according to different local circumstances. Having made the general line clear, the ECCI is sure that the individual communist parties will know how to apply that line in accordance with the conditions prevailing in each country.

17. The principal conditions which are equally categorical for communist parties in all countries are, in the view of the ECCI . . . the absolute independence of every communist party which enters into an agreement with the parties of the Second and the Two-and-a-half Internationals, its complete freedom to put forward its own views and to criticize the opponents of communism. While accepting a basis for action, communists must retain the unconditional right and the possibility of expressing their opinion of the policy of all working-class organizations without exception, not only before and after action has been taken but also, if necessary, *during its course.* In no circumstances can these rights be surrendered. While supporting the slogan of the greatest possible unity of all workers' organizations in every *practical action against the capitalist front,* communists may in

no circumstances desist from putting forward their views, which are the only consistent expression of the defence of working-class interests as a whole.

18. The ECCI considers it useful to remind all brother parties of the experiences of the Russian Bolsheviks, that party which up to now is the only one that has succeeded in winning victory over the bourgeoisie and taking power into its hands. During the fifteen years (1903–1917) which elapsed between the birth of bolshevism and its triumph over the bourgeoisie, it did not cease to wage a tireless struggle against reformism or, what is the same thing, menshevism. But at the same time the Bolsheviks often came to an understanding with the mensheviks during those fifteen years. The formal break with the mensheviks took place in the spring of 1905, but at the end of 1905, influenced by the stormy developments in the workers' movement, the Bolsheviks formed a common front with the mensheviks . . . and these unifications and semi-unifications happened not only in accordance with changes in the fractional struggle, but also under the direct pressure of the working masses who were awakening to active political life and demanded the opportunity of testing by their own experience whether the menshevik path really deviated in fundamentals from the road of revolution. . . . The Russian Bolsheviks did not reply to the desire of the workers for unity with a renunciation of the united front. On the contrary. As a counterweight to the diplomatic game of the menshevik leaders the Russian Bolsheviks put forward the slogan of 'unity from below', that is, unity of the working masses in the practical struggle for the revolutionary demands of the workers against the capitalists. Events showed that this was the only correct answer. And as a result of those tactics, which changed according to time, place, and circumstance, a large number of the best menshevik workers were won for communism.

19. While the Communist International puts forward the slogan of the workers' united front and permits agreements between the various sections of the International and the parties and unions of the Second and Two-and-a-half Internationals, it can itself obviously not reject similar understandings at the international level. The ECCI made a proposal to the Amsterdam International in connexion with relief action for the Russian famine. It repeated this proposal in connexion with the white terror and the persecution of workers in Spain and Yugoslavia. The ECCI is now making a further proposal to the Amsterdam, Second, and Two-and-a-half Internationals, in connexion with the opening of the Washington conference which has shown that the international working class is threatened by a new imperialist slaughter. Up to now the leaders of these Internationals have shown by their conduct that *in fact* they ignore their unity slogan when it comes to *practical action*. In all such cases it will be the task of the Communist International as a whole and of all its sections separately

to explain to the broad working masses the hypocrisy of these leaders who prefer unity with the bourgeoisie to unity with the revolutionary workers, and who, for example, by remaining in the International Labour Office of the League of Nations, form part of the Washington imperialist conference instead of organizing the struggle against imperialist Washington. But though the leaders of the Second, Two-and-a-half, and Amsterdam Internationals reject one or another practical proposal put forward by the Communist International, that will not persuade us to give up the united front tactic, which has deep roots in the masses and which we must systematically and steadily develop. Whenever the offer of a joint struggle is rejected by our opponents the masses must be informed of this and thus learn who are the real destroyers of the workers' united front. Whenever an offer is accepted by our opponents every effort must be made gradually to intensify the struggle and to develop it to its highest power. In either case it is essential to capture the attention of the broad working masses, to interest them in all stages of the struggle for the revolutionary united front.

20. In putting forward the present plan, the ECCI directs the attention of all brother parties to the dangers which it may in certain circumstances entail. Not all communist parties are sufficiently strong and firm, not all have broken completely with the centrist and semi-centrist ideology. Some may overstep the mark, there may be tendencies which would amount in fact to the dissolution of communist parties and groups into the united but formless bloc. To carry out the new tactics successfully for the communist cause it is necessary for the communist parties who put them into operation to be strong and firmly welded together, and for their leaders to possess great theoretical clarity.

21. Within the Communist International itself, there are two tendencies among the groups which may with more or less reason be classed as right or even semi-centrist. One has not really broken with the ideology and methods of the Second International, has not emancipated itself completely from reverence for its former numerical strength, and, half-consciously or unconsciously, is looking for a path of intellectual understanding with the Second International and consequently with bourgeois society. Other elements, who are opposed to formal radicalism, to the mistakes of the so-called 'left', are anxious to give the tactics of the young communist party greater flexibility and manœuvrability, in order to ensure for it the possibility of more rapid penetration among the masses.

The rapid development of the communist parties has occasionally thrust both apparently into the same camp, to some extent into the same group. The use of the methods noted above, which are designed to provide a prop for communist agitation in the united mass actions of the proletariat, is the best way of exposing the really reformist tendencies within the communist parties and if rightly used will contribute in a high degree to their internal revolutionary consolidation, both by educating the impatient and sectarian elements through experience, as well as by ridding the parties of reformist ballast.

22. The united front of the workers means the united front of all workers who want to fight against capitalism, which includes those who still follow the anarchists, syndicalists, etc. In many countries such workers can help in the revolutionary struggle. From the first days of its existence the Communist International has taken a friendly line to these workers, who are gradually overcoming their prejudices and drawing nearer to communism. Communists must pay even greater attention to them now, when the united front of the workers against the capitalists is becoming a reality.

23. In order to give definite form to future work on the lines laid down, the ECCI resolves to convene a meeting of the Executive in the near future at which the parties will be represented by double the usual number of members.

24. The ECCI will follow carefully every practical step taken in the field under discussion, and asks every party to inform the Executive of every attempt and every success, giving full factual details.

EXTRACTS FROM AN ECCI-RILU MANIFESTO ON THE UNITED FRONT

1 *January* 1922   *Inprekorr*, ii, 2, p. 9, 5 *January* 1922

[In a speech on 20 October 1922 Trotsky, explaining the united front policy, said that the third congress had made it clear that the immediate task of communists in Europe was not to capture power, but to win the majority of the working class. 'If we consider that the party is on the eve of the conquest of power and the working class will follow it, then the question of the united front does not arise. But . . . if we become convinced that a certain interval must elapse, perhaps several years, before the conquest of power . . . it is necessary to consider what will happen in the interim to the working class.' At the fourth congress he said that 'the basic idea underlying the decisions of the third congress was as follows. After the war the masses were seized by a revolutionary mood and were eager to take up the battle, but there was no revolutionary party capable of leading them to victory. Hence the defeat of the revolutionary masses in various countries; hence the mood of depression and passivity. Today revolutionary parties exist in all countries, but they rest directly only upon a fraction of the working class. . . . The communist parties must win the confidence of the overwhelming majority of the working class. When experience has convinced them of the correctness, firmness, and stability of communist leadership, the working class will shake off disillusionment, passivity, and dilatoriness. . . . This can and must be achieved in the course of fighting for the workers' transitional demands under the general slogan of the proletarian united front.']

FOR THE UNITED PROLETARIAN FRONT!

Proletarians of all countries!

The Executive Committees of the Communist International and the Red International of Labour Unions have at three meetings examined the world situation and the situation of the international proletariat, and have come to the conclusion that this situation demands the concentration of all the forces of the international proletariat, the establishment of a united front of all parties supported by the proletariat, regardless of the differences separating them, so long as they are anxious to wage a common fight for the immediate and urgent needs of the proletariat. The ECCI is calling an enlarged meeting for 19 February. . . . At the same time it calls on the proletarians of all parties to do everything they can to see that their parties are also ready for joint action. . . .

Six million unemployed in America, two million in England, mounting unemployment in the neutral countries enriched by the war, because they cannot export. While in the ruined countries of central and eastern Europe, in Russia, in the Balkans, in Turkey, there is the greatest poverty. These countries need the products of the industrial countries to set their economy going and to enable them to supply the industrial world with food and raw materials. And, wedged between east and west, there is Germany, working without pause, sending out into the world vast quantities of goods at prices with which the other countries cannot compete. There is practically no unemployment there, but the German workers are worse off than the unemployed in England. Against their will they have become wage reducers for the workers in other countries. . . . Victorious capital is trying to lay the burden of reconstruction costs on to *one* country, and the result is that Germany itself is bound to break down under the burden and become a heap of ruins. And where the bourgeoisie do set about reconstruction, it becomes the object of speculation and exploitation which will give rise to new conflicts.

Three years of civil war and three years of armed intervention by the Allies have laid waste Soviet Russia, Europe's granary, despite its heroic resistance. The drought this summer, which threatens 25 million with death by starvation, makes the question of Russian reconstruction one of life and death for millions of Russian workers and peasants. And it is becoming clear even to the stupid bourgeois that without recognition of the invincible Soviet Government, without the economic reconstruction of Russia, neither the world economic crisis nor the great political tensions can be even temporarily overcome. . . . But the world bourgeoisie leave the hungry millions of the Russian people without help, for they expect hunger to make them more docile. In return for recognition, the Soviet Government is to surrender Russia to a syndicate run by international finance, which would operate in Russia as it has operated in Turkey and China. . . .

It is not only the attitude of world capital to Germany and Russia which represents a source of great new upheavals. The Washington conference, which tried to solve the problems of the Far East, did not solve them. The great Chinese people, 400 million strong, has remained an object of bargaining and of continued rivalry. Aware of their inability to renounce the plundering of China or to partition it, the Allied Powers concluded the four-power treaty, which proves only one thing, that they feel how great the danger of war is, and therefore try to restrain each other from independent action by the frail bonds of a treaty. They did not dare to reduce land armaments even on paper, and all the talk about naval disarmament ended with a limitation on superdreadnoughts while submarine and aircraft armaments increase. . . .

Incapable of uniting for reconstruction, incapable of ensuring bread and peace, the capitalists of all countries are uniting for attack on the working class. . . . The proletariat which during the war, by its labour in the factories and its docility, enabled capital to beat the world into ruins, is now, in peace time, to work harder so that the hyenas of the battlefield may on those ruins live a life of luxury and pleasure. . . .

All the promises of the Second, the Two-and-a-half, and the Amsterdam Internationals have turned to dust. They have all shown themselves incapable of leading you in the struggle even for democracy and reforms, because they are condemned to impotence by their coalition with the bourgeoisie and, whether they want to or not, only help to strengthen the rule of the bourgeoisie. . . .

We know how strong are the chains of the past, the influence of the capitalist school, press, and church. We know how great is the reluctance of large proletarian masses to take power in their own hands and forge their own destiny. We know how great is their fear of the defeats which the communist minorities suffered in the struggles which they waged to save the masses from the fate of slaves. We know how the capitalist press of the entire world seeks to rob you of your courage by pointing to the wounds which the isolated Russian proletariat received in its duel with the entire capitalist world. And therefore we say to you: All right, you do not yet dare to take up the fight for the new, the struggle for power, for the dictatorship, with arms in hand; you are not ready to launch the great offensive on the citadels of world reaction. But at least rally to the fight for bare life, for bread, for peace. Rally for these, struggle in one fighting front, rally as the proletarian class against the class of exploiters. Tear down the barriers erected between you and come into the ranks, whether communist or social-democrat, anarchist or syndicalist, to fight for the needs of the hour.

The Communist International has always demanded that the workers who stand for the proletarian dictatorship and for soviets should form their own independent parties. It does not withdraw a single word of what it said to justify the formation of independent communist parties; it is sure that each day that passes will convince growing numbers how right it was to act as it did. But regardless of everything that separates us, it says: Proletarians of all countries! Close the ranks for the struggle for what unites you, for what you all realize as your common goal.

No worker, whether communist or social-democrat or syndicalist, or even a member of the Christian or liberal trade unions, wants his wages further reduced. None wants to work longer hours, cold and hungry. And therefore all must unite in a common front against the employers' offensive. . . . They all fear being thrown on the scrap heap, and therefore they must join in the fight against everything which increases unemployment. And unemployment will be perpetuated in all industrial countries if the German proletariat is compelled by the Entente and German capital to slave away, exerting pressure on wages throughout the world, so that German capitalists can throw German goods at bargain prices on to the world market and then pay the Versailles tribute. Unemployment will grow if the capitalist world tries to impose conditions of slavery and subjection on Soviet Russia. . . . Therefore unite to fight for the cancellation of war debts and against the strangling of Germany, for the recognition of Soviet Russia and its reconstruction on terms in accordance with the interests of the international proletariat. . . .

The Communist International calls on communist workers, and on all honest workers throughout the world, to come together in their workshops and in their meetings into one family of the working people who stand by each other against capital. . . . Only in this way will all the parties which rely on the proletariat and want the proletariat to follow them, be compelled to come together for the common defensive struggle against capital. Only then will they be compelled to sever their alliance with capitalist parties. . . .

The proletarian giant cannot stretch his limbs, cannot rise to his full height, in the bourgeois chicken-coop. When you begin the fight you will see that you need the sword of dictatorship if you are to triumph. But we know that this dictatorship is possible only if the great majority of the proletariat reach it through their own experience, and that is why the Communist International and the communist parties, in patience and fraternity, wish to march together with all other proletarians, even if they fight on the basis of capitalist democracy. . . .

Firmly convinced that the fighting proletariat will be compelled to take the communist road, we call to you: Proletarians of all countries, unite!

ECCI RESOLUTION ON THE TASKS OF COMMUNISTS IN TRADE UNIONS

February 1922   *Inprekorr*, ii, 30, p. 239, 14 *March* 1922

[The first 'enlarged plenum' of the ECCI, held from 21 February to 4 March 1922, was attended by 105 delegates from 36 sections. It considered *inter alia* the theses on the united front and the proposal from the Vienna Union for a conference of the three Internationals, the war danger and communist work in the trade unions, and the position in the French and British communist parties. The resolution on the Communist Party of Great Britain urged the CPGB to 'seek admission to the Labour Party, thus making possible working-class unity in the political field, particularly in view of the forthcoming elections, with the object of electing a labour government. . . . While affiliating to the Labour Party the CPGB must retain complete freedom of propaganda.' The presidium elected at this meeting consisted of Zinoviev, Radek, Bukharin, Brandler, Souvarine, Terracini, Kreibich, and Carr.

Lozovsky reported on the RILU, and said, *inter alia*: 'Of course we are against splits. But we can in no circumstances conclude from that that we should not make use of splits organizationally when we win the majority in a union.' A union in which the left had won a majority should not remain affiliated to the IFTU. The question of 'liquidating' the RILU was brought up at the fourth Comintern congress later in the year.]

1. The enlarged plenum confirms that there is no need to introduce any change of principle into the decisions of the third Comintern congress on the trade union question. The half-yearly report has shown that the directives on trade union work were correct and appropriate. The present session is dealing with the trade union question only in order to instruct communists that it is necessary in accordance with their increased influence in the unions, to make their work more concrete and to adapt it to the special conditions of the different countries and industries.

2. As a result of the mounting capitalist offensive the trade union movement in all countries is going through a critical period. This is shown in the decline of membership and the exhaustion of trade union funds. On the other hand the growing poverty of the broad masses is exerting an elemental pressure towards unity in the struggle against the capitalist offensive, towards putting an end to the dilatory tactics of the reformist leaders which rob the trade unions of their fighting strength, and, if all else fails, towards defending their basic vital rights by means of united action without the reformist leaders and over their heads.

3. This situation in the international trade union movement is particularly favourable for the further development and deepening of activity to capture the unions and to extend communist influence among the masses. Communists who work in the trade union movement must take this state of affairs as their starting point when they carry on the struggle for the RILU.

4. In some countries the RILU is still only a tendency within the old organizations. In others it embraces the majority of the membership, while in still others it has won the trade union centre. With this in mind it is the task of communists in countries where the RILU is only a tendency to rally all these workers inside each union, national and international, into a strong centre which has the will to take up the struggle against the bourgeoisie seriously and carry it through. Where we have a majority of revolutionary-minded workers in the trade unions, it is the task of communists to advocate adherence of the national trade union movement to the RILU.

5. In the forthcoming period the task of communists is to extend their influence in the old reformist trade unions, to fight the splitting policy of the Amsterdam leaders, and to carry out carefully and consistently the tactics of the united front in the trade union movement. However large the minority within an individual union or trade union federation is, communists must see that this minority stays within its organization and fights for carrying through the programme and tactics of the minority. The adherence of such trade union minorities to the RILU can only be an ideological one, which they must demonstrate by the practical execution of the decisions of the first congress of the revolutionary unions and by following Profintern tactics.

6. Communists are obliged to work in favour of the individual unions affiliated to the RILU remaining inside the international trade and industrial secretariats. If such unions have not already entered these bodies, they must do so. We have put the issue openly and squarely before the international proletariat. We remain inside the national trade union associations and only join the Profintern as organizations if we succeed in winning the majority for the principles of the RILU. At their trade union congress the workers of every country will have to decide whose programme and tactics serve the interests of the working class—those of the Amsterdam International or those of the RILU. This is the only way in which the broad masses will learn who are the splitters, who are hampering the formation of a powerful centre against the powerful employing class. This is the only way in which the masses will recognize that the Amsterdamers are servants of the bourgeoisie who defend bourgeois democracy against the proletarian dictatorship but who trample on proletarian democracy whenever communists by the methods of proletarian democracy try to win a majority in the unions in order to try to change these unions in accordance with the will of the majority from subsidiary agencies of the bourgeoisie into militant bodies fighting against the bourgeoisie.

7. The liquidationist tendencies to be noted in some parties in regard to the RILU arose from a number of misunderstandings and from the false hope that the Amsterdam leaders would turn left. These tendencies must be sharply and categorically condemned. The Amsterdamers will

always vacillate, moving to the left to the extent that the influence of the communist parties in the respective countries increases and the RILU extends its organizational and intellectual influence on the trade union movement. Communists must not count on the leftward turn of the trade union leaders. They must base their tactics on the inevitable revolutionizing of the masses. As social contradictions grow, as the communist parties and the Communist International strengthen their influence, as the working class becomes more revolutionary, the Amsterdam International will make greater efforts to conceal their reformist deeds, their retreat from struggle, even from the struggle for the most urgent daily needs, behind revolutionary phrases.

8. The communist parties and the Communist International which took the initiative in creating the RILU must continue their work by strengthening and developing this organization, which embraces not only communist but also syndicalist and non-party revolutionary elements.

MESSAGE FROM THE ENLARGED ECCI ON THE FOURTH ANNIVERSARY OF THE FOUNDATION OF THE RED ARMY

22 *February* 1922   *Inprekorr*, ii, 2 Sonderbeilage, p. 12, 1 *April* 1922

[At the foundation congress Trotsky assured the delegates that 'the communist workers who form the real kernel of the Red Army, are acting not only as troops defending the Russian socialist republic, but also as the Red Army of the Third International'. Those who fell died not only for Soviet Russia, but for the Third International too. When the call came from their brothers in the west, the Red Army would answer 'We are here, we have learned the use of weapons, we are ready to fight and to die for the cause of world revolution'.

In speaking on the draft programme at the fourth Comintern congress Bukharin said that one of the 'tactical points' that should be included was 'the right to red intervention'. It was, he said, the touchstone for all communist parties. 'We should lay it down in the programme that every proletarian State has the right to red intervention. It says in the *Communist Manifesto* that the proletariat will conquer the whole world. Well, that can't be done with one finger; it has to be done with bayonets.']

The meeting of the enlarged ECCI sends the Red Army of Soviet Russia its warmest congratulations on the fourth anniversary of its existence. The revolutionary vanguard of the proletariat of all countries looks with pride on the brilliant acts of heroism which the Red Army has performed in indescribably difficult conditions. For the first time in history the working masses can regard the victories of an army as their own victories. The Red Army defeated the internal enemies of Soviet Russia one after the other. By a series of powerful blows it accomplished the miracle of hammering into the imperialist Powers of Europe and America, infinitely superior both technically and numerically, the lesson that the Russian bulwark of the world revolution cannot be subdued by arms. But this un-exampled triumph over the power of world imperialism is not the work of guns and bayonets alone. Behind the ranks of the Red Army march the invisible millions of Russian workers and peasants, and millions of workers of all countries.

The alliance of the revolutionary vanguard of the international prole-tariat with the international army of Soviet Russia is a fact of real and tremendous importance; it is not only a political but also a military factor of the first rank. It is this alliance which struck the sword from the hands of the kings of finance and industry of France and America.

Now slowly, now quickly, in almost invisible undermining work, in spontaneous mass outbreaks, in organized actions, along a thousand ways, but steadily and irresistibly the world revolution is advancing. It counts on the Red Army, on its revolutionary spirit, its steadfastness, its unshake-able strength. On the fourth anniversary of the Red Army, the delegates of the sections of the Communist International attending the meeting of the enlarged Executive vow that they will devote their entire strength to extending the alliance between the revolutionary vanguard of the world proletariat and the Red Army, and to making it closer, so that the day may soon come when the red army of the next European Soviet republic will march side by side with the Red Army of Soviet Russia.

Long live the Red Army!

ECCI RESOLUTION ON THE FRENCH COMMUNIST PARTY

2 *March* 1922   *Inprekorr*, ii, 2 Sonderbeilage, p. 6, 1 *April* 1922

[This resolution, drafted and moved by Trotsky, and carried unanimously, sum-marized a long set of theses in which he elaborated the tasks of the French Com-munist Party, and advocated the expulsion of all members who supported a government of the 'left bloc' in France. The ECCI was concerned about the resignation from the central committee at the Marseille congress of Loriot, Treint, Dunois, and Vaillant-Couturier as a mark of protest against the failure to re-elect Souvarine, particularly since these were the strongest advocates of unconditional acceptance of ECCI proposals and policies. Souvarine and Treint were among the French delegates to the ECCI meeting. The delegation under-took to carry out the decisions of the ECCI, and on their return from Moscow the four who had resigned were readmitted to the central committee, which accepted the principle of the united front and submitted the question of the *Journal du Peuple* and the expulsion of Fabre to the conflicts commission. The *Journal du Peuple*, hostile to interference from the ECCI and to the imposition of strict discipline from outside, had protested against 'the Moscow ukase' at the time of the Marseille congress. It had also criticized ECCI action in regard to Serrati. On 12 May, in a long letter to the central committee of the CPF, the ECCI wrote that it had been following developments in the CPF 'with growing alarm'. The party press had refrained from attacking the *Journal du Peuple*; 'on the pretext of maintaining good relations with the trade unions' it had made many grave concessions to them; it was still 'passive and irresolute' about the united front; its relations with the ECCI were 'ambiguous', and the ECCI thought it 'absolutely impossible to maintain relations of this sort in the future'. The problems of the French Communist Party were dealt with again at the subsequent enlarged ECCI in June.]

The great organizational efforts made by the French Communist Party since the congress of Tours have kept within its ranks the best forces of the proletariat and stirred them to political action. The Marseille congress offered the party the opportunity of serious activity in the theoretical field, from which the revolutionary workers' movement will undoubtedly derive the greatest benefit.

In breaking with the parliamentary and political traditions of the old socialist party, whose congresses were merely pretexts for rhetorical duels between the leaders, the communist party called on all militant workers to make a profound study of the theses dealing with the most important questions of the development of the revolutionary workers' movement in France. This has never happened in France before. The organizational crisis in the French party, which it would be incorrect either to exaggerate or to play down, is a factor in the development of the party, in its cleansing, and its rebuilding and consolidation on truly communist foundations.

The split at Tours drew a fundamental line of division between reformism and communism, but it cannot be denied that the communist party which arose from this split retains in certain respects survivals of the reformist and parliamentary past; it can get rid of them and finally discard them by its own efforts and by participation in the struggle of the masses.

These survivals of the past among certain groups in the party can be seen firstly, in a tendency to re-establish unity with the reformists; secondly, in the inclination to form a bloc with the radical wing of the bourgeoisie; thirdly, in the anxiety to replace revolutionary anti-militarism by petty-bourgeois humanitarian pacifism; fourthly, in a false analysis of the relations between party and trade unions; fifthly, in the struggle against a genuinely centralized party leadership; sixthly, in efforts to substitute for international discipline in action a platonic federation of national parties.

After the Tours split these tendencies could neither exert their full effect, nor win any great influence on the party. Under the powerful pressure of bourgeois public opinion, however, the elements inclined to opportunism exert a natural attraction for each other and try to create their own agencies and footholds. Although they have had little success in this, it would be a mistake to underestimate the dangers which their work represents for the revolutionary character and the unity of the party. In no circumstances should communist organizations leave the field clear for these views, which were the essential reasons for the breakaway of the reformists from the party of the working class. Any lack of clarity in this respect would inevitably prejudice in a lasting fashion the work of the revolutionary education of the masses.

The plenary session of the Executive Committee declares that the resolutions of the Marseille congress are permeated with the spirit of the Communist International and create extremely important *points d'appui* for party activity among the working masses both urban and rural.

At the same time the Executive notes with satisfaction the declaration of the French delegation, that within the shortest possible time the party will sever its connection with the *Journal du Peuple*, a paper in which the reformist and confusionist tendencies are concentrated and which takes up an attitude in direct contradiction to the programme of the International, the decisions of the French Communist Party taken at the Tours and Marseille congresses, and to the revolutionary irreconcilability of the class-conscious French proletariat.

The primary significance of the Marseille congress lay in this—that it put before the party as its chief task regular and systematic work within the unions in accordance with the spirit of the party's programme and tactics. This involves final disapproval of the tendency of those party members who on the pretext of fighting for trade union autonomy—which is incidentally not open to question—are really fighting for the autonomy of their own activities within the trade unions without any supervision or direction by the party.

The Executive also notes the declaration of the French delegation that the central committee will take all the necessary measures to see that all party decisions are carried out (in a spirit of strictest unity and discipline) by communists in trade unions under the general control of the central committee of the party.

Since the statutes of the Communist International and all its sections, based on the principle of democratic centralism, adequately guarantee the steady and normal development of each communist party, the plenary session is bound to regard the resignation of various comrades elected to the central committee at the Marseille congress as unjustified, quite apart from the political considerations which provoked their resignation. Resignation from posts to which they have been sent by the party can be interpreted by the broad party masses only as a confession of inability of the representatives of the various tendencies to work together within the framework of democratic centralism, and may give an impulse to the formation of fractions within the party.

The plenary session of the Executive Committee expresses its firm conviction that the fight against the anti-communist tendencies noted above will be carried out by the overwhelming majority of the party and by all its leading bodies.

Since the formation of fractions will inevitably do great harm to the development of the party and injure its authority among the proletariat, the plenary session of the Executive notes with satisfaction the declaration of the French delegation that the central committee is prepared to take the necessary organizational measures to see that the will of the Marseille congress is carried out unchanged and to the end, and that the comrades who handed in their resignation will again take up their work in the party leadership in order to fulfil their task in a friendly and organized fashion.

RESOLUTION OF THE ECCI ON THE EASTERN QUESTION

4 *March* 1922   *Inprekorr*, ii, 2 Sonderbeilage, p. 9, 1 *April* 1922

[In an article published later in 1922 on the work of the ECCI Zinoviev reported that 'with the help of the Executive Committee organized communist parties and groups have been formed in such countries as Japan, China, India, Turkey, Egypt and Persia, that is, in countries where even at the time of the third congress we only had weak circles of supporters. These parties are still weak in numbers, but the kernel is at last there.' The ECCI meeting after the third congress appointed a special committee to reorganize the Turkish Communist Party and re-register its members.]

1. Because of the great importance of the national revolutionary movements which are steadily developing in the colonial countries of the Near East, and in neutral Asia, and especially in Egypt and India, the plenary session of the Executive proposes to all the parties of the countries which are associated with these areas the organization of a systematic campaign in the press, in Parliament, and among the masses for the liberation of the colonies. In particular the English communist party should initiate a well organized and long term action to support the revolutionary movements in India and Egypt.

2. The three parties which are most closely associated with North Africa, Asia Minor, and India, that is, the communist parties of France, Italy, and England, should, following the example of the French party, set up a special colonial commission of the central committee for the purpose of supplying regular information about colonial affairs, of establishing regular contact with the revolutionary organizations of the colonial coun-

tries, and of making this contact practically operative. The Balkan Communist Federation undertakes to concern itself with the organization of the communist movement in Turkey.

3. The Executive Committee proposes to all parties to make use of every possibility of publishing communist literature in the languages of the colonies and so to establish a closer contact with the oppressed colonial masses.

EXTRACTS FROM THE RESOLUTION OF THE ECCI ON THE ENGLISH
QUESTION

4 *March* 1922   *Inprekorr*, ii, 2 Sonderbeilage, p. 8, 1 *April* 1922

[In *'Left-Wing' Communism* Lenin wrote: 'In my opinion the British communists should . . . form a single communist party on the basis of the principles of the Third International and of *obligatory* participation in Parliament. The communist party should propose a "compromise" to the Hendersons and Snowdens, an election agreement . . . and let us retain complete liberty of agitation, propaganda, and political activity. . . . The British communists must absolutely insist on and secure complete liberty to expose the Hendersons and Snowdens.' If the Labour Party agreed, the communists would gain the opportunity of conducting agitation among the masses; if they refused, the gain would be even greater, for this would prove to the masses that the Labour Party leaders preferred good relations with the bourgeoisie to workers' unity. It was when urging communist support for Labour Party candidates that Lenin said they were to be supported 'in the same way as the rope supports a hanged man'. When writing this pamphlet (April 1920), Lenin had not yet made up his mind whether the future CPGB should or should not affiliate to the Labour Party. At the second Comintern congress he said that after talking to a number of comrades he was convinced that it was right for communists to work inside the Labour Party. The question had been fully investigated at a special commission of the congress of which Lenin was chairman. Sylvia Pankhurst and W. Gallacher were the two principal British opponents of affiliation to the Labour Party, on the ground that it would confuse and mislead the working class. They were supported by Serrati. The delegates from the British Socialist Party were in favour of affiliation. The decision to affiliate was passed by 58 votes to 24, with 2 abstentions, at the last plenary session of the second congress. The British Communist Party was formed in August 1920, and voted 115 to 85 for affiliation; its application to affiliate was rejected by the Labour Party.

In a letter to Serrati written from Berlin on 22 October 1920 Zinoviev said 'we shall not surrender lightly to Mr Henderson. We are advising our friends to organize within the unions and the Labour Party communist cells, illegal not only in regard to the police but also, if necessary, in regard to Mr Henderson too.'

In reporting on the work of the ECCI to the fourth congress, Zinoviev suggested that the new Executive would have to pay more attention to Britain.

The CPGB was stagnating, and they could not understand why development there had been so slow. In the discussion Murphy, for the CPGB, said that it was only in October 1922 that the British party had elected a central committee, this having been delayed by the strong syndicalist tendencies within the party. At a meeting in March 1922 they had appointed a commission of three to inquire into the general decline in the party, and on its recommendation the federal structure of the CPGB had been replaced by centralism. At its Edinburgh congress the Labour Party had voted not to admit any party which put forward candidates of its own in opposition to the Labour Party. The CPGB had immediately withdrawn its candidates and announced its acceptance of the Labour Party constitution, but its application for affiliation was again rejected.]

3. Since the Council of Action in 1920, when for the first time in the history of the British labour movement the proletariat was arrayed in a single common front against the bourgeoisie, who were trying to drive the country into war with the Russian workers' republic, the Labour Party has allowed the ranks of the workers to be split up, and to become again incapable of defending themselves against the capitalist offensive. Today the labour movement is not united either industrially or politically, nor centralized enough to counter successfully the united and centralized attacks of the capitalists.

4. The only salvation for the British working class, now more than ever before, is a united front against the bourgeoisie.... Together with preparations for bringing the working class together on a common programme, and for carrying this programme through, the labour movement must be mobilized in a united effort to return a workers' government at the next general election. If the Labour Party approaches the masses with such a programme, it will succeed in creating a united front of the working class which will ensure its victory at the polls.

5. The Communist Party of Great Britain fights for a united working class.... It has tried to organize the unemployed and the ex-servicemen and to make their fight a part of the fight of the entire working class. In the trade unions and workshop organizations the CPGB is making every effort to bring about complete unity among the workers.

6. The General Council elected at the last trade union congress in Cardiff does not have the authority of a Labour General Staff. The situation however demands the centralization and concentration of the workers' movement. Since it was elected, the General Council has not taken a single important step in this direction. The enlarged Executive of the CI therefore demands of the CPGB that it should approach the General Council with the object of establishing the unity of the working class on the programme of minimum demands as formulated above and which are designed to facilitate the formation of a workers' government at the next general election as a means of carrying out such a programme.

7. The Labour Party is the political organization of the trade unions. It includes various political tendencies within the workers' movement, such as those represented by the Independent Labour Party, the Fabians, the Guild Socialists, etc. But the defensive struggle of the working class against the increasing oppression of the bourgeoisie requires that the Labour Party should include within its ranks all the political aspirations of the workers' movement. The Labour Party cannot claim that it unites the working class in the political field if it does not also include the communist party which has long become an undeniable factor in the workers' movement.

The enlarged Executive of the CI suggests that the CPGB seek admission to the Labour Party in order that the unity of the working class in the political sphere can be established with particular reference to the forthcoming general election, the goal of which will be to replace the bourgeois coalition by a workers' government. In seeking admission to the Labour Party the communist party will retain for itself complete freedom of propaganda. On the same basis and with the same object the communist party is asked to support the Labour Party in the general election.

The enlarged Executive of the CI instructs the presidium to work out in detail proposals to the CPGB with regard to adherence to the Labour Party and support for that party in the general election.

EXTRACTS FROM THE ECCI THESES ON THE FIGHT AGAINST THE WAR DANGER

March 1922   *Inprekorr*, ii, 2 Sonderbeilage, p. 2, 1 *April* 1922

[In December 1921 representatives of Finland, Poland, Latvia and Estonia, with French approval, met to draw up a pact of mutual assistance. This was regarded by the Russians as directed against the Soviet Republic. The pact was signed on 17 March 1922 but was not ratified by Finland. In a note to the political bureau of the Russian Communist Party in February 1922 Lenin suggested 'that the question of combating war be brought up at the next enlarged plenum of the ECCI and that a comprehensive resolution be adopted explaining that only a revolutionary party which has been built up beforehand, is well tried, and has a good illegal apparatus can successfully wage a struggle against war, and also that the means of combating war are not a strike against war, but the formation of revolutionary nuclei in the combatant armies'.]

1. The economic and political contradictions among the capitalist great Powers of Europe were not removed by the imperialist war of 1914–18 or the treaties which ended the war. . . . They continue in a changed form and in different circumstances, in the struggle for dominance on the

European and world markets, and new contradictions have also arisen. The contradictions between England, the United States, and Japan are coming rapidly to a head. . . . The national contradictions between the European colonial powers and the peoples subject to or threatened by their rule are growing more pronounced. Soviet Russia is excluded by the blockade from the world market and world economy. . . .

3. . . . France controls the largest deposits of iron ore in Europe, as Germany does of coal. The power to exploit these two—whether by conquest or agreement—would deal a death-blow to England's economic and political position in Europe and elsewhere. Even without this, France is being rapidly transformed into a State with an expanding heavy industry. . . . On the Bosphorus and the Dardanelles, in North Africa, Asia Minor, and Central Asia, the political and economic contradictions between French and English imperialism are growing more and more obvious and conflicting. . . . Under their pressure England is trying to strengthen Italy and Greece at the expense of French imperialism. . . . England and France are competing for precedence in exploiting the natural wealth and the labour power of Soviet Russia. . . .

5. The devastation and spoliation wrought by the capitalist great Powers for four years aroused stormy revolutionary movements in the English colonies . . . which draw courage and strength from the example of the Russian revolution and the existence of Soviet Russia. They are primarily of a nationalist and religious character, but they are also bound up with social revolutionary struggles. . . . From the Atlantic to the Himalayas and to China, the Moslems are stirred up and restive. However various the forms in which this disturbance among the peoples of Asia and Africa is expressed, they are all directed against the capitalist States and are only intensified by the competition among these States. . . .

6. Irreconcilable as are the conflicts of interest between the great capitalist States, these are united as one, armed and ready, to fight Soviet Russia. The concessions which Russia, under the fearful pressure of the present historically-determined calamity, and left in the lurch by the proletarians of the rest of the world, is prepared to make to foreign capitalists, are still not enough for the imperialist States. They are after the unrestricted chance to drain its vast wealth. . . . But above all they are out for the destruction of the Soviet Government itself. The existence of Soviet Russia is a powerful incitement to the workers of all countries to conquer State power, establish their dictatorship and uproot capitalism. . . .

7. . . . The halting development of the proletarian world revolution after its first daring initiative, the Russian revolution, enables the bourgeoisie in the leading capitalist countries to make the attempt to restore the collapsing economy and the shaken State on a capitalist basis. Such restoration involves also the continuation of all the old economic, political,

social, national, and international contradictions and conflicts which will inevitably drive towards world conflict on a titanic scale. . . .

9. . . . The calling of the Genoa conference is an admission that the Versailles peace treaty and the other peace treaties cannot be kept, that they are not a basis for the reconstruction of Europe, but means to its further disruption and impoverishment. The calling of the conference is an admission that the ruling bourgeoisie in the various countries are incapable of bringing order and stability out of the economic chaos left behind by the war, and of bringing a new and better life to flower on the ruins. The conference will prove that this titanic task is too great even for the forces of the united bourgeoisie of Europe and America. It can only be accomplished after the overthrow of bourgeois rule by the revolutionary proletariat. . . .

The projected economic conference is to save, to strengthen, and to improve the edifice of capitalist Europe, shaken to its foundations. It is to square the circle by satisfying the claims of French imperialism on German economy, while at the same time keeping that economy strong enough to provide profitable markets in Germany for English goods, and protecting English industry against cut-throat German competition.

The costs of reconciling the interests of French and English capitalism are to be borne by the German proletarians and, since the fate of the exploited of all countries is linked together, by the proletarians of the entire world. The international bourgeoisie are dreaming of imposing these costs on the State in which the workers and peasants have seized power, Soviet Russia. The question seems to be: Shall a single international mammoth syndicate of capitalists take on the job of Soviet Russia's economic reconstruction, or shall there be several companies. . . .

However uncertain the outcome of the conference, it is already clear that Germany will be the *object* about which the Entente imperialists negotiate. Germany will not even dare to raise the question of a revision of the Versailles treaty, although it is almost palpably obvious that without revision European economy cannot be rebuilt on capitalist foundations. But the Entente imperialists will have to negotiate *with* Soviet Russia, despite the wretched state of its economy. . . . De facto, if not de jure, recognition of the Soviet Government by the invitation to the international economic conference, will aggravate the contradictions between the capitalist States. Just as it is uncertain whether they can reach agreement at Genoa about the reconstruction of Europe, so it is certain that at the most the capitalists there can win no more than a breathing spell; they cannot find salvation. World war or proletarian world revolution—that question will remain on the agenda of history after as before the discussions and decisions of Genoa. . . .

9 [10]. Imperialism is the capitalist reality, bourgeois pacifism the capitalist illusion. Pacifism is as incapable as bourgeois social reform of

overcoming the contradictions, the evils, and the crimes of capitalism. But it will introduce dissension and uncertainty into the ranks of the bourgeoisie, the middle and petty bourgeoisie, and hence weaken the class enemy of the proletariat. Communists must take advantage of any such weakening by using the opportunity of every bourgeois pacifist initiative to lead the working class into struggle, in the course of which they will learn that militarism and imperialism cannot be abolished by the gradual triumph of reason and love of peace. . . . This conviction will counteract any crippling and debilitating effects of pacifism on the revolutionary militant energy of the proletariat, a danger associated with bourgeois pacifist propaganda. . . . The mists of pacifist sentimental hopes must not obscure the recognition that the bourgeoisie rule and exploit thanks to their command of the means of production of life and the means of production of death. The proletariat must take possession of both to liberate themselves from exploitation and bondage. Since they are kept from their freedom by force of arms, they must conquer it and defend it by force of arms.

10 [11]. Proceeding from these facts and considerations, the enlarged Executive of the Communist International declares that the only effective defence against the threatening danger of war is a proletarian revolution. . . . The assembled representatives of 36 nations therefore consider it the duty of all communist parties to prepare ideologically and organizationally for the most intense revolutionary class struggle to avert war. As means to this end they suggest:

1. Systematic education of the working masses, including youth, on the causes and character of wars.

2. Bringing before the court of the broadest masses all problems and decisions concerning foreign policy, armaments, etc.

3. Well-organized legal and illegal propaganda among the forces and armed formations of every kind to enlighten them on these questions.

4. Imbuing the proletariat with the resolve to prevent the transport of troops and army supplies by all means and at whatever cost, should imperialist war break out.

5. Strengthening the revolutionary will of the broadest masses to fight against the outbreak of imperialist war by street demonstrations, general strikes, armed uprisings. . . .

6. The creation of legal and illegal bodies to work for the execution of these tasks.

7. The creation of legal and illegal bodies and institutions to ensure unified and energetic international co-operation of communists in those countries between whom contradictions are most acute.

In regard to the international economic conference of governments at Genoa, this meeting of the enlarged Executive of the Communist

International calls on the toiling and the exploited in every country to put forward, in opposition to the desperate attempt of the international bourgeoisie at economic reconstruction, their demands for. . . .

1. Abrogation of all the treaties ending the imperialist war of 1914–18.
2. Limitation of armaments of every kind.
3. The costs of the war, reparations, and reconstruction to be borne entirely by the bourgeoisie.
4. Hands off Soviet Russia's independence, and establishment of normal political relations with Russia.
5. Wide support by States and private undertakings for the economic development of Soviet Russia.

ECCI STATEMENT ON THE MEETING OF THE REPRESENTATIVES OF THE SECOND, TWO-AND-A-HALF, AND THIRD INTERNATIONALS

2 *April* 1922   *Inprekorr*, ii, 39, p. 312, 3 *April* 1922

[Early in 1922 the Vienna Union proposed a world conference of all workers' organizations, but at the request of the Second International it was decided to hold a preliminary meeting of representatives of the three Internationals (and of the Italian Socialist Party, which was affiliated to none of them) in Berlin on 2 April. The ECCI agreed to the proposal (and suggested that all trade union organizations be invited), since it was in accordance with the recently adopted united front policy; it was opposed by the delegates of the French, Italian, and Spanish parties, who had also opposed the theses on the united front. This statement was read to the conference at its opening session by Klara Zetkin.]

The delegation of the Communist International considers it its duty to make the following declaration at the opening of the negotiations with the representatives of the executives of the Second International and the Union of Socialist Parties.

This is the first time since July 1914, when the last meeting of the International Bureau was held in Brussels and was followed by the world war and the collapse of the Second International, that representatives of all sections of the international labour movement, which once formed a single international association, are to deliberate together at one table. This event cannot be passed over in silence. It cannot take place without our placing on record before the international proletariat the origin of the present split in the working class. This was the fact that some strata of the working class agreed to a temporary community of interest with the imperialist States—a fact expressed in the counter-revolutionary attitude of many working-class parties and organizations.

So long as the working class does not come together in a common struggle for its interests against international capital, so long as it maintains a coalition with the representatives of capitalism, so long as it fails to rise to the struggle for political power, so long will the split endure which is one of capitalism's most important sources of strength. This cannot be changed by regrets or by wishes. Since the working class has not yet risen to this united struggle, since in this struggle it has not yet grasped that capitalism can only be defeated if the great majority of the proletariat conquers power in revolutionary contest and establishes the dictatorship of the working people, we declare that organizational unity of the international proletarian organizations at present based on varying principles would be wholly utopian and therefore injurious. But this does not prevent us from recognizing what the entire world situation imperatively demands. Despite all the deep contradictions dividing the working class they must unite for defensive struggle against the world capitalist offensive. At the end of the war, when the armed and uprooted working masses returned home, there to learn that democracy and the welfare of the people for which they had ostensibly shed their blood, was nothing but a capitalist lie to conceal the struggle of capital for profits, there was a possibility of defeating the capitalist world; but the irresolution of the broad masses of the working class, the democratic illusions which were widespread among them and which were systematically nourished by the reformist parties and their open and tacit coalition with the bourgeoisie, prevented the working class from following the glorious example of the Russian October revolution. Instead they helped world capital to ward off the first proletarian attack. The working masses of the entire world can now feel in their own lives the consequences of this policy. The international bourgeoisie are incapable of bringing order into the world on a capitalist basis or even of ensuring to the proletariat their pre-war standard of living. But the capitalist world, shaken to its deepest foundations, still has enough strength to try to load on to the proletariat the costs of the war.

The world bourgeoisie have not yet given up hope of covering a great part of the costs of the war by intensifying the exploitation of the German proletariat by means of reparations, and of the entire Russian people by means of peaceful penetration into Soviet Russia, which they were unable to overthrow by military means, by exploiting the newly-created States which are being used as instruments of the military and imperialist policy of the great Powers, and by the greater exploitation and oppression of the colonial and semi-colonial peoples (China, Persia, Turkey). But even those circles of the international bourgeoisie who have not yet realized that it is impossible to squeeze hundreds of milliards out of the exhausted masses of the defeated countries, of Soviet Russia, and of the colonies—even they understand that if they were to succeed in reaching this goal, not even their monstrous extortions would be enough to provide means for capitalist reconstruction. That is why throughout the world the bourgeoisie are going over to the offensive against the working class. That is why in every country, despite unemployment, they are trying to lengthen the working day. That is why they are trying to reduce wages. The international working class is to meet all the costs of the war and in addition to provide means for the further consolidation of the capitalist world system.

This situation confronts the international working class with momentous decisions. Either they will now come together for the defensive struggle against all the onslaughts of international capital, either they will advance in solidarity against the attempts to squeeze the life out of the defeated States, Soviet Russia, and the colonies, and also against the wave of lock-outs, either they will rise up to the struggle for the abrogation of the Versailles treaty, for the recognition of Soviet Russia and for its economic reconstruction, for the control of production in all countries, or they will pay with their own lives and health the costs of the peace as they had to pay the costs of the war.

The Communist International calls on the working masses, regardless of their opinion about the road which will lead to final victory and the means of securing this road, to unite for the struggle against the present capitalist offensive and to wage it energetically. That is why the Communist International issued the slogan of the united front for the struggle against the bourgeoisie, and welcomed the initiative of the Vienna Union in calling for an international workers' congress. It regards the proposed congress as a way of unifying the workers' struggles which are now opening.

To make this congress successful the Communist International proposes that all proletarian trade union organizations should be invited to take part. The trade unions cover the majority of the proletariat. They cover the working masses regardless of their political differences. They are concerned with their daily needs. If the international workers' congress is to be more than a mere demonstration, if it is to unify international proletarian action, the trade unions must take part. The split in the central organizations of the proletariat and even in some countries in the mass organizations is no reason for excluding the unions but on the contrary a reason for bringing them in. For it is precisely because the trade unions are organized round two centres that an understanding on action is necessary. We suggest that invitations be sent to the Amsterdam Trade Union International, the Red International of Labour Unions, as well as to the syndicalist organizations which do not belong to those bodies, the American Federation of Labour, and the independent unions.

As to the proletarian parties, we propose that, in addition to the representatives of the parties covered by the three executives, invitations be sent to the parties and political groups which do not belong to any of the international associations. We have in mind in the first place the anarchist and syndicalist organizations. They are not great numerically but they include genuinely revolutionary working-class elements who should be enrolled in the general fighting front of the proletariat. Great differences divide us from these groups. We think it our duty to try to come to an understanding with them on questions of action at a time when the situation makes it necessary to come to an understanding with the reformist parties also whose policy, directed against the interests of the working class, encourages the errors and deviations of these left elements.

We think it essential that the international workers' conference should be convened as quickly as possible. The Genoa conference represents the attempt of world capital, now that its Versailles policy is being more and more shaken by events, to initiate a new partition of the world, a new world capitalist order. During the Versailles conference the international working class remained perplexed and incapable of action. Only Soviet Russia fought weapon in hand against the attempts of Entente capital to enslave the entire world. Today, after three years of capitalist chaos and of progressive capitalist decline, Soviet Russia, victorious in battle, stands untouched. It is however the object of fierce 'peaceful' attacks by world capital. The first State created by the first wave of the world revolution must be helped to resist the attempts to force her to social capitulation. Thanks to the complete capitulation of the German bourgeoisie to the Entente the German proletariat, despite its resistance, has become the wage-reducer of the world proletariat. The struggle against Allied reparations policy is a struggle for the working masses' standard of life in the countries of the Entente, and in America.

Unless the international proletariat opposes with the utmost energy the continuation in force of the Versailles treaty, the attempts to strangle Soviet Russia economically, the plundering of the colonies, the exploitation of the population in the newly created small States, there is no chance of overcoming unemployment and the world economic crisis. That is why the international working class must raise its voice during the Genoa conference. It must try to force the Genoa conference, which is ostensibly concerned with the reconstruction of world economy, to deal with the labour question, with unemployment, and with the eight-hour day. Not as at Versailles, where the representatives of the various workers' organizations, who were not backed up by any militant masses, came hat in hand to request the Entente to consider the interests of the proletariat, but supported by fighting and demonstrating masses—that is how the international representatives of the working class should demand of the representatives of world capital assembled in Genoa to make good the promises they have so shamelessly broken.

The delegation of the Communist International are prepared, without for a moment concealing what separates them from the reformist and

semi-reformist parties, to use all their strength in the common struggle of
the international proletariat. They can do so the more easily since they are
convinced that every day of struggle and every experience in the struggle
will hammer home the lesson to the proletarians of all countries that no
compromise with capital is capable of ensuring peace and a decent worthy
life, that what is essential if this is to be attained is the victory of the
proletariat, who must take control over the ordering of the world into its
own strong hands and construct it in accordance with the interests of the
overwhelming majority of mankind.

For all these reasons the Communist International delegation propose
that at the forthcoming international conference only such questions shall
be dealt with as concern the immediate practical common action of the
working masses, questions which do not divide but unite them. Consequently the Communist International suggests the following agenda for
the international conference:

1. Defence against the capitalist offensive.
2. The fight against reaction.
3. Preparation of the struggle against new imperialist wars.
4. Assistance in re-establishing the Russian Soviet Republic.
5. The Versailles treaty and the reconstruction of the devastated areas.

STATEMENT ISSUED BY THE CONFERENCE OF REPRESENTATIVES OF
THE EXECUTIVES OF THE SECOND AND THIRD INTERNATIONALS AND
THE VIENNA UNION

4 *April* 1922   *Report of the Conference*, p. 83

[At the conference the principal speakers for the ECCI were Klara Zetkin and
Karl Radek. The ECCI delegation included also Bukharin, Rosmer, Frossard,
Katayama and one member each from the Polish, Yugoslav, and Czech communist parties. The discussions were conducted in a tone of bitter recrimination;
Radek taunted the representatives of the Second International with their wartime record, with complicity in the shooting of the 26 Baku commissars, in the
murder of Rosa Luxemburg and Karl Liebknecht, in the Versailles peace treaty,
in colonial oppression. The communists in their turn were charged with aggression in Georgia, Armenia, and the Ukraine, with unscrupulous tactics towards
other labour organizations, and with the imprisonment of socialists.

It is clear from the proceedings that neither the Second nor the Third International was prepared to compromise to establish a united front; only the delegates of the Vienna Union advocated it convincingly.]

The Conference is agreed that, however desirable the unity of the class-
conscious organisations of the proletariat may be, at the present moment

the only thing that can be done is to hold deliberations between all the sections represented at the Conference for the purpose of common action towards a concrete goal. The Conference, therefore, proposes that the Executives should agree to the setting up of an Organisation Committee of Nine, which shall undertake preparations for further conferences of the three Executives, as well as conferences on a wider basis, to include parties which are not affiliated to either of the three international organisations. Each Executive is free to appoint as it thinks fit the three representatives to whom it is entitled. In this Organisation Committee no majority resolutions will be allowed, its task will be to express the general point of view of the three Executives as far as this is declared.

The Conference recommends that this Organisation Committee should try to bring about conversations between the representatives of the Amsterdam Trade Union International and the Red Trade Union International, to consider the question of how the maintenance and restoration of Trade Union unity of front can be secured, nationally and internationally.

The Conference notes the declaration of the representatives of the Communist International that the forty-seven Social-Revolutionaries who are to be tried will be allowed any defenders they wish; that, as already announced in the Soviet press before the Conference, no death sentences will be inflicted in this trial; that, as the trial will be public, representatives of all three Executives will be allowed to attend, to listen to the proceedings, and will be allowed to take stenographic reports for the information of their affiliated Parties.

The Conference declares that all the three Executives have expressed their readiness to collect and examine the material to be submitted by the different sections on the question of Georgia. The Conference authorises the Committee of Organisation to draw conclusions from this examination, and to present a report to a later Conference of the three Executives.

The Conference notes that the representatives of the Second International have declared that they do not consider it possible to hold a general conference in April, that is to say, at the same time as the Genoa Conference. The Conference, however, agrees in principle upon the necessity for calling a general conference as soon as possible. The Executives undertake to inform their affiliated Parties of the progress which the idea of a general conference has made during the Berlin negotiations, and they will give their representatives on the Committee of Organisation full power to conclude favourable negotiations for the calling of a general conference.

As the organisation of the general Conference is impossible this month for the reasons above stated, the present Conference declares that it is an imperative duty, in view of the advance of international imperialist capitalism, to demonstrate the united will of the international class-conscious proletariat. The Conference, therefore, calls upon the workers of every country to organise great mass demonstrations, with as much unity as possible, during the Genoa Conference, either on the 20th of April, or, where this is technically impossible, on the first of May:

For the eight-hour day.

For the struggle against unemployment, which has increased immeasurably on account of the reparations policy of the capitalist powers.

For the united action of the proletariat against the capitalist offensive.

For the Russian revolution, for starving Russia, for the resumption by all countries of political and economic relations with Russia.

For the re-establishment of the proletarian united front in every country and in the International.

STATEMENT OF THE COMINTERN DELEGATION ON THE MANIFESTO ISSUED BY THE CONFERENCE OF THE THREE INTERNATIONALS

5 *April* 1922   *Inprekorr*, ii, 42, p. 339, 6 *April* 1922

[In an article published immediately after the conference, Radek asserted that the Second International had opposed the calling of a world congress of all labour organizations because its watchword would have been 'Down with the Versailles treaty'. Just as the German Government were not allowed to raise the question of the treaty at Genoa, so the German social-democrats did not dare raise it at Berlin because the British and Belgian parties of the Second International were determined to exclude it. (It was at Genoa, ten days after this article was published, that the Soviet and German Governments concluded the treaty of Rapallo, which registered their common opposition to Versailles.) He contended further that the social-democratic parties feared united action at the international level because it would encourage united action within each country. Although they had been compelled to agree to the formation of the committee of nine, which was to consider a world congress, and to joint demonstrations against the capitalist offensive, against reparations, and for the recognition of Soviet Russia, they would probably do everything in their power to sabotage the committee's work. In a manifesto issued a few weeks later, the ECCI singled out the German Social-Democratic Party as primarily responsible for the failure to summon a world congress; the SPD was the only large German party to oppose the Rapallo treaty.]

The delegation of the ECCI decided after the most serious misgivings to agree to the joint declaration put forward by the Vienna Union. Their misgivings arose primarily from the fact that the Second International categorically refused to accept the watchword of workers' demonstrations for the abrogation of the Versailles treaty, which means that a great international workers' association is in this respect far behind intelligent west European liberals. This raised a doubt whether the Second International is really anxious to fight against the danger of a new Versailles peace at Genoa or is prepared to struggle by every means against the capitalist offensive.

The ECCI delegation nevertheless decided to vote for the joint resolution although the proposal to convene an international workers' conference while the Genoa conference is in session was frustrated by the opposition of the Second International.

Despite all these serious misgivings the ECCI delegation voted for the resolution, for they are anxious to promote and not to obstruct even the slightest advance towards a united front. For these reasons they refrained from the demand that this preliminary conference should investigate the murder of Rosa Luxemburg, Liebknecht, Jogiches, and Leviné and all the incidents which accompanied the civil war in Germany. For these reasons they refrained from clearing up the part played by the social-democratic parties in the persecution of communists in Latvia, Poland, Yugoslavia, and Hungary, and they reserve the right to demand the appointment of a commission of investigation under the committee of nine into these and similar cases. For these reasons they refrained from demanding from the German social-democrats at this preliminary conference the liberation of proletarian fighters in Germany. For these reasons they refrained also from demanding at this preliminary conference an investigation of the Labour Party's attitude to Ireland and the colonies, and they reserve the right to raise all these questions subsequently. For they are convinced that unless an end is put to the policy of coalition with the bourgeoisie, which is at the root of all the unprecedented actions mentioned above, a real united front of the proletariat is impossible.

The ECCI delegation decided to agree to the joint declaration and to the feeble beginnings of the united front which it embodies in the firm conviction that the pressure of events will force the proletarian masses to fight and will teach them to compel their reformist leaders to change their policy if they do not wish to be thrust aside by the proletariat.

EXTRACTS FROM THE ECCI STATEMENT ON THE RESULTS OF THE
BERLIN CONFERENCE

April 1922   *Inprekorr*, ii, 55, p. 437, 27 *April* 1922

[The ECCI endorsed the attitude of its delegation to the Berlin conference, although Lenin was extremely critical. In an article published on their return, entitled 'We have paid too dear', he argued that it was wrong to have agreed that no death sentences should be imposed at the forthcoming trial of the Social-

Revolutionaries in Moscow, for this was granting immunity in advance to terrorists. Nor should they have agreed to attendance at the trial of representatives of the Second and Two-and-a-half Internationals. These were 'political concessions by the revolutionary proletariat to the reactionary bourgeoisie', for which nothing had been received in return.]

TO THE CLASS-CONSCIOUS WORKERS OF THE WORLD

The ECCI has attentively examined the results of the Berlin conference of the three Internationals and has unanimously ratified the understanding reached in Berlin. The Executive now requests of the Second and Two-and-a-half Internationals an equally open, clear, and formal ratification of the decision arrived at in Berlin.

But we say to you quite openly that the united front which is just beginning to be formed is in great danger. The leaders of the Second International want to crush it at birth and will leave nothing undone to reach their objective. The course of the Berlin conference proved that up to the hilt.

At Berlin the leaders of the Second International refused to agree to the immediate convening of a world congress of the entire working class. They had the sorry courage to reject the slogan of revision of the predatory Versailles treaty which weighs like an alp on the working class of the entire world. At the moment when the bourgeois rulers of the entire world have assembled in Genoa mainly for the purpose of shunting the costs of the imperialist war on to the backs of the workers, the leaders of the Second International rejected our proposal to bring together the representatives of the working class of the entire world to give expression to the will of the proletarians of all countries. . . .

What is the united front and what should it be? The united front is not and should not be merely a fraternization of party leaders. The united front will not be created by agreements with those 'socialists' who until recently were members of bourgeois governments. The united front means the association of all workers, whether communist, anarchist, social-democrat, independent or non-party or even Christian workers, against the bourgeoisie. With the leaders, if they want it so, without the leaders if they remain indifferently aside, and in defiance of the leaders and against the leaders if they sabotage the workers' united front.

And this genuine united front in the common struggle is bound to come. It must come if the working class wants to defend its most fundamental and elementary interests against the capitalist offensive.

We appeal in particular to the non-party workers and to those who still support the Second and Two-and-a-half Internationals. We say to you: You are not yet communists, many of you are even openly hostile to communism. The time will come when you will recognize the correctness of communist ideas. We will wait patiently until that time comes, which will mark the beginning of the true emancipation of the entire working class. But until then . . . we say: Despite all the differences in our political views, work together with us to organize the united front against the capitalists. . . . Either a united front of all proletarians throughout the world, or starvation and degradation of the working class. That is how the question stands. . . .

Build the united front locally too, without waiting for the permission of the leaders of the Second International, who have been spiritually at one with the bourgeois world too long for them to be able to break quickly with it. In every factory, in every mine, in every district, in every town, the communist workers should arm together with the socialist and non-party workers for the common fight against the bourgeoisie. The communist party remains an independent party; it is convinced that in a short time all honest proletarians will come into its ranks; but everywhere the communist party is ready to fight shoulder to shoulder with any worker against the capitalists.

Once more: Demand the immediate convening of a world congress of the working class. That is the next step towards the united front of all proletarians. The Communist International solemnly declares that it will put aside anything which might prejudice the real unity of all proletarians. . . .

We appeal to the press of the Second and Two-and-a-half Internationals, and of the anarchists, syndicalists, non-party workers, etc., to publish this statement of ours in full, and we are ready to publish in full corresponding statements by the said organizations in our press. The time has come when it must be openly stated who is for and who is against the united proletarian front.

EXTRACTS FROM AN ECCI STATEMENT ON THE GENOA CONFERENCE

19 *May* 1922   *Inprekorr*, ii, 73, p. 563, 22 *May* 1922

[The Genoa conference, convened by the Allied Supreme Council at its meeting in Cannes in January 1922, was held from 10 April to 12 May 1922, to consider questions of European economic reconstruction. Disarmament and reparations were, at Poincaré's request, excluded from the agenda. It was the first general post-war conference to which Germany and Russia had been invited.

Speaking to the Russian Communist Party congress Lenin (who thought the Russian press was exaggerating the importance of the conference) said: 'We are going to Genoa not as communists but as businessmen.' Shortly before the conference opened Radek wrote that it would try to take advantage of the famine to wring concessions from the Russian Government. 'Soviet Russia, its Government, and its masses, pursue a cool *realpolitik*. . . . The Soviet Government knows that the first wave of world revolution has subsided and that the next will mount only slowly. It knows that the Russian economy cannot be restored without the help of European economy. It hoped that it would be the European workers who would supply the Russian workers with machines and the Russian peasants with ploughs. . . . But the European workers are not yet masters in their own house. Therefore the Soviet Government declares: We need world capital and therefore we must give it profits. . . . Fools, who call themselves communists and even left communists, have accused us on this account of treachery to the proletariat. . . . We answer: 'Then show us another way. . . . Split into hostile camps, the capitalist world fears that we shall ally ourselves with the enemies of any State which tries to starve us out. We shall ally ourselves not only with Beelzebub but with his grandmother too if it is a question of defending the rights for which the Russian working class bled and starved.' In another article published a day or two after the conference opened Radek argued that the conflicts among the Allies were too great to be resolved. The only policy on which they were united was the exploitation of Russia. German exports, instead of being admitted to the West as reparations, would be directed to Russia, and thus, through Germany, the Entente would exploit Russia, while Germany would appear to be the exploiter. 'This would ruin Germany's only chance of strengthening itself, not only economically, but also politically, by genuine and equitable co-operation with Russia. Germany would become an industrial colony of the Entente and Russia an agricultural colony.' This plan, he concluded, was however doomed to failure because of the conflict of interests between France and Britain. In a statement published a few days before the end of the conference the ECCI wrote: 'What the Allied Governments are asking of Soviet Russia is directed against the entire international working class. The workers of all countries have fought so that the factories shall belong to the community and not to individual exploiters. At Genoa the main question at issue was nothing else than the demand that the Russian factories, mines, dockyards, should be given back to foreign capitalists. The Russian people were to return to the old slavery. They were to assume in addition the milliards and milliards of debts incurred by Tsarism and the bourgeoisie. Every worker understands that this must be opposed.'

The only practical result of the Genoa conference was the Rapallo treaty signed between Russia and Germany. This was rarely mentioned in the communist press. In an article attacking the German Social-Democratic Party—the only big German party to oppose the treaty—as 'a slave of the Entente and an enemy of the Russian revolution', Thalheimer wrote: 'Excluded from the negotiations between the Entente and Soviet Russia, threatened by the danger that the Entente was seeking agreement with Soviet Russia at Germany's expense, the German Government decided to sign the treaty with Russia. . . . We say to the German workers: It is your duty to see that this step is not followed by a step back, but by further steps in the direction of *Anschluss* with Soviet Russia. . . . The international working class must counter as energetically as possible the hypocritical and malicious campaign of their respective Governments against this treaty.'

At the June 1922 meeting of the ECCI Radek reported that Crispien of the USPD had referred to Rapallo as an alliance with the bourgeoisie, 'the 4 August 1914 of the Third International'. Radek observed later that Russia could neither have remained a great Power nor acquired the economic and technical means for her industrial reconstruction unless she had had, in Germany, a counter-weight to the preponderance of the Allies. At the subsequent world congress the only reference to the treaty—and that an oblique one—was made by Bukharin in his report on the Comintern programme.

Nearly three years before, Chicherin had cautiously suggested that a communist government might have to give weight to considerations which a communist party could ignore.

'The revolutionary Soviet governments themselves are in a rather different position from the revolutionary parties. As actually existing governments, they are compelled to enter into certain relations with other existing governments, and these relations impose obligations with which they must reckon. The Commissar for Foreign Affairs who writes in the journal of the Third International must remember that he is bound by the position of his government, a position which is no longer that of a revolutionary party far removed from power. At the same time, however, the attitude of the revolutionary Soviet government, in virtue of its character and its mission, is the complete antithesis of that of the capitalist governments, and it can in no circumstances take part in their predatory alliances. Its task is to live in peace with all governments, or to try to do so, but to keep itself carefully apart from any coalitions and combinations serving imperialist appetites. All Soviet governments, alike completely opposed to capitalist governments, are necessarily allies of each other, of course allies in the sense of defence, for an aggressive policy is equally alien to all of them. The requirements of national defence, which are the most important factor in the foreign policy of capitalist governments, also come first in the foreign policy of Soviet governments. Where capitalist governments are concerned, the attitude of the revolutionary proletariat to "defence of the fatherland" must be one of absolute rejection. The defence of the Soviet government, on the other hand, is of the utmost importance for the revolutionary proletariat. . . . In the defence of Soviet governments, relations with foreign governments which are aimed at removing the dangers of hostile coalitions have an important part to play. But international relations designed to eliminate the danger of an attack also impose certain obligations. At the present moment in history, when the Soviet governments are surrounded by enemies on all sides and have to battle against incredible difficulties and dangers . . . these requirements of foreign policy must be regarded with the greatest seriousness. Soviet diplomacy is defensive and it is also highly responsible, so that when we speak of the positive tasks of the Third International, we cannot identify the communist parties with the Soviet governments in which these parties predominate.']

THE LESSONS OF GENOA

THE BOURGEOIS ENTENTE IS BREAKING DOWN—SOVIET RUSSIA IS GROWING STRONGER

TO THE WORKERS OF ALL COUNTRIES

The Genoa conference has come to an end. In the intention of its initiators it was to do nothing more nor less than restore the European economic equilibrium which was shattered by the imperialist world war. The braggarts! Nobody can get outside his own skin. The imperialist bourgeoisie cannot save Europe from economic ruin—the Europe which they made into a shambles and which for four years was laid waste and devastated.

GENOA—MIRROR OF THE BOURGEOISIE'S POWERLESSNESS

At Genoa the bourgeoisie revealed their utter powerlessness, their complete impotence. There was a great deal of noise and the prime ministers of the richest bourgeois States attended. . . . And what was the upshot? The talk went on for several weeks. The diplomats beat about the bush and did not stir from the spot and finally they reached a happy ending, moving with God's help from Genoa to The Hague. The petty skirmishes and quarrels of the victor States among themselves have shown the entire world how deep are the contradictions between England and France, between Japan and the United States, between Italy and France, and between the victor States and Germany. The League of Nations is a stinking corpse which the Genoa conference was unable to clear out of the way. The Entente itself is creaking at every seam, junk fit only for the lumber room. The more solemnly Lloyd George and Barthou declared their conviction that the Entente was in good health, that love and harmony reigned between England and France, the more obvious became the outworn hypocrisy and the more clearly can it be seen by every proletarian that the notorious Entente has come to the end of its resources.

Never has the decadence of bourgeois society been exposed so clearly as now. The decay and disintegration of the bourgeois State are proceeding at a gigantic pace. The outward glitter of bourgeois governments is like the hectic flush on the cheeks of a consumptive. A declining class! This is the judgment that will be made by every attentive observer who has followed the course of events at the Genoa conference. The star of the bourgeoisie has set. That is the chief lesson of Genoa.

But the working class is moving up. Its star is rising. The strength of the proletariat will grow irresistibly, slowly at first but then more quickly. The proletariat will succeed the bourgeoisie in power throughout the world. That was proved most clearly by the part played by the Russian delegation at Genoa.

THE SOVIET DELEGATION REPRESENTED THE FUTURE OF MANKIND

The Russian proletarian revolution is in a difficult position. For four years Soviet Russia was tortured and agonized by intervention, conspiracy, and white terror. The country was hit by a serious famine. Nevertheless the Russian revolution is a victorious revolution and this victorious proletarian revolution, the first in the history of the world, proudly confronted the international court of the bourgeoisie. That is why it was only the Soviet delegation which had a consistent programme, a comprehensive outlook, a great historical perspective which served the interests not only of proletarian Russia but all the proletariat of the entire world. Alone in Genoa the Soviet delegation represented the future of humanity while all the bourgeois delegations represented the decaying past.

The first proposal made by the Soviet delegation was for disarmament. ... This proposal was rejected by the English and all the other imperialists.

What conclusions are the workers of the world to draw from this? The conclusion can only be that disarmament is impossible so long as the bourgeoisie remain at the helm. Disarmament is impossible without the victory of the proletarian revolution.

The Soviet delegation's disarmament proposal also hit the representatives of the Second and Two-and-a-half Internationals. These petty-bourgeois philistines have for decades dinned into the ears of the workers their tepid pacifism, and have preached virtue and contentment. According to them the gulf between capital and labour can easily be eliminated. All that needs to be done is to adopt the panaceas of the leaders of the Second and Two-and-a-half Internationals and lo and behold the bourgeoisie will disarm, there will be no more war, and the wolf will lie down with the lamb.

THE LEADERS OF THE SECOND AND TWO-AND-A-HALF INTERNATIONALS ARE LACKEYS OF THE BOURGEOISIE

But what happened at Genoa? Did the leaders of the Second and Two-and-a-half Internationals support the Soviet delegation's disarmament proposals? Of course not. They would not be the servants of the bourgeoisie if at the decisive moment they failed to do what their masters told them to do. On this question the Second and Two-and-a-half Internationals showed that they were really on the side of the bourgeoisie and again every class-conscious worker will have to say, 'If you want disarmament then you must fight for the proletarian revolution; if you want disarmament you must fight for the dictatorship of the proletariat; but if this is what you want you must support the communist party.'

A HANDFUL OF MAGNATES WANTED TO ENSLAVE THE RUSSIAN PROLETARIAT

When the attempt was made in Genoa to despoil Soviet Russia, the first proletarian republic, the bourgeoisie formed a 'united front'. Restitution —that was the battle-cry of the bourgeoisie at Genoa. Restitution for ever! Restitution, the last cry of civilization, no salvation without restitution! . . .

THE TREATY WITH THE GERMAN PEOPLE

Soviet Russia concluded a treaty with the bourgeois German republic. The 'democrats' and 'social-democrats' who are at the helm in Germany resisted for a long time the alliance with Soviet Russia although the entire German working class for two years unanimously demanded this alliance. Only the merciless greed which characterized the attitude of the victor States at Genoa to defeated Germany induced the present German Government to sign a treaty with Soviet Russia. The treaty between Russia and Germany signed at Rapallo is of enormous historical importance. Russia with its one hundred and fifty million population and its predominantly agrarian character, in alliance with Germany with its first-class industry, represents such powerful economic co-operation that it will break through all obstacles. On the German side the treaty was signed by the present bourgeois-menshevik government, but everybody understands that while the position of the bourgeois-menshevik German government is a temporary thing, the German working class remains. The German working class will one day inevitably conquer power in their own country. Germany will become a Soviet republic. And then, when the German-Russian treaty brings together two great Soviet republics, it will provide such unshakeable foundations for real communist construction that the old and outworn Europe will not be able to withstand it for even a few years. In this sense the fate of humanity in the next few years will be determined by the successes of the German working class. The victory of the German proletariat over 'its' bourgeoisie will involve unprecedented changes in the social structure of the whole of Europe. When the German proletariat destroys in its country the influence of the Second and Two-and-a-half Internationals a new chapter will open in the history of mankind.

THE TREACHERY OF THE SECOND AND TWO-AND-A-HALF INTERNATIONALS

The contemptible counter-revolutionary rôle of the Second and Two-and-a-half Internationals has never been so clearly demonstrated as in the weeks when the Genoa conference was being held. The leaders of the two Internationals did everything possible and impossible to prevent the world proletariat from calling its congress and putting forward in the name of the world proletariat a proletarian programme for the reconstruction of Europe and the entire world. The leaders of the two Internationals did everything possible and impossible to facilitate the efforts of the leaders of the bourgeoisie, Lloyd George and Barthou, to despoil the first proletarian republic. At the Berlin conference of the three Internationals the German social-democrats refused to support the demand for the revision of the predatory Versailles treaty. By that alone the treacherous German social-democracy has covered itself for ever in disgrace and ignominy. . . .

COMINTERN—THE GRAVE-DIGGER OF BOURGEOIS SOCIETY

At the end of the Genoa conference the Entente representatives again made an insolent attempt to bring up the question of 'pernicious communist propaganda'. The ECCI declares that the international community of worker communists organized in the Comintern will not let its freedom be hampered by any obligations whatever. We are the deadly enemies of bourgeois society. Every honest communist will fight against bourgeois society to his last breath, in word and in deed and if necessary with arms in hand. Yes, the propaganda of the Communist International will be pernicious for you, the imperialists. It is the historical mission of the Communist International to be the grave-digger of bourgeois society. No offence meant. So long as by your very existence you insult the feelings of every class-conscious worker, so long as your foul breath infects the entire world, so long as a handful of millionaires continue to build their welfare on the bones of the working class, in short so long as your capitalist social system continues to exist, the 'pernicious' propaganda of the communists will not cease. . . .

Workers of France, it is now up to you. Do everything in your power to overthrow Barthou's Government which brings shame on the workers of France. Settle accounts with the reactionary gangs who are destroying France and want to plunder Soviet Russia.

Workers of England, you have been fighting for years for the recognition of Soviet Russia and for years your bourgeoisie, helped by the social traitors, Henderson, MacDonald, and co. have been throwing sand in your eyes. Has not the Genoa conference opened your eyes?

Workers of Japan, even the predatory European Governments found themselves obliged to sign the treaty in which they undertook not to attack Soviet Russia. Only the representatives of your bloodthirsty Government demanded that an exception be made in its case. They want to continue with their daily raids on the working masses of the Far Eastern Republic. Japan is now in a pre-revolutionary period. A significant part even of the Japanese bourgeoisie is opposed to the present regime. Place yourselves at the head of the ripening revolution. Seize the Japanese monarchy by the throat and place your foot on its neck.

Workers of Germany, you must seize power in your country as quickly as possible. In doing so you will remove the weight on the spirit of the world proletariat and accelerate historical progress. The fate of the proletarian revolution is in your hands. Your slogan is, 'Down with the treacherous social-democrats. Down with the power of capital. Long live the workers' government.'

Workers and Red soldiers of Russia, if you still needed proof that only the Soviet Government defends the interests of the proletariat of all countries you received it in incontestable fashion at Genoa. You are living through a difficult time but the worst is already over. Guard the Soviet Government as the apple of your eye. You stand at the outposts of the proletarian world revolution. The proletarian armies of other countries will come to your help. Victory is no longer distant. . . .

EXTRACTS FROM AN ECCI STATEMENT ON THE MEETING OF THE COMMITTEE OF NINE

24 *May* 1922   *Inprekorr*, ii, 77, p. 583, 24 *May* 1922

[The committee of nine set up by the Berlin conference met on 23 May; it failed to reach agreement on joint action, and the ECCI delegates withdrew. Speaking at the June 1922 session of the ECCI, Zinoviev asserted that, despite the failure to establish a united front 'from above', the attempt had been useful because the communist parties could now no longer be accused of being the splitters. Radek said that it marked a step towards the formation of a genuine mass united front 'from below'. Comintern policy after this failure was designed to get members of labour organizations to act jointly with the communist parties in opposition to the declared policy of their organizations. Writing on the dissolution of the committee of nine representing the three Internationals which, he said, marked the end of the first stage of the united front campaign, Radek suggested that it would be a mistake to think that it was only the leaders of the Second International who had sabotaged the united front, while the masses behind them were anxious to fight; it was true that the masses wanted unity, but they did not want the struggle; their attitude was one of passivity. There had also been sabotage within the Comintern itself, from the French party.

At the fourth congress Radek said that the conference of the three Internationals broke down 'not on the question of the world workers' congress. If you analyse the situation you will see that it was wrecked because the Second and Two-and-a-half Internationals had a plan of their own for capitulation, against our plan of defence'.]

THE COMMITTEE OF NINE WRECKED BY THE SECOND INTERNATIONAL
LONG LIVE THE STRUGGLE FOR THE UNITED FRONT FROM BELOW
TO THE WORKERS OF ALL COUNTRIES

What the Communist International feared has happened. The leaders of the Second International have prevented the world workers' congress from meeting. . . . According to them, such a congress could be called only if the communist parties renounced criticism of the policy of the social-democratic leaders and the trade union bureaucracy and if at the same

time the Soviet Government gave the mensheviks and the SRs the opportunity of organizing revolts with impunity. . . .

In reply to the demagogic assertions of the representatives of the Second
International that the Communist International is calling for a world
workers' congress only in order to hitch the world proletariat to the
waggon of Soviet Russian foreign policy, the Communist International
declared, at the request of the Russian Communist Party, that it is ready
to agree that the question of defence of Soviet Russia shall not be placed on
the agenda of the world workers' congress. . . .

The Second International wanted to make the world workers' congress
impossible in any circumstances. But it had no objection to the continued
existence of the commission of nine because that made the communist
struggle against social-democracy more difficult. The Communist International could not allow the social-democrats of all countries and the
trade union bureaucracy to prevent any united proletarian front and at
the same time shield themselves from responsibility for this criminal policy.
For these reasons the Communist International presented the two Internationals with an ultimatum—either cease sabotaging the world workers'
congress or the Communist International will withdraw its representatives
from the commission of nine. . . .

The Vienna International immediately declared that the attitude of the
Second and Third Internationals made the congress impossible. Not content with putting the fight of the communist delegation for the carrying
out of the Berlin decisions on the same footing as the fight of the Second
International against these decisions, Adler, to defend his position, spoke
of the 'differences in the Executive of the Communist International, which
make the convening of the congress more difficult'. And this although he
must have known that the Executive ratified the Berlin decisions unanimously. And at the end of the meeting he even allowed himself to hint that
the communists were now opposed to the world workers' congress because
the Soviet Government was about to reach a compromise with the Entente.
. . . This campaign of lies is designed to conceal the fact that on the 21st
of this month an agreement was reached in Brussels between the French
Socialist Party, which belongs to the Two-and-a-half International, and
the English Labour Party as well as the Belgian Labour Party, two leading
parties in the Second International, on the convening of a world congress
of reformist and semi-reformist parties at The Hague. This agreement
means that the characterless Two-and-a-half International, which cannot
decide between the revolution and counter-revolution, between bourgeois
pseudo-democracy and proletarian dictatorship, has now reached a point
in its see-saw policy which again favours co-operation with the most outright reformists. In view of this there was nothing for the representatives
of the Communist International to do but to leave the commission of nine,

which was to be transformed from an instrument of struggle for the proletarian united front into a bargaining counter for declared and secret reformists in which the communists were to be assigned the part of a screen. . . .

The proletariat without distinction of party has had the opportunity of convincing itself who is for the united front and who is against. The resistance of the leaders of the Second International has frustrated the attempt to organize the proletarian united front from above. That makes it a duty to rally all forces to organize the proletariat for the common struggle in opposition to the leaders of the Second International.

Communist workers, it is your duty to spread the lesson of this first attempt to establish the united front among the broadest masses of the working classes.

Workers of the parties of the Second and Two-and-a-half Internationals! After this experience with your leaders it is your duty to do everything, to omit nothing, to show the leaders of your parties who have forgotten their duty that you will no longer tolerate sabotage of the united front, that you want to unite with the communist workers in the struggle against the capitalist offensive.

The slogan of the world workers' congress will be the slogan of further struggle, but the experience of this first attempt has shown that to be successful it is necessary to break the resistance of the social-democratic leaders, particularly those of Germany and England, that in these countries it is necessary to organize the working masses in the practical daily struggle regardless of their party allegiance into a united front which will then spread to all countries. . . . Fight the leaders of the Second International who are splitting the working class.

Build the united front from below.

EXTRACTS FROM AN ECCI MANIFESTO ON THE NATIONALIST MOVEMENT
IN FRENCH NORTH AFRICA

May 1922   *Inprekorr*, ii, 84, p. 649, 8 *June* 1922

[The Tunisian delegate to the fourth world congress criticized the inactivity of the French Communist Party; it had no colonial action programme and at its Paris congress had postponed discussion of the colonial question for electoral reasons. Communist cells had been organized in Tunis after the Tours congress, and had, according to the speaker, been so successful that the Government had suppressed them and their Arab-language press. In the disorders of April 1922 the Government had been unable to rely on the local garrison and had brought Negro troops into the area. The same delegate was also highly critical of the

Algerian 'pseudo-communists' who, he said, had too much influence on the French party. They believed that liberation could come only as the result of revolution in France, not as the result of local action. They condemned the Comintern appeal as a mistake, because the bourgeois colonial press had used it to stir up public opinion against the communists.]

For the first time since the conquest of North Africa by French capitalism the natives, groaning under the heel of the big planters and the slave-driving officials, are finding strong and reliable allies among the compatriots of their exploiters, who have made the natives' cause their own and will support it until victory is won; that is the party of the proletariat, the Communist Party of France, section of the Communist International. The dawn of emancipation has appeared before the Arab proletarians, subjected to the shameful exploitation of the native aristocracy and the French conqueror. The imperialist war awakened a spirit of unrest in Tunis and Algiers just as it did in Egypt and India. And, together with the nationalist demands, class demands are being mingled, ever more frequently and more urgently.

The rising of the Moslem masses, whom English imperialism was unable to intimidate by its punitive measures, and which was renewed more powerfully than before after every attempt at suppression, cannot be kept within the limits of the English area of occupation, and is already threatening French imperialism.

During the great imperialist war the French colonies paid a heavy tribute in blood. Taking advantage of the ignorance of the masses, and imposing their will on them by terror, the alien rulers of the country formed many native regiments which were then sent to shed their blood on the western front and the Balkans in defence of bourgeois money-bags. . . .

In Africa French civilization is expressed in pitiless oppression, intolerable taxes, unspeakable poverty. Algiers was recently afflicted by a catastrophic famine. For forty years Tunis has been enduring a Tsarist form of rule, cynically called a 'protectorate', exercised under the tricolour.

It is even impossible to publish a communist newspaper in Tunis in the Arab language, and French and Tunisian communists, fraternally united in the struggle against the bourgeois dictatorship, are exposed to the same persecution. . . .

The reprisals in Tunis, now increasing in intensity, will not hold up the tide of freedom. On the contrary, they will make the movement spread, and deepen it until it becomes irresistible. The blows aimed at the communists will increase the prestige of communism, double its influence, and present the communist party to the native masses as the only champion of their rights.

The French proletarians understand that the cause of the African proletarians is their own cause, and accordingly they defend it. . . .

The struggle for the liberation of Algiers and Tunis is only beginning. It will end only when the slaves have triumphed.

The Communist International sends greetings to the French and native comrades persecuted and imprisoned by the ruling caste. . . . It sends greetings to the Communist League of Tunis and the Communist Party of France who are leading the struggle against oppression, and assures them of the complete solidarity of the international proletariat.

The Communist International calls on all the oppressed and exploited in Algiers and Tunis. . . . Unite against your exploiters under the flag of the communist party.

Soldiers and sailors of France!

Do not shoot at your Algerian and Tunisian brothers. Fraternize with the people in their struggle for liberation.

Proletarians of France! Help the African proletariat.

EXTRACTS FROM THE RESOLUTION OF THE ENLARGED ECCI ON THE
FRENCH COMMUNIST PARTY

11 *June* 1922   *Inprekorr*, ii, 122, p. 797, 29 *June* 1922

[The meeting of the enlarged ECCI in June 1922 was attended by 41 delegates, from 17 countries, with voting powers, and 9 delegates with consultative voice. There were in addition 4 representatives of the RILU and 4 from the Youth International, with votes. A later figure gives 60 delegates from 27 countries. The presidium had decided to take part officially in the proceedings at the trial of the Social-Revolutionaries, by putting forward witnesses for the prosecution, and by providing expert testimony on the rôle of bourgeois States and of the mensheviks in intervention. It would also provide defence witnesses for some young former terrorists who had admitted their mistakes and had been accused of treachery by the Second and Two-and-a-half Internationals.

Radek reported on the Berlin meeting of the three Internationals, but the greater part of the time was devoted to discussing the affairs of the French Communist Party.

The presidium elected after this meeting consisted of Bukharin, Radek, Brandler, Souvarine, Gramsci, Smeral, Jordanov, with Cook (North America) and Kuusinen as candidates, and Leiciagué (France) and Jilek (Czechoslovakia) as additional members without votes, while the internal disputes in their parties were being settled.

Between the Marseille congress in December 1921 and March 1922 membership of the French Communist Party had fallen from 120,000 to 60,000. Frossard, the right-wing leader, stated that they would comply with the decision of the conflicts commission of the ECCI to expel Fabre as an opportunist, but urged greater autonomy for the CPF in the future. Similarly, while recognizing the importance of united front tactics, they wanted to be allowed to decide for themselves on their practical application. Souvarine, representing the left, attributed the fall in membership to the inactivity and indiscipline of the CPF. Trotsky endorsed this view, and criticized the 'anti-Moscow' line in part of the French party. Frossard admitted that there was a crisis in the relations between the CI and the CPF.

In regard to the united front Frossard explained that the French delegation were bound by their mandate; it was impossible to seek a united front with those from whom they had so recently split off. He asked the ECCI to leave it to the French party to work out the practical forms that the united front should take in France.

The resolution would be acted upon, he said, 'not from automatic discipline, nor because of the provisions of the CI statutes . . . but because we know that the authority of the International, stemming from its theoretical line and its revolutionary experience, whatever our present reservations, can act only in a salutary way on all parties, including the French party'.

In an article published at this time Trotsky wrote that the objective conditions in France were revolutionary; what was wrong was the development within the party itself, particularly the attempt of the central committee to adapt its policy to the views of the right wing.

Trotsky reported for the commission on the French question which proposed this resolution. In a letter to Ker, of the French central committee, he wrote that the situation in the French party was critical. Unless the central committee took a firm line in regard to discipline and the execution of Comintern decisions, matters would inevitably move towards a split, as in the Italian Socialist Party.]

The chief task of the next communist party congress must consist in the adoption of a programme, tactics, and statutes which correspond fully to the rôle of the party in the present epoch of preparation of the social revolution. Steps must immediately be taken to work out appropriate drafts and to publish them not only in the French party press but throughout the International so that the ideas and experience of all communist parties and the Executive Committee can be drawn on to examine and elaborate the fundamental documents which are designed to secure for the party of the working class the maximum unity and fighting capacity.

STRUCTURE OF THE PARTY

THE CENTRAL COMMITTEE

The constitution of a homogeneous central committee able to ensure that the direction of the party corresponds to the decisions of the national and international congresses must from now on be the object of careful preparation and later be put through by the next congress of the party.

It must be recognized as absolutely essential that more than half of the central committee should consist of workers with genuine ties with the masses; all members of the committee must devote themselves either to party work or to trade union work.

The most essential part of this preparatory work is to select candidates who meet these conditions, to investigate their pasts and their political reliability and to make them known to the local party organizations. Responsibility for this work rests of course on all those members of the present central committee who unreservedly accept the resolutions of the Communist International and are determined to secure their execution.

The majority of members of the central committee established by these means will embody the committee's ties with the local federations, the trade unions, the press, etc. At the same time a permanent political bureau must be set up within the central committee, having its seat in Paris and concentrating the entire conduct of party activities in its hands, preparing all the material necessary to enable the full central committee to reach decisions on the most important questions and supervising the practical execution of these decisions by the general secretariat of the central committee.

DISCIPLINE

The central committee must have the right to declare certain members or groups of members expelled from the party, whenever this is warranted by political considerations.

In cases which require detailed investigation of a violation of discipline or of other offences or crimes against the interests of the party, the central committee may refer the question to the conflicts commission for examination.

Whenever a case occurs in which the political question admits of no doubt and the vital interests of the party require expulsion, the central committee itself decides on expulsion. Appeals against this decision can be made only to the party congress. . . .

The principle of federalism is wholly incompatible with the true interests of a revolutionary organization. Any reference to the federal constitution of the Soviet Republic is utterly misplaced because the structure of the communist party cannot be compared with the structure of the Soviet State. In all the federal republics the party of the communists is one and the same party and is strictly centralized. The communists of the Ukraine, Georgia, etc., are bound to the communists of Moscow and Petrograd not by the bonds of federalism but by strict democratic centralism. It was only thanks to the unity of this centralized organization of the working class that Russia was able to defend its existence victoriously against its innumerable enemies. The International condemns in the most categorical fashion the application of the principle of federalism and local autonomy to a revolutionary party which must act as the lever of revolution. An organization which has at the top a committee with a hundred heads is deprived of resolute and consistent leadership. . . .

THE TRADE UNION QUESTION

The International notes the enormous danger to the labour movement and particularly to the trade union movement represented by the petty-bourgeois individualist elements who are hostile to the spirit of proletarian discipline. . . .

Since there are communists, members of the party, in trade unions which still belong to the CGT, the party must maintain the usual organic contact with these comrades. Communists in the reformist trade unions must organize communist cells which meet regularly and which maintain close contact with the appropriate party bodies. However the relations between the CGT and the CGTU may develop, and whatever action the party takes in its struggle against the reformists, communists must fight to win all CGT bodies from within. . . .

THE UNITED FRONT

The International notes that the press and the leading bodies of the French Communist Party dealt in a wholly incorrect fashion with the meaning and significance of the united front tactics. The International roundly rejects the superficial judgment of journalists who see a rebirth of reformism in what is in fact an intensification of the methods of fighting against reformism. . . .

The most glorious page in the history of the French proletariat, the Commune, was nothing other than a bloc of all organizations and tendencies in the working class against the bourgeoisie. That the Commune, despite the realization of a united front, was quickly crushed, was due primarily to the absence on the left wing of that front of a genuinely revolutionary, disciplined, and resolute organization capable of rapidly taking over the leadership in the fire of events. . . .

The idea of a left bloc can in the given circumstances exercise a spell over a great many workers who have little political experience. The Communist Party of France must give serious consideration to this danger. In its daily propaganda the party must systematically oppose to the idea of the left bloc the idea of a bloc of all workers against the bourgeoisie. Naturally, when it comes to elections, the party must put forward its own independent communist lists. . . .

FRACTIONS

The International notes that in the French party, in addition to other manifestations of crisis, there are symptoms of the rebirth of fractions.

The extreme right wing of the party . . . . has achieved an importance in the party and in the press which is wholly out of proportion to its theoretical and political standing. The failure of the central committee to take decisive measures against this right wing has naturally led to attempts to revive the left wing fraction. The struggle between these two fractions is bound in its turn to undermine the fighting capacity of the party and may in the future endanger its unity. The International is firmly convinced that only the complete concentration of the overwhelming majority of the party against its insignificant right wing and the energetic execution of all decisions of the present conference can cut the ground from under the feet of all fractional groupings.

At the same time the International calls on the left wing never to constitute itself as an independent fraction but, while continuing to uphold revolutionary principles, to confine its activities within the framework of the party's institutions and organizations and to co-operate actively with the solid core of the party in all practical work and particularly in the struggle against the disruptive activities of the reformists, pacifists, and anarcho-syndicalists. . . .

THE NEXT PARTY CONGRESS

The preparations for the next party congress must consist of a campaign for the theoretical and organizational consolidation of the French party against all anarcho-syndicalist and petty-bourgeois pacifist tendencies, against those who only talk of revolution, against the theories which subordinate the action of the proletariat to the stage of maturity reached by the peasants and which are therefore inimical to the class character of the party. Since these various tendencies have already caused the utmost confusion in the party the communist press must establish clarity on all these questions, reminding party members of the relevant resolutions of the Communist International, in particular, the 21 conditions of admission. All these decisions should be explained in the light of the experience of the last year or illustrated by examples of the literary and political statements made by many responsible party fighters which are incompatible with these resolutions.

The date of the congress must be settled by agreement between the central committee of the French party and the presidium of the ECCI.

EXTRACTS FROM AN ECCI STATEMENT ON THE THIRD ANNIVERSARY OF THE VERSAILLES TREATY

24 *June* 1922   *Inprekorr*, ii, 118, p. 787, 28 *June* 1922

[The constant preoccupation of the Soviet Government with the need to prevent 'a united capitalist anti-Soviet front' was reflected in Comintern propaganda against the Versailles treaty, which was designed to keep alive in Germany feelings of resentment against the western Powers. In an interview published in the *Observer* in August, Chicherin, Soviet Foreign Commissar, referring to French hostility to Russia and Germany, asked: 'What is more natural than that the two should be driven into one another's arms?'

In a manifesto published at the end of December 1921 the ECCI called on 'the proletarians of all countries' to protest against the 'pillaging of Germany'. 'In the winter and spring further tribute to the Allies has to be paid by impoverished Germany, where the price of food has doubled in the last few months; the payment of these fresh milliards will bring further ruin to its industry. French imperialism knows that it is impossible, knows that Germany is at the end of its resources. But the capitalist French Government, which spends more than half its income on interest to the war profiteers, does not dare to tax the propertied classes. . . . The international proletariat has no sympathy for the German bourgeoisie, one of those principally responsible for the world war. . . . The international proletariat knows the misery of the towns and villages of Northern France, devastated and burned to the ground. But the international proletariat and above all the French working class must realize that the Allies extort their tribute not from the German bourgeoisie, but from the German proletariat, that they condemn the German proletarian to the life of a coolie, that his cheap labour will compete with the labour of the workers of France, England, and America and lower their standard of living. Therefore we say to the international proletariat, above all to the workers of France: Raise your voice in warning against the preparations for the invasion of the Ruhr. Prepare for the fight against the criminal policy of the French Government. Do not let yourselves be deceived by the negotiations for a moratorium, etc. For such measures will only prolong the crisis and in the end lead to so much the severer conflicts.'

The central political task for French communists, the ECCI wrote in September 1922, was the struggle against the Versailles treaty. The French bourgeoisie were able to maintain their position by ruining and pillaging Germany; reparations enabled them to give a section of the working class a privileged position, and this section naturally supported the reformists. In France the struggle for the social revolution took the form of a fight against French military hegemony and against Versailles.]

The working class let slip the favourable moment when it would have been relatively easy to defeat the bourgeoisie in a bold onslaught. When the war came to an end in 1918, with the ruling capitalist classes in all countries terrified of the revolutionary force of the Russian revolution, while, carried along in the stream of revolutionary enthusiasm, the working class of Germany, Austria, and later of Italy engaged in spontaneous struggles for power, it would have been possible but for the treachery of the social-patriotic war politicians to seize power in a daring attempt. . . . The communists who during the world war began to organize serious struggle against war, who in Russia had overthrown Tsarism and the bourgeoisie, who in various west European countries fought in the front ranks during the spontaneous revolutionary battles of the proletariat, were not strong enough in west Europe to defeat the bourgeoisie because the bourgeoisie had as their best assistants the leaders of the Second International and the trade union bureaucracy. Only in Russia has it so far been possible, despite the furious attacks of the imperialist robber governments helped by the counter-revolutionary trade union bureaucracy of the Second and Two-and-a-half Internationals, to maintain the power of the victorious workers and peasants.

The Communist International has done everything in its power to organize and to lead the struggle against the rule of the bourgeoisie. If this struggle has not so far led to victory it is because the majority of the proletariat could not make up its mind to follow the communist standard without reservation. . . .

Three years after the conclusion of the peace treaty of Versailles we again call on the world proletariat to rally nationally and internationally for the fight against the shameful Versailles peace as we called to you on 28 June 1919 to fight against this treaty.

EXTRACTS FROM AN ECCI MANIFESTO ON THE CONCLUSION OF THE
HAGUE CONFERENCE

22 *July* 1922   *Inprekorr*, ii, 145, p. 925, 25 *July* 1922

[The Genoa conference, which ended its sessions in May, adjourned to The Hague, where a conference of economic experts was held from 26 June to 20 July 1922. The demand for compensation by Russia for nationalized foreign-owned enterprises, and Russia's insistence on credits before the repayment of loans could be contemplated, proved insurmountable obstacles to agreement.]

CAPITALIST PLUNDERING OF SOVIET RUSSIA BEHIND THE MASK OF WORLD
ECONOMIC RECONSTRUCTION

TO THE WORKERS OF ALL COUNTRIES

COMRADES!

The Hague conference has come to an end. The latest effort of the capitalist world to establish 'peace' with Soviet Russia and to initiate the economic 'reconstruction' of Russia has been exposed as a cynical attempt to make the Russian workers and peasants into slaves of world capital. This attempt has foundered against the resolute resistance of the Soviet Government. . . .

It is one of the greatest crimes of the social-democratic parties of the Second and Two-and-a-half Internationals that during the Genoa conference and the Hague conference they did not call on you to exert the utmost pressure on the capitalist States but stabbed the representatives of Soviet Russia in the back. . . .

Having secured the independence of their country, the Russian workers and peasants proposed peace to the capitalist States. They also succeeded in concluding peace with their nearest neighbours, the Polish, Lithuanian, Latvian, Estonian, and Finnish vassals of the Entente, who feared that if they did not conclude peace Soviet Russia would crush them. They have made a provisional trade agreement with England who hoped in this way to hamper Russian revolutionary activity in the Near East. They have made similar trade agreements with the small northern capitalist States who were forced to seek markets in Russia because of the severe economic crisis. Finally they have forced the German bourgeoisie to conclude formal peace with Soviet Russia. However cowardly they are, the German bourgeoisie understood that once their hope of victory over Soviet Russia had suffered shipwreck, and all their attempts to make friends with the Entente had failed, Germany must live in peace with the Russian people if it is ever to liberate itself from exploitation by the Entente.

Soviet Russia knew . . . that if it got stronger economically its importance for the future liberation struggle of the proletariat would be greater. It strove for peace so that the capitalists might have no opportunity to stir up the unconscious working masses against communism with the story that Russia was attempting to impose communism on them by armed force. Soviet Russia sought peace in order to re-establish the trade with the West which is essential for its reconstruction. Since you have not yet seized power, since you are not in a position to supply the Russian workers with machines and tools, Soviet Russia had to try to get them from the capitalists. . . . If you were masters in the economically advanced part of the world you would understand that your own interests require you to support by every means the Russian workers republic so that you could get bread in exchange for your machinery.

The capitalist world is the sworn enemy of Soviet Russia and Soviet Russia knew well that if it was to get help it would have to make sacrifices and pay usurious prices. It declared its readiness to buy peace with the capitalist world by making great concessions. As a condition of peace the capitalist governments demanded recognition of the debts incurred by the Tsarist and Kerensky Governments. They demanded the restitution of the factories and mines which formerly belonged to foreign capitalists and which were made the property of the Russian people by the October revolution. Soviet Russia answered that the Tsarist debts had been incurred without the consent of the Russian working people. They were incurred to enslave and exploit the people. The Russian people has paid these debts in rivers of blood shed on the Allied side for the interests and triumph of the Entente stockjobbers. Without declaring war, the Allies shamefully attacked Soviet Russia and by their intervention destroyed more than was ever owed to them. Their demands therefore are justified by nothing except their power and their exploitation of the famine in Russia and the needs of the Russian people. The Soviet Government takes account of these needs and it is therefore ready to recognize the debts if these are reduced to a reasonable sum and if the Allies by granting credits make it possible for Soviet Russia to re-establish its economy quickly so that it will be in a position to pay the debts.

As to the factories and mines belonging to foreign capitalists, Soviet Russia declares that it will in no circumstances return them. The money with which they were built was sweated out of the labour of foreign workers, and foreign capitalists have drawn enough sweat and blood from the Russian workers in payment. The Russian proletariat cannot return these factories because it is only by developing them that it will be able in future to create the values with which to reconstruct its shattered country, improve agriculture, and find the means to pay the foreign sharks the tribute they demand. . . . But Soviet Russia is ready to pay a certain compensation to the foreign capitalists if by means of credits they now help Russia to rebuild; it is ready to lease some of these factories.

The Soviet Government was prepared to make great sacrifices in order to conclude peace at last with the capitalist States so that the Russian workers and peasants, after the severe fighting, after hunger and poverty, could at last get on with peaceful work.

All these proposals fell on deaf ears. The representatives of the capitalist States demanded unconditional recognition of all the debts of the Tsars and the Russian bourgeoisie and their immediate repayment. They demanded the unconditional return of the factories and mines. They had their eyes on Russia's natural wealth as security for the payment of debts. If Soviet Russia were to agree it would not only make the Russian workers and peasants alive today into slaves of the Entente but it would surrender future generations of the Russian working people to the most extreme exploitation. . . .

If the capitalists stubbornly refuse to grant credits to Soviet Russia, that is only because they fear that the development of nationalized industry in Russia would destroy all their arguments about the impossibility of socialism.

The Soviet Government's fight against the demands of the capitalist world is more than a fight for the further development of the Russian revolution; it is a fight for the development of European socialism, it is your fight. If the Soviet Government is the victor in this struggle then in the near future you in the still capitalist countries will be able when you take up the struggle for socialism to rely on a strong State ruled by the proletariat, whose tremendous economic strength will be put at the service of the proletarian revolution. . . .

The Soviet Republic's struggle will be a difficult one. It is true that the good harvest will make it easier to undertake the indispensable measures to improve the condition of the proletariat and the peasantry, but you should never forget how terribly great Russia's poverty is, how small the help which it has so far received from you. It is the duty of the proletarians in the countries with a sound currency to do everything they can to give material help to their Russian brothers. Follow the example of the American Garment Workers' Union which has established a joint organization with the Soviet Government to improve the Russian garment industry and which is raising a loan of a million dollars for this purpose among trade union members. Nor is it only economic help that is required. After the failure of the Hague negotiations, French imperialism will certainly do everything it can to mobilize its vassals against Soviet Russia again, to organize new conspiracies in Russia, and it will be helped by the SRs, the protégés of the Second and Two-and-a-half Internationals. The counter-revolutionary plots in Russia and the military adventures of the Entente will begin again, and it is your sacred duty, workers of all countries, to work all out for an immediate general peace with Russia, for a peace without loot, without burdens on the Russian people, for a peace which does not throw a halter round the necks of the Russian people but secures them material help.

Organize the proletarian united front for Soviet Russia and you will serve the cause not only of the Russian proletariat and the Russian revolution but your own cause, the cause of your own emancipation.

EXTRACTS FROM AN ECCI MANIFESTO TO THE WORKERS OF ITALY

22 July 1922   Inprekorr, ii, 145, p. 931, 25 July 1922

[Throughout 1922 the power and activities of the fascists were increasing, and violence and disorder spread over the whole country. In a number of cities and rural areas Mussolini's 'squads' were in virtual control, and government forces were unable to provide protection for their victims. After the fall of the Facta government in July 1922, and a number of unsuccessful attempts by various Italian political figures to form a new government, the Socialist Party, which had earlier agreed to support, but not participate in, a bourgeois government, decided for the first time in its history on participation; its offer was not taken up, and Facta was reinstalled. The 'Alliance of Labour', a recently created body founded on the initiative of the railwaymen's union, called a general strike for 31 July 'in defence of civil and trade union liberties'. The fascist council issued an ultimatum: 'We give the State 48 hours to assert its authority. . . . When that time has elapsed fascism will claim full liberty of action and will take the place of the State, which will once more have proved its impotence.' The Alliance decided to end the strike on 3 August. After the strike Mussolini claimed that during its course the fascists had destroyed the headquarters of socialist, trade union, and communist organizations in 43 cities and forced the resignation of several socialist municipal councils. Terracini, of the Italian Communist Party, writing a few days later, attributed the failure of the strike to the conflict between revolutionaries and reformists in the Alliance. At the ECCI meeting in January 1922 Terracini, reporting on the state of parties in Italy, had ignored the fascists.]

What remains of the Italian Socialist Party will be meeting in a few days in a congress that will seal its fate. At this moment we appeal not only to the workers who are members of that party, but to all Italian workers, faced with the public collapse of the Italian Socialist Party, to reflect on the lessons of this collapse and to decide whether it is to be the final defeat of the Italian workers' movement, or the beginning of its rapid recovery. . . .

At the end of the war the Italian bourgeois State was economically shattered; it had no army on which the bourgeoisie could rely; its bureaucracy was dispersed, the proletariat in revolt, the bourgeoisie disheartened. The Italian Socialist Party was the hope of the Italian worker. It alone bore no responsibility for the war which had ruined Italy: on the contrary, it had the glory of having fought against the murderous war. The Italian proletariat rejoiced in the Russian revolution and wanted to follow the Russian example. A flood of strikes swept over the land, the workers occupied the factories, the streets of the towns were in their hands. . . . The sun of the revolution seemed to be rising in Italy. But the majority of the leaders of the Italian Socialist Party did not dare to organize the spontaneous movement of the proletariat and lead it in the attack. And when the proletariat went over to the attack itself, in September 1920, and the bourgeoisie did not dare to use arms against the workers, the trade union leaders, d'Aragona and co., reached an agreement with the bourgeoisie, while the leaders of the party, while Serrati, did nothing to stop them, accepting Giolitti's promise to submit a bill on workers' control of industry to Parliament.

When the bourgeoisie saw how the socialist leaders feared the revolution, they forgot their own fears and organized the fascist squads who instituted a rule of terror throughout the country, killing thousands of revolutionary workers, raiding their homes, and becoming masters of the situation. Serrati undertook to prepare for the revolution by systematic propaganda and organization. What he accomplished was the disorganization of the revolutionary forces and the victory of the fascists. . . .

The Communist International foresaw these developments, and it said to the leaders of the Italian Socialist Party: You maintain that the Italian proletariat is not yet ready to seize power. Well, if that is true, the greater must be the preparation for the struggle for power. And the first step is to break with the reformists, with Turati, Treves, d'Aragona. They are few in number, but they control the proletarian mass organizations, the trade unions and co-operatives, as well as the parliamentary fraction; they are enemies of the proletarian revolution, advocates of class collaboration. . . . Serrati swore that they were not traitors to the proletariat, that they were disciplined comrades who would submit to the will of the party. And he decided to break with the Communist International rather than break with this handful of reformist bureaucrats. . . . Now the parliamentary fraction is rebelling against the central committee and is coming out openly for collaboration with the bourgeoisie, for taking part in the bourgeois government. . . . And Serrati is forced to threaten to break with the reformists, a step which he fought so stubbornly at Leghorn.

What has happened? The attacks of the fascist squads have met with success. The weakest strata of the proletariat, the agricultural labourers, the workers in small towns, abandoned by the passivity of the Italian Socialist Party to the white terror, allowed themselves to be persuaded by the reformist trade union bureaucrats, parliamentarians, and municipal councillors that they would be freed of this terror if the Socialist Party joined the government and got control of the State machine. That is nothing but an illusion. We do not know if the bourgeoisie will still take the Treves, Turatis, Modiglianis, and d'Aragonas into the Government. They do not need them now that they have demoralized the proletariat, have helped the bourgeoisie to disarm the workers. . . . But even if they do take them in, it is ludicrous to think of fighting the fascists with the help of the bourgeois apparatus. The fascists get weapons from the bourgeois-monarchist army, the officials work together with them, and the government is as powerless against the fascists as it is strong with them. . . .

Serrati and his followers are talking of setting up an Independent Socialist Party to fight the reformists. How will he fight them, what will his fight consist of?—that is the question. . . . The reformists can be fought only by mustering the working class for the fight against the fascist attack, by leading the proletariat along the road of struggle. This is the road pointed out by the Italian communists in their proposals to the Alleanza del Lavoro, in which they indicate concretely what the workers should do to save their skins. . . .

If Serrati has really recognized his mistakes, he will have no choice but to reconsider everything that he has said and written against the Communist International. . . . He feared to prepare for the revolutionary struggle, and now he can see that to renounce it was preparation for the victory of the fascists. If it were a question merely of Serrati, we might mock him: 'Tu l'as voulu, Georges Dandin'. But behind Serrati there are still tens of thousands of workers, and so we say: every party can make mistakes, honest workers' leaders can also make mistakes, but they must prove their honesty by recognizing their mistakes, learning from them, and finding the way back to the correct road of struggle marked out for the proletarians of the entire world by the Communist International.

EXTRACTS FROM AN ECCI STATEMENT ON THE DECISION OF THE POALE ZION NOT TO AFFILIATE TO THE THIRD INTERNATIONAL

25 *July* 1922   *Inprekorr*, ii, 148, p. 954, 29 *July* 1922

[At its meeting on 21 September 1920 the ECCI approved the work of the Poale Zion (Socialist Labour Party of Palestine) but affirmed that it was not quite free of bourgeois nationalist prejudices. Its resolution on the question suggested that the Poale Zion put into operation the decisions of the second Comintern congress and change its name. The ECCI would then consider its application to join. The Poale Zion reported in 1921 that it had expelled its reformist and centrist members and again requested admission to the International. The ECCI, at its meeting after the third world congress, stipulated that the Poale Zion should call a congress to decide on the dissolution of the organization, and that within two months of the congress its members should join their national sections of the Comintern. The congress was also to make a radical break with Zionist tendencies and theories, and to disavow Zionist colonial aspirations in Palestine, which served the interests of British imperialism. The communists in Poale Zion resigned at the time of the fourth Comintern congress and enrolled individually in their national communist parties.]

TO THE COMMUNISTS OF ALL COUNTRIES

TO THE JEWISH PROLETARIAT

The congress of the Poale Zion World Federation has taken its decision on the conditions of admission to the Communist International jointly discussed by the ECCI and representatives of the majority and minority in the Federation. The congress rejected these conditions.

That makes the situation clear. Since the third congress the petty-bourgeois, nationalist, and opportunist elements in the majority of the delegations to the Federation have tried to sabotage and damp down the urge of the proletarian and communist elements for amalgamation with the Communist International. . . .

A condition of admission to the Communist International is the abandonment of the nationalist opportunist Palestine programme and the dissolution of the world federation and the entry of the Jewish proletarian communist elements into the national sections, the communist parties. The CI was prepared to make great concessions in the sphere of propaganda and organization in order to facilitate the development of the backward section of the Jewish proletariat towards communism. . . .

The ECCI makes it the duty of the national sections to initiate strong action against the petty-bourgeois sectarians. The theme of Palestine, the attempt to divert the Jewish working masses from the class struggle by propaganda in favour of large-scale Jewish settlement in Palestine, is not only nationalist and petty-bourgeois but counter-revolutionary in its effect, if the broad working masses are moved by this idea and so diverted from an effective struggle against their Jewish and non-Jewish capitalist exploiters. The national sections of the CI must everywhere support the minority of the Poale Zion World Federation in their struggle against the majority in so far as they have accepted the conditions of admission and leave the World Federation in order to adhere to the national sections of the Comintern. . . . The only possible attitude of communists to the Poale Zion Federation after its rejection of the conditions of admission is one of complete hostility.

EXTRACTS FROM AN ECCI MANIFESTO TO THE GERMAN AND FRENCH PROLETARIAT ON THE COLOGNE CONFERENCE OF THE GERMAN AND FRENCH COMMUNIST PARTIES

2 *September* 1922   *Inprekorr*, ii, 177, p. 1172, 7 *September* 1922

[The German and French Communist Parties had held a conference in Cologne in August 1922, to consider the reparations crisis, 'which the London conference had failed to solve'. Their manifesto said that, the bourgeois having failed, it was up to the workers of the two countries to take on the job. The German economy was facing ruin, and the German people starving. The ruin of the German working class would affect the standards of the French, while French ambitions in the Ruhr, which brought France into conflict with England, threatened to start a new war. The slogans issued by the conference were: 'Down with Versailles; no occupation of the Ruhr; no occupation of German territory.' The need for co-operation between the French and German proletariat was specifically noted in the French Communist Party programme; the CPF and the CGTU issued a joint manifesto against the threat of the occupation of the Ruhr. At the fourth Comintern congress, Rosmer complained that the disputes within the French party had preoccupied its energies to such a degree that it had been unable to do anything to carry out the decisions reached at the Cologne conference.]

TO THE GERMAN AND FRENCH PROLETARIAT!

TO THE INTERNATIONAL WORKING CLASS!

MEN AND WOMEN WORKERS!

The Communist International cordially welcomes the joint conference of the communist parties of Germany and France in Cologne and their decision to initiate a joint struggle against the attempt to operate the disintegrating Versailles treaty at the expense of the German and French working class; the German working class would be still further exploited while the French would be driven into new militarist adventures. Only energetic action by the proletarians of both countries can prevent the bourgeoisie, who have demonstrated their complete inability to revise the Versailles treaty in a reasonable fashion, from plunging the world into new military adventures.

The Communist International warns the German and French working class against placing any hopes in the attempts at agreement which the bourgeois governments will certainly again make. They cannot come to an agreement despite their fear of war because their interests differ so widely. While the English bourgeoisie are primarily concerned with the restoration of the European market and are therefore inclined to grant concessions to Germany, the French bourgeoisie, afraid to cover the budget deficit by taxing the peasants (because that would bring about the collapse of the national bloc), and urged forward in their policy of destroying Germany by the greed of French heavy industry which wants to unite the coal of the Rhine–Westphalia district with the iron ore of Briey and Lorraine—which would give it industrial and therefore political hegemony in Europe—are driven to the policy of destroying Germany. They will therefore go on tackling the problem, but they are not in a position to resolve it.

The Communist International warns you against the hope that the diplomats of the Second and Two-and-a-half Internationals and the Amsterdam trade union International are in a position to restrain the bourgeoisie from their criminal policy. . . .

The Communist International calls on you to grasp the necessity of calling a halt to the bourgeois governments by action. It is not a question of a few demonstrations. What is needed is direct energetic agitation in the factories to arouse the sleepy and the irresolute to the realization that the situation is no less serious now than it was in 1914. . . . What the bourgeoisie must learn is that on the day when they attempt to carry out their threats all the wheels will stop.

You can only do that if you close your ranks. More than ever is it necessary for the proletarian united front to be established. The Second and Two-and-a-half Internationals have on their conscience the crime of having sabotaged the world proletarian congress which we demanded at the Berlin conference of the three Internationals in order to organize the proletariat in common for the essential fight. What did not succeed by means of agreement from above must be won by unity from below, by the spontaneous drive of the proletarians of all countries in defiance of the leaders who want to avoid the struggle. . . .

Workers of France!

We summon you to revolutionary struggle against the policy of your Government, against French imperialism, not in order to help German imperialism to get on its feet again, but so that the removal of the military pressure of French imperialism may liberate the forces of the German proletariat for the German revolution.

Workers of Germany!

We summon you to fight against the German bourgeois-social-democratic government, for a proletarian workers' government, which will relieve the French masses of the fear of a resurgence of German militarism and help them to liberate themselves from the spell of nationalism.

ECCI MANIFESTO ON TURKEY

25 *September* 1922   *Inprekorr*, ii, 189, p. 1251, 27 *September* 1922

[Early in 1920 Kemal and his supporters established a centre in Ankara, independent of Constantinople, with a programme of fighting for national independence. Small British forces occupied Constantinople in March. In April 1920 Kemal established a rival government and made friendly overtures to Russia. The Allied peace terms for Turkey, published in May 1920, drew the Kemalists and Bolsheviks closer together.

In the summer of 1921 Greek forces, supported by the British, advanced against the Turks in Anatolia. Kemal's counter-attack, launched in May 1922, ended with the complete defeat of the Greeks, but the British garrison remained in Constantinople.

In their war with Greece the Turks received material and moral support from Russia; the danger of further hostilities was avoided by agreement to negotiate a new peace treaty to replace the Sèvres treaty and a new regime for the Straits. These were concluded at the Lausanne conference in 1923. On 24 September 1922, that is, the day before this manifesto, the Soviet Commissariat for Foreign Affairs had addressed a Note to a number of countries, including Britain and France, interpreting British policy as a threat to Turkey and Russia, and warning them 'against repeating the mistakes which arise from ignoring the vital interests of the States concerned' in deciding the future of the Straits. 'No decision taken without Russia will be final and enduring.'

In an article published early in October 1922 Radek explained that Russia supported Turkey, firstly, because 'everything that strengthens the Eastern peoples, oppressed and exploited by international imperialism, also strengthens Soviet Russia, which is threatened by the same danger', and secondly, because Russia was 'deeply interested in ensuring that the ships carrying grain to Russia (*sic*) and oil from Russia should not be held up by orders from the British Admiralty.']

PEACE TO THE TURKISH PEOPLE

WAR ON EUROPEAN IMPERIALISM

Men and women workers!

Events of the greatest historical import are developing in the Near East. The capitalists of the victorious Entente have condemned the Turkish people to death. They have torn Turkey in pieces and surrounded it with a ring of States which, too weak to exist in their own right, are condemned to be perpetually incited against the Turkish people, hounds acting for the Entente. Constantinople, the Turkish capital, became an Allied war camp. English and French warships trained their guns on it. Turkey was to be for ever at the mercy of Allied arms. But, inspired by the sight of the fighting and triumphant Red Army, the Turkish people, although exhausted by a series of wars, took to the battle and have for three years defended themselves. They put the Greek army, equipped by England, to flight. With the exception of Constantinople and the Dardanelles, Asia Minor has been freed from foreign armies. The victory of the Turkish army demonstrates again that the power of tyrants is not unbounded, and that the chains of slavery forged at Versailles break like glass when nations rise for their freedom.

But the defeat of England's vassal Greece does not mean the final defeat of Entente imperialism. Constantinople and the Dardanelles are still in the hands of the Allies. That means that the Allies can still not only threaten Turkey but use the Dardanelles to send their warships into the Black Sea against Soviet Russia.

English imperialism has the impudence to threaten a new war in the name of the freedom of the seas if Turkey should dare to occupy its capital and the shores of its own country. It is not many years since the blood of English and Australian workers was shed in Gallipoli in order that English imperialism might rule Russia and Turkey. But English imperialism again dares to threaten the world with a new war. If it succeeds in carrying out its threats it will be the blood not only of English and Turkish soldiers but other people's too that will flow. In the last few years France has helped Turkey because as a competitor it wanted to weaken England's position in the East and use this to bargain for freedom to exploit the German people. But if it should come to a showdown, if Turkey were to stretch out its hands to the shores of the Straits, France would be on England's side, because French imperialism fears to lose England's help in the exploitation of Germany. It can demonstrate against England but it cannot break with English imperialism. Thus the French workers too would have to fight again for the joint rule of the Entente. But the war would not be restricted to these peoples. The Entente would drag in Serbia and Rumania, Italy and Greece, and the fire once started in the Balkans would spread further and again make Europe into one vast battlefield. If that were to be avoided by Turkish surrender it would only mean that the war in the Near East would be postponed. Turkey cannot exist with the knife of the Entente in its back, and Russia is not secure so long as its grain and coal areas are within the operational scope of the English navy.

The Turkish Government is not a government of workers and peasants; it is a government of the officer class, a government of intellectuals, a government which certainly does not correspond to our ideals. There is therefore no doubt that as Turkey develops economically the Turkish working class will have to fight against the government. But the Turkish workers understand that, whatever their attitude to this government, Turkey's fight is the fight of a poor peasant people against enslavement by international capital, and the international proletariat must in its own interest and regardless of its attitude to the Turkish government, do everything it can to prevent Entente imperialism from taking up arms again against Turkey and from shedding the blood of the European proletariat once more in the interests of English world domination.

Men and women workers, and, above all, workers of England, France, Italy, Serbia, and Rumania. It is your duty to fight with all your strength against any attempt at military action against Turkey. It is your duty to use all your forces to prevent the Entente from forcing Turkey to abandon the Straits to the Allies which would be the prelude to new wars. The questions now being decided in the Near East are questions of life and death, not only for the people living on the Black Sea but also for the European proletariat.

Down with English imperialism! Freedom and peace to the Turkish people! Down with new imperialist wars! Down with the diplomatic hucksters!

EXTRACTS FROM A LETTER FROM THE ECCI TO THE ITALIAN SOCIALIST
PARTY

October 1922   *Inprekorr*, ii, 197, p. 1323, 10 *October* 1922

[At the Rome congress of the Italian Socialist Party in October 1922, Serrati, with 32,000 votes, split from the right wing, which mustered 29,000 votes, and voted for affiliation to the Third International. Writing at this time, Zinoviev said that 'objectively, Italy is still the country nearest to revolution.' This letter was addressed to the left-wing majority at its opening session after the split.

Bordiga, and other Italian delegates to the fourth Comintern congress, expressed misgivings about accepting Serrati and his followers, known as maximalists, into the Communist Party; the split, he argued, did not denote any change in Serrati's policy, but merely demonstrated its bankruptcy.

At its meeting on 30–31 December 1922, the committee of the Italian Socialist Party decided to accept the fourth congress resolution on the Italian question, and instructed their delegates remaining in Moscow to continue with the practical work of amalgamation. The resolution was cautious in tone, and one group (which included Nenni, at that time editor of *Avanti*) was opposed to fusion with the CPI. Negotiations were not completed when, early in 1923, the leaders of both parties were arrested. Four members of the Italian Socialist Party were present at the fourth congress, with consultative voice.]

The split between maximalists and reformists in Italy has at last been completed. What the Communist International demanded two years ago has inevitably come about. The necessary surgical operation was delayed for two years, the disease was neglected, and that of course has done untold harm to the organism of the Italian Socialist Party. The Italian working class has suffered enormous losses because of the mistakes made in 1920 by the maximalist leaders. The bourgeoisie exploited the mistakes of the socialists to consolidate their own position and to begin an unconcealed and cynical offensive against the Italian working class.

Today every honest maximalist worker realizes that in 1920 the maximalist leaders made a terrible mistake, when he is told that the split is necessary in 1922, but was not yet necessary in 1920 because—as was said at the time—there were no concrete facts to prove the treachery of the reformists. Such a statement is either childish or a blameworthy attempt to conceal the real meaning of events from the workers.

Nobody can claim to be a leader of the proletarian masses who is able to draw the right conclusion only slowly, after the lapse of a few years; a leader of the proletarian masses is one who is able to recognize a new trend at the very beginning, to warn the workers in time of the threatening danger. That is precisely what Marxists are for; they study the course of the class struggle and know how to reach conclusions about it and to fight against dangers as soon as they begin to appear.

At the end of 1922 it is indeed quite easy to see where reformism has led us, for it has already gone over body and soul into the bourgeois camp. The Communist International saw that in good time, but a few maximalist leaders either did not see it or deliberately closed their eyes to the treachery of the reformists. However that may be, the situation of the Italian working class today is so terrible that those whose sole concern is the interests of the proletariat should not spend too much time on arguing who was right and who wrong. The most vital and urgent task in Italy is to unite all revolutionary forces as quickly as possible and to build up the bloc of the proletariat against the bloc of the reformist, fascist, and imperialist forces.

Comrade maximalists!

Two roads lie before you: either you will try to create some kind of middle thing, a so-called independent centre party, and in that case your party will in six months' time or in a year again become the prey of the reformists and the bourgeoisie. In the present conditions in Italy and the present phase of the class struggle, such an independent centrist middle party could for a few years lead a wretched existence but would inevitably be condemned to a shameful end. Or you will take the other road and come out resolutely and without turning aside for unification with the Communist Party of Italy; this is the true road of revolutionary struggle, and to do this you must come back under the banner of the Communist International.

Choose, comrades!

Your congress must consider the significance of the situation and of the choice. Take care. While you have at last broken the rusty chains which bound you to the reformist traitors, the Second and Two-and-a-half Internationals are at the same time uniting. . . . The Two-and-a-half International has ceased to exist, it has capitulated and waits on the mercy of the yellow social-democrats. Is it possible for you to fail to see the enormous significance of this event in the camp of the international labour movement? Is it possible for you still not to see that there are only two roads, the Second International, the two-faced international, and the Communist International, the international of class struggle? . . .

You must choose!

The ECCI is inspired by the sincere desire to do everything it can to facilitate your return to the banner of the Communist International. The situation of the Italian working class is such that you must be given the opportunity to put your point of view to the Third International and to hear its opinions on those questions which are of the most vital importance for the Italian working-class movement.

Recognize the necessity of forming as quickly as possible a joint proletarian committee of action in common with the Italian Communist Party, which is the only representative of the Communist International in Italy today. This action committee should try to organize in the trade union and political field—regardless of the deep differences which still exist—a joint struggle against the bourgeoisie and against the reformists, which would be the best way of preparing the unity of the truly revolutionary forces in Italy.

We repeat: Your fate is in your own hands. Further mistakes, further hesitation and irresolution, would be tantamount in fact to treachery to the Italian working class.

THE ECCI TO THE CONGRESS OF THE FRENCH COMMUNIST PARTY

6 *October* 1922   *Inprekorr*, ii, 197, p. 1323, 10 *October* 1922

[The second congress of the French Communist Party opened in Paris on 15 October 1922 with Manuilsky and Humbert-Droz as ECCI delegates. Attempts made before the opening to get agreement between the left and centre had failed. A joint centre-left (Frossard–Souvarine) resolution on the united front had been agreed on for submission to the congress, but the two groups entered into public controversy before the congress opened. The left had also prepared a resolution on the trade union question, but this was withdrawn when the CGTU made it clear that its acceptance would mean a break between the CGTU and the CPF.

In committee, Manuilsky proposed that the central committee should consist of equal numbers of the left and centre; equal representation should also be established in the political bureau, with the ECCI delegate holding a casting vote. The proposals were not subject to amendment, and Frossard, for the centre, objected to the implied choice between obedience and rebellion, and to the total exclusion of the right wing; it was up to the congress itself to decide the composition of the central bodies. The voting, after a speech by Manuilsky to the plenary session, was 1,516 for his proposal (to accept the ECCI suggestions until the fourth world congress met) against 1,698 for Cachin's list of 24 centrists, with 814 abstentions. The last session continued throughout the night till noon of the following day.

In an earlier letter to the French Communist Party, dated 13 September 1922, the ECCI attributed the internal crisis in the French party to its failure to discard reformist and anarcho-syndicalist ideas. The right wing gained confidence as the proletarian revolution slowed down and Russia's difficulties increased. They challenged the right of the International to intervene, and suggested that Comintern decisions were dictated by passing Russian interests. The new central committee must embody the unification of the left and centre against the right wing, and must have a working-class majority. Verfeuil, elected candidate member of the central committee at the Marseille congress, collaborated with Fabre on the *Journal du Peuple*. He had been expelled by the Seine federation of the CPF.

Following the congress, three leading members of the left wing—Souvarine, Treint, and Dunois—resigned their posts on the ground that the congress decisions implied a break with the International. The new central committee issued an 'appeal to the party' asking the members to wait until the fourth Comintern congress decided whether the French party could be deprived of its right to choose the men who were to lead it.]

On the eve of the opening of the Paris congress of the French Communist Party the situation in the party has become so complicated that the ECCI finds itself compelled, in addition to the documents already published, to address the following remarks to the congress:

1. The ECCI asks the Paris congress to take a formal vote by roll-call

on the 21 conditions accepted by the second world congress of the Comintern. It will be better for the French party as well as for the Comintern to get the position on this question completely clear.

Of course, if the French Communist Party wishes to put before the fourth congress proposals for changing the 21 conditions, the Paris congress has every right to do so. The fourth congress will examine with the utmost care and attention any proposal put forward by the Paris congress.

2. Since the majority of the old central committee—to the astonishment of the Comintern Executive—did not exclude from the party Verfeuil and the comrades who share his views, even after their last flagrantly anti-communist action, the ECCI finds itself compelled to notify the Paris congress that it no longer regards as members of the Comintern Raoul Verfeuil and those who signed the well-known appeal which begins with the words: *La situation dans laquelle le parti se trouve*.

The contents of this appeal completely corroborate the previous statement of the ECCI that Raoul Verfeuil and his adherents are malicious enemies of communism who remained in the communist party of France only in order to disrupt it from within.

Should the Paris congress disagree with the ECCI on this question, the final decision will be left to the fourth world congress of the Comintern.

The ECCI again asks the congress to give a clear appraisal of all the important questions which at present divide the French party. The grave lessons learnt by the Italian party when, after two difficult years full of mistakes and vacillations, it was forced to recognize the correctness of the Comintern's demands, should not be uselessly lost. The Comintern is convinced that the Paris congress will put an end to all hesitations and create a real communist party worthy to lead the heroic French proletariat.

THE FOURTH CONGRESS OF THE COMMUNIST INTERNATIONAL

[Reporting for the mandates commission, Eberlein announced an attendance of 394; of these, 340 had full voting rights, 48 a consultative voice, and six were admitted as guests. Four of these had come from Turkey, where there were two parties; four Koreans had arrived; the dissensions within the Korean party were so wide and persistent that, said Eberlein, it was impossible to discover who were the actual delegates. Two Koreans had been admitted as guests, and two had been turned away. There were also present four members of the Italian Socialist Party, and three members of the opposition within the Czech Communist Party. Two representatives of the foreign bureau of the Persian Communist Party had also arrived, but as this bureau had been dissolved by the ECCI more than six months previously, they were not admitted. Zinoviev in his concluding speech reported 65 delegations from 62 countries; there had been 52 delegations at the third congress. Later reports give the figure of 408 delegates, of whom 343 had voting rights, from 58 countries.

Throughout the congress there was open conflict between the United States delegates. According to one speaker, four thousand left-wing members of the party had been expelled, and another thousand had left of their own accord. In the discussion of the trade union theses the two sides accused each other of misrepresentation, and when the list of nominees for the Executive was put forward Billings, one of the American delegates, protested against the nomination as candidate of Damon; the American delegation, he said, had selected himself for this.

Kolarov presented the list of nominations for the new Executive endorsed by the presidium. Amendments introduced by Norwegian, Dutch, Austrian, and Swiss delegates were rejected, and the entire list was voted unanimously en bloc. Zinoviev rebuked the 'federalist' action of the Dutch, Austrian, and Swiss delegates who had formed a 'bloc' to get a representative on to the Executive.

In his final speech Zinoviev summarized the work of the congress as giving precise and practical content to the more general decisions of former congresses. The Comintern was at last acting as an international party, giving advice and differentiated instructions to its members on all questions relevant to the victory of the world revolution. Reporting in April 1923 to the Russian Communist Party, Bukharin said that nine-tenths of the significance of the fourth congress consisted in this, that it 'interfered' in the affairs of the national sections. The chief defects in the national parties were a deficient degree of internationalism, a lack of tactical flexibility, and a shortage of skilled cadres.

Lenin's speech on 'five years of the Russian revolution and the prospects of the world revolution' was pessimistic in tone. It was devoted largely to an explanation of the 'retreat' to the new economic policy introduced in Russia in the spring of 1921. 'I think we must take note of this . . . from the viewpoint of the Communist International, and of the advanced west European countries.' In drawing up the programme of the Comintern they should not take a final decision at the congress because, inter alia, 'we have given scarcely any thought to the possibility of retreat, and of securing this retreat. In view of the fundamental change that has taken place in the world . . . we cannot absolutely ignore this question. We must not only know how to act when we are passing to the offensive and are victorious. . . . If the enemy possesses sufficient power of endurance, he can rally his forces, and so forth; he can easily provoke us to attack him, and then throw us back for many years. That is why I think that the idea that we must prepare for the possibility of retreat is very important. . . . Even from the practical point of view, all the parties which are preparing to pass to the direct onslaught upon capitalism in the near future must now also think of securing for themselves the possibility of retreat.' At the end of his speech he repeated his appeal for caution and deliberation. 'I think that after five years of the Russian revolution the most important thing for all of us, Russian and foreign comrades alike, is to sit down and study . . . I do not know how long the capitalist powers will permit us to enjoy the opportunity to study in peace. But we must take advantage of every moment of respite . . . to start learning from the beginning. . . . We must tell both the Russian and the foreign comrades that the most important thing in the ensuing period is to study. We are studying in the general sense. They, however, must study in the special sense in order that they may really understand the organization, structure, method, and content of revolutionary activity. If they do that, I am sure the prospects of the world revolution will be not only good, but excellent.']

EXTRACTS FROM A MANIFESTO TO THE ITALIAN WORKERS PASSED AT THE OPENING SESSION OF THE FOURTH COMINTERN CONGRESS

5 *November* 1922   *Protokoll*, iv, p. 18

[A manifesto issued by the Italian Communist Party on 29 October referred to the 'conflict between the constitutional and fascist forces' and said that the workers could not show solidarity 'either with the present system of government with its so-called constitutional democratic guarantees or with the fascist dictatorship'. 'The proletariat must muster its forces and act as an independent participant' against both enemies. 'A bloc between the proletariat and the democrats, that is, a coalition, means the final disarming of the proletariat in its struggle against the rule of the employer.' Anybody who proposed collaboration with other classes was to be denounced as an agent of capitalist exploitation.

Mussolini became Prime Minister on the following day, 30 October 1922. His party held fewer than 10 per cent of the seats in Parliament. Writing a few days later in *Inprekorr*, Terracini contended that the events of 27 October–1 November did not constitute a coup d'état or a revolution; the class situation in Italy was unchanged. The existing state of affairs had been confirmed, hardened, legalized. The fascist action was part of the attempt to re-establish bourgeois State power. Italian parliamentary democracy had accomplished its task of whittling away the post-war gains of the proletariat; the bourgeoisie had had time to pull themselves together, and the bourgeois State had now put an end to an expensive form of dualism. The proletariat was confused and disorganized; the split in the Socialist Party, and the preoccupation both of the Communist Party, which was not unanimously in favour of fusion with the SPI, and of the Socialist Party, with internal affairs, had paralysed the forces of the proletariat. On 28 October the trade union committee of the Communist Party had addressed a letter to all Italian trade unions suggesting united action and proposing a general strike, but the fascist coup had come sooner than they expected, and the communists had now gone over to an illegal system, preparations for which had been made over the past year.]

Dear brothers, comrades, workers, peasants of Italy!

On the solemn opening day of the fourth world congress of the Third International, which coincides with the fifth anniversary of the victory of the proletarian revolution in Russia, the International of communists addresses itself to you, for the events which have occurred during the last few days in your country place your struggle against the naked reaction which is rising against you in the very foreground.

Two years ago the Communist International strongly recommended the leaders of the then united Italian party to go over to the offensive. The Communist International expressly urged that the adherents of compromise, the opportunist wing, should be shaken off, and that, taking advantage of the panic among the bourgeoisie and of the mounting revolutionary sentiments among the working masses after the trials of the war and the disappointments of the peace, a decisive blow be dealt at the old order.

But the opinion of those who inclined to half-measures and prudence gained the upper hand. . . .

The fascists have become masters of the situation; they have established a dictatorship, and trodden underfoot democracy and legality, those false decorations which won the naïve admiration of the feeble leaders of Italian socialism. With fire and sword they are completing the destruction of the workers' organizations, against which, with the support of the State which they now completely control, they had already waged an unrelenting struggle.

But do not despair!

The fight is not yet lost; your victory is certain if you act resolutely and correctly.

In the most important industrial centres, Turin, Milan, Venice, and Trieste, the forces of the proletariat are still unbroken, and can get ready for defence comparatively quickly.

The Italian Communist Party, having broken in time with those irresolute elements which behind the mask of maximalism pursued tactics of weakening and of concessions which a year ago went as far as a treaty of peace with the fascist gangs—the Communist Party holds high the red flag, and will summon not only all socialists who are still capable of revolutionary action, not only all the working masses and the class-conscious peasants, but also all honest people who regard the approaching black cloud of reaction with horror, to rally to that banner.

You must remember that, while the revolutionary forces in Italy are not so weak as the panic-mongers say, the fascist forces are much weaker than their friends and admirers maintain. Not only will a substantial part of the radically-minded democracy turn away from them; in the camp of your direct class enemies itself there is no unity.

The fascists are, primarily, a weapon in the hands of the large landowners. The industrial and commercial bourgeoisie are following with anxiety the experiment of ferocious reaction, which they regard as black bolshevism.

On the other hand, apart from such politically indeterminate elements —which are, however, energetic when it comes to a direct fight—as the reactionary students, demobilized officers, and simple rogues, the fascists also have battalions composed of workers, rural proletarians, and part of the peasantry. These elements will soon realize how deceptive were the promises which attracted them into this counter-revolutionary adventure and turned them into an army of the landlords against their kindred.

Finally, fascism means an adventurist foreign policy. Fascism, which has no programme and no ideals, no firm and uniform class basis, will very soon create a movement of public indignation against itself. We must direct this movement into our own channels. . . .

The entire Communist International is with you, dear comrades; it is carefully watching the different stages of your difficult and responsible struggle, it is drawing the attention of the proletarians of all countries to the serious tactical errors of opportunism and semi-opportunism, and it will be happy to refer to the later history of your movement as an example of how such mistakes can be corrected. The Communist International is ready to support you in this struggle, to give you all the help in its power.

RESOLUTION OF THE FOURTH COMINTERN CONGRESS ON THE REPORT
OF THE ECCI

November 1922   *Thesen und Resolutionen*, iv, p. 5

[Zinoviev reported for the ECCI. What had become clear, he said, was that although the bourgeoisie were demonstrably incapable of ruling, the proletariat was not yet ready to take their place. The International had been described as an International of action, but it would require years and years to accomplish the action. In a later speech Radek said that 'the broad masses of the proletariat have lost belief in their ability to conquer power in any foreseeable time . . . the conquest of power as an immediate task of the day is not on the agenda.' Zinoviev dealt with the relations between the ECCI and the major parties. Contact with the German party was maintained better than with any other; the third congress had not been severe enough with the French party; it was to the left wing in that party that the Comintern owed its moral support; the ECCI still had serious differences with the Italian party, where abstentionist and anti-parliamentary tendencies had not yet been eliminated. If the Italian party had seized power in the autumn of 1920, it might have suffered Hungary's fate, but it had come out too late with the slogan of a workers' government.

The ECCI had held 30 meetings since the third congress, and the presidium had met 75 times. The problems of the French party had been on the agenda 42 times, of the Italian party 31 times, of the German party 27, and of the Russian party once. The Executive had considered in advance the theses and resolutions to be submitted to national party congresses. Since the third congress the presidium had sent 54 delegates to various countries. 'The numerous divisions and conflicts within some sections,' Bukharin said later, 'the struggles of fractions and groups, required the most authoritative intervention.'

In the commission the report of the ECCI had been passed against the votes of two delegations; in the full congress it was passed against 1 vote, with 16 abstentions. The abstentions included the Italian delegation, who disapproved both of the united front policy and the attitude to the Italian question.]

The fourth world congress of the CI fully approves the political work of the ECCI which has correctly carried out during the last 15 months the decisions of the third world congress and correctly applied them to individual political situations. In particular the congress fully approves the tactic of the united front as formulated by the ECCI in the theses of December 1921 and in the subsequent Executive documents on this question.

The fourth CI congress approves the attitude adopted by the ECCI in the French CP crisis, in the events in the Italian workers' movement, in the Norwegian and the Czechoslovakian communist parties. Purely practical questions of detail concerning these parties will be dealt with in special commissions whose decisions will be subsequently examined by the congress.

Bearing in mind the events which have occurred in some parties, the fourth congress again notes and confirms that in the periods between world congresses the ECCI is the supreme body of the entire communist movement and that its decisions are binding on all affiliated parties. It follows from this, in particular, that any violation of the decisions of the Executive on the pretext of an appeal to the next congress is an open breach of discipline. For the CI to allow such behaviour would be tantamount to the complete frustration of any systematic and unified activity by the CI.

As to the doubts expressed in the French CP about the interpretation of article 9 of the CI statutes, the fourth congress declares that this article gives the ECCI the unconditional right to expel individuals and groups who, in the opinion of the ECCI, are hostile to communism, from the CI and consequently from their own national sections also.

It is obvious that the ECCI is compelled to apply article 9 of the statutes if the national party in question does not display, through its leading bodies, the necessary energy and vigilance in protecting the party from non-communist elements.

The fourth congress of the CI again confirms the 21 conditions elaborated by the second congress, and instructs the next Executive to supervise their effective execution very strictly. More than ever before the ECCI must in future be an international proletarian organization which relentlessly fights any kind of opportunism, an organization built on the principles of the strictest democratic centralism.

OPEN LETTER TO THE COMMUNISTS AND WORKING PEOPLE OF TURKEY
ADOPTED AT THE FOURTH COMINTERN CONGRESS

20 *November* 1922   *Thesen und Resolutionen*, iv, p. 119

[For a brief period the Turkish Government had permitted the Turkish Communist Party to exist legally; it was outlawed in October 1922. Having defeated Greece, and gained the acquiescence of the Allied Governments to the abrogation of the Sèvres treaty, the Turkish Government was no longer in need of Russian diplomatic support, and was anxious not to arouse antagonism before the Lausanne conference by maintaining close ties with Russia. The Turkish delegate who moved the resolution gave a long account of Kemal Pasha's betrayal and persecution of the Turkish communists. In the debate on the theses on the eastern question Radek said: 'We do not for a moment regret telling the Turkish communists that their first task after the formation of the party was to support the national liberation movement. . . . Even now, with the persecutions, we say to our Turkish comrades, do not let the present moment blind you to the near future. Defend yourselves against your persecutors . . . but do not forget that historically the time has not yet come to take up the decisive battle; you have still far to go.' At the twelfth congress of the Russian Communist Party Bukharin said that, despite the persecution of the communists, Turkey was playing a revolutionary part because it was an instrument in the destruction of imperialism.]

The fourth congress of the Third International, which coincides with the fifth anniversary of the great proletarian revolution, sends its warmest greetings to the workers and peasants of Turkey on the success of their heroic struggle for independence against western imperialism. Turkish comrades! It is you who have given the entire enslaved East and all colonial countries the living example of a revolutionary independence movement.

But the latest events have shown that the nationalist bourgeois Government wishes to appropriate to itself the fruits of this victory won at the cost of your immense sacrifices. The nationalist Government in Ankara is ready to come to terms with the imperialists for the sake of certain concessions in favour of the Turkish grand bourgeoisie.

It is inaugurating this new policy by dissolving the party, suppressing all its organizations, making mass arrests, treating the arrested comrades barbarously, and finally by closing down the Turkish workers' union in Constantinople. The Communist Party of Turkey has always supported the bourgeois national Government in the struggle of the working masses against imperialism. The Communist Party of Turkey even proved its readiness, faced by the common enemy, to make temporary sacrifices in regard to its programme and ideals.

The attitude of the Government towards the Communist Party can be explained by the fact that they want to get rid of the class-conscious representatives of the working class and the peasantry, who will demand the fulfilment of the promises of democratic reforms made in order to win our support, and to appear at the Lausanne conference as a truly bourgeois Government. The bourgeois Government of Turkey dares to commit crimes against you and your representatives which are bound to arouse the greatest indignation among the entire world proletariat, at whose head stands the Russian proletariat who, at the most difficult moment, when all the imperialist and capitalist classes joined forces to strangle the working people of Turkey, shrank from no material sacrifice.

In preparation for an understanding with imperialism, the nationalist Government wants to annihilate your real representatives and separate them from your friends outside.

The fourth congress of the Communist International protests emphatically against this barbarous act and considers it its duty to declare solemnly that it is willing to support any government or political party which does not play the part of a gendarme of imperialism, which will continue the fight against imperialism and reaction, and will bring about democratic reforms in favour of the Turkish working masses.

Arrested comrades! The Communist International, as the general staff and defender of the entire world proletariat, greets in you with the greatest warmth the class-conscious and most devoted representatives of the Turkish working masses.

Do not forget, comrades, that the darkness of prison can never blot out the sun of revolution.

Do not forget, comrades, that on the eve of the victory of the revolution the powerlessness of the ruling class is expressed in their greater brutality. At the moment when capitalism is breaking down under the weight of its own internal contradictions, and the conflicts within imperialism reach their highest point, the international bourgeoisie double their persecutions of the protagonists and builders of the new communist society.

But no white terror can intimidate those who believe in inevitable and final victory. And in the place of every comrade thrown into prison or shot, hundreds of comrades come forward from the ranks of the exploited proletarian masses to carry on the struggle for liberation with greater strength.

Comrades! The Third International considers it its most important task to do everything it can to rescue you from your executioners.

THESES ON THE EASTERN QUESTION ADOPTED BY THE FOURTH COMINTERN CONGRESS

November 1922   *Thesen und Resolutionen*, iv, p. 42

[The theses were drafted by the delegations from the eastern countries in collaboration with members of the ECCI. They were introduced by Ravesteyn (Holland). The contradictions between Russian and British imperial interests, he said, submerged during the war when Russia, hoping for Constantinople, was on the British side, had again come to the surface. The Russian interest in favour of the freedom of the Straits was also in the interest of the international proletariat. 'The freedom of the Straits means nothing but that this world traffic centre shall not be dominated by British imperialism.' Since tribute from the East was a main source of capital accumulation 'the independence of the eastern world as a whole, the independence of Asia, the independence of the Moslem peoples . . . means in itself the end of western imperialism, and pre-eminently of British imperialism', which was the most powerful enemy of all eastern, and particularly of the Moslem peoples. 'The Moslem peoples have it in their power to destroy the bridges which keep the British empire together.' Speaking at an earlier session of the congress Malaka (Java) had asked whether and how far communists should support local boycott movements and pan-Islamic movements. Until they quarrelled in 1921 the Javanese communists, numbering 13,000, had worked with the Moslem association Sarekat Islam, which had millions of members, and had persuaded them to adopt communist slogans. The hostility to pan-Islam expressed by the second congress had damaged the position of the communists. Sarekat Islam was founded in 1912; the Indonesian Communist Party was founded in May 1920 and in December voted to affiliate to the Comintern. The delegate from Tunis criticized the British and French parties because of their inactivity in the colonial question; he was in favour of support for pan-Islam, because it was an association of all Moslems against their oppressors.

Roy (India) said that, since the second congress, the Comintern had realized that different action was required in different countries. There were colonies with a fairly strong indigenous bourgeoisie, others where capitalism was only in its initial stages, and others that were still quite primitive. Bourgeois-nationalist movements in the colonies were objectively revolutionary, but if they were directed only against the foreign bourgeoisie and not against native feudalism they represented not a class struggle, but capitalist competition. 'Revolutionary national movements in those countries where millions and millions are pining for national liberation, and which must free themselves economically and politically from imperialism before they can make further progress, will not succeed under the leadership of the bourgeoisie.' Leadership would have to be taken over by the communist parties when the bourgeoisie deserted and betrayed the national revolution, as they were bound to do.

The same argument had been put forward at the meeting of the ECCI in January 1921; the bourgeois nationalists were uncertain and unreliable allies; the Comintern should base its activities on the industrial workers in countries like India, and on the peasants in less developed countries like Persia and Afghanistan.

The Japanese delegate thought that a Japanese workers' insurrection was possible in the near future, and the Egyptian delegate that the red flag would soon be waving over the pyramids. Lin Yen-chin (China) said in the course of the discussion: 'On the assumption that the anti-imperialist united front is necessary to get rid of imperialism in China, our party has decided to form a national front with the national revolutionary party of the Kuomintang. Members of the Communist Party joined the Kuomintang as individuals. . . . If we do not enter this party we shall remain isolated, preaching a communism which is, it is true, a great and sublime ideal, but which the masses do not follow. . . . If we enter the Kuomintang we shall be able to show the masses that we too are for revolutionary democracy, but that for us revolutionary democracy is only a means, although we do not ignore the daily demands of the masses. . . . We can rally the masses round us and split the Kuomintang party.' Safarov, and the delegates from Turkey and Persia, reproached the communist parties with having done too little about the colonial question. Radek, replying to the discussion, suggested that some of the speakers had been too optimistic. The second congress theses which spoke of support for the movements in the East did not refer to class struggles. Marx, too, advocated support of the bourgeoisie so long as it was revolutionary. By carrying out their historical task of supporting the liberation movements, communists gained a firm foothold among the masses. In his report for the ECCI Zinoviev said that the 'nucleus' of parties had been formed in China, Egypt, and Turkey. They were quite small, but represented a positive advance. The theses were passed unanimously. During the course of the debate the Japanese and Chinese delegates introduced a resolution condemning the Japanese occupation of North Sakhalin.]

I. GENERAL THESES

The second Comintern congress drew up a general statement of principles on the national and colonial question in the epoch of the protracted struggle between imperialism and the proletarian dictatorship, taking as its basis Soviet experience in the East and the advance of national revolutionary movements in the colonies.

Since then the struggle against imperialist oppression in the colonial and semi-colonial countries has become far more acute as the result of an intensification in the political and economic post-war crisis of imperialism. Evidence of this is seen in:

1. the failure of the Sèvres treaty for the division of Turkey, and the possibility of the complete restoration of Turkey's national and political independence;

2. the tempestuous growth of the national revolutionary movement in India, Mesopotamia, Egypt, Morocco, China, and Korea;

3. the hopeless internal crisis of Japanese imperialism, which is provoking in that country a rapid growth in the elements of the bourgeois-democratic

revolution and the movement of the Japanese proletariat towards independent class struggle;

4. the awakening of the workers' movement in all countries of the East
and the formation in practically all of them of communist parties.

The facts enumerated are synonymous with a change in the social basis
of the colonial revolutionary movement; this change leads to an intensification of the anti-imperialist struggle, whose leadership is no longer solely in
the hands of the feudal elements and the national bourgeoisie who are prepared to compromise with imperialism.

The imperialist war of 1914–18 and the subsequent continuing crisis
of imperialism—above all European imperialism—have weakened the
economic hold of the great Powers over the colonies.

On the other hand the same factors which have narrowed the economic
basis and the political influence of European capitalism have sharpened
imperialist competition for colonies and thus disturbed the balance of the
imperialist world system as a whole (the struggle for oil, the Anglo-French
conflict in Asia Minor, Japanese-American rivalry in the Pacific, etc.).

Precisely this weakening of imperialist pressure on the colonies, together
with the steady intensification of the rivalry between the various imperialist
groups, has facilitated the development of indigenous capitalism in the
colonial and semi-colonial countries; it has outgrown the narrow and
restricting limits of the imperialist rule of the great Powers, and this process
is continuing. Until now great Power capital has striven to isolate the
backward countries from world trade, and thus make sure of its monopoly
rights to super-profits from the commercial, industrial, and fiscal exploitation of these countries. The demand for national and economic independence advanced by the national movement in the colonies expresses the
needs of bourgeois development in these countries. The progress of indigenous productive forces in the colonies thus comes into irreconcilable
conflict with the interests of world imperialism, for the essence of imperialism consists in exploiting the different stages of development of the
productive forces in the different areas of world economy to gain monopoly
super-profits.

II. THE CONDITIONS OF STRUGGLE

The backwardness of the colonies is expressed in that variety of national-
revolutionary movements against imperialism which reflects the different
stages of transition from feudal and feudal-patriarchal relations to capitalism. This variety gives a special stamp to the ideology of this movement.
To the extent that capitalism in the colonial countries arises on feudal
foundations, and develops in distorted and incomplete transitional forms,
which give commercial capital predominance, the differentiation of
bourgeois democracy from the feudal-bureaucratic and feudal-agrarian

elements frequently proceeds in a devious and protracted manner. This represents the chief obstacle to a successful mass struggle against imperialist oppression, for in all backward countries alien imperialism makes the feudal (and in part also semi-feudal, semi-bourgeois) upper class of native society into an instrument for the exercise of its rule (the military governors —Tuchuns—in China, the native aristocracy and the land-tax farmers— —zemindars and talukdars—in India, the feudal bureaucracy and aristocracy in Persia, the more or less capitalist plantation owners in Egypt, etc.).

That is why the ruling classes among the colonial and semi-colonial peoples are unable and unwilling to lead the struggle against imperialism in so far as that struggle assumes the form of a revolutionary mass movement. Only where feudal-patriarchal relations are not sufficiently disintegrated to separate the indigenous aristocracy completely from the masses—as, for example, among nomads and semi-nomads—can the representatives of these upper strata come forward as active leaders in the struggle against imperialist oppression (Mesopotamia, Mongolia).

In Moslem countries the national movement at first finds its ideology in the religio-political watchwords of pan-Islam, and this enables the officials and diplomats of the great Powers to exploit the prejudices and ignorance of the broad masses in the struggle against this movement (English imperialism's game with pan-Islamism and pan-Arabism, English plans to transfer the Khalifate to India, French imperialism's playing on its 'Moslem sympathies'). But to the extent that the national liberation movements grow and expand, the religio-political watchwords of pan-Islam are increasingly replaced by concrete political demands. The struggle recently waged in Turkey to deprive the Khalifate of temporal power confirms this.

The chief task which is common to all national revolutionary movements is to bring about national unity and achieve political independence. The real and logically consistent solution of this question depends on the extent to which such a national movement is able to break with the reactionary feudal elements and to win over the broad working masses to its cause, and in its programme to give expression to the social demands of these masses.

Taking full cognizance of the fact that those who represent the national will to State independence may, because of the variety of historical circumstances, be themselves of the most varied kind, the Communist International supports every national revolutionary movement against imperialism. At the same time it does not forget that only a consistent revolutionary policy, designed to draw the broadest masses into active struggle, and a complete break with all adherents of reconciliation with imperialism for the sake of their own class domination, can lead the oppressed masses to victory. The bond between the indigenous bourgeoisie and the feudal-reactionary elements enables the imperialists to exploit to the full feudal anarchy, the rivalry between different leaders and races, the antagonism between village and town, the struggle between castes and religious sects, in order to disorganize the national movement (see China, Persia, Kurdistan, Mesopotamia).

III. THE AGRARIAN QUESTION

In most eastern countries (India, Persia, Egypt, Syria, Mesopotamia) the agrarian question is of primary importance in the struggle for emancipation from the yoke of the great Powers' despotism. By exploiting and ruining the peasant majority of the backward nations, imperialism deprives them of their elementary means of existence, while industry, which is only poorly developed and confined to a few centres, is incapable of absorbing the resulting surplus agricultural population, who are also deprived of any opportunity to emigrate. The impoverished peasants remaining on the land become bondsmen. In the advanced countries before the war industrial crises played the part of regulator of social production; in the colonies this part is played by famine. Since imperialism has the strongest interest in getting the largest profits with the least capital outlay, in the backward countries it supports as long as possible the feudal-usurer forms of exploiting labour power. In a few cases, e.g. India, it takes over the native feudal State's monopoly of the land and turns the land tax into tribute to great Power capital and its servants—the zemindars and talukdars; in others it makes sure of its groundrents by acting through the native organizations of the large landowners, e.g. in Persia, Morocco, Egypt, etc. The struggle to free the land from feudal dues and restrictions thus assumes the character of a national liberation struggle against imperialism and the feudal large landowners. Examples of this were provided by the Moplah rising against the feudal landowners and the English in India in the autumn of 1921 and the Sikh rising in 1922.

Only the agrarian revolution, whose object is to expropriate the large estates, can set in motion the enormous peasant masses; it is destined to exercise a decisive influence on the struggle against imperialism. The bourgeois nationalists' fear (in India, Persia, Egypt) of the agrarian watchwords, and their anxiety to prune them down as far as possible, bear witness to the close connexion between the native bourgeoisie and the feudal and feudal-bourgeois landlords, and to the intellectual and political dependence of the former on the latter. These vacillations and hesitations must be used by all revolutionary elements for the systematic criticism and exposure of the timidity of the bourgeois leaders of the nationalist movements. It is precisely this timidity which places obstacles in the way of organizing and rallying the working masses, as the bankruptcy of the non-co-operation tactics in India shows.

The revolutionary movement in the backward countries of the East cannot be successful unless it relies on the action of the broad peasant masses. Therefore the revolutionary parties of all Oriental countries must formulate a clear agrarian programme, putting forward the demand for the complete abolition of the feudal system and survivals of it in the form of large landownership and tax farming. To draw the peasant masses into active participation in the struggle for national liberation they must conduct propaganda for a radical change in the legal basis of land ownership, and it is also necessary to compel the bourgeois-nationalist parties to adopt as much as possible of this revolutionary agrarian programme.

IV. THE LABOUR MOVEMENT IN THE EAST

The young labour movement in the East is a product of the recent development of native capitalism. Until now the working class in those countries, even their most advanced elements, have been in a transitional stage between craft and artisan labour and the large capitalist factory. As the bourgeois-nationalist intelligentsia draws the revolutionary working-class movement into the struggle against imperialism, its representatives at first also take the lead in the newly formed trade union organizations and their activities. At first the proletariat, in these activities, does not go beyond the framework of the 'general national' interests of bourgeois democracy (as in the strikes against the imperialist bureaucracy and administration in China and India). As the second Comintern congress pointed out, it often happens that the representatives of bourgeois nationalism, taking advantage of the political authority of Soviet Russia and adapting themselves to the class instincts of the workers, clothe their bourgeois-democratic aspirations in a 'socialist' or 'communist' garb, in order—although they themselves may not always be conscious of this—to divert the embryonic proletarian associations from the direct tasks of a class organization (for example, the communist colouring given by the Eshil-ordu party in Turkey to its pan-Turanianism, and the 'state socialism' preached by some leaders of the Kuomintang party in China).

Nevertheless both the trade union and the political movement of the working class in the backward countries has made great progress in the last few years. The formation of independent proletarian class parties in practically all countries of the East is a significant fact, although the overwhelming majority have still a great deal to do to rid themselves of dilettantism, sectarianism, and many other defects. The fact that the Communist International from the very beginning gave due value to the future possibilities of the labour movement in the East is unusually significant, for it eloquently expresses the genuine international unification of the proletarians of the entire world under the banner of communism. Up till now the Second and the Two-and-a-half Internationals have found no adherents in a single one of these backward countries, precisely because they are only acting as the 'employees' of European and American imperialism.

V. THE GENERAL TASKS OF COMMUNIST PARTIES IN THE EAST

While the bourgeois nationalists regard the workers' movement from the standpoint of its importance for their victory, the international proletariat appraises the young workers' movement of the East in the light of its revolutionary future. Under capitalist rule the backward countries cannot share in the achievements of modern technology and culture without paying, by savage exploitation and oppression, enormous tribute to great Power capital. The alliance with the proletariat of the advanced countries is dictated not only by the interests of the common struggle against imperialism but also by the fact that it is only from the victorious proletariat of the advanced countries that the workers of the East can get disinterested help for the development of their backward productive forces. Alliance with the proletariat of the West will clear the way for the international federation of Soviet republics. For backward countries the Soviet system represents the most painless transitional form from primitive conditions of existence to the advanced communist culture which is destined to replace capitalist methods of production and distribution throughout the world economy. This is proved by the experience of the Soviet structure in the liberated colonies of the Russian empire. Only the Soviet form of government is able to ensure the consistent execution of the peasant agrarian revolution. The specific conditions of agriculture in certain parts of the Orient (artificial irrigation) formerly maintained by the special organization of a collective labour community on a feudal-patriarchal basis, and later undermined by the system of capitalist piracy, also demand a State organization which is able to meet social needs in a planned and organized manner. In view of the special climatic and historical conditions, co-operatives of small producers will have an important part to play in the transition period throughout the East generally.

The objective tasks of the colonial revolution go beyond the limits of bourgeois democracy if only because a decisive victory for this revolution is incompatible with the rule of world imperialism. At first, the indigenous bourgeoisie and intelligentsia are the champions of the colonial revolutionary movements, but as the proletarian and semi-proletarian peasant masses are drawn in, the bourgeois and bourgeois-agrarian elements begin to turn away from the movement in proportion as the social interests of the lower classes of the people come to the forefront. There is a long struggle ahead of the young proletariat of the colonies, a struggle covering an entire historical epoch, against imperialist exploitation and their own ruling classes, who are trying to monopolize and keep to themselves all the advantages of industrial and cultural development, while keeping the broad working masses firmly in their former 'prehistoric' condition.

This struggle for influence over the peasant masses must serve the indigenous proletariat as training for the part of political leadership. Only when they have mastered this job and won influence over the social strata nearest to them will they be in a position to come out against bourgeois democracy which, in the conditions prevailing in the backward East, is far more hypocritical in character than it is in the West.

The refusal of the communists in the colonies to take part in the struggle against imperialist tyranny, on the ground of the ostensible 'defence' of their independent class interests, is opportunism of the worst kind, which can only discredit the proletarian revolution in the East. Equally injurious is the attempt to remain aloof from the struggle for the most urgent and everyday interests of the working class in the name of 'national unity' or of 'civil peace' with the bourgeois democrats. The communist workers' parties of the colonial and semi-colonial countries have a dual task: they fight for the most radical possible solution of the tasks of a bourgeois-democratic revolution, which aims at the conquest of political independence; and they organize the working and peasant masses for the struggle for their special class interests, and in doing so exploit all the contradictions in the nationalist bourgeois-democratic camp. By putting forward social demands they release the revolutionary energy for which the bourgeois-liberal demands provide no outlet, and stimulate it further. The working class of the colonies and semi-colonies must learn that only the extension and intensification of the struggle against the imperialist yoke of the great Powers will ensure for them the rôle of revolutionary leadership, while on the other hand only the economic and political organization and the political education of the working class and the semi-proletarian strata of the population can enlarge the revolutionary surge of the struggle against imperialism.

The communist parties of the colonial and semi-colonial countries of the East, which are still in a more or less embryonic stage, must take part in every movement which gives them access to the masses. They must none the less wage an energetic struggle against patriarchal and craft prejudices and against the bourgeois ideology which prevails in the workers' unions, in order to safeguard these undeveloped forms of trade union organization from reformist tendencies and transform them into militant mass bodies. They must make every effort to organize the numerous agricultural labourers and apprentices of both sexes on the basis of the defence of their day-to-day interests.

VI. THE UNITED ANTI-IMPERIALIST FRONT

In the conditions prevailing in the West, where the transitional period is characterized by an organized gathering of forces, the slogan put forward is that of the proletarian united front, but in the colonial East the slogan that must be emphasized at the present time is that of the anti-imperialist united front. The *expediency* of this slogan follows from the prospect of a prolonged and protracted struggle with world imperialism which demands the mobilization of all revolutionary elements. This mobilization is the more necessary as the indigenous ruling classes are inclined to effect compromises with foreign capital directed against the vital interests of the masses of the people. And just as in the West the slogan of the proletarian united front has helped and is still helping to expose social-democratic betrayal of proletarian interests, so the slogan of the anti-imperialist united front will help to expose the vacillation of various bourgeois-nationalist groups. This slogan will also promote the development of the revolutionary will and the clarification of the class consciousness of the working masses and put them in the front ranks of those who are fighting not only against imperialism, but also against the survivals of feudalism.

The workers' movement in the colonial and semi-colonial countries must first of all win for itself the position of an independent revolutionary factor in the anti-imperialist front as a whole. Only when its importance as an independent factor is recognized and its political independence secured, are temporary agreements with bourgeois democracy permissible and necessary. The proletariat supports, and itself puts forward, partial demands, for example, the demand for an independent democratic republic, for abolishing the unequal legal status of women, etc., in so far as the existing relation of forces does not allow it to make the realization of its Soviet programme the immediate task. At the same time it seeks to put forward slogans which promote the creation of political ties between the peasant and semi-proletarian masses and the industrial workers' movement. It is one of the most important functions of the anti-imperialist united front tactic to make clear to the broad working masses the necessity of an alliance with the international proletariat and the Soviet republics. The colonial revolution can triumph and maintain its conquests only side by side with the proletarian revolution in the highly developed countries.

The danger of an agreement between bourgeois nationalism and one or several rival imperialist Powers is far greater in the semi-colonial countries like China or Persia, or in the countries which are fighting for their independence by exploiting inter-imperialist rivalries, like Turkey, than it is in the colonies. Every such agreement means a wholly unequal division of power between the indigenous ruling classes and imperialism, and, under the cloak of formal independence, leaves the country in its former position as a semi-colonial buffer State in the service of world imperialism. The working class acknowledges that it is permissible and necessary to make partial and temporary compromises in order to win a breathing space in the revolutionary struggle for liberation against imperialism, but it must be absolutely and irreconcilably opposed to any attempt at an open or tacit division of power between imperialism and the indigenous ruling classes designed to maintain the class privileges of the latter. The demand for a close alliance with the proletarian Soviet republic is the device of the anti-imperialist united front. In addition to putting forward this slogan, the most resolute struggle must be waged for the broadest possible demo-cratization of the political system, in order to deprive the most politically and socially reactionary elements of their support in the country and to secure for the workers organizational freedom in the struggle for their class interests (the demands for a democratic republic, agrarian reform, fiscal reform, the reorganization of administration on the basis of com-prehensive local self-government, labour legislation, protection of juveniles, maternal and child welfare, etc.). Even in independent Turkey the work-ing class does not enjoy freedom of association, which is an index to the attitude of the bourgeois nationalists towards the proletariat.

VII. THE TASKS OF THE PROLETARIAT IN THE COUNTRIES OF THE PACIFIC

The need to organize the anti-imperialist united front is dictated, further, by the continuing and uninterrupted intensification of imperialist rivalry. This has now reached such an acute stage that a new world war, which will be fought out in the Pacific, is unavoidable, unless it is fore-stalled by the international revolution.

The Washington conference was an attempt to eliminate the threaten-ing danger, but in fact it only deepened and sharpened imperialist contra-dictions. The recent struggle between Wu Pei-fu and Chang Tso-lin in China was a direct consequence of the failure of the attempt of Japanese and Anglo-American capital to harmonize their discordant interests. The new war which threatens the world will involve not only Japan, America, and England, but also other capitalist States (France, Holland, etc.). It threatens greater destruction even than the 1914–18 war.

The task of the communist parties in the colonial and semi-colonial countries of the Pacific is to conduct vigorous propaganda to make the danger clear to the masses, to call on them to struggle actively for national liberation, and to orient themselves towards Soviet Russia as the bastion of all the oppressed and exploited masses.

The communist parties of the imperialist countries, America, Japan, England, Australia, and Canada should not restrict themselves, in face of the threatening danger, to propaganda against war, but must make every effort to eliminate the factors which disorganize the workers' movement in these countries and make it easier for the capitalists to exploit the antagonisms between nations and races. These factors are: the immigration question and the question of cheap coloured labour power.

Even today the contract system of indentured labour is the chief means of recruiting coloured workers on the sugar plantations of the south Pacific area, to which workers are brought from China and India. This induces the workers in the imperialist countries to demand legislation prohibiting immigration and hostile to the coloured workers, both in America and Australia. Such legislation deepens the antagonism between the coloured and white workers, and splits and weakens the workers' movement.

The communist parties of America, Canada, and Australia must conduct an energetic campaign against laws prohibiting immigration and must explain to the proletarian masses of these countries that such laws, by stirring up race hatred, will in the end bring injury to themselves.

The capitalists on the other hand are prepared to dispense with laws against immigration, in order to facilitate the free entry of cheap coloured labour power and thus lower the wages of white workers. Their intentions can only be successfully frustrated by one thing—the immigrant workers must be enrolled in the existing trade unions of white workers. At the same time the demand must be made that the wages of coloured workers must be raised to the level of the wages of white workers. Such a step by the communist parties will expose the intentions of the capitalists and at the same time clearly show the coloured workers that the international proletariat knows no race prejudice.

To carry out these steps the representatives of the revolutionary proletariat in the countries of the Pacific must convene a conference to work out the correct tactics and to devise the appropriate organizational forms for the real unification of the proletariat of all races in the Pacific.

VIII. THE COLONIAL TASKS OF THE METROPOLITAN PARTIES

The extreme importance of the colonial revolutionary movements for the international proletarian revolution makes it necessary to intensify work in the colonies, in the first place by the communist parties of the imperialist Powers.

French imperialism bases all its calculations on the suppression of the proletarian revolutionary struggle in France and Europe by using its colonial workers as a reserve army of counter-revolution. English and American imperialism still continue to split the workers' movement by getting the labour aristocracy on to their side by promising them a certain share of the super-profits drawn from colonial exploitation.

Every communist party of the countries possessing colonies must take over the task of organizing systematic moral and material assistance for the proletarian and revolutionary movement in the colonies. The quasi-socialist tendencies towards colonialism of some categories of well-paid European workers in the colonies must be firmly and stubbornly combated. European communist workers in the colonies must try to organize the indigenous proletariat and win their confidence by concrete economic demands (raising the wages of native workers to that of European workers, labour protection, social insurance, etc.). The creation of separate European communist organizations in the colonies (Egypt, Algiers), is a concealed form of colonialism and only helps imperialist interests. The creation of communist organizations on this national basis is incompatible with the principles of proletarian internationalism. All parties of the Communist International are obliged to explain to the broad working masses the great importance of the struggle against imperialist rule in the backward countries. The communist parties which work in the great Power countries must set up standing colonial commissions consisting of members of their central committee to pursue the said objects. The Communist International can be of assistance primarily by helping to found a local press and by the publication of periodicals and newspapers in the local languages. Particular attention must be paid to work among the European workers' organizations and the occupation troops in the colonies. The communist parties of the great Power countries must not let slip any opportunity of exposing the predatory colonial policy of their imperialist governments and of the bourgeois and reformist parties.

TELEGRAM FROM THE FOURTH COMINTERN CONGRESS TO THE ALL-INDIA TRADE UNION CONGRESS AT LAHORE

28 *November* 1922   *Protokoll*, iv, p. 782

[The Indian Communist Party was not founded officially until 1925, but the influence of individual communists in the young Indian trade union movement was considerable. The All-India Trade Union Congress was established in 1920, but did not affiliate to the RILU. In his report on the work of the ECCI to the fourth congress, Zinoviev stated that successful work had been done in India, and the communist forces there would soon be brought together into an organization.]

Comrades! the proletariat of the West sends you its sincere congratulations on the struggle which you have waged in the last few years for improving the economic position of the Indian working class. The fourth congress of the Communist International sends you its most cordial greetings. Comrades, while assuring you of our sympathy and promising you our fullest support for the victory of your cause, we must remind you that your task is very great, and that it should not be underestimated. The Indian working class is not fighting only for a wage in accordance with the work done. The economic emancipation of the Indian workers and peasants depends on national political freedom. No improvement in the conditions of life is possible within the framework of imperialist exploitation. For this reason you will be playing an important part in the struggle for national independence. Prepare yourselves for this historic part. The advanced proletariat of the 52 countries represented at this congress are with you. Beware of the false friendship and the misleading advice of the workers' leaders who abet imperialism.

With fraternal greetings,
The fourth world congress of the Comintern

EXTRACTS FROM THE AGRARIAN ACTION PROGRAMME ADOPTED BY THE FOURTH COMINTERN CONGRESS: DIRECTIVES ON THE APPLICATION OF THE AGRARIAN THESES PASSED BY THE SECOND CONGRESS

30 *November* 1922   *Protokoll*, iv, p. 831

[The second congress theses, Varga said, had been drafted with the idea of an immediate seizure of power in mind. That having been postponed, the job now was to win wider adherence in the countryside. Although bourgeois agrarian reforms might damp down revolutionary sentiments, communists had to support them, because a negative attitude would be incomprehensible to the peasantry. Such support must be accompanied by warnings that no bourgeois reform could give the land-hungry or landless peasantry what they really wanted. The ideal would be for the peasants to receive their land from the proletarian dictatorship, but meanwhile the communist parties had to compete for the peasants' allegiance with the peasant parties, and they must always go one better than them.

In reporting back from the commission to which the theses were referred, Varga said they had been guided in their work by a letter from Lenin in which he urged them to avoid giving the slightest impression that there was any real or apparent discrepancy between the agrarian action programme and the second congress theses which would give their enemies the opportunity of saying that they changed their minds every two years. The commission had compared the programme with the theses and had made the necessary changes whenever it seemed that misunderstanding might arise.

A Rumanian delegate said that he had asked Varga whether he thought that large-scale industrialized agriculture was more productive than small-scale peasant farming, and Varga had replied that he did not know. This suggested that the International had not devoted sufficient study to the agrarian question. It was in replying to this discussion that Varga, who complained that the speakers had kept to generalities instead of analysing their experience, referred to the speech of a British delegate about England's dependence on imports and its bearing on the revolution. A German professor, Varga said, had proved that

England could manage without imports if it cultivated its uncultivated lands and caught more fish. Radek interjected that Britain could not survive without imports, and Varga replied: 'Of course, hunger would be very severe, but the people of England would not die of hunger if the dictatorship were left to its own resources for a while.' The theses were adopted unanimously.]

The bases of our attitude to the rural working masses were laid down in the agrarian theses passed by the second congress. At the present stage of the capitalist offensive the agrarian question becomes more important. The fourth congress exhorts all parties to work hard to win the working masses of the countryside, and issues the following directives for this work.

1. The great mass of the rural proletariat and poor peasants, who do not have enough land of their own and must work partly for wages, or who are exploited in other ways by large landowners or capital, can only be finally liberated from their present bondage and from the wars[1] inevitable under capitalism by a proletarian revolution, a revolution which confiscates the land of the large landowners together with all the means of production, without compensation, and places them at the disposal of the labouring people; which, in place of the State of large landowners and capitalists, establishes the social State of proletarians and working peasants, and thus builds the road to communism.

2. In the fight against the landlords' and capitalists' State, the poor working peasants and small tenants are the natural allies of the agricultural and industrial proletariat. The adherence of their revolutionary movement to the struggle of the proletariat in town and country helps substantially to overthrow the bourgeois State; while the urban proletariat seizes political power and dispossesses the bourgeoisie of the means of production, the rural proletariat and the poor peasants seize the land, drive out the large landowners, and put an end to the rule of the agrarians and bourgeoisie in the country.

3. In order to win not only the agricultural labourers, but also the poor peasants (those with dwarf or small holdings, small tenants, and part of the poorer peasants) for the cause of the revolution, and to ensure the benevolent neutrality of the middle peasants, these sections must be rescued from the influence and leadership of the large peasants who are bound to the large landowners. They must be brought to realize that, since their interests coincide not with those of the large peasants, but with those of the proletariat, only the revolutionary party of the proletariat, the communist party, can be their leader in the fight. In order to accelerate this separation of the poor peasants from the leadership of the landowners and large peasants, it is not enough to put forward a programme or carry on propaganda; the communist party must prove by *constant action* in the interests of these strata that it really is the party of all working and oppressed people.

[1] Other texts give 'want' instead of 'wars'.

4. Therefore the communist party places itself at the head of every struggle waged by the rural working masses against the ruling classes. Using their day-to-day demands as a rallying point, the communist party unites the scattered forces of the land workers, stimulates their will to fight, and supports the fight by bringing to bear the forces of the industrial proletariat, always putting forward new objectives which lead in the direction of the revolution. The struggle waged in common with the industrial workers, the fact that, under the leadership of the communist party, the industrial workers fight for the interests of the rural workers and poor peasants, will convince them that: (1) it is only the communist party which really takes their cause seriously while all other parties, agrarian as well as social-democratic, only want to dupe them with demagogic phrases and are really at the service of the large landlords and capitalists; (2) no permanent improvement in their position is possible within capitalism.

5. Our concrete fighting demands must be adapted to the various forms of dependence and oppression to which the agricultural workers, the poor and middle peasants, are subjected by the landlords and capitalists, as well as to the interests of the different strata.

In the colonial countries with an oppressed native peasant population the national liberation movement is composed either of the entire population, as for example in Turkey, in which case the struggle of the oppressed peasantry against the landlords inevitably begins after the victory of the liberation struggle; or the feudal landlords are allied with the imperialist robbers, and in these countries, for example India, the social struggle of the oppressed peasants takes place at the same time as the struggle for national liberation.

In those areas where strong survivals of feudalism remain on the land, where the bourgeois revolution has not been completed, where land ownership is still bound up with feudal privileges, these privileges must be cleared away in the course of the struggle for the land, which is in this case of decisive importance.

6. In all countries where there is a real agricultural proletariat, this stratum is destined to be the most important factor in the revolutionary movement on the land. . . . To accelerate the process by which the rural proletariat becomes revolutionary, and to train them for the struggle for the dictatorship of the proletariat, which alone can finally liberate them from exploitation, the CP supports the agricultural proletariat in their fight for higher real wages, for improvement in working, housing, and cultural conditions, complete freedom of association, of meetings, of trade unions, of strikes, of the press, etc.; for at least the same rights as the industrial workers possess. . . .

7. Until the peasants are finally freed from their bondage by the social revolution, the communist party fights against all forms of exploitation of

the poor and middle peasantry by capital, against exploitation by loan and usury capital, which forces the poor peasants into debt bondage; against exploitation by commercial and speculative capital, which buys up the small production surplus of the poor peasants cheaply and sells it to the urban proletariat at high prices. The CP advocates the elimination of this parasitic speculative capital, and the establishment of direct connexions between co-operatives of small peasants and the consumers' co-operatives of the urban proletariat. It opposes exploitation by industrial capital, which uses its monopoly position to keep the prices of industrial goods artificially high. We therefore fight for cheap supplies of the means of production (artificial manures, machinery, etc.) to poor peasants. The factory councils should collaborate in this through price control. We fight against exploitation by the private transport monopoly, such as occurs above all in the Anglo-Saxon countries, against exploitation by the capitalist State which through its fiscal system imposes one-sided taxes on the poor peasants for the benefit of the large landlords. We demand complete exemption from taxation for poor peasants.

8. But the most severe exploitation of the land-hungry population in all non-colonial countries arises from the large landlords' private property in land. If they are to use all their labour power, and in general be able to live at all, the land-hungry peasants are forced to work for the large landlords at starvation wages, or to rent or buy land at a high price; thus part of the wages of the working peasantry is filched by the large landlords. Insufficient land forces the poor peasants into modern forms of medieval serfdom. The CP therefore fights for the confiscation of the land with all its installations and equipment, and for placing the land at the disposal of those who really work it. Until this has been accomplished by the proletarian revolution, the CP supports the fight of the land-hungry peasants for: a. an improvement in the living conditions of share-croppers by reducing the landowner's share; b. a reduction in the rent of leased small holdings, full compensation at the end of his tenancy for improvements made by the tenant, etc. . . . c. allocation of land, cattle, and means of production to all land-hungry peasants on terms which ensure progress; not scraps of land which keep their owners tied to the soil, while forcing them to seek work at starvation wages from neighbouring landowners or large peasants, but enough land for complete subsistence. In this connexion special attention should be paid to the interests of agricultural labourers.

9. By bourgeois agrarian reforms, by distributing land to the leading elements of the peasantry, the ruling classes are trying to damp down the revolutionary character of the land movement. They are succeeding in bringing about a temporary ebb in the revolutionary movement. But every bourgeois agrarian reform comes up against the barriers of capitalism; land can only be handed over with compensation, and only to those people

who already own the means of production to work it. Bourgeois agrarian reform has absolutely nothing to offer the purely proletarian and semi-proletarian elements. The onerous terms inevitably imposed on those who receive land under a bourgeois land distribution and which therefore lead to no improvement in their situation, but only to debt bondage, provide the basis for carrying the revolutionary movement further and for sharpening the contradictions between the rich and poor peasants, as well as the agricultural labourers who receive no land and lose the chance of work when the large estates are divided up.

10. The complete emancipation of all workers on the land can only be brought about by a proletarian revolution. . . . The workers on the land will themselves decide the way in which the land confiscated from the landlords is to be worked. . . .

In organizational matters all communists who work in agriculture and in the industrial concerns connected with agriculture, must join the land workers' organizations, and rally and lead the revolutionary elements with the object of changing these organizations into revolutionary instruments. Where there are no unions, the communists must see that they are organized. In the yellow, fascist, and Christian counter-revolutionary organizations they must carry on persistent educational work with the object of disintegrating these counter-revolutionary unions. On the large agricultural undertakings they must establish estate councils to . . . prevent the introduction of extensive agriculture. They must summon the industrial proletariat to support the struggles of the land workers and conversely draw the latter into the industrial factory council movement.

Because of the tremendous importance of the poor peasants for the revolutionary movement, it is absolutely essential for communists to join their organizations (producers, consumers, and credit co-operatives), to revolutionize them, to eliminate the apparent opposition of interests between wage workers and land-hungry peasants, which is artificially magnified by the landlords and large peasants and placed in the forefront, and to bring the movements and actions of these organizations into close association with those of the rural and urban proletariat.

THESES OF THE FOURTH COMINTERN CONGRESS ON THE NEGRO QUESTION

30 *November* 1922   *Thesen und Resolutionen*, iv, p. 53

[In the debate on the theses on the national and colonial question at the second congress John Reed (United States) spoke on the position of the Negroes and emphasized the importance of getting them into joint organizations with white workers. At the final session of the third congress on 12 July 1921 the South

African delegation proposed that the Executive should consider the Negro question, and the suggestion was adopted.

The theses were introduced by Billings (United States). The problem, he said, was primarily economic, and was aggravated by friction between black and white workers. 'The racial question, although it derives from the class prejudices of certain social groups, still plays an important part.' American Negroes were a source of cheap labour power, and would provide forces for the counter-revolution in the event of insurrection, and that was why organizations like the Rockefeller Foundation gave large sums to Negro schools and associations whose members could then be used as strike-breakers. One reason why they could be used for this purpose was that white unions would not admit them. McKay (United States) said he had encountered race prejudice among many white comrades, who did not really want to grapple with the Negro problem. The theses were passed unanimously.]

During and after the war a movement of revolt against the power of world capital developed among the colonial and semi-colonial peoples which is still making headway. The penetration and intensive colonization of the areas inhabited by the black races is the last great problem on the solution of which the further development of capitalism itself depends. French capitalism has clearly recognized that the power of French post-war imperialism can be maintained only by the creation of a French African empire connected with the motherland by a railway across the Sahara. America's finance magnates (who already exploit 12 million Negroes in the United States) have now begun on the peaceful penetration of Africa. England's fear of the threat to its position in Africa is shown clearly in the extreme methods used to suppress the Rand strike. Just as the danger of a new world war has become acute in the Pacific, as a result of the competition between the imperialist Powers there, so there are menacing signs that Africa is becoming the object of their rival aspirations. Moreover, the war, the Russian revolution, and the powerful movements of revolt among the Asiatic and Moslem peoples against imperialism, have awakened the race consciousness of millions of Negroes, who have for centuries been oppressed and humiliated by capitalism not only in Africa, but also, and perhaps to a greater degree, in America.

The history of the Negroes in America qualifies them to play an important part in the liberation struggle of the entire African race. Three hundred years ago the American Negro was dragged from his homeland, brought in indescribably horrible conditions on board ship, and sold into slavery. For 250 years he worked as a slave under the lash of American overseers. His labour cleared the forests, built the roads, planted the cotton, laid the railways, and kept the aristocracy of the south. His wages were poverty, ignorance, humiliation, and wretchedness. The Negro was not a docile slave; his history is rich in revolts, disturbances, and subterranean methods of gaining freedom. But all his struggles were savagely suppressed. He was forced into subjection by torture, and the bourgeois press and religion justified his enslavement. Slavery then became an obstacle to American development on a capitalist basis; personal slavery came into conflict with wage slavery, and personal slavery was bound to go under. The civil war, which was not a war to free the Negroes, but a war to maintain the industrial predominance of capital in the northern states, confronted the Negro with the choice between slavery in the south and wage slavery in the north. The longings, the blood, and the tears of the 'emancipated' negroes were a part of the fabric of American capitalism. As America, which had meanwhile risen to the position of a world Power, was inevitably dragged into the maelstrom of the world war, the Negro was declared to be equal in rank to the whites. He had to kill and be killed for 'democracy'. Four hundred thousand coloured workers were enrolled in the army and organized in Negro regiments. Immediately after the terrible sacrifices of the world war the returning Negro was met with racial persecution, lynching, murder, deprivation of franchise, inequalities between him and the whites. He defended himself and had to pay dearly for it. Negro persecution became more intense and widespread than before the war, until he learned to forget his 'presumption'. The postwar industrialization of the Negro in the north, and the spirit of rebellion provoked by persecution and brutality after the war (which, although suppressed, still flared up in protest against such atrocities as the events in Tulsa), give the American Negro, particularly in the north, a place in the vanguard of the fight against oppression in Africa.

The Communist International notes with satisfaction the resistance of the exploited Negro to the exploiters' attack, for the enemy of his race and the enemy of the white workers are one and the same—capitalism and imperialism. The world struggle of the Negro race is a struggle against capitalism and imperialism. The Negro movement throughout the world must be organized on this basis; in America, the centre of Negro culture around which the Negro protest crystallizes; in Africa, the reservoir of human labour power for the further development of capitalism; in Central America (Costa Rica, Guatemala, Colombia, Nicaragua, and the other 'independent' Republics) where American imperialism rules; in Porto Rico, Haiti, San Domingo, and the other islands of the Caribbean, where the brutal treatment of our black fellow beings by the American occupation troops has aroused a protest from the conscious Negro and the revolutionary white workers throughout the world; in South Africa and the Congo, where increasing industrialization of the Negro population has led to various outbreaks; in East Africa, where the penetration of world capital is driving the native population to active resistance against imperialism.

It is the task of the Communist International to bring home to the

Negroes that they are not the only people suffering from the oppression of imperialism and capitalism, that the workers and peasants of Europe, Asia, and America are also victims of the imperialist exploiter, that in India and China, in Persia and Turkey, in Egypt and Morocco the oppressed coloured workers are defending themselves heroically against the imperialist exploiters, that these peoples are revolting against the same intolerable conditions which drive the Negroes themselves to desperation —racial oppression, social and economic inequality, intense industrial exploitation; that these peoples are fighting for the same objects as the Negroes—political, economic, and social emancipation and equality.

The Communist International, which embodies the world-embracing struggle of the revolutionary workers and peasants against the power of imperialism, which is not only the organization of the enslaved white workers of Europe and America, but also the organization of the oppressed coloured peoples of the world, regards it as its duty to support and promote the international·organization of Negroes in their struggle against the common enemy.

The Negro problem has become a vital question of the world revolution; the Communist International, which has already realized what valuable help the Asiatic coloured peoples in the semi-colonial countries can give to the proletarian world revolution, considers the collaboration of our oppressed black fellow beings absolutely essential for the proletarian revolution and the destruction of capitalist power. For these reasons the fourth congress declares it the special duty of communists to apply the '*Theses on the colonial question*' to the Negro problem also.

1. The fourth congress recognizes the necessity of supporting every form of the Negro movement which undermines or weakens capitalism, or hampers its further penetration.
2. The Communist International will fight for the equality of the white and black races, for equal wages and equal political and social rights.
3. The Communist International will use every means at its disposal to force the trade unions to admit black workers, or, where this right already exists on paper, to conduct special propaganda for the entry of Negroes into the unions. If this should prove impossible, the Communist International will organize the Negroes in trade unions of their own and use united front tactics to compel their admission.
4. The Communist International will take steps immediately to convene a world Negro congress or conference.

EXTRACTS FROM THE RESOLUTION OF THE FOURTH COMINTERN CON-
GRESS ON THE FRENCH QUESTION

2 *December* 1922   *Thesen und Resolutionen*, iv, p. 75

[Twenty-four delegates of the CPF attended the fourth Comintern congress. The
French commission included Trotsky, Zinoviev, and Bukharin (Lenin, appointed
a member of the commission, was unable to attend). The commission proposed
that the central committee be composed according to the voting at the Paris
congress, to which the French delegation agreed. Reporting for the French commission, Trotsky said that the crisis in the CPF was marked by loss of membership, declining circulation of the party press, and the existence of fractions in
bitter conflict with each other. There was in fact no party apart from these
fractions. 'In a country where only a dwindling minority of the working class
is organized, where the trade unions are split, the working class can only regain
self-confidence if its struggles are taken up under the slogan of the united front.'
The French party had not yet carried out the decisions of the third congress; its
right-wing leaders said they were 'torn between loyalty to the Comintern' and
the interests of the French party, as though there could be any conflict between
the two. There had been a prolonged correspondence between the ECCI
and the CPF; Frossard and Cachin had been invited to Moscow more than once,
but had not come. The agreement on a centre-left bloc reached by a large
majority at the June session of the ECCI had been broken, at the Paris congress,
by the centre fraction, on the ground that it violated party sovereignty. The left
had also made mistakes, but of a less serious kind; it was the only tendency within
the CPF which had the right attitude towards Comintern decisions.

The resolution of the French commission of the fourth congress, passed against
two votes, with one abstention, settled ('as an exception') the composition of the
French central committee and politburo as between left, right, and centre,
taking the voting at the Paris congress as a guide. The lists were approved by the
congress 'as the only way out of the crisis', and were to be submitted in January
to a specially convened national council of the French party with the powers of
a congress. The leading representatives of the left and centre wings were to
remain in Moscow as delegates to the ECCI for at least three months, until the
crisis in the French party was surmounted. Some of the French delegates
(including Cachin, speaking for the centre) expressed their misgivings, but all
agreed to observe discipline and to prevent fractional struggles. The commission's proposals were approved, against the vote of the Brazilian delegate.

The central committee of the French party, meeting in December 1922,
before all the delegates had returned from Moscow, passed a resolution, with
three abstentions, affirming their loyalty to the International and their intention to observe discipline.

There was no debate on Trotsky's report, since all the points at issue had been
thoroughly discussed in the commission. The leaders of the various groups, including Cachin for the centre and Souvarine for the left, endorsed the resolution.
Renaud Jean, leader of a small group, thought the selection of the central committee by the fourth congress set a dangerous precedent and might create new

difficulties. Trotsky replied that the list had not been forced on the French party, but had been proposed by the French delegates themselves; it was to be submitted to, not imposed on, the French party. The Brazilian delegate voted against the resolution because he had had no chance to speak to it. The organizational proposals were passed against two votes (one French, one Brazilian) and one abstention. In the course of the congress Bordiga attacked those who 'regarded the International as though it stood as something apart from the parties . . . the International is often forced to have its fractions in the parties, whereas the parties should be at its service.'

Graziadei, an Italian delegate, had in 1920 wished to include 'no freemasonry' among the conditions of admission, but this had been rejected as 'too obvious'. Writing at the time of the fourth congress, Trotsky described freemasonry as basically a petty-bourgeois imitation of Catholicism, feudal in its roots, with bankers, lawyers, deputies, and journalists in place of cardinals and abbots. Externally non-political, as was the Church, its function was to attract working-class leaders, to soften their minds and weaken their wills. Freemasonry, said Trotsky, was a bridge leading to the bourgeois camp, and it had to be blown up; it embodied the spirit of careerism, pelf, and place. Some of the leaders of the French Communist Party (notably Frossard) were automatically excluded by the resolution on freemasonry. A programme of action for the CPF approved by the fourth congress on 5 December included among its objectives the united front, trade union unity, adherence of the CGTU to the RILU, the struggle against the Versailles treaty, communist penetration of the army, and support for the demand of the French colonies for independence.]

The fourth congress of the Communist International notes that the evolution of the French party from parliamentary socialism to revolutionary communism is proceeding with extraordinary slowness. This cannot be explained only by objective conditions, traditions, the workers' national psychology, etc. etc., but primarily by the outright and at times extremely stubborn resistance of the non-communist elements which are still very strong at the top of the party, and particularly in the centre fraction, into whose hands the party leadership largely passed after the Tours congress.

The chief reason for the present acute crisis in the party is the indecisive, wavering, waiting policy of the leading centrist elements who, confronted with urgent demands concerning party organization, are trying to gain time, thus putting up a cover for their policy of outright sabotage on the question of the trade unions, the united front, party organization, etc. The time thus gained has been time lost to the revolutionary development of the French proletariat.

The congress instructs the ECCI to follow with the closest attention the internal life of the French Communist Party so that, relying on its unquestionable revolutionary-proletarian majority, it can free the party from the influence of those elements responsible for the crisis and who continually make it more acute.

The congress dismisses the very thought of a split, which is not in the least called for by the state of affairs in the party. The overwhelming majority of its members are sincerely and deeply devoted to the cause of communism. It is only the still inadequate clarity of consciousness in the party which has allowed its conservative centrist and semi-centrist elements to sow such deep confusion and to breed fractional groups. . . . The party must be cleansed of those elements who, while in the party, are bound by their entire way of thought and life to the customs and habits of bourgeois society, and are incapable either of understanding a genuine revolutionary policy or submitting to revolutionary discipline. This is a prerequisite for preserving the party's health, cohesion, and capacity for action. . . .

The congress notes that the effort of the ECCI to mitigate the organizational aspects of the crisis by creating equal membership of the two chief fractions, the centre and the left, in the leading party bodies, was frustrated by the centre, under the influence of its most conservative elements, who always gain the upper hand in the centre whenever the centre comes out in opposition to the left.

The congress thinks it necessary to explain to all members of the French Communist Party that the efforts of the ECCI to bring about a preliminary agreement between the two leading fractions were designed to facilitate the work of the Paris congress, and were not in any way an infringement of its indisputable rights as the supreme body of the French Communist Party.

The congress thinks it necessary to state that, whatever mistakes the left may have made, it has at bottom tried to carry out the policy of the Communist International, both up to and during the Paris congress, and on important questions of the revolutionary movement—such as the united front and the trade unions—has taken up a correct position. . . .

The incompatibility of freemasonry and socialism was generally recognized in most parties of the Second International. The Italian Socialist Party excluded freemasons in 1914, and this was undoubtedly one of the reasons why the party was able during the war to conduct an anti-war policy, while the freemasons, acting as instruments of the Entente, urged intervention.

The second congress of the Communist International did not include a special point on the incompatibility of communism and freemasonry among the conditions of admission only because the principle had already been embodied in a special resolution passed unanimously by the congress. The fact which has come to light at the fourth congress, that a considerable number of French communists belong to freemasons' lodges, is in the view of the Communist International most striking and most lamentable proof that our French party has not only retained the psychological heritage of the epoch of reformism, parliamentarianism, and patriotism, but keeps up quite material connexions, highly compromising to the leadership, with the secret political and careerist institutions of the radical bourgeoisie. While the communist vanguard is mustering the forces of the proletariat for unrelenting struggle against all the groups and parties of bourgeois society in the name of the proletarian dictatorship, a number of responsible party workers—deputies, journalists, and even members of the central committee—retain close connexions with the secret organizations of our enemy. . . .

The International thinks it essential to put an end once and for all to these compromising and demoralizing connexions between leading members of the communist party and political organizations of the bourgeoisie. It is a point of honour for the French revolutionary proletariat to cleanse all its class organizations of elements which are anxious to belong at one and the same time to the two mutually hostile camps.

The congress instructs the central committee of the French Communist Party to sever, not later than 1 January 1923, all connexions of the party, in the person of individuals or groups, with freemasonry. Any communist who is also a freemason, and who has not by 1 January openly announced to his organization and published in the party press, his complete break with freemasonry, is thereby automatically expelled from the communist party and is for ever barred from membership. . . .

In order to give the party a genuinely proletarian character, and to eliminate from its ranks those elements who see in it merely a corridor to Parliament, to the local councils, etc. it must be laid down as an inviolable rule that the list of party candidates at elections must consist of at least 90 per cent of worker communists, members actually working in factory or farm; members of the liberal professions may be included only in strictly limited numbers . . . and it is essential to exercise the utmost care in selecting candidates from the liberal professions (thorough investigation by special commissions composed of proletarians of their political record, their social connexions, reliability, fidelity and devotion to the cause of the working class, etc.). . . .

The fourth congress again directs attention to the extreme importance of correct and systematic work by the party in the colonies. . . . Only irreconcilable struggle by the communist party of the metropolitan country against colonial slavery, coupled with systematic revolutionary work in the colonies themselves, can weaken the influence of the extreme nationalist elements of the oppressed colonial peoples on the labouring classes, attract the labouring classes to the cause of the French proletariat, and thus deprive French capital, at the time of revolutionary proletarian insurrection, of the possibility of using the colonial natives as the last reserves of counter-revolution.

EXTRACTS FROM AN OPEN LETTER TO THE SECOND INTERNATIONAL
AND THE VIENNA LABOUR UNION, TO THE TRADE UNIONS OF ALL
COUNTRIES AND TO THE HAGUE INTERNATIONAL TRADE UNION AND
CO-OPERATIVE CONGRESS

4 *December* 1922   *Protokoll*, iv, p. 1029

[The IFTU conference in Rome had passed a resolution calling for a general
strike in the event of war, and had instructed its management committee to
promote a campaign for peace and disarmament. The conference to discuss how
the resolution could be put into effect was held at the Hague from 10 to 15
December 1922. It was attended by 600 delegates, and advocated public control
of the armaments industry, revision of the Versailles treaty and the carrying
through of its disarmament provisions, the settlement of disputes by arbitration,
etc.

In a note dated 4 December 1922 with suggestions for the Russian delegation
to the Hague congress, Lenin outlined the strategy they should follow and the
chief points they should make in their speeches. 'On such a question not only a
mistake, but even incompleteness on any essential matter, will be intolerable.']

THE SLOGAN OF THE FOURTH CONGRESS: UNITED FRONT!

The fourth congress of the Communist International, representing 62
parties in Europe, America, Asia, and Australia, most decisively confirmed
what the enlarged ECCI had twice decided, that it is the duty of all communist parties to do their utmost to resist the world capitalist offensive
against all working-class positions by a firm united front. In doing so the
supreme organ of the communist parties approved the content and aim of
our work in the past year, and issued as the slogan for future work: fight
for the united front of the world proletariat, fight for the unity of all proletarians in common defence regardless of their political affiliation and
attitude.

In the spring the Communist International appealed to the Second
International and the Vienna Labour Union to organize through a world
workers' congress this joint struggle for the maintenance of the eight-hour
day, against wage reductions, against the attack on the achievements of
the trade unions, against new armaments, against the danger of a new
war. At the Berlin conference of the delegates of the three executives the
Comintern representatives put forward a reasoned statement of these
proposals. They were rejected by the parties of the Second International....

SIX MONTHS OF CAPITALIST OFFENSIVE

Six months have passed since the failure of our proposal to establish the
proletarian united front and organize the defensive struggle. During that

time the bourgeois attack has gone forward uninterruptedly in all countries. . . .

In Germany the coalition government of social-democracy and bourgeoisie has publicly proclaimed that the only way to stabilize the mark is to squeeze more surplus labour out of the underfed proletarian masses. It has openly proclaimed the abolition of the last vestiges of economic control, it has given the most ruthless speculators a free hand. The new government of Cuno is a government of the captains of industry, the precursor of the open dictatorship of the coal and steel barons. Its character is so frankly large-capitalist, so frankly directed against the most elementary interests of the working class, that the social-democrats had to refuse to enter it. From Bavaria extreme counter-revolution is preparing an armed onslaught on the last vestiges of the November revolution, on the republic. It has been encouraged in its designs by the victory of Italian fascism which, without the least resistance from the democratic bourgeoisie, proclaimed the dictatorship of the sword, turned parliament into a cipher, and whose object is to strengthen the rule of the bourgeoisie by forcing the working class into complete subjection to capital. . . .

TOWARDS NEW WARS

But the capitalist offensive is directed not only at increasing the exploitation of the proletariat; the danger of a new imperialist world war has again come clearly into the picture. Until now not a single capitalist State has started to carry out the agreement on the reduction of naval armaments reached by the Washington conference. Not a single warship has been scrapped. The building of new warships has not been stopped.

The Russian Soviet Government's proposal at Genoa for disarmament, or at least the reduction of land armaments, was rejected by all the capitalist Powers. The League of Nations is powerless to do the least thing in this field, even if it wanted to. Its decisions must be unanimous, and require ratification by the governments which are opposed to disarmament.

Europe is bristling with weapons, even more than before the war. In September, during the eastern crisis, the world saw what that meant. Only the renunciation by the Turkish Government of its right to occupy its capital and to cross the Dardanelles, which give access to it—only this renunciation by the Turkish Government of its right to self-determination saved Europe from a new war. . . .

The fourth congress of the Communist International asks the workers of the Second and the Vienna Internationals, the millions of workers throughout the world organized in trade unions, their leaders, and the Hague conference: Do you want to stand idly by and watch the eight-hour day, the prime condition for the advance of the working class, being abolished? The workers' standard of living in the oldest industrial countries depressed to the level of the Chinese coolie's living standards? The most elementary rights of the workers, through which after all you hoped to find by peaceful means emancipation from the capitalist yoke, annulled? The dictatorship of capitalism established? Will you stand idly by and watch how triumphant capitalism, freed from all restraints, brings about a new war, in which you will once again shed your blood for the interests of capital?

The fourth Comintern congress calls on all its member parties, and all the trade unions in all countries which sympathize with it, to put these questions to all labour parties and to challenge them to a common struggle against the legal or factual abolition of the eight-hour day, against the reduction of wages, against the abrogation of the working class's freedom of movement, against new armaments, against the war danger; for the eight-hour day, for the workers' minimum wage, for complete freedom of organization for the working class, for disarmament, and for peace among the peoples.

THE CHALLENGE OF THE FOURTH COMINTERN CONGRESS

The fourth Comintern congress puts a plain question to the Second and the Vienna Internationals: Are they willing, now that their policy has still further worsened the position of the working class, to offer their hand to establish the common front of the international proletariat for the struggle for the basic rights and interests of the working class?

It asks the Amsterdam International whether it is willing to stop splitting the trade unions, stop excluding communists from the unions, willing to help in a united front to lead the proletariat in struggle.

The fourth Comintern congress asks the Hague conference of trade unions and co-operators, meeting at a time when in Lausanne the Entente capitalists, after the bankruptcy of Versailles, are forcing a new Versailles on the Turkish people and so preparing the ground for new wars, whether it is willing to act together with us in showing the bourgeoisie by the mobilization of the working class that the international proletariat is no longer willing to be dragged unresisting to new battlefields.

As we said at the Berlin conference, the Communist International does not expect the parties of the Second International, the Vienna Labour Union, and the Amsterdam trade union leaders to fight for the dictatorship of the proletariat, which was and is our goal. But we ask them whether they want to fight against the dictatorship of capital, whether at least they want to use what remains of democracy to organize resistance to the triumph of that same capital which turned the world into a mass grave and is now digging new mass graves for our proletarian youth.

The Communist International has spoken. It has given its parties their fighting slogans. . . . It is now the turn of the Second International, the Vienna Labour Union, the Amsterdam Trade Union International and its Hague congress to speak!

EXTRACTS FROM THE DIRECTIVES FOR COMMUNIST ACTION IN THE TRADE UNIONS ADOPTED BY THE FOURTH COMINTERN CONGRESS

December 1922   *Thesen und Resolutionen*, iv, p. 28

[In the German party, Zinoviev said in his report for the Executive, there had been serious discussion of the question whether it had been premature to found the RILU, and whether it should not be dissolved. The Executive had intervened in the discussion in favour of the RILU, and 'liquidationism' had been eradicated. It was the IFTU who were the splitters. 'We need the unity of the working-class movement, the Amsterdamers need a split. The more influence we win, the stronger will be their desire to split the unions, and the harder we must fight them. . . . But if they force us to organize independently, as they have done in France and Czechoslovakia, and as they are trying to do in Germany and other countries, we must in our propaganda demonstrate that those of our unions which were born as a result of this split were born with the cry for unity on their lips.' The reformists, he added later, acted as though they had received direct orders from the bourgeoisie to smash the unions to smithereens rather than let them be won by the communists. This was greater treachery even than August 1914.

In introducing the theses, Lozovsky said the trade union question had been discussed at the second and third congresses as well as at the enlarged ECCI meeting in June 1922; the suggestion that the RILU should be dissolved made it necessary to bring the question up again; those who believed in liquidating the RILU would, he said, soon come to believe in the liquidation of the Comintern itself. The communists were for unity, but they could not sacrifice communism to that unity. It was not merely a question of the communist cells within the unions; the RILU was not required for that work, which was in the hands of the Comintern. The RILU was required to provide a centre for the non-communist revolutionary members of the trade unions, and to keep them united with the Comintern. Otherwise the basis of international communist action would be narrowed, and this would lead logically to the dissolution of the Communist International. 'The split in the trade unions was not caused by us communists. . . . We tried to fight within the unions, to direct them along a new path, to revolutionize them, but our watchword was winning the unions, not destroying them.' The unity of the trade union movement, he asserted, was the most important question for all communist parties. The disorganizing and demoralizing activities of the reformists were driving millions of workers out of the unions. Amsterdam's splitting policy had been supported by the anarchists, including the IWW in the United States, the anarchists in France, the syndicalists in Italy, and the anarcho-syndicalists in Spain.

In the discussion Tasca (Italy) said that the RILU was no more than a propaganda bureau; if it wanted to be more than that it would have to ac-knowledge that it aimed at splitting the world trade union movement. At the time of the twelfth Russian Communist Party congress in April 1923 Bukharin noted that important concessions had been made to conciliate the French syndicalists; instead of the Comintern being a body superior to the Profintern, the two had been made formally equal. His figures of a membership of 20 million for the IFTU and of 6–7 million for the RILU, were challenged by Lozovsky, who said that, given communist trade union policy, support counted for more than formal membership. The IFTU had 14–15 million supporters, the RILU 13 million.]

I. THE STATE OF THE TRADE UNION MOVEMENT

1. In the course of the last two years, characterized by the general capitalist offensive, the trade union movement in all countries has grown markedly weaker. With a few exceptions (Germany, Austria) the trade unions have lost a large proportion of their members. This decline is explained both by the powerful bourgeois offensive and by the powerless-ness of the reformist unions to put up serious opposition to the capitalist attack and to defend the most elementary interests of the workers.

2. Disillusioned both by the capitalist offensive and the continuation of class co-operation, some of the working masses are attempting to establish new organizations, while a great number of less class-conscious workers are leaving their organizations. For many the trade union has ceased to be a centre of attraction because it did not resist, and in many cases did not want to resist the capitalist offensive and to defend the positions already won. The barrenness of reformism has been made clear in practice.

3. In all countries the trade union movement gives evidence of an inner instability. Fairly numerous groups of workers are constantly breaking away, while the reformists zealously carry on with their policy of class collaboration on the pretext of 'using capital for labour's benefit'. In reality however capital has always made the reformist organizations serve its interests by using them to reduce the standard of living of the masses. . . .

II. AMSTERDAM'S ATTACK ON THE REVOLUTIONARY UNIONS

4. While yielding to bourgeois pressure all along the line, the reformist leaders began their attack on the revolutionary workers. Since they saw that their lack of will to organize resistance to capital had aroused intense bitterness in the working masses, and were determined to cleanse the organizations of revolutionary elements, they started a systematic attack on the revolutionary trade union movement with the object of disinte-grating and demoralizing the revolutionary minorities by all the means in their power, and of helping to consolidate the shaken rule of the bourgeoisie.

5. To maintain their authority, the Amsterdam leaders did not hesitate

to exclude not only individuals or groups, but entire organizations. At any price they do not want to be in a minority, and if faced by a threat of the revolutionary elements, adherents of the RILU and the Communist International, they are determined to provoke a split, provided that they can keep in their hands the administrative machinery and the funds. . . .

6. Simultaneously with the reformist attack in the different countries, the attack on a world scale also opened. The international secretariats which adhere to Amsterdam systematically excluded the corresponding national revolutionary unions or refused to admit them. Thus the international congresses of the textile workers, clerical employees, skin and leather workers, woodworkers, building workers, and post and telegraph employees refused to admit the Russian unions and the other revolutionary unions because they belonged to the RILU.

7. This campaign of the Amsterdamers against the revolutionary unions is one facet of the campaign of international capital against the working class. It pursues the same aims: to reinforce the capitalist system with the bones of the working masses. Reformism is hastening towards its end; by expulsions and by cutting off the most militant elements, it seeks to weaken the working class, in order to make them incapable of conquering power and the means of production.

III. ANARCHISTS AND COMMUNISM

8. At the same time an 'offensive', somewhat similar to that of the Amsterdamers, was launched by the anarchist wing of the workers' movement against the Communist International, the communist parties, and the communist cells in the unions. A certain number of anarcho-syndicalist organizations openly proclaimed themselves enemies of the Communist International and the Russian revolution, despite their solemn adherence to the Communist International in 1920 and their declaration of sympathy for the Russian proletariat and the October revolution. . . .

9. In the name of trade union autonomy certain syndicalist organizations (the National Secretariat of Dutch Workers, the IWW, the Italian Syndicalist Union, etc.) excluded the adherents of the RILU in general and the communists in particular. Thus the slogan of independence, once super-revolutionary, has become anti-communist, that is, counter-revolutionary, and this suits Amsterdam, which pursues the same policy under the banner of independence, although it is no longer a secret to anybody that it is wholly and entirely dependent on the national and international bourgeoisie.

10. The action of the anarchists against the CI and RILU and the Russian revolution has brought division and confusion into their own ranks. The best elements of the working class have protested against this ideology. Anarchism and anarcho-syndicalism have split into a number

of groups and tendencies, which are waging a bitter struggle for or against the RILU, for or against the proletarian dictatorship, for or against the Russian revolution.

IV. NEUTRALITY AND AUTONOMY

11. Bourgeois influence on the proletariat is expressed in the theory of neutrality: the trade unions are to stick to purely craft, narrowly economic aims, and not general class aims. Neutrality has always been a purely bourgeois theory, energetically combated by revolutionary Marxism. Trade unions which have no class aims, i.e. which are not bent on the overthrow of the capitalist system, are, despite their proletarian composition, the best defenders of the bourgeois order of society.

12. This theory of neutrality has always been based on the argument that the trade unions should interest themselves only in economic questions, and not mix in politics. The bourgeoisie always tend to separate politics from economics for they realize very well that if they manage to confine the working class within the frame of craft interests their rule is not seriously endangered.

13. The same frontier between economics and politics is drawn by the anarchist elements in the trade union movement, in order to divert the workers' movement from the political path on the pretext that all politics are directed against the workers. This theory, in essence purely bourgeois, is presented to the workers as the theory of trade union autonomy, which is then interpreted as hostility of the trade unions to the communist parties and as a declaration of war on the communist workers' movement, still on the notorious pretext of independence and autonomy.

14. . . . . Autonomy in all its forms, whether anarchist or anarcho-syndicalist, is an anti-communist theory, and must be most decisively resisted, for, at the best, it results in independence from communism and antagonism between trade union and communist party, if it does not lead to a bitter struggle of the unions against the communist parties, communism, and the social revolution.

15. The theory of autonomy, as it is set forth by the French, Italian, and Spanish anarcho-syndicalists, is by its very nature the battle-cry of anarchism against communism. Communists must conduct from within the trade unions an energetic struggle against this attempt to smuggle in anarchist refuse under the flag of autonomy, and to split the workers' movement into sections at war with each other in order to hamper and delay the triumph of the working class.

V. SYNDICALISM AND COMMUNISM

16. The anarcho-syndicalists confuse trade unions and syndicalism by representing their anarcho-syndicalist party as the only genuinely revo-

lutionary organization capable of conducting proletarian action to the end. Syndicalism, while a tremendous advance on trade unionism,[1] nevertheless embodies many errors and bad aspects, which must be most resolutely combated.

17. Communists may not and should not, in the name of abstract anarcho-syndicalist principles, give up their right to organize 'cells' inside the trade unions of whatever colour. Nobody can deprive them of this right. Naturally, communists who struggle within the unions must link their action with those syndicalists who have learnt from the experiences of the war and the revolution.

18. Communists must seize the initiative in forming within the unions a bloc with revolutionary workers of other tendencies. Those who are closest to communism are the syndicalist-communists, who acknowledge the necessity of the proletarian dictatorship, and, as opposed to the anarcho-syndicalists, defend the principle of the workers' State. But joint action presupposes an organization of communists. Communists acting individually would not be in a position to collaborate with anyone, since they would represent no serious force.

19. While putting their principles into practice in the most energetic and consistent manner, and combating the anti-communist theories of autonomy and the separation of politics and economics, which is a conception very injurious to the revolutionary advance of the working class, communists must make every effort within the unions, of whatever tendency, to co-ordinate their activities in the practical struggle against reformism and the sham militancy of the anarcho-syndicalists, with all the revolutionary elements who are in favour of the overthrow of capitalism and the dictatorship of the proletariat. . . .

VI. THE STRUGGLE FOR TRADE UNION UNITY

21. The slogan of the Communist International against the splitting of the unions must still be applied with undiminished energy, despite the furious persecution of communists by the reformists everywhere. The reformists resort to expulsions in order to provoke splits. By systematically driving the best elements out of the unions, they hope that the communists will lose their heads, leave the unions, and so give up the deeply considered plan to win the trade unions from within. . . .

22. The splitting of the trade union movement, particularly in present conditions, is the greatest danger to the entire workers' movement. It would throw the working class back for several years, for the bourgeoisie could then easily recapture what the workers have won. Communists must prevent the splitting of the unions with all the means at their disposal, with

[1] Trade unionism in the original to imply a narrow, purely industrial, non-political outlook.

all the strength of their organization; they must check the criminal frivolity with which the reformists are breaking up trade union unity.

23. In countries where there are two trade union federations (Spain, France, Czechoslovakia, etc.) communists must fight for the fusion of the dual organizations. Given this goal of merging the unions which are already split, it is not reasonable to detach individual communists and revolutionary workers from the reformist unions in order to bring them into the revolutionary unions. No single reformist union should be robbed of the communist yeast. Energetic work by the communists in both organizations is indispensable to the re-establishment of unity. . . .

24. . . . Every communist must bear in mind that the splitting of the unions not only endangers the immediate gains of the working class, but also threatens the social revolution. The attempts of the reformists to split the unions must be killed in the bud, but this can only be done by vigorous organizational and political work among the working masses.

VII. THE FIGHT AGAINST THE EXPULSION OF COMMUNISTS

25. The expulsion of communists is intended to confuse the revolutionary movement by separating the leaders from the working masses. That is why communists can no longer restrict themselves to the forms and methods of struggle which they have used up to now. The world trade union movement has reached a critical point. The reformists have become more eager to split the unions; our desire for unity has been attested by numerous facts, and in the future communists must demonstrate practically the value they place on the unity of the trade union movement.

26. The more obvious the splitting tendencies of our enemies become, the more vigorously must we raise the question of trade union unity. No single factory, workshop, or workers' meeting should be overlooked; protests against the tactics of Amsterdam must be made everywhere. The question of splitting the trade unions must be put before every trade unionist, not merely at the moment when a split is imminent, but when it is being prepared. The question of the exclusion of communists from the trade union movement must be placed before the entire trade union movement of all countries. The communists are strong enough not to allow themselves to be choked off without a word. The working class must know who is for splitting and who is for unity.

27. The exclusion of communists after their election by local organizations is more than a matter for protest against interference with the will of the electors; it should be met by firm and well-organized resistance. Those excluded should not be dispersed. It is most important for the communist parties not to allow the excluded elements to be scattered. They must organize themselves in trade unions of the excluded and make their readmission into the unions the central point of their political work.

28. The fight against expulsions is in fact a fight for the unity of the trade union movement. In this connexion all steps are good which are aimed at the re-establishment of unity. Those excluded should not remain isolated and cut off from the opposition as a whole, or from the existing revolutionary independent organizations. The expelled groups should at once attach themselves closely to the opposition in the unions and to the revolutionary organizations in the country concerned in order to wage a joint struggle against expulsions and ensure community of action in the struggle against capital.

29. Practical measures of struggle can and should be worked out and changed in accordance with local conditions and peculiarities. It is important for communist parties to make their hostility to splitting clear, and to do everything in their power to stop the wave of expulsions which has become noticeably stronger in connexion with the early stages of the fusion of the Second and Vienna Internationals. There are no universal and definitive ways and means in the fight against expulsions. All communist parties have the opportunity of fighting with the weapons which seem best to them to reach their object, to win the trade unions and to restore trade union unity.

30. Communists must develop an energetic struggle against the exclusion of revolutionary unions from the international trade federations. Communist parties cannot and will not stand idly by while the revolutionary unions are systematically expelled merely because they are revolutionary. The international committees for factory propaganda established by the RILU must be vigorously supported by the communist parties so that all the available revolutionary forces are put into operation to fight for the creation of international and unified trade federations.

This entire struggle must be waged under the slogan of admitting all unions, of whatever tendency, and regardless of their political complexion, into a single organization for the industry.

CONCLUSION

In following its path of winning the trade unions and of fighting the splitting policy of the reformists, the fourth Comintern congress most solemnly declares that, whenever the Amsterdamers do not resort to expulsions, whenever they give the communists the opportunity of fighting with ideological weapons for their principles within the trade unions, communists will fight as disciplined members within the ranks of the one organization, and in all conflicts and clashes with the bourgeoisie will stand in the front ranks.

The fourth congress of the Communist International makes it the duty of every communist party to do everything in its power to prevent the splitting of the trade unions, to restore the unity of the trade union movement where it has been destroyed, and to strive for the adherence of the trade union movement of the country in question to the Red International of Labour Unions.

EXTRACTS FROM THE THESES ON TACTICS ADOPTED BY THE FOURTH COMINTERN CONGRESS

5 *December* 1922   *Thesen und Resolutionen*, iv, p. 6

[The theses, drafted and presented by Zinoviev, were an elaboration of the December 1921 theses of the ECCI. They attempted to reconcile the views of those (such as Radek and the German right wing) who wanted a 'united front from above', and of those (such as Zinoviev and the German left) who advocated the 'united front from below'. The theses were adopted unanimously.

The discussion of Zinoviev's ECCI report, and of Radek's report on 'the capitalist offensive', was concerned primarily with problems of the united front and the slogan of a workers' government. The united front, Zinoviev said, did not mean an electoral alliance, or amalgamation with the reformists. It was the common struggle for the daily demands of the working class. This had universal validity, but the slogan of a workers' government was more restricted in scope. It was applicable only in those countries where the problem of government was in the forefront, both inside and outside parliament. It had little relevance in the American situation, but might at any time be relevant for Germany or Italy. If it arose from the parliamentary situation alone it was worthless; it could not replace the class struggle, and in countries where parliamentary traditions were strong there were dangers in its use that would have to be anticipated. Radek, answering the German left who criticized the negotiations between the KPD and the SPD, asserted that the German communists were not strong enough on their own to take action against the monarchists. (This referred to the 'Rathenau action' after the assassination of the German Foreign Minister.) A workers' government, he said, was not the dictatorship of the proletariat, but a transition stage towards it, and the transition was necessary because in the West (unlike Russia), the workers were not politically amorphous. A workers' government was not a historical necessity, but a historical possibility. Meyer (KPD), suggested that a workers' government was not a government but a slogan which might win wide adherence and so inaugurate a period of severe class struggle and civil war. Duret (France) argued that the tactics of the united front could be used by strong but not by weak parties. If a workers' government relied not on parliament but on the masses, it was tantamount to Soviets. In France there was only a parliamentary context for the slogan, and that was why the French party had rejected the united front tactics. Bordiga (Italy) said that if 'workers' government' were merely a verbal substitute for proletarian dictatorship he would not oppose it, although this desire to conceal the real programme smacked of opportunism. If, however, it meant that relations between the working class and the State could be settled otherwise than by armed struggle for power he would oppose it. He had, he said, been given dozens of explanations of what a workers' government was not, but not one explanation of what it was. Domski (Poland) said the slogan of a workers' government was unnecessary. A workers' government would come, if at all, as the result of a number of forces and conflicts, and the communist party should stick to its own slogan of proletarian dictatorship; if a workers' government were merely another name for proletarian dictatorship, he would point out that battles were not won by pseudonyms. No communist should proclaim a watchword in which he did not believe and for which he would not fight.

The ambiguities of the slogan for a workers' government particularly perplexed the French party. One of its delegates to the congress complained that he still could not understand it, although Radek and Thalheimer had sent long explanatory letters. There had been a severe crisis in the KPD over the united front tactics, particularly in regard to the possibility of a 'workers' government' in Saxony.

Bukharin informed the Russian party congress that shortly before the fourth Comintern congress the ECCI had sent out a questionnaire: 69 per cent. of the replies from France expressed opposition to united front tactics, 40 per cent. of those from Germany, 26 per cent. from Italy, and 24 per cent. from England. 'For us', he said, 'the united front tactics are primarily a great strategic manœuvre designed to destroy the influence of social-democracy.'

The fusion of the Second and Two-and-a-half Internationals, Zinoviev said in his ECCI report to the fourth congress, was a defeat for the Vienna Union. The Second International was an enemy of the working class, and the amalgamation of the two would accelerate the split in the working-class movement; the proletariat could only gain. The most urgent task of the day, perhaps of the epoch, was to defeat social-democracy, which was the strongest factor of international counter-revolution. This fight was not a fractional struggle within socialism, but the last and decisive fight of the international working class against the last advocate and agent of international capitalism. In its letter to the French Communist Party of 13 September 1922 the ECCI explained that the merging of the two Internationals, while they appeared to strengthen the opposition to the Comintern, would in fact work to its advantage, for the members of the old Two-and-a-half International would restrain the social-democrats from fulfilling their 'bourgeois' mission, while the members of the Second International would restrain the Independents from playing their part as an opposition to reformism; the disappearance of this sham opposition would reveal the communist party as the sole genuine opponent of the bourgeoisie. Trotsky had made the same point in a speech in Moscow on 20 October 1922. 'At first this unification means an accession of strength for the social-democrats. But if we look at it from a longer view, it is a colossal political gain for us, because . . . the Two-and-a-half International, which served as a buffer between communists and social-democrats, obscured the real relations and confused the minds of a certain number of the workers. . . . When we have on one side the social-democrats linked with the bourgeois State, and on the other side only the communists as the real opposition, then the power of the communist party to attract the workers is bound to grow.'

Answering Meyer (KPD), who interpreted the fusion of the SPD and the USPD as a victory for the KPD, Domski (Poland) suggested that many such victories would bring the KPD to the grave.]

1. ENDORSEMENT OF THE RESOLUTIONS OF THE THIRD CONGRESS

The fourth world congress first of all notes that the resolutions of the third world congress

1. on the economic crisis and the tasks of the Comintern, and
2. on the tactics of the Comintern, have been completely borne out by the course of events and the development of the labour movement in the period between the third and fourth congresses.

2. THE PERIOD OF CAPITALIST DECLINE

After an appraisal of the world economic situation the third congress could declare with complete certainty that capitalism, having fulfilled its mission of promoting the development of production, had reached a stage of irreconcilable conflict with the needs not only of historical development, but also of the most elementary conditions of human existence. . . .

The general picture of the decay of capitalist economy is not mitigated by those unavoidable fluctuations of the business cycle which are characteristic of the capitalist system both in its ascendancy and in its decline. The attempts of bourgeois and social-democratic economists to explain the improvement which began in the second half of 1921 in the United States, to a much less extent in Japan and England, and to some extent also in France and other countries, as a sign that capitalist equilibrium has been restored, rest partly on the desire to falsify the facts, partly on the lack of insight of these lackeys of capital. . . . The next cyclical crisis, which will operate in the same direction as the general trend of capitalist decay, will intensify all its manifestations and thus make the revolutionary situation far more acute.

Capitalism will be subject to cyclical fluctuations till the hour of its death. Only the seizure of power by the proletariat and the socialist world revolution can save mankind from the catastrophe provoked by the existence of present-day capitalism.

What capitalism is passing through today is nothing but its death throes. The collapse of capitalism is inevitable.

3. THE INTERNATIONAL POLITICAL SITUATION

The international political situation also reflects the continuing breakdown of capitalism.

The reparations question is still unsettled. While one conference of the Entente States after another is held, Germany's economic collapse is proceeding unchecked and threatens the existence of capitalism throughout central Europe. The catastrophic deterioration in Germany's economic situation will either force the Entente to renounce reparations, which will aggravate the economic and political crisis in France, or it will lead to the creation of a Franco-German industrial bloc on the continent, and this will make England's economic situation and its position on the world market worse; it will place England and the continent in political opposition to each other.

In the *Near East* Entente policy has suffered complete bankruptcy. The treaty of Sèvres was torn up by Turkish bayonets. The war between Turkey and Greece, and the events associated with it, have made palpably clear how unstable the present political equilibrium is. The spectre of a new imperialist world war became plainly visible. Having, because of competition with England, helped to overthrow the joint work of the Entente in the Near East, imperialist France has now been driven back by its capitalist interests into the common capitalist front against the eastern peoples. Thus capitalist France has demonstrated once again to the peoples of the Near East that they can wage their struggle against oppression only at the side of Soviet Russia and with the support of the revolutionary proletariat of the whole world.

In the *Far East* the victorious Entente States tried at Washington to revise the Versailles treaty. But they were only able to give themselves a breathing space, cutting down *one* form of armaments only, the number of big battleships to be built in the next few years. They did not reach any solution to their problem. The struggle between America and Japan continues and is stoking up the civil war in China. The shores of the Pacific remain as before the burning focus of great conflicts.

The example of the national liberation movements in India, Egypt, Ireland, and Turkey shows that the colonial and semi-colonial countries are hotbeds of a growing revolutionary movement against the imperialist Powers and represent inexhaustible reservoirs of revolutionary strength which in the given situation work objectively against the entire existence of the bourgeois world order.

The *Versailles treaty* is being liquidated by events. It is not, however, being replaced by a general understanding among the capitalist States, by the abandonment of imperialism, but by new contradictions, new imperialist alignments, and new armaments. In the given situation the reconstruction of Europe is not possible. Capitalist America is unwilling to make sacrifices to restore capitalist European economy. Capitalist America watches like a vulture the breakdown of capitalism in Europe, to which it will be heir. America will enslave capitalist Europe if the European working class does not seize political power and set about clearing away the ruins of the world war and beginning the construction of a federal Soviet republic of Europe. . . .

At the same time the international political position of *Soviet Russia*, the only country where the proletariat has defeated the bourgeoisie, and which has for five years maintained power against the onslaughts of the enemy, has grown immeasurably stronger. At Genoa and at The Hague the Entente capitalists tried to force the Russian Soviet Republic to abandon the nationalization of industry and to impose on it a burden of debt which would have made Soviet Russia in fact a colony of the Entente. The proletarian State was however strong enough to resist these arrogant intentions. Amidst the chaos of the crumbling capitalist State system, Soviet Russia, from the Berezina to Vladivostok, from Murmansk to the Armenian mountains, is a factor of growing power in Europe and the Near and Far East. Despite the attempt of the capitalist world to strangle Soviet Russia by a financial blockade, it is in a position to go on with its economic reconstruction. For this purpose it will make use not only of its own economic resources, but also of the competition of the capitalist States among themselves, which will force them to conduct negotiations separately with Soviet Russia. One-sixth of the earth is in the hands of the Soviets. The mere existence of the Russian Soviet Republic represents a permanent element of weakness in bourgeois society; it is the most important factor in the world revolution. The greater the improvement in Soviet Russia's economic strength, the more powerful will be the influence of this most pre-eminent revolutionary factor in world politics.

4. THE CAPITALIST OFFENSIVE

Since the proletariat of all countries, with the exception of Russia, failed to exploit the weakness of capitalism created by the war for decisive battles, the bourgeoisie were able, with the help of the social-democrats, to defeat the militant revolutionary workers, to re-establish their own political and economic power, and to open a new offensive against the proletariat. All the efforts of the bourgeoisie to set international production and distribution of commodities going again after the storms of the world war were made solely at the cost of the working class. . . .

The capitalist offensive, which in these last years has assumed gigantic proportions, forces the working class in all countries to fight in defence. Thousands and thousands in the most important industries have taken up the fight. New groups of workers are constantly joining in—railwaymen, miners, engineers, public and municipal employees. So far the majority of these strikes have had no direct success, but the struggle itself is creating among multitudes of formerly backward workers undying hatred of the capitalists and the State power which protects them. These battles, forced on the proletariat, are destroying the policy of collaboration with the employers pursued by the social-reformists and trade union bureaucrats. These struggles show even the most backward sections of the proletariat the obvious connexion between economics and politics. Today every big strike becomes a big political event. They show that the parties of the Second International and the leaders of the Amsterdam trade unions not only gave no help to the working masses engaged in severe defensive struggles, but left them in the lurch and betrayed them to the employers and to the bourgeois governments.

It is one of the duties of the communist parties to expose publicly this shameful and continued treachery and to bring it home to the workers in their daily struggles. It is the duty of the communist parties of all countries to extend and to deepen the numerous industrial strikes which are breaking out and if possible to let them develop into political strikes and struggles. It is obviously the duty of the communist parties so to strengthen the defensive struggles and the revolutionary understanding and militancy of the proletarian masses that, when they are strong enough, they will pass from defence to attack.

The steady intensification of the contradictions between proletariat and bourgeoisie is inevitable as these struggles extend. The situation remains objectively revolutionary, and even the slightest occasion can today become the starting point of great revolutionary struggles.

5. INTERNATIONAL FASCISM

Closely connected with the capitalist offensive in the economic sphere is the political offensive of the bourgeoisie against the working class, expressed most grossly in international fascism. As growing impoverishment revolutionizes the masses, reaches the middle strata, including public employees, and shakes the confidence of the bourgeoisie in the absolute docility and adequacy of the bureaucracy as their instrument, the legal methods at their command no longer satisfy the bourgeoisie. They are therefore resorting everywhere to the creation of special white guards for use particularly against all the revolutionary efforts of the proletariat and to a growing degree for the defeat by brutal means of every attempt by the workers to improve their lot.

The characteristic feature of Italian fascism—'classic' fascism, which has for the present triumphed throughout the country—consists in this, that the fascists not only form strictly counter-revolutionary fighting organizations, armed to the teeth, but also try by social demagogy to gain a footing among the masses, among the peasantry, the petty bourgeoisie, and even among some sections of the working class, cleverly using the inevitable disappointment in so-called democracy for their own reactionary purposes. There is a danger of fascism now in many countries, in Czechoslovakia, Hungary, practically all the Balkan countries, Poland, Germany (Bavaria), in Austria and America, and even in countries like Norway. Nor is fascism impossible, in one form or another, in countries like France or England.

It is one of the most important tasks of the communist parties to organize resistance to international fascism, to lead the entire working class in the struggle against the fascist gangs, and to make vigorous use in this field also of the united front tactics; *in this struggle methods of illegal organization are absolutely essential.*

But the frenzied fascist organization is the last card in the bourgeoisie's hand. The unconcealed rule of the white guards is directed against the very foundations of bourgeois democracy. The broadest masses of the working people will be convinced by this fact that the rule of the bourgeoisie is possible only in the form of an undisguised dictatorship over the proletariat.

6. THE POSSIBILITY OF NEW PACIFIST ILLUSIONS

The characteristics of the present international political situation are fascism, the state of emergency, and the rising wave of white terror against the working class. But that does not exclude the possibility that in the near future in some very important countries open bourgeois reaction will be succeeded by an era of 'democratic-pacifism'. In England (where the Labour Party increased its vote at the last elections), in France (where the so-called 'left bloc' is sure to come in) such a democratic-pacifist period of transition is probable and can in its turn give rise to a revival of pacifist hopes in bourgeois and social-democratic Germany. Between the present period of the rule of open bourgeois reaction and the complete victory of the revolutionary proletariat over the bourgeoisie various stages and various temporary episodes are possible. The Communist International and its sections must keep these possibilities in mind. They must know how to defend their revolutionary positions in *any* situation.

7. THE SITUATION WITHIN THE LABOUR MOVEMENT

While the working class is being driven to the defensive by the capitalist offensive, the parties of the centre (the Independents) are drawing nearer to and finally fusing with the open social-traitors (the social-democrats). When the revolutionary wave was rising even the centrists, under the pressure of mass sentiment, declared themselves in favour of the proletarian dictatorship and approached the Communist International. With the ebbing of the revolutionary wave, which is however only temporary, these centrists are again falling back into the social-democratic camp, from which they had never genuinely broken away. During the revolutionary mass struggles they always took up a delaying and vacillating position; now they renounce the defensive struggle and return to the camp of the Second International, which was always consciously anti-revolutionary. The centrist parties and the entire centrist Two-and-a-half International are breaking down. The best revolutionary workers now in the centrist camp will come in time to the Communist International. Here and there (as in Italy) this movement has already begun. The overwhelming majority of the centrist leaders, who are now allied with Noske, Mussolini, etc. will on the other hand become hardened counter-revolutionaries.

Objectively the fusion of the parties of the Second and the Two-and-a-half Internationals can only be of advantage to the revolutionary labour movement. The fiction of a second revolutionary party outside the communist camp is at an end. Within the working class there will now be only two groups contending for the majority of the workers, the Second International, which represents the influence of the bourgeoisie within the working class, and the Communist International, which has raised the banner of the socialist revolution and the dictatorship of the proletariat.

8. THE TRADE UNION SPLIT AND THE PREPARATIONS FOR WHITE TERROR AGAINST COMMUNISTS

The amalgamation of the parties of the Second and Two-and-a-half Internationals is undoubtedly designed to create a 'favourable atmosphere' for a systematic anti-communist campaign. One part of this campaign is the deliberate splitting of the trade unions by the leaders of the Amsterdam International. They recoil from any struggle against the capitalist offensive and are more concerned to continue their policy of collaboration with the employers. In order not to be disturbed by the communists in this alliance with the employers, they are trying to eliminate communist influence in the trade unions. Since however in many countries the communists have already won a majority in the trade unions, or are about to do so, the Amsterdamers do not shrink from expulsions, or even from officially splitting the unions. Nothing weakens the forces of proletarian resistance to the capitalist offensive so much as splitting the unions. The reformist trade union leaders are well aware of this, but since they are also aware that they are losing ground, and that their bankruptcy is both unavoidable and near, they are anxious to split the unions, which are the irreplaceable instrument of the proletarian class struggle, so that the communists will inherit only the fragments and splinters of the old trade union organizations. The working class has witnessed no greater treachery since August 1914.

9. THE TASK OF WINNING THE MAJORITY

In these circumstances the basic directive of the third world congress, 'of winning communist influence among the majority of the working class and leading the decisive section of this class in struggle' retains full validity.

Even more than at the time of the third congress, it is true today that, with the present precarious equilibrium of bourgeois society, the most severe crisis may quite suddenly break out as the result of a large-scale strike, a colonial revolt, a new war, or even a parliamentary crisis. That is precisely why the 'subjective' factor is of such tremendous importance, that is, the degree of consciousness, of militancy, the level of organization in the working class and in its vanguard.

To win the majority of the American and European working class—that is, now as before, the Comintern's cardinal task.

In the colonial and semi-colonial countries the Comintern has a dual task: (1) to create a core of communist parties which represent the interests of the proletariat as a whole, and (2) to support to the utmost the national revolutionary movement which is directed against imperialism, to become the vanguard of this movement, and to emphasize and expand the social movement within the national movement.

10. UNITED FRONT TACTICS

The necessity of the united front tactic follows from all this. The slogan of the third congress 'to the masses' is now more than ever appropriate. Only now is the struggle for the formation of the proletarian united front beginning in a great number of countries. Only now are the difficulties of the united front tactic beginning to be overcome. The best example is France, where the course of events has convinced even those who a short time ago were on principle hostile to this tactic of the necessity of its employment. The Comintern requires all communist parties and groups to carry out the united front tactic strictly, because in the present period that alone can give communists a sure road to winning the majority of the workers.

The reformists need a split. The communists are interested in rallying all the forces of the working class against capitalism.

The united front tactic means that the communist vanguard must take the lead in the day-to-day struggles of the broad working masses for their most vital interests. In these struggles the communists are even ready to negotiate with the treacherous social-democratic and Amsterdam leaders. The attempts of the Second International to represent the united front as the organizational fusion of all 'workers' parties' must of course be decisively rebutted. The attempts of the Second International, under the cloak of the united front, to absorb workers' organizations further to the left (for example the unification of the socialists and independent socialists in Germany) mean in practice nothing but the opportunity for the social-democratic leaders to surrender further sections of the working masses to the bourgeoisie.

The existence of independent communist parties and their complete freedom of action in regard to the bourgeoisie and the counter-revolutionary social-democracy is the most significant historical achievement of the proletariat, which communists will in no circumstances whatever renounce. Only the communist parties fight for the interests of the pro-letariat in its entirety.

Nor does the united front tactic mean so-called upper level 'electoral alliances' which pursue some parliamentary purpose or other. The united front tactic is the offer of a joint struggle of communists with all workers who belong to other parties or groups, and with all non-party workers, in defence of the basic interests of the working class against the bourgeoisie. . . .

In executing the united front policy it is especially important to achieve not only agitational, but also *organizational* results. No single opportunity should be missed of creating organizational footholds among the working masses themselves (factory councils, supervisory commissions of workers of all parties, and of non-party workers, committees of action, etc.).

The most important thing in the united front tactic is and remains the agitational and organizational rallying of the working masses. Its true realization can come only 'from below', from the depths of the working masses themselves. Communists however must not refuse in certain cir-cumstances to negotiate with the leaders of the hostile workers' parties, but the masses must be kept fully and constantly informed of the course of these negotiations. Nor must the communist parties' freedom to agitate be circumscribed in any way during these negotiations with the leaders.

It is obvious that the united front tactic is to be applied in different ways in different countries, according to the actual conditions prevailing there. Where, in the most important capitalist countries, objective conditions are ripe for the socialist revolution and where the social-democratic par-ties—with their counter-revolutionary leaders—are deliberately working to split the working class, the united front tactic will be decisive for a new epoch.

II. THE WORKERS' GOVERNMENT

The slogan of a workers' government (or a workers' and peasants' govern-ment) can be used practically everywhere as a general propaganda slogan. But as a *topical political slogan* it is of the greatest importance in those coun-tries where bourgeois society is particularly unstable, where the relation of forces between the workers' parties and the bourgeoisie is such that the decision of the question, who shall form the government, becomes one of immediate practical necessity. In *these* countries the slogan of a workers' government follows inevitably from the entire united front tactic.

The parties of the Second International are trying to 'save' the situation in these countries by advocating and forming a coalition government of bourgeois and social-democratic parties. . . . To this open or concealed bourgeois-social-democratic coalition the communists oppose the united front of all workers and a coalition of all workers' parties in the economic and the political field for the fight against the bourgeois power and its eventual overthrow. In the united struggle of all workers against the bourgeoisie the entire State apparatus must be taken over by the workers' government, and thus the working class's positions of power strengthened.

The overriding tasks of the workers' government must be to arm the proletariat, to disarm bourgeois, counter-revolutionary organizations, to introduce the control of production, to transfer the main burden of taxation to the rich, and to break the resistance of the counter-revolutionary bourgeoisie.

Such a workers' government is only possible if it is born out of the struggle of the masses, is supported by workers' bodies which are capable of fighting, bodies created by the most oppressed sections of the working masses. Even a workers' government which is created by the turn of events in parliament, which is therefore purely parliamentary in origin, *may* provide the occasion for invigorating the revolutionary labour movement. It is obvious that the formation of a real workers' government, and the continued existence of a government which pursues a revolutionary policy, must lead to a bitter struggle, and eventually to a civil war with the bourgeoisie. The mere attempt by the proletariat to form such a workers' government will from the outset encounter the sharpest opposition of the bourgeoisie. The slogan of a workers' government is therefore suitable for concentrating the proletariat and unleashing revolutionary struggles.

In certain circumstances communists must declare themselves ready to form a workers' government with non-communist workers' parties and workers' organizations. But they can do so only if there are guarantees that the workers' government will really conduct a struggle against the bourgeoisie in the sense mentioned above. The conditions on which communists participate in such a government are:

1. communists may take part in a workers' government only with the consent of the Comintern;

2. the communist members of such a government are under the strictest control of their party;

3. the communists chosen to take part in the workers' government must be those who have the closest contact with the revolutionary organizations of the masses;

4. the communist party retains without any restrictions its own identity and complete independence of agitation.

With all its great advantages, the slogan of a workers' government also has its dangers, just as the united front tactic as a whole conceals dangers. In order to avoid these dangers, the communist parties must bear in mind that while every bourgeois government is a capitalist government, not every workers' government is a really proletarian government, that is, a revolutionary instrument of power. The Communist International must consider the following possibilities:

1. Liberal workers' governments, such as there was in Australia; this is also possible in England in the near future.

2. Social-democratic workers' governments (Germany).

3. A government of workers and the poorer peasants. This is possible in the Balkans, Czechoslovakia, Poland, etc.

4. Workers' governments in which communists participate.

5. Genuine proletarian workers' governments, which in their pure form can be created only by the communist party.

The first two types are not revolutionary workers' governments, but in fact coalition governments of the bourgeoisie and anti-revolutionary labour leaders. Such governments are tolerated by the enfeebled bourgeoisie in critical times as a means of deceiving the proletariat about the real class character of the State, or to ward off, with the help of the corrupt workers' leaders, the revolutionary offensive of the proletariat and to gain time. Communists cannot take part in such governments. On the contrary, they must vigorously expose to the masses the real character of these pseudo-workers' governments. But in the present period of capitalist decline, when the most important task is to win the majority of the proletariat for the revolution, even such governments may objectively help to accelerate the process of disintegration of bourgeois power.

Communists are however prepared to act together with those workers who have not yet recognized the necessity of the proletarian dictatorship, social-democrats, members of Christian parties, non-party syndicalists, etc. They are thus ready, in certain conditions and with certain guarantees, to support a workers' government that is not communist. . . . The two types numbered 3 and 4, in which communists may take part, do not represent the dictatorship of the proletariat, they are not even a historically inevitable transition stage towards the dictatorship. But where they are formed they may become an important starting point for the fight for the dictatorship. The complete dictatorship of the proletariat is represented only by the real workers' government (the fifth on the above list) which consists of communists.

13. THE FACTORY COUNCIL MOVEMENT[1]

No communist party can be considered a seriously and solidly organized communist mass party unless it has strong communist cells in the factories, workshops, mines, railways, etc. In present conditions a movement cannot be regarded as a systematically organized proletarian mass movement if the working class and their organizations do not succeed in creating factory councils as the backbone of that movement. In particular the struggle against the capitalist offensive and for the control of production

---

[1] [*Sic.*] There is no paragraph 12.

is hopeless if the communists have not at their disposal firm footholds in all factories and if the working class have not created their own proletarian combat groups in the factories (factory councils, workers' committees).

The congress therefore considers it one of the chief tasks of all communist parties to get a firmer anchorage in the factories and to support the factory council movement or to take the initiative in establishing that movement.

14. THE COMINTERN AS A WORLD PARTY

While proceeding to develop its organization as a world communist party, the Communist International as such must also engage to an increasing extent in political affairs; in particular it must aim at gaining the leadership in important actions undertaken in entire groups of countries.

15. INTERNATIONAL DISCIPLINE

In order to carry out the united front tactic internationally and in each individual country, the strictest international discipline is more than ever necessary in the Comintern and in each of its sections.

The fourth congress categorically demands of all sections and all members the strictest discipline in carrying out the tactical line, which can only bear fruit if it is done unanimously and systematically in all countries, not only in words, but also in deeds.

Adherence to the 21 conditions involves the carrying out of all tactical decisions of the world congresses and of the Executive as the organ of the Comintern between world congresses. . . . Only the sharply defined revolutionary tactics of the Comintern ensure the earliest possible victory of the international proletarian revolution.

The congress decides to attach the text of the December (1921) theses of the Executive on the united front as an appendix to this resolution, as the present theses explain the united front tactic correctly and in detail.

RESOLUTION OF THE FOURTH COMINTERN CONGRESS ON THE VERSAILLES PEACE TREATY

5 *December* 1922   *Protokoll*, iv, p. 1002

[Although the treaty of Rapallo was not mentioned at the congress, its impact can be seen in the emphasis on the Versailles treaty; the third congress tactical theses had talked of the struggle against the German Government, but this objective is omitted from the fourth congress decisions. In introducing the resolution Cachin (France) said it was the duty of the French Communist Party to demand the abrogation of the treaty, and its actions must be brought into harmony with those of the German Communist Party. Smeral (Czechoslovakia) said that a great many of his compatriots, including proletarians, thought the Versailles treaty historically progressive because it was to that treaty that their country owed its birth. The resolution was passed unanimously.

The programme of action of the French Communist Party approved at the fourth Comintern congress stated that 'the struggle against the Versailles treaty and its consequences must remain in the forefront of the party's entire activity'. The French party was to inform the French workers and soldiers of 'the tragic plight of their German brothers'. The French workers themselves would be seriously affected by the competition of cheap German labour and the stimulus to German exports provided by currency depreciation. 'The party press must constantly describe the sufferings of the German proletariat, the real victims of the Versailles treaty, and demonstrate the impossibility of executing the treaty.']

The world war ended with the downfall of three imperialist Powers: Germany, Austria-Hungary, and Russia. Four great robber States remained victorious on the battlefield: the United States, England, France, and Japan.

The peace treaties, whose kernel is formed by the Versailles treaty, are an attempt to stabilize the world domination of these four victorious Powers; politically and economically, by coercing all the rest of the world into their sphere of colonial exploitation; and socially, by ensuring the rule of the bourgeoisie both over the proletariat in their own countries and over the victorious revolutionary proletariat of Russia by an alliance between the bourgeoisie of all countries. For that purpose a wall of small vassal States around Russia has been erected and armed, to strangle Soviet Russia when a suitable opportunity occurs. The defeated States are moreover to pay full compensation for the material losses suffered in the war by the victor states.

Today it is clear to everybody that all the assumptions on which the peace treaties were based were false. The attempt to establish a new equilibrium on a capitalist foundation has failed. The history of the last four years shows continuous fluctuation, constant insecurity, economic crises, unemployment and surplus labour, cabinet crises, party crises, crises in foreign policy. At innumerable conferences the imperialist Powers have tried to stay the breakdown of the world system established by the peace treaties and to conceal the bankruptcy of Versailles.

The attempts to overthrow the dictatorship of the proletariat in Russia miscarried. The proletariat of all capitalist countries are coming out more and more emphatically for Soviet Russia. Even the leaders of the Amsterdam International had to declare publicly that the downfall of proletarian rule in Russia would mean the victory of world reaction over the entire proletariat.

Turkey, as vanguard of the revolutionary East, successfully resisted by force of arms the execution of the peace treaty. At the Lausanne conference the solemn burial of an important part of the peace treaty system is taking place.

The continuing economic crisis has shown that the economic conception of the Versailles peace treaty is untenable. The leading European imperialist Power, England, who is in the highest degree dependent on world trade, cannot consolidate its economic basis unless Germany and Russia are re-established. The United States, the strongest imperialist Power, has turned completely away from the peace and is trying to build its world imperialism by itself. In this endeavour it has gained the support of important parts of the English world empire, Canada and Australia.

The oppressed colonies of England, the foundation of its world power, are in rebellion; the entire Moslem world is in open or latent insurrection.

All the presuppositions of the peace have become untenable, except one: the proletariat of all bourgeois countries are still to carry the burdens of the war and of Versailles.

FRANCE

On the surface France got the greatest increase in power of all the victor States. Apart from gaining Alsace-Lorraine, the occupation of the left bank of the Rhine, the claim to untold milliards in German war indemnities, it has in fact become the strongest military Power on the European continent. With its vassal States (Poland, Czechoslovakia, Rumania), whose armies are trained and led by French generals, with its own large army, with its submarines and its air force, it dominates the continent, playing the part of guardian of the Versailles peace treaty. But France's economic basis, its small and declining population, its tremendous internal and external indebtedness, and its consequent economic dependence on England and America, are not an adequate foundation for a boundless imperialist appetite for expansion. As a Power it is narrowly restricted by England's dominion over all important naval bases, and by the English and American oil monopoly. Economically, the acquisition of iron ore under the Versailles treaty was lessened in value because the Ruhr coal necessary for its working remained in Germany. The hope of bringing order into shattered French finances by German reparation payments has proved deceptive. All financial experts of the world are agreed that Germany cannot pay the sums which France needs to clear up its finances. The only road remaining open to the French bourgeoisie is to lower the standards of the French proletariat to the level of the German. The hunger of the German workers today prefigures the French workers' poverty of tomorrow. The depreciation of the franc, which is being deliberately encouraged by certain sections of French heavy industry, will be used to shunt the burdens of war—now that Versailles has proved useless—on to the shoulders of the French proletariat.

ENGLAND

The world war gave England the opportunity to unite its colonial world empire from the Cape of Good Hope, across Egypt and Arabia, to India. It has kept all the important ocean approaches in its possession. By concessions to its settlement colonies it is trying to build up an Anglo-Saxon world *imperium*.

But despite the flexibility of the English bourgeoisie, despite stubborn efforts to regain the world market, it transpires that in the world situation created by the Versailles peace treaty England cannot make progress. The English industrial State cannot exist if Germany and Russia are not economically re-established. This sharpens the antagonism between England and France; England wants to sell goods to Germany, which the Versailles treaty makes impossible; France wants to exact enormous sums from Germany as war costs, which destroys Germany's purchasing power. Hence England is in favour of reducing reparation obligations, while France is carrying on a concealed war against England in the Near East in order to force it to yield on the reparations question. While the English proletariat is carrying the burdens of the war in the form of millions of unemployed, the bourgeoisie of England and France are coming together again at Germany's expense.

CENTRAL EUROPE AND GERMANY

Central Europe, the new colonial sphere of the imperialist robbers, is a most important part of the Versailles peace handiwork. Riven into innumerable small States, divided into a number of areas incapable of supporting themselves economically, these regions cannot pursue an independent policy. They have sunk to being colonies of English and French capital. They are incited against each other according to the changing interests of these great Powers. Czechoslovakia, carved out of an economic area of 60 million population, is in a state of permanent economic crisis. Austria has shrunk to a lifeless creature, which continues to lead an ostensibly independent political existence only because of the mutual jealousies of the neighbouring countries. Poland, which was given large territories with a non-Polish population, is France's furthest outpost, a caricature of French imperialism. In all these countries the proletariat has had to pay the costs of the war by a reduction in the standard of life or by heavy unemployment.

But it is Germany which is the most important *object* of the Versailles peace treaty. Disarmed, deprived of every possibility of defence, it is at the mercy of the imperialist Powers. The German bourgeoisie try to ingratiate themselves now with the English, now with the French bourgeoisie. They hope by the severe exploitation of the German proletariat to satisfy a part of French claims and at the same time secure with foreign help their own domination over the German proletariat. But even the most intense exploitation of the German proletariat, the reduction of German workers to Europe's coolies, the incredible poverty into which the German proletariat have sunk as a result of the Versailles treaty, still do not make it possible to pay reparations. Germany is therefore being converted into a plaything in the hands of England and France. The French bourgeoisie want to settle the question by force by occupying the Ruhr. England is still opposed to this. Only the intervention of the strongest economic Power, the United States, would have made it possible to compose in some degree the conflicting interests of England, France, and Germany.

THE UNITED STATES OF AMERICA

The United States however has long withdrawn from the Versailles system by refusing to ratify the treaty. The United States, which emerged from the world war as the strongest Power, economically and politically, and to which the European imperialist Powers are heavily indebted, showed no desire to enable France to overcome its financial crisis by granting further large credits to Germany. United States capital is turning away more and more from the chaos in Europe, and is trying most successfully to build a large colonial empire in Central and South America and the Far East, while protecting the exploitation of the home market for its own ruling class by protective tariffs. While thus leaving continental Europe to its fate, it encounters on the other hand the conflicting interests of England and Japan. By using its economic superiority in regard to naval construction it compelled the other imperialist Powers to sign the Washington agreement. But in doing so it destroyed one of the most important pillars of Versailles, England's superiority at sea, and thus destroyed any reason for England to adhere to the alignment of Powers contemplated at Washington.

JAPAN AND THE COLONIES

The youngest imperialist world Power, Japan, keeps itself aloof from the chaos in Europe created by the Versailles treaty. But its interests have been strongly affected by the growth of the United States into a world Power. It was forced at Washington to dissolve the alliance with England, thus destroying another most important pillar of the division of the world established at Versailles. At the same time not only are the oppressed peoples rebelling against the rule of England and Japan, but England's settlement colonies are trying to secure their interests in the approaching struggle between the United States and Japan by closer ties with the United States. The structure of British world imperialism is thereby still more shaken.

TOWARDS A NEW WORLD WAR

The attempt of the imperialist great Powers to create a firm foundation for their world rule has failed lamentably because of their conflicting interests. The great edifice of peace lies in ruins. The great Powers and their vassal States are arming for a new war. Militarism is stronger than ever. And although the bourgeoisie are terribly afraid of a new proletarian revolution as the outcome of a world war, the inherent laws of the bourgeois order of society are driving inexorably towards a new world conflict.

THE TASKS OF THE COMMUNIST PARTIES

The Second and Two-and-a-half Internationals are trying to support the radical wing of the bourgeoisie, who represent primarily the interests of commercial and banking capital, in their ineffective struggle to reduce reparations. In this, as in every question, they act together with the bourgeoisie. The task of the communist parties, above all those of the victor countries, is to explain to the masses that Versailles shunts all the burdens, in the victorious as in the defeated countries, on to the proletariat, that the proletarians of all countries are the real victims of the bourgeoisie's peace. On this basis the communist parties, particularly those of France and Germany, must wage a *common fight* against the Versailles peace treaty. The German communist party must emphasize the willingness of the German proletariat to help the proletarians and peasants in the devastated areas of northern France to rebuild their homes, and must at the same time wage a sharp struggle against the German bourgeoisie, who are ready to adopt, in agreement with the French bourgeoisie, a policy of reparations fulfilment (Stinnes agreement) at the cost of the German proletariat and yield Germany as a colony to the French bourgeoisie, if only their class interests are safeguarded. The French Communist Party must fight with all its strength against the imperialist aspirations of the French bourgeoisie, against the attempt to enrich the French bourgeoisie by the more intense exploitation of the German proletariat; it must fight for the immediate annulment of the occupation of the left bank of the Rhine, against the occupation of the Ruhr, against the dismemberment of Germany, against French imperialism. Today it is not enough to fight in France against the defence of the fatherland; today it is necessary to fight the Versailles peace at every step. The communist parties in Poland, Czechoslovakia, and the other vassal States of France have the duty of combining the fight against their own bourgeoisie with the fight against French imperialism. By jointly conducted mass actions it must be made clear to the proletariat that the attempt to execute the Versailles treaty is bound to plunge the entire European proletariat into the deepest poverty, and that the fight against it is the common interest of the proletariat of all countries.

EXTRACTS FROM THE RESOLUTION OF THE FOURTH COMINTERN CONGRESS ON THE ITALIAN QUESTION

December 1922   *Thesen und Resolutionen*, iv, p. 87

[The majority of the Italian party, Zinoviev said in his report to the congress for the Italian commission, were opposed to the immediate fusion of the Italian Communist and Socialist Parties, although in the end they agreed to accept and carry out the decision. Unity was essential to encourage the psychology of resistance to fascism and willingness to enter the Communist Party in the conditions prevailing in Italy was a sign of courage and honesty. The programme for the united party was to establish a united front politically and industrially, to unite all those who opposed fascism, to agitate for a workers' government, and to join the fascist trade unions because there were many workers inside these bodies and the genuine working-class unions might be dissolved. Bordiga for the Communist Party majority, Graziadei for the minority, and Serrati for the Italian Socialist Party endorsed the resolution. The Socialist Party delegates were not empowered to accept the resolution, and some had therefore returned to Italy to get the endorsement of their central committee for the proposed organizational arrangements, so that no difficulties might be encountered on the delegation's return. The resolution was passed unanimously.]

At the close of the imperialist world war the situation in Italy was objectively revolutionary. The reins had fallen from the hands of the bourgeoisie. The machinery of the bourgeois State was broken. The ruling classes felt uncertain. The working masses were filled with indignation against the war and were in open insurrection in various parts of the country. Large sections of the peasantry were beginning to rise against the landlords and the State and were ready to support the working class in revolutionary struggle. The soldiers were against the war and ready to fraternize with the workers.

The objective prerequisites for a victorious revolution were at hand. The only thing missing was the most important subjective factor—a resolute, militant, conscious, revolutionary workers' party, that is, a genuine communist party, to assume resolute leadership of the masses.

At the end of the war the situation in practically all the belligerent countries was in broad outline the same. If the working class in the decisive countries did not triumph in the years 1919 and 1920, that can be ascribed to the absence of a revolutionary workers' party. This was particularly obvious in Italy, where revolution was closest, and which has now fallen into the deepest abyss of counter-revolution.

The occupation of the factories by the Italian workers in the autumn of 1920 was a decisive moment in the development of the class struggle in Italy. The Italian workers moved instinctively towards a revolutionary solution of the crisis, but the absence of a revolutionary workers' party decided the fate of the working class, sealed their defeat, and prepared the present victory of fascism. Without an adequate revolutionary leadership, the working class, though at the height of its strength, showed that it was not resolute enough to seize power. Thus it happened that after the lapse of a certain time the deadly enemy of the working class, the bourgeoisie, in the person of their most energetic wing, the fascists, laid the working class low and established their dictatorship. The Italian example is of the greatest significance. Nowhere has it been more palpably demonstrated than in Italy how great is the historical rôle of a communist party for the world revolution. It has shown how the absence of such a party can turn the course of history in favour of the bourgeoisie.

It is not that in these decisive years there was no workers' party in Italy. The old socialist party had a large membership and seen from the outside a great influence, but it carried within it reformist elements who crippled its action at every step. Despite the first split which occurred in 1912 and which expelled the extreme right and the second split in 1914, there were in 1919 and 1920 a great number of reformists and centrists in the SPI. In all decisive situations the reformists and centrists acted as a leaden weight on the party. Nowhere was it so clear as in Italy that the reformists are the most dangerous tools of the bourgeoisie in the working-class camp. They left nothing untried to betray the working class to the bourgeoisie. Such treachery as that of the reformists during the occupation of the factories in 1920 is not to be found often in the history of reformism, although it is an unbroken chain of treachery. The real precursors and pioneers of fascism are undoubtedly the reformists. The treachery of the reformists is primarily responsible for the dreadful sufferings of the Italian working class. If the Italian working class is now once more only at the beginning of its revolutionary advance and still has a long and difficult road ahead, that is because the reformists were tolerated too long in the Italian party....

In view of the decision taken by the SPI in October 1922 to exclude the reformists and to adhere unconditionally to the Communist International, the fourth world congress of the Communist International resolves . . .

1. The general situation in Italy, particularly after the victory of fascist reaction, imperatively demands the widest possible unification of all proletarian revolutionary forces. The Italian workers will breathe again if, after their defeats and splits, a new mustering of all revolutionary forces begins.

2. The Communist International . . . is completely convinced of the sincerely revolutionary frame of mind of the SPI, freed from the reformists, and resolves to admit the SPI to the Communist International. . . .

4. The fourth world congress instructs the central committee of the SPI to expel from the party all those who make any reservations to the 21 conditions of admission.

5. Since under the statutes of the Communist International there can be only one section in each country, the fourth world congress resolves that the Communist Party of Italy and the Socialist Party of Italy shall immediately amalgamate. The united party shall be called the United Communist Party of Italy (section of the Communist International).

6. To effect this amalgamation the fourth congress shall appoint a special organization committee consisting of three members of each party under the chairmanship of a member of the Executive. . . . Disputed questions shall be decided by the ECCI. . . .

9. At the same time a joint trade union committee shall be immediately set up whose task shall be to convince the trade union federation of the treachery of the Amsterdamers and to win a majority for the Profintern. This committee will be composed of two members of each party under the chairmanship of a comrade to be appointed by the ECCI or the organization committee. The trade union committee shall work under the instruction and supervision of the organization committee.

10. In towns where there are a communist and a socialist newspaper these shall be amalgamated by 1 January 1923. The editorial board of the central organ for the forthcoming year shall be appointed by the ECCI.

11. The united congress shall be held not later than the first fortnight of March 1923.

12. In present-day Italy illegal work has become absolutely essential. The SPI comrades must make up for what they have so far failed to do in this respect. . . .

13. The congress shall publish a manifesto on the amalgamation of the two parties.

DECISIONS OF THE FOURTH COMINTERN CONGRESS ON THE
REORGANIZATION OF THE ECCI AND ON ITS FUTURE ACTIVITIES

December 1922   *Protokoll*, iv, p. 994

[Writing on the opening of the congress, Zinoviev said that the Executive in its work had felt the need for some serious reforms. 'It is probable that the Executive will have to set up a number of sections . . . on the lines of the Central Committee of the Russian Communist Party.' The Executive was not to be regarded as a conciliation commission. 'It is obvious that the Executive must "interfere" in the affairs of practically every party. . . . It took an active part in the preparations for every congress and conference of its principal parties. . . . Representatives of the Executive attended practically every important congress and gave them ideological direction.'

The object of the reorganization, said Eberlein, reporting for the ECCI, was to eliminate the remaining traces of federalism, to make the ECCI the leadership of a centralized world party in which no individual or section could sabotage decisions. The sections had been very casual in this respect, and the Executive had not been strict enough in enforcing discipline. It was intolerable that sections should fail to publish ECCI documents because they disagreed with them. Greater centralization (and again closer approximation to the model of the Russian Communist Party, despite Lenin's criticism) would also be achieved by the practice of direct election of the Executive at the congress not as delegates of sections (although the sections were free to make nominations) but as individuals. The decision that national party congresses should be held after the world congress had been opposed by some parties; its advantages were, first, that it would eliminate the practice of delegates turning up with binding mandates, which on some questions might make it difficult for the world congress to reach agreement; second, difficulties would be created if the world congress reached decisions that differed from the decisions of national congresses. Parties would then be faced with the alternative of observing discipline and annulling the decisions, or coming into conflict with the Comintern. As to the membership of the ECCI, it was obvious that the Executive could not do its job properly unless it consisted of the best and most responsible people, not those who were at the beck and call of the sections. Although the enemies of the International alleged that it did just what the Russians wanted it to do, it was obvious that in the future as in the past 'the Russian comrades on the presidium and the ECCI must be accorded the greatest weight, for they have the greatest experience in the field of international class struggle; they are the only ones who have really carried out a revolution and they are therefore far superior in experience to all delegates from other sections. . . . But it is essential for the other parties to collaborate more and more in running the CI, and to send their most able representatives.' The presidium, Eberlein continued, would act as 'a kind of politburo'; the organization bureau would undertake tasks not previously carried out, such as dealing with organizational questions in the affiliated sections, and keeping track of and assisting their illegal work, which had so far made little progress. An eastern department was necessary because the parties in eastern countries were still only in the initial stage, and the work would at first have to be carried out mainly by members of stronger and more stable parties. Correspondence and the sending of delegates to Moscow by the sections had proved inadequate for their purpose, and were to be reinforced by the despatch of delegates from the ECCI to the sections. These would have explicit instructions, and would supervise the execution of the 21 conditions of admission and other Comintern decisions. The eastern department had a bureau in Vladivostok.

The theses were accepted against the vote of the delegate from Brazil.

The fourth world congress, Trotsky said shortly after its conclusion, 'in electing the Executive Committee created for the first time a central organ not on federal principles, not composed of representatives delegated by the various parties, but a body elected by the congress itself.'

The obstacles to centralization which they were trying to overcome, Bukharin said later, were in part due to outside causes, but many of them could be eliminated by the apparatus itself. He listed in particular defective contact between the CI and its sections, the inadequacy of the representatives sent to

Moscow, the overloading of the national sections with directives, instructions, letters, and appeals, and the failure to exchange opinions before decisions were taken, giving rise to conflicts which might have been avoided.]

WORLD CONGRESS

The world congress shall be held, as before, every year. The date shall be decided by the enlarged Executive. All affiliated sections are obliged to send delegates. Their number will be determined by the Executive. The costs shall be borne by the parties. The number of votes for each section shall be determined by the congress in accordance with the membership and the political circumstances of the country. Binding mandates are not allowed and will be annulled in advance, for such mandates are incompatible with the spirit of an international, centralized, proletarian party.

EXECUTIVE

The Executive is elected by the congress. It consists of the president, 24 members, and 10 candidates. Of the Executive, at least 15 members must be constantly in Moscow.

ENLARGED EXECUTIVE

As a rule meetings of the enlarged Executive shall be held once every 4 months. It shall be composed as follows:

1. The 25 members of the Executive;

2. three representatives of each of the following parties: Germany, France, Russia, Czechoslovakia, and Italy, as well as the Youth International and the Profintern;

3. two representatives each for England, Poland, America, Bulgaria, and Norway;

4. one representative from each other section entitled to vote.

The presidium is obliged to submit all important questions of principle which permit of delay to a meeting of the enlarged Executive. The first meeting of the enlarged Executive shall take place immediately after the world congress.

PRESIDIUM

At its first meeting the enlarged Executive elects the presidium, which shall include one representative of the YCI and of the Profintern, each with consultative voice; it shall establish the following departments:

1. An eastern department, whose work for the coming year shall receive the special attention of the Executive; the head of the eastern department must be a member of the presidium. In political work this department is subject to the presidium; its relation to the orgburo is arranged by the presidium.

2. An organization department (orgburo), to which at least 2 members of the presidium must belong. The orgburo is subordinate to the presidium.

3. An agitation-propaganda department, which shall be under the direction of a member of the Executive. This department is also directly subject to the presidium.

4. A statistical and information department, which is under the orgburo. The Executive has the right to set up further departments.

DIVISION OF LABOUR AMONG THE MEMBERS OF THE EXECUTIVE

A precise division of labour is to be introduced among the members of the Executive and of the presidium. The presidium shall appoint a responsible rapporteur for each of the most important countries to prepare the work of the individual sections. As a rule he shall be a member of the Executive, or, if possible, of the presidium. Rapporteurs who are not members of the Executive or the presidium work under the supervision of a member of the presidium.

The presidium shall organize a general secretariat, to work under the direction of a general secretary. He shall be given two deputies by the Executive. The secretariat does not have the function of an independent political organization; it is only an executive organ of the presidium.

The Executive is instructed to see that a similar division of labour, taking into account the conditions and the situation in each country, is introduced in all parties.

DELEGATES

In special cases the Executive shall send a delegate to the individual countries, who shall be drawn from the most highly qualified comrades of the sections. These representatives shall be endowed by the Executive with the most comprehensive powers. In special cases the functions of these envoys, their rights and duties, and their relation to the party in question, shall be precisely set down in writing.

The Executive is empowered to supervise with special emphasis the effective application of the 21 conditions and the execution of decisions of the world congress. Its envoys are to be explicitly entrusted with this supervision. The envoys must report on the results of their work at least once a month.

INTERNATIONAL CONTROL COMMISSION

The international control commission shall remain in being. Its functions are the same as those formulated by the third world congress. Each year the world congress shall choose two neighbouring sections, whose central committees shall each choose three members of the control commission from among their own number; their names must be approved by the Executive. For the coming year the world congress allots this function to the German and French sections.

TECHNICAL INFORMATION BUREAU

The technical information bureaux remain in being. Their job is to provide technical information and their work is under the control of the Executive.

'THE COMMUNIST INTERNATIONAL'

The Communist International is the organ of the Executive; the editorial board is chosen by and subject to the Executive.

PUBLICATIONS OF THE EXECUTIVE

The congress confirms that all communist organs are obliged as before to publish immediately all Executive documents (appeals, letters, resolutions, etc.) if the Executive so requests.

MINUTES OF THE NATIONAL PARTIES

The central committees of all sections are obliged to forward the minutes of all their sessions regularly to the Executive.

RECIPROCAL REPRESENTATION

It is desirable that the most important sections, where the countries are neighbours, shall maintain reciprocal representation for the purpose of keeping each other informed and co-ordinating their work. The reports of these representatives shall be sent also to the Executive. It is further desirable that such representatives shall be appointed in agreement with the Executive.

CONGRESSES OF THE SECTIONS

As a rule party conferences, or enlarged national committees, shall meet before the world congress of the CI, and shall deal with preparations for the world congress and the selection of delegates. Party congresses shall be held after the world congress. Exceptions can be made only with the consent of the Executive.

Such procedure will ensure that the interests of the individual sections are best safeguarded and at the same time provide the opportunity for the entire experience of the international movement to be appraised from 'below to above.'

At the same time this procedure gives the Communist International the opportunity, as a centralized world party, of transmitting to the individual parties from 'above to below', by means of democratic centralism, directives based on international experience as a whole.

RESIGNATIONS

The congress decisively condemns the instances of resignation which have occurred in the case of individual comrades of various party centres and of entire groups of such members. The congress regards these resignations as the greatest disorganization of the communist movement. Every leading office in a communist party belongs not to those holding the office, but to the Communist International as a whole.

The congress decides: Elected members of central bodies of a section can lay down their mandates only with the consent of the Executive. Resignations accepted by a party centre without the agreement of the Executive are invalid.

ILLEGAL WORK

In accordance with the decision of the congress, in which it was noted that a number of the most important parties are to all appearances approaching a period of illegality, the presidium is instructed to devote greater attention to the preparation of the parties in question for illegal work. Immediately after the congress the presidium shall begin discussions on this subject with all the parties concerned.

INTERNATIONAL WOMEN'S SECRETARIAT

The international women's secretariat remains as before in being. The Executive appoints the secretary and in agreement with her takes all further organizational measures.

REPRESENTATION ON THE YOUTH EXECUTIVE

The congress instructs the Executive to establish regular representation of the Comintern in the Youth International. The congress considers it one of the most important tasks of the Executive to promote the work of the youth movement.

REPRESENTATION ON THE PROFINTERN

The congress instructs the Executive to work out jointly with the Profintern central committee the forms which the connexion between the two bodies shall take. It points out that, particularly in the present period, the industrial struggle is most closely bound up with the political, and therefore requires specially close co-ordination of the forces of all the revolutionary organizations of the working class.

REVISION OF STATUTES

The congress confirms the statutes adopted by the second congress and instructs the Executive to redraft and supplement these statutes on the basis of the decisions taken. This work must be carried out promptly, submitted to all parties for preliminary discussion, and finally confirmed by the fifth world congress.

RESOLUTION OF THE FOURTH COMINTERN CONGRESS ON
PROLETARIAN HELP FOR SOVIET RUSSIA

5 *December* 1922   *Protokoll*, iv, p. 935

[The resolution was moved by Münzenberg and passed unanimously without discussion.]

1. The workers of all countries, without distinction of political or trade union attitude, are interested in the survival and consolidation of Soviet Russia. Apart from the deeply-rooted feeling of proletarian solidarity, this more than anything else has made all workers' parties ready to support action for the relief of the famine in Soviet Russia, and inspired millions of workers in all countries to make the greatest sacrifices with enthusiasm. With the help of this proletarian relief action, which grew into the biggest and most prolonged international solidarity action in the history of the workers' movement, Soviet Russia survived the most difficult days of famine and triumphed over hunger.

But even during this famine relief action, large sections of the workers' organizations which took part in it realized that more was needed to help Soviet Russia than the provision of food. The economic war of the imperialist States on Soviet Russia continues, the trade blockade continues in the form of a refusal of credit, and whenever capitalist groups do start to do business with Soviet Russia, this is done with the object of exploiting and profiting from Soviet Russia.

As in all other conflicts between Soviet Russia and its imperialist enemies, it is the duty of the workers of all countries to intervene in favour of Soviet Russia in the economic war also, against its imperialist enemies, and to support Soviet Russia actively and practically with every means, including economic assistance.

2. The best support for Soviet Russia in the economic war is the political revolutionary struggle of the workers and their pressure on the government of every country to recognize the Soviet Government and establish favourable trade relations with Soviet Russia. With the importance that Soviet Russia has for all workers, the maximum economic, as well as the political, power of the world proletariat must be mobilized in its support.

Every factory and workshop which Soviet Russia gets going with the support of the workers without capitalist credits, is effective help for Soviet Russia in the struggle against the imperialist robber policy, and every strengthening of Soviet Russia, the first workers' State in the world, strengthens the international proletariat in the struggle against their class enemy, the bourgeoisie.

The fourth congress of the Communist International therefore declares that it is the duty of all workers' parties and organizations, above all of communists, to give immediate and practical support to Soviet Russia in the reconstruction of its economy, not only through their political revolutionary struggle, but also by a campaign for economic aid among the broadest masses.

3. The most important task of proletarian economic assistance outside Soviet Russia consists in collecting funds for the purchase of machinery, raw materials, tools, etc., for Soviet Russia. In addition to the methods already used, collections, special exhibitions, etc., attention should be paid to participation by party groups, trade unions, co-operatives, and other workers' circles, in workers' loans for Soviet Russia.

Propaganda for proletarian economic help at the same time offers the opportunity of carrying on the best agitation for Soviet Russia. It should therefore be carried out in closest connexion with the sections in the individual countries.

Since the question of economic support for Soviet Russia is of general importance for the entire working class, it is necessary to create special committees or societies to organize and carry out this campaign, composed of delegates from all kinds of workers' organizations, similar to the workers' famine relief committees. These committees or societies should interest and win the support of the broadest workers' circles for this economic aid. They shall be subject to the control of the Communist International.

4. The use of the funds collected by these committees and societies is to be decided in closest consultation with the appropriate Russian economic bodies, either of the State or of workers' organizations.

5. In the present state of Russian economic life the mass immigration of foreign workers would not help but rather hamper reconstruction, and should in no circumstances be encouraged. The immigration of foreign workers into Russia should be restricted to individual specialist workers, who are urgently required in certain industries. But even in these cases the agreement and consent of the Russian trade unions must first be obtained.

6. Proletarian economic aid must aim at bringing into harmony two ideals: the concentration of international workers' solidarity on help for the first proletarian State in the world, and the attainment of tangible economic results.

7. In accordance with the principles of socialist co-operation and economic management, any surplus funds collected may be used only to expand the scope of the activities in question.

EXTRACTS FROM THE RESOLUTION OF THE FOURTH COMINTERN
CONGRESS ON 'FIVE YEARS OF THE RUSSIAN REVOLUTION'

5 *December* 1922   *Thesen und Resolutionen*, iv, p. 35

[The resolution was moved by Klara Zetkin and passed unanimously.]

. . . The fourth world congress of the Communist International observes
that Soviet Russia, the proletarian State, now that it is no longer forced to
defend its bare existence by force of arms, has turned with unexampled
vigour to the construction and development of its economy, keeping steadily
in sight the transformation to communism. The separate stages and
measures leading to this goal, the transitional steps of the so-called new
policy, are the outcome, on the one hand, of the particular given objective
and subjective historical conditions in Russia, and, on the other, of the
slow rate of development of the world revolution and of the isolation of the
Soviet republic in the midst of capitalist States. . . .

The fourth world congress reminds the proletarians of all countries
that the proletarian revolution can never triumph completely within a single
country; rather must it triumph internationally, as world revolution.
The labour of Soviet Russia, its struggle for existence, for the achievements
of the revolution, is the fight for the liberation of the proletarians, the
oppressed and exploited of the whole world, from the chains of slavery.
The Russian proletarians have more than done their duty as the revolutionary protagonists of the world proletariat. The world proletariat must
at last do theirs. In all countries the workers, the disinherited, and the
enslaved, must proclaim their most active solidarity, moral, economic, and
political, with Soviet Russia. Not merely international solidarity, but their
own most fundamental interests demand that for this purpose they must
take up the sharpest fight against the bourgeoisie and the capitalist State.
In every country their battle-cry must be: Hands off Soviet Russia! De
jure recognition of Soviet Russia! Active support of every kind for the
economic construction of Soviet Russia! Every strengthening of Soviet
Russia means a weakening of the world bourgeoisie. The five years of
Soviet Russia's existence is the most severe blow that world capitalism
has ever received, and one from which it will not recover.

RESOLUTION OF THE FOURTH COMINTERN CONGRESS ON THE
PROGRAMME OF THE COMMUNIST INTERNATIONAL

December 1922   *Protokoll*, iv, p. 542

[A programme had been drafted by Bukharin, who stated at the outset that it
had not yet been considered even by the Russian party. The Bulgarians and

Germans had also submitted drafts, on which Kabakchiev and Thalheimer spoke. It was in the course of his speech analysing the draft programme that Bukharin said: 'when we were a revolutionary opposition party, we could not of course consider for a single moment taking money from any bourgeois State for our revolutionary activities. That would have been too stupid. The moment we took any money from a hostile power, our cause would have been completely discredited. That was why the bourgeoisie were from their point of view acting quite rightly when they tried to prove that we were the agents of German imperialism. . . . But now that a proletarian State exists and can raise a loan in a bourgeois State, it would again be stupid if we were to reject this on principle. . . . When the bourgeoisie speak of defending the country, they mean defence of the bourgeois State apparatus; when we speak of it, we mean defence of the proletarian State. We must therefore make it quite clear in the programme that the proletarian State should and must be defended not only by the proletariat of that State, but by the proletarians of all countries. . . . Secondly, should proletarian states, proceeding from considerations of the strategic aims of the entire proletariat, form military blocs with bourgeois States? There is no difference of principle between a loan and a military alliance. And I maintain that we have now grown so strong that we can conclude a military alliance with the bourgeoisie of another country in order to use it to smash another bourgeoisie. . . . This is nothing but a question of pure strategic and tactical expediency.'

Where such an alliance exists, he went on, it was the duty of the comrades in the partner country to help it forward to victory. This is the only reference—oblique, it is true—to the Rapallo treaty in the published proceedings of the congress.

After the three speakers had finished, there was a discussion whether the debate should continue, and one of the drafts be selected, or postponed to the fifth congress. The Russian delegation asked for time to consider this. At a later session, Zinoviev introduced the resolution, saying that this was preferable to a hurried and crippled discussion. The Italian delegation wanted the programme discussed and adopted then, even if it meant that final revision and editing were postponed. The resolution, put forward by the congress presidium, was carried unanimously; the Italian delegates adding a statement, 'for the record', that while voting for the resolution they would have preferred an outline programme to be debated and adopted at the Congress.

The programme of the Communist International was not adopted until its sixth and penultimate congress in 1928.]

1. All draft programmes shall be submitted to the Executive of the Communist International, or to a commission appointed by it, for study and detailed elaboration. The Executive is obliged to publish all draft programmes which it receives as quickly as possible.

2. The congress confirms that those national sections of the Communist International which do not yet have national programmes, are obliged to begin at once on the drafting of their programmes, which shall be submitted to the Executive at least three months before the fifth congress for ratification by the next congress.

3. The programmes of the national sections must clearly and decisively establish the necessity of the struggle for transitional demands, making the necessary reservations about the dependence of these demands on the concrete circumstances of time and place.

4. The theoretical basis for all transitional and partial demands must be clearly stated in the general programme, and the fourth congress likewise decisively condemns the attempt to depict the inclusion of transitional demands in the programme as opportunism, as well as all attempts to gloss over or replace the fundamental revolutionary tasks by partial demands.

5. The general programme must clearly explain the basic historical types of the transitional demands of the national section, in accordance with the basic differences in the economic and political structure of the different countries, for example England on the one hand, and India on the other.

EXTRACTS FROM A MANIFESTO OF THE COMMUNIST INTERNATIONAL TO
THE ITALIAN PROLETARIAT

December 1922   *Inprekorr*, ii, 241, p. 1820, 21 *December* 1922

[Speaking on the report of the ECCI Zinoviev said, inter alia: 'I come now to Italy, and think I can say that it is on the verge of revolution. . . . Viewed historically, what has just happened in Italy is a comedy.' The fascist rise to power had been made possible by the Italian Socialist Party. Radek took a gloomier view: 'I see in the triumph of fascism the greatest defeat which socialism and communism have suffered since the beginning of the era of world revolution. . . . How was the victory of fascism possible, what was it based on?' He traced its rise to the support of the petty bourgeoisie who since the war had been unable to maintain their place in Italian society. They were hostile to the socialists not merely because of their natural anti-socialism, but also because the socialist party had been opposed to the war and paid no attention to the ex-servicemen and the disabled. But although the bourgeoisie had failed, through inner disintegration, to retain the support and confidence of officials and of the petty bourgeoisie, Mussolini would have to carry out a capitalist programme; fascism had no programme of its own. In another speech he said that the fascist victory was a greater defeat than the fall of the Hungarian Soviet Government, because it was a sign of the temporary spiritual and political bankruptcy of Italian socialism and of the entire Italian labour movement.

Bordiga described fascism as the instrument of the shrewdest and most class-conscious section of the bourgeoisie, which would subordinate sectional interests to the general interests of the capitalist class. Trotsky attributed the fascist victory to the fiasco of the Italian revolution, for which everything had been present except a revolutionary party.

The manifesto was signed by the presidium of the fourth congress and the delegates from the Italian Communist and Socialist Parties.]

Workers! Comrades!

In 1920 the Italian working class was on the point of seizing power; the workers were in occupation of the factories; even the more backward sections of the peasantry were caught up in the movement and took forcible possession of the landowners' estates; the first germs of a proletarian red guard came spontaneously to life, revolution was bursting into flame throughout the land. The working class, which felt that to it belonged the leading part in history, was ready for the greatest and most heroic sacrifices. But precisely at that moment the most dangerous enemies of the proletariat rose up within the ranks of our party itself . . . the entire pack of reformists and centrists tore victory from your hands and saved the bourgeoisie.

You did not succeed in seizing power in 1920, and therefore in 1922 the fascists were able to march on Rome and set up their dictatorship. The reformists tried to justify their sabotage of the revolution by serving up at every opportunity the long tale of unheard-of sacrifices which the revolution would have demanded. But have the reformists managed to spare the working class the bloodiest sacrifices? Hundreds and thousands of victims have already fallen; tens and tens of thousands of proletarians and peasants are condemned to misery and despair; the fascist hordes terrorize the country; the capitalist offensive against the economic and political institutions of the working population is being mercilessly continued.

The working class, weakened and disunited, watches all this desolation, virtually powerless. The reorganization of proletarian forces is a necessity that cannot be postponed or delayed.

The true features of the Italian reformists have now been revealed to all the workers with the greatest clarity: the reformists are nothing but tools of the bourgeoisie. As could be easily foreseen, their tactics of a government coalition with the left wing of the bourgeoisie in order to bring about the gradual realization of socialist reforms has failed lamentably. Democracy has allied itself openly and unreservedly with reaction. All constitutional guarantees and achievements are being stamped out by the fascist dictatorship and the terror. The reformists did not want red violence; and consequently what they did was to help unleash reactionary violence. In vain they implored the bourgeoisie to allow them to co-operate in the reconstruction of Italy. In vain they threw themselves devoutly at the feet of the monarchy, and tried to persuade the working class to do the same. In order to put their own class on its feet again, the bourgeoisie destroyed the workers' organizations. Despite Signor Turati's sage advice, the monarchy threw itself into Mussolini's arms, gave him full powers to work on public opinion by means of the censorship and the confiscation of newspapers, and to reorganize the national economy by the taxation of wages, the abolition of the eight-hour day, the protection of parasitic capitalism, and to impose by force majority proportional franchise instead of universal franchise. It was in this way that the bourgeoisie accepted the services humbly offered by Messrs. Turati and company: The reformists have been turned out like unwanted servants.

Comrades!

The lessons of the past still have their use.

The Rome congress of the Italian Communist [Socialist] Party expelled the reformists and resolved to join the Communist International by accepting the 21 points without reservation, a decision which involved fusion with the Communist Party. The Rome congress showed that the Italian socialists genuinely want to take the road of communism; they have admitted the dangerous mistakes they made and have stated their readiness to correct them. The fourth congress of the Communist International dealt in full and careful detail with the new situation which has thus been created in the Italian workers' movement. It agreed unanimously on the immediate fusion of the Italian Socialist Party and the Communist Party of Italy, under the name of 'United Communist Party of Italy' (section of the Communist International). The statutes of the International provide that there can be only one communist party in any country, only one section of the Communist International. The fourth congress appointed a special commission consisting of three representatives of the communist party and three of the socialist party under the chairmanship of a member of the ECCI. We call on all of you to support this commission confidently and enthusiastically, to establish the most favourable conditions for its work, to exert all your efforts so that the fusion can be accomplished quickly and smoothly.

The period of splits is over. A new historical period is opening for the Italian proletariat, the period of the reorganization of the forces of the proletariat. All truly revolutionary workers, all elements of the Italian labouring population determined to fight, will enter the ranks of the United Communist Party of Italy. The United Communist Party must become the organizational centre of all class-conscious Italian proletarians. They must unite all their efforts to defeat the reformists, to liberate the trade unions from the 'Amsterdam' traitors, to fight energetically against the latest attempts of the reformists to kill any spirit of struggle in the trade union organizations through a so-called party of labour and to turn them into an instrument of co-operation with the fascist bourgeoisie. The firm unity of the trade union organizations must be maintained, but they must also be enlivened by a revolutionary spirit and brought over to the ranks of the Red International of Labour Unions.

Workers! Peasants!

The United Communist Party of Italy will be the vanguard in the fight of all workers against cursed fascism; around its banner the best and most conscious elements of the working class and peasantry must rally. Make systematic and energetic use of the united front tactics in the trade unions as well as the political field. If there is one country where these tactics are necessary to strengthen the position of the working class, it is in the Italy ruled by fascism.

The treachery of the reformists has been paid for in the best blood of the Italian working class. New fighters must spring up from this blood. The fascist yoke will not last for ever. The more frightful the reaction, the more savage the dictatorship of the bourgeoisie, the more numerous will be those who remain true to the red flag and fight for the goal of the proletarian dictatorship.

To the masses! In spite of all the difficulties you will find in your way because of fascist violence and the cunning intrigues of the reformists, go to the masses. Communists must work among every group of workers; they must educate their class brothers, move them to struggle. Communists must penetrate everywhere where the bourgeoisie and their servants are trying to coerce our class brothers into associations which they will use as tools in the interests of capital. We must be present wherever there are workers, to educate them and win them for the common cause.

'We want a workers' government.' That is the slogan which must capture the consciousness of the Italian workers. Only a government of workers and peasants can rescue Italy from its present wretchedness. Only a government of workers and peasants can 'put Italy on its feet again'. All workers, even those who fight in no party, or even in hostile parties, must be summoned to create the proletarian united front.

Do not lose courage! Resist! Defend the cause of communism among the working masses, by legal methods if possible, by illegal if necessary. Go to the masses and tell them that the time of splits is past, and that the fourth world congress of the Communist International has begun on the work of concentrating all the workers' forces of Italy.

Long live true revolutionary socialism!

Long live communism!

Long live the United Communist Party of Italy!

Long live the Italian working class!

Long live the Communist International!

EXTRACTS FROM AN ECCI-RILU MANIFESTO ON THE HAGUE PEACE
CONGRESS

19 *December* 1922   *Inprekorr*, ii, 244, p. 1842, 28 *December* 1922

[The Russian co-operatives and trade unions were invited to the conference, but, said Zinoviev at the fourth congress, the reformists had been afraid to invite the

International. The Russian delegates were Radek, Lozovsky, and Rothstein. They put forward a 14 point programme (which was rejected) proposing the establishment, nationally and internationally, of committees of action against war. Lozovsky, the first Russian speaker, protested against the exclusion of the Comintern and RILU, the absence of delegates from the colonial and Far Eastern countries, and the presence of delegates from bourgeois pacifist societies. Radek, speaking in a conciliatory tone about the need to prepare beforehand for anti-war action, was applauded, although his speech concluded with the threat: 'We offer you, frankly and fearlessly, the hand of friendship and co-operation. Reject that offer, and the outstretched hand of friendship will be turned against you.'

The Russian delegates voted against all the resolutions of the congress, which included one protesting against sanctions and coercive measures in the reparations question, one on the revision of the peace treaties, the control of armaments, the admission of Germany to the League of Nations, and the abolition of secret diplomacy, and a final resolution on the tasks of the labour movement in the war against war.]

'PEACE ON EARTH'

Men and women workers!

Between the 10th and 15th December the congress of the Amsterdam trade union International and of the Second and Two-and-a-half Internationals was held in The Hague. It was called to discuss how the international working class can avert the danger of a new imperialist war. Never was such a congress more timely. . . . While the situation of the workers is growing steadily worse, while there is no money to give the unemployed even a piece of bread, while expenditure on cultural needs is being steadily reduced, the capitalist States are spending more on armaments than they did before the war. Among the masses of workers the feeling is growing that things cannot go on any longer in this way, and all bourgeois politicians are speaking openly of the danger of a new world war.

The Hague congress had a great task before it—to rally all the forces of the working class so that the proletariat should not again become the cannon fodder of capitalism. Unfortunately, however, the representatives of the Amsterdam and the Second and Two-and-a-half Internationals renounced in advance the mobilization of all the forces of the working class for this struggle. Although there can be no struggle for peace while the popular masses of the Near and Far East do not take part in it, and capitalist and militarist cliques have a free hand in their countries, the leaders of the Amsterdam trade unions, of the Second and Two-and-a-half Internationals, did not for a moment dream of inviting the representatives of the working-class organizations of these countries. There are trade unions in Constantinople, in Japan, China, and India, which have already led great strikes and which are imbued with the will to struggle for the interests of the working class, but the supercilious representatives of the west European labour aristocracy did not lift a finger to attract them to the congress. Moreover, they deliberately kept out of the congress three million members of the communist parties, although these parties were formed of precisely those elements which during the war fought most boldly for peace. They deliberately excluded from the congress the millions of workers who support the Red International of Labour Unions. Only the Russian trade unions were invited.

The representatives of the Russian trade unions immediately proposed the admission of representatives of all communist parties and red trade unions and they said to the Amsterdamers and the social-democrats, 'We are divided from you by great differences, but if you want to fight against war we shall be there. We are ready to conclude an alliance for the fight against the war danger, despite all your sins, for in the face of this danger all other differences retreat into the background.' The Amsterdamers answered with insults against the communists who allegedly split the trade unions. The Russian trade union representatives thereupon replied, 'Every child knows that we are opponents of splitting the trade unions and it is not we but you who throw the minorities who have different opinions out of the unions, but whoever may be guilty of splitting the unions we offer our help in overcoming this split; for in the struggle against war strong and united unions are necessary. We propose the formation of a committee of action which shall eliminate the split in each country and make further splits impossible. If only you give us the opportunity of agitating for our ideas in the unions we shall submit to trade union discipline in the struggle against capitalism.' The Amsterdamers rejected this proposal with scorn.

At the same moment as they were preventing the formation of the proletarian united front against imperialism they concluded an alliance with the bourgeois pacifists. For the first time in the history of the modern workers' movement there was a joint congress of trade unions and political workers' organizations with the representatives of a part of the bourgeoisie, who were thus given the opportunity of helping to decide the most important question of the workers' movement. This was justified on the ground that all forces hostile to war must be rallied for the fight against war. But this argument is a sheer swindle. The Amsterdamers have rejected an alliance with the revolutionary workers who are the only real opponents of imperialist war. They ally themselves only with the bourgeois pacifists who during the war went over just like the Amsterdamers into the capitalist camp and helped imperialism to mangle the body of the proletariat.

In rejecting the proletarian united front and concluding an alliance with the bourgeois groups the three Internationals passed sentence on the Hague conference. People who reject joint action with the revolutionary

THE COMMUNIST INTERNATIONAL

proletariat and prefer a bourgeois alliance have no real desire to fight against war. Imperialist war serves the interests of the bourgeoisie and whoever allies himself with the bourgeoisie unnerves and debilitates the working class and makes it impossible for them to fight against the war danger. . . .

Instead of organizing the fight against the war danger now, the Amsterdamers threatened the bourgeoisie with an international strike in the event of war. The Russian trade union delegates replied that an international strike against war involves a trial of strength which requires thorough preparation. When war breaks out, nationalist passions are unleashed, emergency legislation is introduced, and the proletariat will be able to defend itself only if it has been equipped and trained by years of unbroken class struggle. How can they be armed for revolutionary struggle against war if they have for years been hitched to the wagon of the bourgeoisie by a coalition policy . . . if they have no illegal organizations, if all the weapons are left in the hands of the bourgeoisie? . . .

The Hague congress has shown that the leaders of the Amsterdam, and Second and Two-and-a-half Internationals have no desire to fight against the growing war danger but on the contrary are doing everything to make this fight impossible. If you do not want to be dragged helpless on to the battlefield once more and be annihilated in your millions you must come together into a common fighting front, in opposition to the will of your leaders, in factory and mine, in town and in country. . . . You must reject the crippling influence of the reformist leaders who are splitting your ranks in order to join the bourgeoisie. . . . The working masses of the victorious capitalist countries must understand that they are no less defeated than the masses of the defeated capitalist countries. They must understand that if they do not oppose the robber campaigns of their governments it is not the bourgeoisie of the defeated countries but the masses who will pay tribute, that their situation will become that of Chinese coolies and that they will be driven by poverty to work in conditions of slavery which will permit the bourgeoisie of the victorious countries to force their workers to accept starvation wages. The workers of the defeated capitalist countries must understand that the chains of Versailles, Trianon and Neuilly can be broken if they act not with their own bourgeoisie but with the proletariat of the victorious countries. The entire international proletariat must rally round Soviet Russia, the only proletarian State which opposes to the robber policy of international imperialism the organized strength of one hundred and fifty million people.

APPENDIX

THE EXECUTIVE COMMITTEE OF THE COMMUNIST INTERNATIONAL

THE first Comintern congress did not elect an Executive Committee. It was to consist of delegates from the communist parties of Russia, Germany, German Austria, Hungary, the Balkan Communist Federation, Switzerland, and Scandinavia.

The ECCI reported to the second congress that, with the exception of Russia and Hungary, none of these parties had been able to send a permanent delegate. The Russian party had been represented by Balabanova, Berzin, Bukharin, Vorovsky, Zinoviev, and Klinger. Lenin and others had attended important meetings. At various times the following had taken part in ECCI meetings: Rudas (Hungary); Sadoul (France); Reed, Anderson (United States); Rutgers (Holland); Pak (Korea); Liao Chao (China); Friis (Norway); Kilbom, Grimlund (Sweden). The Polish, Yugoslav, Finnish, and Latvian parties had sent permanent representatives: Markhlevsky, Milkich, Sirola, Stuchka.

Balabanova, Berzin, Vorovsky, and Radek had acted as secretary, in that order.

The Executive Committee elected at the second congress consisted of:

Russia: Tomsky, Zinoviev, Radek, Bukharin, Kobetsky; Candidates: Lenin, Trotsky, Berzin, Tsiperovich, Stalin, Pavlovich
Germany: Meyer; Candidate: Levi
France: Rosmer
Britain: Quelch
United States: Reed, Gurvich (N. Hourwich)
Italy: Serrati; Candidate: Cesare
Czechoslovakia: Gula
Austria: Steinhardt
Scandinavia: Friis
Bulgaria: Shablin
Yugoslavia: Milkich
Far East: Pak
Near East: Sultan-Zade
Finland: Manner
Poland: Radek
Holland: Wijnkoop, Jansen
Latvia: Stuchka (candidate)
Hungary: Rudniansky
Georgia: Tskhakaya
Java: Maring
Youth: Shatskin

The little bureau elected by this Executive consisted of: Zinoviev, Bukharin, Rudniansky, Meyer, and Kobetsky. The bureau was later enlarged; at the time of the third congress it consisted of the above five and, in addition, Bela Kun, Rosmer, Koenen, and Radek.

The third congress did not directly elect an Executive Committee, but decided that parties with forty votes at the congress (of which there were four) should send two delegates, and those with twenty to thirty votes (of which there were fourteen) should send one delegate. The Russian Communist Party was to send five delegates. Other parties were to have a consultative voice on the Committee. As constituted after the congress, the Executive consisted of the following members:

Germany: Heckert, Frölich
France: Souvarine
Czechoslovakia: Burian, Kreibich
Italy: Terracini
Russia: Bukharin, Zinoviev, Lenin, Radek, Trotsky
Ukraine: Shumsky
Poland: Glinsky
Bulgaria: Popov
Yugoslavia: Markovich
Norway: Scheflo
Britain: Bell
United States: Baldwin
Spain: Merino-Gracia
Finland: Sirola
Holland: Jansen
Belgium: Van Overstraaten
Sweden: Kilbom
Rumania: Bodulescu
Switzerland: Arnold
Austria: Koritschoner
Latvia: Stuchka
Youth: Münzenberg, Lekai

Some changes were subsequently made, and at the time of the fourth congress Germany was represented by Eberlein and Zetkin, France by Leiciagué and Henriet, Czechoslovakia by Neurath and Smeral, Italy by Ambroggi, Poland by Prukhniak, Bulgaria by Jordanov, the United States by Carr (L. E. Katterfeld) and Cook (J. P. Cannon), Finland by Manner and Kuusinen, Switzerland by Humbert-Droz, and the Youth International by Schüller. In addition Katayama represented the Japanese Communist Party, and Lozovsky the Profintern.

Members with a consultative voice included:

Azerbaijan: Mussabekov
Georgia: Tskhakaya
Lithuania: Angareitis
Luxemburg: Jansen
Persia: Sultan-Zade
Turkey: Salikh
Estonia: Pögelmann

Denmark: Jurgensen
India: Roy
Greece: Dimitros
South Africa: Johns
Korea: Khananchen
Armenia: Kassian
China: Chan
Iceland: Valenius

At the time of the fourth congress Johns had been replaced by Banting, and in addition Australia was represented by Earsman and South America by Penelon.

The presidium elected by the Executive consisted of Zinoviev, Bukharin, Radek, Heckert, Souvarine, Gennari, Kun, and Humbert-Droz.

The first enlarged plenary session of the ECCI elected to the presidium Zinoviev, Radek, Bukharin, Brandler, Souvarine, Terracini, Kreibich, and Carr, with Valetsky and Kuusinen as candidates.

At the second enlarged plenum Terracini, Kreibich, and Carr were replaced by Gramsci, Smeral, and Jordanov. Cook and Kuusinen were elected candidate members, and Leiciagué (France) and Jilek (Czechoslovakia) as additional members without votes while the disputes in their parties were being settled. At the time of the fourth congress the presidium consisted of Zinoviev, Bukharin, Radek, Brandler, Souvarine, Jordanov, Carr, Ambroggi, Kuusinen, and Shatskin.

The secretariat, consisting of Kuusinen, Rakosi, and Humbert-Droz after the third congress, had five members when the fourth met: Kuusinen, Kon, Eberlein, Rakosi, and Minkin.

The fourth congress elected the following Executive Committee, nominated by the presidium and voted *en bloc*: Zinoviev (President); Frossard, Souvarine (France); Zetkin, Hörnle (Germany); Bukharin, Radek (Russia); Smeral, Neurath (Czechoslovakia); Gennari, Gramsci (Italy); Schüller, Shatskin (Youth); MacManus (Britain); Carr (United States); Höglund, Scheflo (Scandinavia); Prukhniak (Poland); Kuusinen (Finland); Kolarov (Balkans); Garden (Australia); Stirner (South America); Andrews (South Africa); Katayama, Safarov (eastern countries). Candidate members: Duret (France); Böttcher (Germany); Lenin, Trotsky (Russia); Muna (Czechoslovakia); Bordiga (Italy); Newbold (Britain); Damon (United States); Makkavei (Balkans); Roy (eastern countries).

The presidium consisted of Zinoviev, Bukharin, Radek, Zetkin, Smeral, Gennari, Souvarine, Kuusinen, Kolarov, Katayama, MacManus, and Shatskin, with Hörnle, Neurath, and Gramsci as candidate members. There was a five-man secretariat: Kolarov, Piatnitsky, Stoecker, Kuusinen, and Rakosi.

[The accuracy of a few of these names is doubtful; here, as elsewhere in this volume, it has been impossible to establish their authenticity.]

SOURCES

Full title   *Abbreviated title*

Balabanov, A., *My Life as a Rebel*. London, 1938

Bericht über die Verhandlungen des 2. Parteitages der Kommunistischen Partei Deutschlands, abgehalten in Jena vom 22 bis 26 August 1921. Berlin, 1922

Berichte zum zweiten Kongress der Kommunistischen Internationale. Hamburg, 1921

Borkenau, F., *The Communist International*. London, 1938

Carr, E. H., *The Bolshevik Revolution 1917–1923*, vol. III. London, 1953

Desiat Let Kominterna v Resheniakh i Tsifrakh, ed. by A. Tivel and M. Kheimo. Moscow, 1929

Desiatyi S'ezd RKP(b). Moscow, 1933

Deviatyi S'ezd RKP(b), Mart-Aprel 1920 g. Moscow, 1934

Der I Kongress der Kommunistischen Internationale: Protokoll der Verhandlungen in Moskau vom 2 bis zum 19 [6] März 1919. Hamburg, 1921   *Protokoll, i*

Dvenadtsatyi S'ezd RKP(b): Stenograficheskii Otchet. Moscow, 1923

Der ferne Osten: Der erste Kongress der kommunistischen und revolutionären Organisationen des fernen Ostens. Moskau, Januar 1922. Hamburg, 1922

Fischer, R., *Stalin and German Communism*. Harvard, 1948

Flechtheim, O. K., *Der KPD in der Weimarer Republik*. Offenbach a. M., 1948

Frossard, L. O., *De Jaurès à Lénine*. Paris, 1930

Die Gründung der dritten Internationale. Vienna, 1919

International Press Correspondence (October 1921–). English edition of ECCI periodical. Berlin   *Inprecorr*

Internationale Presse-Korrespondenz (September 1921–). German edition of ECCI periodical. Berlin   *Inprekorr*

Kommunisticheskii Internatsional (May 1919–). Periodical publication of the ECCI. Petrograd–Moscow   *K.I.*

Lazitch, B., *Lénine et la IIIe Internationale*. Neuchâtel, 1951

Lenin, V. I., *Sochinenia*. 2nd ed. Moscow, 1930–5

Levi, P., *Unser Weg wider den Putschismus*. Berlin, 1921

Manifest, Richtlinien, Beschlüsse des ersten Kongresses: Aufrufe und offene Schreiben des Exekutivkomitees bis zum zweiten Kongress. Hamburg, 1920   *Beschlüsse des ersten Kongresses*

Odinnadtsatyi S'ezd RKP(b). Moscow, 1936

I S'ezd Narodov Vostoka. Baku 1–8 Sent. 1920 g. Stenograficheskie Otchety. Petrograd, 1920

Protokoll des III. Kongresses der Kommunistischen Internationale (Moskau, 22 Juni bis 12 Juli 1921). Hamburg, 1921   *Protokoll, iii*

Protokoll des IV. Kongresses der Kommunistischen Internationale. Petrograd-Moskau vom 5. November bis 5. Dezember 1922. Hamburg, 1923   *Protokoll, iv*

Reichenbach, B., 'Zur Geschichte der KAPD', in *Archiv für die Geschichte des Sozialismus und der Arbeiterbewegung*. Vol. XIII. Leipzig, 1928.

Report of the International Peace Congress held at The Hague under the auspices of the International Federation of Trade Unions, December 10–15, 1922. Amsterdam, [1923]

Rosmer, A., *Moscou sous Lénine*. Paris, 1953

Rossi, A., *The Rise of Italian Fascism, 1918–1922*. Eng. transl. London, 1938

The Second and Third Internationals and the Vienna Union: Official Report of the Conference between the Executives, held at the Reichstag, Berlin, on the 2nd April, 1922, and following days. London, 1922   *Report of the Conference*

Thesen und Resolutionen des III. Weltkongresses der Kommunistischen Internationale. Hamburg, 1921   *Thesen und Resolutionen, iii*

Thesen und Resolutionen des IV. Weltkongresses der Kommunistischen Internationale. Hamburg, 1923   *Thesen und Resolutionen, iv*

Trotsky, L. D., *The First Five Years of the Communist International*. 2 vols. New York, 1945, 1953

Vosmoi S'ezd RKP(b), 19–23 Marta, 1919 g. Moscow, 1933

Walter, G., *Histoire du Parti Communiste Français*. Paris, 1948

Zetkin, K., *Reminiscences of Lenin*. London, 1929

Der Zweite Kongress der Kommunist. Internationale: Protokoll der Verhandlungen vom 19 Juli in Petrograd und vom 23 Juli bis 7 August 1920 in Moskau. Hamburg, 1921   *Protokoll, ii*

INDEX